Natural Resources and the Environment Series
Volume 8

The World Environment 1972–1982

NATURAL RESOURCES AND THE ENVIRONMENT Series

SERIES DIRECTORS
Margaret R. Biswas and Asit K. Biswas.

EDITORIAL BOARD
Essam El-Hinnawi, Nairobi; Huang Ping-Wei, Beijing; Mohammed Kassas, Cairo; Victor A. Kovda, Moscow; Walther Manshard, Freiburg; W. H. Matthews, Hawaii; M. S. Swaminathan, New Delhi.

Volume 1: THE ENVIRONMENTAL IMPACTS OF PRODUCTION AND USE OF ENERGY
Essam El-Hinnawi, United Nations Environment Programme.

Volume 2: RENEWABLE NATURAL RESOURCES AND THE ENVIRONMENT: PRESSING PROBLEMS IN THE DEVELOPING WORLD
Kenneth Ruddle and Walther Manshard. United Nations University.

Volume 3: ASSESSING TROPICAL FOREST LANDS: THEIR SUITABILITY FOR SUSTAINABLE USES
Richard A. Carpenter, Editor, East-West Center.

Volume 4: FUELWOOD AND RURAL ENERGY PRODUCTION AND SUPPLY IN THE HUMID TROPICS
W. B. Morgan and R. P. Moss, United Nations University.

Volume 5: ECONOMIC APPROACHES TO NATURAL RESOURCE AND ENVIRONMENTAL QUALITY ANALYSIS
Maynard M. Hufschmidt and Eric L. Hyman, Editors, East-West Center.

Volume 6: RENEWABLE SOURCES OF ENERGY AND THE ENVIRONMENT
Essam El-Hinnawi and Asit K. Biswas, Editors.

Volume 7: GLOBAL ENVIRONMENTAL ISSUES
Essam El-Hinnawi, Editor, United Nations Environment Programme.

Volume 8: THE WORLD ENVIRONMENT 1972–1982
Martin Holdgate, Mohammed Kassas, Gilbert White, Editors; *Essam El-Hinnawi*, Study Director, United Nations Environment Programme.

Volume 9: ENERGY ALTERNATIVES IN LATIN AMERICA
Francisco Szekely, Editor. United Nations Environment Programme.

Volume 10: INTEGRATED PHYSICAL SOCIO-ECONOMIC AND ENVIRON-MENTAL PLANNING
Yusuf J. Ahmad, Editor. United Nations Environment Programme.

Volume 11: THIRD WORLD AND THE ENVIRONMENT
Essam El-Hinnawi and Asit K. Biswas, Editors.

Volume 12: DEVELOPMENT WITHOUT DESTRUCTION: EVOLVING ENVIRONMENTAL PERCEPTIONS
Mostafa K. Tolba.

Volume 13: LONG DISTANCE WATER TRANSFER IN CHINA
Asit K. Biswas, Zuo Da-kang, J. Nickum and Liu Chang-Ming. United Nations University.

The World Environment 1972 – 1982

A Report by
The United Nations Environment Programme

Edited by
MARTIN W. HOLDGATE
MOHAMMED KASSAS
GILBERT F. WHITE

with the assistance of
DAVID SPURGEON

Study Co-ordinator
ESSAM EL-HINNAWI

Published for the UNITED NATIONS ENVIRONMENT
    PROGRAMME
by TYCOOLY INTERNATIONAL PUBLISHING LIMITED,
    DUBLIN

HC
79
.E5
W668
1982 | 45,116

Tycooly International Publishing Ltd.
6, Crofton Terrace,
Dun Laoghaire,
Co. Dublin,
Ireland

First edition 1982

© Copyright 1982 UNITED NATIONS ENVIRONMENT PROGRAMME

Typeset by Brunswick Press Ltd., Dublin and
printed by Irish Elsevier Printers Ltd., Shannon, Ireland.

ISBN 0 907567 13 4 Hardback.
ISBN 0 907567 14 2 Flexicover.

CONTENTS

		Page
Contents		v
List of Tables		ix
List of Figures		xiii
Foreword		xv
Preface and Acknowledgements		xix
List of Contributors		xxiii
Editors' Preface		xxxi

Chapter 1	INTRODUCTION	1
	The Events Leading to the Stockholm Conference	4
	The Stockholm Conference	6
	The Stockholm Action Plan	8
	Developments since the Stockholm Conference	11
	References	17

Chapter 2	ATMOSPHERE	19
	The Atmosphere and Climate	22
	Atmospheric Trends over Recent Decades	30
	Observed changes in Climate over the Past Decade	51
	The Impacts of Climatic and Atmospheric Changes on Man	57
	Future Prospects	64
	References	67

Chapter 3	THE MARINE ENVIRONMENT	73
	The Physical, Chemical and Biological Features of the Oceans	75
	The State of the Marine Environment in the 1970s	78
	The Use and Conservation of Marine Resources	98
	International Action for Environmentally Sound Marine Development	105
	Future Prospects	109
	References	112

Chapter 4	INLAND WATERS	121
	Water Quantity: Supply and Demand	124
	Changes in Water Quality	139
	Changes in Fresh Water Biota	152
	Major New Water Bodies	156
	Planning, Legislation and Shared Water Resources	158
	Future Prospects	161
	References	164

		Page
Chapter 5	**LITHOSPHERE**	171
	The Geological Background	174
	The Occurrence and Nature of Mineral Resources	177
	Production of Minerals	183
	Environmental Impacts of Mineral Production	184
	Selected Trends and Issues in Mineral Resources in the 1970s	188
	Geological Hazards	199
	References	206
Chapter 6	**TERRESTRIAL BIOTA**	209
	Changing Impact of Man	212
	The Biomes of the World	217
	Zonobiomes and their Changes during the Decade	218
	Recent Actions to Conserve Terrestrial Biota	230
	Future Prospects	241
	References	245
Chapter 7	**AGRICULTURE, FORESTRY AND THE ENVIRONMENT**	249
	Agricultural and Forest Productivity	252
	Changes in Bioproductive Systems	265
	Environmental Effects of Agricultural Chemicals and Pollutants	277
	Losses in Food Production	286
	Future Prospects	290
	References	293
Chapter 8	**POPULATION**	299
	Demographic Trends of the 1970s	301
	International Migration	316
	People and Food	318
	People, Resources, Environment and Development: a Broadened View	320
	References	325
Chapter 9	**HUMAN SETTLEMENTS**	327
	Changes in Settlement Patterns	330
	Impacts of Urbanization	338
	Conditions of the People	341
	Public Action	345
	Future Prospects	352
	References	354
Chapter 10	**HEALTH AND THE ENVIRONMENT**	357
	Changes in Communicable Diseases During the Decade	363
	Pollution and Health	372

Cancer and Environmental Exposure   380
Nutrition and Health   386
Diseases Associated with Life-styles   391
Mental Health and the Environment   394
Future Prospects   396
References   399

Chapter 11   INDUSTRY   405
               Development of Environmental Concerns in Industry   408
               Developments in the 1970s   412
               A Cross-sectoral Overview   421
               Changes in Economic and Political Factors   428
               Environmental Considerations in the Location
                 of Industry   438
               Future Prospects   440
               References   444

Chapter 12   ENERGY AND THE ENVIRONMENT   447
               Energy Consumption and Economic Growth   449
               Energy and Environment   466
               Energy Conservation   487
               Future Prospects   489
               References   493

Chapter 13   TRANSPORT   499
               Transport Modes and Systems   501
               Trends in Transport during the 1970s   503
               The Impact of Transport on the Environment   517
               The Regulation and Management of Transport   530
               Future Prospects   537
               References   539

Chapter 14   TOURISM   543
               World Trends   545
               Economic and Cultural Aspects   549
               Environmental Aspects   552
               Future Prospects   555
               References   558

Chapter 15   ENVIRONMENTAL EDUCATION AND PUBLIC
                 UNDERSTANDING   561
               Environmental Education at the Pre-Primary and
                 Primary Levels   567
               Environmental Education at the Secondary Level   568
               Environmental Education at the University and
                 Professional Level   570
               Teacher Training   574

		Page
	Education and Public Participation	576
	Perceptions and Attitudes	579
	Future Prospects	585
	References	587
Chapter 16	PEACE AND SECURITY	591
	Environmental Impacts of War	594
	The Environmental Hazards of Possible Future Wars	605
	The Responses of the International Community	610
	Future Prospects	613
	References	616
Chapter 17	CONCLUSIONS	621
Index		633

List of Tables

Table   Page

1—1   Groupings of Recommendations in the Stockholm Action Plan   10
1—2   Topics Treated in Annual State of The Environment Reports   13
2—1   The Composition of the Atmosphere Near the Earth's Surface   23
2—2   Man-made Sulphur Dioxide Emissions for Various Classes of Sources in
       Selected Countries   32
2—3   Emission of Sulphur Dioxide by Regions by the Beginning of the 1970s   33
2—4   Estimated Emissions of Sulphur Dioxide and Particulates in 1978–1980   34
2—5   Suspended Particulate Matter Emissions to the Atmosphere from
       Different Sources   34
2—6   Average Concentrations of Suspended Particulate Matter (SPM) and
       Sulphur Dioxide (SO$_2$) During 1973–77 in Seven Cities   35
2—7   All-Time Worldwide Man-made Emissions of Trace Metals   43
2—8   Selected Extreme Atmospheric Events During the 1970s   55
3—1   Major Salt Constituents of Seawater   77
3—2   Sources of Pollution in Various Regions of the World Ocean   80
3—3   Estimated Inputs of Contaminants to the Oslo Commission Area   82
3—4   Estimated input of Contaminants to the Mediterranean   83
3—5   Concentrations of Contaminants in Various Oceanic and Inshore Waters   84
3—6   Metal Concentrations in Fish from Various North Atlantic and
       Mediterranean Waters   86
3—7   Mercury Concentrations in Fish from Various Waters   87
3—8   DDT and PCB Concentrations in Fish and Marine Mammals from
       Various Localities   88
3—9   Oil Spilled into Oceans Following Incidents Involving Tankers in which
       5,000 tonnes or more were shed   90
3—10 Comparison of Estimates for Petroleum Hydrocarbons Annually
       Entering the Ocean, 1969–1971   91
4—1   Average Annual Surface Run-off according to Different Sources   126
4—2   Increase of Water Withdrawal Over the World   131
4—3   Water Withdrawal and Consumption in the USSR and USA   133
4—4   Irrigated Areas in Major Regions   134
4—5   Estimated Service Coverage for Drinking Water Supply in
       Developing Countries 1970–1980   136
4—6   Water Supply Coverage, Urban and Rural, by Region for Countries
       Reporting Both in 1970 and 1980   136
4—7   Estimated Service Coverage for Sanitation in Developing Countries,
       1970–1980   137
4—8   Annual Mean Concentrations of Nitrates, in Selected Rivers, 1965–1975   141
4—9   Acidification of Soft-Water Lakes in Scandinavia and North America   142
5—1   Ratio of Cut-off Grade to Average Crustal Abundance for Selected Elements   176
5—2   Reserves and Resources of Selected Metals and Minerals, 1980   180
5—3   Production of Selected Non-Metallic Mineral Raw Materials, 1970–1980   184
5—4   World Production of Selected Minerals and Metals, 1970–1979   185
5—5   Major Mineral Producers in 1979   186
5—6   Recent Estimates of First Generation Mine Sites   189
5—7   Potential Contribution of Ocean Mining to World Supply in the
       Mid-1980s   190
5—8   Use Intensity of Mineral Materials in the USA in 1972   194
5—9   Estimated "Lifetimes" for Selected Metal Resources   195
5—10 Imports of Strategic Materials, USA, 1980   197
5—11 Price Trends for Selected Metals and Minerals, 1970–1980   198

Table		Page
5—12	Seismic Energies Released Worldwide and Earthquake Deaths During 1970–1980 compared with Previous Years	200
5—13	Volcanic Eruptions that caused more than 9 Deaths During 1970–1979	201
6—1	Multilateral Agreements Affecting Terrestrial Biota	231
6—2	Reserves in Tropical Rain Forest	234
6—3	Protected Areas in Zonobiomes	235
6—4	Nature Reserves in the USSR	240
7—1	Estimated Use of Ice-Free Land Surface of the World—1975	253
7—2	Areas Under Cultivation in Developing Countries	254
7—3	Projected Changes in World Land Use and Land Productivity	257
7—4	World Crop Production	258
7—5	World and Regional Indices of Food Production	259
7—6	World Forest Production	261
7—7	Growth in Value of Agricultural Production, 1970–1979	262
7—8	Estimates of Present Annual Global Rates of Soil Displacement	266
7—9	Distribution of Salinity and Alkalinity in Countries Most Extensively Affected	268
7—10	Arid Lands Affected by Desertification	272
7—11	World Fertilizer Production	279
7—12	World and Major Regional Fertilizer Consumption	280
7—13	Estimates and Projections of Minimum Post-Harvest Food Losses in Developing Countries	287
8—1	Population Trends in the Eight Major Areas of the World, 1950–2000	302
8—2	Average Annual Rate of Population Growth	303
8—3	Crude Birth Rate Decline, from 1965 to 1975 in 94 Developing Countries	311
8—4	Estimated Number of Refugees	319
9—1	Urban Populations of The World	331
9—2	Average Annual Growth Rates of Urban Populations	334
9—3	Proportions of Population Living in Urban Areas	334
9—4	Population and Number of Cities In a Particular Size Class	337
10—1	Life Expectancy at Birth by Region	361
10—2	Age-standardized Mortality Rates for Chronic Bronchitis and Emphysema for Various Countries	377
10—3	Aflatoxin Ingestion and Liver Cancer Incidence in some countries	384
10—4	Average Daily Energy Supply per Head	387
10—5	Estimated Proportion of People with Daily Energy Intake less than the Critical Limit	388
10—6	Age-standardized Death Rates for Lung Cancer 1965 and 1975	392
10—7	Age-standardized Mortality Rates for Coronary Heart Disease in Various Countries	393
11—1	Production of Chemicals and Apparent Consumption per Capita, Selected Countries	410
11—2	Some World Development Indicators	413
11—3	Average Annual Growth of Labour Force	414
11—4	Some Examples of Low- and Non-Waste Technologies	424
11—5	Costs and Benefits of Non-Waste Technologies	425
11—6	Some Examples of Recycling and Residue Utilization in Industry	427
11—7	Examples of Substitution of Resources	428
11—8	Percentage Price Increase in the USA due to Pollution Control	430
11—9	Pollution Abatement Costs in Ten Industrialized Countries	432
12—1	World Energy Consumption	456
12—2	Per Capita Energy Consumption	459

Table		Page
12—3	Fuel Consumption	459
12—4	Energy Source-Activity Matrix for Pura Village, India	460
12—5	World Resources of Solid Fossil Fuels	462
12—6	Cumulative Production, Reserves, Resources, and Ultimate Recovery of Oil	465
12—7	World Natural Gas Resources	467
12—8	Emissions From Fossil Fuel Operated Power Stations	469
12—9	World Annual Cumulative Requirements for Natural Uranium	473
12—10	World Hydropower	478
12—11	Estimate of Coastline Wind Potentials	481
12—12	Electricity Costs for a Typical Tanzanian Village	482
12—13	Capacity of Renewable Sources to Meet Forecast Demand in Western Europe	492
13—1	Freight Movement by Mode in Selected Countries	505
13—2	Merchant Shipping in the 1970s	515
13—3	World Movement of Oil by Sea	516
13—4	Total Road Networks	518
13—5	Energy Consumption in the Transport Sector	519
13—6	Illustrative Costs of Urban Travel by Different Modes	521
13—7	Representative Composition of Exhaust Gases (Heavy Vehicles)	522
13—8	Population Exposed to Aircraft and Road Traffic Noise	526
13—9	Road, Rail and Air Casualties in the United Kingdom, 1968–1978	528
13—10	EEC Automative Noise Legislation	533
14—1	Structure of International Tourism Arrivals	546
14—2	Growth of Internal and International Tourism in CMEA Countries	548
15—1	Pilot Projects in Environmental Education	565
16—1	Civilian Deaths and Displacements in Some Recent Major Wars	595
16—2	Public Expenditure on Education, Health and Foreign Economic Aid	601
16—3	The Potential Lethal Impact of Some Modern Weapons	606
16—4	The Environmental Impact of the One-Megaton Nuclear Explosion	607
16—5	Some Effects of Ground-Burst Nuclear Weapons Within 24 Hours of Detonation	608
16—6	Hostile Environmental Modification Techniques Feasible in 1980	609
16—7	The Principal International Arms-Regulation or Disarmament Agreements Currently in Force	614
16—8	International Arms-Regulation or Disarmament Agreements Under Active Negotiation or Awaiting Entry Into Force in 1980	615

List of Figures

Page

Figure 1–1 The framework of the Stockholm Action Plan 9
Figure 1–2 Theoretical relationship between damage costs, control costs and pollution abatement 15
Figure 2–1 Physical structure of the lower atmosphere 24
Figure 2–2 Schematic illustration of the climatic system 27
Figure 2–3 Annual mean concentration of sulphate in precipitation in Europe 39
Figure 2–4 Excess sulphate at two groups of Scandinavian EACN stations 40
Figure 2–5 Long-term variations of annual concentrations of nitrates in precipitation 41
Figure 2–6 Isopleths showing annual average pH for precipitation in eastern North America 42
Figure 2–7 Maximum in the stratospheric aerosol mixing ratios versus time from balloon soundings at Laramie, Wyoming 46
Figure 2–8 Mauna Loa monthly averages of atmospheric CO_2 concentrations 48
Figure 2–9 The annual release of CO_2 to the atmosphere by the combustion of fossil fuels, cement production and the flaring of natural gas 50
Figure 2–10 Temperature variation for Northern and Southern Hemispheres and the World as a whole 52
Figure 2–11 Smoothed time series of mean difference in thickness between 1000 and 5000 MB pressure surfaces for area of Earth North of 25°N 53
Figure 3–1 Marine pollution around the World 93
Figure 3–2 The global catches of Sperm, Minke, Sei, Fin and other whales 103
Figure 3–3 Geographic coverage of UNEP Regional Seas Programme 108
Figure 4–1 Distribution of withdrawals among major categories of water uses; selected countries, 1965 132
Figure 4–2 Acidification of Norwegian and Swedish lakes 143
Figure 4–3 Domestic waste water treatment; selected countries, 1965–1975 145
Figure 4–4 Annual mean levels of biological oxygen demand (BOD), selected rivers, 1965–1975 148
Figure 4–5 Annual mean concentration of nitrates, selected rivers, 1965–1975. 149
Figure 4–6 Inland water fishery landings, 1970–1976 155
Figure 5–1 Tectonic map of Earth showing boundaries of major lithospheric plates 175
Figure 5–2 Scrap metals recycled; USA data for 1974 and UK data for 1978. 192
Figure 5–3 Major destructive earthquakes 1970–1979 202
Figure 6–1 World desertification map 222
Figure 7–1 Changes in manpower, farm machinery and use of commercial fertilizers, 1965–1975 263
Figure 7–2 World fertilizer consumption 279
Figure 8–1 Growth of World population and shares of more developed, and less developed regions, 1800–2000 304
Figure 8–2 World population density 306
Figure 8–3 Birth and death rates and population increase 308
Figure 8–4 Percentage decline in crude birth rate, 1950–1955 through 1975. 309
Figure 8–5 Distribution of population, 1970–2000 314
Figure 8–6 Population growth by sex and age groups, 1970–2000. 315
Figure 9–1 Trends in urbanization 332
Figure 9–2 Regional trends of urbanization 335
Figure 9–3 Rural population, 1950–2000, in major areas 336
Figure 10–1 Relationship between life expectancy at birth and GNP; 1975 362
Figure 12–1 World consumption of commercial energy 450
Figure 12–2 Relationship between GNP and per capita commercial energy consumption 451

Figure 12–3 Relation between GNP per capita and energy consumption in the USA, 1972–1978   452
Figure 12–4 Oil prices, 1972–1980   453
Figure 12–5 Commercial energy consumption   457
Figure 12–6 Per capita commercial energy consumption   458
Figure 12–7 Proved World recoverable oil reserves   464
Figure 12–8 World oil production, 1960–1979   466
Figure 12–9 New nuclear reactors ordered per year   472
Figure 12–10 Average radiation exposure from different sources   474
Figure 12–11 Average annual dose to the population of the UK   475
Figure 13–1 Some of the main interactions in transport   502
Figure 13–2 Transport-land relationship   503
Figure 13–3 Growth in railway traffic   506
Figure 13–4 Growth in World motor vehicles   508
Figure 13–5 Regional growth of passenger cars   509
Figure 13–6 Growth of passenger cars/1000 population in different regions   510
Figure 13–7 Total length of oil pipeline in Europe   512
Figure 13–8 Merchant shipping fleets   512
Figure 13–9 Growth of international and domestic air passenger traffic   513
Figure 13–10 International and domestic air transport of goods in the 1970s   516
Figure 13–11 The traffic noise system   524
Figure 13–12 Percentage changes in the total of injury accidents between 1975 and 1979   529
Figure 14–1 Growth of international tourism   547
Figure 14–2 Components of the Obergurgl Model   557
Figure 15–1 Environmentally oriented articles in periodicals between 1953 and 1969   580
Figure 15–2 New York Times articles dealing with environmental topics.   581
Figure 15–3 Awareness of environmental issues   582
Figure 16–1 World military expenditure   598
Figure 16–2 The importers and exporters of major weapons, 1970–1979   599
Figure 16–3 Military expenditure and productivity   602

Foreword

THERE is no doubt that since the United Nations Conference on the Human Environment convened in Stockholm in 1972 there have been considerable changes in our understanding and perception of environmental issues. Most of the attention devoted to environmental matters previously had been mainly concerned with direct assaults on human welfare and, more particularly, with acute rather than chronic manifestations. Land and natural resources had been exploited without restraint; and wastes discharged freely into air and water, which nobody owned. The 1970s brought into focus the general realization that the different physical components of the environment have limited assimilative and carrying capacities and that pollution control measures must be instituted to safeguard the environment and the quality of human life. More important has been the growing realization that the natural environmental resources of water, soil, plant and animal life constitute the natural capital on which man depends to satisfy his needs and achieve his aspirations for development. The wise management of these resources has demanded positive and realistic planning that balances human needs against the potential the environment has for meeting them.

It is gratifying to note that environmental policies are no longer focussing simply on the control of pollution and the abatement of nuisances but indeed on more positive actions directed at the improvement of the quality of life that depends on the health and viability of the natural and man-made environments. Preventive rather than curative actions have been gaining momentum and wide acceptance. Good management avoids pollution and the wastage of resources by irreversible damage; to prevent such types of environmental degradation is more challenging and certainly more efficient than to redress them after they have occurred.

The 1970s brought into focus the importance of international co-operation – which may be regional, between groups of developing countries "South-South Linkages" or between developed and developing countries "North-South Linkages"—not only to solve world development problems but also to safeguard the environment for future generations. It is true that countries are at many stages of development with different economic, social and environmental priorities. But it is not enough to deduce that poverty defiles the environment in many developing regions; it is necessary to know exactly how this happens – and how over-consumption creates other threats elsewhere. Moreover, nations are not isolated; the actions of one country may affect the environment in a neighbouring one. The ratification in the 1970s of a number of international and regional conventions on matters relating to the environment is an encouraging sign on the road of international co-operation. The interest Governments have shown in environmental matters, demonstrated by the establishment of national environmental machineries in many countries and by the enforcement of environmental protection measures, is further evidence of concern for environmentally-sound development.

Since its establishment in 1972, the United Nations Environment Programme has been keeping under review the world environmental situation to ensure that environmental problems of wide significance receive appropriate consideration. In this respect, UNEP has produced over the past years a number of in-depth reviews of different environmental subjects and an annual State of the Environment Report which concentrated on selected emerging topics. On the occasion of the tenth anniversary of Stockholm, in 1982. I found it appropriate to take stock of the developments of the 1972–1982 decade and to undertake a major study analysing the changes that have taken place in the human environment over this period. As I pointed out in the 1977 State of the Environment Report, 1982 will be for the United Nations Environment Programme a year of audit. We need to evaluate carefully and critically the problems that have been solved during the past ten years, the others that have appeared, and above all the effectiveness of the World's community at international, regional and national level in dealing with these matters.

The present volume is the result of an extensive effort undertaken over the past four years to review the state of the world environment in the decade after Stockholm. The effort has been a truly international one and there are few countries or relevant intergovernmental bodies within or outside the United Nations system that have not participated at some stage or other. The important thing for me to stress here is that it is a *scientific* volume, not a formal intergovernmental report, and for this reason the participants have interacted as individual specialists arguing over the validity of their conclusions, and the meaning to be attached to data. This process of debate does not lead to certainty; indeed it frequently reveals far greater weaknesses in knowledge and analysis than would the formal process of compilation of an intergovernmental policy report. It is however a uniquely valuable way to assemble a truly world–wide document. In this respect, I must emphasize that it has never been our intention to present an encyclopaedic study; the main focus has been on the changes (positive and/or negative) that occurred in the different components of the environment with particular attention to the interacting processes between these components. I hope that this Study will be found to give a balanced assessment of the world environmental situation as viewed by the United Nations organ responsible for the safety of the environment at the global level. In this connection the gaps in the report may prove of even greater importance than the areas where coverage of information is complete. Ten years after Stockholm it is clear that we still have a very imperfect knowledge of the state of the major components of our environment and of the interacting mechanisms. It is my sincere hope that the scientific community will pick up these inadequacies and accelerate the efforts to fill these gaps. In this respect, it is appreciated that several policy-makers faced with long-term environmental problems often argue that they cannot afford to worry about the remote and abstract when surrounded by the immediate and concrete: that potential climatic and genetic instabilities are of academic interest in a world full of actual war, famine, disease and ignorance. This thesis cannot be fully accepted. The problems which overwhelm us today are precisely those which, through a similar approach we failed to solve decades ago; problems which have built-in perpetual and responsive delays of many years. These delays ensure that such an approach can only defer or disguise problems, not solve them.

Many scientists participated in this Study either by contributing background reports or by taking part in the review of the different drafts—or both. To all of them, I would like to express my gratitude. My appreciation goes also to the Governments, United Nations bodies, Inter-governmental and non-governmental organizations and to the scientific institutions that provided information and/or helped in the review process. Special thanks are due to the Senior Scientific Advisory Board which formulated the contents of the Study and followed it throughout with most valuable suggestions and contributions. My deep gratitude goes to Martin W. Holdgate, Mohammed Kassas and Gilbert F. White who went far beyond the normal editorial process and indeed re-wrote large sections of the text.

Mostafa Kamal Tolba
Executive Director
United Nations Environment Programme

Nairobi, December 1981

Preface and Acknowledgements

ONE of the main functions of the Governing Council of the United Nations Environment Programme as directed by the General Assembly of the United Nations in its resolution 2997 (XXVII) of 15 December, 1972 is to:

"Keep under review the world environmental situation in order to ensure that emerging environmental problems of wide international significance receive appropriate and adequate consideration."

To assist in this task the Executive Director of UNEP was requested to prepare each year a report on the state of the environment.

At the fourth sesion of the Governing Council (1976), the Executive Director of UNEP pointed out that it would be more meaningful to restrict the annual state of the environment reports to some selected emerging issues and to carry out a comprehensive assessment of the state of the global environment every five years. The Governing Council endorsed this suggestion and it was decided that the first comprehensive report should cover the period from 1972 to 1982, i.e. ten years after the United Nations Conference on the Human Environment held in Stockholm.

The present Study has, therefore, been undertaken with the following main objective: "assessment of the state of the world environment in the decade after the Stockholm Conference". It attempts to identify, analyse and interpret the different changes in various aspects of the environment and environmental situations, according to available information. It displays the interrelationships among the different aspects of the subject and identifies trends which would indicate current and possible future changes in the different ecosystems.

In order to carry out this Study, the Executive Director of UNEP established in 1978 a Senior Scientific Advisory Board (SSAB) to advise the UNEP Secretariat on the approach and the implementation of the project. The members of the SSAB were:

Asit K. Biswas
Director, Biswas and Associates
Oxford

Frank Fenner
Australian National University
Canberra

Martin W. Holdgate
Chief Scientist
Departments of the Environment
and Transport
London

Mohammed Kassas
Professor of Botany
Cairo University
Cairo

Y. A. Mageed
Associated Consultants
Khartoum

David Munro
Former Director-General
IUCN
Gland, Switzerland

B. D. Nagchaudhuri
Professor of Physics
Saha Institute of Nuclear Physics
Calcutta

I. Nazarov
Professor
Institute of Applied Geophysics
Moscow

T. Odhiambo
Director
International Centre of Insect
   Physiology and Ecology
Nairobi

Leon de Rosen
Former Director
UNEP Industry Programme
Paris

C. Suarez
Professor
Instituto de Economia Energetica
San Carlos de Bariloche
Argentina

T. Suzuki
Deputy Director-General
Institute of Public Health
Tokyo

A. Buzzati-Traverso
Senior Advisor
UNEP

G. F. White
Professor of Geography
Institute of Behavioural Science
Boulder, Colorado

A detailed plan of the Study was formulated in 1978 by the SSAB with contributions from some experts. In accordance with the Study Plan a number of institutions and experts were selected by the Executive Director in 1979 to prepare background reports on different subjects. The hardest work — the consolidation of these background reports or their revised versions into a single draft — was done by the Editors of this volume, assisted by David Spurgeon of the State of the Environment Reports Unit of UNEP. In addition, the Editors themselves prepared drafts of the introductory and concluding chapters. The background papers were reviewed by a number of experts; the consolidated draft was reviewed by a number of United Nations and other organizations and was circulated to all governments for comments. The Study benefitted enormously from the contributions and comments received. Furthermore, the consolidated draft was reviewed at an International Workshop convened in Nairobi from 16 to 27 March, 1981.

The names of the contributors, reviewers and those who participated at the Workshop are given on the following pages.

A great deal of credit goes to the Editors of this volume who brought the pieces of the Study together in final form. I was personally responsible for drafting six background reports for the Study and for revising and putting into shape the final manuscript for publication. Dr. Manzur H. Hashmi and Mr. Edmundo F. Ortega of the State of the Environment Reports Unit (UNEP) helped greatly in the organization of the different meetings of the SSAB and the International Workshop and in the different stages of the preparation of the different drafts and final manuscript. P. Ayew, A. Fernandez, N. Hansraj, J. Kanza, W. Musani and G. Njoroge were responsible for typing the different drafts and the final manuscript and managed to work with admirable patience under endless pressures; their efforts are gratefully acknowledged.

Grateful acknowledgements are due to Cambridge University Press, World Energy Conference, W. H. Freeman and Co., D. Reidel Publishing Co., Royal Swedish Academy of Sciences, OECD, Rand McNally and Co., Chicago, American Association for Advancement of Sciences, International Road Federation and the Stockholm International Peace Research Institute for permissions to redraw and use figures and tables from their publications.

Essam El-Hinnawi
Study Co-ordinator
Chief, State of the Environment Reports Unit
United Nations Environment Programme

Nairobi, October 1981.

List of Contributors

I Contributors to the Study Plan, Background Reports and Revised Texts

I. H. Abdel Rahman
Advisor to the Prime Minister
Cairo

M. Alamgir
Visiting Fellow
Harvard Institute for
     International Development

M. Alexander
Professor of Agronomy
Cornell University
Ithaca, U.S.A.

H. Z. Benitez
Philippine Women's University
Metro Manila

M. E. Berlyand
Institute of Applied Geophysics
Moscow

V. G. Boldyrev
Institute of Applied Geophysics
Moscow

M. I. Budyko
Institute of Applied Geophysics
Moscow

R. C. Bunker
South Australian Institute of Technology
Adelaide, Australia

CEFIGRE
Centre de Formation Internationale a la
Gestion des Ressources en Eau Valbonne,
France

Essam El-Hinnawi
United Nations Environment Programme
Nairobi

L. M. Filippova
Institute of Applied Geophysics
Moscow

G. Fresco
Turconsult Italia
Rome

G. Gallopin
Fundacion Bariloche
San Carlos de Bariloche
Argentina

R. Gambell
Secretary, International Whaling
     Commission

K. von Gehlen
Professor, Institut für Geochemie
     Petrologie und Lagerstättenkunde
Frankfurt M.

G. Goodman
Director
Beijer Institute
Stockholm

C. N. Gruza
Institute of Applied Geophysics
Moscow

M. N. Htun
UNEP Industry Programme
Paris

IUCN
International Union for Conservation of
  Nature and Natural Resources
Gland, Switzerland

Yu A. Izrael
Institute of Applied Geophysics
Moscow

A. Jedraszko
Research Institute for
Environmental Development
Warsaw

I. L. Karol
Institute of Applied Geophysics
Moscow

R. L. Kintanar
Director, PAGASA
Quezon City
The Philippines

K. V. Krishnamurthy
Director, Hydro-consult Intern.
New Delhi

G. Kullenberg
Professor of Physical Oceanography
University of Copenhagen

A. Laquian
Professor, College of
  Public Administration
University of the Philippines
Metro Manila

J. W. M. La Riviere
International Institute for
  Hydraulic and Environmental
  Engineering
Delft, The Netherlands

C. E. Law
Executive Director
Canadian Institute of
  Guided Ground Transport
Queen's Univ., Kingston, Ontario

London School of Hygiene
and Tropical Medicine

Y. Mageed
Associated Consultants
Khartoum, Sudan

R. E. Munn
Institute for Environmental Studies
University of Toronto

B. D. Nagchaudhuri
Saha Institute of Nuclear Physics
Calcutta

M. Naito
National Institute for Environmental Studies
Japan Environment Agency
Tokyo

S. H. Ominde
University of Nairobi
Kenya

M. E. D. Poore
Professor
Department of Forest Science
Oxford University

V. A. Popov
Institute of Applied Geophysics
Moscow

L. de Rosen
Former Director, UNEP Industry
  Programme,
Paris

F. Ya. Rovinsky
Institute of Applied Geophysics
Moscow

M. G. Royston
Centre d'Etudes Industrielles
Conches-Geneva

A. G. Ryaboshapko
Institute of Applied Geophysics
Moscow

I. Sachs
International Research Centre
on Environment and Development
Paris-Cedex

J. F. Talling
Freshwater Biological Association,
Ambleside, United Kingdom

United Nations Centre for Disarmamemt
New York

M. Waldichuk
West Vancouver Marine Lab.
Canada

K. J. Walton
Office of Secretariat Services for
Social and Economic Matters
United Nations, New York

A. Williams
Department of Pathology
University College
Ibadan, Nigeria

A. F. Yuakovlev
Institute of Applied Geophysics
Moscow

II Workshop Participants and Reviewers

J. Amyot
Chulalongkorn University
Bangkok

A. A. Arbatov
USSR Commission for UNEP
Moscow

C. Averous
OECD
Paris

F. Barnaby
Stockholm International Peace
Research Institute (SIPRI)

S. Bergstrom
Karolinska Institute
Stockholm

R. J. H. Beverton
The Royal Society
London

C. F. Bird
University of Melbourne
Victoria, Australia

A. K. Biswas
Director, Biswas and Associates
Oxford

B. Bolin
Professor of Meteorology
University of Stockholm

E. Bordas-Rubies
Consultur
Barcelona

M. Boutros-Ghali
UNDP
New York

D. J. Bradley
London School of Tropical Medicine

J. Bugnicourt
ENDA
Dakar, Senegal

R. C. Bunker
South Australian Institute
  of Technology
Adelaide, S. Australia

Y. Burmistrov
UNIDO
Vienna

D. R. Cawthorne
Transport and Road Research Lab.
United Kingdom

D. F. Cornelius
Department of Transport
London

I. Corpuz
College of Agriculture
University of Philippines
Los Banos
Laguna

C. Costa Ribeiro
Centro de Technologia Promon
Rio de Janeiro

P. J. Crutzen
Max Planck Institut für Chemie
Mainz
Federal Republic of Germany

R. Davies
Department of Transport
London

L. H. Day
Research School of Social Science
Australian National University
Canberra

R. Dickinson
National Centre for Atmospheric
  Research
Boulder, Colorado

E. Eckholm
IIED
Washington, D.C.

P. R. Ehrlich
Leland Stanford University
Stanford, California

Essam El-Hinnawi
United Nations Environment Programme
Nairobi

I. Everson
British Antarctic Survey
Cambridge, United Kingdom

R. Frosch
Former Administrator, NASA
USA

D. S. Galanos
Department of Food Chemistry
National University of Athens
Athens, Greece

R. Gambell
International Whaling Commission

R. Geldiay
University of EGE
Izmir, Turkey

I. P. Gerasimov
USSR Commission for UNEP
Moscow

F. B. Golley
National Science Foundation
Washington, D.C.

G. Goodman
Beijer Institute
Stockholm

S. Gotoh
National Institute for Environmental Studies
Environment Agency of Japan
Tsukuba Ibaraki

K. Grasshoff
Institut für Meereskunde
Kiel
Federal Republic of Germany

N. J. Graves
Institute of Education
University of London

Lim Guan Soon
Malaysian Agriculture Research
    and Development Institute
Serdang, Selangor
Malaysia

L. E. Herrera
Centro de Investigacion
    y Desarrollo
Filial de Petroleos de Venezuela
Los Teques, Edo Miranda
Venezuela

M. W. Holdgate
Chief Scientist
Departments of Environment and
    Transport
London

M. Hudec
Federal Ministry of Technological
Development and Investments
Prague

K. H. Ir Yap
Centre for Management and
Industrial Development
Rotterdam

Y. A. Isakov
Institute of Geography
USSR Academy of Sciences
Moscow

P. Jacobs
Faculté de l'Amenagément
Universite de Montréal
Montreal

J. G. James
Department of Transport
London

J. N. R. Jeffers
Institute of Terrestrial Ecology
Grange-over-Sands
Cumbria, United Kingdom

M. A. Karim
Director
Environment Pollution Control
    Department
Dacca, Bangladesh

K. Kartawinata
National Biological Institute
Bogor, Indonesia

M. Kassas
Department of Botany
Faculty of Science
Cairo University

W. W. Kellogg
National Centre for
  Atmospheric Research
Boulder, Colorado

A. Keynan
Hebrew University
Jerusalem

H. C. Kim
Planning and Co-ordination Bureau
Office of the Environment
Seoul

A. King
IFIAS
Paris

V. Kodat
Ministry of Health
Prague

L. A. Kosinski
Department of Geography
University of Alberta
Edmonton, Canada

J. Kostrowicki
Institute of Geography and
  Spatial Organization
Warsaw

V. A. Kovda
Institute of Agrochemistry
  and Soil Science
USSR Academy of Sciences
Moscow

S. Krishnaswamy
School of Biological Sciences
Madurai Kamaraj University
Madurai, India

P. Lagos
National Council for Physical
  Planning and Environment
Athens

J. W. M. La Riviere
International Institute for
  Hydraulic and Environmental
  Engineering
Delft, The Netherlands

Lin Feng
Research Institute of Petroleum
  Processing
Peking

R. C. Loehr
Environment Studies Programme
Cornell University
Ithaca, New York

Y. A. Mageed
Associated Consultants
Khartoum

W. H. Mathews
Environment and Policy Institute
East-West Centre
Honolulu

W. J. Maunder
New Zealand Meteorological Service
Wellington, New Zealand

D. Munro
Former Director-General
IUCN

B. D. Nagchaudhuri
Saha Institute of Nuclear Physics
Calcutta

M. Naito
National Institute for Environmental Studies
Environment Agency of Japan
Tsukuba Ibaraki

I. Nazarov
USSR Commission for UNEP
Moscow

R. A. Novikov
USSR Commission for UNEP
Moscow

M. Numata
Faculty of Science
Chiba University
Chiba-Shi, Japan

J. S. Oguntoyinbo
Faculty of Social Sciences
University of Ibadan
Ibadan, Nigeria

D. Pimentel
Cornell University
Ithaca, New York

A. Podniesinski
Institute of Environment and Development
Warsaw

Ph. Polk
Laboratorium voor Ekologie en Systematiek
Vrije Univ. Brussel
Brussel

J. G. Port
Department of Transport
London

J. Prats-Llaurado
FAO
Rome

A. Preston
Fisheries Laboratory
Lowestoft
United Kingdom

S. Z. Qasim
National Institute of Oceanography
Dona Paula
Goa, India

R. Risebrough
University of California

F. Y. Robinsky
Institute of Applied Geophysics
Moscow

L. de Rosen
UNEP Industry Programme
Paris

D. Rudd
Department of Transport
London

A. M. Ryabchikov
Moscow State University

I. Sachs
International Research Centre
   on Environmental and Development
Paris-Cedex

F. Sai
University of Ghana
Legon, Accra

B. Schuster
Federal Ministry of Interior
Bonn

A. K. Sharma
Department of Botany
University of Calcutta
Calcutta, India

V. G. Sokolovsky
USSR Commission for UNEP
Moscow

W. Stapp
School of Natural Resources
University of Michigan
Ann Arbor, Michigan

Y. A. Starikov
USSR Commission for UNEP
Moscow

F. B. Straub
Institute of Biochemistry
Budapest

J. O. Stromberg
Marine Biological Station
Kristineberg, Sweden

C. Suarez
Instituto de Economia Energetica
San Carlos de Bariloche
Argentina

M. S. Swaminathan
Ministry of Agriculture and
Irrigation
New Delhi

K. Szesztay
Institute for Water Management
Budapest

J. F. Talling
Freshwater Biological Association
Far Sawrey, Ambleside
Cumbria, United Kingdom

D. Thery
International Research Centre on
Environment and Development
Paris-Cedex

N. Tuntawiroon
Faculty of Environment and
Resource Studies
Mahidol University
Bangkok

J. R. Vallentyne
Canadian Centre for Inland Waters
Burlington, Ontario
Canada

F. Vallespinos Riera
Fisheries Research Institute
Barcelona

W. J. Veening
Ministry of Health and
  Environmental Protection
Leidschendam
The Netherlands

A. K. Ventura
Scientific Research Council
Kingston, Jamaica

M. Waldichuk
West Vancouver Marine Lab.
West Vancouver, Canada

A. H. Westing
School of Natural Science
Hampshire College
Amherst, Massachusetts

G. F. White
Institute of Behavioural Science
Boulder, Colorado

F. E. Wielgolaski
Botanical Laboratory
University of Oslo

J. de Wilde
Agricultural University
Wageningen, The Netherlands

A. Williams
Department of Pathology
University College Hospital
Ibadan, Nigeria

J. Williams
Climate Consultant
Karlsruhe
Federal Republic of Germany

G. Woldeghiorghis
National Energy Commission
Addis Ababa

P. C. Wood
Fisheries Laboratory
Lowestoft
United Kingdom

M. M. Zahran
Beirut Arab University
Beirut, Lebanon

A. Zaitsev
WMO
Geneva

Editors' Preface

THE Senior Scientific Advisory Board (SSAB) (see Preface and Acknowledgements) recommended that this Report should not only contain chapters dealing with sectors of the physical environment such as the atmosphere, oceans and seas, or inland waters but also cover human populations, health and settlements and the many activities by which people altered the environment. Conceptual aspects – such as the nature of basic human needs or of environmental quality – were to be considered alongside physical, biological and technical issues. It was agreed at the outset that the Report must focus on the changes that had taken place since the Stockholm Conference and should not provide the kind of descriptions of environmental systems available in any good textbook. Only short background descriptions should be included, to the extent necessary for the interpretation of changes. Wherever possible, changes were to be quantified – in terms of their geographical scale, regional variation, rate, and variation during the decade. The causes of change were to be described, natural and man-made factors being distinguished wherever possible. It was recognized that if it was to be in the hands of the readers by early 1982 – in time for the Session of Special Character to be held that year by the Governing Council of UNEP – the Report would have to be completed by mid-1981, and could not deal with events after 1980. In order to provide a decade of coverage, the period between 1970 and 1979 (with such information as became available for 1980) was chosen. It was also recognized that while changes in this period should receive special emphasis, they would need to be placed in context by discussion of the sequence of events over earlier decades, and indeed, in some cases would prove to be part of longer trends or cycles covering centuries or millenia.

As Editors, we have endeavoured to follow the original guidelines laid down by the SSAB. This report is neither a textbook nor an encyclopedia. Where it describes features of the world like the layers of the atmosphere, the circulation of the oceans or the aggregation of land plants and animals into biomes, this is so that the pattern of change and human impact can be understood. It is selective in its choice of examples, concentrating on global or regional international phenomena: for this reason numerous pieces of information about the situation in individual countries have been omitted. Nor is the book a chronicle of environmental events: indeed we have deliberately excluded accounts of important but well-known environmental events like the mercury poisoning at Minamata or the London smogs that belong to decades before the 1970s.

The Editors cannot manufacture data where none exist, and cannot hope to know about all the many subjects covered in a review of this breadth. We have had to rely on colleagues – fellow members of the SSAB, contributors to the study, Workshop participants, reviewers and UNEP staff – to supply statistical and other data for inclusion. Likewise, while we have made an effort to include as much relevant information as possible from countries outside Europe and North America, our ability to do so has been limited by the data supplied to us by such colleagues or by Governments. We have used most of the high-quality numerical information about trends that was supplied to us. We have made a point of indicating the origins of such data through bibliographic references, although we must stress that time has not allowed us personally to check all these original sources to ensure that every quotation or interpretation is valid. We have had to rely on the accuracy of statements transmitted by Governments and individuals, only querying with them or with scientific authorities those that were inconsistent, contradictory or apparently at variance with the general body of scientific understanding. We have, however, been cautious about accepting assertions that were not supported by references especially when they did not appear compatible with other evidence that was traceable to its primary sources. If there are some gaps in coverage of important issues this is because we did not have information on which we felt we could rely to fill them.

In one sense, however, our work has involved much more than scientific editing commonly implies. At the outset, the Executive Director of UNEP and the SSAB determined that the Report should not exceed some 700 pages in length. The volume of textual and tabular material supplied to us was more than twice that length. Condensation has therefore occupied a great deal of our time, and the process has involved the rewriting of almost all the text, some parts of it several times over. We have made every endeavour to retain the balance and scientific judgement of expert contributions, but recognize that in shortening and simplifying we may from time to time have allowed distortions to occur. We accept that the final text is our responsibility.

No group of three individuals could have done this work unaided. We are glad to take this opportunity of thanking all those colleagues, whose names appear in the lists given on previous pages, for the enormous help they have given us. We trust they will forgive us if we give especial mention here to the support and encouragement we have received throughout from Dr Mostafa K. Tolba, Executive Director of UNEP, the Study Co-ordinator, Dr Essam El-Hinnawi (with his colleagues Dr Manzur H. Hashmi and Mr Edmundo F. Ortega) and our Assistant Editor David Spurgeon who has ensured editorial conformity between texts prepared in parallel on three continents, and interchanged on various time scales at the whim of the world's telecommunications and postal services!

Martin W. Holdgate
Mohammed Kassas
Geneva, August 1981   *Gilbert F. White*

CHAPTER 1

Introduction

THIS volume reviews the state of knowledge about changes in the world environment since 1970. It concentrates on events known to have occurred. While the final section of each Chapter looks at the implications of what happened in the 1970s, the Report is not primarily concerned with forecasting (or speculating about) the future.

It is in three parts. The first (Chapters 2 to 7) is concerned with sectors of the physical environment – the atmosphere, marine waters, inland waters, the lithosphere and the minerals it supplies, the life of the land and the production of food, fibre, timber and fuel by agriculture and forestry. Trends in pollution, productivity, human use and other major features are noted: environment systems are evaluated and the actions taken nationally and internationally to safeguard the environment are described. The second part of the volume (Chapters 8, 9 and 10) looks directly at the human situation: at population distribution and growth, the changing patterns of health and disease and human settlements. Finally, the third part (Chapters 11 to 14) reviews the major human activities affecting the environment: industrial development, the generation and use of energy, transport and tourism. It is evident that the process of environmentally sound development demands not only improvement in the wealth of a community but also education so that better practices can be introduced. Environmental education and public understanding are therefore reviewed in Chapter 15. It is also evident that peace and security are vital if development is to proceed, and that preparations for war are currently wasting resources that, if redeployed, could do much to remedy poverty and improve the environment of millions of people. These issues are discussed in Chapter 16.

The duality of the human situation was summed up by Ward and Dubos (1972) in their book *Only one Earth*, written as background for the United Nations Conference on the Human Environment held in Stockholm in 1972:

"Man inhabits two worlds. One is the natural world of plants and animals, of soils and airs and waters which preceded him by billions of years and of which he is a part. The other is the world of social institutions and artefacts he builds for himself, using his tools and engines, his science and his dreams to fashion an environment obedient to human purpose and direction."

The last ten years have emphasised that development cannot be secured without conservation or conservation without development. That is the central message of the World Conservation Strategy written near the end of the period reviewed in this volume (IUCN/UNEP/WWF, 1980). The concept of *environment* and the pattern of action – national and international – to safeguard it, evolved in the years leading up to the Stockholm Conference, were given new form and direction there, and have continued to develop subsequently. Much of the remainder of this Introduction is devoted to tracing this evolution. Brief summaries stand at the head of each Chapter, while Chapter 17 draws general conclusions from the whole volume.

The Events Leading to the Stockholm Conference

THE international 'environmental movement' that generated the Stockholm Conference has a long history and no sharp beginning. In part, it is the successor to the great voyages of discovery and exploration that made people aware of the shape of the world and the diversity of its lands and waters, rocks, vegetation, faunas and cultures. Another of its roots is in international science, which gained strength during the 1960s and 1970s. The International Geophysical Year (IGY) of 1957-58 gave international cooperation a major impetus, because it demonstrated conclusively that world-wide scientific problems could be tackled successfully in this way – and that, indeed, there was no other way to secure simultaneous worldwide observations of the upper atmosphere or the co-ordinated study of remote areas like the Antarctic, where the geological, geophysical, meteorological and biological research programmes of fourteen nations have since been coordinated by the Scientific Committee on Antarctic Research (SCAR). The IGY was also the direct inspiration of the International Biological Programme (IBP) which ran between 1964 and 1974 and had as its central theme 'biological productivity and human welfare'. Much of the understanding of world environmental systems which underlies the reviews in the chapters of the present volume developed during these international programmes, or related ones. These latter included the Upper Mantle Project (1964–70), which yielded new insights into the properties of the lithosphere (Chapter 5), the Global Atmospheric Research Programme (1970–80), a joint effort between the World Meteorological Organization (WMO) and the International Council of Scientific Unions (ICSU) (highly relevant to Chapter 2) and the various projects of the ICSU Scientific Committee on Problems of the Environment (SCOPE) (reviewed, with other ICSU environmental activities, by Holdgate and White, 1977). The United Nations Educational, Scientific and Cultural Organization (UNESCO) programme on Man and the Biosphere (MAB) – (operational since 1970) – and the programmes of the Food and Agriculture Organization of the United Nations (FAO), the World Health Organization (WHO), the United Nations Environment Programme (UNEP), WMO, the United Nations Regional Commissions, and the International Union for the Conservation of Nature and Natural· Resources (IUCN) have also brought substantial advances in understanding.

The other major evolution in recent years has been in the wider public's appreciation of environmental issues. In the developed countries – the USA, USSR, and many Western European nations – a conservation movement appeared in the last decade of the nineteenth and first decades of the twentieth centuries. It was concerned with both the efficient management of natural resources and the preservation of natural habitats and human monuments. National forestry and agriculture societies provided a forum for the first kind of activity, while the second was stimulated by bodies like the Moscow Society of Nature Investigators (USSR), the National Audubon Society, Wilderness Society and Sierra Club (USA), the National Trust (UK) and the societies that now make up the Fédération Française des Sociétés de Protection de la Nature, the Landelijk Milieu Overleg (Netherlands) and their Swedish, Swiss and Federal German counterparts.

But the widening of the 'environment movement' in the second half of the twentieth century brought three developments of major importance. First, the scientific and nature protection components grew together, especially under the influence of professional ecologists. Second, appreciation of the environment grew in many countries outside Europe and North America. Third, and most important, the character of the approach changed (Morrison et al., 1972). A much broader conception of the environment was adopted. The movement became concerned with all aspects of the natural environment: land, water, minerals, all living organisms and life processes, the atmosphere and climate, the polar icecaps and remote ocean deeps, and even space. It also turned towards the human situation, at the level both of whole communities and of individual needs for housing and living, and emphasized the relationship between man-made and natural environments.

This new movement had a broader and scientifically more sophisticated perception of the relationship between man and environment. Not only was it concerned with the condition of natural resources but with values, institutions, technology, social organization, and, in particular, with the way the population influenced the use and conservation of those resources. Whereas the earlier nature protection movement was concerned with safeguarding certain natural resources against overuse or destructive change on the general grounds of prudence or aesthetics, the new environmental movement, while including this, went beyond it. It became concerned with a much wider range of environmental phenomena on the ground that the violation of ecological principles had reached the point where, at best, the quality of life was threatened and at worst the long-term survival of humanity could be imperilled.

These developments were strengthened during the 1950s and 1960s by a number of demonstrations of the damage unwise environmental management could do – the air pollution episodes in London and New York beween 1952 and 1966, the fatal instances of mercury poisoning at Minamata and Niigata between 1953 and 1965, the reductions in aquatic life in some of the North American Great Lakes, the deaths of birds caused by the unexpected side-effects of DDT and other organochlorine pesticides, and the massive oil pollution from the wreck of the *Torrey Canyon* in 1966. These widely-publicised events caused many people in the developed countries to fear that pollution was already jeopardising the human future – and the revelation, at about the same time, of the upward trend in atmospheric carbon dioxide concentrations and of possible mechanisms whereby human activities might perturb stratospheric ozone concentrations added force to these concerns.

The Stockholm Conference

IT IS not surprising therefore that representatives of the developed, industrialized countries approached the Stockholm Conference with environmental pollution problems weighing heavily on their minds; and with the need for a worldwide conservation programme to safeguard the planet's genetic and natural resources (documented in the IBP) as a strong second concern. Experience in these countries had demonstrated that environmental deterioration could threaten their citizens' health and well-being, and damage ecosystems and species important to their quality of life. There were also fears that more subtle and widespread effects could modify the global environment over a longer period, at great cost to the whole of humanity. The accelerating consumption of resources by industrialized societies, their ever-mounting demand for energy, and the pressure on resources generated by the rapid rise in human populations suggested to many that continuing economic growth could be jeopardized by environmental constraints.

Such people believed that the central lesson of ecology – that the numbers of any species were limited by interactions with the environment – had to be applied to man. They argued that curative measures had to be found urgently if disaster was to be avoided (Meadows et al., 1972). The Stockholm Conference was accordingly expected to lead to a global campaign to curb pollution, conserve resources (including wildlife) and lay the foundation for a more careful management of these resources.

But the developing countries approached Stockholm with a different perspective. In these countries energy and resource consumption was not high, and their industrial pollution problems were localized if present at all. But with them poverty was rife, expectation of life was poor, infectious diseases took a terrible toll, and human settlements commonly failed to provide the basic essentials of adequate shelter, clean drinking water, and safe disposal of human body wastes. They were also deliberately engaged in stimulating rapid change with far too few financial resources to go round and a desperate shortage of skilled people. If therefore, they accepted, intellectually, the thesis that pollution prevention was cheaper than cure there was nonetheless a temptation to industrialize by the cheapest route first and cure the resulting pollution afterwards.

Moreover, it could be argued that if the capacity of the environment to disperse wastes was itself a natural resource, it was one in which developing countries were rich and one they could exploit by accepting industries intolerable in the more congested environments of the developed world. Environmental concern was therefore often dismissed as the business of the rich countries (which caused most of the pollution and moreover had the wealth to cure it). "Debates on doomsday theories, limits to growth, the population explosion, and the conservation of nature and natural resources were thought of as largely academic, of no great interest to those faced with the daily realities of poverty, hunger, disease and survival. Indeed, arguments were presented to show that environmental concerns could well retard development efforts in the third world" (UNEP, 1978, a, b).

An important event in the preparation for the Stockholm Conference was a Seminar on Development and Environment, held at Founex, Switzerland, in June 1971. This meeting began to clarify the links between environment and development, destroyed the false idea that they were necessarily incompatible, and began to convince the representatives of the developing countries that environmental concerns were both more widespread and more relevant to their situation than they had appreciated. For example, developing countries in the arid zones and humid tropics have always had to deal with environmental problems such as droughts or water-borne diseases, which have materially affected their development; and they have evolved certain traditional techniques of water management and shifting cultivation that, properly applied, are environmentally sound.

Another link was forged by the recognition that many problems confronting developing countries had been encountered earlier by developed countries, whose mistakes could be avoided. Resource deterioration, squalid housing and lack of sanitation, affecting poor people throughout the world and generally resulting from under-development, were seen to be as much environmental problems as those caused by industrial emissions. At Founex and Stockholm the phrase 'the pollution of poverty' came into use to describe the worst of all the world's environmental problems, and it was recognized that the skills of all nations were needed to tackle it.

The Founex meeting thus began to bridge the gap in understanding. There was general recognition that virtually all countries needed to undergo further development, so that sound approaches to environmental planning and management would be required everywhere. Environmental concerns should not be a barrier to development, but should be a part of the process, since development that is sound environmentally is likely also to be enduring and to avoid unforseen and unwelcome side effects. 'Ecodevelopment' – a word coined to describe this process of ecologically sound development, a process of positive management of the environment for human benefit – emerged as a central theme from Stockholm. These re-defined concepts made the Stockholm Conference more attractive to developing countries.

The Stockholm Conference was, however, a focus for, rather than the start of, action on environmental problems. Major United Nations agencies (FAO, WHO, WMO, UNESCO) and IMCO, the Inter-Governmental Maritime Consultative Organization had well-established programmes by the start of the 1970s. The United Nations Economic Commission for Europe (ECE), other Regional Commissions, IUCN, and non-UN bodies like the Organization for Economic Co-operation and

Development (OECD), the Council for Mutual Economic Assistance (CMEA) and the European Economic Community (EEC) were active. Many nations had established Departments of the Environment or national environmental agencies. The United States Council on Environmental Quality and Environmental Protection Agency date from 1970, as do the United Kingdom Royal Commission on Environmental Pollution and Department of the Environment, and the Canadian Department of the Environment. The Swedish National Environmental Protection Board is older (1969). The Environment Agency of Japan dates from 1971, while France established a Ministry for the Environment and the Protection of Nature in 1971. Further Departments or Agencies were set up after the Stockholm Conference in many countries. The period saw a burst of legislation among OECD nations: whereas only four major national environmental laws were passed in the five years 1956–60, ten in 1961–65 and eighteen in 1966–70, between 1971 and 1975 thirty-one such measures were adopted, and a further twenty-five followed in the four years 1976–79 inclusive (OECD, 1979a). By the end of the 1970s regular statistics or reports on the state of the environment (or both) were being produced in many countries particularly in Austria, Canada, Finland, France, FRG, GDR, Italy, Japan, Luxembourg, the Netherlands, Norway, the Philippines, Spain, Sweden, the United Kingdom, the United States and Yugoslavia.

The Stockholm Action Plan

THE Stockholm Conference produced an Action Plan for the Human Environment, submitted in the report of the Conference to the United Nations General Assembly in the autumn of 1972, and endorsed in General Assembly Resolution 2994 (XXVII) of 15 December 1972. The Recommendations in the Plan fell into three groups concerned respectively with environmental assessment, environmental management and supporting measures (Figure 1–1).

The first, (the 'Earthwatch' function) demanded a process of evaluation and review, providing a world 'intelligence service' describing the state of the world environment, and providing a means for international exchange of knowledge of environmental situations, problems, and management techniques. For this reason one of the key components was seen to be an International Referral System (now called INFOTERRA), to be designed

Figure 1–1 ˋThe Framework of The Stockholm Action Plan (UNEP, 1978a).

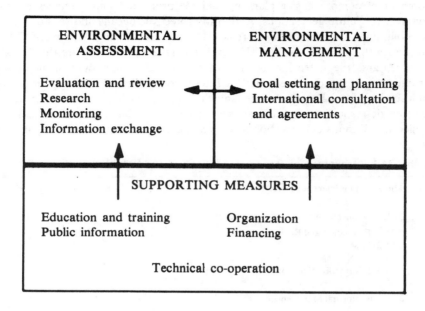

as a kind of switchboard. An applicant needing information – say a Government agency in a tropical country concerned about soil conservation in a region where shifting cultivation was merging into continuous agriculture – would be put in touch with laboratories or agencies notified to a central Secretariat by their national Government as expert in this field. The surveillance of the environment was to be the concern of a Global Environmental Monitoring System (GEMS), again conceived as a network, drawing upon the information many governments collected for their own purposes and assembling the data to give a coherent picture of regional or global trends. It was recognized that gaps in the coverage of the world might need to be filled, especially in developing countries and remote oceanic and polar zones. A special network of about ten baseline atmospheric stations in remote areas and a hundred regional stations away from immediate sources of environmental contamination was to be established under the auspices of WMO. Marine pollution, radioactive waste discharges, food contamination and changes in ecosystems and animal and plant populations that might indicate potential problems, were also to be monitored. Another component in the information system was to be an International Register of Potentially Toxic Chemicals (IRPTC) – again compiled by drawing on information supplied by governments and UN agencies. The information provided from these and other sources was to be assessed critically, so that the significance of the changes detected could be evaluated, and governments alerted to actions that might be needed. This process of information-gathering and evaluation was recognized as the heart of the Earthwatch function of UNEP. It was to be supported by research, where this was necessary in order to create new knowledge and so enhance the evaluations.

10

THE WORLD ENVIRONMENT 1972–1982

The second area, Environmental Management, had as its broad objective the development of comprehensive planning and the protection and enhancement of the environment for future generations. Action to protect the oceans and seas of the world against pollution was given priority: a regional Convention on the Dumping of Wastes at Sea in the north-east Atlantic had already been signed at Oslo before the Stockholm Conference, and the extension of this to the world oceans was strongly urged. Governments were urged to strengthen the International Whaling Commission and work within it for a ten-year ban on commercial whaling. International action to preserve the world's genetic resources, vital as a source for new crop plants and domestic livestock was called for. Various conservation initiatives including a convention to regulate trade

Table 1–1. Groupings of Recommendations in the Stockholm Action Plan.

I Under Action Plan Categories[a]		Number of Recommendations
1. Environmental Assessment (Earthwatch)		137
1.1 Evaluation and Review	29	
1.2 Research	42	
1.3 Monitoring	30	
1.4 Information Exchange	36	
2. Environmental Management		66
3. Supporting Measures		77
3.1 Education, Training and Public Information	17	
3.2 Organizational Arrangements	27	
3.3 Financial and Other Assistance	33	
II Under Conference Categories		
1. Planning and Management of Human Settlements for Environmental Quality		·9
2. Environmental Aspects of Natural Resources Management		51
3. Identification and Control of Pollutants of Broad International Significance		25
(a) Pollution generally	16	
(b) Marine pollution	9	
4. Educational, Informational, Social and Cultural Aspects of Environmental Issues		7
5. Development and Environment		8

Source: UNEP (1978 a).

[a] Some of the 109 recommendations appear more than once in the categories in section 1.

in endangered species (CITES), and a World Heritage Convention developed by UNESCO, were supported.

The third area, of Supporting Measures, had three components. The first was education, training and public information, for it was recognised that there was a great need for specialists, multi-disciplinary professionals and technical personnel in many countries. The second subject was organizational arrangements, and the third, financial and other forms of assistance.

Table 1–1 indicates the numbers of recommendations (not necessarily a guide to the importance assigned to the various topics) in each of the above categories and sub-categories and also under the alternative series of headings that were used to group the proposals during the Conference itself.

These activities were to constitute the U.N. Environment Programme, and it is important to stress that this programme was conceived of as drawing together and giving added strength to the environmental activities of the whole United Nations system. To service the programme, the Stockholm Conference recommended the establishment of a small United Nations Environment Secretariat, and this was also endorsed by the General Assembly in Resolution 2997 (XXVII) which established a fifty-eight nation Governing Council for the programme, a voluntary Environment Fund (with a target of US$100 million over the first five years), and an Environment Co-ordination Board under the Chairmanship of the Executive Director of the United Nations Environment Programme, to ensure co-operation and co-ordination among all UN bodies. By resolution 3004 (XXVII) the General Assembly decided to locate the UNEP secretariat in Nairobi, Kenya.

Developments since the Stockholm Conference

The detailed actions following the Stockholm Conference are reviewed in a separate background UNEP report for the Session of Special Character to be held in 1982 (UNEP, 1982). The main Chapters of the present volume deal only briefly with the principal international organizational developments of the decade. It is evident, however, that the context and the conception of environmental action have changed during this period. The 1960s had been a decade of substantial economic growth – between 4 and 5 per cent annually in the developed countries of North America and Europe and as much as 10 per cent in Japan. In the 1970s this slowed to under 3 per cent (and 5 per cent in Japan). In developing countries the change was less marked, with an average growth in GNP of 5.6 per cent between 1960 and 1970, falling to around 5 per cent between 1975 and 1979 (World Bank, 1980). The price of oil rose markedly, shaking some of the assumptions on which many countries had planned their development (as Chapter 12 explains). These changes brought home to many people the finite (and generally inadequate) financial resources available for development and the need to plan carefully so that waste was avoided. It was increasingly recognized that the environmental component of development must be properly evaluated within the total planning process.

In 1973 the United Nations initiated a major study of economic trends, taking into account such matters as the availability of natural resources, pollution, and the economic impact of pollution abatement. The UN Secretariat commenced 'Project 2000' to examine alternative patterns of development up to that year, and their policy implications. Environmental considerations were built into the programmes of many United Nations, intergovernmental and national bodies concerned with development strategies. The theme of Environment and Development singled out by the Governing Council of UNEP at its first session in 1973 as a subject of high priority became a central strand in UNEP thinking (UNEP 1978 b, c).

The systems approach to development planning demanded a fusion of environmental science, characterizing the physical and biological resources available and the way they might respond to new human actions, of economics and of social understanding of the needs of people and communities. One manifestation of this approach was the development of formal environmental impact assesment methods, with or without simulation models (see, for example, Holling, 1978); another, the proposal of indicators of environmental quality (Perloff, 1969; Dansereau, 1971, 1977; Bugnicourt, 1979). The recognition that socio-environmental systems extend widely and that the developed countries had a direct interest in the development of others gained ground during the decade and was illustrated in such studies as the OECD Interfutures Study (OECD, 1979 b) and the Report of the Brandt Commission (1980). The World Conservation Strategy, published by IUCN in co-operation with UNEP and the World Wildlife Fund (IUCN/UNEP/WWF, 1980), emphasized that the conservation of the resources of the biosphere is at the heart of environmentally-sound development and that without development resources are unlikely to be available for protection of the world's wildlife and natural environments. The 1970s were the decade during which the colonial pattern that had dominated the twentieth century came almost to its end, yet in 1980 it was evident that a new pattern of interdependence had not grown to take its place, and this was affecting both political and environmental stability.

Something of the range of environmental concerns in the world community can be judged by the themes chosen by the Governing Council for the annual State of the Environment Reports provided by the Executive Director each year since 1974 – especially after the first three years, when the Governing Council decided that it would prefer a selective approach (Table 1–2). It is evident that the Governing Council had people very much at the centre of its concerns. The human impacts of diseases whose prevalence depends especially on environmental factors, the effects on people of

Table 1–2. Topics Treated in Annual State of the Environment Reports

Subject Area	Topic	Year
The atmosphere	Climatic changes and their causes	1974*, 1976, 1980
	Possible effects of ozone depletion	1977
The marine environment	Oceans	1975*
Freshwater environment	Water resources and quality	1974*, 1976
	Ground Water	1981
Land environment	Land resources	1974*
	Raw materials	1975*
	Firewood	1977
Food and agriculture	Food shortages, hunger, and losses of agricultural land	1974*, 1977, 1976
	Use of agricultural and agro-industrial residues	1978
	Resistance to pesticides	1979
Environment and health	Toxic substances and effects	1974*, 1976*
	Heavy metals and health	1980
	Cancer	1977
	Malaria	1978
	Schistosomiasis	1979
	Biological effects of ozone depletion	1977
	Chemicals in Food Chain	1981
Energy	Energy conservation	1975*, 1978
	Firewood	1977
Environmental pollution	Toxic substances	1974*
	Chemicals and the environment:	
	—possible effects of ozone depletion	1977
	—chemicals and the environment	1978
	Noise pollution	1979
Man and environment	Human stress and societal tension	1974*
	Outer limits	1975*
	Population	1975*, 1976*
	Tourism and environment	1979
	Transport and the environment	1980
	Environmental effects of military activity	1980
	The child and the environment	1980
Environmental management achievements	The approach to management	1974*, 1976
	Protection and improvement of the environment	1977
	Legal and institutional arrangement	1976*
	Environmental economics	1981

*Indicates brief treatment in early reports.

chemicals in the environment and the ways in which human activities influence the
environment, account for the bulk of the list. The condition of the physical environment,
so obviously a focus of emphasis in the years leading up to Stockholm, has become of
lesser concern to those commissioning these reviews.

As the chapters of the present volume reveal, this shift of emphasis does not mean
that there have not been significant changes in the physical environment. Carbon dioxide
concentrations in the atmosphere continued to rise, concern about acid rains grew, and
fears about man's impact on stratospheric ozone remained. The pollution of the oceans
and inland waters and the loss of soil and of productivity through erosion, desertification
and salinity, were at the forefront of attention. The depletion of genetic resources,
especially in the tropical forests, was much debated. The volume and number of
manufactured chemicals reaching the environment increased enormously: in 1975
industrial production stood at 1.4 times the 1965 level, and during the 1970s at least
30,000 substances were in use and the figure was increasing by 1,000 to 2,000 a year
(UNEP, 1978d; Miller, 1978).

However, the changes in the nature and scale of impact on the physical
environment in the past decade may well have been less important than the parallel
changes in human institutions and perceptions. There was an 'information explosion'
among scientific journals (Brown, 1971). The decade saw rapid advances in the capacity
of computers, and rapid reductions in the costs of electronic data storage and retrieval
systems. Satellites brought the prospect not only of improved intercontinental
communications, but of more efficient surveillance of changes on the earth and in the
atmosphere. New instruments greatly enhanced the resolution of chemical analysis.
Computerized data banks holding scientific results, abstracts and information offered a
possibility, yet to be realized in 1980, of making INFOTERRA, IRPTC and GEMS
more comprehensive and more responsive than was contemplated at Stockholm –
because (assuming the software is compatible) UNEP might be able to link directly with
a swelling host of national and international data centres.

The decade witnessed not only a massive expansion in available information, but
major advances in understanding of the workings of environmental systems. Ecological
science, building upon the IBP, MAB, and other studies, began to build more credible
mathematical models of the behaviour of populations, and (to a lesser extent) of
ecosystems (see, for example, May, 1976; Frenkiel and Goodall, 1978; Bennett and
Chorley, 1978). These have given insights into the life strategies of species and the
optimum techniques for control of particular pests (Conway, 1976), and improved ways
of evaluating the likely impact of alternative management techniques on complex
environmental systems (Holling, 1978).

The increasing rigour and numeracy of ecology and other environmental sciences
had two consequences. First, they have demanded changes in the kinds of data collected
about the environment, generally in the direction of more precise, quantitative
information suited to a particular type of analysis. Second, much of the anecdotal
information about the environment that satisfied the needs of the past is tending to be
rejected as not reliable enough for making decisions about environmental management
today. This Report provides examples of both. In the late 1970s, observations from
satellites were raising questions over the truth of assertions about rates of forest

clearance inferred from ground observations. New analytical methods had led marine scientists to disregard data on the concentration of trace substances in the sea acquired before 1972–74. Paradoxically, these advances hampered comparisons that might have revealed changes in the world environment between 1970 and 1980 because they cast doubt on so much of the earlier information.

At the end of the decade of the 1970s, therefore, despite very great increases in knowledge, it was possible to ask the same central question as at the beginning— "is the world environment changing in ways that could be seriously detrimental in the long term to the well-being of humanity?" – and still not be sure of the answer. There was also uncertainty over the most effective ways of harnessing international scientific knowledge and turning it into practical action at the many levels from international treaties through regional and national laws, standards and codes of practice, to practical action to assist the people on the ground through whose activities the environment was modified.

Figure 1–2   Theoretical relationship between damage costs, control costs and pollution abatement (arbitrary units). The dotted line is the sum of the two curves and indicates total cost. If damage estimates are increased or if control costs are lowered, for example by new technology, the optimum shifts towards higher abatement: the opposite happens if the damage is shown to be less than feared or if control costs rise (after Holdgate, 1979).

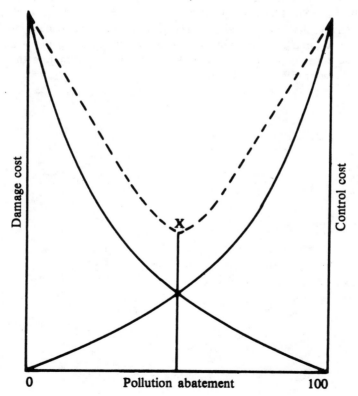

The economic constraints that are universally present in developing countries, and were felt in developed countries late in the decade, accentuated this search for operational efficiency. UNEP itself reviewed the theme of environmental economics in the 1981 Annual State of the Environment Report. The kind of relationship illustrated in Figure 1–2 in which the cost of protecting the environment needs to be balanced (however difficult this may be) against the perceived benefits obtained gained wider recognition. The search for means of judging priorities brought with it views on the possibility of securing wider acceptance of particular indicators of environmental and social well-being. However, many doubts were expressed about universal yardsticks of this kind when human needs and environmental conditions vary so widely.

The environmental topics discussed in this book need to be judged on many planes. At the most basic level, wise environmental management should be an evident act of self-interest, and what is needed is education and training to help people judge the true scale of the problems that confront them, and find the best solution. They need also to be aided to avoid "poverty traps" in which imperatives for survival lead to actions like cutting the last wood on slopes prone to erosion, to secure warmth and cooking for the present, even though it means that crops and fuelwood for the future are at risk. At a more subtle level environmental questions have a strong ethical content. The responsibility of States (or individuals) not to engage in actions that may damage the environment of other states (or people), or of the "international commons" beyond the limits of national jurisdiction was stated clearly in the Stockholm Declaration. There is a danger, as the world's economic problems intensify, that this ethical base and its logical consequence – international or national action to manage environmental resources in an integrated way – may be blunted. These considerations need to be kept in mind in evaluating the state of the environment between 1972 and 1982.

References

Bennett, R. J. and R. J. Chorley (1978), *Environmental Systems; Philosophy, Analysis and Control,* Methuen, London.

Brandt Commission (1980), *North-South; A Program for Survival,* MIT Press, Cambridge, Massachusetts.

Brown. H. (1971), *Science Information Today – a Scientist's View,* Final Report of the Intergovernmental Conference for the Establishment of a World Science Information System (UNISIST), UNESCO, Paris.

Bugnicourt, J. (1979), Three Futures for Africa. *Mazingira,* 10, 19.

Conway, G. R. (1976), Man Versus Pests, In R.M. May (Editor), *Theoretical Ecology,* Blackwell, Oxford.

Dansereau, P. (1971), Dimensions of Environmental Quality, *Sarracenia,* 14,1.

Dansereau, P. (1977), An Ecological Framework for the Amenities of the City, *Diogenes,* 98,1.

Frenkiel, R. N. and D. W. Goodall, Editors (1978), *Simulation Modelling of Environmental Problems; SCOPE 9,* John Wiley, New York.

Holdgate, M. W. (1979), *A Perspective of Environmental Pollution,* Cambridge Univ. Press.

Holdgate, M. W. and G. F. White, Editors (1977); *Environmental Issues; SCOPE 10,* John Wiley, London.

Holling, C. S., Editor (1978), *Adaptive Environmental Assessment and Management,* John Wiley, Chichester.

IUCN/UNEP/WWF (1980), *World Conservation Strategy,* International Union for the Conservation of Nature and Natural Resources, United Nations Environment Programme and World Wildlife Fund, IUCN, Gland, Switzerland.

May, R. M., Editor (1976), *Theoretical Ecology,* Blackwell, Oxford.

Meadows, D. H. *et. al.* (1972), *The Limits to Growth,* Universe, New York.

Miller, D. R. (1978), General Considerations, In G. C. Butler (Editor), *Principles of Ecotoxicology; SCOPE 12,* John Wiley, Chichester.

Morrison, D. E. *et al.* (1972), The Environmental Movement, Some Preliminary Observations and Predictions, In W. R. Burch *et al.* (Editors), *Social Behaviour, Natural Resources and the Environment.* Harper and Row, New York.

OECD (1979a), *The State of the Environment in OECD Member Countries,* Organization for Economic Co-operation and Development, Paris.

OECD (1979b), *Interfutures; Final Report of the Research Project on the Future Development of Advanced Industrial Societies in Harmony with that of Developing Countries,* Organization for Economic Co-operation and Development, Paris.

Perloff, H. S. (1969), A Framework for Dealing with the Urban Environment, In H. S. Perloff (Editor), *The Quality of the Urban Environment,* Resources for the Future, Washington, D.C.

UNEP (1978a), *Compendium of Legislative Authority,* United Nations Environment Programme, Nairobi.

UNEP (1978b), *Review of the Areas of Environment and Development and Environmental Management,* UNEP Report No. 3, United Nations Environment Programme, Nairobi.

UNEP (1978c), *Survey of Activities in the Areas of Environment and Development and Environmental Management,* UNEP Report No. 4, United Nations Environment Programme, Nairobi.

UNEP (1978d), *The State of the Environment – Selected Topics,* United Nations Environment Programme, Nairobi.

UNEP (1982), *Review of the Implementation of the Stockholm Action Plan,* United Nations Environment Programme, Nairobi.

Ward, B. and R. Dubos (1972), *Only One Earth: The Care and Maintenance of a Small Planet,* André Deutsch, London.

World Bank (1980), *World Development Report,* World Bank, Washington, D.C.

CHAPTER 2

Atmosphere

All life on Earth depends in some way on the atmosphere, yet it is only in comparatively recent times that mankind has become aware of the extent to which human activities can interfere with this vital resource. The alterations these activities are causing are difficult to identify and measure, but during the 1970s a number of conclusions could be drawn:

(a) Carbon dioxide concentrations were slowly and steadily increasing, chiefly as a result of the increasing use of fossil fuels and forest clearing. This phenomenon has important – but as yet incompletely understood – implications for world weather conditions and agriculture, because it could alter temperature and precipitation patterns and the distribution of snow and ice cover.

(b) Acid rain was established as a phenomenon that resulted from the long-distance transport of sulphur oxides and nitrogen oxides produced primarily by fossil fuel combustion. Its adverse effects, such as acidification of inland waters, which were of increasing concern during the decade, are discussed in Chapters 4 and 7.

(c) The depletion of ozone postulated early in the decade as a result of supersonic transport and increasing releases into the stratosphere of chlorofluorocarbons from such sources as spray cans and refrigerators was undetectable with current methods. There was, therefore, uncertainty over whether or not the process was occurring and whether its predicted environmental consequences, one of which was an increase in human skin cancers, were likely.

(d) Photochemical oxidants, which cause smog, decreased in cities with effective controls, and increased where controls were absent or ineffective or where automobile use increased.

(e) Sulphur dioxide and suspended particulate matter concentrations were decreasing in most cities with control policies, but increasing elsewhere, especially in developing countries.

(f) Stratospheric particulates appear to have increased somewhat, with possible undetermined effects on climate.

While local climatic changes occurred (as in heat islands and hazy areas), the question of whether long-term climatic changes were in progress, and if so at what rate, remained controversial. It was apparent that, because of lack of understanding of the basic global cycles of carbon, sulphur and associated elements, long-term climatic changes could not be predicted with confidence. Therefore, if the postulated general warming due to the increase in carbon dioxide concentrations were actually to take place, it would be impossible to forecast its full effects on climate patterns - and all the more so its economic and social consequences. The climate changes probably would not be uniform, and the social and economic consequences would be likely to benefit some areas and work to the *detriment of others. There was agreement that if a general warming is at present taking place, it will be detected within a decade or two.*

Despite the occurrence of extreme atmospheric events in various parts of the world during the 1970s (severe droughts, disastrous floods, consecutive cold winters and tropical storms), there is no evidence of marked changes in the variability of weather over recent decades. Variability is the norm in weather, and the fact that extremes occur does not necessarily mean that the climate is changing.

A number of challenges emerged during the decade. These included the need to improve long-term weather forecasts. One of the period's major successes in understanding global systems resulted from international co-operation within the Global Atmospheric Research Programme, and this advance together with those achieved by the World Climate Programme offered hope that reliable forecasts for longer than five days could be made. But the problems are extremely complex.

Another challenge for the future is the critical appraisal that needs to be made of the climatic implications of governmental energy policies, particularly if they include increased reliance on coal. The environmental impacts of large-scale expansion of this source remained uncertain at the end of the decade.

The atmosphere is an important resource, which is subject to wide natural variation and human modification. It provides fresh water supply, transferring it from oceans to continents and de-salting it on the way by evaporation. It disperses pollutants, while rapidly diluting them. The atmosphere shields plants and animals from harmful wavelengths and intensities of solar radiation, moderates temperature extremes on Earth, transports heat from the equator to the poles, and moves nutrients and seeds from place to place. Yet at times, extremes of atmospheric processes endanger human lives and property through hurricanes, droughts, heat waves, blizzards or floods.

On the whole people have learned to live with climate, exploiting its beneficial features and developing ways of coping — more or less successfully — with its hazards. Agricultural production, for example, is tuned to the annual cycle of climate, with some assistance from irrigation works, frost-protection schemes, shelter belts and other protective devices, although these cannot adjust to all extremes.

But while the atmosphere thus modifies peoples' lives, people can also modify the atmosphere. There are basically three ways in which they can do this, either deliberately or inadvertently: by changing the concentration of substances (including water); by releasing heat; and by changing the physical and biological properties of the earth's surface.

As a result of these changes, people and other living organisms may be exposed to harmful levels of toxic pollutants transported by the atmosphere. Droughts and desertification may occur. Changes in the concentration of ozone in the stratosphere may alter the amount of solar ultraviolet light reaching the surface of the earth, with possible effects on the health of humans and other species. Or the climate may be altered, with either beneficial or detrimental consequences. All such possibilities caused concern during the decade, and, as is characteristic of atmospheric environmental problems, they were regional and global in scale and hence affected large numbers of people.

The present chapter considers: (1) The basic structure and circulation of the atmosphere, the climatic system, and the components subject to human modification; (2) Atmospheric trends during recent years; (3) The resulting effects on mankind and the biosphere; (4) The responses of human society to these changes and impacts; and (5) The likely course of future events.

The Atmosphere and Climate

THE COMPOSITION OF THE ATMOSPHERE

The atmosphere consists mainly of nitrogen (78 per cent), oxygen (21 per cent) and argon (0.9 per cent), with trace amounts of other gases, liquid droplets and solids. For the quasi-constant components listed in the first part of Table 2–1, the composition is almost constant to 100 km height. For the active gases and aerosols, there are important variations seasonally, geographically and vertically. For example, clouds occur mainly in the troposphere while the main ozone layer is in the stratosphere.

The impact of mankind on the composition of the atmosphere is limited to possible changes in the concentrations of those trace gases and aerosols listed in the lower half of Table 2–1. The recently expressed concern that oxygen concentrations may become depleted is unfounded: the amount available in the global atmosphere is so great that the impact of mankind is unimportant. In contrast, the quantity and distribution of gases like ozone (O_3) and carbon dioxide (CO_2) can more readily be upset.

THE PHYSICAL STRUCTURE OF THE ATMOSPHERE

The atmosphere contains four main layers: the troposphere, stratosphere, mesosphere and thermosphere, defined in terms of altitude and temperature regime.

Table 2–1. The Composition of the Atmosphere near the Earth's Surface.

Gas	Concentration (Percentage by Volume)
	Quasi-constant components
Nitrogen (N_2)	78.11 ± 0.004
Oxygen (O_2)	20.953 ± 0.001
Argon (Ar)	0.934 ± 0.001
Neon (Ne)	$(18.18 \pm 0.04) \, 10^{-4}$
Helium (He)	$(5.24 \pm 0.004) \, 10^{-4}$
Krypton (Kr)	$(1.14 \pm 0.01) \, 10^{-4}$
Xenon (Xe)	$(0.087 \pm 0.001) \, 10^{-4}$
Hydrogen (H_2)	0.5×10^{-4}
Nitrous oxide (N_2O)	$(0.3 \pm 0.1) \, 10^{-4}$
	Chemically and /or radiatively thermodynamically active admixtures
Water (H_2O)	$0 - 7$
Carbon dioxide (CO_2)	$0.01 - 0.1$ (average 0.034)
Total Ozone (O_3)	$0 - 10^{-4}$ (average 3×10^{-5})[a]
Sulphur dioxide (SO_2)	$0 - 10^{-4}$
Methane (CH_4)	1.6×10^{-4}
Nitrogen dioxide (NO_2)	$0 - 2 \times 10^{-6}$
Liquid and solid aerosols	very small (20–50 micrograms per cubic metre background)

Source: Khrgian (1978).
[a]The upper values are only encountered under extreme conditions.

Figure 2–1 indicates the structure of the lower zones, where human impacts are concentrated. The heights given are averages, and considerable variability is found, depending on latitude, season and meteorological situation. The lower region of the troposphere, from 1 to 1.5 km thick, is termed the planetary boundary layer. The troposphere is a zone with well-defined climatic features determined by latitude, season, the rotation of the earth, the distribution of continents and oceans, and altitude. The stratosphere is located above a transitional zone (the tropopause). It is virtually cloudless. Its upper boundary is the stratopause, where temperature increases rapidly; another transition layer, at an altitude of about 82km, separates the mesosphere from the overlying thermosphere.

Most of the mass of the atmosphere is in the troposphere (the proportion varying from 70 per cent in temperate and high latitudes to 90 per cent in lower ones (Khrgian, 1978)). The troposphere — and especially the planetary boundary layer — is the zone where pollutant concentrations are highest. Particulate matter and chemically active gases such as sulphur dioxide (SO_2) and nitrogen dioxide (NO_2) emitted into the troposphere remain there for only a few days on average. Within one hemisphere, and

Figure 2–1. Physical structure of the Lower Atmosphere.

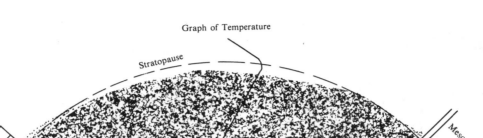
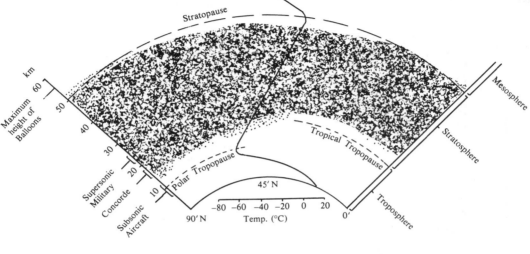

Ozone Layer

After U.K., 1976.

particularly in the temperate zones, trace substances are often transported and mixed over distances of 1000km in a few days.

However, exchange between the two hemispheres is believed to proceed rather slowly, taking of the order of 6–12 months. In contrast, substances reaching the stratosphere may remain there for many years if their reactivity is low, because there is very little interchange between the stratosphere and the layers below it. Fine particulates and chlorofluorocarbons (which are only slowly decomposed by solar radiation) are particularly long lasting.

It is mainly in the stratosphere, however, that strong ultra-violet (UV) radiation from the sun dissociates oxygen molecules to release oxygen atoms which then combine with other oxygen molecules to form ozone. Ozone absorbs UV and effectively shields the surface of the earth from most of the more harmful radiation. Besides being created in the stratosphere, ozone is also destroyed there through reactions with natural and man-made stratospheric trace substances. These include some oxides of nitrogen, hydrogen radicals (H, HO and HO_2) and the chlorine atoms and halogen radicals formed by the breakdown by solar radiation of chlorofluorocarbons and other chlorine-containing compounds (Thrush, 1979). Downward transport, and local processes including the reactions in 'photochemical smog' described later, also cause ozone to occur in the planetary boundary layer.

THE CLIMATE SYSTEM

The general features of the climate system are now well established, and are represented in simple form in Figure 2–2 (Bolin, 1975), which emphasizes the importance of coupling between atmosphere, ocean and land biota. Numerical models can reproduce these climatic features, but it is not possible to validate the simulation with data sets for conditions other than those experienced in the last thirty years. The two major components of this system interact by:

(a) micro-scale processes in the thin layer of air overlying the oceans. Here there is an exchange of particles, gas, heat, and momentum, thus contributing to interactions on a larger scale;

(b) medium-scale processes, which determine the properties and peculiarities of the boundary layers, such as inversions and thermoclines in water bodies;

(c) large-scale, three dimensional processes, notably the general atmospheric circulation and the system of ocean currents, which depend both on the configuration of the continents and oceans, and on heat exchanges between them.

There is a continual exchange of carbon dioxide between the ocean and atmosphere. Carbon dioxide solubility is related to ocean chemistry and temperature, tending to decrease as the temperature rises. Hence a cold ocean may serve as a sink for carbon dioxide, and a warm one be a source (Monin and Shiskov, 1979). It is currently believed that solution processes predominate, and that the oceans as a whole are a sink for carbon dioxide released from other sources but the processes, rates and proportions are not well understood (Bolin *et al.,* 1979; see also Chapter 3).

Present investigations of the ocean-atmosphere interactions involve two concepts. The first is derived from numerical experiments with equations developed to describe the major interactions (Marchuk, 1979; Marchuk *et al.,* 1979). These experiments suggest that regions in the ocean may significantly affect large-scale atmospheric processes over the continents, with a time-lag of 4–8 months.

The second concept is a hypothesis that may help explain climate variability and large-scale weather anomalies. It assumes that water masses with abnormal temperatures may persist for long periods, can reach deep waters and migrate for long distances, and under certain conditions may reappear at the surface and induce large-scale anomalies of atmospheric circulation several months, or more probably, years later (Stommel, 1958).

With so many factors involved in these interactions, it is perhaps surprising that climatic variability is not even greater, No ice age or melting ice cap has occurred in the last 10,000 years. This has led some climatologists to speculate that the atmosphere is in one of its stable states, and that this stability is not likely to be affected by mankind. On the other hand, there are climatologists who worry that the atmosphere may be triggered into seeking a new stable state different from the present one, the shift remaining undetected in its early stages because of:

(a) the natural variability of climate that makes trends difficult to detect;

(b) the presence of feedback mechanisms that impede the interpretation of trends (for example, tropospheric warming could cause changes in atmospheric pressure patterns, bringing cooling to some regions, and confusing the calculation of the rise in surface temperature averaged over the globe).

To assist in overcoming these difficulties, the World Meteorological Organization (WMO) and research institutes in many countries sought during the decade to improve numerical models of climate. By 1980, these computer simulations had already provided clues to the probable effects of such changes as a doubling of atmospheric carbon dioxide concentrations, or a reduction of the world forest cover. However, the models did not yet have the required sophistication or spatial resolution and did not adequately incorporate oceans, ocean-atmosphere coupling, and cloud cover. Hence the predictions could not be used with confidence as effective environmental management tools. A major goal of the 1980s is to produce better models.

THE IMPACT OF HUMAN ACTIVITIES

Additions of trace substances to the troposphere

People introduce substances into the troposphere by:

(a) emitting gases and particulates, particularly from fossil fuel combustion, domestic and industrial sources and transport;

(b) burning stubble and starting forest and grassland fires (some fires are also touched off by lightning);

(c) ploughing and overgrazing, releasing dust that rises in dry windy weather and augments that naturally present in the atmosphere;

(d) releasing particulates that act as condensation and freezing nuclei.

The introduced substances of most importance are the traditional pollutants of towns: suspended particulates, sulphur oxides, nitrogen oxides, carbon monoxide, hydrocarbons, lead, hydrogen sulphide, mercaptans and other odorous compounds and fluoride. Some of these are long-lived toxic substances, such as heavy metals (and their compounds) or pesticides, which are transported by the atmosphere to areas where they may accumulate in organisms, soils, water bodies or glaciers. Others are photochemically reactive gases, notably nitrogen oxides and hydrocarbons, whose reactions in the presence of sunlight produce oxidants such as ozone. Sulphur oxides and nitrogen oxides also produce sulphate and nitrate aerosols, some of which are later scavenged by precipitation hundreds of kilometres downwind of source regions, causing acid rain (OECD, 1978). Others, such as ammonia and sulphur oxides, can react to

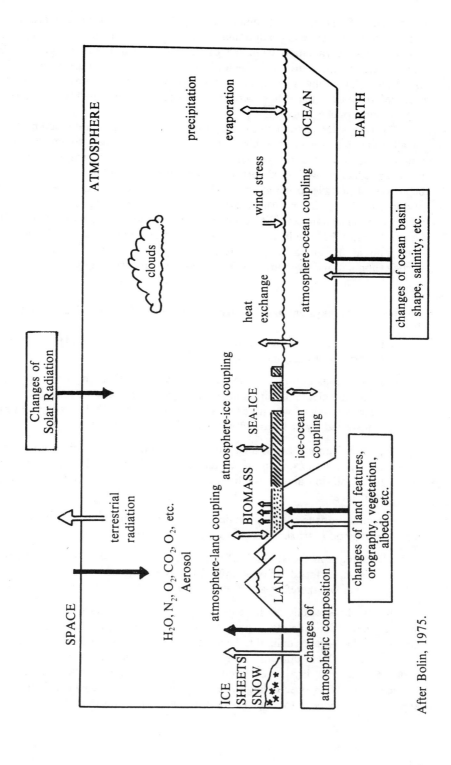

Figure 2–2. Schematic Illustration of the Climatic System. Full Arrows Indicate Examples of External Processes; Open Arrows Internal Processes.

After Bolin, 1975.

create hazes. Still other gases (mainly carbon dioxide, but also the chlorofluorocarbons, nitrous oxide, methane and ammonia) do not attenuate the sun's rays significantly but absorb outgoing radiation from the earth in several infra-red bands, thereby raising tropospheric temperatures and creating the so-called greenhouse effect. Aerosols and particulates (including the sulphates and nitrates mentioned above) may also affect the radiation balance of the atmosphere and influence climate. Finally, some gases affect the stratospheric ozone layer.

The role of the 'greenhouse gases' was reasonably well understood by the end of the decade (it is discussed later in this chapter). The role of suspended particulates, however, remained somewhat controversial. Part of the uncertainty was due to the fact that particles reflect as well as absorb radiation from the sun and the Earth. The radiative behaviour of particles originating in a desert might be expected to be different from that of particles originating in urban and industrial areas. Kellogg (1977) suggested that an increase in particulate concentrations would warm industrial regions such as Europe and North America but might cool the oceanic parts of the Northern Hemisphere. In any case, simulations of particulate effects on climate are not realistic unless they treat particle populations over the continents and oceans separately.

Changes in the physical and biological properties of the Earth's surface

The atmosphere can be affected both by human activities and by natural changes in the surface of the Earth, including:

(a) alterations in forest cover, irrigation or desertification, snow clearance on land and ice clearance in shipping lanes and the construction of towns, roads or airports, all of which can change the fractions of solar radiation reflected and absorbed by the ground surface;

(b) modifications, again including deforestation and swamp drainage, that reduce evaporation from an area, alter the apportionment of available energy used for evaporation and convection, and so change the energy balance at the Earth's surface;

(c) alterations to the hydrological cycle, for example through water storage works, irrigation, grazing practices, or the diversion of rivers;

(d) changes in the strength of natural sources and sinks of trace substances (for example, forests play an important role in the carbon cycle: a change in forest cover will therefore affect atmospheric CO_2 concentration).

Many of these activities have been going on for 5000 years or more. They can affect microclimates, for example, if particles are deposited on a snow surface, reducing the amount of short-wave sunlight reflected and increasing the amount of energy available to melt the snow. Developments such as irrigation, which increase evapo-transpiration, cool the air so that daytime convection may be suppressed at the surface. If the Earth's surface is modified over a large area, regional climate may be affected. There is no experimental evidence to establish that human impact on the surface of the Earth has changed the climate on a continental or global scale, although some observers argue that it may (Sagan *et al.*, 1979).

Releases of heat and water vapour into the atmosphere

Large quantities of heat are released into the atmosphere directly, for example from chimneys, space heating or air conditioning, or indirectly through systems such as cooling ponds and towers. This contributes to the well-known urban heat island effect described later.

When averaged over the globe, the heat generated by mankind is a trivial fraction of the heat from net solar radiation at the Earth's surface. Even the heat from large metropolitan complexes like the Washington-New York-Boston corridor is not expected to affect global climate in the foreseeable future. However, because this heat comes from point sources, considerable local effects can be produced in the cities themselves.

Water vapour is also released from industry, transport and space heating. Local climatic effects are most likely during cold weather in temperate and sub-polar regions. In Fairbanks, Alaska, ice fog may be formed in winter. The growth of the city of Edmonton, Alberta, between 1949–50 and 1968–69 was accompanied by a substantial increase in winter fogginess (Hage, 1972). Over isolated tall chimneys, a single cumulus cloud may develop.

However, the regional and global effects of such events are negligible. Similarly, there is as yet no evidence that intentional cloud seeding has any effect on regional climate. At the decade's end, the WMO was co-ordinating a detailed study in Spain on the feasibility of modifying precipitation through cloud seeding (PEP: the Precipitation Enhancement Programme).

Human activities that might affect the stratosphere

One of the chief concerns during the decade was that the ozone layer in the stratosphere might be perturbed by various natural and man-induced events. While this would be unlikely to have a significant effect on global climate, it might substantially increase the penetration of biologically damaging UV–B radiation. The principal natural factors are volcanic eruptions and solar flares. On the other hand, people may modify the system, either through the direct release of material into the stratosphere from aircraft and nuclear explosions, or via upward movement from the troposphere of chlorofluorocarbons, carbon tetrachloride, nitrous oxide, methyl chloroform, carbon dioxide, methane, particulates and water that they have caused to be released on Earth. Complex mathematical models, which include photochemistry, radiation and stratospheric dynamics, are used to predict their effects. However, the models cannot easily be validated and many difficult problems remain to be solved before reliable predictive calculations can be made.

Atmospheric Trends Over Recent Decades

DIFFICULTIES IN IDENTIFYING AND INTERPRETING TRENDS

Atmospheric conditions vary greatly from place to place and from time to time. Some of the variations, such as the daily and yearly cycle and the weekly variation in urban air pollution, are predictable on average. Other variations, like the general west-to-east movement of low and high pressure areas in the temperate zones, show some signs of regularity. Still other fluctuations are not predictable from present models.

In classical statistics, an increase in the number of independent observations of an element causes the calculated mean value of that element to converge towards its true mean. In the atmosphere (and other complex environmental systems), however, as longer time series are analysed, fluctuations with longer periods are revealed. This creates difficulties in identifying and interpreting trends (Munn, 1980). The scientist analyzing data now available cannot be certain whether the detected change is part of a long-period oscillation or a new trend.

Another problem arises because time series do not extend back very far in time. Surface weather observations have, of course, been made for more than two centuries. However, many early weather stations were established in towns, and those set up in the 1930s and 1940s were located mainly at airports. Weather records, therefore, are confused by the effects of increasing urbanization. Networks of upper air stations were established in the 1940s which means that only about thirty years of data were available for three-dimensional analysis of the atmosphere during the decade.

A further difficulty stems from the uneven distribution of both surface and upper air stations, with dense coverage over the continents and few stations over the oceans particularly in the Southern Hemisphere. It is therefore difficult to obtain unbiased estimates of average global and hemispheric values in the meteorological elements. An alternative is to study trends obtained from a single station or from a group of stations in the same region; these trends may, however, reflect a short-term shift (lasting only a few years) in the strength or orientation of the atmospheric general circulation in that part of the world, rather than a shift in global mean values. Natural changes in circulation may also explain events that might otherwise be ascribed as human activities. For example, Pittock (1977) was able to relate an increase in precipitation on the west-coast of North America between 1941 and 1970 to an anomaly in the annual mean latitude of maximum sea level pressure above the west coast, without having to postulate that emissions of cloud condensation nuclei from industrial sources had increased these during this thirty-year period.

Measurements of urban pollution (total suspended particles and sulphur dioxide) began in the last century. In the 1950s there was a substantial increase in the number of cities and pollutants monitored; carbon monoxide, for example, being measured at seven stations in Los Angeles since 1955 (Tiao et al., 1975). A few measurements of background levels of trace substances in rural and remote areas in Europe were also made before the middle of the present century. However, the results are often confusing because the analytical and calibration procedures were not generally comparable with those used today. Because of these problems, most of the time series available for study are short, the following being the most significant:

1. *Carbon dioxide:* the record dates back to 1957 at Mauna Loa, Hawaii, and in Scandinavia some stations operated from 1955 to 1960, with other baseline stations being established in the 1970s.

2. *The chemical constituents of precipitation:* a special observation network began in Europe in 1954 under the auspices of Stockholm University's International Meteorological Institute. There is information, for example, about the sulphate content of rainfall in Norway, the Federal Republic of Germany, the USSR and eastern Europe, from this time. Systematic observations of chemical constituents of precipitation began in the USSR in 1957, and by 1980 samples were taken at 70 stations over the whole country (Petrenchuk, 1980). In the United States, a network of stations was operated for a short period in 1955–56 and the data have been widely used for comparison with later measurements beginning in one small basin in 1964 and across North America in the 1970s. Recently networks were established in Canada, and in 1978 a special network was set up to monitor long-range sulphur transport in Europe.

3. *Background monitoring of trace substances:* In 1970 the WMO decided to organize a Background Air Pollution Monitoring Network (BAPMoN) which includes sampling of the chemical constituents of precipitation, and in 1980 this comprised about 110 stations in about 60 countries. The United States associated with BAPMoN its own network of baseline stations (GMCC: Geophysical Monitoring for Climate Change) located at Mauna Loa, Hawaii; Point Barrow, Alaska; Samoa; and the South Pole (see for example, GMCC, 1978). Other national baseline stations, including those at Cape Grim, Australia, and Mount Kenya, were also associated with the network.

In the USSR, BAPMoN stations were established in 1972–73 (Berlyand, 1980). Intercalibration of analytical methods was conducted with the participation of Bulgaria, Czechoslovakia, the German Democratic Republic, Hungary, Poland and the USSR.

Systematic observations under an integrated monitoring programme providing
determination of particles, sulphur dioxide, 3, 4–benzpyrene, mercury, lead, cadmium,
and arsenic in the atmosphere began in the USSR in 1976. By 1980 the total number of
first-stage integrated background stations in co-operating socialist countries reached
twenty-two; eight of them are located in different geographical zones of the USSR
(Rovinsky et al., 1980).

Finally, the stratospheric data available for trend analyses are the meteorological
elements (e.g. temperature and wind) and ozone. In the latter case, measurements began
in the 1930s using the ground-based Dobson spectrophotometer, supplemented by
balloon observations (ozonesondes) beginning in the 1950s. On behalf of the WMO,
Canada has been publishing ozone data since 1957 (the International Geophysical
Year). These are the data sets for trace substances available for trend analyses.

CHANGES IN THE CONCENTRATION OF TRACE SUBSTANCES IN THE TROPOSPHERE

Changes in source strengths

One of the developments of the 1970s was the growing attempt to estimate both
natural and man-made source strengths. Semb (1978), for example, published a sulphur
dioxide emission inventory for western Europe. In the USSR annual inventories of air
pollution emissions have been prepared since 1975. This will make it possible in future
decades to relate ambient air quality trends directly to emission trends. But so far there is
only limited information available about trends in source strengths.

Table 2–2. Man-made Sulphur Dioxide Emissions for Various Classes of Sources in
Selected Countries (in Per Cent).

Class of Source	U.S.A.	U.S.S.R.	England	Federal Republic of Germany
Energy production	55.1	52.8	53.0	58.5
Oil refining	8.6	2.1	6.9	5.8
Ferrous and non-ferrous metallurgy	20.8	26.2	7.8	10.8
Industry	4.7	4.8	17.8	24.9
Coal processing		3.7	3.0	
Other	10.8	10.4	11.5	

Source: Reay (1973); EPA (1975); Berlyand (1977).

Sulphur dioxide enters the atmosphere through the burning of fossil fuels, which contain from 0.05 to 8 per cent sulphur (natural gas having the lowest and coal the highest concentrations), and from metal smelting (the sulphur content of pyrite ores can be as high as 45 per cent). Table 2–2 shows the main sources of sulphur dioxide emissions in several countries. Energy production is the most important source, and for this reason emissions in temperate and cool latitudes are highest in winter.

Table 2–3 shows the geographic distribution of man-made sulphur dioxide emissions at the beginning of the 1970s. The contribution of developing countries is small. It can also be seen that emissions are much higher in the Northern than in the Southern Hemisphere (145.5 and 5.5 million tonnes/y respectively). Between 1970 and 1980 global man-made emissions of sulphur dioxide grew at about 5 per cent per year, to give a total increase of 40–50 per cent over the decade. Total emissions of anthropogenic SO_2 reached 196 ± 30 million tonnes annually at the end of the 1970s. This volume was nearly twice as high as the natural emission of sulphur compounds to the atmosphere of the continents (Ivanov and Freney — in press).

Table 2–3. Emission of Sulphur Dioxide by Regions by the Beginning of the 1970s. (Million tonnes/y).

North America	45
Europe (without the USSR)	37
Asia (without the USSR)	35
USSR	27
North Africa	1.5
South Africa	2
South America	2
Australia	1.5
Total:	151

Source: Ivanov and Freney (in press).

Table 2–4 compares estimated aerosol (dust) emissions from some major industrial regions in 1978 and 1980. Table 2–5 gives more details of global particulate emissions. Human activities emit 65 million tonnes of sulphur per year as sulphur dioxide, out of a total of 144 million tonnes — i.e., about half. However, in industrial zones the proportion emitted is much higher — probably over 90 per cent. It is because man-made emissions are concentrated in industrial and urban areas, which cover less than 1 per cent of the Earth's surface, that health problems arise.

The world's 270 million automobiles contribute more than 200 million tonnes/y of carbon monoxide, but the situation is different in different regions. In the United States, automobiles contribute some 75 per cent of urban carbon monoxide emissions, whereas in the USSR the figure is from 25–50 per cent (Berlyand, 1977). However, natural sources are now thought to release a much greater quantity of carbon monoxide — perhaps as much as 3,500 million tonnes/y. Automobiles are also a major source of

Table 2–4. Estimated Emissions of Sulphur Dioxide and Particulates in 1978–1980.

Country	Sulphur dioxide (million tonnes)	Aerosol (dust) (million tonnes)
USA	27.0	73.3
USSR	24.5	22.5
Japan	14.0	6.5
EEC (except Luxembourg and Ireland)	19.0	2.4

Source: ECE (1981); Data are for 1978 or more recent year.

Table 2–5. Suspended Particulate Matter Emissions to the Atmosphere from Different Sources (million tonnes/y).

Man-made sources	Mean	Deviation ±	Natural sources	Mean	Deviation ±
	Primary aerosols				
Fuel combustion	30	24	Marine salt	700	400
Industrial emissions	15	12	Soil erosion	300	250
Land ploughing	5	4	Forest fires	200	160
			Volcanic eruptions	80	70
Total	50	40	Total	1,280	880
	Secondary aerosols				
Sulphates from (SO_x)	170	40	Nitrates (from NO_x)	250	200
Hydrocarbons	50	40	Ammonium salts (from NH_3)	170	90
Nitrates (from NO_x)	30	5	Sulphates from (H_2S)	170	40
Total	250	85	Total	730	400
Grand Total	300	125	Grand Total	1,320	730

Source: Berlyand (1975).

oxides of nitrogen and hydrocarbons: in the United Kingdom they account for about 25 per cent of emissions of the former (power stations and industry being the dominant source) and 40 per cent of the latter (DOE, 1980).

Total sulphur oxide emissions in the United States remained relatively stable over the decade (OTA, 1979) although the pattern of sources changed, with a decline in urban emissions. In the United Kingdom total sulphur dioxide emissions declined from 6.12

million tonnes in 1970 to 5.00 in 1976, but rose to 5.26 in 1979 (DOE, 1980). Hydrocarbons and oxides of nitrogen emitted by U.K. motor vehicles rose somewhat from 0.27 and 0.23 million tonnes respectively to 0.36 and 0.31 million tonnes; oxidants were not monitored but are likely to have risen also. These two trends — towards stable or declining sulphur emissions, especially in urban zones, but rising oxidant concentrations — are likely to be widespread in western Europe.

Trends in smoke and sulphur oxides concentrations

Neither sulphur oxides nor aerosols accumulate indefinitely in the atmosphere. The health problems they have created in the past arose from exposure to high local concentrations in urban areas where fossil fuels were burned inefficiently. In urban zones today, annual mean sulphur dioxide concentrations of 50 micrograms per cubic metre (μg/m^3) are still common (see Table 2–6), whereas in rural regions figures of below 10 μg/m^3 are typical. Sulphate aerosol concentrations similarly range from 5–15 μg/m^3 in cities to under 2 μg/m^3 in rural areas. For smoke particles, typical values range from 20 to 100 μg/m^3 and below 10 μg/m^3 respectively. In unpolluted oceanic situations still lower values are to be expected. These figures do not reflect the pollution of indoor environments. The latter conditions received more attention during the decade (CEQ, 1980; see also Chapter 10). Urban air quality trends can be estimated from networks of monitoring stations or may be inferred qualitatively from economic data relating to fuel and power production, etc. Using the second approach, Brimblecombe (1977) inferred that smoke and sulphur dioxide concentrations in London rose steadily from 1600 AD to the late nineteenth century, and then slowly declined with the introduction of more efficient methods of combustion, cleaner fuels, smoke removal equipment and taller chimneys. No serious pollution episodes have been reported in London since the early 1960s.

Table 2–6. Average Concentrations of Suspended Particulate Matter (SPM) and Sulphur Dioxide (SO$_2$) During 1973–77 in Seven Cities (amounts in μg/m^3).

City	Commercial		Residential		Industrial	
	SPM	SO$_2$	SPM	SO$_2$	SPM	SO$_2$
Brussels	24	87	20	71	18	91
Calcutta	397	14	392	18	298	7
London	24	126	23	75	29	69
Madrid	170	116	44	47	214	112
Prague	170	108	112	100	133	49
Tokyo	43	68	47	42	52	77
Zagreb	147	117	112	40	144	49

Source: Akland *et al.* (1980).

The London experience is typical of cities in developed countries. In cities where control policies have not been implemented, pollution has naturally increased with population growth. In Ankara the incomplete combustion of coal and lignite had raised both sulphur dioxide and smoke concentrations to over $250 \, \mu g/m^3$ by the late 1960s and the situation continued to deteriorate during the 1970s. In the cities of the developing world, smoke concentrations in urban areas also remained high because of the use of wood as a home fuel and because of the many open incinerators. Table 2–6 shows that suspended particulate concentrations in Calcutta were much higher than in any other city listed. In countries like Bangladesh the smoke concentrations continued high as a result of inefficient burning of fossil fuels, the popularity of firewood for fuel, and the prevalence of coal-burning brickfields.

First results of the World Health Organization/United Nations Environment Programme (WHO/UNEP) urban air monitoring project (Akland et al., 1980) showed that the changes between 1973–75 and 1975–77 in the concentrations of suspended particulate matter and sulphur dioxide in seven cities were mainly downward. However, the period of record was rather short. A longer time series (1970–1976) for sulphur dioxide in twenty four localities, most of them cities, published by OECD (1979) showed comparable results, with a halving or more of concentrations in Montreal, Toronto, Tokyo, Osaka and Nagoya and a deterioration in only three places. In the USSR, records from more than 350 cities showed that the maximum concentration of particles and sulphur dioxide varied between 150–300 and 80–160 $\mu g/m^3$ respectively at the beginning of the 1970s, and had decreased considerably by the end of the decade.

The effects of these changes on human health and on biological productivity are discussed elsewhere in this volume (Chapters 10 and 7). One effect not discussed there which claimed special attention during the 1970s is the corrosion of stone and metal on historical monuments: a particularly serious problem was the deterioration of marble in the Acropolis at Athens (Greece, 1981).

Trends in photochemical oxidant concentrations

Photochemical oxidant smog is formed in urban areas as a result of reactions between nitrogen oxides and reactive hydrocarbons in the presence of sunlight. Ozone and numerous organic compounds are produced. The phenomenon was first investigated in Los Angeles during the 1950s. Since then it has been found in many parts of the world, especially in towns with high traffic densities and warm, sunny climates. Mexico City and Lima, Peru, for example, have frequent episodes. Significant oxidant concentrations were also reported in Tokyo, Sydney and Melbourne in Australia, London and other cities in northern Europe, Edmonton in Canada, and the north-eastern United States. In some of these areas, the photochemical pollution considerably reduces visibility, and the aerosol in the polluted air mass has been observed to reduce the intensity of sunlight reaching the ground to one-tenth of the incident value.

It was formerly believed that photochemical oxidants give rise only to a local problem in the large urban areas because of either topography or population distribution.

However, recent evidence from field studies conducted in Europe and Eastern North America has established that photochemical pollutants and their precursors can be transported up to several hundred kilometres. This long-range transport implies that emission control on a local scale may be grossly insufficient in Europe and Eastern North America (OECD, 1978).

General conclusions about oxidant trends over the last two decades are difficult to make. The data are sparse, particularly from rural areas and from cities in developing countries. In addition, measurement techniques changed during the period. It is likely, however, that oxidant levels rose:

(a) in areas where automobile use increased substantially;

(b) in areas with strong control programmes for suspended particulates (e.g. emissions from open incinerators) without a corresponding programme to reduce oxides of nitrogen and reactive hydrocarbons. (This was the case in some European cities.)

In contrast, where effective controls had been imposed, concentrations fell. In 1965 the average monthly maximum oxidant concentration in downtown Los Angeles was 0.27 parts per million (ppm); in 1974 it was 0.17 ppm. In the San Francisco Bay region the concentrations fell from 0.13 to 0.09 ppm during the same period (CEQ, 1976). In Japan, the number of days when the hourly average of photochemical oxidant concentrations exceeded the threshold at which "warnings" were issued (0.12 ppm) peaked at 330 alerts in 1973, and fell to around 150 warnings in 1978 and to 84 in 1979 (EAJ, 1980). No alarms for concentrations of 0.24 ppm or higher were issued in the latter year.

Sulphate and nitrate hazes

During fine summer weather the emissions of sulphur dioxide and nitrogen oxides from tall chimneys (power stations, smelters) are gradually converted to sulphate/nitrate hazes, which augment the haze and organics from forests, and sometimes cover areas as large as Western Europe and Eastern North America.

There were many personal testimonies to the lessening of occurrences of exceptionally high visibilities in the fifty years preceding the decade. These recollections were supported by analyses of visibility records at weather stations (Vickers and Munn, 1977; Husar et al., 1979). For example, the frequency of summer haziness in the Canadian Atlantic Provinces increased sixfold since the 1950s, with winds blowing from the states of New York and New Jersey; with north-east winds off Newfoundland and Labrador, there was no change in the frequency of summer haziness (Vickers and Munn, 1977). Special attention was being given to this problem in the United States (Costle, 1980) but successful control strategies had not been developed by the end of the decade. Summer haziness was also reported from a variety of other countries, including Bangladesh.

A haze layer of interest to atmospheric chemists occurred over the Arctic Ocean from time to time (NIAR, 1977; Rahn *et al.*, 1979; Larssen and Hanssen, 1980). The haze was imported from more southerly regions but the dynamics of the phenomenon were not yet fully understood.

Acid rain

One of the environmental concerns voiced at the Stockholm Conference was the increasing acidification of Swedish lakes and rivers. The Swedish Case Study to the Stockholm Conference (1972), suggested that atmospheric long-range transport carried sulphur, nitrogen oxides, sulphates and nitrates across international boundaries. These gases and particles were subsequently scavenged by clouds and precipitation, causing acid rain.

In the past ten years it has been clearly established that transport over distances of 1,000 km and upwards is common in western Europe (OECD, 1977) and Eastern North America (NAS, 1978; Altschuller ,and McBean, 1980). As transport proceeds, sulphur dioxide is removed from the atmosphere in three main ways: absorption by underlying surfaces ("dry deposition"); solution in rain or cloud droplets; and oxidation to sulphuric acid, which is in turn liable to "wet deposition" in rainfall and snow. Both wet and dry deposition must be included in any analysis of the acid rain problem. Nitrogen oxides are likewise liable to deposition as nitrate and nitric acid. Although these transformation and removal processes were understood in broad qualitative terms by 1980, the coefficients of transformation had not been established precisely and this was a source of error in regional modelling.

Between 1955 and 1965 the network of Swedish and nearby Norwegian precipitation stations reported a rise in sulphate and nitrate concentration and in acidity. In Eastern North America similar concerns were expressed a few years later, and it was shown during the decade that there had been an increase in acidity over a period of 25 years (NAS, 1978; Likens *et al.*, 1979; Ontario, 1980). Acid precipitation was accordingly identified as a "major global environmental problem" in the preparations for a United States federal research program.

Figure 2–3 shows the average sulphur concentrations in precipitation over Western Europe in 1954–59 (De Bary and Junge, 1963) and in 1972–76 (Wallén, 1980*). In his comparison of the two figures, Wallén remarked that:

(i) in the most northern part of Scandinavia, there was hardly any increase in sulphur content from the 1950s to the 1970s;

(ii) in southern Scandinavia, the increase was of the order of 50–100 per cent, from 1.0 to 1.5–2.0 milligrams of sulphur per litre (mg S/l);

(iii) in the maximum area in Central Europe, there was an increase of 100 per cent, i.e. from about 2.3 to 5.0 mg S/l;

---

* According to Wallén, it is incorrectly stated that the values in Figures 1 and 2 of his publication (Wallén, 1980) are for sulphates.

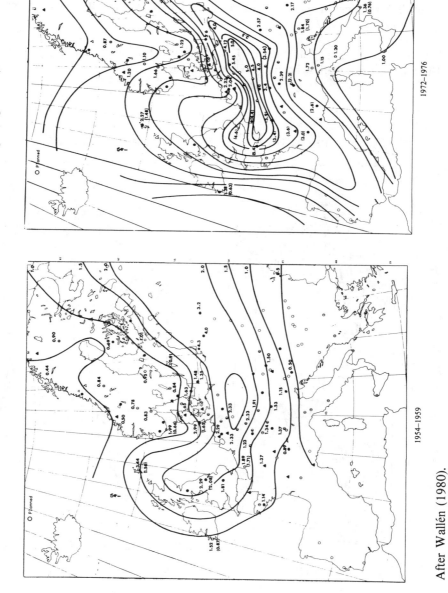

Figure 2–3. Annual mean Concentration of Sulphate in Precipitation in Europe (mg S/litre).

After Wallén (1980).

(iv) in south-central Europe, the order of the increase also was around 100 per cent, i.e., from about 1 to 2 mg S/l;

(v) the mean value for Europe as a whole based upon the data used from De Bary and Junge was 1.28 mg S/l compared with 1.88 mg S/1 for the BAPMoN data, indicating an average increase for the whole area of about 50 per cent.

However, inspection of detailed records suggests that the pattern was not one of simple linear change. Figure 2–4 shows how sulphate ion deposition and concentration

Figure 2–4. Excess Sulphate at Two Groups of Scandinavian EACN Stations (European Atmospheric Chemistry Network Stations). After: Chester et al: 11th World Energy Conference, Munich, 3,347 (1980).

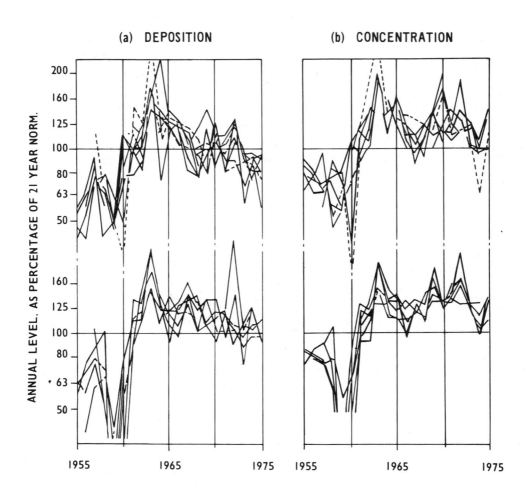

Figure 2–5. Long-term Variations of Annual Weighted Mean Concentrations of Nitrate in Precipitation at Three EACN Stations in Norway (After OECD: Long-range Transport of Air pollutants; OECD, 1979).

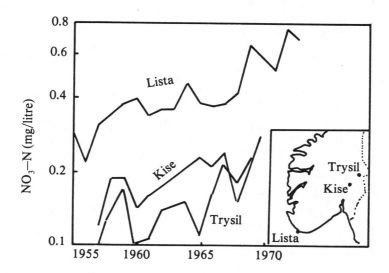

in rainfall at two groups of Scandinavian stations was reported to rise sharply between the mid–1950s and mid–1960s but subsequently levelled off or even declined (Granat, 1978). (How much this was due to a change in analytical method is not clear.) Nitrate concentrations at the other stations rose steadily (Figure 2–5). It is tempting to relate these curves to those for sulphur emissions in Europe, which rose some 50 per cent between the mid–1960s and 1972 but then peaked. Somewhat comparable changes were reported in Eastern North America between 1955–1956 (Junge, 1960) and 1975–76 (Likens et al., 1979) (Figure 2–6). Here too, detailed scrutiny of the data suggests that sulphate concentration trends from 1964 to 1974 were slightly downwards while nitrate in precipitation increased (Likens, 1976; Johannes et al., 1980).

Petrenchuk (1980) discussed the chemical composition of precipitation at a number of stations in the USSR from the late 1950s to 1976. At remote sites, he reported little change. In the western part of the European territory of the USSR, in contrast, there was an increase not only in sulphate concentrations but also in basic salts such as ammonium and calcium ions, which neutralize the acids. Thus the pH of precipitation remained unchanged. There were a few data of this type from other parts of the world.

Toxic chemicals

The atmosphere is one of several pathways by which toxic substances reach humans and the biosphere. Many of the substances are long-lived (e.g., heavy metals,

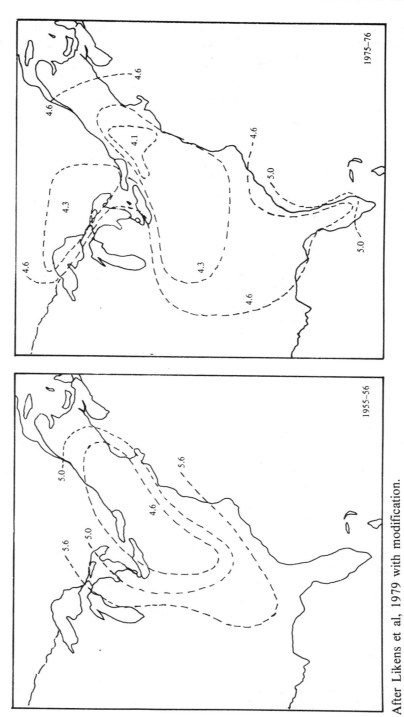

Figure 2–6. Isopleths showing Annual Average pH for Precipitation in Eastern North America.

After Likens et al, 1979 with modification.

pesticides) and thus accumulate in receptor media over years or decades. The list of toxic chemicals is long and growing. Atmospheric monitoring for these substances during the decade was generally limited to locations known to be affected, and local sampling programmes were usually terminated once a source had been controlled. There was therefore no information on general trends in atmospheric concentrations, although a few anecdotal measurements were available, e.g., of lead in Greenland and Antarctic ice, and of metal pollution in the sediments of the Palace Moat in Tokyo (Goldberg *et al.*, 1976). Some inferences as to trends were also derived from an examination of crustal enrichment factors, which provided an indication of the atmospheric concentrations of a trace element if it had originated locally in the soils and rocks. (See, for example, Rahn and McCaffrey, 1979).

From various types of economic and industrial data, trends in regional and global emissions of various toxic substances may be inferred. In this way, Nriagu (1979) compiled the information contained in Table 2–7, which shows an increase in the emissions of all the metals listed. The values quoted for lead were considered by some investigators to be low by several orders of magnitude (Patterson, in NAS, 1980).

Table 2–7. All-Time Worldwide Man-made Emissions of Trace Metals.

	Cd	Cu	Pb	Ni	Zn
			(millions of kilograms)		
Pre–1850	63	319	2,420	–	2,804
1850–1900	19	92	1,100	12	841
1901–10	8.9	53	471	8.2	392
1911–20	11	80	493	21	493
1921–30	14	96	1,120	21	622
1931–40	17	116	1,639	49	746
1941–50	22	169	1,672	80	959
1951–60	34	230	2,694	140	1,514
1961–70	54	435	3,704	257	2,372
1971–80	74	585	4,265	415	3,252
Total (all time)	317	2,175	19,578	1,003	13,995

Source: Nriagu (1979).

With respect to the last decade, the following qualitative statements can be made:

1. In many of the industrialized countries, there was a reduction in the lead content of gasoline and in the use of non-degradable pesticides and herbicides, while increasingly stringent controls were imposed on secondary lead smelters and other point sources of toxic chemicals. On the other hand, the use of lead and cadmium increased over the world as a whole (Table 2–7).

2. In many of the developing countries, there were some local problems, but there was little information on trends or on how concentrations compared to standards.

CHANGES IN THE CONCENTATION OF SUBSTANCES IN THE STRATOSPHERE

The changes in stratospheric trace constitutents that attracted most attention during the decade were those of ozone and fine particulate matter, and of the substances interacting with ozone, notably chlorofluorocarbons (CFCs) 11 and 12.

The latest predictions for releases of CFC 11 and 12 during the decade came from the UNEP Co-ordinating Committee on the Ozone Layer (UNEP, 1981a). The committee estimated that continued releases at the 1977 rate would eventually deplete the stratospheric ozone layer by about 10 per cent. This estimate was less than that of a committee of the U.S. National Academy of Sciences (NAS, 1979), which put the figure at 16.5 per cent. The overall uncertainty, according to the NAS committee, was such that there was believed to be one chance in forty that ozone depletion would be less than five per cent and one chance in forty that it would be more than 28 per cent: the question remained as to whether uncertainty limits were in fact quantifiable.

The Chemical Manufacturers Association reported in 1980 that world production of CFCs 11 and 12 had fallen by 17 per cent between 1974 and 1979. During the same period, according to the UNEP committee, there was a reduction in their combined use for aerosols and open cell foam from 608,800 tonnes to 365,500 tonnes but an increase in the amounts used for refrigeration and closed cell foams (which delay release of CFCs) from 203,800 to 282,100 tonnes.

The model used by the UNEP committee calculated that a total ozone depletion of about one per cent should have already occurred, but such a small amount could not be directly detected with technology available at the time, as it was well within the range of natural variation. However, it should be recognized that the predicted depletion of about 10 per cent is only that attributable to CFCs 11 and 12. Other CFCs, methyl chloroform, and carbon tetrachloride emissions appeared to be on the increase worldwide, and their impact could more than offset gains achieved through reduction in use of CFCs 11 and 12.

It was argued late in the decade that the effect of aircraft emissions was likely to be small (DOT, 1979), or that they might even increase ozone concentration in the upper troposphere. However, the latest evaluation by UNEP (1981a) concluded that the data were insufficient for meaningful assessment of this possible impact. The effect of nitrogen fertilizer releases was uncertain (see for example CAST, 1976; Crutzen, 1976; and Wang and Sze, 1980). The effect of chlorofluorocarbon dissociation in reducing ozone might be partly counteracted by rising concentrations of carbon dioxide and nitrogen oxides (UNEP, 1981a).

The key question at the end of the decade was whether these hypothetical effects had actually occurred. There were indications that chlorofluorocarbon concentrations had risen: measurements of $CFCl_3$ (trade name Freon 11) at Cape Grim, Tasmania, for example, revealed an upward trend after 1976 and there was supporting evidence from other locations (CSIRO, 1978; DOE, 1976). But other analyses (e.g. Angell, 1979) provided no evidence for human modification of ozone concentrations between 1969 and 1979.

In other studies, Angell and Korshover (1979) and Penner and Chang (1978) showed that stratospheric ozone concentrations were responsive to the eleven-year solar cycle, the quasi-biennial oscillation in the tropical southern hemisphere and volcanic eruptions. However, the latter effect could have been an instrumental error: Dobson spectrophotometer observations are degraded by stratospheric dust veils. These factors created tremendous difficulties in searching for a trend caused by chlorofluorocarbons or other factors. In fact, if mankind were to wait for experimental evidence of ozone depletion of five per cent with 95 per cent confidence, by the time this was established it would be too late to prevent an extended period of such conditions.

It is commonly accepted that the main effect of the depletion of stratospheric ozone would be an increase in the amount of ultraviolet radiation reaching the earth's surface. Countries have established networks of stations to monitor UV–B only recently, (Berger, 1978) and no trends had been reported by the end of the decade. However, because there was no detectable downward trend in stratospheric ozone levels during the decade, there is not likely to have been a change in surface UV–B radiation. Theoretically, it should be possible to estimate the UV–B increase for a given ozone depletion. The relationship turns out to be rather complex, depending on latitude, season and time of day. The numerical model by Pyle and Derwent (1980) predicted that for a global ozone depletion of 13 per cent, the global increase in UV–B would be 12 per cent but a 2:1 ratio is commonly cited by other scientists.

Turbidity measurements made at high-altitude observatories over several decades as well as series of balloon soundings reveal the persistence of volcanic dust for many years after an eruption. An example is shown in Figure 2–7, which presents the stratospheric aerosol concentrations, expressed as mixing ratios for the altitudes at which the maxima were observed in each flight (Hoffmann and Rosen, 1980). The effect of the Fuego (Guatemala) eruption is evident. Hoffman and Rosen (1980) estimated that when the volcanic contribution was removed, the data suggested an increase of nine per cent per year, with an error margin of ± 2 per cent in background levels of stratospheric particulates.

The recent eruption of Mt St Helens provided an opportunity to trace the spread of particulates and gases directly, rather than to deduce their likely behaviour from the observation of radioactive fall-out (NASA/DOT, 1980).

Figure 2–7. Maximum in the Stratospheric aerosol Mixing Ratios Versus Time from 87 Balloon Soundings at Laramie, Wyoming. *r* is particle adius. The Enhancement in Late 1974 is due to Fuego Eruption; Guatemala.

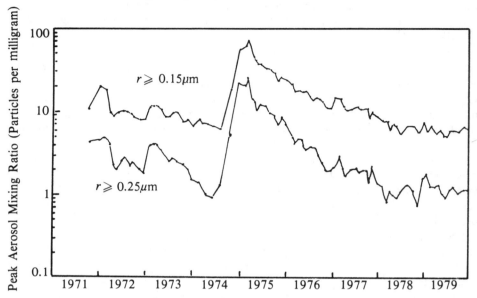

After Hofmann and Rosen, 1980.

CHANGES THAT MAY AFFECT CLIMATE

Changes at the Earth's surface

As indicated in a previous section, mankind continues to modify the surface of the Earth in ways that affect local climate. The main effects are three-fold. Firstly, the ratio of solar radiation reflected from and absorbed by the Earth's surface is changed. Secondly, the ratio of convective and evaporative heat released from the Earth's surface is changed. Finally, the hydrologic cycle is modified.

There is little quantitative information on global trends over the last several decades in any of the factors listed above. However, Flohn (1977) believed that man's activity over the past 2,000 years increased global annual evaporation by only about 3.5 per cent; the world oceans cover such a large area that they reduced the net impact of mankind. It was suggested frequently during the decade that the accelerating rate of destruction of the tropical forest could affect convective/evaporative heat transfer rates in the tropics as well as the global carbon dioxide cycle. These claims were believed by some to be exaggerated (Abelson, 1980). FAO/UNEP statistics, supported by LANDSAT observations, suggested that downward trends in areas of natural forest cover were continuing but that the rates might be expected to decline (UNEP/FAO, 1981; Chapter 6).

On a much more local scale the weather conditions in and around some urban areas are affected by direct discharges of heat, or "thermal pollution". Increasing attention was given during the decade to the growth of "heat islands" in cities: differences of about 1°C in mean annual air temperature were apparent between some cities and their surrounding areas. Night-time differences of an average of 1–2°C – and in certain areas as much as 8°C – were observed (Berlyand, 1975). Urban pollution was also associated with changes in rainfall. Increases of 10–15 per cent in precipitation downwind of some cities were believed to be explained by the abundance of hygroscopic particles and enhancement of lower layer instability (Berlyand, 1975). Shaeffer (1975) reported a case downwind of Buffalo, USA, where the city's heat and water vapour developed snow flurries. Downwind effects on air quality were traced for distances of several hundred kilometres, but the mechanism of urban impact on precipitation formation remained in controversy.

Changes brought about by trace substances

Carbon dioxide is the most widely studied gas that contributes to the so-called greenhouse effect, but ozone, nitrous oxide, water vapour, methane and the chlorofluorocarbons may also be important. (This could turn out to be a reason for reducing emissions of chlorofluorocarbons, in addition to the usual concern about stratospheric ozone depletion.)

It was commonly stated that before 1850 the concentration of CO_2 in the atmosphere was between 265 and 290 ppm by volume (Bolin, 1979; UNEP, 1980). At the Mauna Loa baseline station, the concentrations of CO_2 rose steadily at the rate of about 1 ppm per year after 1957, as seen in Figure 2–8 (Keeling and Bacastow, 1977). This upward trend was also observed at other sites (Antarctica, Samoa, Weather Ship Papa, Point Barrow, Alaska and in central Europe). A reason for the increase was not difficult to find. Figure 2–9 shows the upward trend in estimated annual global emissions of CO_2 by the combustion of fossil fuels, cement production and the flaming of natural gas (Rotty and Weinberg, 1977). About 25 per cent of this total was estimated to come from the United States; North America, Europe (east and west) and the USSR together accounted for 75 per cent (Rotty, 1978).

Carbon dioxide was also released when forests were cleared. This occurred more rapidly if the standing crop of timber was burned and the soil humus layers were oxidized, but the scale of this input, relative to that from fossil fuel combustion, was in some dispute (UNEP, 1980; WMO/UNEP/ICSU, 1980). The atmospheric CO_2 increases shown in Figure 2–8 were only about half what would have been expected if all the CO_2 emitted by burning fossil fuel had remained in the atmosphere. The major sink is presumably the ocean, but there has recently been debate about whether the net absorption of CO_2 into this sink is large enough to account for the difference between the

Figure 2–8. Mauna Loa Monthly Averages of Atmospheric CO$_2$ Concentrations.

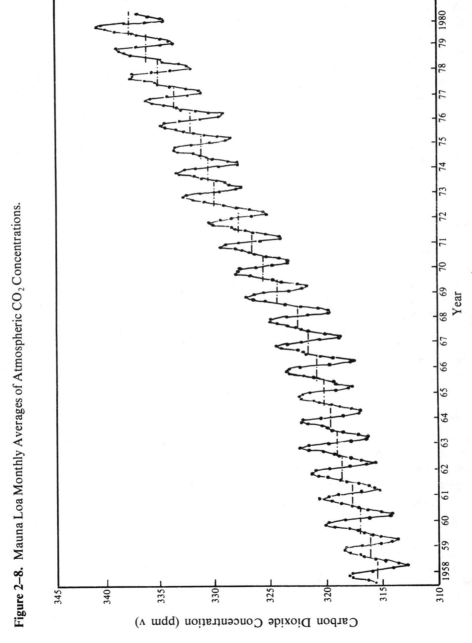

After NOAA, 1981 Personal Communication; Data subject to change.

additions of CO_2 by man to the atmosphere and the observed yearly increase in atmospheric CO_2 concentration. Other sinks have also been proposed, including accelerated plant growth and peat accumulation.

The other greenhouse gases were not monitored to the same extent as CO_2. However, as reported above, there is evidence of an upward trend in chlorofluorocarbon concentrations. Trends in particulate matter are difficult to quantify. Indirect measurements since 1910 in the Northern Hemisphere indicated that the mass of aerosols had increased about 1.5 times while the number of particles had more than doubled. Mention has already been made of the increase in summer haziness that took place in Eastern North America and Europe and over Africa, South Asia, and the Atlantic. At the same time, however, there was an improvement in winter visibility in many areas as a result of smoke control measures.

For other parts of the world, there was little published information on trends of suspended particulate matter. The WMO–UNEP BAPMoN network programme includes atmospheric turbidity measurements; the data will soon be sufficient to permit trend analysis for a few locations.

It seems likely that the injection of particles and aerosols (or of gases like SO_2 that are subsequently converted into aerosols) into the stratosphere from aircraft will not have a significant effect on climate, but that volcanic eruptions may be of major significance (Schneider and Mass, 1975). Bryson and Dittberner (1976) and Hansen et al., (1978) published explanations of global climatic anomalies lasting several years in terms of volcanic activity.

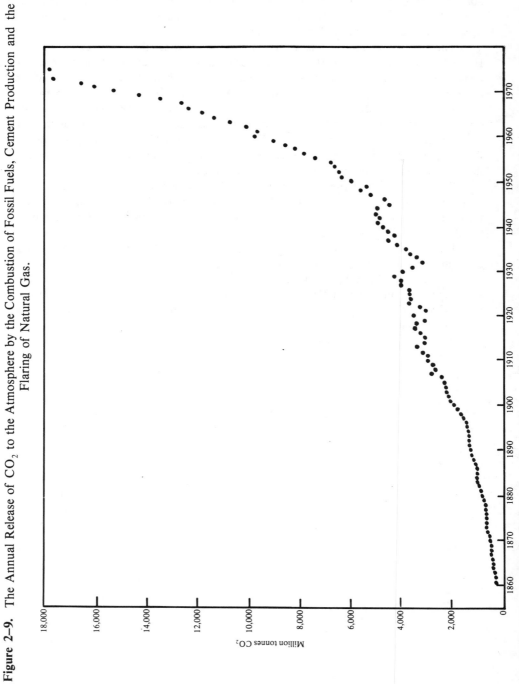

Figure 2–9. The Annual Release of CO_2 to the Atmosphere by the Combustion of Fossil Fuels, Cement Production and the Flaring of Natural Gas.

After Rotty and Weinberg, 1977

Observed Changes in Climate Over the Past Decade

Recent research on climate variations (e.g. Borzenkova *et al.*, 1976) was reviewed at the 1979 World Climate Conference, where the summary (Hare, 1979) suggested several changes had occurred. From 1880 until about 1938 mean surface air temperatures rose in the northern hemisphere, the average increase being 0.6°C, with the largest values in hight latitudes. They then fell by about 0.4°C into the middle 1960s, when the fall appeared to reverse briefly.

Some papers (Vinnikov *et al.*, 1980) suggested a linear upward trend from the middle of the 1960s. It was not clear whether this temperature rise was the beginning of a new trend or a short-term perturbation on a decreasing curve. The extreme cold of 1976 may support the latter view but cooling appears to have halted in intertropical latitudes where conditions since 1963 have been very variable. These trends were largely obscured by striking changes from year to year. Average northern hemisphere temperature in successive years may differ by ± 0.4°C or more — as much as was achieved by the downward trend between 1938 and 1975.

Such slow trends of hemispheric temperature are also small by comparison with strong, persistent spatial anomalies. Mean charts of temperature and pressure over fifteen-year periods show very large areas of positive or negative anomalies, which tend to be quite different in successive periods. The temperature anomalies are closely related to persistent anomalies of prevailing winds and are clearly caused by disturbances of the general circulation of the atmosphere and oceans.

Accurate and representative precipitation measurement is very difficult, and is almost impossible at sea. Available long-term rainfall and snowfall records show no consistent global or regional trend over the past two centuries.

Some illustrative data on trends are given in Figures 2–10 and 2–11. Figure 2–10 shows air temperatures averaged for the whole globe and by hemisphere, for the surface of the Earth, for the troposphere layer from the surface to 100 millibars (0–16 km), and for the low stratosphere in the range of 16–24 km (Angell, in press). The values are deviations from the mean for 1958–80. The two lower layers were warmer in 1980 than any previous year. This reflected a continuing warming trend in the tropics, with recent

Figure 2–10. Temperature Variation for Northern and Southern Hemispheres and the World as a Whole; The Eruption of Mt. Agung is Indicated by Arrows at bottom (After Angell; in Press).

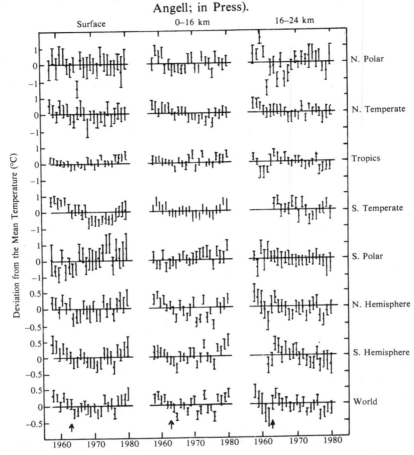

warming in the south temperate latitudes and in the south polar latitudes. The north polar latitudes did not appear to change. In the lower stratosphere there was a cooling trend, particularly in the southern hemisphere, after the eruption of Mt Agung in 1963. The correspondence between tropospheric warming and statospheric cooling was expected, but the distribution of warming did not appear to conform to that modelled for CO_2 effects. Figure 2–11 shows, for 1949 to 1975 for the area north of 25°N, the mean difference in the thickness or height between the 1,000 and 5,000 millibars pressure surfaces (Boer and Higuchi, 1979). This is an indicator of the mean temperature of the atmosphere from the earth's surface to a height of about 5–6 km. A larger thickness corresponds to a higher temperature. Contrary to popular belief, the variability in climate (as measured by variance among eddies) has not changed in recent years.

Finally, it should be emphasized that hemispheric or global values of the meteorological elements may obscure economically important regional or seasonal

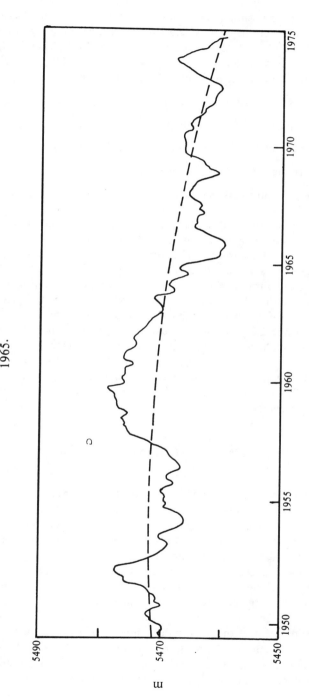

Figure 2–11. Smoothed (12 Month Running Mean Filter) Time Series of Mean Difference in Thickness Between 1000 and 5000 MB Pressure Surfaces for the Area of the Earth North of 25°N. Data for the Pacific Ocean South of 55°N were Missing Prior to 1965.

After Boer and Higuchi; 1979.

anomalies. For example, a below-normal mean temperature could result from either a cold winter + normal summer, or a normal winter + cool summer; the latter combination could have more serious consequences for agriculture, although rainfall anomalies need also to be considered. As an example, Harley (1980) examined the surface-to-500 millibars thickness patterns over the years 1949–1978 for various regions of the Northern Hemisphere. In particular, he found evidence for:

    (a) cooling in East Asia in all seasons except winter;

    (b) cooling in Eastern North America in winter;

    (c) cooling in the Central Atlantic in spring and summer; and

    (d) warming in the Caspian Sea area in spring.

In other regions and seasons, there was no evidence for trends.

The various studies described above suggest that human activities had either not affected the global climate by the end of the decade, or if there was an effect, it was obscured by the background of natural variability in climate. Taking variations in volcanic aerosols and solar luminosity into account, Hansen *et al.,* (1981) concluded that man-made CO_2 warming should be distinguishable from natural variability by the end of the century and that there was a high probability of warming in the 1980s. Madden and Ramanathan (1980) considered that there were indications already of a climate change due to increasing CO_2 but that because of a lag in atmospheric response it was unlikely to be measurable before the year 2000 at the latest. They also suggested some critical indicators that could be useful, possibly within the next decade. In particular, because radiative absorption occurs in selected wavebands, changes in infra-red fluxes should be monitored for the wavebands of importance, separately for CO_2 and for the chlorofluorocarbons.

WEATHER AND CLIMATE ANOMALIES IN THE 1970s

Climatic variability is a natural phenomenon, characteristic of both warm and cold periods of the earth's history. The occurrence of extremes is no evidence of climatic change, although their increasing frequency or severity may be. Table 2–8 lists a selected number of extremes recorded during the 1970s. These include severe winter cold, prolonged drought, rare floods, and tropical storms,

Widespread and damaging droughts were a conspicuous feature of the record. The continuing one in the Sudano-Sahelian region of Africa had a larger impact than other similar droughts in the past because of changes that had taken place in land-use practice (Glantz, 1977). The drought of 1975 in the USSR reduced cereal yields by half, and affected 70 per cent of the land under cultivation. The European drought of 1976 also caused serious damage to agriculture, and that of 1979 caused a collapse in foodgrain production in the USSR. Records of high, intense precipitation followed by flooding, and of tropical cyclones accompanied by storm surges also appear in Table 2–8.

Table 2–8. Selected Extreme Atmospheric Events During the 1970s.

Year	Region	Event
1976/77–1978/79	USA	Consecutive cold winters, unprecedented in the available 85-year record.
1978/79	Western Europe, European part of USSR	Severe winter cold
1968–1974	Sudano-Sahelian belt of Africa extending from the Sahara to the Equatorial forest	Very severe drought
1970	Australia	One of severest recorded droughts
Jan–April 1972	USSR, Yugoslavia, German Democratic Republic, Federal Republic of Germany, Switzerland	Very low rainfall coupled in USSR with temperatures 3–4°C below normal: deep frost penetration into soil
May–June 1972	European USSR	Severe drought
1975	European USSR, Northern Kazakhstan, Southern areas of West Siberia	Most severe drought for 100 years
Mid 1970s	Western United States and Canada	Severe drought
1976	Europe, from Scandinavia to N. Italy and France, Central Europe, North-East Brazil, East Africa	Abnormally low rainfall for 6 months, severe droughts
1979	European USSR	Severe drought
1979	India	Failure of monsoon
1980	Central and Southern USA	Severe heatwave and drought
May 1970	Northern Romania	Disastrous floods, heaviest recorded
June–Aug 1971	Northern India, East Pakistan (now Bangladesh)	Heavy floods, claiming over 1,000 lives: severe damage
Jan-Feb 1971	Buenos Aires, Argentina	Heaviest rainfall of century
Jan and Feb 1976	Australia (various stations)	5 times normal precipitation in January: 10 times normal in February
	Northern New South Wales: Southern Queensland	Over 500,000 square kilometres flooded
May–Aug 1976	Reykjavik, Iceland	70% more precipitation than normal
1976	USSR; Gorky, Kuibyshiev and Saratos	Very heavy rainfall
	Alma Ata	September rainfall over 3 times normal
	Tashkent	September rainfall nearly 4 times normal
August 1977	USA: Southern California	Very high rainfall due to tropical storm Doris
	: San Diego	2 days rainfall more than twice that recorded since 1873
	: Los Angeles	Rainfall 4 times greater than previously recorded in August
June–Oct 1980	Southern Asia	Heavy monsoon: one-fifth of population without shelter due to flooding

Table continued

Table 2–8. Selected Extreme Atmospheric Events During the 1970s—cont'd.

Year	Region	Event
Autumn 1970	Philippines	Many lives lost: Severe damage due to typhoons
November 1970	Bangladesh	200,000 lives lost in very severe tropical storm: tidal bore with surge up to 4m caused widespread flooding
October 1971	India, Orissa State	10,000 lives lost, 6 million people suffered damage due to floods and wind
June 14–23, 1972	USA: East Coast	120 lives lost, damage estimated at US$ 3.5 billion due to Tropical Storm Agnes
1970	Madagascar	Two tropical storms, one (Clotilda 5–17 January) the most severe recorded in the country, caused considerable damage

Such natural disasters had provoked calls at the Stockholm Conference for concerted action to promote, through existing national and international organizations, an effective world-wide natural disaster warning system with special emphasis on tropical cyclones and earthquakes. The World Weather Watch and the WMO Tropical Cyclone Project were expected to contribute. The need for more research on forecasting the periodicity and intensity of droughts was recognized. A beginning was made in designing early warning indicators for food shortages. During the 1970s, advances were made in the development of measuring equipment for rainfall and snowfall, determining the effects of snow cover by satellite, and precipitation assessment by radar and automatic data reporting networks. Models of flow in major river basins, including the Danube, Volga and Tennessee, were constructed thereby allowing changes to be forecast as the data is collected. Various other advances in flood management were developed (these are discussed in Chapter 4). The numerous international actions to combat desertification are described in Chapter 7.

The Impacts of Climatic and Atmospheric Changes on Man

THE NATURE AND SCALE OF IMPACTS

As the preceding sections have demonstrated, the effects of mankind on the atmosphere during recent decades have been limited. Man-induced influences on climate have been small or undetectable, except on the local scale. Trends in stratospheric substances and processes have also been small or undetectable. In the troposphere, there has been a downward trend in many major pollutants in the air over the cities of many industrialized countries, while there are insufficient data to establish trends for those of developing countries. There has been an indication that the wet deposition of nitrates and sulphates in parts of Europe and North America, and the acidity of precipitation, are greater than twenty to thirty years ago.

The resulting impacts on mankind and on the biosphere have been little studied. Certain consequences of air pollution for people are discussed in the chapter on Health, and those for biota and water are reviewed in Chapters 7 and 4 on Agriculture and Forestry and Inland Waters. The effects of increasing wet deposition of sulphates and nitrates and the increasing acidity of precipitation in Scandinavia and Northeastern North America are thought to have impacted on sensitive receptors (poorly buffered water bodies) in ways discussed elsewhere in this report (Chapter 4; Drabløs and Tollan, 1980). It is possible, of course, that other irreversible long-term trends have begun (e.g., due to carbon dioxide increases and ozone depletion) that cannot yet be detected within the natural variability of atmospheric conditions.

ACTIONS TAKEN DURING THE DECADE

Mankind responded in various ways to the atmospheric threats and challenges of the decade. Priorities were established by a process of consensus in which governments, intergovernmental bodies, the scientific community, industry and the news media all played a part. Internationally, the World Health Organization (WHO), UNEP and ICSU as well as regional groups such as the United Nations Economic Commission for Europe (ECE), the Council for Mutual Economic Assistance (CMEA) and the Organization for Economic Cooperation and Development (OECD), were particularly active. The main atmospheric challenges of the last decade were:

1. Improved weather and climate prediction.

2. Coping with natural hazards (floods, droughts, etc.).

3. Air pollution control.

4. Acid rain.

5. CO_2 climate warming.

6. Stratospheric ozone depletion.

Improved weather and climate prediction

One of the decade's major successes in deepening understanding of global systems was the international collaboration within GARP (the Global Atmospheric Research Programme). GARP began officially in October 1967 with the signing of an agreement between WMO and ICSU. This set up a Joint Organizing Committee (JOC) and defined its objective as study of "those physical processes in the troposphere and the stratosphere that are essential for an understanding of:

(a) the transient behaviour of the atmosphere as manifested in the large-scale fluctuations that control changes of the weather; this would lead to increasing the accuracy of forecasting over periods from one day to several weeks;

(b) the factors that determine the statistical properties of the general circulation of the atmosphere that would lead to a better understanding of the physical basis of climate".

Points (a) and (b) became known as the GARP first and second objectives, respectively. The JOC was subsequently renamed the JSC (Jont Scientific Committee for the World Climate Research Programme).

To achieve the first objective, a number of large-scale field programmes were undertaken, including:

— GATE (Global Atlantic Tropical Experiment) 1975.

— FGGE (First GARP Global Experiment) 1979.

The data are still being analyzed but there is no doubt that the observational programmes were successful.

To achieve the second objective, a planning conference was convened in 1974 (Bolin, 1975), and a Climate Dynamics Subprogramme was created in 1975. Subsequently WMO sponsored a World Climate Conference (February 1979) and in May 1979 adopted a World Climate Programme (WCP). WCP has four inter-related components, each with its lead agency:

1. World Climate Research Programme (WMO/ICSU);

2. World Climate Application Programme (WMO);

3. World Climate Impact Study Programme (UNEP: ICSU/WMO);

4. World Climate Data Programme (WMO).

The JSC provides scientific guidance for the first component, in which UNESCO and IOC participate.

Coping with natural hazards

Increasingly in the last twenty years, there was recognition that civilization was becoming more vulnerable to losses from weather and climate extremes. This was due to a number of socio-economic factors such as:

(a) the desire to optimize cost-effectiveness under normal weather conditions, thus failing to protect against extremes (for example in agriculture, energy production and industry);

(b) the desire to optimize short-term profits at the expense of long-term degradation (e.g., overgrazing);

(c) population growth leading to expansion into areas vulnerable to drought, hurricane, and riverine flooding.

Vulnerability increased particularly rapidly in those areas where folk cultures were in the transitional stage of adopting new technology in place of older, more varied adaptations to extremes. Even if the climate were to remain unchanged, the societal impacts of rare events would become greater. The need to study the vulnerability of mankind to weather and climatic extremes was recognized by the establishment of the second and third components of the World Climate Programme (involving UNEP, WMO, UNESCO, UNDRO, FAO, United Nations Research Institute for Social Development (UNRISD) and other agencies, together with the ICSU and the Scientific Committee on Problems of the Environment.

Air pollution control

Major achievements of the last decade in the understanding and technology of air pollution control included:

(a) increased public awareness in developed countries of both air pollution problems and of the need for controls;

(b) the development and wide adoption of crankcase gas recirculation and the catalytic converter, which reduced reactive emissions from automobiles;

(c) the reduction of lead in gasoline;

(d) continued advances in the technology for reducing air pollution from industrial processes (Chapter 11);

(e) the development of multiple-source urban air pollution climatological models facilitating land use planning;

(f) development of episode forecasting and alert systems, which became operational in some cities (e.g. Tokyo, Toronto);

(g) major improvements in monitoring equipment and organization (including international co-operation to monitor trans-boundary pollution).

At the beginning of the decade, the height of chimneys being constructed was constantly increasing. This solved local problems (e.g., at Sudbury, Canada where a 375m chimney was erected) but did not reduce discharge, and in some cases created problems at sites some distance away to which pollutants were transported. Although technological solutions for sulphur removal became available they were not widely implemented for financial and environmental reasons. In the United States, limestone scrubbing of stack gases was recommended, the sulphate products being dumped into lagoons. However, this merely transferred the problem from the air to the land. In the Sudbury, Canada, International Nickel Co. Ltd. case, 90 per cent of the sulphur was removed at source but the emissions still amounted to about 2,500 tonnes/day. Most of this excess could be captured in the form of sulphuric acid or elemental sulphur but there was no market for such large quantities, and no sites where the material could be safely dumped.

The scale of interest in air pollution control increased considerably during the decade, with environmental management spanning national borders. Air quality standards for sulphur dioxide were established in such diverse countries as Canada, Israel, Poland, Sweden, Turkey, Finland, the Netherlands, Rumania, Switzerland and the European Economic Community (Holdgate, 1979). The Netherlands and the Federal Republic of Germany cooperated on air pollution problems (Morawa, 1978). The EEC adopted an Environment Programme under which concerted action on air pollution problems was developed. CMEA member countries collaborated in developing improved pollution control equipment and in reducing discharges in the atmosphere (CMEA, 1981 a, b). In the United Kingdom the Clean Air Acts of 1954 and 1962 and continuing control of industrial emission under older legislation had led by the beginning of the decade to substantial improvement in air quality, and those trends have continued (Holdgate, 1979; DOE, 1980). In the United States the 1963 Clean Air Act was amended in 1970 and two deadlines were established: to attain air quality standards adequate to protect human health by 1 July 1975 and to attain more stringent standards that would, *inter alia,* eliminate most damage to vegetation and crops by 1 July 1977 (CEQ, 1976). Although the energy crisis and recession slowed progress and prevented those deadlines from being met, much was done, especially in curbing emissions from motor vehicles (the main source of the ingredients of oxidant smog). In the USSR in 1980 the Atmosphere Protection Act was adopted.

Episode forecasting and alert systems were linked to arrangements for voluntary reduction of emissions during periods of high pollution in many countries: in the State of North Rhine Westphalia in the Federal Republic of Germany, alert and control systems were established by law. However, in developing countries air quality deteriorated in many areas, partly because of the existence of many poorly-maintained internal combustion engines.

In 1972, WHO published a tentative air quality criterion value for urban areas of 0.06 ppm ozone. In 1976, WHO convened a Task Group to produce an updated air quality criteria document. The no-effect value for ozone was found to be 0.1 to 0.2 ppm. The Task Group reached a consensus that a one-hour mean ozone concentration of 0.05 to 0.1 ppm, not to be exceeded more than once per month, should be a guideline for the protection of public health (WHO, 1978).

There also were important observational studies of the air pollution of cities and areas downwind. For example, Project METROMEX was carried out in and around St. Louis, Missouri, USA (Berry and Beadle, 1974).

Acid rain

Concern about the effects of long-range transport of air pollutants increased after the late 1960s in both Europe and North America (Drabløs and Tollan, 1980). In 1972 the OECD began a "Cooperative Technical Programme to Measure the Long-Range Transport of Air Pollution (LRTAP)", which included extensive monitoring and modelling activities. The final report (OECD, 1977) confirmed that long-range transfers did occur and that scavenging of sulphates and nitrates by precipitation was causing acid rain.

Because the OECD suggested that Eastern and Western Europe should be examined as a single region with respect to long-range transport, the ECE originated in October 1977 the "Cooperative Programme for Monitoring and Evaluation of the Long-Range Transmission of Air Pollutants in Europe". This programme continues with the support of WMO and UNEP. In 1979, a multi-nation convention was signed committing the parties to use exchanges of information, consultation, research and monitoring to develop without undue delay policies and strategies to serve as a means of limiting and as far as possible gradually reducing and preventing air pollution, including long-range trans-boundary air pollution (ECE, 1979; CMEA, 1981 a, b).

In 1976, the Canadian government identified acid rain as a high priority environmental problem. Because of its transboundary nature, a United States-Canada Research Consultation Group was established, which produced its first report in 1979 (US–Canada, 1979). In 1980 a Memorandum of Intent was agreed upon (US–Canada, 1980), relating to research, monitoring, exchange of scientific information and gradual reduction in sulphur emissions, and Ontario announced proposed regulations for substantive reduction of sulphur dioxide and nitrogen dioxide emissions from coal-fired electric generating plants (Ontario, 1980).

In the USA, the Environmental Protection Agency, in collaboration with other federal agencies, established a fifty-station network, including the ten existing US regional BAPMoN stations, for a National Atmospheric Deposition Project (NADP) to help elucidate long-term trends in acid precipitation.

Carbon dioxide climate warming

The potential warming due to increasing concentrations of carbon dioxide has been understood since the 1930s and had been a matter of much earlier speculation. Arrhenius in 1896 and Chamberlin in 1899 suggested that the apparent warmth and luxuriant plant life of the Carboniferous period was associated with the 'greenhouse' effect of high CO_2 levels (Lamb, 1977). There is also evidence, from CO_2 trapped in the Greenland ice sheet, of considerable variations during the past 25,000 years, although these do not appear to coincide with known glacial variations (Thompson and Schneider, 1981).

However, it was only in the middle 1960s that there was general realization that the carbon dioxide concentrations at Mauna Loa were actually increasing. This led to an intensification of studies of world carbon cycle by Bolin, Keeling, Machta and others; a research activity that continues to this day (Bolin et al., 1979, Bolin et al., 1981). The advances of the past decade have included the development of mathematical models that explore the relationship between CO_2, temperature and climatic patterns.

In 1974 Budyko, using a simplified temperature model, estimated that the mean global temperature of the troposphere would rise by 2.5 to 3.5°C if atmospheric carbon dioxide were to double. In 1975 Manabe and Wetherald, using a general circulation model, predicted that a doubling of atmospheric carbon dioxide concentrations would cause a rise in mean global tropospheric temperatures of about 2°C. The latest evaluations (CEQ, 1981) conclude that such a doubling could eventually increase average annual global surface temperatures by about 3°C (but by as much as 7–10°C in the north polar region during winter). Wind, ocean current and precipitation patterns would be expected to alter, and some scientists have speculated that if the warming were large and persistent enough it could cause melting of part of the West Antarctic Ice Sheet and a rise in global sea level of 5 to 6 metres, on an uncertain time scale (Bentley, 1980). The climatic variations could manifestly affect agricultural patterns and ecological systems over large areas and the impacts – both detrimental and beneficial – on the socio-economic structure of the world could be considerable. However, present climate models and observations do not permit prediction of the magnitude and location of such disruptions (Kellogg and Schware, 1981).

These analyses stimulated action in two main areas: energy planning and research. A number of reports have evaluated the likely climatic implications of increases in the burning of fossil fuel in coming decades, such as are currently contemplated in many countries (e.g. OTA, 1979; Robinson, 1979; WMO/UNEP/ICSU, 1980; Kellogg and Schware, 1981; CEQ, 1981). In the United States it was concluded that a high priority must be given to incorporating the CO_2 issue into national energy policy planning, and that an upper limit of tolerable atmospheric CO_2 concentration should be defined (CEQ, 1981). The problem was also recognized as giving added importance to energy conservation and to the development of alternative energy sources (see also, Chapter 12).

The CO_2 question was undoubtedly the largest outstanding environmental problem confronting the world at the end of the 1970s. Major uncertainties remained, especially concerning the role of living organisms in the carbon cycle, the interactions of the carbon cycle with other biogeochemical cycles, and the regional climatic impacts of an increase in atmospheric CO_2 concentrations. Accelerated research was recognized as necessary, including the detailed assessment of deforestation and soil destruction rates and the associated fluxes of CO_2 in the atmosphere. Further information on historic trends in these processes and changes in living organisms that could influence atmospheric CO_2 was also sought. UNEP supported the WMO-BAPMoN CO_2 Reference Laboratory at the Scripps Institute of Oceanography in California, which provided calibration standards for all BAPMoN stations measuring carbon dioxide. At the end of the decade SCOPE had established an active programme on biogeochemical cycling, while WMO and UNEP supported a programme of research and monitoring related to carbon dioxide and possible climate change (WMO, 1979). The research needs, as seen in the United States, were published in an agenda by the Department of Energy (US DOE, 1980).

A WMO/UNEP/ICSU Workshop concluded that five areas in particular required the attention of a major international inter-disciplinary research effort:

1. Critical evaluation of the likely consumption of fossil fuel over the next century;

2. Analysis of likely trends in biosphere management, and especially of the conversion of forests to grazing and agricultural land;

3. Clarification of the carbon cycle, and quantification of the partitioning of CO_2 between the atmosphere, oceans and biosphere;

4. Better models of the climatic response to increasing atmospheric CO_2 concentrations;

5. Analysis of the potential impact of climatic change, especially on agriculture and fisheries, but also on water supplies and natural ecosystems.

Stratospheric ozone depletion

Following predictions in 1974 that chlorofluorocarbons as well as various other chemicals, diffused to the altitudes of the ozone layer, would lead (as described above) to the layer's depletion, a group of experts prepared a World Plan of Action on the Ozone Layer. Under it a Co-ordinating Committee on the Ozone Layer (CCOL) was established, which subsequently produced assessments of ozone layer depletion and its impacts.

Among the highlights of the CCOL report in 1980 were:

1. Prediction, as noted above, that continued releases of CFCs 11 and 12 at the 1977 rate would eventually reduce the ozone layer to 10 per cent less than if no CFCs were released;

2. Recognition that many other factors such as lightning, methyl chloroform, and fertilizers may increase or decrease global ozone amounts;

3. Increasing indications of sunlight as a causative factor in skin cancer;

4. Recognition of the need for further investigation of the effects on organisms of changed levels of UV–B radiation.

One of the outcomes was the suggestion by one government that scientific knowledge had advanced to such a stage that it should be translated promptly into policy action on the global level.

Future Prospects

Through the WMO and its predecessor the IMO there has been a long tradition of international collaboration among atmospheric scientists. More recently, linkages have been strengthened between atmospheric scientists and environmentalists in other disciplines (oceanography, hydrology, geography, agronomy, forestry, etc.), partly due to the encouragement given by UNEP, SCOPE, and various national groups (DOE, 1980). This trend will continue, permitting the application of comprehensive approaches to the outstanding atmospheric problems of the current decade. The prospects are therefore favourable that proper research priorities will be set and that appropriate governmental and intergovernmental actions will follow. Three of the major atmospheric challenges for the decade of the 80s will be mentioned in the following subsections. Two of these relate to forecasting and monitoring, and the third to the question of energy alternatives.

THE NEED FOR LONG-RANGE WEATHER AND CLIMATE FORECASTS

Three-dimensional numerical models of the atmosphere greatly simplify the atmosphere – ocean – biosphere – cryosphere coupled system. Even so they are exceedingly complex. For this and other reasons, the development of long-range (more than five days) weather and climate forecasts proved to be an intractable problem over the last century. However, current activities within GARP and the World Climate Programme offer some hope of extending forecast ability, with attendant economic benefits.

INTEGRATED MONITORING SYSTEMS

Near the end of the decade, Izrael (1979, 1980) and Izrael *et al.*, (1978, 1980) in the USSR emphasized the importance of integrated monitoring systems, in which observations are made in all media and are co-ordinated in space and time. This approach was said to be cost-effective as well as to provide a framework for harmonizing different kinds of monitoring programmes (UNEP, 1981 b).

Thirty to forty land stations and up to ten marine stations are believed to be sufficient for global coverage. They would best be located in biosphere reserves established within the UNESCO/MAB Programme (See Chapter 6), with co-ordination by UNESCO, WMO and UNEP. The basic principles of the integrated monitoring system are that observations of concentrations and pathways of primary pollutants occur in all media; the responses of natural systems to man-made impacts are measured; and that maximum use is made of available stations under the aegis of WMO, UNESCO, IOC, ECE, CMEA, UNEP and other international and national programmes and projects. It should assist national governments to manage natural resources better. All types of monitoring in space and time, and compatible techniques and methods of observation, data processing and interpreting would be used as far as possible.

Before such a system is established, a few pilot projects may be carried out to provide a basis for more general application. The first such project is planned for the Bereszinsky Biosphere Reserve in the USSR, starting in 1981. So far as the atmosphere is concerned, monitoring would include background levels of substances; solar radiation; thermal balance components; meteorological elements; and hydrological components. Still other types of monitoring can be of significant scientific interest. Monitoring of the past could include measurements of pollutant concentration in dated samples (of peat, ice, arboreal layers, museum specimens, etc.). Monitoring of the future will call for storage of samples in banks for future analysis. One of the challenges of the 1980s will be to implement these ideas on a global scale, providing one basis for a continuing *earthwatch* of the planet's atmosphere.

ENVIRONMENTAL IMPACTS OF ENERGY ALTERNATIVES

A major preoccupation of governments and scientists at present is the question of energy alternatives, particularly the environmental aspects of the expanding nuclear industry and increasing coal utilization in many countries. This leads to growing concern about the problems of acid rain and carbon dioxide climate-warming.

Atmospheric scientists have given high priority to these questions, and the research programmes currently in place are needed. However, the prediction of impacts is still rather uncertain and has insufficient space and time resolution. Attention should also be directed to comparative risk assessments of various alternative management strategies to provide a more solid foundation for national and international policy analysis. Atmospheric scientists should work more closely with social scientists seeking means to quantify not only the biogeophysical changes in the environment but also the socio-economic benefits and disbenefits, clearly identifying the affected parties.

An important common element of both the acid rain and the carbon dioxide questions is the biogeochemical cycling of trace substances through the environment. For example, the atmospheric components of the sulphur and nitrogen cycles are linked, which means that control of sulphur emissions alone would not necessarily have the expected effect (Rodhe *et al.,* 1979).

Special tasks for the next few years include:

1. Development of improved experimental and empirical methods of estimating the transfer rates of trace gases and suspended particulate matter between the atmosphere and the Earth's surface;

2. Development of improved methods of estimating emission rates of trace substances from both man-made and natural sources;

3. Improved understanding and modelling of atmospheric chemical transformations;

4. Refinement of methods of studying health and ecological effects of low-level exposure;

5. Refinement of methods for estimating climate change, including shifts of precipitation patterns, from mounting atmospheric carbon dioxide.

References

Abelson, P. H. (1980), The Global 2000 Report, *Science*, 209, 760.

Akland, G. *et al.* (1980), Air Quality Surveillance; Trends in Selected Urban Areas, *WHO Chronicle*, 34, 147. World Health Organization, Geneva.

Altschuller, A. P. and G. A. McBean (1980), *Second Report of the United States – Canada Research Consultation Group on the Long-Range Transport of Air Pollutants.*

Angell, J. K. (1979), Some Preliminary Results of Study Trends in Ozone Concentrations, Appendix to UNEP/CCOL III/3.Add.3, United Nations Environment Programme.

Angell, J. K. (In press), *Trends in Surface and Upper Air Temperatures*, NOAA Air Resources Laboratories, Silver Spring.

Angell, J. K. and J. Korshover (1979), Comparison of Ozone Variations Derived from Ozonesondes and Umkher Measurments for the Period 1969–76, *Mon. Weather Rev.*, 107, 559.

Bentley, C. R. (1980), *Response of the West Antartic Ice Sheet to CO_2- Induced Climatic Warming*, Report of a US Department of Energy Sponsored Meeting, June 1980.

Berger, D. (1978), *Ultraviolet Erythema Global Measuring Network* 1978, GMCC Summary Report 1978, Env. Res. Labs., NOAA, Department of Commerce, Washington, D.C.

Berlyand, M. E. (1975), *Present-Day Problems of Atmospheric Diffusion and Pollution*, Gidrometeoizdat, Leningrad.

Berlyand, M. E., Editor (1977), *Standardization and Control of Industrial Emissions to the Atmosphere*, Gidrometeoizdat, Leningrad.

Berlyand, M. E. (1980), *Problems of Atmospheric Pollution Monitoring*, Proc.Int.Symp. on Integrated Global Monitoring of Poll. of Nat. Envir., Riga, USSR, 1978, Gidrometeoizdat, Leningrad.

Berry, E. X. and R. W. Beadle (1974), Project METROMEX, *Bull. Amer. Meteor. Soc.*, 55, 86.

Boer, G. J. and K. Higuchi (1979), *A Study of Climatic Variability*, Report No. 79–14, Canada Climate Centre, AES, Downsview, Ontario, Canada.

Bolin, B. (1975), *The Physical Basis of Climate and Climate Modelling*, GARP Publication No. 16, World Meteorological Organization, Geneva.

Bolin, B. (1979), *Global Ecology and Man*, World Climate Conference, World Meteorological Organization, Geneva.

Bolin, B. *et al.*, Editors (1979), *The Global Carbon Cycle SCOPE* 13, John Wiley, Chichester.

Bolin, B. *et al.* (1981), *Global Carbon Modelling; SCOPE* 16, John Wiley, Chichester.

Borzenkova, I. I. *et al.* (1976), Changes of Air Temperature in the Northern Hemisphere for the period of 1881–1975, *Meteorologia i Gidrologia*, No. 7.

Brimblecombe, P. (1977), London Air Pollution, 1500–1900, *Atmos. Environ.*, 11, 1157.

Bryson, R. A. and G. J. Dittberner (1976), A Non-Equilibrium Model of Hemispheric Mean Surface Temperature, *J. Atm. Sci.*, 33, 2094.

CAST (1976), *Effect of Increased Nitrogen Fixation on Stratospheric Ozone*, Report No. 53, US Council for Agriculture, Science and Technology, Washington, D.C.

CEQ (1976), *Environmental Quality*, 7th Annual Report of the Council on Environmental Quality, Washington, D.C.

CEQ (1980), *The Global* 2000 *Report to the President*, Council on Environmental Quality, Washington, D.C.

CEQ (1981), *Global Energy Futures and the Carbon Dioxide Problem*, Council on Environmental Quality, Washington, D.C.

CMEA (1981 a), *Information on Co-operation Between the CMEA Member Countries in the Field of Environmental Protection and Improvement and the Related Use of Natural Resource*, Council for Mutual Economic Assistance, Moscow.

CMEA (1981 b), *Description of the Overall Expanded Programme of Co-operation of the CMEA Countries for* 1981–85 *in the Field of Environment Protection and Improvement and the Related Use of Natural Resource*, Council for Mutual Economic Assistance, Moscow.

Costle, D. M. (1980), Visibility Protection – A Proposal, *J. Air Poll. Control Assoc.*, 30, 632.

Crutzen, P. J. (1976), Upper Limits on Atmospheric Ozone Reductions Following Increased Application of Fixed Nitrogen to the Soil, *Geophys. Res. Letters*, 3, 169.

CSIRO (1978), *Atmospheric Chemistry Research*, CSIRO Division of Atmospheric Research, Mordialloc, Victoria, Australia.

De Bary, E. and C. Junge (1963), Distribution of Sulphur and Chlorine Over Europe, *Tellus*, 15, 370.

DOE (1976), *Chlorofluorocarbons and Their Effect on Stratospheric Ozone*, Department of the Environment, HMSO, London.

DOE (1980), *Digest of Environmental Pollution and Water Statistics*, No. 3, Department of the Environment, HMSO, London.

DOT (1979), *Second Biennial Report Prepared in Accordance with the Ozone Protection Provision of the Clean Air Act Amendments of* 1977, FAA High Altitude Pollution Programme, FAA–EE–79–24, US Department of Transportation, Washington, D.C.

Drabløs, D. and A. Tollan, Editors (1980), *Ecological Impact of Acid Precipitation*, Proc. Int. Conf., Sandefjord, Norway, March 1980. SNSF Project, Oslo.

EAJ (1980), *Quality of the Environmental in Japan* –1980, Environment Agency, Tokyo.

ECE (1979), *Convention on Long-Range Transboundary Pollution*, Economic Commission for Europe, Geneva.

ECE (1981), *New Developments with Regard to Strategies and Policies for the Abatement of Air Pollution Caused by Sulphate Compounds*, Economic Commission for Europe, ECE/ENV/IEB/R. 13, Geneva.

EPA (1975), *Position Paper on Regulation of Atmospheric Sulphates*, US Environmental Protection Agency, 450/2–75–007 I, XIX 1–88, Washington, D.C.

Flöhn, H. (1977), Man-induced Changes in Heat Budget and Possible Effects on Climate. In W. Stumm (Editor), *Global Chemical Cycles and their Alterations by Man*, Abakon Verlagsgesellschaft, Berlin.

Glantz, M., Editor (1977), *Desertification; Environmental Degradation in and around Arid Lands*. Westview Press, Boulder, Colorado.

GMCC (1978), *Summary Report* 1978, *Geophysical Monitoring for Climatic Change*, No. 7, Environmental Research Labs, NOAA, Department of Commerce, Washington, D.C.

Goldberg, E. D. *et al.* (1976), Metal Pollution in Tokyo as Recorded in Sediments of the Palace Moat. *Geochem. J.*, 10, 165.

Granat, L. (1978), Sulphate in precipitation as observed by the European Atmospheric Chemistry Network, *Atmos. Environ.*, 12, 413.

Greece (1981), *Problems and Protection Measures for Monuments; The Acropolis Case*, Greek Review of Environmental Policies, Reference Document Submitted by Ministry of Co-ordination, Athens.

Hage, K. D. (1972), Urban Growth Effects on Low Temperature Fog in Edmonton, *Boundary-Layer Meteorology*, 2, 334.

Hansen, J. E. *et al.*, (1978), Mount Agung Eruption Provides Test of a Global Climatic Perturbation, *Science*, 199, 1065.

Hansen, J. *et al.*, (1981), Climate Impact of Increasing Atmospheric CO_2, *Science*, 213, 957.

Hare, F. K. (1979), *Climate Variation and Variability: Empirical Evidence from Meterological and Other Sources*, Extended Summary of Papers Presented at the World Climate Congress, World Meterological Organization, Geneva.

Harley, W. S. (1980), The Significance of Climatic Changes in the Northern Hemisphere 1949–1978, *Mon. Weather Rev.*, 108, 235.

Hoffmann, D. J. and J. M. Rosen (1980), Stratospheric Sulphuric Acid Layer: Evidence for an Anthropogenic Component, *Science*, 208, 1368.

Holdgate, M. W. (1979), *A Perspective of Environmental Pollution*, Cambridge University Press, Cambridge.

Husar, R. B. *et al.*, (1979), *Trends of Eastern US Haziness Since* 1948, 4th Symposium on Atmospheric Diffusion and Air Pollution, American Meterological Society, Boston, Mass.

Ivanov, M. V. and J. R. Freney, Editors (In press), *The Global Biogeochemical Sulphur Cycle and Influence on it of Man's Activities*, John Wiley, Chichester.

Izrael, Yu. A. (1979), *Ecology and Control of the State of the Natural Environment*, Gidrometeoizdat, Leningrad.

Izrael, Yu. A. (1980), *Basic Principles of Monitoring of Natural Environment and Climate*, Proc. Int. Symp. on Integrated Global Monitoring of Poll. of Nat. Envir., Riga, USSR 1978. Gidrometeoizdat, Leningrad.

Izrael, Yu. A. *et al.*, (1978), On the Programme of Integrated Background Monitoring of the State of the Natural Environment, *Meteorology and Hydrology*, No. 9, 5.

Israel, Yu. A. *et al.*, (1980), *Atmosphere; Background Report*, Prepared for the United Nations Environment Programme.

Johannes, A. H. *et al.*, (1980), *Snow Pack Storage and Ion Release*, Proc. International Conference on Ecological Impact of Acid Precipitation, Sandefjord, Norway, SNSF Project, Oslo.

Junge, C. (1960), Sulphur in the Atmosphere, *J. Geophys. Res.*, 65, 227.

Keeling, C. D. and B. B. Bacastow (1977), Impacts of Industrial Gases on Climate. In *Energy and Climate*, National Academy of Sciences, Washington, D.C.

Kellogg, W. W. (1977), *Effects of Human Activities on Global Climate*, Technical Note 156, World Meterological Organization, Geneva.

Kellogg, W. W. and R. Schware (1981), *Climatic Change and Society; Consequences of Increasing Atmospheric Carbon Dioxide*, Westview Press, Boulder, Colorado.

Khrgian, A. P. (1978), *Physics of the Atmosphere, Part I*, Gidrometeoizdat, Leningrad.

Lamb, H. H. (1977), *Climate; Present, Past and Future*, Methuen, London.

Larssen, S. and J. E. Hanssen (1980), *Annual Variation and Origin of Aerosol Components in the Norwegian Arctic-Subarctic Region*, Proceedings WMO Technical Conference on Regional and Global Observation of Atmospheric Pollution; Report No. 549, World Meteorological Organization, Geneva.

Likens, G. E. (1976), Hydrogen Ion Input to the Hubbard Brook Experimental Forest, New Hampshire, During the Last Decade, *Water, Air and Soil Pollution*, No. 6, 435.

Likens, G. E. *et al.*, (1979), Acid Rain, *Scientific Amer.*, 241, 43.

Madden, R. A. and V. Ramanathan (1980), Detecting Climate Change Due to Increasing CO_2, *Science*, 209, 763.

Manabe, S. and R. T. Wetherald (1975), The Effects of Doubling the CO_2 Concentration on the Climate of a General Circulation Model. *J. Atmos. Sci.*, 32, 3.

Marchuk, G. I. (1979), A Modelling of Climatic Changes and the Problem of Early Weather Forecasting, *Meteorologia i Gidrologia*, 7, 25.

Marchuk, G. I. *et al.*, (1979), The Global Model of General Circulation of the Amosphere, *Izv. AK.SSR, Fizika Atmosfery i Okeana*, 15, 5.

Monin, A. S. and Yu. A. Shiskov (1979), *History of Climate*, Gidrometeoizdat, Leningrad.

Morawa, C. (1978), *Co-operation Between the Netherlands and the FRG on Air Pollution Problems*, Kleindienst, Offsetdruk, Berlin.

Munn, R. E. (1980), *The Estimation and Interpretation of Air Quality Trends, Including Some Implications for Network Design*, Proceedings WMO Technical Conference on Regional and Global Observation of Atmospheric Pollution, Report No. 549, World Meteorological Organization, Geneva.

NAS (1978), *Sulphur Oxides*, National Academy of Sciences, Washington, D.C.

NAS (1979), *Stratospheric Ozone Depletion by Halocarbons; Chemistry and Transport*, Panel on Stratospheric Chemistry and Transport, National Academy of Science, Washington, D.C.

NAS (1980), *Lead in the Human Environment*, National Academy of Sciences, Washington, D.C.

NASA/DOT (1980), *Upper Atmospheric Programs Bulletin*, Issue No. 80–3. Washington, D.C.

NIAR (1977), *Sources and Significance of Natural and Man-made Aerosols in the Arctic*, Report of a workshop, Norwegian Institute for Air Research, Lillestrøm, Norway.

Nriagu, J. O. (1979), Global Inventory of Natural and Antropogenic Emissions of Trace Metals to the Atmosphere, *Nature*, 279, 409.

OECD (1977), *Co-operative Technical Programme to Measure the Long-Range Transport of Air Pollutants*, Organization for Economic Co-operation and Development, Paris.

OECD (1978), Photochemical Oxidants and their Precursors in the Atmosphere. *Env.*, 78, 6, Organization for Economic Co-operation and Development, Paris.

OECD (1979), *The State of the Environment in OECD Member Countries,* Organization for Economic Co-operation and Development, Paris.

Ontario (1980), *The Case Against the Rain,* A Report on Acidic Precipitation and Ontario Programs for Remedial Action, Ministry of the Environment, Ontario.

OTA (1979), *The Direct Use of Coal,* Office of Technology Assessment, US Congress, Washington, D.C.

Penner, J. E. and J. S. Chang (1978), *Possible Variations in Atmospheric Ozone Related to 11-Year Solar Cycle,* WMO Rept. No. 511, World Meteorological Organization, Geneva.

Petrenchuk, O. P. (1980), *The Chemical Composition of Precipitation Studies at Background Stations,* Proc. Int. Symp. on Integrated Global Monitoring of Poll. of Nat. Envir., Riga, USSR, 1978. Gidrometeoizdat, Leningrad.

Pittock, A. B. (1977), On the Causes of Local Climate Anomalies, with Special Reference to Precipitation in Washington State, *J. Applied Meteorology,* 16, 223.

Pyle, J. A. and R. G. Derwent (1980), Possible Ozone Reductions and UV Changes at the Earth's Surface, *Nature,* 286, 373.

Rahn, K. A. *et al.,* (1979), Long-Range Impact on Desert Aerosols on Atmospheric Chemistry: Two Examples, In C. Moreles (Editor), *Saharan Dust; SCOPE* 14. John Wiley and Sons, Chichester.

Rahn, K. A. and R. J. McCaffrey (1979), Compositional Differences Between Arctic Aerosols and Snow. *Nature,* 280, 479.

Reay, J. S. S. (1973), *Air Pollution Monitoring in the United Kingdom,* Design of Environmental Information Systems, HMSO, London.

Robinson, F. A., Editor (1979), *Environmental Effects of Utilizing More Coal,* Royal Society of Chemistry, London.

Rodhe, H. *et al.,* (1979), *Formation of Sulphuric and Nitric Acid in the Atmosphere During Long-Range Transport,* Proceedings of the Symposium on Long-Range Transport of Pollutants, Sofia, Bulgaria. World Meteorological Organization, Geneva.

Rotty, R. M. (1978), Atmospheric CO_2 Consequences of Heavy Dependence on Coal. In J. M. Williams (Editor), *Carbon Dioxide, Climate and Society.* Pergamon Press, Oxford.

Rotty, R. M. and A. M. Weinberg (1977), How long is Coal's Future? *Climat. Change,* 1, 45.

Rovinsky, F. Y. *et al.,* (1980): *Materials of Background Integrated Monitoring of Natural Media Pollution,* Proc. Int. Symp. on Integrated Global Monitoring of Poll. of Nat. Envir., Riga, USSR, 1978. Gidrometeoizdat, Leningrad.

Sagan, C. *et. al.,* (1979), Anthropogenic Albedo Changes and the Earth's Climate, *Science,* 206, 1363.

Schaeffer, V. J. (1975), The Inadvertent Modification of the Atmosphere by Air Pollution. In S. F. Singer (Editor), *The Changing Global Environment,* Reidel Publ. Co., Dordrecht, Holland.

Schneider, S. H. and C. Mass (1975), Volcanic Dust, Sunspots and Temperature Trends. *Science,* 190, 741.

Semb, A. (1978), Sulphur Emissions in Europe. *Atm. Env.,* 12, 455.

Stommel, H. (1958), *The Gulf Streams; A Physical and Dynamical Description*, Univ. California Press, Berkeley, California.

Thompson, S. L. and S. H. Schneider (1981), Carbon Dioxide and Climate; Ice and Ocean, *Nature*, 292, 9.

Thrush, B. A. (1979), Aspects of the Chemistry of Ozone Depletion, *Phil. Trans. Roy. Soc. London*, A.290, 505.

Tiao, G. C. *et al.*, (1975), A Statistical Analysis of the Los Angeles Ambient Carbon Monoxide Data 1955–1972, *J. Air. Poll. Control Assoc.*, 25, 1129.

UK (1976), *Chlorofluorocarbons and their Effect on Stratospheric Ozone*, Pollution Paper No. 5, Department of the Environment, HMSO, London.

UNEP (1980), *The State of the Environment – Selected Topics*, United Nations Environment Programme, Nairobi.

UNEP (1981 a), *Environmental Assessment of Ozone Layer Depletion and Its Impact*, Ozone Bulletin No. 6, United Nations Environment Programme, Nairobi.

UNEP (1981 b), *Selected Works on Integrated Monitoring*, GEMS/PAC Info. Series No. 2, United Nations Environment Programme, Nairobi.

UNEP/FAO (1981), *GEMS Global Assessment of Tropical Forest Resources*, Food and Agriculture Organization of the United Nations, Rome.

US/Canada (1979), *The LRTAP Problem in North America; A Preliminary Overview*, State Department, Washington, D.C.

US/Canada (1980), *Memorandum of Intent Between the Government of Canada and the Government of the United States of America Concerning Trans-Boundary Air Pollution*, State Department, Washington, D.C. and External Affairs, Ottawa.

US DOE (1980), *Carbon Dioxide Effects; Research and Assessment Program*, US Depart. of Energy, Washington, D.C.

Vickers, G. G. and R. E. Munn (1977), A Canadian Haze Climatology, *Climat. Change*, 1, 97.

Vinnikov, K. Ya. *et al.*, (1980), The Present-Day Changes of Climate in the Northern Hemisphere, *Meteorologia i Gidrologia* No. 6, 5–17.

Wallén, C. C. (1980), A Preliminary Evaluation of WMO-UNEP Precipitation Chemistry Data, *MARC Rep.* No. 22, MARC, Chelsea College, London.

Wang, W. C. and N. D. Sze (1980), Coupled Effects of Atmospheric N_2O and O_3 on the Earth's Climate, *Nature*, 286, 589.

WHO (1978), *Environmental Health Criteria, No. 7, Photochemical Oxidants*, World Health Organization, Geneva.

WMO (1979), *WMO Project on Research and Monitoring of Atmospheric CO_2*, Rep. No. 2, World Meteorological Organization, Geneva.

WMO/UNEP/ICSU (1980), *On the Assessment of the Role of CO_2 on Climate Variations and their Impact*, Joint WMO/UNEP/ICSU Meeting of Experts, Villach, Austria, November, 1980.

CHAPTER 3

The Marine Environment

During the 1970s considerable advances were made in scientific understanding of the physical and chemical properties of the oceans, and of the circulation of their waters – important features because they determine the dispersion of pollutants and the productivity of fisheries. But the monitoring of pollution and of ecosystems was confined to a few localities, making it impossible to define trends for the oceans as a whole. The best data came from the Baltic, the North Sea, some North American and Australian estuaries and coastal waters, and the Mediterranean. By the end of the decade, the Regional Seas Programme of the United Nations Environment Programme (UNEP) was collecting information about other seas as well.

In most of these areas the pollution that caused most concern was due to sewage, agricultural chemicals, oil, and metals. Metal concentrations were clearly elevated in coastal waters, and in fish and shellfish living there. In some areas mercury levels in species such as tuna were high enough to make these fish undesirable as human food but some of this mercury came from natural processes rather than pollution. Overall, chemical contamination of the oceans appeared to be localized, with the worst conditions in estuaries and land-locked coastal seas in industrial regions, and here ecological changes were apparent.

Some of this pollution came via rivers: the amount of iron, manganese, copper, zinc, lead, tin and antimony that reached the sea this way was far greater than would be supplied by natural geological processes. Other contaminants came through atmospheric deposition: the importance of this pathway for metals and synthetic chemicals was first recognized during the decade.

Mineral resources of the sea-bed – especially oil – were increasingly exploited during the decade. Coastal zone developments affected extensive areas of mangrove swamp and coral reef. Oil pollution killed thousands of sea-birds, fouled beaches and affected tourism. Although tanker accidents were the source of only about 5 per cent of all the oil entering the sea, they released large volumes in small areas and were especially damaging for this reason.

Organochlorine pesticides and polychlorinated biphenyls (PCBs) were found to be widely distributed in the sea and marine life. However, the concentrations of DDT and related pesticides fell in coastal waters of north-west Europe and North America, and PCBs also showed some indication of decline. Except in the most highly polluted coastal localities, there was no evidence that marine productivity or fish stocks had been reduced through chemical contamination, or that floating oil had affected the recruitment rates of fish or shellfish. However, many scientists were cautious in their reaction to this generally reassuring picture because there were deficiencies in monitoring and because they were uncertain over the possible long-term effects of ecosystem exposure to contamination.

World fishery yields rose during the 1960s and 1970s, with a dip in the production curve in 1972/73. Some populations – notably of Peruvian anchoveta and North Atlantic herring – were depleted, with over-exploitation commonly blamed. Some argued that world *landings in 1980 were 15–20 million tonnes less than they would have been had good management prevailed. By the end of the decade, however, there were hopes of recovery in several fish stocks as a result of tighter controls. Looking ahead, substantial increases in marine food production appeared possible, partly through mariculture, which expanded greatly, especially in China and South-East Asia.*

The decade saw continuing concern over marine mammals. Population estimates of species that have formed the basis of the commercial whaling industry this century in the North Pacific and the Southern Hemisphere suggest that there is now only about 48 per cent of the total stock remaining. A ban on all commercial whaling, proposed at the Stockholm Conference, had not been achieved by the decade's end, but a new management procedure was implemented by the International Whaling Commission in 1975, under which catches have been greatly reduced.

Much international activity took place during the decade. Conventions to control marine pollution were adopted. Action plans were in operation or planned for ten regions. Coastal and marine national parks and reserves were extended.

The Physical, Chemical and Biological Features of the Oceans

The productivity of the marine environment and its capacity to receive and disperse pollutants depend on its physical and chemical properties. The transport of pollutants and their rate of dilution or deposition in sediments is determined by motion in the sea, at all scales from the oceanic to the molecular.

The surface layer of the sea is directly influenced by the atmosphere. Above a certain wind speed, the wind-induced motion generates a surface mixed layer, and in shallow shelf seas wind and tidal action together prevent stratification of the water and ensure that pollutants are fairly rapidly interchanged between surface and bottom waters. In the open ocean, however, the surface mixed layer is generally separated from colder, deep water by a relatively shallow zone of sharp transitional temperature or salinity (thermocline, halocline) or both. The circulations of the upper and deep waters are markedly different and contaminants injected into them follow different routes, on different time scales.

The strongest currents are at the western boundaries of the oceans (the Gulf Stream in the North Atlantic, Kuroshio in the North Pacific, Agulhas Current in the South Indian Ocean and East Australian Current in the South Pacific). They transport water at velocities around 100–200 cm/sec away from the equatorial regions, turning to a more eastward flow at around latitudes 40° North and South. Slower currents flowing towards the equator on the eastern sides of the oceans feed the equatorial currents and establish circular flow patterns (gyres) in the subtropical regions: other gyres with an opposite direction of circulation occur in higher latitudes (Munk, 1950; Stommel, 1965). The combination of wind and surface current has a dominant influence on the dispersion of oil and other pollutants in the upper layers of the sea.

The circulation of the deep and bottom waters is very different. Cold, deep water is formed, especially in the Weddell Sea (Antarctica), and spreads northwards into the Atlantic where it drives the deep circulation and influences the whole world ocean. Other deep water is formed in the Norwegian/Greenland Sea. At an intermediate depth of around 2,000 m in the North Atlantic there is a southward flow beneath the Gulf Stream with velocities less than 20 cm/sec which extends across the equator to 30° or 40° South latitude and eventually forms part of a warm intermediate layer which rises to the surface in a zone of upwelling around the Antarctic. Because these deep currents flow slowly over great distances, substances injected into them may re-emerge in the surface layers after very long intervals.

The circulation pattern in semi-enclosed and shelf seas is more complicated than in the open ocean and is subject to seasonal variations. In the Baltic and Black Seas there is only weak vertical mixing, so that the bottom water stagnates and tends to become depleted of oxygen and to accumulate pollutants. In the Mediterranean, in contrast, high evaporation at the surface creates a weak convective circulation so that oxygen concentrations in the deeper waters are sustained — although land-locked areas like the northern Adriatic are not well scoured. Such variations make it necessary to study the circulation patterns of seas of this type in some detail if the pattern of contaminant dispersion and biological production within them is to be understood.

At the sea surface there is a boundary microlayer about 100 microns thick, through which exchanges between atmosphere and ocean must pass. The microlayer has higher concentrations of many substances (including lipids) than the waters beneath: some pollutants (such as dichlorodiphenyltrichloroethane (DDT) and other organochlorines) accumulate there and it is also high in bacteria and plankton and has enhanced biological activity. Its micro-organisms may be important in the breakdown of oil slicks.

The oxygen concentration at the surface is governed primarily by interchange with the atmosphere, but is affected by biological oxygen consumption. Vertically, there is an oxygen minimum at around 600m to 1000m, and relatively high concentrations at depth. The dissolved carbon dioxide (CO_2) in the sea is in approximate equilibrium with atmospheric CO_2, the sea being an important sink for the CO_2 added to the air by man (Chapter 2). Photosynthesis in the surface layers removes CO_2, which is returned when the dead organic matter is oxidized. Dissolved CO_2 is also removed from the surface waters as bicarbonate, ultimately accumulating in carbonate sediments which are the largest pool of carbon in the total biosphere (Bolin et al., 1979). The rates of transfer are critical, equilibrium between the atmosphere and the upper mixed layers of ocean being attained in a matter of five to ten years, whereas the exchange time between the upper waters and the deep sea is of the order of 500—2,000 years.

Table 3–1 lists the major components of sea water. About 25 billion tonnes of material are added to the ocean each year, over 90 per cent via rivers. Besides the substances listed, the sea contains considerable quantities of silicon (important biologically), some 61 trace elements, and various radioactive isotopes. Some trace elements are removed from the water and concentrated a thousandfold or even a hundred thousandfold by organisms. Metals and some synthetic contaminants (such as organochlorine pesticides and polychlorinated biphenyls) are prone to behave in this way.

Table 3–1. Major Salt Constituents of Seawater [a]

Component		Concentration	% of Total Salt
Chloride	(Cl^-)	18.980	55.04
Sodium	(Na^+)	10.543	30.61
Sulphate	(SO_4^{2-})	2.465	7.68
Magnesium	(Mg^{2+})	1.272	3.69
Calcium	(Ca^{2+})	0.400	1.16
Potassium	(K^+)	0.380	1.10
Bicarbonate	$(HCO_3^-)^b$	0.140	0.41
Bromide	$(Br^-)^b$	0.065	0.19
Boric acid	(HBO_3)	0.024	0.07
	Total	34.455	99.95

Source: Fairbridge (1972).

[a]values in g/kg ($^o/_{oo}$) (per thousand) based on chlorinity of 19$^o/_{oo}$.
[b]varies to give equivalent CO_3^{--} depending on pH.
value given is essentially true for pH 7.50 at 20°C.

Biological productivity and biomass (standing stock) are very much influenced by physical conditions (light, temperature and salinity) and by the availability of nutrients (Riley and Skirrow, 1975). Areas near the coasts where water containing dissolved nutrients rises to the surface from depth (upwelling) and zones where water masses converge or diverge are generally rich, while the central areas of oceanic gyres have low biomass (although production rates may remain high). Silicon, phosphorus and nitrogen are the most important nutrients and are commonly depleted during summer months, although not necessarily to the point where they limit growth. Although some 200 million tonnes of organic carbon reaches the oceans each year via rivers, and a comparable amount through the atmosphere, this is only equivalent to about two per cent of the total net primary production, 90 per cent of which is due to phytoplankton and almost all the remainder to benthic algae (algae growing on the sea bed). In temperate regions, the amount of carbon entering the food chain as a result of photosynthesis can range from

50–170 grams per square metre (g/m^2) per year in coastal waters and 60–100 g/m^2 offshore. In highly productive zones of upwelling as much as 5–10 g/m^2 of carbon can be fixed per day. Overall, 20 billion to 60 billion tonnes of carbon per year are fixed by oceanic photosynthesis — a total comparable to that on land.

The marine biological system differs from the terrestrial in that the phytoplankton of the open sea is eaten nearly as fast as it is produced, nearly all the plant material in the ecosystem passing to the herbivores (whereas only about 10 per cent does so on land). The herbivores are highly efficient at transferring energy through the food chain from plants to primary carnivores (Steele, 1974). Herbivore faeces rather than dead plant material are the main nutrient source for animals living on the sea bottom. The high fishery yield from upwelling zones is due to the harvesting of species such as anchovy which are predominantly herbivorous.

Shallow coastal waters, including estuaries and swamps, are enriched by nutrients coming from the land and from upwelling and are especially productive of many species important to man. They are also the breeding and nursery grounds for fish species that are commercially important offshore. These are the areas where human influence is most profound, and where damage from pollution and changes in the use of coastal lands are concentrated, and it is therefore logical that monitoring has also focussed on them (GESAMP, 1980 b).

The State of the Marine Environment in the 1970s

THE MEASUREMENT OF CHANGES IN THE MARINE ENVIRONMENT

There are three essential components in any estimation of changes in the contamination of the marine environment. First, standards are required against which the significance of detected changes can be assessed. These may be provided by a baseline study defining the situation at the start of the period under consideration. Second, the input of contaminants by man needs to be determined and related to the natural flux of the same materials, including their uptake by organisms. Third, the distribution of these substances in the environment must be monitored in order to detect and follow subsequent changes in contaminant concentrations in ecosystems. It is essential that analytical techniques are inter-calibrated (ICES, 1978 c) and that agreed sampling and storage procedures are followed over a common time period (UNESCO, 1976).

Judged against these criteria, there were serious deficiencies in knowledge of the state of the oceans and seas in 1970–80, although information about some shallow seas and estuaries was increasing rapidly. While the general characteristics of the world oceanic circulation, sea-water composition and biological production have been broadly established, the monitoring of pollutants and ecosystems has been highly localized and time series data are lacking for most areas. Existing data on pollutant concentrations obtained by different laboratories are not always comparable because methods, standards and sampling techniques differ. Intercalibration exercises on contaminants in biota and sea water carried out by the International Council for the Exploration of the Sea (ICES), (1978 c), the Inter-Governmental Oceanographic Commission (IOC) and the International Laboratory of Marine Radioactivity of the International Atomic Energy Agency (IAEA) at Monaco have demonstrated the seriousness of this problem (IAEA, 1981). Trends in the concentration of pollutants between 1970 and 1980 can therefore only be established in a few limited areas such as the Baltic or the North Sea. Similarly, biological changes in the major oceans cannot be ascertained because of insufficient monitoring. Fishery and whaling statistics do, however, allow comments on the state of species and stocks in some regions. More general evaluations have been made by some international groups of experts such as the Group of Experts on Scientific Aspects of Marine Pollution (GESAMP), (GESAMP, 1981), and the Food and Agriculture Organization of the United Nations (FAO), (FAO, 1971).

CHEMICAL CONTAMINATION

Sources of pollution

Table 3–2 summarizes the main activities liable to cause marine pollution in different regions of the world. It is evident that most contamination reaches the sea through rivers, direct coastal out-falls, drainage from human settlements and agricultural land, and deposition from the atmosphere. Some potential pollutants are, however, discharged from shipping and offshore structures such as oil rigs. Most of the detailed information about marine contamination comes from the Northern Hemisphere, and from estuaries, bays and land-locked seas such as the Mediterranean, Baltic and North Seas and certain estuaries in North America. In the Southern Hemisphere, Port Philip Bay in Australia and various coastal waters around southern Africa have been examined.

Much of the suspended particulate matter in the sea originates from the land, and the particle-rich plumes of great rivers like the Amazon can be traced for as much as 2000 km (Jerlov, 1958; Pak et al., 1970; Gibbs, 1974). Particles of biological origin generally disintegrate in the top 500 m, but some detritus and faecal pellets along with part of the atmospheric fall-out reach the deep ocean floor (Rex and Goldberg, 1958). Such sediments are important transporters of pollutants, especially metals. The amount of iron, manganese, copper, zinc, lead, tin and antimony reaching the sea today through river discharges is an order of magnitude greater than would be supplied by natural geological processes. Smelting and other industries may also contribute substantial quantities via the atmospheric pathway. Persistent solid wastes also enter the sea from urban areas, and 6.4 million tonnes are dumped annually from shipping: of this the proportion of plastic is currently low (under one per cent) but is expected to increase unless controls are applied (UNEP, 1981 f).

Table 3–2. Sources of Pollution in Various Regions of the World Ocean

Water Discharge or other Process of Activity Potentially Causing Contamination	Baltic Sea	North Sea	Mediterranean Sea	Persian Gulf	West African Areas	South African Areas	Indian Ocean Region	South-east Asian Areas	Japanese Coastal Waters	North American Areas	Caribbean Sea	South-west Atlantic Region	South-east Pacific Region	Australian Areas	New Zealand Coastal Waters
Sewage	x	x	x	x	x	x	x	x	x	x	x	x	x	x	x
Petroleum Hydrocarbon (Maritime Transport)	x	x	x	x	x	x	x	x	x	x	x	x			
Petroleum Hydrocarbon (Exploration and Exploitation)		x			x	x		x		x	x	x	x		
Petrochemical Industry		x	x	x						x	x	x			
Mining		x						x		x			x	x	
Radioactive Wastes	x	x	x					x		x	x		x		
Food and Beverage Processing	x	x	x			x				x	x	x	x	x	x
Metal Industries		x	x		x					x	x		x		x
Chemical Industries	x	x	x							x	x				
Pulp and Paper Manufacture	x			'	x					x			x	x	x
Agriculture runoff (Pesticides and Fertilizer)			x		x		x	x		x					x
Siltation from Agriculture and Coastal Development						x	x	x			x				
Sea-salt Extraction							x				x				
Thermal Effluents							x	x		x	x	x	x		
Dumping of Sewage Sludge and Dredge Spoils		x								x	x				

Source: GESAMP (1981).

Tables 3–3 and 3–4 summarize the pollutant inputs to the Oslo Commission area (the north-eastern Atlantic between 63°30' East and 42° West, North of Latitude 36°N) and the Mediterranean, studied respectively by ICES (1978 a, b) and by a co-ordinated investigation called the Mediterranean Action Plan (MEDPOL), under the auspices of the United Nations Environment Programme (UNEP) Regional Seas Programme (UNEP, 1978a, 1978b, 1979, 1981a; Keckes, 1977). The Table for the Oslo Commission area illustrates the importance of the atmospheric pathway for metals and some synthetic chemicals – something recognized only recently (ICES, 1974; Goldberg, 1975, 1976; Duce et al., 1976; GESAMP, 1980a). Production of DDT and polychlorinated biphenyls (PCBs), for example, have been located mainly in the Northern Hemisphere while their use has been concentrated between 45°N and 45°S. But such pollutants have spread widely through the atmosphere, so that DDT has reached detectable concentrations in Antarctic organisms (Risebrough, 1977). Through scavenging by settling particles, DDT takes a fairly direct path to the deep waters and even to the deep-sea benthos (the organisms living on the sea bed).

Preliminary studies in the Caribbean by UNEP and the Inter-Governmental Maritime Consultative Organization (IMCO), (UNEP, 1981 b, c), and the Cooperative Investigation of the Caribbean and Adjacent Regions (CICAR) including IOC, FAO and UNEP (UNESCO, 1977), indicated that oil pollution was a growing threat to the region's ecological and marine economic resources in the late 1970s. Organic pollution from domestic sources, agricultural wastes (including those from sugar refineries) and effluent from pulp and paper plants caused severe localized problems, and mining and chemical wastes were significant in some places. Overall the Caribbean in 1980 had not experienced the same severity of pollution as the Mediterranean or Baltic, but its similarly land-locked nature and the rapid development around it make concerted action essential (UNEP, 1981 b).

In East Asian waters sewage from urban areas, dredging spoil, industrial effluents, oil, pesticides (including DDT and other organochlorines used in agriculture and forestry) and particulates were the major contaminants (IOC/FAO/UNEP workshop, reported in UNESCO, 1976 and Hann et al., 1981). In Japan (which has land-locked seas and bays receiving much urban effluent) oil pollution, industrial chemical discharges and sewage created many environmental problems in the early 1970s (EAJ, 1976, 1977, 1978). Some details of discharges to the south-east Pacific along the coasts of Ecuador, Peru and Chile also confirm the importance of direct and indirect discharges of organic and industrial wastes, and also of oil and pesticides locally (Arriaga, 1976).

These examples are extended by a number of local studies of estuaries and bays, including Raritan Bay on the lower Hudson River (possibly the most heavily polluted major embayment in the north-eastern United States) (Pearce, 1979a); Long Island Sound (Reid, 1979); various British estuaries and coastal seas (Royal Commission, 1972; Porter, 1973) and Port Philip Bay, Australia (Anon., 1973). All show enrichment with nutrients from sewage effluent, and in many of them the accumulation of heavy metals and organochlorines have caused considerable concern.

Estuaries present special problems. The fresh water entering them from rivers tends to form a layer above the saline marine waters and mix only slowly with them. The banks confine lateral spread and the water mass as a whole tends to surge in and out with the tide. Pollutants can therefore be trapped and exert a disproportionate influence (Porter, 1973).

Table 3.3. Estimated Inputs of Contaminants to the Oslo Commission Area

	Domestic sewage	Industrial waste	Domestic + Industrial	Rivers	Dumping	Atmospheric deposition
Total flow (million m^3/y)	5,664	3,432	9,393	316,514	—	—
Contaminant (tonnes/y):						
Nitrogen	109,999	70,255	202,481	973,010	22,202	(400,000)[a]
Phosphorus	29,759	25,042	56,249	94,794	13,048	(~2,000)[b]
Suspended solids	388,000	9,354,100	9,893,100	5,188,000	—	—
BOD	452,000	395,000	1,125,000	938,000	—	—
Iron	4,958	16,051	28,336	246,588	—	(105,000)[c]
Manganese	310	—	—	30,207[d]	—	(4,100)[c]
Cadmium	43[d]	38	80[d]	421[d]	89	(530)[c]
Copper	598[d]	891	1,492	2,786[d]	2,426	(4,900)[c]
Chromium	176[d]	170	381[d]	2,678[d]	2,712	(720)[c]
Nickel	219[d]	173	391[d]	2,417[d]	527	(1,650)[c]
Lead	246[d]	785	1,726	3,831[d]	4,248	(5,600)[c]
Zinc	1,279[d]	11,053	13,719	19,275	9,131	(14,500)[c]
Mercury	17	6.3	23.3	36.4	35	(5.6)[c]

Source: ICES (1978b) except as noted below. Data are in most cases for 1974 or 1975. No data for France, Spain, Portugal or for inputs to the Oslo area from North America.

[a] Estimated input to the Baltic alone, by Rodhe et al. (1980). These authors estimated the airborne inputs of other substances to the Baltic as: mercury 30; lead 2,400; zinc 6,000; copper 1,400; cadmium 80 tonnes.

[b] For the Baltic.

[c] Inputs to the North Sea alone, from ICES (1978b). Cambray et al. (1979) estimated inputs in rainwater as: iron 11,000; zinc, 16,000; lead, 5,800; copper, 5,600; chromium, 740 tonnes. There may also be significant inputs of PCBs, DDT and HCH (hexachlorocyclohexane) (Wells and Johnston, 1975).

[d] The compiler of the ICES tables estimated these figures.

Concentrations of contaminants in the sea and in marine life

Data on metal concentrations in oceanic waters in the North Atlantic were summarized by ICES (1974; 1977 a, b; 1978 b; 1981). Soviet scientists also monitored the background pollution in the North Atlantic, and its implications for marine life (Kirillova and Orlova, 1979). The first phase of the coordinated research and monitoring programme within MEDPOL has recently been concluded. Numerous sampling programmes have been carried out elsewhere by national marine research organizations. The results of these surveys are summarized in the following paragraphs and tables.

A survey of metals (lead, cadmium, zinc, copper and nickel), radio-nuclides (plutonium–239 and –240, plutonium–238 and –241, and caesium–137), halogenated

Table 3.4.   Estimated Input of Contaminants to the Mediterranean

	Domestic	Agricultural	Industrial	Rivers	Total
Contaminant (tonnes/y):					
BOD	500,000	100,000	900,000	1,800,000	3,300,000
COD	1,100,000	1,600,000	2,400,000	3,500,000	8,600,000
Phosphorus	22,000	30,000	5,000	300,000	360,000
Nitrogen	110,000	65,000	25,000	800,000	1,000,000
Mercury[a]	0.8	—	7	120	130
Lead	200	—	1,400	3,200	4,800
Chromium	250	—	950	1,600	2,800
Zinc	1,900	—	5,000	18,000	25,000
Others[b]					

Source: Helmer (1977); UNEP (1979).

[a]The estimate of industrial mercury is based on insufficient data, and therefore is unreliable. The figure for mercury in domestic discharges is almost certainly too low.

[b]Estimated inputs of other substances include 60,000 tonnes of detergents, 12,000 tonnes of phenols, 350 million tonnes of total suspended solids, and 90 tonnes of organochlorine pesticides.

hydrocarbons and petroleum hydrocarbons in the tissues of mussels (*Mytilus*) and oysters (*Ostrea*) in coastal areas of the United States was begun in 1976 (Goldberg *et al.*, 1978). This 'mussel watch' takes advantage of the fact that bivalves accumulate such pollutants in their tissues, making them a convenient natural sampling device. Provided that various inter-comparison problems can be solved and the uptake processes defined, such a survey could be used to indicate baseline levels and to identify areas with high concentration of industrial metals requiring detailed study.

Table 3–5 summarizes results of the analysis of various oceanic and coastal waters. The variation is considerable, but metal concentrations are clearly lower in the open oceans than in many coastal waters, and the highest values are from land-locked seas and inlets with known industrial discharges. Recorded oceanic mercury concentrations, for example, range from 0.005 to 1.09 micrograms per litre (μg/l) (Jones, 1975; Fitzgerald, 1976) with the highest figures for bottom water over the Mid-Atlantic Ridge, possibly in an area where water naturally rich in mercury emerges from submarine vents. Most oceanic waters contain less than 0.05 μg/l, whereas enclosed seas range between 0.05 and 0.11 μg/l, with highest concentrations in contaminated coastal waters. Other metals (e.g. cadmium) show a comparable pattern.

There is no reason to suppose that *oceanic* metal concentrations have been raised substantially above background levels by human activities, except perhaps for lead, whose flux through the atmosphere has been increased by an order of magnitude due to its use as an anti-knock agent in gasoline (UNEP, 1981 f). Even in coastal waters, natural erosion and upwelling may be more important locally than human actions as a cause of enhanced metal concentrations. Tables 3–6 and 3–7 summarize data on metal

Table 3–5. Concentrations of Contaminants in Various Oceanic and Inshore Waters (Quantities ($\mu g/$ 1))

Location	Copper	Zinc	Cadmium	Lead	Nickel	Iron	Manganese	Mercury	DDT	PCBs	Reference
Oceanic waters											
Central Atlantic (mean)	0.39	1.07	0.04	—	0.23	1.8	0.04	0.005	0–0.018[a]	0.001–0.03[b]	ICES (1980a)
Coastal waters											
Global range of means	0.5–3.0	1.8–8.8	0.05–0.8	—	0.4–1.0	0.2–12.0	0.3–1.8	0.001–0.01	—	—	Yeats et al.(1978)
Eastern Irish Sea	—	49.1	1.2	2.4	9.8	24.7	25.5	—	—	—	Preston et al.(1973)
								0.06	—	—	Baker (1977)
Firth of Clyde	11.0	25.0	1.2	19.0	—	24.0	—	—	—	—	Halcrow et al.(1973)
Southern North Sea	—	15.6	6.2	—	—	18.4	38.4	—	—	—	Dutton et al.(1973)
Inner German Bight	6.0	—	—	11.0	5.5	1050	130	—	—	—	Schmidt (1976)
N.W. Mediterranean	<0.04–5.8	0.02–10.0	<0.02–0.70	—	—	—	—	0.008–0.03	—	—	UNEP (1981a)
S.W. Mediterranean	<0.04–0.60	0.02–6.0	<0.02–0.51	—	—	—	—	0.005–0.03	—	—	UNEP (1981a)
S. Levantin Mediterranean	<0.04	0.3–1.3	<0.02–0.11	—	—	—	—	0.012–0.02	—	—	UNEP (1981a)
Mediterranean	—	—	—	—	—	—	—	—	[c]	0.0001–0.0025	UNEP (1981a)

[a] Soviet data for the surface waters of the North Atlantic. DDT varied from zero to 0.018 $\mu g/$ 1, dichlorodiphenyldichloroethylene (DDE) from 0 to 0.006 $\mu g/$ 1 and dichlorodiphenyldichloroethane (DDD) from 0 to 0.004 $\mu g/$ 1.

[b] Data from Harvey et al. (1974). The upper figure is suspect.

[c] In the Mediterranean waters sampled in MEDPOL organochlorine pesticide concentrations were too low for measurement.

concentrations in a variety of fish, the second table giving details for mercury. Clearly, fish from the open ocean commonly contain an order of magnitude less mercury than those from coastal areas of land-locked seas. There are also species differences, tuna (*Thunnus thynnus*) having higher concentrations than the others sampled. The gradient is likely to be due to higher mercury input to coastal seas both from pollution (the plastics, paint, paper and chemical industries and also agriculture have been important sources) and from the natural erosion of mercury-containing rocks (the sulphide ore of the metal, cinnabar, is widely distributed). In the water column and marine sediments inorganic mercury is liable to conversion to the more toxic methyl form, which enters food chains and is especially prone to accumulate in fish and so become a hazard to human consumers. Methyl mercury was the cause of the tragic outbreak of 'Minamata disease' in Japan, where mercury concentrations in fish reached around 5 to 15 mg/kg (Ui, 1969). The inter-species differences in Table 3–7 probably reflect variations in this bioaccumulation process, whose critical elements have been summarized by a SCOPE Expert Group (in Holdgate and White, 1977). Tuna from the Mediterranean contain around 1.26 mg/kg mercury, while Atlantic fish range from 0.2 to 0.3, Pacific fish average around 0.3 and Indian Ocean fish 0.06 to 0.4 mg/kg (UNEP, 1981 a), and this variation is also likely to be largely due to natural factors.

Organochlorine pesticides and PCBs are widely distributed in the sea and in marine life, and some data are set out in Table 3–5, and 3–8. Detailed studies (e.g. Gardner, 1979) indicate that DDT and its metabolites dichlorodiphenyldichloroethylene (DDE) and tetrachlorodiphenylethane (TDE) are most abundant, with dieldrin in lesser quantities. Such pesticides accumulate especially in fish liver, the ratio of concentrations between liver and muscle varying from around 2:1 to 100:1 in different species. The maximum concentration of dieldrin observed in any sample was 0.4 mg/kg in cod liver from the Southern Bight of the North Sea. Concentrations in edible muscle tissue were, however, much lower (0.017 mg/kg in plaice from the North Sea). Persistently high concentrations have also been recorded in Clyde herrings. In North Atlantic surface waters the ratio of DDT to PCBs is generally less than 0.05:1 despite the higher production of DDT, suggesting that PCBs are more stable in the marine environment or are produced there by natural transformations (Maugh, 1973; Goldberg, 1975). In Atlantic fish the ratio of DDT to PCBs is usually around 1:2 and always less than unity. In the North Sea PCB concentrations generally exceed total DDT by a factor of 2, the highest values being found in fish and shellfish off the coasts of the Netherlands, Sweden and south-east England. Very high concentrations can occur in polluted waters: for example, eels (*Anguilla rostrata*) from the Hudson Estuary, United States, contained up to 60 mg/kg dry weight of PCBs (Reid, 1979). Marine mammals and seabirds also accumulate these substances, especially in fat, and Table 3–8 gives some data for DDT and PCBs in the blubber of Baltic seals: similar values have been found in California, but off Greenland concentrations are lower (Johansen *et al.*, 1980). Organochlorine concentrations are also raised in white whales resident in the Gulf of St Lawrence (Sergeant, 1980).

Other oceanic pollutants that have received study include polynuclear aromatic hydrocarbons such as 3,4–benzpyrene (a potential carcinogen whose wide distribution in unpolluted waters suggests airborne dispersal, perhaps of materials formed in forest fires)

Table 3–6. Metal Concentrations in Fish From Various North Atlantic and Mediterranean Waters (in mg/kg wet weight)

Location	Species	Mercury	Cadmium	Zinc	Copper	Reference
Baltic	Cod (*Gadus merluccus*)	0.02–0.88	2–50	1.2–9.2	0.08–2.4	} ICES, 1977 a
	Herring (*Clupea harengus*)	0.004–0.9	2–72	3.2–32	0.3–1.9	
North Sea	Cod	0.03–0.58	0.02–0.5	2.4–7.0	1.1–2.6	} ICES, 1977 a
	Herring	0.02–0.24	0.02–0.7	3–17	0.6–3.6	
Atlantic	Cod (muscle)	0.02–0.1	—	1.9–7.3	0.1–2.1	ICES, 1977 b
	(liver and kidney)	—	—	2.4–36	2.4–12.5	
	Herring (muscle)	0.01–0.03	—	3.3–7.5	0.76–1.8	
Mediterranean	*Mullus barbatus*	0.2–(0.05–1.3)	0.017–0.069	3.06–5.06	0.15–0.092	} UNEP, 1978a, 1981a
	Merluccius merluccius	0.1	0.05	3.0	1.0	
	Sardina pilchardus	0.2	0.02	10.0	1.0	

Table 3–7. Mercury Concentrations in Fish from Various Waters (mg/kg wet weight)

Locality	Species	Tissue Muscle	Tissue Unspecified	Size of sample	Reference
Western Australia	Shark (4 spp)	~0.17	—	—	Caputi et al. (1979).
	blue grenadier	<1.6	—	—	Marine Poll. Bull. (1980)
Indian Ocean	Shark [a]	0.2	0.09–0.21	—	Kureishy et al. (1973)
Mediterranean	Engraulis encrasicholus	—	0.25	171	Thibaud (1971); Stoeppler et al. (1977);
	Merluccius merluccius	—	0.12	5–6	Bernhard and Renzoni (1977);
	Sardina pilchardus		0.22	79	Cumont et al. (1972).
	Scomber scombrus		0.29	26	
	Mullus barbatus [b]		0.59±0.94	492	UNEP (1981a): Area II
	Thunnus thynnus [b]		1.096±0.94	176	UNEP (1981a): Area II
Atlantic Ocean (mainly NE)	Engraulis encrasicholus	—	0.07	42	Thibaud (1971); Stoeppler et al. (1977);
	Merluccius merluccius		0.05	5–6	Bernhard and Renzoni (1977);
	Sardina pilchardus	—	0.06	78	Cumont et al. (1972).
	Scomber sp.	—	0.07	19	
	Thunnus thynnus		0.48	285	
North Atlantic, (Greenland, Norwegian Sea)	Cod, Gadus merluccus	0.02–0.04	—	20	ICES (1977b)
(various waters)	Cod [c]	0.03–0.26	—	—	ICES (1981)
	Plaice [c]	0.05–0.30	—	—	ICES (1981)

[a] Mercury content in liver, gonads and muscle ranged from 0.09–0.21 mg/kg with highest values in sharks, followed by tuna, dolphin and seer fish. See also Yamanaka et al. (1972).

[b] The ranges of variation cited are standard deviations. Area II, the north-west Mediterranean is one of the more polluted areas.

[c] Maximum concentrations in cod in the 1978 survey reported in this publication reached 0.7–0.9 mg/kg in the Southern Bight of the North Sea and off the north coast of Norway. The highest concentration in plaice was 0.65 mg/kg in the Irish Sea.

(Johnston, 1976). Benzpyrenes in the Bering Sea reach highest concentrations in surface waters and accumulate in organisms to attain levels over 2,000 times greater than in the water. Radioisotopes such as strontium–90, caesium–137, plutonium–239 and plutonium–240 have entered the sea primarily from nuclear weapons testing, but to a lesser extent from nuclear power production. About 0.1 per cent of the total radionuclides in the ocean are of artificial origin (Goldberg, 1976). Concentration gradients about points of discharge (such as Windscale, on the Irish Sea coast) are steep, and several radionuclides including plutonium, zirconium, niobium and ruthenium appear to be removed rapidly from the water column to sediments through absorption onto settling particles (Jefferies *et al.*, 1980). Caesium–137, however, persists in sea water and has consequently been distributed widely in western European shelf seas. Sufficient radioactive material remains in the water to allow effluents of this kind to serve as a tracer for water movements, and such material released from Windscale has been followed around the north coast of Scotland, southward into and across the North Sea, and round the margins of the Norwegian Sea to western Spitsbergen.

Table 3–8 DDT and PCB Concentrations in Fish and Marine Mammals from Various Localities (in mg/kg wet weight)

Location	Species and Tissues	DDT	PCBs	Reference
Baltic (Bornholm-Gotland)	Herring (extractable fat)[a]	18–26	4.2–31	ICES (1978 a)
(North Baltic)	Herring (extractable fat)[a]	7–37	6.1–27	
(Central Baltic)	Ringed Seal and grey seal (blubber)	420	140	Helle *et al.* (1976 a, b)
North Sea	Herring (tissues)	0.1	0.001–0 48	ICES (1977 b)
	Cod (liver)	~10	~10	
	Mussels (*Mytilus*)(tissues)	0.003–0.088	0.02–0.39	
North Atlantic	Cod (muscle)	<1–10	—	ICES (1977 a)
Gulf of St. Lawrence	Cod	1.8	—	
Greenland	Cod	0.18–0.3	0.44–4.1	
	Cod (liver)		1.7	ICES (1981)
Barents Sea	Cod (liver)	<1.3	0.8–15	ICES (1981)
Various, 1978	Herring, pilchard, mackerel (muscle)	0.008–0.026	—	
Mediterranean, Area II[b]	*Mullus barbatus*	0.028 ± 0.035	0.814 ± 1.49	UNEP (1981 a)
	Engraulis encrasicholus	0.045 ± 0.022	0.385 ± 0.151	UNEP (1981 a)

[a] These figures, being for concentrations in extractable fat, are not directly comparable with others in the table.

[b] Area II is the north-western Mediterranean, and organisms there have higher concentrations of many contaminants than are found in other regions of the sea.

MINERAL EXPLOITATION AND TRANSPORTATION

During the 1970s, there were dramatic advances in the technology for exploiting the resources of the sea bed, and the process seems likely to continue in the 1980s. Offshore oil and gas production accounted for about 90 per cent of the value of mineral resources recovered from the sea bed. In 1973 about 18 per cent of world petroleum production and 10 per cent of total gas production were recovered from the sea. During the decade offshore production rose steadily, penetrating into deeper waters and into many different areas of the ocean, including Indonesian waters, the Persian Gulf, Gulf of Mexico and the North Sea. The speed of development is well illustrated by events in Scottish waters. Exploratory drilling began in 1967, increasing dramatically by 1970: production started in 1975 with proven reserves over 1,000 million tonnes, and production in 1980 was around 100 million tonnes per year. The development has demanded facilities on land with a corresponding need for environmental planning (Affolter, 1976; SVEAG, 1976).

Sand and gravel, heavy mineral sands, phosphorite and manganese nodules are among the resources of the unconsolidated sediments on the sea bed (Chapter 5). Current exploitation by dredging is limited to about 30 to 50 m depth. Sand and gravel exploitation is the most important and demands for offshore sources are increasing in certain areas (e.g. the North Sea, Japan, the United States). Among metals, tin mining is important in East Asia. Techniques for recovering deep sea manganese nodules on an industrial basis have been developed. Minerals, especially salt, magnesium and bromide, are also extracted from sea water. De-salination plants are important in some areas not only for the salt obtained but also as a significant source of local water supplies. In recent years there has been considerable interest in obtaining energy from the ocean from waves, currents, tides, temperature and salinity gradients (see Chapter 12).

The impacts of mineral exploitation

The environmental impacts of these activities were examined by GESAMP (1977 c) and ICES (1979 b). The former were concerned with the effects of sand and gravel extraction on fisheries, and in particular on nursery grounds, which are generally located in shallow coastal waters. Such effects are local, producing alterations of topography, wave climate, water circulation and sediment transport, and increased turbidity. Beaches and coastal configurations can be affected, as can existing or potential mariculture since it normally requires water of particularly good quality.

Offshore structures such as platforms, wellheads and pipelines restrict fishing activities and may also lead to local re-distribution of fish populations. Dumping of debris from the platforms — but not of materials that arise as a result of drilling activities — is covered by dumping conventions. Disposal of cuttings and losses of drilling mud could taint fish feeding in the area, but there is no documentary evidence of this, although the large-scale use of oil-based muds may be a cause for concern. Limited field evidence available in 1976 did not suggest any harmful effects of dumped drilling mud and cuttings on marine organisms other than those due to highly localized blanketing of bottom fauna. Generally speaking, the operation of these structures does not appear to pose serious environmental problems so long as accidents — especially blowouts — do not happen.

Transportation and its impacts

Transportation and associated operations constitute a major use of the ocean, yielding a revenue of some US$40 billion in 1975 — considerably more than the fishing industry's and comparable to the offshore oil industry's (UN, 1975). In the period 1965–1975 the world's merchant fleet nearly doubled in tonnage, oil tankers comprising a large part of the fleet (about 40 per cent in 1975) (Chapter 13). These trends were accompanied by the development of new ports capable of receiving large special carriers, some of them in areas of previously undisturbed environment or on artificial islands. Careful siting and planning has been needed in order to avoid severe local environmental stress.

Petroleum hydrocarbons were produced and transported in increasing quantities during the decade. In 1970 about 1.26 billion tonnes of oil were transported annually by sea, and by 1975 the total had risen to 1.50 billion (Sasamura, 1977). The number of reported accidental oil spillages at sea undoubtedly increased during the decade (Table 3–9). However, estimates suggest that shipping is the source of less than half of all the oil reaching the oceans and that tanker accidents account for only some 10 per cent of the input from shipping — and hence under five per cent of the overall total (Table 3–10; see also Chapter 13). Transportation is, however, the largest single source (if the speculative estimate of atmospheric input in SCEP (1970) is disregarded), with river drainage and natural seepage next in order. Some evaluations have concluded that the total amount of oil introduced into the oceans in 1980 was not substantially greater than in the early 1970s (UNEP, 1981 f).

Table 3–9. Oil Spilled into Oceans Following Incidents Involving Tankers in which 5,000 Tonnes or More Were Shed[a]

Year	Incidents	Spillages
1970	11	212,120
1971	4	121,250
1972	1	65,000
1973	3	58,000
1974	2	61,000
1975	6	123,000
1976	8	150,000
1977	6	134,500
1978	5	264,000 [b]

Source: IMCO (1979).

[a]These figures are certainly underestimates. Not only may some incidents have been missed but many spillages of under 5,000 tonnes are omitted.

[b]The *Amoco Cadiz* contributed some 220,000 tonnes towards this total.

Table 3–10. Comparison of Estimates for Petroleum Hydrocarbons Annually Entering the Ocean, circa 1969–1971

Source	Authority (Millions of tonnes per Annum)		
	SCEP Report (1970)	USCG Impact Statement (1973)	NAS Workshop (1973)
Marine transportation	1.13	1.72	2.133
Offshore oil production	0.20	0.12	0.08
Coastal oil refineries	0.30	—	0.2
Industrial waste	—	1.98	0.3
Municipal waste	0.45	—	0.3
Urban runoff	—	—	0.3
River runoff[a]	—	—	1.6
Sub-total	2.08	3.82	4.913
Natural seeps	?	?	0.6
Atmospheric rainout	9.0[b]	?	0.6
Total	11.08	?	6.113

Source: NAS (1975).

[a]PHC input from recreational boating assumed to be incorporated in the river runoff value.

[b]Based upon assumed 10 per cent return from the atmosphere.

The Integrated Global Ocean Station System (IGOSS) Marine Pollution (Petroleum) Monitoring Project collected a considerable amount of information about visible slicks and tar at sea (Kohnke, 1979; Levy, 1979). Slicks were most frequently reported along the major tanker routes from the Middle East to Europe and Japan, and between Venezuela and Europe. More than 10,000 visual observations between 1975 and the end of 1978 were processed to show that the most polluted regions were the Red Sea (where 31 per cent of observations reported oil), the Straits of Malacca, the Mediterranean and the Caribbean (about 20 per cent) and the South China Sea (15 per cent) (Kohnke, 1979). In the North Atlantic, the most polluted waters are in the tropical and sub-tropical zones between 10° and 50°N., within and to the south of the Gulf Stream. North and west of the latter current, slicks and tar occur rarely. Similarly in the Pacific tar has generally been observed in the western boundary current of the Kuroshio. In the Southern Hemisphere, the waters around southern Africa are likely to be the most polluted. In 1977 about 650 million tonnes of petroleum — about 38 per cent of the oil transported by sea in the world — passed around the Cape of Good Hope, and it has been estimated that between 60,000 and 600,000 tonnes may be released annually to the marine environment in this region (Anon., 1979). The widening and deepening of the Suez Canal will reduce the volume of this traffic but may increase the chronic oil pollution in the Red Sea and Gulf of Aden.

Actual oil hydrocarbon concentrations in the North Atlantic and adjacent seas range from 0.2 to 15 μg/l in the surface microlayer, with values around 1–8 μg/l in enclosed and polluted waters such as the Gulf of St Lawrence or the Baltic (Levy and Walton, 1974; Goldberg, 1976; Levy, 1980 a). In the Pacific, oil hydrocarbon concentrations reach 380 μg/l in parts of the south-western ocean and the Sea of Japan and 200 μg/l in areas of the north-western and south-western ocean. In the Mediterranean surface waters, oil hydrocarbon concentrations fall in the range 4–2,000 μg/l. Concentrations diminish with depth: for example, one station near Bermuda had a surface maximum of 6 μg/l, diminishing to about 3 μg/l at 100 m, 1 μg/l at 1,000 m, and zero below 2,000 m. Sediments can accumulate oil hydrocarbons, and in New York Harbour an average of 39 μg/l has been observed over a six-month period.

Worldwide, oil pollution continued to be a potential threat to marine life and habitats in the 1970s, both as a result of major accidents and through persistent chronic pollution at specific localities. The report of Britain's Advisory Committee on Oil Pollution of the Sea (ACOPS) for 1978 showed that it was the worst year on record for pollution from incidents around the coasts of the United Kingdom, with over 500 spills, plus five major incidents including the grounding of the *Amoco Cadiz* off the coast of Brittany. At least 175 of the oil spills in the United Kingdom involved heavy fuel oil.

TRENDS IN POLLUTION AND ITS EFFECTS

GESAMP (1976) analyzed the extent to which sewage, pesticides, inorganic wastes, radioactive materials, oil, organic chemicals, organic industrial wastes and other materials created hazards in the 1970s to human health or living resources, hindrance to maritime activities, or reduction of amenities. But neither their analysis nor most of the studies reviewed in the preceding sections of this chapter allowed trends in pollutant input or concentration to be established quantitatively. However, they do suggest that the broad regional pattern of pollution at the end of the decade differed little from that at the beginning, summarized in Figure 3–1. The input of organic matter and nutrients in sewage and other effluents has been increasing in many areas (although there was an increase in the proportion of sewage receiving primary treatment). In 1979 some Mediterranean and western European beaches were found to be so contaminated with coliform bacteria that they were closed to the public (Marine Pollution Bulletin, 1979 a, b). In other areas, such as Raritan Bay, the Adriatic Sea, the Seto Inland Sea and other land-locked Japanese seas, local over-enrichment may account partly for an increasing number or intensity of plant plankton blooms which can have undesirable effects on the composition of fish faunas. However, long-term climatic changes are believed to be equally or more important in changing the biological characteristics of some areas, including the northern Adriatic (Degobbis *et al.*, 1979).

Organic pollution may also lead to oxygen depletion in coastal waters, especially where they are further stressed by climatic extremes. Although the oxygen content of the

Figure 3–1. Marine Pollution Around the World

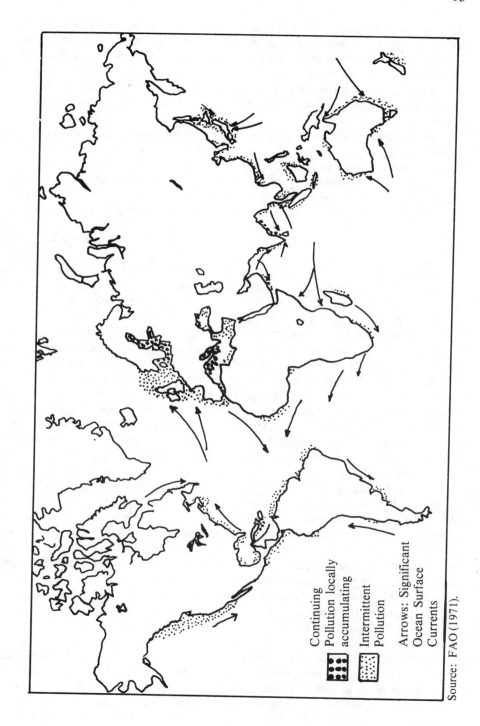

Continuing
Pollution locally
accumulating

Intermittent
Pollution

Arrows: Significant
Ocean Surface
Currents

Source: FAO (1971).

deep and bottom waters of the Baltic Sea has fallen throughout the present century, and the area of 'benthic desert' (the sea bottom devoid of animal life) has increased from about 26,000 km² in 1959 to 84,000 km² in 1975 (Jansson, 1978), natural fluctuations in the rate of renewal of bottom waters, and changes in the temperature and salinity of the inflowing deep and bottom water are likely to have been the major factors. Oxygen-free bottom water is clearly shown by sediment cores to have existed in the Baltic before the present century.

Over recent years, there has been a decline in the input of many potentially toxic substances to the sea through the dumping of wastes, as the various international conventions have come into effect. DDT concentrations in coastal waters off the United States and in the Baltic also declined, no doubt as a result of reduced production and use since the early 1970s (Goldberg, 1975, 1976). DDE concentrations also fell, and the reproductive success of fish-eating birds rose in the Long Island Sound area (Spitzer et al., 1978). On the California coast, DDT concentrations in black perch and kelp bass fell by a factor of about 3 between 1972 and 1977 when inputs of the pesticide to the area decreased by a factor of about 30 (Smokler et al., 1979). However, concentrations are not declining in Dover sole, which feeds on invertebrates living in the sediments where the pesticide has persisted. Moreover, the use of organochlorine pesticides has not fallen markedly in tropical areas (and has increased in some regions such as South America), so that concentrations in southern seas may be expected to increase.

PCB residue levels are also falling slowly in some areas, although elsewhere they are rising even though inputs are known to have decreased (possibly because PCBs may be formed naturally in the sea by the oxidation of organochlorine pesticides) (Maugh, 1973). Mercury concentrations can also be expected to fall as a result of tighter controls on industrial emissions and dumping. The persistence of many metals and organic compounds in sediments, and the slow rate of renewal of the water in many land-locked seas mean, however, that problems are likely to remain in such areas for some time after inputs are cut back (although mercury levels in several United Kingdom inshore areas fell fairly rapidly when inputs were reduced). Metal concentrations generally are known to have risen in oysters on the Connecticut coast of the United States by 50 per cent to 100 per cent between 1933–35 and the 1970s, but trends over the decade are not clear. In the North Atlantic and Baltic Seas, only mercury among metals was found during the decade to attain concentrations in fish or molluscs approaching those regarded as too high for human consumption (set by many governments at 0.5 or 1.0 ppm, with further advisory limits on the frequency with which fish was eaten, the goal being to keep intake below the World Health Organization (WHO) provisional tolerable weekly limit of 0.3 mg total mercury per person) (WHO, 1972). Even in these areas, however, no species was found to have a general mean mercury concentration above these limits. In the North Atlantic area generally, data from Belgium, Canada, the United Kingdom, France, the Federal Republic of Germany, Ireland, the Netherlands, Norway, Portugal and the United States for 1975–1978 were reviewed by ICES (1981) and do not appear to indicate any trend in the concentrations of heavy metals or organochlorines in fish or shellfish. There is, however, evidence that mercury concentrations in feathers of a seabird, the black guillemot (Cepphus grylle) rose considerably in the Baltic between 1940 and 1973, and to a lesser degree in the Faeroes, and that people in the latter area who have a traditional seafood diet may be nearing the WHO limit (Somer, 1981).

Although some North Atlantic seal populations increased during the decade (for example the grey seal, *Halichoerus grypus* in Britain), those in the Baltic declined, and in northern regions there was evidence of reduced fertility in the ringed seal (*Pusa hispida*). Only 27 per cent of a sample of females of reproductive age were pregnant, compared with 80–90 per cent in regions of low pollution like Ochotsk Sea (Helle *et al.*, 1976 a, b), and it has been suggested that this may be due to PCBs or some substances interacting with PCBs. The Dutch population of the harbour seal (*Phoca vitalina*) also declined rapidly during the past decade, with raised juvenile mortality, but the cause of the phenomenon is not clear, although Duinker *et al.*, (1979) report high concentrations of organochlorines and metals. Just before the decade under review, PCBs were also found in high concentrations in guillemots (*Uria aalge*), which died in large numbers in the Irish Sea. This event too was ascribed to a fairly complicated series of interacting factors, including PCBs, the physiological stress of moulting, and climate (Holdgate, 1969).

There are considerable uncertainties over the impact of chemical contamination on fisheries. On the one hand it can be argued that yields generally do not show declining trends that can be correlated with pollution — whereas there are definite signs that overfishing has caused serious depletion of many stocks. Moreover, there is no evidence that the concentrations of metals (except lead) in the open oceans have been raised above background levels or that concentrations of synthetic pollutants and oils there are anywhere near the threshold of likely deleterious effect. On the other hand, it can be argued that pollution, climatic variables and over-exploitation are likely to affect marine stocks in quite different ways, climatic change causing natural fluctuations, overfishing producing population reductions that are (at least potentially) readily reversible, but pollution imposing new stresses that could hamper the recovery of depleted stocks, make organisms more sensitive to climatic extremes, and have unpredictable long-term ecological impacts. The relationship between pollution and fish diseases has recently attracted attention (Newman *et al.*, 1979; Murchelano and Ziskowski, 1979; Jensen *et al.*, 1979; ICES, 1980 b).

Pollution concentrations are highest in coastal areas and land-locked seas. Although these, together with the relatively small areas of oceanic upwelling, represent only about 10 per cent of the total ocean area, they yield over 90 per cent of the world's marine fish catch. Molluscan and crustacean stocks, and the breeding and nursery grounds for many fish, are concentrated in estuaries, bays and the shallowest seas, and migratory fish (such as salmonids) must pass through these waters in order to reach their freshwater spawning sites. About 60 per cent of the total commercial fish catch in the United States and 97 per cent of the commercial fishery in the Gulf of Mexico comes from species that depend on the estuarine environment. Yet it is here that discharges of sewage, petroleum hydrocarbons, synthetic chemicals, metals, radioactive discharges, waste heat, urban wastes and dredging spoils are most concentrated. Long before the impacts of pollution are detected in offshore waters, inshore resources could be seriously damaged. About eight per cent of the total value of the fin fish and shellfish catch in the Gulf of Mexico and the United States Atlantic coast is said to have been lost through pollution (Kumpf, 1977), especially as a result of fish kills due to reduced water quality, and to habitat changes. In Japan, 'red tides', oil and other pollution have caused fisheries losses.

In the north-eastern Pacific and the Sea of Japan, concentrations of radionuclides (especially strontium–90 and caesium–137) declined between 1964–65 and 1974–77 (observations by the Soviet Hydrometeorological Service). This trend (which is paralleled in other areas, and on land) no doubt reflects the reduction in fall-out from the atmosphere following the Partial Nuclear Test Ban Treaty. However, as the number of nuclear power stations (and plants reprocessing nuclear fuel) continues to increase in the coastal zones of developed countries, emissions of radionuclides from these sources can be expected to rise, as will discharges of waste heat from these and conventional power stations.

During the decade, the impact of oil pollution on seabirds and marine ecosystems continued to cause widespread concern, and generated numerous studies. There were major blow-outs in the Ekofisk field of the North Sea in 1977 and in the Gulf of Mexico in 1979. The former had only local acute effects, temporarily reducing primary production significantly for a few square nautical miles around the platform (ICES, 1977c). Dead copepods were also observed in this area, but apart from this no obvious differences were observed in plankton composition and distribution. Nor were changes in fish distribution or abundance detected. The impact of this event was probably localized in this way because winds and currents caused rapid spreading, the most volatile and toxic compounds evaporated efficiently, and the dissolved hydrocarbons were quickly mixed and diluted. Moreover, the oil did not drift onto beaches. The blowout in the Gulf of Mexico may well have more marked acute effects (*Oil Spill Report,* 1980). However, a thorough review by GESAMP (1977 a) concluded emphatically that "no evidence has been found in the literature that floating oil has ever affected the recruitment to any fish or shellfish stock". The acute effects of spills from shipwrecks were studied following accidents to the *Torrey Canyon, Metula, Monte Urquiola, Argo Merchant* and *Amoco Cadiz* (which released 50,000–200,000 tonnes of oil) and smaller incidents like the release of 8,000 tonnes from the *Tsesis* in the Stockholm archipelago (Linden *et al.,* 1979) or 5 to 6,000 tonnes from the *Antonio Gramsci* in the Baltic in 1979. As a result. the general pattern of impact is now fairly well established (see Fylion-Myklebust and Johannessen, 1980 for bibliography). Although the environmental consequences immediately after a spill can be serious, recovery occurs over a period of months or years in most cases.

Chronic pollution around terminals and refineries in some areas increased the proportion of green algae and modified populations of limpets, barnacles and other molluscs (Baker, 1976a, b). The repeated use of detergents reduced worm (*Arenicola*) populations (Levell, 1976) with implications for sediment stability. Inter-tidal salt marshes were destroyed, and even when pollution was reduced and recovery followed, the original ecosystem was not necessarily restored (Dicks, 1976). The scale of the impact apparently depends on the frequency and scale of pollution and the quality of dispersion in a coastal locality: impacts are worst on shores with poor dispersion, repeatedly subject to pollution.

Oil pollution can cause massive mortality to seabirds, both in inshore waters and at sea. In 1978 over 10,000 birds, mostly auks and sea ducks, died as a result of oil pollution around Britain, excluding the minimum of 4,149 (probably only one-third of the actual total) recovered after the *Amoco Cadiz* accident. A recent analysis showed that over the previous nine years at least 46,000 oiled birds had been found dead around the coasts of Britain — 35,000 of them from 88 separate major incidents (ACOPS, 1978). Seals are also occasionally affected by oil pollution but the resultant mortality is insignificant by comparison. The terrestrial ecosystem is affected at the land/sea interface, where damage may be caused to salt-marshes and other coastal habitats. The littoral fauna and flora, particularly in estuaries and sheltered cover, often suffer severe local damage from the direct smothering effect of the oil.

Even small oil spills can cause many deaths, as evidenced by the incident off the coast of northern Norway in March 1979, when an estimated 10,000 birds were killed. In January 1979 some 400 tonnes of fuel oil leaked from a grounded tanker in the Kattegat, Denmark, and resulted in the death of at least 35,085 birds. There is some evidence that oil pollution can act synergistically with climatic stress to produce death in seabirds. Levy (1980b) found a number of lightly oiled birds dead on the Nova Scotia coast during the winter following the *Argo Merchant* incident in December 1976. He concluded that very small amounts of oil were enough to disturb behaviour and impair survival in a high-latitude winter. There are parallels here with the mass mortality of guillemots in the Irish Sea in 1969 (Holdgate, 1969).

Petroleum fractions interact with the marine biota at many levels. The marine microorganisms are the agents that eventually degrade the non-volatile fractions. The process proceeds at a rate greatly influenced by surface area temperature and the availability of nutrients (especially nitrogen and phosphorus). Thus oil might persist longer in polar than in tropical waters. Whilst major incidents may cause obvious large-scale mortality among seabirds or widespread damage to coastal habitats, some biologists consider that chronic pollution may have the more serious long-term impact on the marine ecosystem. Low concentrations of hydrocarbon pollutants in one area over a long period of time may well lead to the slow degradation of the ecosystem. Prolonged exposure to oil and some other substances is said by Soviet specialists to lead to a decline in primary productivity and a shift in the composition of the phytoplankton, with reduced diatom numbers and an increased frequency of blue-green algae and flagellates (Gerasimov; personal communication). Pelagic food chains are modified, and medusae increase at the expense of fish, with reductions in fishery potential. Such changes have been detected recently in the Black Sea and the Sea of Azov, and also near the Atlantic coast of the United States. Exposure to increasing quantities of benzpyrenes and other carcinogens and mutagens might also have long-term effects on marine species and populations.

It has been shown experimentally that aromatic hydrocarbons have deleterious effects on early life stages of fish. Under natural conditions, the acute toxicity of the oil decreases considerable after 24–72 hours. But in experiments using dispersants the toxicity remained almost unchanged over this period, perhaps because only limited dilution could take place (in contrast to the situation in the field). Baltic herring larvae in these conditions appeared 50 to 100 times more sensitive to an oil dispersion obtained by adding so-called non-toxic dispersants than to natural oil (Linden, 1975, 1976). Uncertainty over the effects of dispersants remained during the 1970s, with a widespread view that they should only be used when undispersed oil was likely to cause an even greater problem such as damage to seabirds, amenity beaches or shellfish beds.

Oil that has been at sea for some days before coming ashore will have lost the volatile toxic fractions due to evaporation. In the *Amoco Cadiz* incident, 6 months after the pollution about 30 per cent of the fauna and five per cent of the flora were destroyed locally, although the only commercial fishery to be harmed was the oyster fishery. The kelp harvest was put back only one month. Studies in 1978 of the longer-term effects of the *Amoco Cadiz* spill on finfish (plaice, sole, dab) showed quantitative effects of the pollution as a lack of recruitment in 1978, and qualitative effects in the form of reduced growth of plaice, fin erosion and the presence of bent fin rays (ICES, 1980b).

The world-wide increase in offshore oil exploration and production operations, which are moving into ever deeper waters and into environmentally more dangerous and sensitive areas such as the polar seas, will certainly lead to increased ecological hazards over the next ten to twenty years. Although a good deal is now known about the effects of chronic low-level hydrocarbon pollution on the community structure of adjacent regions, and their rate of recovery from both acute and chronic pollution, more research is still needed in order to predict the full consequences of hydrocarbon pollution of the marine and coastal environment.

The Use and Conservation of Marine Resources

THE STATUS OF FISH STOCKS

Fish provide mankind with considerable quantities of protein. Thirty-two countries get 34 per cent or more of their animal protein from sea food, and another eleven consume double the world average (FAO 1977; IUCN/UNEP/WWF, 1980). Between 1900 and 1962 the total annual catch from marine and fresh waters combined rose by a factor of 8, to about 40 million tonnes (Idyll, 1970), the sea providing about 90 per cent of this. Production from marine fisheries increased markedly in the years following the Second World War, from 19.4 million tonnes in 1948—1952 to 61.5 million tonnes in 1976, but appeared to level off at around 60–65 million tonnes in the mid-1970s. Total fishery landings exceeded 70 million tonnes in 1970/71, dropped in 1972/73, but again rose above this figure in 1976. In 1976, 18 per cent of the animal protein consumed worldwide or six per cent of the total protein consumed, came from fish. Herring, sardine, anchovy, cod and haddock accounted for about 32 per cent of the catch in 1970 and 25 per cent in 1975. In 1975, marine fisheries yielded a total of 34 and 26 million tonnes in the Pacific and Atlantic Oceans respectively, with about 60 per cent of the catch coming from the northern areas in both oceans. The growth rate has slowed in recent years. Some yields have indeed declined dramatically; catches of Peruvian anchoveta fell from about 12 million tonnes in 1970 to 4 million tonnes in 1972 and have not recovered since (the sardine population off California suffered a similar decline in the late 1940s). The herring fishery in the North Atlantic has also decreased severely in recent years, after a period of rising catches up to the mid-1970s. The cause of these declines is generally considered to be over-exploitation, possibly combined with natural changes in environmental factors (the Peruvian coastal fishery is particularly sensitive to variations in the current and nutrient pattern offshore) (Glantz, 1979). In Northern Europe several periods of rich herring fishery, interspersed with periods when the fish almost disappear, have been known since the Middle Ages. Proper fisheries management clearly demands an understanding of the interactions between biological and physical conditions on various scales of time and space so that trends can be predicted and regulations imposed.

The fisheries in the *North-east Atlantic* area have received particularly detailed study under the auspices of the North-east Atlantic Fishery Commission (NEAFC) now the North Atlantic Fishery Organization (NAFO) and the associated scientific organization (ICES). Most of the resources were fully exploited (i.e. cropped at sustainable yield), or even temporarily over-exploited by the early 1970s (FAO, 1974). Exceptions were blue whiting, sand eels and squid. There were considerable short-term variations in catches of individual species. For example, there was a massive outburst of gadoid species in the late 1960s and early 1970s, with a doubling of cod, whiting and pout catches and a quadrupling of saithe yields. Such changes can mainly be ascribed to variations in year-class strength, but increased exploitation, encouraged by favourable variations of this kind, has had serious consequences. For example, catches of Atlanto-Scandian herring rose to 1.6 million tonnes in 1966 but subsequently declined to virtually zero in 1972—74, and in 1976 a fishery for this stock was totally prohibited. Since then the catch remained at zero in 1977 and 1978, apart from catches of around 10,000 tonnes per year of small herring in Norwegian inshore waters. ICES recommended that the ban be maintained in 1979 and 1980 (ICES, 1979a). A similar trend occurred in the North Sea herring stocks. For these and other species strict regulation of the fisheries, including catch quotas, were imposed. Unilateral national extension of fishing limits, closing some areas (e.g. the Arcto-Norwegian and Icelandic cod grounds) to traditional fleets, was a feature of the decade.

Detailed analysis of the catch statistics for 1976 (ICES, 1979 c) by Cole (1980) has revealed a number of very interesting details. The total catch increased by about 10 per cent compared with 1975, but the catch of invertebrates decreased and was 10 per cent below the record level in 1973. The composition of the catch shifted, with a big increase in the proportion of fish used mainly for industrial purposes. Capelin made up 24 per cent of the catch, cod 14.9 per cent, sprat 7.2 per cent, herring 7.2 per cent, mackerel 6.3 per cent and haddock 3.9 per cent. In 1962 the order had been herring 33.3 per cent, cod

23 per cent, haddock 5.7 per cent and mackerel 2.2 per cent. In the late 1970s there were further changes, with mackerel increasing in importance and blue whiting making up a substantial proportion of the catch. Factors such as availability and value of the catch per unit effort have become more important than the public preference for particular species.

This analysis also showed that the catches in the ICES area have grown more rapidly since 1962 — by 73.2 per cent — than in other parts of the world, where the growth since 1962 was 68.6 per cent. The North Sea was in 1976 still the most productive area, yielding 26.6 per cent of the total, compared to 22.6 per cent in 1962. The next highest was the Barents Sea, with 20.8 per cent of the total. The Baltic provided 7 per cent in 1976, compared to 6.2 per cent in 1962 and 7.9 per cent in each of the years 1973, 1974 and 1975. The information available does not give any evidence for damage by pollution to offshore living resources, although equally it does not prove that there has been no effect (the crash in Peruvian fisheries in 1974 and the over-fishing of Iceland's herring undoubtedly raised the relative importance of North Sea and Baltic fisheries in the period under review).

In the north-west Atlantic, cod, haddock and redfish were mostly fully exploited at the beginning of the 1960s (FAO, 1974) and many of the stocks had become over-exploited by the early 1970s. Many have, however, subsequently improved as a result of the rigorous control of fishing following the adoption of the two hundred miles jurisdictions. The measures adopted included periodic closing of fisheries, mesh regulations and catch quotas applied to developing as well as established fisheries, and in most areas controls on the total catch of all species and the licensing of fishing vessels.

The *North-west Pacific* region has always supported important fisheries but it has never had an infra-structure of international coordination comparable to that in the north Atlantic. As a result, although there has been considerable research, a reliable comprehensive assessment of the state of the stocks is hampered by a lack of statistical data (FAO, 1974). It appears that heavy fishing combined with deterioration of spawning grounds, has led to a depletion of salmon. Many other stocks are probably fully exploited. In the waters around Japan some species, e.g. Japanese sardine and herring, which in the past yielded great catches, have almost disappeared, while others, for instance mackerel, have greatly increased. Such changes are probably due to variations in both oceanographic conditions and fishing.

In the *North-east Pacific*, fisheries for salmon and halibut have for a long time been subject to controls and management, and halibut stocks have responded well. Newer fisheries developments have, however, switched from species to species, making assessment difficult. Most stocks appear to be fully exploited. The British Columbia herring was depleted for a time, but appears to have recovered, probably due to strict controls imposed in the 1967/68 season. Bilateral agreement and national controls have been imposed.

The *Western-central Atlantic* menhaden and shrimp fisheries were fully exploited in the early 1970s, but several other available stocks were only lightly exploited (FAO, 1974). Menhaden catches along the United States Atlantic coast fell drastically at the end of the 1960s, but have since increased again. Menhaden catches in the Gulf of Mexico peaked in 1971, decreasing in 1972. Most of the shrimp stocks in the Gulf are heavily exploited, but not so much that the productivity or total yield have been affected significantly. However, there has been concern over the likely effects on the shrimp stocks of alternative uses of the marine environment, and the loss of coastal wetlands.

FISHERIES PROSPECTS AND TRENDS

The 1970s saw development of new fisheries outside traditional areas. Non-traditional species such as capelin, squid and blue whiting were increasingly introduced to the market. In the early 1970s various scientific estimates (Moiseev, 1970; Gulland, 1970) indicated that Antarctic krill (*Euphausia superba*) might have a sustainable yield of between 50 and 100 million tonnes per year as human or animal food, thereby virtually doubling world fishery production. These figures are now regarded as much too high, possibly by an order of magnitude. Experimental fishing by Soviet, Japanese and German expeditions confirmed that catching rates as high as 20 tonnes per hour could be sustained in krill swarms for short periods. By the end of the decade some fifteen nations were either engaged in research on krill and in experimental fishing, or planning to do so (Mitchell and Tinker, 1980). Recorded catches rose from about 20,000 tonnes in 1973/74 to just under 130,000 tonnes in 1977/78 (FAO, 1979). The whitefish stocks of some remote southern localities were also being examined and Soviet vessels took substantial catches of southern blue whiting (*Micromesistius australis*) from Burdwood Bank.

Total global fish production has been estimated at 240 million tonnes wet weight, divided between coastal zones in general and upwelling areas (Ryther, 1969). Traditional species can yield 100 million tonnes per year, and there are unexploited reserves such as squid, estimated at 100 million tonnes per year. Deep-living myctophids have also been considered (Ackefors, 1977). Some authors (e.g. Ackefors, 1977) calculate that through proper management the world-wide catch of 70 million tonnes could be increased by a factor of 2 to 3. A more reasonable recent FAO estimate is that marine catches could be raised by 20 to 30 million tonnes (Robinson, 1979). The World Conservation Strategy (IUCN/UNEP/WWF, 1980) argued that had stocks not been damaged by overfishing, world yields in 1980 would have been 15 to 20 million tonnes higher than they were. Others believe that the krill resources of the Southern Ocean could be yielding at least 10 million tonnes per year by 1990. But there are considerable scientific uncertainties and successful exploitation will in the end depend on market values in relation to the cost of fishery as much as on the size of the resource.

Rational exploitation of these resources requires international agreements and regulations; the extension of economic zones to 200 nautical miles will not provide adequate conditions for protection or rational exploitation of these resources unless combined with international agreements and regulations. Proper assessment of the potential yield is a vital prerequisite to successful management, setting a balance between stock recruitment and catch potential. Assessment can be done indirectly by considering the production in the oceans, or directly by egg and larval surveys, acoustic surveys, exploratory fishing surveys and analysis of the age — length content of commercial catches (Ackefors, 1977). Nations must agree on techniques, fishing gear and quotas, like those first introduced in 1974 for fishing in the North-east Atlantic (NEAFC area), regulating the total catch of herring, cod, haddock, whiting, plaice and sole in the North Sea, and such agreements must be enforced (in 1981 disputes within the European Economic Community were once again placing fish stocks at risk).

Such projections imply a shift from traditional species to other faster-growing, faster-maturing and relatively short-lived ones. Their successful marketing will demand adjustments in the attitude and fish consumption habits of the consumer. It is also likely that mariculture will increase. In China in 1978, 148,000 ha were already being utilized in this way, 65,000 ha under intensive culture, with a production of 450,000 tonnes, 60 per cent as algae and almost all the remainder from molluscs (Zhu De-Shan, 1980). In the years 1970–78 kelp (*Laminaria japonica*) yields rose from 88,000 to 251,000 tonnes. In Indonesia, the Philippines and other areas of Southeast Asia, milkfish (*Chanos chanos*) culture in brackish water yielded some 200,000 tonnes in the early 1970s, and mullet (*Mugil*), groupers, snappers, bass, seabreams and other inshore species were being reared in floating pens. Seabass (*Dicentrarebus labrax*) culture also began in Italy and France in the 1970s (Mistakidis, 1977).

THE STATUS OF MARINE MAMMALS

The decade also saw continuing concern over the status of various cetacean species. Marine mammals, including whales, porpoises, dolphins, seals, sea lions, sirenians, sea otters and polar bears, have historically been subject to severe hunting. This has caused serious depletion and has even endangered a number of species, although where conservation measures have been applied (as with grey seals (*Halichoerus grypus*) in the British Isles and fur seals in the Antarctic) recovery has sometimes occurred (e.g. in grey seals) to the point where a local conflict with fisheries has developed (ICES, 1979c).

Whaling has concentrated successively on single species of whales and technological development has assured that the whales, once located, cannot readily avoid capture. Estimates of the original and current population of the ten species of large whales that have formed the basis of the commercial whaling industry this century in the North Pacific and Southern Hemisphere suggest that there is now only about 48 per cent of the total stock of these whales remaining (Allen, 1980). This average figure conceals the fact that while some stocks and species have actually increased during this period due to reduced inter-specific competition some have been reduced to five per cent or less of their former abundance by whaling. The International Whaling Commission (IWC) has attempted responsible management and has had some success in limiting whaling. A ban on all commercial whaling, proposed at the Stockholm Conference and at subsequent meetings of the IWC since then, has still not been achieved, but did result in the implementation of a new management procedure by the IWC in 1975. Under this regime, the global catches of whales were considerably reduced (Figure 3—2).

Figure 3—2. The Global Catches of Sperm, Minke, Sei, Fin and other Whales

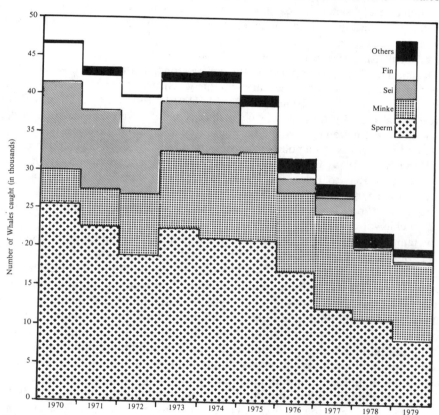

Source: R. Gambell, International Whaling Commission; private Communication.

A basic problem for proper management of whales, as with all marine fishery resources, is the lack of precise data on populations, as well as incomplete knowledge of whale behaviour and population dynamics. Consequently, some countries now prohibit whaling within their economic zones, and are intensifying pressure for a total ban. Whaling outside IWC control, which was a serious problem because the potentially unlimited catches included otherwise protected sizes and species of whales, has been stopped by the effectiveness of the IWC resolutions (Allen, 1980).

DEVELOPMENTS IN THE COASTAL ZONE

Mangroves (*Rhizophora, Avicennia* etc.) dominate the intertidal zone in many tropical areas where sediments, especially loose mud, provide good rooting conditions. They not only provide shelter against coastal erosion, but build productive biological communities which serve as nursery grounds for commercially important fish, shellfish, prawns and crabs, and support a rich diversity of other aquatic organisms and birds. In other tropical areas salt marshes and coral reefs also support extremely diverse and important plant and animal communities. Coral reefs shelter the coasts and for this reason are crucial to the environmental stability of many oceanic islands. They are the scene of local fisheries and are major tourist attractions.

During the 1970s, development in the coastal zones of many regions caused local changes in these formations, which are extremely sensitive to disturbance (Ferguson-Wood and Johannes, 1974; Hann *et al.,* 1981; UNEP, 1981 c). Coastal urbanization damaged coral reefs by depositing a blanketing sediment from construction works in Hawaii. The construction of port and harbour installations, and the increasing exposure of reefs and mangroves to oil pollution caused concern in the Caribbean and South East Asia (Hann *et al.,* 1981; UNEP, 1981c). Large areas of mangrove in South-East Asia have been converted to fish ponds, while on the east coast of Sumatra and East Kalimantan (eastern Indonesian Borneo) mangroves are being exploited for charcoal and firewood, for poles exported to Singapore as a building material and to Japan as a source of chipwood.

In temperate regions, intertidal salt marshes and mud flats support very large numbers of wading birds, geese and ducks, especially in winter when many species that breed in the Arctic migrate south to habitats on the coasts of Europe and North America. During the 1970s the protection of such areas received much attention and a number were listed under the Ramsar Convention (Chapter 6). The intertidal zone has traditionally been important for ecological teaching and research, and the aesthetic value of coastal areas is widely attested in art and literature.

In many parts of the world the coastal zone is also becoming increasingly important for recreation, which will almost certainly bring more boats, harbours, marinas, coastal residential development, sewage and pollution. In the Mediterranean coastal zone some 100 million inhabitants had to absorb a comparable number each year by the late 1970s (Chapter 14). Enclosing coastal areas to form carefully managed pools for mariculture also causes great changes in their ecology. Artificial reefs are being built on a large scale in Japan to attract fish (*Marine Pollution Bulletin,* 1979c).

The conservation of coastal landscapes and living resources in marine parks and nature reserves received increasing attention during the 1970s. IUCN became active in this work in the early 1970s initially promoting overall reviews of the subject and developing a classification as a framework for conservation (Björklund, 1974; Ray, 1975 a, b). In 1976 a major conference was held in Tokyo (IUCN, 1976). Action in the Mediterranean followed under the regional Action Plan (UNEP, 1980, 1981d, 1981g). A protocol for the establishment of a series of specially-protected areas was worked out between 1977 and 1980, and is likely to be signed in 1982, general criteria for selection being devised by IUCN (UNEP, 1977, 1980, 1981g). The Caribbean has also been the scene of considerable activity by UNEP in cooperation with IUCN (UNEP, 1981 c, 1981 e). Special attention was given to the protection of whales, cetacean sanctuaries being established in the Indian Ocean, off Mexico, Argentina, Hawaii and Japan and a number more being actively debated (IUCN, 1979). IUCN also developed guidelines for the establishment of coral reef reserves (Salm, 1980).

The various uses of coastal regions noted above are in potential conflict, and further conflicts exist between them and the exploitation of such regions for industry and as a source of energy. Major power plants (including nuclear power stations) are increasingly located on the coast because of their need for large quantities of cooling water. Oil terminals and refineries, pulp mills and chemical works are common near shorelines. Lately there has been mounting discussion of possible uses of tidal and wave power, the former in places such as the Bay of Fundy (Canada-United States), the Severn Estuary (United Kingdom), (Department of Energy, 1981) and in France, Alaska, the USSR, Argentina, Australia, India and Korea. Such plants can cause substantial ecological changes (Gordon and Longhurst, 1979), including those due to increased siltation (Risk and Buckley, 1979).

Careful management can limit disturbances and minimize conflicts, but it demands thorough scientific analysis and contact between all types of prospective users of the marine environment.

International Action For

Environmentally Sound Marine Development

Some international agreements to protect the marine environment and manage its resources date from well before the Stockholm Conference. These include:

— The Convention on the High Seas (1958);

— The Convention on the Continental Shelf (1958);

— The Convention on Fishing and Conservation of the Living Resources of the High Seas (1958);

— International Conventions for the Prevention of the Pollution of the Sea by Oil (1954, amended in 1962, 1969 and 1971, but the latter amendment not in force by early 1981) (IMCO, 1981);

— The Convention on Third Party Liability in the Field of Nuclear Energy (1963);

— The Treaty Banning Nuclear Weapons Tests in the Atmosphere, Outer Space and Underwater (1963);

— Conventions arising from the Third Law of the Sea Conference;

— The International Convention Relating to Intervention on the High Seas in Cases of Oil Pollution Casualties (1969);

— The International Convention on Civil Liability for Oil Pollution Damage (1969);

— The Agreement on Cooperation in Dealing with the Pollution of the North Sea by Oil (1969);

— International Convention on the Establishment of an International Fund for Compensation for Oil Pollution Damage (1971).

In the preparatory period for the Stockholm Conference, an Inter-Governmental Working Group began the preparation of a convention to curb the dumping of wastes at sea. Marine pollution was a major concern of the conference itself. In the decade under review the following important actions were taken:

— The Convention for the Prevention of Marine Pollution by Dumping from Ships and Aircraft (a regional convention) signed at Oslo in 1972;

— The Convention on the Dumping of Wastes at Sea (global) signed at London in 1972;

— The Convention on the Protection of the Marine Environment of the Baltic Sea Area signed at Helsinki in 1974;

— The Convention on the Prevention of Marine Pollution from Land-Based Sources signed at Paris in 1974;

— The Convention on the Protection of the Mediterranean Sea against Pollution signed at Barcelona in 1976. Protocols under this convention cover dumping from ships and aircraft, accidental oil spills and land-based sources of pollution. A draft Protocol on Marine Protected areas was due for signature in 1981 (UNEP, 1981 g), and a regional action plan for the protection and development of the Mediterranean has been in operation since 1975;

— The Kuwait Regional Convention for cooperation on the Protection of the Marine Environment from Pollution signed in Kuwait in 1978, covering a regional Action Plan for the Convention Area which came into operation in 1978 (UNEP, 1978 c);

— The Convention for cooperation in the Protection and Development of the Marine and Coastal Environment of the West and Central African Region (UNEP, 1981 h): a regional Action Plan also came into operation in 1981;

— Regional Action Plans were also agreed for the Red Sea and Gulf of Aden (1976), the Wider Caribbean (1981), and East Asian Seas (1981), while plans for the South-East Pacific, South-West Pacific, East Africa and the South-West Atlantic are in the process of negotiation (Figure 3—3). The South Asia Cooperative Environment Programme (SACEP) is expected to undertake coordinated regional studies on marine and related ecosystems;

— A Convention on Antarctic Marine Living Resources was signed in 1980;

— Concern over fisheries resources remains the business of Regional Fisheries Commissions. For example the Baltic Fish Commission (1974) meets annually and recommends fishing quotas for the Baltic Sea area;

— Pollution from shipping (reviewed by Moore, 1976; Abecassis, 1978 and M'Gonigle and Zacher, 1979) is the concern of IMCO, which in 1969 decided to convene in 1973 an International Conference on Marine Pollution. The Conference adopted two instruments (IMCO, 1974):

    (i) International Convention for the Prevention of Pollution from Ships, 1973 (not in force by early 1981);

    (ii) Protocol relating to intervention on the high seas in causes of marine pollution by substances other than oil, 1973 (not in force by early 1981);

— IMCO convened a Conference on Tanker Safety and Pollution Prevention in February 1978. This conference adopted two protocols relating to the International Convention for the Safety of Life at Sea, 1974, and the International Convention for the Prevention of Pollution from Ships. The latter convention is modified by the 1978 protocol, and the two instruments need to be read together, but the 1978 protocol was not in force by early 1981;

— The exploitation of marine mammals was the subject of concern: the Inter-governmental Whaling Commission gave total protection to certain species and reduced quotas for others (see above). A Convention on Antarctic seals was signed in 1972. The CITES Treaty prohibits trade in a number of endangered marine species. Certain whale products were added to the first schedule of this convention in 1980.

— An evaluation and categorization of noxious substances transported by ships (other than oil) was carried out by GESAMP (1973). The substances were evaluated on the basis of bio-accumulation, damage to living resources, hazard to human health and hazard to amenities such as recreational uses and aesthetics;

— An evaluation was made by GESAMP of harmful substances in the marine environment (GESAMP, 1977b), each substance being briefly discussed in

Figure 3–3. Geographic coverage of UNEP Regional Seas Programme

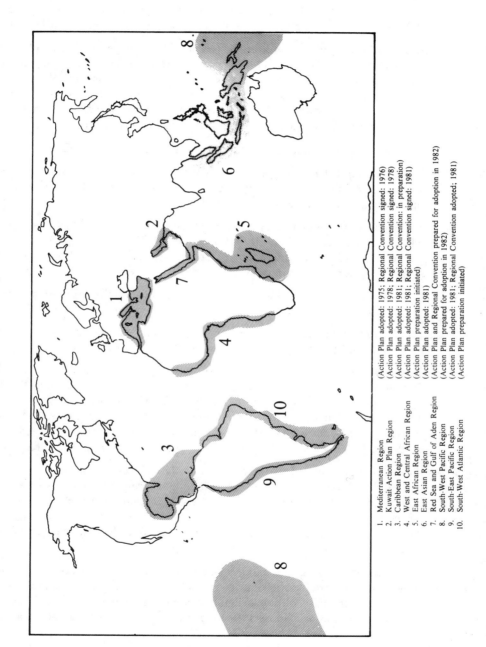

1. Mediterranean Region   (Action Plan adopted: 1975; Regional Convention signed: 1976)
2. Kuwait Action Plan Region   (Action Plan adopted: 1978; Regional Convention signed: 1978)
3. Caribbean Region   (Action Plan adopted: 1981; Regional Convention: in preparation)
4. West and Central African Region   (Action Plan adopted: 1981; Regional Convention signed: 1981)
5. East African Region   (Action Plan preparation initiated)
6. East Asian Region   (Action Plan adopted: 1981)
7. Red Sea and Gulf of Aden Region   (Action Plan and Regional Convention prepared for adoption in 1982)
8. South-West Pacific Region   (Action Plan prepared for adoption in 1982)
9. South-East Pacific Region   (Action Plan adopted: 1981; Regional Convention adopted: 1981)
10. South-West Atlantic Region   (Action Plan preparation initiated)

terms of sources, pathways and risks. In all, GESAMP (1971) listed 167 *Category I* substances, liable to cause serious problems in the marine environment and 229 *Category II* substances judged less hazardous.

Future Prospects

At first sight the data on contaminant levels in various areas of the marine environment and its biota presented in this chapter seem to imply that noticeable pollution is confined to coastal areas, and generally concentrated there in "hot spots", whereas contaminant concentrations in the open oceans are not raised significantly above background levels. Marine contamination thus appears to be a localized problem. However, much caution is necessary because of the limited data base. The analytical and sampling techniques used during most of the 1970s were very coarse; much data obtained before about 1974 should be discarded; the techniques can only resolve for identification a very few of the synthetic chemical compounds known to be present; and knowledge of factors influencing concentration levels in biota is limited. Moreover, the ecological effects likely to result from chronic exposure to pollutants at low concentrations are far from clear.

The data do not permit trends to be established, except for a few substances in a few areas. For example, it was shown that DDT levels in Baltic Sea biota decreased during the 1970s, and that inputs of some pollutants from land-based sources and through marine dumping also declined in some areas. National legislation had some effect in decreasing pollution in most industrialized countries by concentrating especially on coastal and estuarine waters. These seem likely to continue to be the focal points for action in the next decade, and indeed this is natural since this is where human impacts are concentrated and the potential for control exists (UNEP, 1981 g). However, the initial steps in pollution abatement have probably been easier than the work that will have to be accomplished during the 1980s.

The yield from renewable living marine resources steadily increased up to the 1970s, but it seems to have levelled off in the latter part of this decade. Although some species increased even in heavily fished areas, most of the traditional fishing grounds and species were over-exploited in the mid-1970s. Introduction of quotas led to some species recovering, while others still declined. Over-fishing, natural fluctuations in environmental conditions and perhaps pollution in some coastal waters combined to cause a severe decline in many traditional fisheries. This was largely compensated for by new fishing grounds, development of deep-water fishing techniques and catches of non-traditional species. Increasing energy prices put a severe stress on commercial fisheries, and are leading to development of low-energy fishing methods. In coming decades, demand for fishing for direct human consumption is expected to continue to rise, perhaps by 18 million tonnes by 1990, and the fish meal industry for livestock feed is also likely to go on growing (Robinson, 1979). FAO estimates of potential production suggest that it should be possible to take world production from 75 million tonnes in 1980 to 84.7 in 1990 and 92.5 in 2000. But this will demand a broad-based approach including much more effective management of resources, improved utilization of caught fish to reduce post-harvest losses, which may currently amount to some 20 per cent of all fish taken, and increased attention to species not now exploited and to mariculture (Mistakidis, 1977).

Exploration and exploitation of non-living marine resources, in particular petroleum, steadily increased during the 1970s. There was also an increasing demand on coastal areas for industry, shipping, processing, and tourism or recreational uses. The conflicts of interest are apparent, but have not been resolved, and are likely to intensify in the 1980s.

Proper management and control will go a long way to prevent the increasing use of coastal areas having disastrous consequences, but some harmful effects may be unavoidable on a local scale (GESAMP, 1980 b). Marine nature reserves – already established in a number of countries during the 1970s – are likely to become more numerous and extensive (Dunnet, 1979; Cole, 1979). Future projects to help maintain or increase living resources may include increased construction of artificial reefs and islands. The relative importance of mariculture will increase if land erosion and the destruction of agricultural land in various areas are not checked. The potential of mariculture is very large, but its implementation requires relatively unpolluted waters and a systems-oriented approach (Weatherby and Cogger, 1977).

International action will remain necesary in two areas: scientific and regulatory. While there is no present evidence that pollution has caused any general decline in oceanic productivity, it is clearly important that monitoring of the state of the oceans and the ecological systems they support continues, since if serious and widespread damage were to become apparent it would be too late to adopt preventive measures. International reviews of the best available information about the health of the oceans (like that prepared by GESAMP, 1981), and about the risks posed by particular substances in particular areas, remain essential. Such global overviews need to be complemented by regional action like that undertaken through UNEP's Regional Seas Programme, and under the various conventions and protocols. The MEDPOL programme of monitoring, and the programme undertaken by ICES in the north-east Atlantic and its coastal sea and by national scientists elsewhere, remain of first importance.

At the regulatory level, the adoption of regional conventions had undoubtedly been one of the environmental successes of the decade: the extension of such agreements to cover all major areas of the world ocean, subject to pollution by several nations, remains of high priority. Such agreements need to be backed by national controls on discharges to the marine environment by all routes – dumping, direct discharge from coastal and estuarine outfalls, and indirect discharge via rivers. At the global level, the 1970s saw the achievement of the London Convention on Dumping of Wastes, and agreements to curb pollution from shipping negotiated in IMCO, but although the Law of the Sea Conference met for most of the period it had not achieved final success by summer 1981. Nonetheless, a number of the aims of the Conference had been carried forward by regional and national actions. International action to negotiate special regimes protecting vulnerable areas of the environment, such as the Antarctic Seas, from overcropping and uncontrolled mineral exploitation was also in train at the end of the decade (Antarctic Treaty, 1979) and international cooperation was playing an increasingly important part in the development of fishery resources.

The continuing expansion of offshore oil and gas production, moving into deeper waters and remote seas (including ice-beset polar regions) will undoubtedly stimulate continuing demands for international action both to protect the marine environment and to develop an agreed basis for compensation when actions under the jurisdiction of one government cause ecological damage to the resources of another. Nearer inshore, an increase in sand and gravel extraction is projected for the 1980s in Europe (ICES, 1979 b), and off the north-east coast of the United States (Pearce, 1979 b). ICES has expressed strong concern about the possible impact on fisheries, urging careful management of such activities to avoid nursery grounds, and careful consideration of the effects of suspended matter generated through large-scale dredging operations.

Exploitation of deep-sea mineral resources such as manganese nodules has not yet started, although the potential is there and several national laws to control such activities have been passed. At international level, the management of this resource has been a particular concern of the United Nations Conference on the Law of the Sea. The potential environmental impacts requiring consideration have been discussed by GESAMP (1977 c).

References

Abecassis, D. W. (1978), *The Law and Practice Relating to Oil Pollution from Ships*, Butterworths, London.

Ackefors, E. (1977), Production of Fish and Other Animals in the Sea, *Ambio*, 6, 4, 192–200.

ACOPS (1978), *Annual Report of Advisory Committee on Oil Pollution of the Sea*, London.

Affolter, M. T. (1976), North Sea Oil Development: Some Related Environmental Planning Considerations in Scotland, *Ambio*, 5, 1, 3.

Allen, R. J. (1980), The Inadequacy of Existing Chlorophyll Phosphorus Concentration Correlations for Assessing Remedial Measures for Hypertrophic lakes, *Environ. Pollut.*, Ser. B. 1, 217–321.

Anon. (1973), *Environmental Study of Port Philip Bay*, Report on Phase I, 1968–1971, Melbourne, 372 pp.

Anon. (1979), *The Transfer of Pollutants in Two Southern Hemisphere Oceanic Systems*, Proceedings of a Workshop, South African National Scientific Programmes Rept. No.39.

Antarctic Treaty (1979), *Report of the 10th Antarctic Treaty Consultative Meeting*, Department of State, Washington, D.C.

Arriaga, M. (1976), Contaminacion en el Oceano Pacifico Surrorriental (Ecuador–Peru–Chile) *Rev. Com. Perm. Pacifico Sur*, 5, 3–62.

Baker, J. M., Editor (1976 a), *Marine Ecology and Oil Pollution*, Applied Science Publishers, Barking, U.K.

Baker, J. M. (1976 b), Ecological Changes in Milford Haven during its History as an Oil Port. In J. M. Baker (Editor), *Marine Ecology and Oil Pollution*, Applied Science Publishers, Barking, U.K.

Baker, C. W. (1977), Mercury in Surface Waters of Seas Around the United Kingdom, *Nature*, 270, 230–232.

Bernhard, and Renzoni (1977), In UNEP (1978a).

Björklund, M. I. (1974), Achievements in Marine Conservation, I. Marine Parks, *Environmental Conservation*, 1, 3, 205–224.

Bolin, B. *et al.*, Editors (1979), *The Global Carbon Cycle: SCOPE* 13, J. Wiley and Sons, Chichester.

Cambray, R. S. *et al.* (1979), The Atmospheric Input of Trace Metals to the North Sea. *Mar. Res. Comm.*, 5, 175–194.

Caputi, N. *et al.* (1979), Mercury Content of Shark from South-West Australian Waters, *Mar. Poll. Bull.*, 10, 11, 337.

Cole, H. A. (1979), Marine Nature Reserves, *Mar. Poll. Bull.*, 10, 12, 364.

Cole, H. A. (1980), Change in North Atlantic fisheries, *Mar. Poll. Bull.*, 11, 2, 31.

Cumont, G. *et al.* (1972), Contamination Des Poissons de Mer par le Mercure. *Rev. Int. Oceanog. Med.*, 28, 95–127.

Deggobis, D. *et al.* (1979), Increased Eutrophication of the Northern Adriatic Sea, *Mar. Poll. Bull.*, 10, 10, 298.

Department of Energy (1981), *Tidal Power from the Severn Estuary*, Vol. 1 Energy Paper No. 46. HMSO. London.

Dicks, B. (1976), The Effects of Refinery Effluents: Case History of a Saltmarsh. In J.M. Baker (Editor), *Marine ecology and Oil Pollution*, Applied Science Publishers, Barking, U.K.

Duce, R. A. *et al.* (1976), Trace Metals in the Marine Atmosphere: Source and Fluxes. In H. L. Windom and R. A. Duce (Editors) *Marine Pollutant Transfer*, Lexington, New York.

Duinker, J. C. *et al.* (1979), Organochlorines and Metals in Harbour Seals (Dutch Wadden Sea), *Mar. Poll. Bull.*, 10, 12, 360.

Dunnet, G. M. (1979), Nature Conservation in the Marine Environment, *Mar. Poll. Bull.*, 10, 11, 318.

Dutton, J. W. R. *et al.* (1973), Trace Metals in the North Sea, *Mar. Poll. Bull.*, 4, 9, 135.

EAJ (1976), *Annual Report of the Environment Agency of Japan*, Tokyo.

EAJ (1977), *Annual Report of the Environment Agency of Japan*, Tokyo.

EAJ (1978), *Annual Report of the Environment Agency of Japan*, Tokyo.

Fairbridge, R. W., Editor (1972), *Encyclopedia of Geochemistry and Environmental Sciences*, Van Nostrand Reinhold, New York.

FAO (1971), *Pollution: An International Problem for Fisheries*, Food and Agriculture Organization, Rome.

FAO (1974), *Review of the Status of Exploitation of the World Fish Resources*, FAO Fisheries Circular No. 328, Food and Agriculture Organization, Rome.

FAO (1977), *Provisional Food Balance sheets. 1972–1974 Average*, Food and Agriculture Organization, Rome.

FAO (1979), *Yearbook of Fishery Statistics: Catches and Landings*, Food and Agriculture Organization, Rome.

Ferguson-Wood, E. J. and R. E. Johannes (1974), *Tropical Marine Pollution*, Elsevier, Oceanography Series 12, Amsterdam.

Fitzgerald, W. F. (1976), Mercury Studies of Seawater and Rain: Geochemical Flux Implications, In H. L. Windom and R. A. Duce (Editors), *Marine Pollutant Transfer*, Lexington, New York.

Fylion-Myklebust, C. and K. I. Johannesson (1980), *Biological Effects of Oil Pollution in the Marine Environment: A Bibliography*, The Norwegian Marine Pollution Research and Monitoring Programme. ICES C.M. 1980/E:31.

Gardner, B. D. (1979), *The Halogenated Pesticides in the Marine Environment of Natal, Transkei and the South Eastern Cape*, Contribution to Workshop on Transfer of Pollutants in Two Southern Hemisperic Oceanic Systems, Plettenburg Bay, South Africa.

GESAMP (1971), IMCO/FAO/UNESCO/WMO/WHO/IAEA Joint Group of Experts on the Scientific Aspects of Marine Pollution (GESAMP), Rep. 2nd Sess., UNESCO. Paris.

GESAMP (1973), Group of Experts on the Scientific Aspects of Marine Pollution, Rep. 5th Sess., IAEA, Vienna.

GESAMP (1976), Review of Harmful Substances, Reports and Studies No. 2, Food and Agriculture Organization, Rome.

GESAMP (1977a), Impact of Oil on the Marine Environment, Reports and Studies, No.6.

GESAMP (1977b), Review of the Harmful Substances in the Marine Environment, Reports and Studies, No.2.

GESAMP (1977c), Scientific Aspects of Pollution Arising From the Exploration and Exploitation of the Sea-Bed, Reports and Studies, No.7.

GESAMP (1980a), Marine Pollution Implications of Coastal Area Development, Reports and Studies, No.10.

GESAMP (1980b), Monitoring of Biological Variables Related to Marine Pollution, Reports and Studies, No.12.

GESAMP (1981), *The Health of the Oceans* (In Press).

Gibbs, R. J., Editor (1974), *Suspended Solids in Water*, Marine Science Series 4, Plenum Press, New York.

Glantz, M. H. (1979), Science, Politics and Economics of the Peruvian Anchoveta Fishery, *Marine Policy*, July, 201–210.

Goldberg, E. D. (1975), Synthetic Organochlorides in the Sea, Proc R. Soc., Lond. B. 189, 227.

Goldberg, E. D. (1976), *The Health of the Oceans*, The UNESCO Press, Paris.

Goldberg, E. D. *et al.* (1978): The Mussel Watch, *Environmental Conservation*, 5, 2, 101.

Gordon, D. L. and A. R. Longhurst (1979), The Environmental Aspects of a Tidal Power Project in the Upper Reaches of the Bay of Fundy, *Mar. Poll. Bull.*, 10, 2, 38.

Gulland, J. (1970), In M. W. Holdgate (Editor), *Antarctic Ecology*, Academic Press, London.

Halcrow, W. *et al.* (1973),The Distribution of Trace Metals and Fauna in the Firth of Clyde in Relation to the Disposal of Sewage Sludge, *J. Mar. Biol. Ass.*, UK, 53, 721–739.

Hann, R. W. *et al.* (1981), *The Status of Oil Pollution and Oil Pollution Control in the South East Asia Region*, Texas A and M University.

Harvey, G. R. *et al.* (1974), Observations of the Distribution of Chlorinated Hydrocarbons in Atlantic Ocean Organisms, *J. Mar. Res.*, 32, 103.

Helle, E. *et al.* (1976a), DDT and PCB Levels and Reproduction in Ringed Seals from the Bothnian Bay, *Ambio*, 5, 4, 188.

Helle, E. *et al.* (1976b), PCB Levels Correlated With Pathological Changes in Seal Uteri, *Ambio*, 5–6, 261.

Helmer, R. (1977), Pollutants from Land-based Sources in the Mediterranean, *Ambio*, 6, 6, 312–316.

Holdgate, M. W. (1969), *The Sea Bird Wreck in the Irish Sea*, Natural Environment Research Council, London.

Holdgate, M. W. and G. F. White, Editors (1977), *Environmental Issues; SCOPE* 10, J. Wiley and Sons, Chichester.

IAEA (1981), Intercalibration of Analytical Methods on Marine Environmental Samples. UNEP/WG.46/INF.7. United Nations Environment Programme, Experts Meeting to Evaluate the Pilot Phase of MEDPOL and to Develop a long-term Monitoring and Research Programme for the Medit. Action Plan, Geneva, Jan. 1981.

ICES (1974), Report of Working Group for the International Study of the Pollution of the North Sea and its Effects on Living Resources and Their Exploitation, International Council for the Exploration of the Sea (ICES), *Co-op. Res. Rept. No.39*, Copenhagen.

ICES (1977a), Studies of the Pollution of the Baltic Sea, by ICES/SCOR. Working Group on the Study of Pollution of the Baltic Sea. International Council for the Exploration of the Sea, *Co-op. Res. Rept. No.63*.

ICES (1977b), A Baseline Study of the Level of Contaminating Substances in Living Resources of the North Atlantic, International Council for the Exploration of the Sea, *Co-op. Res. Rept.* No.69.

ICES (1977c), The Ekofisk Bravo Blow-out – Compiled Norwegian Contribution, International Council for the Exploration of the Sea, c.m. 1977/E55.

ICES (1978a), Assessment of the Marine Environment of the Baltic Sea, Mimeo, 43 pp. International Council for the Exploration of the Sea.

ICES (1978b), Input for Pollutants to the Oslo Commission Area, International Council for the Exploration of the Sea, *Co-op. Res. Rept.* No.77.

ICES (1978c), Report on International Analyses in ICES North Sea and North Atlantic Baseline Studies, International Council for the Exploration of the Sea, *Co-op Res. Rept. No.* 80.

ICES (1979a), Report of the Working Group on Atlanto-Scandian Herring. C.M. 1979/H:8, Mimeo, International Council for the Exploration of the Sea.

ICES (1979b), Report of the ICES Working Group on Effects on Fisheries of Marine Sand and Gravel Extraction. C.M. 1979/E.3, International Council for the Exploration of the Sea.

ICES (1979c), Report of the ICES Advisory Committee on Fishery Management. International Council for the Exploration of the Sea.

ICES (1980a), A Review of Past and Present Measurements of Selected Free Minerals in Sea Water in the Oslo Commission and ICNAF (NAFO) Areas, International Council for the Exploration of the Sea, *Co-op Res. Rept. No.* 97.

ICES (1980b), Report of the ICES Working Group "Pathology and Diseases in Marine Organisms", C.M. 1980/E.33. International Council for the Exploration of the Sea.

ICES (1981): The ICES Co-ordinated Monitoring Programme 1978. International Council for the Exploration of the Sea, (In Press).

Idyll, C. P. (1970), *The Sea Against Hunger,* Thomas Y. Cromwell Co., New York.

IMCO (1974), International Conference on Marine Pollution, 1973, Inter-Governmental Maritime Consultative Organization, London.

IMCO (1979), Where the Oil was Spilled: 1962–1978. *IMCO News,* 1,12. Inter-Governmental Maritime Consultative Organization, London.

IMCO (1981), Status of International Convention Relating to Marine Pollution of which IMCO is Depository or is Responsible for Secretarial duties, Paper MEPC/XV/2, Inter-Governmental Maritime Consultative Organization, London.

IUCN (1976), An International Conference on Marine Parks and Reserves, International Union for the Conservation of Nature and Natural Resources, *Publication No.* 37 (New Series), Gland, Switzerland.

IUCN (1979), Proceedings, Workshop on Cetacean Sanctuaries, Tijuana and Guerrero Nego, B.C. Mexico. International Union for the Conservation of Nature and Natural Resources, Gland, Switzerland.

IUCN/UNEP/WWF (1980), World Conservation Strategy, International Union for the Conservation of Nature and Natural Resources; United Nations Environment Programme, World Wildlife Fund, Gland, Switzerland.

Jansson, B.O. (1978), The Baltic; A Systems Analysis of a Semi-enclosed Sea, In H. Charnock and G. Deacon (Editors), *Advances in Oceanography,* Plenum, New York.

Jefferies, D. F. *et al.* (1980), Transport Processes in the Irish Sea as Indicated by the Measurement of Radionuclides Released from Windscale, International Council for the Exploration of the Sea, C.M. 1980/Gen 5.

Jensen, N. J. *et al.* (1979), The Ulcus-Syndrome in Cod (*Gadus-Morrhua*) III. A Preliminary Virological Report, *Nord. Vet. Med.,* 31, 436.

Jerlov, N. G. (1958): Distribution of Suspended Material in the Adriatic Sea, *Arch. Oceanog. Limnol.,* 11, 227.

Johansen, P. *et al.* (1980), Heavy Metals and Organochlorines in Marine Mammals from Greenland, International Council for the Exploration of the Sea, C.M. 1980/E.32.

Johnston, R. (1976), *Marine Pollution,* Acadamic Press, London.

Jones, P. G. W. (1975): Review of the Distribution of Selected Trace Metals in the Water of the North Atlantic, In ICES/ACMP Report, *Co-op. Res. Rept. No.50,* Annex 3, International Council for the Exploration of the Sea, Copenhagen.

Keckes, S. (1977), The Co-ordinated Mediterranean Monitoring and Research Programme. *Ambio.* 6, 6, 327.

Kirillova, E. P. and I. G. Orlova (1979), Pollution of the North East Atlantic (Based on materials of 23rd Expedition), Proc. of State Oceanographic Inst., Gidrometeoizdat, Moscow, 26–31.

Kohnke, D. (1979), Preliminary Analyses of Data from Visual Observations and Tar Ball Collections Submitted to RNODC's. Unpublished Report, Intergovernmental Oceanographic Commission/World Meteorological Organization, IOC/WMO-MAP-MOPP, 11/6.

Kumpf, H. E. (1977), Economic Impact of the Effects of Pollution on the Coastal Fisheries of the Atlantic and Gulf of Mexico Regions of the USA. Food and Agriculture Organization, Rome.

Kureishy, T. W. *et al.* (1973), Total Mercury content in Some Marine Fish from the Indian Ocean, *Mar. Poll. Bull.,* 10, 12, 357.

Levell, D. (1976), The Effect of Kuwait Crude Oil and the Dispersant BP–1100X on the Lugworm *Arenicola marina* L. In J. M. Baker (Editor), *Marine Ecology and Oil Pollution,* Applied Science Publishers, Barking, UK.

Levy, E. M. (1979), The IGOSS Pilot Project on Marine Pollution (Petroleum) Monitoring: Its Evolution and a Personal Viewpoint, *Mar. Poll. Bull.,* 10, 1, 5.

Levy, E. M. (1980 a), Oil Pollution and Seabirds: Atlantic Canada 1976-77 and Some Implications for Northern Environments, *Mar. Poll. Bull.,* 11, 2, 51.

Levy, E. M. (1980 b), *Transfer Processes and the Global Distribution of Petroleum Pollution in the Marine Environment,* Elsevier, Amsterdam. (In press).

Levy, E. M. and A. Walton (1974), Dispersed and Particulate Petroleum Residues in the Gulf of St. Lawrence (abstract). In *Rapports et Process-Verb,* 167, International Council for the Exploration of the Sea.

Linden, O. (1975), Acute Effects of Oil and Oil Dispersant Mixture on Larvae of Baltic Herring. *Ambio*, 4, 3, 216.

Linden, O. (1976), The Influence of Crude Oil and Mixtures of Crude Oil/Dispersants on the Ontogenic Development of Baltic Herring, *Clupea harengus* Membras, *Ambio*, 5, 3, 136.

Linden, O. *et al.* (1979), The Tsesis Oil Spill: Its Impact on the Coastal Ecosystem of the Baltic Sea, *Ambio*, 8, 6, 244.

Marine Poll. Bull. (1979a), Bathing Ban in Italy, *Marine Poll. Bull.*, 10, 8, 217.

Marine Poll. Bull. (1979b), Wastes on Spanish Beaches, *Marine Poll. Bull.*, 10, 9, 249.

Marine Poll. Bull. (1979c), Man-made Reefs, *Marine Poll. Bull.*, 10, 1, 4.

Marine Poll. Bull. (1980), High Mercury Levels in Australian Commercial Fish. Vol., 11, 1, 2.

Maugh, T. H. (1973), DDT: An Unrecognized Source of Polychlorinated Biphenyls. *Science*, 180, 578–9.

M'Gonigle, R. M. and M. W. Zacher (1979), *Pollution, Politics and International Law*, University of California Press, Berkeley, Calif.

Mistakidis (1977), Culture of Marine Fishes in the Third World, FAO Fisheries Circular No. 104, Food and Agriculture Organization, Rome.

Mitchell, B. and J. Tinker (1980), *Antarctica and Its Resources*, Earthscan, London.

Moiseev, P. A. (1970), Some Aspects of the Commercial Use of the Krill Resources of the Antarctic Seas. In M. W. Holdgate (Editor), *Antarctic Ecology*, Academic Press, London.

Moore, G. (1976), Legal Aspects of Marine Pollution Control. In R. Johnston (Editor); *Marine Pollution*, Academic Press, London.

Munk, W. H. (1950), On The Wind-driven Ocean Circulation. *J. Meteorol.*, 7.

Murchelano, R. A. and J. Ziskowski (1979), Fin Rot Disease-sentinel of Environmental Stress, International Council for the Exploration of the Sea C.M./E:25.

NAS (1973), Background Papers for a Workshop on Inputs, Fates and Effects of Petroleum in the Marine Environment, 2 Vols. Ocean Affairs Board, National Academy of Sciences, Washington, D.C.

NAS (1975), *Petroleum in the Marine Environment*, National Academy of Sciences, Washington, D.C.

Newman, M. W. *et al.* (1979), *Aetiology of Spinning Disease of Menhaden*, International Council for the Exploration of the Sea.

Oil Spill Report (1980), Special Report, IXTOC 1, Oil Spill Intelligence Report, Vol. 3, No. 1, 4 January.

Pak, H. *et al.* (1970), The Columbia River as a Source of Marine Light Scattering Particles, *J. Geophys. Res.*, 75, 4570.

Pearce, J. B. (1979a), *Raritan Bay - a Highly Polluted Estuarine System*, International Council for the Exploration of the Sea, ICES/C.M. 1979/E:45.

Pearce, J. B. (1979b), Marine Sand and Gravel Production in Areas off the Northeast Coast of the United States, *Mar. Poll. Bull.*, 10, 1, 14.

Porter, E. (1973), *Pollution in Four Industrialised Estuaries*, HMSO, London.

Preston, A. *et al.* (1973), British Isles Coastal Waters; The Concentration of Selected Heavy Metals in Sea Water, Suspended Matter and Biological Indicators – A Pilot Survey, *Environ. Poll.*, 3, 69.

Ray, G. C. (1975 a), A Preliminary Classification of Coastal and Marine Environments, IUCN Occasional Paper No. 14, International Union for Conservation of Nature and Natural Resources, Gland, Switzerland.

Ray, G. C. (1975 b), Conservation of Marine Biota with Particular Reference to the Role of Marine Parks and Reserves, Paper IUCN/TM/75/10, 13th Technical Meeting, Kinshasha, Zaire, International Union for Conservation of Nature and Natural Resources, Gland, Switzerland.

Reid, R. N. (1979), *Contaminant Concentrations and Effects in Long Island Sound*, International Council for the Exploration of the Sea, C.M. 1979/E: 47.

Rex, R. W. and E. D. Goldberg (1958), Quartz Contents of Pelagic Sediments of the Pacific Ocean, *Tellus*, 10, 153.

Riley, J. P. and G. Skirrow, Editors (1975), *Chemical Oceanography*, 2nd Edition, Vol. 1–4, Academic Press, London.

Risebrough, R. W. (1977), Transfer of Organochlorine Pollutant to Antarctica, In G. A. Llano (Editor), *Adaptations Within Antarctic Ecosystems*, Smithsonian Institution, Washington, D.C.

Risk, M. J. and D. E. Buckley (1979), Viewpoint on a Viewpoint: Comments on Tidal Power Plant Developments, *Mar. Poll. Bull.*, 10, 8, 219.

Robinson, M. A. (1979), Prospects for World Fishing to 2000, FAO Fisheries Circular No. 722, Food and Agriculture Organization, Rome.

Rodhe, H. *et al.* (1980), Deposition of Airborne Pollutants on the Baltic. *Ambio*, 9, 3–4, 168–173.

Royal Commission (1972), *Pollution in Some British Estuaries and Coastal Waters*, Third Report of the Royal Commission on Environmental Pollution, HMSO, London.

Ryther, J. H. (1969), Relationship of Photosynthesis to Fish Production in the Sea, *Science*, 166, 72.

Salm, R. V. (1980), Guidelines for the Establishment of Coral Reef Reserves, Final Draft Report, Project WWF/IUCN 1700. International Union for the Conservation of Nature and Natural Resources, Gland, Switzerland.

Sasamura, Y. (1977), *Environmental Impact of the Transportation of Oil*, Inter-Governmental Maritime Consultative Organization, London.

SCEP (1970), Study of Critical Environmental Problems. *Man's Impact on the Global Environment: Assessment and Recommendations for Action*, MIT Press, Cambridge, Mass.

Schmidt, D. (1976), *Distribution of Seven Trace Metals in Sea Water of the Inner German Bight*, International Council for the Exploration of the Sea, Doc. CM 1976/C.10.

Sergeant, D. E. (1980), Levels of Mercury and Organochlorine Residues in Tissues of Sea Mammals from St Lawrence Estuary, International Council for the Exploration of the Sea, C.M. 1980/E.55.

Smokler, P. E. D. R. *et al.* (1979), DDTs in Marine Fishes Following Termination of Dominant California Input, 1970–77, *Mar. Poll. Bull.*, 10, 11, 331.

Somer, E. (1981), Mercury; Interaction of Scientific Experiences and Administrative Regulation in Denmark, Paper presented to the First Conference on the Scientific Bases for Environmental Regulatory Actions, Rome, May 1981.

Spitzer, P. R. *et al.* (1978), Productivity of Ospreys in Connecticut-Long Island Increases as DDT Residues Decline. *Science* 202, 333–335.

Steele, J. H. (1974), *The Structure of Marine Ecosystems,* Blackwell, Edinburgh, UK.

Stoeppler, M. *et al.* (1977), Mercury in Marine Organisms of the Mediterranean and other European Seas, XXVth Congress and Plenary Assembly (Split, Oct. 1976) Chemical Committee 2 (Preprint).

Stommel, H. (1965), *The Gulf Stream,* University of California Press, Berkley.

SVEAG (1976), *Oil Terminal at Sullom Voe; Environmental Impact Assessment,* Thuleprint, Sandwick, Shetland.

Thibaud, Y. (1971), Teneur en Mercure dans Quelques Poissons de Consommation Courante, *Sci.Pêche* 209, 1–10.

Ui, J. (1969), A short History of Minamata Disease and the Present Situation of Mercury Pollution in Japan, *Norsk. Hyg. Tidskr.,* 50, 2, 139–146.

UN (1975), Marine Questions: Uses of the Sea, United Nations Economic and Social Council E/5650.

UNEP (1977), Report of Expert Consultation on Mediterranean Marine Parks and Wetlands, Tunis, Jan. 1977, Paper UNEP/WG 6/5, United Nations Environment Programme, Nairobi.

UNEP (1978a), Preliminary Report on the State of Pollution of the Mediterranean Sea. UNEP/IG 11/INF.4, Intergovernmental Review Meeting of Mediterranean Coastal States on the Med. Action Plan, Monaco, Jan. 1978, United Nations Environment Programme, Nairobi.

UNEP (1978 b), Pollutants from Land-based Sources in the Mediterranean. UNEP/IG 11/INF.5, Intergovernmental Review Meeting of Mediterranean Coastal States on the Med. Action Plan, Monaco, Jan. 1978. United Nations Environment Programme, Nairobi.

UNEP (1978c), Final act of the Kuwait Regional Conference of Plenipotentiaries on the Protection and Development of the Marine Environment and Coastal Areas, United Nations Environment Programme, Nairobi.

UNEP (1979), Pollutants from Land-based Sources in the Mediterranean. Paper UNEP/WG.18/INF.4, Meeting Technical Experts on Draft Protocol for Protection of Mediterranean Sea Against Pollution from Land-based Sources, Geneva, June 1979. United Nations Environment Programme, Nairobi.

UNEP (1980), Report of the Intergovernmental Meeting on Mediterranean Specially Protected Areas, Athens, October, 1980, UNEP/IG/20/5. United Nations Environment Programme, Nairobi.

UNEP (1981a), Co-ordinated Mediterranean Pollution Monitoring Programme UNEP/3/WG 46/3, Part I. Meeting Experts Evaluate Pilot Phase Med. Pol, Geneva, Jan. 1981, United Nations Environment Programme, Nairobi.

UNEP (1981b), The State of Marine Pollution in the Wider Caribbean Region, UNEP/CEPAL/WG.48/INF.5, Second Meeting of Government nominated Experts to Review Draft Action Plan for the Wider Caribbean Region, Managua, Feb. 1981, United Nations Environment Programme, Nairobi.

UNEP (1981c), The Status of Oil Pollution and Oil Pollution Control in the Wider Caribbean Region, UNEP/CEPAL/WG.48/INF.6, Second Meeting of Government nominated Experts to Review Draft Action Plan for Wider Caribbean Region, Managua, Feb. 1981, United Nations Environment Programme, Nairobi.

UNEP (1981d), Draft Environmental Quality Criteria, Meeting of Experts to Evaluate the Pilot Phase of MED POL., Geneva, Jan. 1981, UNEP/WG. 46/7, United Nations Environment Programme, Nairobi.

UNEP (1981e), A Strategy for the Conservation of the Living Marine Resources and Processors of the Caribbean Region, UNEP/CEPAL/WG.48./INF.17. Second Meeting of Government nominated Experts to Review Draft Action Plan for the Wider Caribbean Region, Managua, Feb. 1981, United Nations Environment Programme, Nairobi.

UNEP (1981f), Marine Pollution, Report of Executive Director. UNEP/GC.9/Add.3. United Nations Environment Programme, Nairobi.

UNEP (1981g), Principles, Criteria and Guidelines for the Selection, Establishment and Management of Mediterranean Marine and Coastal Protected Areas, UNEP/IG.23/INF.7. Second Meeting Contracting Parties to Convention for Protection Mediterranean Sea against Pollution, Cannes, March 1981, United Nations Environment Programme, Nairobi.

UNEP (1981h), Conference on Plenipotentiaries – West and Central African Region, Abidjan, 1981, Final Act, United Nations Environment Programme, Nairobi.

UNESCO (1976), International Workshop on Marine Pollution in Asian Waters, IOC Workshop Rep.8., UNESCO, Paris.

UNESCO (1977), Contributions to International Workshop on Marine Pollution in the Caribbean and Adjacent Region, IOC Workshop II and Supplement, UNESCO, Paris.

USCG (1973), Draft Environmental Impact Statement: US Coast Guard, for International Convention for the Prevention of Pollution from Ships.

Weatherby, A. H. and B. M. G. Cogger (1977), Fish Culture: Problems and Prospects. *Science,* 197, 4302, 427.

Wells, D. F. and S. J. Johnston (1975), The Occurence of Organochlorine Residues in Rain Water, *Nat. Air and Soil Poll.,* 9, 271–280.

WHO (1972), Evolution of Certain Food Additives and the Contaminants – Mercury, Lead and Cadmium, Technical Report Series No. 36. World Health Organization, Geneva.

Yamanaka, S. *et al.* (1972): Mercury Concentration in Tuna, and in Hair of Tuna-Fishermen II. *Jap. J. Hyg.,* 27, 117.

Yeats, P. A. *et al.* (1978), Sensitivity of Coastal Workers to Anthropogenic Trace Metal Emission, *Mar. Poll. Bull.,* 9, 264–268.

Zhu, De-Shan (1980), A Brief Introduction to the Fisheries of China. FAO Fisheries Guide No. 726, Food and Agricultural Organization, Rome.

CHAPTER 4

Inland Waters

Fresh water is one of the necessities of life, but for millions of people during the 1970s it was a scarce and hard-won commodity. Among the reasons were that inland waters occur in strictly limited volume (less than 0.01 per cent of global waters flow in rivers and their associated lakes and swamps), they undergo both seasonal and yearly fluctuations, and they are subject to man-made changes in their physical and biological qualities.

Considerable international activity was aimed at solving such problems. The International Hydrological Decade (IHD) programme (1965-74) and the International Hydrological Programme (IHP) that followed brought improved knowledge of hydrological processes. Great advances were made in assessment of water stocks, even before the United Nations Water Conference in 1977. The need for better management of water resources, and for treatment of river basins as unitary systems, received wider recognition, and there were advances in ground water assessment and applications of advanced technologies for surveying aquifers.

Of the three major uses of water (domestic supplies, industry and agriculture), agriculture made the major demand, for irrigation; and the decade saw further extension of irrigation (and improved drainage) to newly reclaimed lands, especialy in arid regions. Industrial uses increased during the decade, but savings were also made through increased efficiency. In Japan, for example, total industrial withdrawals increased from about 50 million cubic metres daily in 1965 to 120 million cubic metres in 1974 – but by the mid–1970s two-thirds of this was recycled water compared with one-third in 1965.

Spurred on by recurrent floods and droughts, engineers and scientists made progress in flood management through both structural (i.e., dykes and barrages) and non-structural techniques (land-use zoning, flood-proofing, flood insurance and land treatment through afforestation or soil conservation). Some research advances were made in augmenting water supplies through weather modification, evaporation suppression, desalination and recycling. Research advances were also made in development of models of river systems and ground water.

The large number of people with no access to safe, clean water and no sanitary services was a matter of deep concern to the world during the 1970s. This concern was expressed at the United Nations Conferences on Human Settlements (1976) and on Water (1977). These shortages were most pronounced in rural areas: in 1970 only 14 per cent of people there had access to safe water supplies. By 1980 that proportion had risen to only 29 per cent. Rural people were even worse off for sanitary facilities: by 1980 only 13 per cent had them. The picture was different for urban dwellers: in 1970, 67 per cent had access to safe water supplies and 71 per cent to sanitary facilities, while by 1980, 75 per cent had safe water but those with sanitary facilities had dropped to 53 per cent. As a result of the world-wide interest in improving this situation, the current decade (1980–1990) was named the United Nations International Drinking Water Supply and Sanitation Decade.

Inland water bodies suffered pollution and over-enrichment (eutrophication) caused by discharges from industries, drainage from agricultural and domestic chemicals and wastes, and acidification from acid rain. Underground aquifers deteriorated. But technologies for waste water treatment and recycling advanced to such an extent that for many rivers and lakes the deterioration was reversed and they were biologically revived (for example, the Thames in London, to which fish have returned). Nevertheless, the damage done by acid rain to life in lakes in North America and Scandinavian countries caused increasing concern.

Inland fisheries catches increased from about 5.2 million tonnes in the 1950s to about 10 million tonnes between 1973 and 1976. Creation of new inland fisheries in man-made lakes contributed to this growth. Aquaculture showed much promise, increasing production by 5–6 per cent in some countries and as much as 10 per cent in others.

One issue that received much attention during the decade was the environmental effect of large, man-made lakes. Because of the seriousness of some of their adverse impacts, the economic justification for some of these lakes was questioned.

In some places and in some ways, the world's water resources were worse off in 1980 than at the time of the United Nations Conference on the Human Environment (Stockholm, 1972). But there were some more positive aspects during the decade. Planning benefited from more and better data and improved understanding, stemming from research. Flood forecasting became more accurate and some major rivers became less polluted. Irrigation practices were improved and extended. And some national water development plans went into action, while internationally, agencies were set up to assist in co-operative development of shared water resources.

Water from surface and underground sources provides sustenance to plants and animals, constitutes the habitat for aquatic organisms, and meets important agricultural and industrial needs. Ocean water is drawn for some industrial cooling purposes and in a few places it is desalinated for drinking and manufacturing. But the waters of the continents, displaying tremendous differences in occurrence, seasonality and quality, are the essential resource for development on the land.

For much of the land surface the critical problems of water use are related to its limited volume or to the fluctuations in its flow from season to season or over the years. Regulation and storage works are designed to even out stream flow, but they also alter channel characteristics and sub-surface drainage and create new aquatic environments. Withdrawals of groundwater need to be limited to the average replenishment rate, or they may deplete the aquifer.

Through withdrawals and the use of water courses for navigation or waste disposal, water quality is changed, sometimes for the better but more often detrimentally. All human management of water has some effect upon its quantity or quality or both, and the record of the decade may be assessed in terms of those changes and how people sought to turn them to human benefit or to minimize the harm they might do to the environment.

Whilst its distribution varies in space and time, the total stock of freshwater remains fixed on the global scale. Greater human activity tends to deplete locally available supplies, and the continued growth of world population and acceleration in water use to meet increasing human demands had by 1970 already begun to strain the water resources of some areas, even in humid regions. The strain was made more acute by deterioration in water quality brought about by agricultural and industrial use and by waste disposal.

Accordingly, the decade saw increasing recognition of the need for better management of water resources by treating river basins as unitary systems (Whitton, 1975; White, 1977; OAS, 1978). The conservation of water and its biota was recognized as desirable for practical reasons (to sustain biological resources, especially fisheries) as well as aesthetic ones. Other topics of concern during the 1970s were the special problems and opportunities raised by the creation of man-made lakes, and the impacts of recent scientific and technological development. Water-borne diseases remained of great concern, especially in tropical developing countries (Chapter 10).

Water Quantity: Supply and Demand

THE WORLD'S STOCK OF WATER

Evaluation of water resources

The launching by the United Nations Educational, Scientific and Cultural Organization (UNESCO) of the International Hydrological Decade IHD (1965–1974), followed by the International Hydrological Programme (IHP), brought improved knowledge of hydrological processes. Great advances were made in assessment methods and by the time the United Nations Water Conference (UNWC) was held in 1977 there was a sound base for estimating the dimensions of the world's stock of water and for examining surface and ground water as a unified system.

In addition to the conventional observations and assessment of precipitation, streamflow and ground water, the Global Observation System (GOS) of the World Meteorological Organization (WMO) Weather Watch Programme produced valuable meteorological and related environmental data for operational and research purposes.

Advances were made in developing equipment for measuring rainfall and snowfall, assessing the water equivalent of snow through gamma radiation methods, and assessing precipitation by radar and automatic data reporting networks. Satellites, with their broad synoptic coverage, facilitated rapid data communication, and prepared the ground for advances in remote sensing technology. Snow cover assessment was greatly improved as a result. But basic data continued to come from ground observations in areas where the necessary instrument networks were maintained.

A mid-decade survey showed that a large number of countries, chiefly in Africa and Latin America, still had not achieved a minimum capability to assess their water resources on a continuing basis (UNWC, 1978 p. 953).

The decade saw major developments in ground water assessment and enhancement techniques. New information was acquired on the dynamics of ground water movement within aquifers, interconnections between aquifers, and interrelations between ground water and surface water. Other gains included:

(a) advances in space and aerial photography, which improved geomorphological and geological analysis, and the use of aerophotographic maps in estimating the location of supplies;

(b) improvement of geophysical prospecting equipment;

(c) improvement in the knowledge of water movement by the use of chemical tracers and environmental isotope analysis (UNWC, 1978 p. 857);

(d) advances in drilling techniques.

Whilst techiques improved for measuring sediment transport in rivers and sediment distribution within large reservoirs, the measuring techniques for suspended matter and bed-load continued to fall short of needs. There was growing concern over the relation between sediment and water quality, especially with regard to heavy metals and other contaminants such as polychlorinated biphenyls (PCBs) which are stored and transported in river-borne materials.

The collection of larger masses of data about water, data storage and retrieval and their use in models that permit analysis and forecast became more important. Computers for processing and storing hydrological data came into more general use. These were coupled with mathematical and modelling techniques for analysis, planning and forecasting. Modelling for surface water quantity was advanced, and was widely used in the operation of reservoir systems (Biswas, 1976). Water quality models for surface water were less satisfactory (Biswas, 1981). Similarly, the models for ground water movement were more reliable than those for diffusion and transport of contaminants underground (NRC, 1981).

The decade witnessed substantial progress in hydrologic forecasting techniques. In developed countries this involved expanding and improving existing river forecasting services. In several developing countries, international support assisted in intensifying basic networks so as to allow river forecasting. Operation of water control works was thereby made more efficient, and flood and low-flood predictions became more timely and accurate. The number of hydrological models describing water movement for forecasting purposes multiplied. An international critical comparison of some of these models was conducted by WMO.

Global water balance

The IHD brought together the results of research on global, regional and national water balance and water resources, including appraisals of changes in water quantity and quality generated by human activities. Global and continental water balances were computed, and the proportions of the main flows and withdrawals could be recognized (UNWC, 1978, p. 14).

According to recent estimates the total water volume on earth is about 1,400 million cubic kilometres (km³), more than 97 per cent being ocean water. An estimated 77.2 per cent of the fresh water is stored in ice caps and glaciers, 22.4 per cent is ground water and soil moisture, 0.35 per cent is in lakes and swamps, 0.04 per cent is in the atmosphere and less than 0.01 per cent is in the streams (UNWC, 1978, p. 5). The flow of surface water is roughly as shown in Table 4-1, with more than one-half of the annual run-off to the sea occurring in Asia and Latin America. In contrast, the overwhelming flow of sediment is carried by Asian rivers, as described in Chapter 7.

Table 4.1. Average Annual Surface Run-off (in 1,000 km³), according to different sources

	USSR Monograph (1974)	Lvovich (1974)	Baumgartner and Reichel (1975)
Europe	3.0	3.1	2.8
Asia	14.1	13.2	12.2
Africa	4.6	4.2	3.4
Australia	2.5	2.0	2.4
N. America	8.2	6.0	5.9
S. America	12.2	10.4	11.1
Antarctica	2.3	—	2.0
Total Land Areas	47	41[a]	40

Source: UNWC (1978; p. 14).

[a] Value adjusted upwards to include Antarctica for comparison with corresponding volumes derived by the other two authors.

More data were assembled on changes in the thermal regime and hydrological cycle. For example, measurement of the rate of lowering of the Caspian Sea (by three metres between 1882 and 1972) permitted estimates of the effects of changes in weather, land use, and water consumption in its drainage area. These and other alterations in the hydrologic cycle are noted in later parts of this chapter.

Ground water

It is less easy to estimate the precise occurrence of ground water. It is known to occur in many strata, but the extent, depth, rate of flow through the aquifer, quality, and rate of replenishment from surface sources are difficult to determine. Certain of the reserves are no longer replenished and as "fossil" supplies are, in effect, mined when used. Two-thirds of all ground water lies at depths greater than 750 metres and therefore is accessible only by deep wells, entailing expensive pumping costs. The ground water situation was reviewed in *the State of the Environment Report* for 1981 (UNEP, 1981a).

Surface water and ground water of any region may be closely related. Ground water is recharged by leakage from river channels in certain geological situations. Linkages between wetlands and ground water may go in either direction. The size of the linkages between ground and surface water varies with local geology and season (UN, 1975). Ground water is highly valued because of certain properties not generally possessed by surface water. It does not suffer evaporative loss while stored; it is free of mud and sediment; it is biologically clean (if uncontaminated by human actions); it remains cool in summer and warm in winter, relative to conditions at the land surface; and it is generally accessible to land overlying an aquifer at no cost of conveyance from its source. The main constraints on its use are mineralization, the persistence of contamination, and cost of pumping it to the surface, especially after recent rises in energy prices.

With improved assessment, and advances in well-drilling and pumping techniques, the demands made upon ground water increased considerably during the decade. In some areas there was environmental damage as a result of overpumping, subsidence due to compaction following pumping, intrusion of saline water into freshwater aquifers, and contamination through recharge or through direct discharge from municipalities or industry into wells. Some of these changes are irreversible or can be corrected only over very long periods of time.

There was evidence that ground water in some arid and semi-arid areas was decreasing as a result of expansion of pump irrigation. Permanent depletion of aquifers proceeded at a rapid rate in a number of areas. Regulation of withdrawals was encouraged in western Australia and in some countries of the Economic Commission for Europe (ECE) rigid licensing requirements were adopted. Subsidence due to pumping was halted in Venice and the Osaka and Tokyo metropolitan areas as well as some other centres of industrial use, but continued in numerous areas elsewhere. The ground water situation varied greatly, and, as noted in a later section, a wide range of administrative devices were employed to deal with it (UNWC, 1978, p. 2179). The pursuit of more refined and economical methods of survey and exploitation gained urgency. Significant advances were made in methods to predict ground water quality and occurrence (Kovacs, 1977).

FLOODS AND DROUGHTS

Climatic variations during the 1970s are described in Chapter 2, where selected extremes of rainfall and drought are included in Table 2–10. There is no evidence of widespread change in the occurrence of large floods of very low frequency on great rivers, or in the extreme peaks of smaller streams. However, the volume of discharge from floods of high and intermediate frequency (say 5 per cent, or with a twenty-year recurrence interval) was observed to mount in two types of drainage areas: lands subject to rapid upstream urbanization with its spread of paved streets and parking lots and roofs, where the flood discharge as much as doubled in some instances (UNWC, 1978, p. 2505); and rural areas subject to widespread removal of forest or plant cover and to rapid advance of gully erosion, as in the Terai of the Indian sub-continent.

The decade witnessed considerable progress in flood management technologies. Areas of flood risk were defined through flood frequency analysis, and stage-damage curves were produced as a basis for evaluating the costs and benefits resulting from application of possible flood damage management techniques. Many conceptual models and some physically based deterministic models and integrated catchment models were developed and used operationally for hydrological forecasting. In basins such as the Danube, Tennessee, and Volga it became possible to provide an on-the-line forecasting system in real time coupled with observation, transmission, processing and forecasting facilities. Flood control measures, national legislation, and international flood control agreements advanced, especially in developed countries. The international agreements covered information exchange and joint plans for the construction or operation of protection works. The Rio Grande (Mexico and United States), Danube and Senegal rivers were treated in this way.

Several non-structural techniques including land-use zoning, flood-proofing, flood insurance and land treatment through afforestation and soil conservation, found wider acceptance during the decade. At the same time there were advances in methods of reducing the risks of flooding in newly urbanized areas through sound land-use planning and the design of buildings and roads to withstand flood damage or reduce run-off (UNWC, 1978, p. 1261, 2071). France, Japan and the United States gave special attention to non-structural measures. In many countries, however, losses from flood damage increased because of intensive development and increases in property values in flood plains. In some areas the problem arose through false confidence in control works that could not contain very large, rare flows, as in the Damodar Valley, India. A number of developing countries, such as Sri Lanka, suffered enlarged flood damage following modernizations that rendered croplands more vulnerable to losses from overflow (Burton et al., 1978).

One of the common structural ways to reduce damage from flood crests is to build detention or storage dams. In the 1970s the trend was towards construction of multi-purpose reservoirs operated for some combinations of power generation, flood control, irrigation, navigation and water supply. These were commonly sited in the upper reaches of a catchment and discharged water unevenly so as to balance out fluctuations in flow due to varying rainfall: the bed of the river served as a natural culvert for supply to users downstream. Other prevalent ways to prevent floods are to build levees or by-passes and to enlarge, clean and line river channels. Careful analysis of flood magnitude and periodicity is crucial at the design stage, and proper maintenance of such structures is also essential. All structural measures require considerable investment and therefore a cost/benefit analysis is important.

As mentioned in Chapter 2, severe droughts were a special problem during the 1970s. As one consequence the importance of water management strategies and of linking water planning with land-use planning, was recognized. For example, additional bore holes or surface water supplies would not necessarily prevent suffering in times of rainfall shortage. Evidence from areas in the Sudano-Sahelian region showed that additional water supplies led to augmented livestock populations and destruction of nearby grazing lands. What is required is a careful combination of many measures, including water supply, regulation of grazing density and patterns, improved cultivation and cropping practices, and production of forage in irrigated lands.

The point was evident in the plains area of North America where precipitation deficiencies in the 1970s caused less distress than those of the 1930s because changes in farming practice, cultivation techniques, supplemental irrigation, and other adjustments had been made during the intervening years.

AUGMENTATION OF WATER SUPPLIES

The growing demands on already strained water supplies, especially in arid and semi-arid areas, intensified the search for new sources. In addition to surface and ground sources, non-conventional ones were sought through intervention in the chemical and physical characteristics of the hydrological cycle (UNWC, 1978, pp. 87, 346, 1017, 2489). Measures examined included weather modification, evaporation suppression, desalination and aquifer re-charge. New ideas, as yet untested, also emerged during the decade: for example, transporting icebergs from polar regions and hauling water by supertankers.

Weather modification

Experimentation and research continued on the controversial question of rain-making through cloud seeding. Although knowledge of both cloud dynamics and microphysics are not yet sufficient to permit confident predictions of the effects of seeding in many areas, simplified cloud models are beginning to provide useful insights into many physical details. The development of numerical models encompassing all the physical processes and interactions taking place in and around the cloud system may enable physical evaluations to be made. Attempts were made to test the possibilities of seeding warm clouds. United States studies show that seeding of cold clouds in favourable years is believed by some observers to increase the annual run-off of the Upper Colorado River by 15 per cent at costs varying from US$1.50 to US$3 per 1,200 cubic metres (m^3) (USBR, 1976). A contrary view is found in Morel-Seytoux and Restrepo (1977).

The interest of many governments in weather modification and the emergence in the late 1960s of commercial rain-making enterprises led the WMO to issue the statement, 'Present State of Knowledge and Possible Practical Benefits in Some Fields of Weather Modification'. This was followed in 1975 by the launching of a WMO weather modification programme of which a major feature was the Precipitation Enhancement Project (PEP) in Spain.

Evaporation suppression

As a result of new water storage, the volume of water evaporated from lakes and reservoirs was estimated to double (70 to 140 billion m^3; CEFIGRE, 1980). Research on different methods of reducing evaporation from water bodies, ranging from windbreaks and floating covers to molecular films, continued but without conspicuous success. The substances used included white perlite ore, polystyrene beads, chopped styrofoam, white hydrophobic amorphous powder, cetyl and stearyl alcohol, and other chemical films. Experiments conducted for certain materials under still conditions gave reductions reaching as high as 50 per cent, but when the wind velocity exceeded 10 km/h the reduction became insignificant (Frenkiel, 1965). Moreover, it was not clear what effects radiation-reflecting materials might have on the passage of oxygen through the surface of water bodies.

Desalination

Desalination of sea water and brackish water, especially in arid areas, went into large-scale operation at a few favourable sites. The cumulative installed capacity of land-based desalination plants increased from about 900 million litres per day in 1970 to about 2,200 million litres per day in 1977. It is estimated that this capacity would reach almost 3,000 million litres per day in 1982 (Wood, 1978). Most installations were based on multi-stage flash processes, which proved to be reliable technically and economically. Major installations were made in Abu Dhabi, Hong Kong, Kuwait, Sardinia and Saudi Arabia. They are commonly used for the dual purpose of meeting demands of water and electric power. Experiments on the reverse osmosis method revealed advantages over evaporation methods, especially for treating brackish water, and it requires only one-fifth of the energy. Brackish water was also used directly in agriculture and industry on an increasing scale. By 1974, for example, 9 per cent of Israel's water withdrawals were brackish (UNWC, 1978, p. 2284).

Recycling

The decade witnessed increasing research on, and demonstrations of, sewage and industrial waste water recycling and the application of urban organic waste on land. Disposal of municipal sewage on agricultural land, although long practised in various parts of the world, came into more prominence during the 1970s as a means of handling waste without polluting streams and with less loss of nutrients. Schemes to apply sewage, as distinct from industrial waste with its burden of metals and toxics, were adopted on a wide scale and with considerable debate as to their health consequences (UNWC, 1978, pp. 110; 2601).

Practically every water-use pollutes water. The pollutants may be valuable materials, but they are called wastes because they are often present in very diluted form or at the wrong place. When economically possible, water engineers aim at retrieving both water and pollutants in such a form that they can be re-used.

In many river basins in the world, water is being used successively by one city after another as it passes downstream. This recycling demands effective treatment of waste water prior to discharge, and of abstracted water prior to use. In certain very isolated locations (e.g. Windhoek, Namibia) where water is scarce, almost total water recycling is being practised at high cost, involving sophisticated physico-chemical processes. As water prices soared, many industries, through internal recycling, reduced their water consumption per unit product during the decade (Chapter 11).

WATER DEMAND

General pattern of demand

Recent estimates placed the total water use in 1980 in the order of 2,600 to 3,000 km^3/y; this is projected to reach 3,750 km^3 in 1985 – about 8 to 10 per cent of the average run-off in all continental river basins. Accurate data for withdrawals are not available but rough estimates for the three major uses in terms of volume of water taken from the source are presented in Table 4–2: irrigation accounted for 73 per cent, industry 21 per cent and the remainder went to domestic, livestock, recreational and other uses. The proportion withdrawn and returned to its supply source, or the "consumptive use", is large in the case of agriculture where as much as 80–90 per cent may be lost by evaporation and transpiration, and is usually small for domestic and industrial uses.

Table 4.2. Increase of Water Withdrawal Over the World (in km^3/y)

Water Used	1970	1975	Estimated percentage used consumptively
Domestic water supply	120	150	1–15
Industry	510	630	0–10
Agriculture	1,900	2,100	10–80
Totals	2,530	2,880	

Source: USSR (1978)

The differing national patterns of water withdrawals are illustrated by the data for 16 countries at the beginning of the decade (Figure 4–1). Some, such as Czechoslovakia, the German Democratic Republic, the Federal Republic of Germany and Poland, made their greatest demands in the industrial sector. Others, such as India and Mexico, withdrew most heavily for irrigation. In all but a few the domestic sector withdrawal was low. Records of withdrawals by two of the larger users – the USSR and the USA – are given in Table 4–3: irrigation in the USSR and industry in the USA made major claims. Withdrawal and consumptive use are identical for reservoirs that lose the water by evaporation and seepage.

Figure 4–1. Distribution of Withdrawals Among Major Categories of Water Uses; Selected Countries, 1965

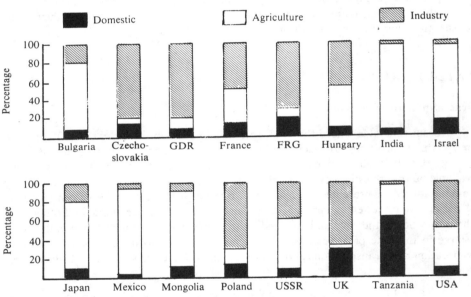

Source: UNWC (1978)

The Organization for Economic Co-operation and Development (OECD) reported in 1979 that "in certain countries, while domestic withdrawals increased markedly between 1965 and 1975, growth now seems to have slowed due to reduced rates of urban expansion and small growth in the use of household appliances. Furthermore, there is evidence that the increasing cost of freshwater is beginning to affect industrial abstraction, except for cooling, and is leading to increased recycling sometimes in association with pollution control" (OECD, 1979). Figures for 1975 presented to the UN Water Conference by fourteen governments from developed countries and seven from countries with centrally planned economies indicated that all but two of them estimated that in the period 1981–2000 their annual percentage increase in all water use would be less than during 1970–1980 (UNWC, 1978, p. 486). Sweden estimated in that connection that its annual water use would decline by 4 per cent during the 1980s, and only the German Democratic Republic and the Federal Republic of Germany predicted increases in their annual rate of change.

Table 4.3. Water Withdrawal and Consumption in the USSR and USA (in km³/y)

	USSR			United States		
	1965	1970	1975	1965	1970	1975
Public utilities						
Withdrawal (full use)	6.0	9.7	14	33	37	42
Consumptive use (irrecoverable use)	1.1	1.7	2.3	6.5	8.0	10
Industry						
Withdrawals (full use)	46.0	66.0	83.0	179	242	305
Consumptive use (irrecoverable use)	2.0	2.8	3.9	5.4	7.5	9.6
Agriculture						
Withdrawal (full use)	123	149	181	157	169	181
Consumptive use (irrecoverable use)	74	90	107	94	101	108
Reservoirs						
Withdrawal (full use)	12	14	16	9	13	16
Consumptive use (irrecoverable use)	12	14	16	9	13	16
Total Withdrawal	187	238.7	294	378	461	544
Consumptive use	89.1	108.5	129.2	114.9	129.5	143.6

Source: USSR (1978).

Irrigation

Growth in the use of water for irrigation was linked to two factors. First and most important, the area served by regular water supplies was expanded by numerous large projects and by individual pump installations drawing upon ground water. In all regions the area of land reported to be served by irrigation increased by at least 15 per cent during 1968–1978 (Table 4–4). The largest absolute gains were in Asia, principally in China and India, and the largest percentage gain in the USSR (62.7 per cent).

The stability of food production was enhanced thereby to the extent that land supplied by a water delivery system was actually cultivated. There is often a considerable time interval between the construction of a major water storage or delivery scheme and the completion of the distribution system, the preparation of the soil for cultivation, and the provision of suitable drainage. Thus, surveys made of irrigation projects in Africa south of the Sahara in 1965 and 1975 showed that the irrigation potential of the projects increased from 2.1 million to 3.04 million ha but that the actual cultivated acreage was less, and that in the event of full development the systems could reach 4.3 million ha (UNWC, 1978, p. 536). In some developing countries the costs and difficulties of land development impeded or even reversed the expansion of irrigation. In developed countries in Europe and North America, much of the enlargement of irrigated land was through the installation of spray and similar pumping rigs for supplemental supply to lands already cultivated.

Table 4.4.   Irrigated Area in Major Regions (in 1,000 ha)

Region	1961–65	1968	1978	Per cent change 1968–1978
World	149,474	162,634	200,913	23.5
Africa	5,870	6,772	7,831	15.6
North and Central America	18,606	20,366	23,543	15.6
South America	4,862	5,403	6,663	23.3
Asia	100,363	108,184	130,950	21.0
Europe	8,957	10,266	13,670	33.2
Oceania	1,198	1,443	1,656	14.8
USSR	9,618	10,200	16,600	62.7

Source: FAO (1980a)

The second factor affecting the expansion of irrigation was the extent to which techniques of application and land management allowed economies in the amount of water required and the avoidance of environmental hazards. The development of deep wells and application systems that did not require extensive distribution channel networks reduced costs, and in many cases also became more efficient in the sense of requiring less water for a given crop output. However, the pump and spray systems made it possible to deplete ground water at a rapid rate. Where the rates exceeded the natural re-charge the aquifers were depleted. Such "mining" of the supply occurred in areas like the high plains of the western United States. The gains in crop production were therefore temporary.

The lifetime of other irrigation projects was jeopardized by water-logging and salinization resulting from inadequate design or operation and maintenance. The significance of these situations for biological productivity is discussed in Chapter 7, but several trends affecting them deserve note here. On a large scale there was recognition, spurred on by the Food and Agriculture Organization of the United Nations (FAO), of the necessity to provide suitable drainage facilities and this was expressed in the project reviews of the World Bank and the United Nations Development Programme (UNDP).

There was substantial rehabilitation of waterlogged land in the Indus valley. The intensity of use of irrigated land was estimated to have risen between 1965 and 1975 from 77 per cent to 89 per cent in Latin America, from 80 per cent to 95 per cent in the Near East, and from 119 per cent to 129 per cent in Asia (UNWC, 1978, p. 912). Sophisticated techniques such as drip irrigation and measures to reduce water losses by canal lining, scheduling of water delivery in relation to soil moisture measurements, and other improved farm management systems spread slowly during the decade (UNWC, 1978, p. 91). In the Federal Republic of Germany, new spray techniques made it possible to irrigate in 1976, with only 210 million m^3 of water, the same area of land that in 1958 required 1,230 million m^3.

Industry and energy

Industrial water withdrawals, as already noted for OECD countries, were on the increase, but with a marked trend in efficiency of water use. Water withdrawn per unit of manufacturing output decreased in many places, and greater attention was given to re-use within the plant for reasons which will be discussed in Chapter 11. Pulp and paper plants began to employ processes that discharged little or no water and drew fresh supplies only to make up for evaporation and product losses (UNWC, 1978, p. 2456). In Japan the total industrial water withdrawal moved from about 50 million m^3 daily in 1965 to 120 million m^3 in 1974, but by the mid-1970s two-thirds of the water was recycled in contrast to one-third at the beginning of the period (UNWC, 1978, p. 2440).

A large part of the additional use in many areas was for cooling thermal power installations. Air cooling was a substitute adopted in a number of plants. Where, however, major new power plants were in prospect the demand for water was massive. In Ghana, for example, withdrawals were expected to grow 500-fold when the country supplemented its Volta River hydroelectric plant with a thermal installation (UNWC, 1978, p. 543). There were also substantial new hydro-power developments (Chapter 12), and in several countries there was debate over their environmental impact, especially on rivers prized for their scenery and sport fisheries.

Domestic

The domestic water supply picture varied. Whereas the proportion of the urban population in developing countries with access to safe water supply rose from 67 per cent in 1970 to 77 per cent in 1975 and then declined slightly to 75 per cent in 1980 (as shown in Table 4–5), the proportion of rural people served by safe water supply increased from 14 per cent in 1970 to 29 per cent in 1980 (UN, 1980). During that period the number of countries reporting changed, and enumeration methods varied. The data therefore are of uneven quality and when aggregated as shown in Table 4–6 may be misleading. A less rough picture of changes may be gained from comparing countries reporting in both 1970 and 1980. Table 4–5 excludes the developing country members of the ECE. Among the major regions, only the Economic and Social Commission for Asia and the

Table 4.5. Estimated Service Coverage for Drinking Water Supply in Developing
Countries 1970–1980[a]

	1970		1975		1980	
	Population served (in millions)	Percentage of total population	Population served (in millions)	Percentage of total population	Population served (in millions)	Percentage of total population
Urban	316	67	450	77	526	75
Rural	182	14	313	22	469	29
Total	498	29	763	38	995	43

Source: UN (1980).

[a] Figures do not include the People's Republic of China.

Table 4–6. Water supply Coverage, Urban and Rural, by Region for countries
Reporting Both in 1970 and 1980[a]

Region	Number of countries	1970			1980			
		Total population (millions)	Water coverage (millions)	Percentage of total population	Total population (millions)	Water coverage (millions)	Percentage of total population	Change in percentage covered
Africa (ECA members)								
urban	29	62.8	51.5	82	96.2	78.9	82	0
rural	23	187.8	40.2	21	239.6	64.6	27	+6
Latin America (ECLA members)								
urban	18	153.1	115.6	76	212.6	157.8	74	−2
rural	15	110.6	25.2	24	129.1	27.8	22	−2
Western Asia (ECWA members)								
urban	9	13.9	13.3	96	22.5	19.8	88	−8
rural	7	18.0	6.1	34	18.4	6.2	34	0
Asia and the Pacific (ESCAP members)								
urban	14	220.5	130.2	59	300.3	209.5	70	+11
rural	12	737.3	77.6	11	917.3	298.6	32	+21

Source: WHO (1973) and UN (1980).

[a] The European (ECE members) region countries qualifying for technical assistance under UNDP
procedures are not included as only one country reported in both years, and the figures listed for it for 1970
are not consistent.

Pacific (ESCAP) members – the most numerous in population – reported significant gains in the proportion of both urban and rural populations covered by safe water supply. The Economic Commission for Africa (ECA) members reported an extension of coverage for rural dwellers but no increase in urban coverage. In Latin America and Western Asia the proportions remained the same or declined (see Table 4–6).

Although the estimates are rough (and are not based on a uniform definition of what constitutes safe water and reasonable access) a few aspects of domestic supply became apparent as the decade drew to a close. Massive improvements were made in the availability of supply. The number of rural dwellers served increased by 157 per cent. The urban dwellers served expanded by 66 per cent. However, considering the total population in need of service, the urban gains were modest, and while the rural proportion doubled it still left more than two-thirds without safe service. In only one major region was the rate of improvement in excess of the rate of population growth. A continuation of the 1970–1980 trends would leave the total population only slightly better off. A disturbing aspect of the situation not revealed by the statistics (and indeed not precisely documented) was the probably large number of rural improvements that had fallen into disrepair. In addition many urban systems, such as those in Nepal and Pakistan, provided only intermittent service (ESCAP, 1980).

The waste water situation was even less heartening. While a high proportion of the developed urban populations had adequate services, the proportion of developing country urban population served by sewers, latrines or other sanitary measures for excreta disposal declined during the decade from 71 per cent to 53 per cent (Table 4–7).

Table 4.7. Estimated Service Coverage for Sanitation in Developing Countries 1970–1980[a]

	1970		1975		1980	
	Population served (in millions)	Percentage of total population	Population served (in millions)	Percentage of total population	Population served (in millions)	Percentage of total population
Urban	337	71	437	75	372	53
Rural	134	11	209	15	213	13
Total	471	27	646	33	585	25

Source: UN (1980).

[a] Figures do not include the People's Republic of China.

In rural areas the numbers served were 11 per cent in 1970 and little better in 1980. Regional data are so incomplete that comparisons between 1970 and 1980 are not warranted. In 1980, however, it appeared that the proportion of urban populations covered was: Africa 56 per cent, Latin America 54 per cent, Western Asia 70 per cent and Asia and the Pacific 50 per cent. For the rural populations the estimates were: Africa 15 per cent, Latin America 23 per cent, Western Asia 20 per cent, and Asia and the Pacific 10 per cent. Urban sanitation efforts clearly had not kept up with population growth (the special problem of squatter settlement is discussed in Chapter 9), and rural improvement had barely kept pace.

Inland navigation

The importance of inland waters for transport, both historically and today, is discussed in Chapter 13. Inland navigation on international rivers has been acceptable for decades, because of the evident mutual interests of riparian countries and because of its non-consumptive use of water. However, with the increasing demand for water for other purposes this situation is gradually changing and great effort and cost are involved in harmonizing the different interests.

The decade witnessed increasing awareness of the environmental impact of inland navigation and developed new techniques to prevent possible pollution. The measures taken included the provision of facilities to retain sewage on board boats, for later discharge ashore. Care was taken to minimize pollution from oil spillage and leaks, bilge water tank refuse, and water liquids. In many cases these were being reclaimed and recycled. The disposal of dredged material from channel beds in the course of routine annual maintenance was another major environmental concern. Research was undertaken in a number of countries, especially the United States, to evaluate its environmental impact and develop improved dredging and disposal techniques.

Recreation

The use of inland waters for recreation, and in particular bathing and fishing, gained popularity during the last ten years. In most industrial countries this brought demands for improvement in the quality of inland waters, to make more of them "fishable" and "swimmable". The formulation of minimum health or environmental quality standards enabled sites to be more easily protected for bathers and facilitated measures to control pollution caused by indiscriminate waste discharge from factories and conurbations. Many governments also supported action to preserve or improve fishing. Because the presence of fish in inland waters is one of the better indices of the quality of the aquatic environment, the concerns of advocates of water-based recreation and of water quality management frequently converged. The importance of inland wetlands for wildlife conservation is widely recognized (Chapter 6).

Changes in Water Quality

NATURAL WATER QUALITY

'PURE WATER', in a scientific sense, is not found in nature. Even the most dilute freshwaters contain dissolved material, including major inorganic ions, (e.g. phosphate), dissolved gases (e.g. oxygen), and complex organic compounds (humic and fulvic acids). In addition, there is a variable quantity of suspended particulate material, including silt, and of microorganisms.

The variability of these constituents between water bodies in immense. In extreme cases concentrations can become high enough to eliminate many freshwater communities or render the water unfit for direct use by man. Reasonably low salinity is a particularly desirable quality. An unfavourable increase in salinity (salinization) can occur naturally in basins of closed drainage due to evaporation, contamination from pre-existing salt deposits, or incursions of too much sea water. The first case is illustrated by what happened in Lakes Chad (Sikes, 1972) and Chilwa (Kalk et al., 1979) in Africa, in which periods of low rainfall during the 1970s led to very great diminution of water volume and enhanced salinity. Salinization in the Egyptian Lake Qarun (Faiyum Depression), long a feature of this water body, accelerated during the 1970s, with unfavourable consequences for fisheries (Bishai and Kirollos, 1980; Boraey, 1980). A recent counter-measure – diversion of drainage into a separate depression nearby (Wadi Rayan) – is creating a new saline lake.

A global project for water quality monitoring was established in 1976 (Helmer 1981). By the end of the decade more than 388 stations had been identified in sixty-two countries and a global data centre was operating in Burlington (Ontario, Canada).

OVER-ENRICHMENT (EUTROPHICATION)

Although plant nutrients are a natural and essential foundation of biological production in inland waters, continued man-made additions often result in heavy growths of microscopic plants (algae) that are undesirable from several points of view. Examples of such over-enrichment were widespread between 1960 and 1980, and can generally be traced to nutrient supply from drainage containing agricultural fertilizers and from domestic sewage.

The key role played by phosphorus in the over-enrichment of fresh-waters was amply demonstrated during the decade (e.g. Thomas 1973; Schindler 1977). Since the mid-1950s there has been a marked increase in the concentration of phosphate in the inland waters of many countries. In large part this rise reflects inputs from phosphorus-containing detergents, although agricultural fertilizers can also be important. Concomitant increases in biotic abundance, notably of planktonic algae, have occurred (often assessed by concentrations of chlorophyll). During the decade many authors examined correlations between summer phytoplankton abundance and the preceding concentrations of total phosphorus (e.g. Dillon and Rigler, 1974; Jones and Bachmann 1976; Hrbáček et al., 1977; Nicholls and Dillon 1978; Hickman 1980), although the predictability may fall short of usefulness for remedial measures (Allen 1980). It is not known how far such phosphorus-chlorophyll relationships are applicable to tropical freshwaters, where concentrations of inorganic nitrogen are often low and possibly limit plant growth (e.g. Talling and Talling, 1965). Few major tropical freshwaters have received large man-induced inputs of phosphorus.

The modifications caused by nutrient enrichment are naturally greatest in heavily populated and developed countries. Illustrative surveys were published for Europe by OECD (1970), for North America by Vallentyne (1974), for the Netherlands by Parma (1980), for Britain by Collingwood (1977), and for South Africa by Toerien (1975). Among large lakes, changes in the Bodensee (Lake Constance) and in Lake Washington (USA) were especially well documented (e.g. Edmonson, 1970; Lehn 1973, 1975). Lake Washington provides an excellent example of the rapid reversibility of eutrophication, after diversion (by canal) of the main sewage input. Another example of reversion in a large lake, the Swedish Lake Vattern, was described by Olsen and Willen (1980), while the general principle was discussed by Hasler (1969) and Schindler (1974). However, in shallow lakes reversal following the reduction of inputs may be prevented by massive accumulations of nutrients in the sediments. The 'restoration' of Lake Trummen in Sweden was achieved by the large-scale removal of such sediments during 1970 and 1971 (Bjork 1972; Anderson et al., 1973; Gelin and Ripl 1978). Such a remedy is economically feasible only for small lakes. Examples of the wide range of techniques for lake restoration were listed by Dunst et al., (1974). In general, the extreme anxiety felt during the 1960s regarding the extent, pace and consequences of over-enrichment had lessened by 1980, at least in some major regions. Lake Erie is a relevant example (Arnold, 1969; Charlier, 1969; Symposium on Lake Erie, 1976). Nevertheless, many disturbing cases undoubtedly remain.

Concern of another type was often expressed during the 1970s over the widespread increase of nitrate concentrations in many rivers and ground waters (e.g. Bolin and Arrhenius, 1977; Commoner, 1977; Magee, 1977). The increase mainly derives from the agricultural application of nitrogenous fertilizers. Concentrations in human drinking water above approx. 10–12 mg NO_3 nitrogen per litre involve some danger to health, especially to bottle-fed babies (discussed in Chapter 10). Such concentrations are, for example, occasionally approached or exceeded in some lowland English rivers (Tomlinson, 1970), but were not a problem some ten or twenty years earlier (Table 4–8).

POLLUTION

With continued economic growth, population increase, urbanization and technical development, more and more waste materials were discharged into water bodies. During

Table 4–8 Annual Mean Concentrations[a] of Nitrates in Selected Rivers 1965–1975

Country	River	1965	1970	1975
Japan	Tama	2.87	1.96	3.31
Austria[b]	Drau	1.8	2.0	2.6
Belgium[c]	Maas	—	3.9	9.4
	Scheldt	—	3.9	7.75
France[d]	Seine	—	7.5	18.5
	Loire	—	7.0	6.4
Federal Republic of Germany	Rhone	—	3.6	4.2
	Rhine	10.1	11.7	13.8
Netherlands	Rhine	1.7	2.5	2.8
United Kingdon	Lee[e]	9.0	15.0	19.7
	Wear	1.94	2.13	3.85
	Irwell and Mersey[f]	0.6	1.0	2.3

Source: OECD (1979)

[a] Measured in ppm, at mouth of river or national boundary (downstream).
[b] 1966 data in column 1965.
[c] 1972 data for river Maas in column 1970; 1971 data for river Scheldt in column 1970.
[d] 1971 data in column 1970; 1976 data for river Seine in column 1975.
[e] 1967 data in column 1965.
[f] Data in column 1965 is an average figure for 1967/1968.

the decade extensive efforts were made in the developed countries to arrest this pollution by treating the growing volume of waste water. A variety of regulations and incentives were tried. These were moderately effective in checking a deteriorating trend, and in a few countries the trend was reversed and an improvement in water quality resulted. In some countries industries were taxed for discharging wastes into public waters and sewers, and hence given an incentive to install their own waste treatment plants. In others, standards specified the maximum concentrations of pollutants permitted in an individual discharge or a type of industrial emission. Reduction of water pollution was also one motive for reducing the use of fertilizers and chemical pesticides by substituting biological nitrogen fixation and biological pest control.

Thermal pollution by discharges from the cooling systems of power plants has in some areas affected the aquatic ecosystem to various degrees (Biswas, 1980; UNEP, 1981b). Heat influences all biological activity, ranging from feeding habits and reproduction rates of fish via metabolism to changes in nutrient levels, photosynthesis, eutrophication and degradation rate of organic material. In several instances (as in the Federal Republic of Germany) the maximum capacity for power generation in plants along a river has been limited by government restrictions. These warm water discharges can, however, be put into beneficial use (for example, for residential and industrial space heating; in hot houses for growing tropical or sub-tropical crops in temperate regions; in aquaculture etc; see, UNEP, 1981b).

The decade saw great progress in development of new instrumentation for measuring and monitoring water quality, for example, in the form of gas chromatography and ion-selective electrodes which, when coupled to remote sensing of thermal pollution, computerized data storage and mathematical modelling, increased the capability to assess and predict water quality. One result of this advance in instrumentation was the detection of low concentrations of hundreds of chemical pollutants (micropollutants) in rivers like the Rhine, resulting from industrial waste discharges. These pollutants are differentially modified by chemical interaction, partial degradation and chlorination after passing through a municipal water supply system.

Pollution via the atmosphere

One of the major concerns identified at the Stockholm Conference was the possible environmental impact of the long-range transport of sulphur and nitrogen oxides deposited as strong mineral acids in precipitation. In the 1970s, a number of major research programmes confirmed the reality of this phenomenon (Chapter 2). Several international conferences (Ohio, USA, 1975; Telemark, Norway, 1976; Toronto, Canada, 1978; Sandefjord, Norway, 1980) and many regional conferences considered the problem during the decade. These conferences have documented that atmospheric transport of sulphur compounds and other acidifying components has led to extensive regional acidification of water courses in areas such as Southern Scandinavia (Table 4–9, Figure 4–2) and parts of eastern North America (Likens et al., 1979) that are not far from centres of industry and where there is little natural buffering. Sulphur oxides and nitrogen oxides derived from fossil fuel combustion both contribute appreciably to the acidity of precipitation.

Table 4–9. Acidification of Soft-Water Lakes in Scandinavia and North America

Region	No. of Lakes	Past Values		Recent Measurements	
		pH	Year	pH	Year
Scandinavia					
Central Norway[a]	10	7.4 ± 0.8	1941	5.8 ± 0.7	1975
	6	6.6 ± 0.2	1933–35	5.4 ± 0.8	1971
Westcoast of Sweden	8	6.8 ± 0.4	1942–49	5.6 ± 0.9	1971
West-central Sweden	5	6.3 ± 0.3	1937–48	4.7 ± 0.2	1973
South-central Sweden	5	6.2 ± 0.2	1933–48	5.5 ± 0.7	1973
Southernmost Sweden	51	6.76± 0.14	1935	6.23±0.44	1971
North America					
La Cloche Mtns. Ontario	7	6.3 ± 0.7	1961	4.9 ± 0.5	1972–73
	8	5.0 ± 0.7	1969	4.8 ± 0.5	1972–73
North of La Cloche	7	6.6 ± 0.8	1961	5.9 ± 0.7	1971
Mtns. Ontario	19	6.7 ± 0.8	1968	8.4 ± 0.8	1971
Adirondack Mtns. New York	8	6.5 ± 0.6	1930–38	4.8 ± 0.2	1969–75

Source: Wright and Gjessing (1976).

[a]Still lower pH values in 1975 in Southern Norway.

There is a particularly rich documentation for Sweden (Dickson, 1975; Almer *et al.*, 1978) and Norway (Drabløs and Tollan, 1980; Overrein *et al.*, 1980). About 10,000 Swedish lakes were estimated to have been acidified to a pH below 6.0, and 5,000 lakes to below pH 5.0 (Dickson, 1975). Some lakes have shown a decline in pH values of as much as 1.8 units since the 1930s – that is, hydrogen ion concentration has increased almost a hundred fold. Elsewhere in Europe the acidification of surface waters has been reported in Belgium, the Netherlands, Denmark, Italy, and also in the United Kingdom (Drabløs and Tollan, 1980). In North America, changes are also well documented, especially in the Adirondack Mountains and areas of Canada including those near the smelting industry at Sudbury, Ontario (Gorham, 1976; Likens *et al.*, 1979; NRCC, 1981).

Figure 4–2. Acidification of Norwegian and Swedish Lakes

Source: Wright and Gjessing (1976).

Acid precipitation causes changes in freshwater chemistry by mobilizing heavy metals in soils, rocks and sediments. These are subsequently leached by drainage and enter surface and ground waters (Hultberg and Wenbald, 1980). Elevated concentrations of cadmium, lead, aluminium, manganese, zinc, copper and nickel (these last five being toxic to living organisms in the 0.3 to 10 ppm range) have frequently been observed in acidified lakes (Dickson, 1975; Wright and Gjessing, 1976). Greatly raised levels of aluminium ions have been reported in the United States (Schofield and Trojnar, 1980), Norway (Muniz and Leivestad, 1980) and Sweden (Dickson, 1978). The mobilization of mercury is also increased by acidification (Almer et al., 1978; Bloomfield et al., 1980), and the formation of methyl mercury and its entry into food chains may be increased (Fagerström and Jernělov, 1972; Jernělov, 1980).

There is evidence that acidification reduces the diversity of plant plankton and affects a number of other organisms in the aquatic food web (Dochinger and Seliga, 1976; Braekke, 1976; Hendrey et al., 1976). The growth of rooted plants is reduced, and the abundance of bog moss (*Sphagnum*), growing as benthic carpets, increased. The rate of decomposition of organic matter declines and fungal felts may develop over sediments, mineralizing nitrogen and phosphorous much more slowly than the normal bacteria. Productivity of the lake ecosystem is reduced. Fish populations declined during the 1960s and 1970s in lakes over an area of 33,000 km^2 in southern Norway (Overrein et al., 1980), in the Adirondack Mountains in the United States (Schofield, 1976), and in several areas in Canada (Harvey, 1980). Heavy metal (especially mercury) accumulation in fish was, at the end of the decade, causing concern over their fitness for human consumption in some areas (Jernelǒv, 1980).

Pollution from urban and industrial discharges and land drainage

The most critical problems of water pollution arise in the vicinity of centres of high population density and extensive industrial development. Waterborne sewage, storm drainage from city streets, and effluents from smaller industries combined to flow from municipal outfalls in mounting volumes. Industries frequently referred to as being significant polluters of water include pulp and paper, chemical works and food industries. Their progress or failure in coping with waste is described in Chapter 11.

Among industrial pollutants, mercury caused particular alarm during the late 1960s and the 1970s because of its conversion to the more toxic methyl form by bacteria in freshwater (and marine) sediments and accumulation in animal tissues. In several regions accumulations above a minimum safety level were detected in freshwater fish, which had to be withdrawn from human consumption. In Sweden, a ban imposed in 1967 on the use of mercury in the pulp and paper industries was followed by reductions in environmental concentrations (Olsson, 1976). In Lake Erie, Canada, the mercury originated from mercury-cell chlor-alkali works, and could be detected in sediments and fish (Thomas and Jaquet, 1976). Examples elsewhere in the world are given by D'Itri and D'Itri (1977).

In the early years of the decade, emphasis was placed upon urban and industrial sources of freshwater pollution, but by 1980 attention was turning to non-point sources as the cause of more intractable problems. This general trend was well illustrated by experience in OECD countries which reported that (1) levels of suspended solids and oxidizable matter (as measured by biological oxygen demand, BOD) commonly levelled off or decreased while micropollutants, pathogenic micro-organisms and thermal pollution caused increasing concern; and (2) while pollution from point sources was

Figure 4–3. Domestic Waste Water Treatment; Selected Countries, 1965–1975

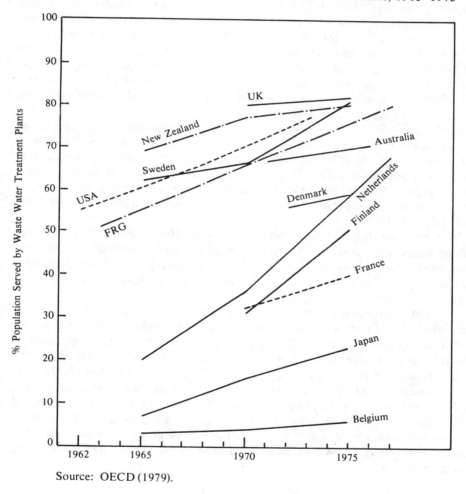

Source: OECD (1979).

under progressively better control, non-point pollution was on the increase (OECD, 1979). The intensive use of fertilizer was a major factor in eutrophication. Other problems arose from the mis-application of pesticides and careless storage and handling of manure.

Another growing source of water pollution resulted from the expanding use of petroleum and petroleum products. Rapidly increasing road travel, the mechanization of agriculture, and the increased transport of oil on inland waters contributed to further pollution of both surface and ground water. A potential future source of pollution is spills from vulnerable pipelines at high latitudes, as in Canada, although these have not yet been serious (Sage, 1980; see also Chapter 13).

The most readily available indicator of effluent loading is provided by the statistics on the proportion of population in selected industrial countries served by some kind of waste water treatment. Figure 4–3 shows the 1965–1975 trends in 12 countries. In all of them the percentage increased, but the proportion of population served ranged from less than 10 per cent in Belgium to more than 80 per cent in the United Kingdom. No distinction is made as to type of treatment or the nature of the receiving water and these are crucial in determining the effects upon the aquatic system. In the developing countries about half of the urban population were covered by sewer service (Table 4–7). Only scattered data are available on treatment facilities for the existing sewer systems, but treatment beyond the primary stage of removal was rare.

In OECD countries the biological oxygen demand and nitrate load of selected major streams in industrial countries changed as shown in Figure 4–4 and Figure 4–5. BOD decreased between 1970 and 1975 in many streams, but mounted in the Scheldt, Tagus, Rhone and lower Rhine. Nitrate concentrations increased in all the selected streams except the Red and Nelson in Canada, and the Loire. As a consequence in those countries "almost all important freshwater bodies deteriorated during the 1965–1975 period" (OECD, 1979)

In many United States streams, non-point pollution from nitrogen and phosphorus increased, whereas coliform bacteria, oxygen-demanding organic materials, and the level of suspended solids, salinity and acidity showed a decreasing trend. More rivers were moderately polluted in this decade than in the last decade, but fewer rivers were highly polluted.

The United Kingdom reported improvement in the quality of non-tidal rivers in recent years. The Thames was notable for restoration of quality as reflected in the re-establishment of fish populations. The improvement of water quality is attributed to intensified construction of purifying plants and facilities. In Sweden 99 per cent of the sewage from urban areas was treated by 1975 (UNWC, 1978, p. 1965) and BOD levels had decreased after peaking in the previous decade. The biochemical oxygen demand in the Rhine rose between 1965 and 1975 but then fell and in 1978 was only 74 per cent of the 1965 figure. On the other hand, the salinity of the Rhine increased. Large lakes respond to treatment very slowly. It was estimated, for example, that it would take thirty years for Lake Varen in Sweden to respond fully to the present day reduction of industrial pollution.

Pollution of ground water

Ground water, in its percolation through soil and rocks, leaches out soluble salts; it is thus typically mineralized, and sometimes heavily so. The vulnerability of ground water to contamination is determined by the hydrological setting of the aquifer, the nature of the contaminant and the effectiveness of regulatory action. Of all the activities of man that influence the quality of ground water, agriculture is probably the most important, as a diffuse source of pollution from fertilizers, pesticides and animal wastes. Of the main nutrients in nitrogen, phosphorus and potassium fertilizers, nitrogen in the form of nitrate is the most common cause of degradation of ground water near agricultural lands (UNEP, 1981a). Industrial wastes include a wide spectrum of materials from all types of industry, and contain many organic and inorganic chemicals which are potential pollutants. Industrial wastes reach ground water from impoundments or lagoons, spills, pipeline breaks and land disposal sites.

Septic tanks and cesspools contribute filtered sewage effluent directly to the ground, and are the most frequently reported sources of ground water contamination, especially in rural, recreational, and suburban areas. An increasing percentage of the municipal sewage is, however, now being processed in primary and secondary sewage treatment plants. In many areas, the solid residual material known as sewage sludge – which contains a large number of potential contaminants – is spread on agricultural land. In some regions liquid sewage that has not been treated or that has undergone partial treatment is sprayed on the land surface. Such application of liquid sewage and sewage sludge to the land provides valuable nutrients such as nitrogen and phosphorus to the soil, with benefits to agriculture. However, the waste water or sludge can add to the contamination of ground water. The soil profile shows a considerable ability to remove or detoxify several of the compounds found in the waste water, but some may nonetheless affect ground water quality. The soil may also effectively eliminate the pathogenic bacteria through filtration and soil microbiological processes, but survival of viruses is still an open question.

WATER QUALITY MANAGEMENT

Pollution prevention

Despite the efforts made during the decade in pollution control, a number of difficulties and constraints were encountered including:

(a) continued reluctance to change traditional views of water as an abundant and free commodity;

(b) lack of adequate data on quality and quantity, especially in developing countries;

(c) slow improvement in actions to reduce water needs and water pollutants;

(d) delay in adopting new and more efficient methods of recycling and re-use;

(e) failure to evaluate economic losses due to inadequate water quality and so reveal the social benefits from improvement;

(f) the need for international and bilateral agreements to regulate shared river basins.

Figure 4–4. Annual Mean Levels of Biological Oxygen Demand (BOD), Selected Rivers, 1965–1975

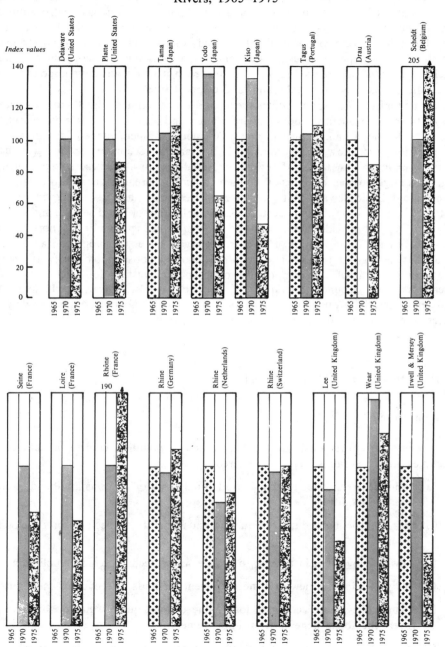

Source: OECD (1979).

Figure 4–5. Annual Mean Concentration of Nitrates, Selected Rivers, 1965–1975

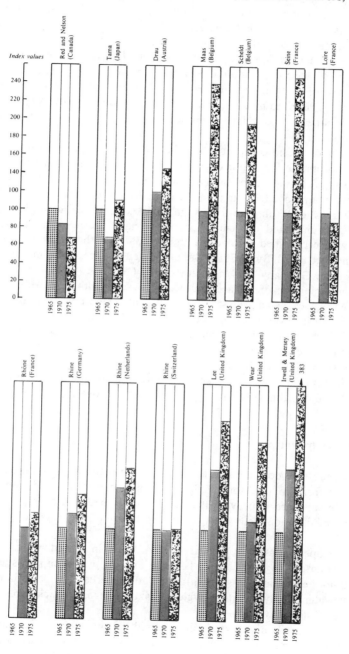

Source: OECD (1979)

Major advances were made in legislation to improve the adequacy of water pollution control in some countries and regions of the world. During the years after Stockholm, major new water pollution control statutes were enacted in the United States, New Zealand, the Federal Republic of Germany, Greece, Ireland, Italy, the Netherlands, Spain, the United Kingdom (OECD, 1979) and the USSR. The difficulty facing many countries by 1980 was the question of how *pure* the water should be. Financial resources to support improvements in water quality were limited, and the evaluation of costs and benefits naturally received much attention. This, as well as the diversity of land use and aquatic environment, was reflected in the variety of standards and methods for classifying water uses.

A number of countries approached the problem by specifying the water quality considered appropriate for major categories of use, including human potable supplies, food processing, fisheries, agricultural supplies, recreation and industrial use. Economic incentives were employed by many countries to protect the quality of the water, including charges for discharges to sewage networks and treatment plants, indemnities for discharging untreated effluent into public water sources, and penalties for not complying with established regulations and standards. Other incentives include loans, subsidies and tax relief. By 1979, pollution-related charges were in force in Canada, Finland, France, Germany and the Netherlands (OECD, 1979).

The contamination of surface and ground waters with toxic substances released from dumped wastes, as canisters corroded long after dumping had taken place, was a cause of concern in several countries including the United States, the Netherlands and the United Kingdom. In the latter, legislation was introduced to require all dumping sites to be licensed by a competent authority that would satisfy itself that the substances and method of disposal involved posed no hazard to water systems. In the Netherlands and the United States costly remedial measures had to be adopted to remove contaminated soil from old dumps that had subsequently been built over.

Drinking water treatment

The decade saw considerable advances in the technology for producing potable water supplies from polluted sources. Methods of chlorination, ozonation and activated carbon treatment were improved and came into extended use, in combination with coagulation and filtration methods. More plants were automated. Water prices inevitably increased.

As developed countries learned to live with increased water pollution, the developing countries lagged behind, because existing water supply systems in large cities could not be extended in step with population increase. This led in many cases to intermittent water supply, creating hygienic hazards through back-syphonation during low-pressure spells.

During the decade it was gradually realized that installing in developing countries piped water supply and sewage of the conventional Western type on a scale that matched rising needs would demand prohibitive amounts of money (Kalbermatten *et al.*, 1980). Thus new approaches emerged, such as the use of stand-pipes to supply clusters of dwellings, and utilization of local materials like bamboo waterpipes and hydraulic rams for pumping. Biological slow sand filtration received attention (Huisman and Wood, 1974) and more emphasis was placed on well protection. It was further realized that water supply and sanitation should be dealt with in an integrated manner. More studies of water provision in rural areas of developing countries were undertaken, focussing on special local problems, like the time and energy expended in fetching water over long distances in Africa (White, *et al.*, 1972) and on the organization of effective self-help programmes (Van Wijk-Sijbesma, 1980). Another important trend was towards dealing with all water quality aspects of a river basin through one responsible river authority (UK, FRG, USA) permitting improved strategic planning of water supply, use for other purposes and for waste treatment.

In some countries there was debate over the desirability of adding fluoride to drinking water supplies, as a means of improving dental health. Boiled down to their essentials, the debates were over two principles:

(a) the propriety of public authorities introducing any extraneous substances into drinking water,

(b) the possible ill effects to general health from the artificial introduction of fluoride to drinking water supplies.

Although natural waters in which fluoride concentrations are high enough to have damaging consequences are rare ((Kilham and Hecky, 1973), and moderate fluoride levels are known to reduce tooth decay, augmenting sub-optimal concentrations met with widespread opposition and much avoidable damage to dental health resulted. Towards the end of the decade the recognition that hardness of water and the incidence of coronary heart disease were associated in some fashion led certain countries to discuss measures for deliberately increasing the hardness of some water supplies.

Waste water treatment and utilization

Technological innovations emerging in sewage treatment during the decade included tertiary treatment, consisting of biological and chemical removal of phosphates, nitrates and ammonia to reduce eutrophication of receiving waters. Deep shaft aeration, the carousel version of the oxidation ditch, chlorination of treated effluents and use of pure oxygen instead of air were all practised and more plants were automated. Recovery of chemical wastes by industry became more effective and sophisticated as legislation tightened. In the developing countries in the tropics oxidation ponds or lagoons (Arceivala *et al.*, 1970; Oswald, 1973) found further application.

The mounting prices of energy and fertilizers stimulated research and development efforts towards *utilization* rather than defensive *treatment* of domestic and agricultural wastes, which dilutes and dissipates the valuable ingredients contained in them. It was in the developing countries, harder pressed as they were, that most of the new trends emerged during the decade. Methodologies for improved composting of human excreta were elaborated in China (McGarry and Stainforth, 1978) and elsewhere. Arid lands were irrigated with nutrient-rich waste effluents, while the health hazards of long-standing sewage farming received new attention. Oxidation ponds and lagoons, in which the wastes form a substrate for algal growth, were combined with fish ponds, whose productivity is discussed in the next section. This development follows the practice of many Southeast Asian villages where village ponds have long served as public toilets as well as fish-rearing units. When handled with proper sanitary precautions, these can be considered models of modern waste recycling rather than out-dated practices to be abandoned.

Another form of waste utilization is via anaerobic digestion through which biogas (a mixture of methane and carbon dioxide) is produced (see Chapter 12). The effluent and sludge remaining after digestion has taken place, is a rich and effective fertilizer. It is claimed that the use of biogas slurry as a fertilizer had led to an increase in the yield of some crops by 10 to 28 per cent in the People's Republic of China and India as compared to the use of excreta (Van Buren, 1979). The use of biogas slurry can also give protection to crops during prolonged drought and also reduce the weeding cost as fertility of weeds is destroyed in the fermentation process. Experiments in the Philippines have shown that rice fertilized with commercial urea had an average yield of 6.5 tonne/ha whereas rice fertilized with manure sludge produced 8.3 tonne/ha (Eusebio and Rabino, 1978). The effluents can be used also for growing algae that can be used as animal feed and input material to the digester; the water from the algae ponds can be used to feed fish ponds. Yields of *Tilapia* of over 7 tonne/ha were achieved in field experiments (other species of fish can also be produced). Anaerobic digestion provides, therefore, a means for environmentally sound management of organic wastes and leads to considerable reduction of the pathogens in the waste, thus reducing health hazards (El-Hinnawi and El-Gohary, 1981).

Changes in Fresh Water Biota

INTRODUCTION AND EXPLOSIVE SPREAD OF SPECIES

INLAND water systems appear to be particularly susceptible to invasion and massive spread of some aquatic plants and animals, usually with undesirable effects. From the 1950s onwards, the accidental introduction and multiplication of several floating aquatic plants that form surface mats has greatly interfered with normal uses such as navigation and fishing in various tropical rivers and reservoirs. Thus the water hyacinth (*Eichhornia crassipes*), a native of South America, spread over 1,600 km on the Congo (Zaire) River in the early 1950s; it entered the White Nile system of the Sudan in the late 1950s, where in 1980 it was still a massive pest, only partially controlled by expensive spraying with herbicides (Pirie, 1960; Obeid *et al.*, 1975; Wolverton and McDonald, 1979). Species of water fern, *Salvinia auriculata* and *S. molesta*, are similar pests in Sri Lanka and in Lake Kariba on the Zambesi River. The water lettuce (*Pistia stratiotes*) had become troublesome in Lake Volta (Ghana), although this is normally not the case over the greater part of its wide tropical range. On the whole, there were fewer primary invasions by such aquatic species in the 1970s than in the preceeding two decades, and in several places (e.g. Sudan, Lake Kariba, Lake Volta) the area occupied by them lessened appreciably – in part due to natural factors.

Accidental and deliberate introductions of fish species have occurred in several regions since 1960. The results are sometimes unfavourable as with the rapid spread in Australia of the European carp, *Cyprinus carpio*. This now threatens the environment of native and introduced sport species, mainly because it causes water turbidity which affects the productivity of aquatic plants. The introduction of the Nile Perch, a large fish-predator, into Lake Victoria, where it has spread greatly during the decade, is more controversial (Fryer, 1972). Species of small clupeid fish from Lake Tanganyika were deliberately introduced into Lake Kariba to increase the fishing potential there (Balon and Coche, 1974).

EFFECTS OF OVER-ENRICHMENT (EUTROPHICATION)

The effects on water quality already described are mainly due to the enhanced growth and subsequent decomposition of microscopic algae. These may discolour the water, alter its chemical characteristics (e.g. oxygen content), and unfavourably affect its use in water supply and recreation. Benthic growths (those that grow at the bottom of a water body) of larger algae can also have undesirable effects, especially on recreation. The growth of blanket weed (*Cladophora*) in enriched streams, and on the shores of lakes (e.g. Lake Michigan), was one cause of concern during the decade (Whitton, 1970). Besides changes in quantity, over-enrichment commonly modifies the composition of the algal flora towards dominance by vigorous species of blue-green algae which readily form scums and other local accumulations and aggravate environmental problems.

Animal communities also show qualitative and quantitative changes associated especially with declining oxygen concentrations. The benthic fauna of deep lakes and reservoirs often change progressively, with declining diversity and a replacement of insect larvae by aquatic worms (oligochaetes). If anoxic conditions are complete and prolonged, species can be eliminated, as has happened to mayfly larvae over large areas of Lake Erie. Among fish communities of temperate regions, more desirable salmonid species are often displaced by less edible coarse fish such as cyprinids.

EFFECTS OF POLLUTION

The impact of acidification has already been discussed. Toxic substances and heavy organic loads usually have a more severe local impact than nutrient over-enrichment. This is especially true of smaller waterbodies, such as streams, where the composition of invertebrate communities has been used to derive practical indices of pollution severity (reviewed in Hellawell, 1978). Fish also provide sensitive indicators.

A particularly insiduous effect of pollution occurs when toxic materials accumulate within the tissues of a species used as food. Such materials include PCBs and mercury, as described elsewhere in this chapter. Fish in the Lower Rhine accumulate sufficient quantities of phenol for this to be detectable by taste.

EFFECTS ON INLAND FISHERIES AND AQUACULTURE

The percentage contribution of inland fisheries to the total world catch changed very little between the 1950s and the period between 1970 and 1976, remaining at around 14–15 per cent throughout. The actual quantity landed, however, rose from around 5.2 million tonnes in the earlier period to about 10 million tonnes in 1973–1976 (Figure 4–6). Recent FAO statistics (FAO, 1980 b) confirm a further increase in nominal catches from 1976 to 1979 although the detailed figures differ from those cited by Gulland (1978), giving 7.1 million tonnes as the 1976 catch and 7.48 million tonnes for 1979. These discrepancies presumably arise because the figures have a different base. The creation of several new inland fisheries in man-made lakes contributed to this growth in production. Catches in Asia made up over 70 per cent of the world total throughout the 1970s, with Africa next in importance at around 14 per cent and the USSR third at 7–9 per cent.

There were indications in 1976 that most fish stocks in Africa were nearly fully exploited, although the resources of the Okavanga Swamp in Botswana and the Sudd Swamp in Sudan were under-developed (Gulland, 1978). New lakes had created fisheries in Lakes Volta, Kariba and Kainji. The Aswan High Dam created a new fishery in Lake Nubia–Nasser but reduced downstream catches including those of the Nile Delta coast and the eastern Mediterranean fisheries. Overfishing had caused serious damage in several large lakes, especially Lake Victoria where progressively finer gill nets were used in the 1960s and 1970s and commercial trawling had been introduced (Fryer, 1972). In some areas such as the Kaverondo (Winam) Gulf a rich original fishery for *Sarotherodon* (*Tilapia*) *esculenta* had been virtually eliminated.

North American waters contributed only a small proportion of the world total catch. About 60 per cent of them were considered to have inherently low productivity, while others showed signs of damage by pollution. In contrast, South American freshwater yields appeared capable of a two-to three-fold increase and a Commission for Inland Fisheries in Latin America (COPESCAL) was established to promote their development. In Asia, also, traditional catches from rivers and flood plains were extended by reservoir development, but there were also some losses in production from rice fields due to more intensive husbandry (double-cropping) and the increasing use of pesticides. In Europe, catches increased slightly, but remained very low and sport fisheries were of greater importance generally than commercial fisheries (Gulland, 1978).

Figure 4–6. Inland Water Fishery.Landings, 1970–1976

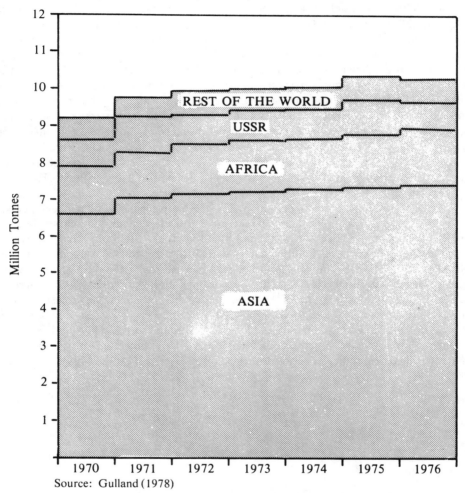

Source: Gulland (1978)

Over-enrichment and pollution remained the cause of damage to several European fisheries. For example, of eleven migratory species of fish that formerly occurred in the Rhine, nine (including salmon and trout) had virtually or totally disappeared by 1976 and practically no commercially useful fisheries remained (Wolff, 1978). In contrast, pollution control measures eliminated summer deoxygenation in the Thames which had formerly been a barrier to migratory species, and these began to re-enter the river in increasing numbers (Holloway, 1978).

Although the overall rate of growth in production between 1972 and 1976 was only around 1 per cent per annum, within this total aquaculture grew at 5 to 6 per cent per annum generally and in some countries, including Indonesia, the Philippines and Thailand, it was as high as 10 per cent. The status, problems and potential of freshwater aquaculture were reviewed in 1976 by an FAO Technical Conference at Kyoto, Japan (FAO, 1979 a, b), and regional workshops were subsequently organized by the FAO/UNDP Aquaculture Development Co-ordination Programme in Africa, Latin America and Asia. Under natural conditions the productivity of fisheries normally varies from 10–20 kg/ha in temperate lakes to 100–200 kg/ha in tropical waters. In very small lakes stocked artificially and provided with supplementary feeding, 500 kg/ha can be obtained. All these figures can be improved substantially, and in small ponds 10,000–20,000 kg/ha or more are attainable – but only with costly inputs of materials and expertise. In developing countries under more traditional systems of fish culture, production of 500 kg/ha or even less is normal, because of shortages of young fish as seed, fertilizers and knowledge. In India and some other areas, yields were increased around 2,000 kg/ha through polyculture and more effective use of locally available material (FAO, 1979 a). Further improvement appeared unlikely without changes in infrastructure.

In 1978 FAO was executing about 40 aquaculture projects – a 60 per cent increase since 1973. Bilateral and multi-lateral cooperative projects were also numerous. In Asia, the FAO Regional Office for Asia and the Far East, the Indo-Pacific Fisheries Commission (IPFC), the South East Asian Fisheries and Development Centre (SEAFDEC), the Association of South East Asian Nations (ASEAN) and the South China Sea Fisheries Development and Co-ordination Programme (SCSP) were all active. Through the joint efforts of the People's Republic of China, the largest producer of fish through aquaculture, FAO and UNDP, the recent experience of China in polyculture and integrated fish, crop and livestock farming was brought to wide attention through study tours and training courses. The FAO Committee on Fisheries reviewed the whole field and indicated priorities for action in 1979 (FAO, 1979a).

Major New Water Bodies

ALTHOUGH many smaller impoundments or reservoirs have been established for hundreds of years, the creation of very large man-made lakes (some over 1,000 km²) was an especially prominent feature of the 1950s and 1960s, during which the characteristics of earlier lakes often changed appreciably. Similarly, although local water transfer by canalization is of considerable antiquity, very large-scale transfers between watersheds were increasingly contemplated during the decade (Golubev and Biswas, 1979), and are likely to become a feature of the 1980s.

While man-made lakes contribute significantly to economic and social well-being through flood control, provision of water for irrigation, domestic and industrial use, hydropower generation, and fisheries development, their construction has major effects on the delicately balanced natural resources of river basins and their ecological systems (Ackermann et al., 1973; UNWC, 1978, pp. 352, 1792, 2015, 2261; Biswas, 1981; UNEP, 1981 b). People are flooded out through inundation of substantial portions of land, and may receive inadequate recompense or re-settlement. Animals and their habitats are shifted or destroyed. Ground water resources are affected and in some cases the impounded water may cause seismic disturbances. Climate can be modified locally; for example, some such lakes have made fog more frequent. Man-made lakes may also promote greater biological productivity, evidenced by the explosive growth of aquatic weeds, especially during the first decade after impoundment (Obeng, 1969; Mitchell, 1973; Gaudet, 1979), and the spread of water-borne diseases (Stanley and Alpers, 1975; Obeng, 1977).

The global distribution of large man-made lakes is very uneven, with the most extensive developments in Africa, the USSR and North America. The impoundment of Cabora Bassa in Mozambique, Kossou in the Ivory Coast and Argyle in Australia, were the more important events during the decade in tropical areas.

Ecological changes were reviewed on a world-wide basis by Obeng (1969), Baxter (1977), Biswas (1981) and UNEP (1981), for tropical examples by Petr (1978), and for African examples by McLachlan (1974) and Davies (1980). The Cabora Bassa ecology was described by Davies et al., (1975) and Bond et al., (1978). Changes affecting vegetation were examined by Bond and Roberts (1979), and those affecting fish stock by Balon and Coche (1974) and Balon (1978). The qualitative aspects of transition from river to lake fish fauna are also important, and were documented during the 1970s at Lake Kainji in Nigeria (Blake, 1977).

Other environmental problems of large impoundments can arise from sedimentation within the basins, especially in rivers bearing heavy silt loads (e.g. the Nile; Entz, 1978). Experience with the silting of reservoirs in some other areas focused interest on the need for initiating watershed treatment upstream before the construction of storage work (UNWC, 1978, pp. 352, 1792, 2015, 2261).

In the 1970s the economic justification and environmental impacts of large storage works were widely questioned. Analyses of the ecological issues at Lake Nasser above Aswan are given by Rzóska (1976) and El-Hinnawi (1980); for Lake Volta by Obeng (1977); and for Lake Kariba by Balon (1978). Attention was directed toward understanding and predicting the full consequences of man-made dams. This led to the adoption of new procedures of evaluation in advance of construction by some national governments and by intergovernmental financial agencies such as the World Bank and UNDP.

Increasing emphasis was given to the multiple use of large and small reservoirs. Although most were originally created for one predominant use (e.g. hydroelectric power or water storage for irrigation), multiple benefits can almost always be obtained. Thus no major man-made lake has been created primarily to provide a fishery, yet this is obviously an important benefit. In developed countries, the older attitude that reservoirs supplying drinking water should be kept "sterile" was giving way to a greater tolerance of recreational activities.

During the 1960s and 1970s discussions arose about major environmental development such as the creation of inland seas in Africa or the USSR, and the diversion of Soviet rivers to augment the shrinking reserves of the Caspian and Aral Seas. These developments provoked discussion also because of their possible effects on climate.

Planning, Legislation and
Shared Water Resources

ALTHOUGH water had always been recognized as an essential resource, its role in national development took on greater weight in the 1970s. The provision of adequate water was an essential element in the expansion of rice production. Reduction of extreme variations in crop harvests depended in some countries upon irrigation. The threats to public health and amenities from water pollution were widely recognized and attacked. The rights of the world population to potable supplies were enunciated for the first time. Against this background of changing attitudes the United Nations designated the 1980s the "Drinking Water and Sanitation Decade" and stressed the importance of national water planning and international co-operation in managing shared resources.

NATIONAL POLICY, PLANNING AND MANAGEMENT

The rise in demand for water, the complexity of meeting these demands quantitatively and qualitatively, the interaction of conflicting uses, the interrelations between water and land and other natural resources, and the delicate balance between water and other environmental components all received greater attention. Accordingly, new stress was placed upon national organization and management, and many of the contributions to the UN Water Conference dealt with planning objectives for multiple uses and their reconciliation, and emphasized protection of the natural environment (UNWC, 1978, pp. 1163, 1173).

A number of advances that became available during the decade – for example in information systems and mathematical modelling, and in the use of computers and the development of management techniques, including systems analysis – helped in the appraisal of planning options and management strategies on an interdisciplinary basis. Many countries began long-range planning based on demand projections, comprehensive river basin planning and water economy budgets. Examples were Argentina, Egypt, Mexico and Romania (UNWC, 1978, pp. 336, 339).

Parallel to this broadened approach, many countries experimented with new institutional frameworks for integrated water assessment, research and management. There was evidence of a growing trend to establish river basin authorities, (e.g. the Sokota Rima basin in Nigeria and the Volta basin in Upper Volta (UNWC, 1978, p. 568). National water councils and ministries responsible for water development were established in a number of countries (UNWC, 1978 p. 1063). Among the special examples was the establishment of regional water authorities responsible for water supply, river conservation and waste water treatment in the United Kingdom.

Water law gained importance in both developed and developing countries (UNWC, 1978 pp. 993, 1041; Teclaff, 1978). It has been estimated that at least one-third of the countries of the world revised their administrative and statutory arrangements for water resources over the decade. These embraced water rights, water and land control, pollution and waste disposal. In the USSR water legislation, including water quality standards, was developed from 1972. A detailed study is given by Kaverin (1977).

Many countries also enlarged their use of indigenous research and educational capabilities. Among the institutes that emerged were the Water Research Centre in the United Kingdom, the Institute of Water Economics, Legislation and Administration (INELA) in Latin America (regional), and the International Training Centre for Water Resources Management (CEFIGRE) in France.

Two further trends in water management deserve note. One was the growing acknowledgement of public participation in decisions on the location, design and operation of new water projects, particularly for domestic water supplies. The other was the growing interest in developing local and appropriate technologies as a tool to expedite economic development and improve the conditions of the world's poor. This was especially noticeable in connection with domestic water supply, sanitation, and small-scale irrigation questions.

GROUND WATER RESOURCES

Preparations for the United Nations Conference on Desertification held in Nairobi in 1977 canvassed the feasibility of regional cooperation for ground water resource survey and development in the Arabian Peninsula and North-East Africa. Subsequently, a project for the development of the ground water resources of the Nubian Sandstone formation, shared by Egypt and the Sudan, was implemented with support from the United Nations Conference on Trade and Development (UNCTAD) and UNEP.

During the past fifteen years, the United Nations ground water exploration and development programme, under the aegis of the Centre for Natural Resources, Energy and Transport has involved over 100 projects, bringing substantial benefits to fifty-seven developing countries. It contributed to the improvement of agricultural production through supplemental irrigation from ground water and to the alleviation of water shortages in urban and industrial areas through construction of supply wells. Assessment of ground water resources was carried out in most United Nations projects. Ground water maps covering areas ranging from 5,000 km^2 to more than 10,000 km^2 were prepared in more than twenty-five countries. Some 150 fellowships for training abroad were granted to technical and professional personnel associated with United Nations ground water projects (Taylor, 1979).

During recent years, FAO and the World Bank funded large-scale ground water development projects for irrigation or livestock water supply, for example in Pakistan, India and the Middle East. WHO was concerned with the protection of rural and urban water supplies against disease vectors. UNESCO was concerned with scientific and educational exchange on ground water geology and hydrology, and undertook studies of large regional aquifer systems such as the Nubian Sandstone formation and the Chad Basin.

SHARED WATER RESOURCES

In 1970 the United Nations General Assembly recommended that the International Law Commission (ILC) study the law on non-navigational uses of international water courses with a view to codifying and developing it. Thereafter in their response to questions by the ILC, several states stressed the importance of the subject but disagreed on the definition of an international river. In general, they supported the classification of fresh water uses into agricultural, economic, commercial, domestic, and social categories (the latter including flood control and erosion control and pollution prevention).

UNEP's intergovernmental Working Group of Experts on Natural Resources Shared by Two or More States sought to draft principles of conduct for the guidance of states in the conservation and harmonious exploitation of shared environmental resources. Other efforts included the recommendation of the Interregional Seminar on River Basin and Interbasin Development (Budapest 1975) and the activities of non-governmental bodies on international law.

A major event in the development of shared water resources was the declaration of the United Nations Water Conference in 1977 that 'it is necessary for states to co-operate in the case of shared water resources in recognition of the growing economic, environmental and physical interdependencies across international frontiers'. The conference further recommended that national policies should take into consideration the right of each state sharing the resource to utilize it equitably.

There was increasing collaboration in joint studies and exchange of data between states sharing water resources, as in the River Nile, Rio de la Plata, the Senegal Basin, and along the Canadian-United States boundary (UNWC, 1978, p. 2525). Co-operation in research in the area of pollution control, nuclear water contamination, disposal of thermal wastes, and water management methods gained importance in international relations. Yet despite these encouraging attitudes, the decade failed to see resolution of critical conflicts between states with regard to water in more than a few basins. In all major regions new instrumentalities were organized to deal with water problems involving two or more countries, but while the list is impressive, the record of achievement was uneven: some instrumentalities existed only on paper and others were limited to data collection, while still others commanded effective study and operating agreements. In Europe in 1977 there were at least forty bilateral, six trilateral, and one five-member agreements affecting boundary waters, in addition to the international commissions on the Danube, Rhine, Mosel and Saar rivers (UNWC, 1978, p. 514).

Future Prospects

EFFORTS towards international co-operation accelerated during the 1970s, but the record was not one of unmixed improvement. In some places and in some ways the water resource was worse off in 1980 than when the Stockholm Conference called for a reversal of the then prevailing trends. Although water accessibility and quality improved in some regions, the absolute numbers of people without access to safe water grew. A rough balance of gains and losses suggests that the trends were generally – albeit slightly – favourable to the sustained use of the basic resource. As indicated in the preceding review, the major changes can be summarized as follows.

ON THE POSITIVE SIDE

— Understanding of the distribution, volume and quality of water on the surface and underground was enhanced by research on basic processes, expanded hydrologic observations, and improved means of measurement and exploration.

— Much of the rapidly accumulating data was used to arrive at local, regional and global water balances. Many developing countries made comprehensive assessments of their water resources.

— Further analysis of the data, to define needs and prescribe corrective action, was strengthened by sophisticated data processing and by development of models for surface water flow, ground water movement, surface water quality, and water consumption. Planning benefited from more and better data, and more effective ways of analyzing it, including techniques for dealing with inadequate data and persistent uncertainty.

— The forecasting of flood, average, and low flows became more accurate and was extended over larger areas.

— On a number of the major rivers draining modern industrial areas the load of polluting substances decreased.

— The international navigable waterway networks were extended.

— Large new water bodies were created or matured as valuable water resources.

— Greater, more systematic attention was given by international and some national agencies to anticipating and curbing undesirable consequences of large man-made lakes.

— The means of coping with the extremes of flood and shortage encompassed to a larger degree a mix of measures such as land-use management, warnings, and organization to prevent the expansion of urbanization and uneconomic land-use into vulnerable areas.

— Recognition was given on a global scale to the need to provide drinking water and suitable sanitation to the entire human family.

— Drainage and improved irrigation practice was extended to a good many systems threatened by waterlogging and salinity.

— New national plans for water development were translated into action in a few countries.

— International commissions or other similar agencies were established to assist in the co-operative development of water resources shared by two or more countries.

— Standards, regulations or incentives were established in many countries, mostly industrialized, to reverse the growing flow of wastes into water bodies.

ON THE NEGATIVE SIDE

— Many low-income countries lacked the infrastructure to apply the new data and advanced techniques to the lasting solution of their local water problems. Technical assistance was no substitute for indigenous capacity to make water plans in co-operation with the affected population and to carry them out.

— In numerous countries the targets for the Drinking Water and Sanitation Decade will not be attainable if the rate of progress shown during the 1970s were to continue. This is particularly the case for the mushrooming squatter settlements on the edges of tropical cities.

— Deterioration of irrigated lands because of inadequate drainage and cultivation practices continued on a scale about equal to the rate at which new lands were opened up. This meant that rehabilitation measures would have to be stepped up and new planning improved if net gains in productivity were to be achieved rapidly.

— Water quality continued to degrade in many streams and lakes, especially in low-income countries with new industrialization, and under administrations that looked only at effluent levels in relation to human health, without regard for aquatic ecosystems.

— Even in some industrial countries with extensive programmes for treating waste from cities and manufacturing plants the volume of pollutants from non-point sources mounted substantially, and technically feasible methods for reducing manufacturing waste were not being practised.

— The task of maintaining water quality was complicated by increasing amounts of evidence that minute doses of organic substances could injure human health. Refinements in detecting minute quantities of pollutants had helped uncover the evidence.

The events of the 1970s thus emphasized the opportunity to marshal national and international forces in the direction of wiser, more stable water use and control. The balance is complicated, but some trends are clearly directed towards a sustained environment.

References

Ackermann, W. C. *et al.*, Editors (1973), *Man-made Lakes: Their Problems and Environmental Effects*. Amer. Geophys. Union, Washington.

Allen, R. J. (1980), The Inadequacy of Existing Chlorophyll/Phosphorus Concentration Correlations for Assessing Remedial Measures to Hypertrophic Lakes, *Environ. Pollution*, Ser. B, 1, 217.

Almer, B. *et al.* **(1978), Sulfur Pollution and the Aquatic Ecosystem, In J. O. Nriagu (Editor),** *Sulfur in the Environment*, John Wiley, New York.

Anderson, G. *et al.* (1973), Planktonic Changes Following the Restoration of Lake Trummen, Sweden, *Ambio*, 2, 44.

Arceivala, S. J. *et al.* (1970), *Waste Stabilization Ponds*, Central Public Health Engineering Research Institute, Nagpur, India.

Arnold, D. E. (1969), The Ecological Decline of Lake Erie, N.Y. *Fish Game J.*, 16, 27.

Balon, E. K. (1978), Kariba: The Dubious Benefits of Large Dams, *Ambio*, 7, 40.

Balon, E. K. and A. G. Coche (1974), *Lake Kariba: A Man-made Tropical Ecosystem in Central Africa*, Junk, The Hague.

Baxter, R. M. (1977), Environmental Effects of Dams and Impoundments, *Ann. Rev. Ecol. Syst.*, 8, 255.

Bishai, H. M. and S. Y. Kirollos (1980), The Water Budget of Lake Qarun and Its Physico-Chemical Characteristics, *Water Supply and Management*, 4, 93.

Biswas, A. K., Editor (1976), *Systems Approach to Water Management*, McGraw-Hill, New York.

Biswas, A. K. (1980), Non-Radiological Environmental Implications of Nuclear Energy, In E. El-Hinnawi (Editor), *Nuclear Energy and the Environment*, Pergamon Press, Oxford.

Biswas, A. K. Editor (1981), *Models for Water Quality Management*, McGraw-Hill, New York.

Bjork, S. (1972), Swedish Lake Restoration Program Gets Results. *Ambio*, 5, 153.

Blake, B. F. (1977), Lake Kainji, Nigeria: A Summary of the Changes Within the Fish Population Since the Impoundment of the Niger in 1968, *Hydrobiologia*, 53, 131.

Bloomfield, J. A. *et al.* (1980), Atmospheric and Watershed Inputs of Mercury to Cranberry Lake, St. Lawrence County, New York. In T. Y. Toribara *et al.* (Editors), *Polluted Rain*. Plenum, New York.

Bolin, B. and E. Arrhenius, Editors (1977), Nitrogen – An Essential Life Factor and a Growing Environmental Hazard, *Ambio*, 6, 96.

Bond, W. J. *et al.* (1978), The Limnology of Cabora Bassa, Mozambique, During Its First Year, *Freshwat. Biol.*, 8, 433.

Bond, W. J. and M. G. Roberts (1979), The Colonization of Cabora Bassa, Mozambique, A New Man-made Lake, by Floating Aquatic Macrophytes, *Hydrobiologia*, 60, 243.

164

Boraey, F. A. (1980), Studies on the Changes of Some Ecological Factors Affecting Fish Life in Lake Qarun, Faiyum, Egypt, *Water Supply and Management*, 4, 99.

Braekke F. H. (1976), Impact of Acid Precipitation on Forest and Freshwater Ecosystems in Norway. Research Report No. 6. 6. Aas, Norway.

Burton, I. *et al.* (1978), *The Environment as Hazard*, Oxford Univ. Press.

CEFIGRE (1980), Inland Waters. Report Prepared for the United Nations Environment Programme by the International Training Centre for Water Resources Management (CEFIGRE), France.

Charlier, R. M. (1969), Crisis Year for the Great Lakes, *New Scientist*, 44, 593.

Collingwood, R. W. (1977), A Survey of Eutrophication in Britain and Its Effects on Water Supplies, Tech. Rep. Wat. Res. Centre, TR40, 41 pp.

Commoner, B. (1977), Cost-Benefit Analysis of Nitrogen Fertilization – A Case History, *Ambio*, 6, 157.

Davies, B. R. (1980), Stream Regulation in Africa; A Review. In J. V. Ward and J. A. Stanford (Editors), *The Ecology of Regulated Streams*, Plenum Press, New York.

Davies, B. R. *et al.* (1975), Some Ecological Aspects of the Cabora Bassa Dam, *Biol. Conserv.*, 8, 189.

Dickson, W. (1975), The Acidification of Swedish Lakes, Rep. Inst. Freshwat. Res. Drottningholm, No. 54.

Dickson, W. (1978), Some Effects of the Acidification of Swedish Lakes, *Verh. Internat. Verein. Limnol.*, 20, 851.

Dillon, P. J. and F. H. Rigler (1974), The Phosphorus-Chlorophyll Relationship in Lakes. *Limnol. Oceanogr.*, 19, 767.

D'Itri, P. A. and F. M. D'Itri (1977), *Mercury Contamination: A Human Tragedy*. John Wiley, New York.

Dochinger, L. S. and T. A. Seliga (1976), Workshop Report on Acid Precipitation and the Forest Ecosystem. USDA Forest Service, Gen. Techn. Rept. NE–26 Northeast For. Exp. Sta. Upper Darby, Pa.

Drabløs, D. and A. Tollan, Editors (1980), *Ecological Impact of Acid Precipitation*, Proceedings of an International Conference, Sandefjord, Norway, March 1980. Oslo–As. SNSF Project.

Dunst, R. C. *et al.* (1974), Survey of Lake Rehabilitation Techniques and Experiences, Tech. Bull. No. 75, Dep. Nat. Res., Madison, Wisconsin.

Edmonson, W. T. (1970), Phosphorus, Nitrogen and Algae in Lake Washington After Diversion of Sewage. *Science*, 169, 690.

El-Hinnawi, E. (1980), The State of the Nile Environment: An Overview, *Water Supply and Manag.*, 4, 1.

El-Hinnawi, E. and F. El-Gohary (1981), Energy From Biomass. In E. El-Hinnawi and Asit K. Biswas (Editors), *Renewable Sources of Energy and the Environment*, Tycooly International Publishing Ltd., Dublin.

Entz, B. (1978), Sedimentation Processes Above the Aswan High Dam in Lake Nasser – Nubia (Egypt – Sudan), *Verh. Int. Verein. Theor. Agnew, Limnol.*, 20, 3, 1667.

ESCAP (1980), Economic and Social Commission for Asia and the Pacific, United Nations, Document E/ESCAP/7/1.

Eusebio, J. and B. Rabino (1978), Recycling System in Integrated Plant and Animal Farming, *Compost Science*, March/April, 24.

Fagerström, T. and A. Jernělov (1972), Some Aspects of the Quantitative Ecology of Mercury. *Water Research* 6, 1193.

FAO (1979a), Aquaculture Development, Committee on Fisheries, 13th Session, Paper COFI/79/5. Food and Agriculture Organization of the United Nations, Rome.

FAO (1979b), Summary Report, FAO Technical Conference on Aquaculture, Kyoto, May, 1976. FAO, Rome.

FAO (1980a), 1979 *Production Yearbook*, FAO, Rome.

FAO (1980b), 1979 *Yearbook of Fishery Statistics*, FAO, Rome.

Frenkiel, J. (1965), *Evaporation Reduction. Physical and Chemical Principles and Review of Experiments*, UNESCO Arid Zone Research, vol. 27. UNESCO, Paris.

Fryer, G. (1972), Conservation of the Great Lakes of East Africa: A Lesson and a Warning, *Biol. Conserv.*, 4, 256.

Gaudet, J. J. (1979), Aquatic Weeds in African Man-made Lakes, *PANS*, 25, 279.

Gelin, C. and W. Ripl (1978), Nutrient Decrease and Response of Various Phytoplankton Size Fractions Following the Restoration of Lake Trummen, Sweden, *Arch. Hydrobiol.*, 81, 339.

Golubev, G. N. and A. K. Biswas, Editors (1979), *Interregional Water Transfers*, Pergamon Press, Oxford.

Gorham, E. (1976), Acid Precipitation and Its Influence upon Aquatic Ecosystems, Proc. Int. Symp. Acid Precip. Forest Ecosystems, 1975, 425–458.

Gulland J. A. (1978), Review of The State of World Fishery Resources, FAO Fisheries Circular No. 710. FAO, Rome.

Harvey, H. H. (1980), Widespread and Diverse Changes in the Biota of North American Lakes and Rivers Coincident with Acidification. Proc. Int. Conf. Ecological Impact Acid Precipit., Sandefjord, Norway.

Hasler, A. D. (1969), Cultural Eutrophication is Reversible, *Bioscience*, 19, 425.

Hellawell, J. M. (1978), *Biological Surveillance of Rivers. A Biological Monitoring Handbook*, Water Research Centre, Stevenage.

Helmer, R. (1981), Water Quality Monitoring; A Global Approach, *Nature and Resources*, 17, 7.

Hendrey, G. R. *et al.* (1976), Acid Precipitation; Some Hydrological Changes. *Ambio*, 5, 224.

Hickman, M. (1980), Phosphorus, Chlorophyll and Eutrophic Lakes, *Arch. Hydrobiol.*, 88, 2, 137.

Holloway, T. (1978), The Restoration of the River Thames, *Environment*, 20, 6.

Hrbáček, J. *et al.* (1977), Observations on the Relation Between Phosphorus and Chlorophyll in a Small Reservoir, Klivaca, Bohemia, *Int. J. Ecol. Environ. Sci.*, 3, 9.

Huisman, L. and W. E. Wood (1974), *Slow Sand Filtration*. WHO, Geneva.

Hultberg, H. and A. Wenblad (1980), Acid Groundwater in Southwestern Sweden, Proc. Inter. Conf. Ecological Impact Acid Precipitation, Sandefjord, Norway.

Jernělov, A. (1980), The Effects of Acidity on the Uptake of Mercury in Fish. In T.Y. Toribara *et al.* (Editors) *Polluted Rain*, Plenum, New York.

Jones, J. R. and R. W. Bachmann (1976), Prediction of Phosphorus and Chlorophyll Levels in Lakes, *J. Water Poll. Control Fed.*, 48, 9, 2176.

Kalbermatten, J. M. *et al.* (1980), *Appropriate Technology for Water Supply and Sanitation; A Planner's Guide*, World Bank, Washington, D.C.

Kalk, M. *et al.* (1979), Lake Chilwa; Studies of Change in a Tropical Ecosystem, *Monog. Biol.*, 35, 462 pp.

Kaverin, A. M. (1977), *Pravovaya okhrana vod ot zagryazneniya*, Yuridicheskaya Literatura, Moscow.

Kilham, P. and R. E. Hecky (1973), Fluoride: Geochemical and Ecological Significance in East African Waters and Sediments, *Limnol. Oceanogr.*, 18, 932.

Kovacs, G. (1977), Human Interaction with Groundwater, *Ambio*, 6, 1, 22.

Lehn, H. (1973), *Phytoplanktonänderungen im Bodensee und Einige Fölgerprobleme*, Verhandl. Gesellsch. für Ökologie, Saarbrucken, 225.

Lehn, H. (1975), Entwicklung des Bodensee-pelazials seit 1920, *Schrift-Reihe Gesell. Wass. Forsch.*, 116, 170.

Likens, G. E. *et al.* (1979), Acid Rain, *Scientific Amer.*, 241, 43.

Magee, P. N. (1977), Nitrogen as a Health Hazard, *Ambio*, 6, 123.

McGarry, M. C. and J. Stainforth (1978), Compost, Fertilizer and Biogas Production from Human and Farm Wastes in P. R. China, *IDRC Pub. No. TS8e*, Ottawa.

McLachlan, A. J. (1974), Development of Some Lake Ecosystems in Tropical Africa, with Special Reference to the Invertebrate, *Biol. Rev.*, 49, 395.

Mitchell, D. S. (1973), Aquatic Weeds in Man-made Lakes. In W. C. Ackermann *et al.* (Editors), *Man-made Lakes: Their Problems and Environmental Effects*, Amer. Geophys. Union, Washington.

Morel-Seytoux, H. J. and J. Restrepo (1977), *Weather Modification on Runoff in the State of Colorado*, Colorado State Univ., Fort Collins, Colorado.

Muniz, I. P. and H. Leivestad (1980), Toxic Effects of Aluminium on the Brown Trout, *Salmo trutta L.*, Proc. Int. Conf. Ecological Impacts of Acid Precipit., Sandefjord, Norway.

Nicholls, R. H. and P. J. Dillon (1978), An Evaluation of Phosphorus - Chlorophyll-Phytoplankton Relationships for Lakes, *Inter. Rev. Hydrobiol. Hydrogr.*, 63, 141.

NRC (1981), *Outlook for Science and Technology: The Next Five Years*, A Report prepared for the National Science Foundation, National Research Council, Washington, D.C.

NRCC (1981), *Acidification in the Canadian Aquatic Environment: Scientific Criteria for an Assessment of the Effects of Acidic Deposition on Aquatic Ecosystems*. Public. No. 18475. National Research Council of Canada.

OAS (1978), *Environmental Quality and River Basin Development: A Model for Integrated Analysis and Planning*, Organization of American States, Washington D.C.

Obeid, M. *et al.* (1975), *Aquatic Weeds in the Sudan*, The National Council for Research, Khartoum.

Obeng, L. E., Editor (1969), *Man-made Lakes: The Accra Symposium*, Ghana Univ. Press, Accra.

Obeng, L. E. (1977), Should Dams Be Built? The Volta Lake Example, *Ambio*, 6, 46.

OECD (1970), *Eutrophication in Large Lakes and Impoundments*, Organization for Economic Co-operation and Development, Paris.

OECD (1979), *The State of the Environment in OECD Member Countries*, Organization for Economic Co-operation and Development, Paris.

Olsen, P. and E. Willen (1980), Phytoplankton Response to Sewage Reduction in Vattern, A Large Oligotrophic Lake in Central Sweden, *Arch. Hydrobiol.*, 89, 171.

Olsson, M. (1976), Mercury Level as a Function of Size and Age in Northern Pike, One and Five Years After the Mercury Ban in Sweden. *Ambio*, 5, 73.

Oswald, W. J. (1973), Complete Waste Treatment in Ponds. In S. H. Jenkins (Editor), *Progress Water Technology*, Vol. 3, Pergamon Press, Oxford.

Overrein, L. N. *et al.* (1980), *Acid Precipitation – Effects on Forest and Fish*, SNSF Project, Norway, 175p.

Parma, S. (1980), The History of the Eutrophication Concept and the Eutrophication in the Netherlands. *Hydrobiol. Bull.*, 14, 5.

Petr, T. (1978), Tropical Man-made Lakes – Their Ecological Impact, *Arch. Hydrobiol.*, 81, 368.

Pirie, N. W. (1960), Water Hyacinth: A Curse or a Crop? *Nature*, 185, 116.

Rzóska, J., Editor (1976), The Nile, Biology of an Ancient River, *Monographiae Biol.*, 29, Junk, The Hague.

Sage, B. (1980), Rupture in the Trans-Alaska Oil Pipeline: Causes and Effects, *Ambio*, 9, 262.

Schindler, D. W. (1974), Eutrophication and Recovery in Experimental Lakes: Implications for Lake Management, *Science*, 184, 897.

Schindler, D. W. (1977), Evolution of Phosphorus Limitation in Lakes, *Science*, 195, 260.

Schofield, C. L. (1976), Acid Precipitations: Effects on Fish. *Ambio*, 5, 228.

Schofield, C. L. and J. R. Trojnar (1980), Aluminium Toxicity to Brook Trout (*Salvelinus fontinalis*) in Acidified Waters, In T. Y. Toribara *et al.* (Editors), *Polluted Rains*, Plenum, New York.

Sikes, S. K. (1972), *Lake Chad*, Methuen, London.

Stanley, N. F. and M. P. Alpers, Editors (1975), *Man-made Lakes and Human Health*, Academic Press, London.

Symposium on Lake Erie (1976), Proceedings of a Symposium on Lake Erie, *J. Fish. Res.*, Canada, 33, 3.

Talling, J. F. and I. B. Talling (1965), The Chemical Composition of African Lake Waters, *Inter. Rev. Hydrobiol. Hydrogr.*, 50, 421.

Taylor, G. C. (1979), The United Nations Ground Water Exploration and Development Programme – A Fifteen Year Perspective, *Natural Resources Forum,* 3, 147.

Teclaff, L. (1978), Harmonizing Water Use and Development with Environmental Protection, In A. Utton and L. Teclaff (Editors), *Water In a Developing World,* Westview Press, Boulder, Colorado.

Thomas, E. A. (1973), Phosphorus and Eutrophication, In E. P. Griffith *et al.* (Editors), *Environmental Phosphorus Handbook,* John Wiley, New York.

Thomas, R. L. and J. M. Jaquet (1976), Mercury in the Surfacial Sediments of Lake Erie, *J. Fish. Res., Canada,* 33, 404.

Toerien, D. F. (1975), South African Eutrophication Problems, *Water Pollution Control,* 74, 134.

Tomlinson, T. E. (1970), Trends in Nitrate Concentrations in English Rivers in Relation to Fertilizer Use, *J. Soc. Wat. Treatm. Exam.,* 19, 277.

UN (1975), Ground Water Storage and Artificial Recharge, *Natural Resources, Water Series No.* 2, United Nations, New York.

UN (1980), *International Drinking Water Supply and Sanitation Decade; Present Situation and Prospects,* A/35/367, United Nations, New York.

UNEP (1981a), *The State of the Environment – Selected Topics –* 1981, United Nations Environment Programme, Nairobi.

UNEP (1981b), *Environmental Impacts of Production and Use of Energy,* Study Director: E. El-Hinnawi, Tycooly International Publishing Ltd., Dublin.

UNWC (1978), *Proceedings of the United Nations Water Conference, Mar del Plata, Argentina,* 1977, 4 vols, Pergamon Press, Oxford.

USBR (1976), *Colorado River Basin Pilot Project: Comprehensive Evaluation Report,* US Bureau of Reclamation, Gobeta, California.

USSR (1978) *World Water Balance and Water Resources of the Earth,* USSR Committee for the International Hydrological Decade 1974. English Translation published by UNESCO, 1978.

Vallentyne, J. R. (1974), The Algal Bowl: Lakes and Man. Dept. Environ, *Fish. Mar. Serv., Misc. Spec. Publ.* 22. pp 186, Ottawa.

Van Buren, A. (1979), *A Chinese Biogas Manual,* Intern. Techn. Publ., London.

Van Wijk-Sijbesma, C. (1980), *Participation and Education in Community Water Supply and Sanitation Programmes; A Literature Review.* Techn. Paper No. 12, WHO Intern. Reference Centre for Community Water Supply, The Hague.

White, G. F., Editor (1977), *Environmental Effects of Complex River Development,* Westview Press, Boulder, Colorado.

White, G. F. *et al.* (1972), *Drawers of Water: Domestic Water Use in East Africa,* University of Chicago Press.

Whitton, B. A. (1970), Biology of *Cladophora* in Freshwaters, *Water Research,* 4, 457.

Whitton, B. A. (1975), *River Ecology,* Univ. California Press.

WHO (1973), *World Health Statistics Report* 26, 11, World Health Organization, Geneva.

Wolff, W. J. (1978), The Degradation of Ecosystems in the Rhine. In M. W. Holdgate and M. J. Woodman (Editors), *The Breakdown and Restoration of Ecosystems*. Plenum, New York.

Wolverton, B. C. and R. C. McDonald (1979), The Water Hyacinth; From Prolific Pest to Potential Provider. *Ambio, 8, 2*.

Wood, F. C. (1978), The Status of Desalting, *Aqua, 4, 23*.

Wright, R. F. and E. T. Gjessing (1976), Acid Precipitation: Changes in the Chemical Composition of Lakes. *Ambio 5, 219*.

CHAPTER 5

Lithosphere

The outer layer of the Earth is a source of mixed blessings to mankind; both enormous wealth and disastrous upheavals originate there. During the decade man exploited the one and suffered from the other. The minerals extracted in ever-growing amounts provided a physical basis for economic advances. The earthquakes, volcanoes and landslides that occurred from time to time retarded these advances.

During the decade, the elaboration of the theory of plate tectonics helped scientists increase their understanding of how and where minerals are formed and how crustal movements take place. This theory explains how major surface features of the earth were shaped by the movement of large solid pieces (plates) of crustal material over the plastic layer of the mantle. These processes, still operating today, are responsible not only for catastrophic phenomena such as earthquakes or volcanic eruptions, but also for mineral formation. The theory thus facilitated exploration of various types of mineral deposits. It was also important for environmental policies aimed at husbanding finite resources.

The definition of resources and reserves and their classification were advanced during the decade, emphasizing the tentative nature of many resource estimates and the fact that at any one time such estimates are strongly influenced by investment factors. Much argument occurred during the 1970s over the increase in mineral consumption and the possibility of depleting mineral resources. In an absolute sense the Earth cannot run out of mineral raw materials since mankind's use of them shifts them from place to place rather than destroys them, though it does increase, often prohibitively, the technical difficulty and economic expense of recovering them.

Annual production of almost all major non-metallic minerals expanded during the decade. With a few exceptions, metal production increased at a moderate rate, but annual volumes and prices fluctuated widely as a result of economic and political conditions.

Important improvements were made in the methods used to reduce deleterious effects of mining, treatment and transport of both metallic and non-metallic minerals. Advances occurred chiefly in dust control, the reclamation of open pits, reduction of acid drainage and treatment of tailings and liquid waste. One estimate, made in mid-decade, suggested that 40–60 per cent of lands disturbed by mining were either in the course of natural restoration or were being reclaimed.

Recycling and substitution of mineral raw materials received renewed attention during the 1970s, but some thought their role might have been over-stated: they are not new ideas, and they are not magic solutions to scarcity. Midway in the decade, however, the amounts of some scrap metals being recycled in the United Kingdom and the United States were equivalent to a substantial proportion of world production for that year.

Some industrialized countries continued to depend heavily on the importation of a few strategic minerals, so that minerals formed an integral part of international diplomacy. For example, the United States between 1976 and 1979 imported 94 per cent of its bauxite, 97 per cent of its manganese, and all of its columbium and titanium. Supply, demand and price fluctuations of strategic minerals sometimes seriously disrupted the economies of producer countries dependent on such exports.

172

Earthquakes, volcanoes and landslides claimed their tolls of lives and damaged property during the 1970s, as they had in previous decades. The Tangshang earthquake of 27 July 1976 was a catastrophe with an intensity reached only a few times in recorded history: it killed at least 242,000 people and injured a comparable number. The decade also saw the first successful prediction of a major earthquake: in the Haicheng area of the People's Republic of China in 1975. More reliable warning systems seemed possible, and some progress was made in managing land use and building design and construction in such a way as to reduce human activities on areas vulnerable to earth movements.

This chapter deals with a particular group of natural resources — minerals — the majority of which are non-renewable in character. Mineral resources represent the physical heritage of the planet in the form of raw materials for construction and industry. In the decade of the 1970s they were the subject of fierce debate, particularly with regard to their possible scarcity, cost or availability in the future, given current rates and patterns of consumption. This debate, in turn, focused attention on the nature, occurrence and distribution of mineral resources and the impact of their use on the environment, including their role in the economic future of developing countries.

Geophysical theory is analyzed in this chapter only where it has had a direct bearing on issues in mineral resources: a good example here would be the use of plate tectonics to select areas within which to concentrate exploration for minerals. Soils as a natural resource, and energy resources as a particular sub-group of natural resources, are not treated here (see Chapters 7 and 12 respectively). Following a short introduction dealing with the broad geophysical background as it affects mineral resources, the chapter focuses on trends in the production and use of particular minerals as raw materials in the modern economy and on the growing environmental impact of these activities. The subsequent use of mineral resources in the form of industrial commodities is treated in Chapter 11. Finally, the chapter concludes with a brief and self-contained summary of the main geophysical events that created a hazard to human life or property during the decade.

The Geological Background

THE lithosphere is the solid earth: its surface is the setting for human activity and from it are obtained all inorganic raw materials as well as virtually all energy resources. The lithosphere can be divided into several layers. An outer layer, known as the "crust", varies in thickness from 6–8 km beneath the ocean floor to between 30 and 75 km beneath the continents. The crust covers a denser zone, the "mantle", in the middle of which occurs a yielding plastic layer — the asthenosphere — whose rocks are near the melting point. The crust and the harder upper layer of the mantle make up the lithosphere, although geologically this term is also used in a more general application to describe the entire solid earth. Below the mantle lies the core of the earth, itself divided into an outer molten zone and an inner solid core, composed largely of iron and nickel, at extremely high temperatures and under great pressure.

From an environmental point of view rather than a geophysical one, human interest in the lithosphere is limited to its surface and near-surface features. Millions of years of geophysical, geomorphological and geochemical processes have contributed to a continuous reworking and reshaping of these crustal features. Many of the gross physical features of the planet are a result of long-term tectonic processes, the motion of large solid pieces of the crustal portion of the lithosphere, known as "plates", moving over the viscous asthenosphere at rates of a few centimetres a year (Figure 5–1). Over long periods of geological history, these movements have produced large-scale displacements, some of thousands of kilometres. The decade of the 1970s was marked by an increase in knowledge of such basic structural processes which have shaped the present configuration of the earth's surface, including its continents. Not only are these new ideas important in geoscience, but they are relevant to an understanding of the nature and occurrence of minerals and of the processes that lead to their formation and distribution, which is of direct economic and environmental interest (Wilson, 1972).

Three particular aspects of tectonic processes merit attention in connection with mineral resources and geological hazards: divergent plate boundaries, convergent plate boundaries, and parallel plate boundaries (Rona, 1976). In some areas, for example the mid-Atlantic, adjacent crustal plates are moving apart and new crustal material or magma is upwelling and solidifying to form new crust, by the phenomenon known as seafloor spreading. By contrast with such divergent plate boundaries, in other areas one crustal plate may be driven under another into the asthenosphere along a convergent plate boundary, as for example along the western edge of South America.

Heat produced in these "subduction zones" melts crustal rock into magma, which in turn feeds volcanic activity at the surface. These boundaries of collision between plates are also characterized by steep mountain chains, deep ocean trenches and strong earthquake activity. Along parallel plate boundaries, such as that marked by the San

Figure 5–1. Tectonic map of Earth showing boundaries of major lithospheric plates.

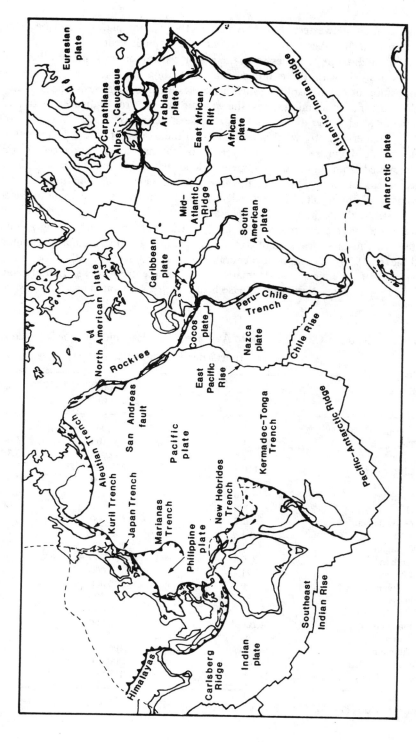

After Head and Solomon, Science, 213, 62, 1981.

Andreas fault in western North America, the crustal plates move past each other, producing earthquakes with extensive surface displacement.

Although tectonic forces form the major crustal features, many other geophysical processes work with these movements over time to contribute to the shape and composition of the lithosphere. Such processes include orogenesis, the uplifting of parts of the crust into mountain ranges; the wearing down of rock surfaces by the weathering actions of wind, water and chemical processes; the transportation of rock particles and soil through erosion by wind and water; and the formation and transformation of new rocks from sedimentary material. Over geological time-spans, large volumes of material are removed from higher elevations and deposited in lowland areas and on the ocean margins and floors. The accumulation of sediments and the tectonic process of subsidence — the result of larger-scale crustal movements — contribute to the sinking of the crust. At the same time, in other areas, crustal uplift compensates for the loss of materials through erosion and weathering of the continents. The folding and contortion of the crust in these ways results in a wide variety of topographical phenomena (Press and Siever, 1974). As sediments accumulate at depth, pressure and temperature induce a physical and chemical transformation into sedimentary rocks, notably sandstones, limestones or shales. Similarly, intense heat and pressure, often associated with volcanic

Table 5–1. Ratio of Cut-off Grade to Average Crustal Abundance for Selected Elements
(parts per million)

Element	Average crustal abundance	Cut-off grade (1975)	Ratio
Mercury	0.089	1,000	11,200
Tungsten	1.1	4,500	4,000
Lead	12	40,000	3,300
Chromium	110	230,000	2,100
Tin	1.7	3,500	2,000
Silver	0.075	100	1,330
Gold	0.0035	3.5	1,000
Molybdenum	1.3	1,000	770
Zinc	94	35,000	370
Uranium	1.7	700	350
Carbon	320	100,000	310
Lithium	21	5,000	240
Manganese	1,300	250,000	190
Nickel	89	9,000	100
Cobalt	25	2,000	80
Phosphorus	1,200	88,000	70
Copper	63	3,500	56
Titanium	6,400	100,000	16
Iron	58,000	200,000	3.4
Aluminium	83,000	185,000	2.2

Source: Cook (1976).

activity, may produce metamorphic rocks, such as slate or marble. More abundant in the crust are those rocks formed by the cooling and resolidifying of magma — the igneous group of rocks. Melting, migration and resolidification of the materials in the lithosphere over long periods of time have led to a general division between underlying denser materials and lighter materials on the top of the crust. Granitic rocks rich in silica and alumina predominate in the upper layer of the continental crust, while basaltic rocks, denser and containing iron in addition to silica and alumina, are prevalent in the lower layer of the continental crust and in the oceanic crust.

The operation of some of these processes can be disruptive rather than beneficial in human terms. Natural catastrophic phenomena, earthquakes or volcanic eruptions for example, can cause considerable interference with ecosystems and pose environmental hazards to humans in particular areas. On the other hand, the occurrence and distribution of mineral resources in concentrations richer than their average crustal abundance (see Table 5–1) is a geological fact of enormous economic importance, representing an endowment of the physical environment that is critical to prospects for industrial and economic development. Particular mineral resources tend to be clustered in metallogenic or geochemical provinces from which other minerals are excluded: some areas of the earth are rich in mineral raw materials, others are relatively poor. No part of the earth, even on a continental basis, is entirely self-sufficient in all critical mineral metals (Mason, 1966; Skiro, 1969). A widespread critical examination of the nature of this geological legacy and of the rates at which human consumption is depleting it gathered force in the 1970s.

The Occurrence and Nature of Mineral Resources

THE concept of plate tectonics and associated geophysical theory led to the introduction in the 1970s of a framework within which the evaluation of mineral resources advanced. This has helped to explain the known distribution of various types of mineral deposits. For example, many copper and molybdenum deposits occur on the overthrust continental margins of convergent plates. Copper, nickel, manganese and other metals have been detected at mid-ocean rifts where new lithosphere is forming. Other types of deposits, such as lead, zinc, fluorite, vanadium, titanium and iron ores rich in phosphorus (associated with igneous origins) are formed in continental interiors: several of them appear to be associated with crustal fractures related to fragmentation of the continental plates. Plate tectonics has thus stimulated theories of ore deposition worldwide — but it is only a first step. The largest deposit of ore is extremely small compared with an orogenic chain or continental plate; also, knowing the reason for the location of a particular deposit in a particular region does not help to identify precisely the location of a buried deposit. It is therefore essential to follow-up these broader theories with particular concepts and techniques of exploration, adjusted to the search for particular deposits.

Since mineral ore deposits result from a variety of igneous, metamorphic, sedimentary and biological processes, their size, extent, shape and host environments are extremely diverse. The discovery of deposits of great lateral size, which are by nature often syngenetic (formed with their host rocks) or concentrated by weathering processes at or near the surface, poses few problems once their overall environment is recognized. Their existence can be established by relatively simple exploration methods and technology or, if they outcrop at the surface, by traditional prospecting. Deposits of many metals and minerals, especially the rarer ones, are epigenetic (formed later than their host rocks) and hypogenetic (formed by gases or solutions migrating upwards to deposit their metals in restricted "pockets" or locations near but beneath the surface). In some cases, erosion may have uncovered such deposits, but more usually particular geological, geochemical or geophysical exploration methods and techniques have to be used to determine their nature and extent. The geologist studies the gamut of the observable characteristics of the deposit and its geological setting, whereas the geochemist measures traces of elements in rocks, soils, water or flora that may indicate the proximity of a buried deposit: the geophysicist may probe magnetic, seismic, gravity, electrical or electro-magnetic anomalies that are indicative of ore deposits buried at depth. Modern scientific exploration combines many techniques, which are designed to delineate target areas for the physical exploration that follows to evaluate the size, content, structure, extent and value of a deposit. There is no universal method in exploration for all metals or ores, or for all environments, or for all types of deposits (Guild, 1976).

This brief background is relevant for environmental policies that are focused on the prudent husbandry of finite resources, because it is important to realize the uneven, irregular distribution of geological resources over the surface of the globe and the difficulties of precise assessment of *how much of what is where?* and *how long will it last?*

An examination of environmental aspects of mineral resources in the lithosphere thus should begin with the recognition that there is a wide variation in the concentrations of metals or ores that can or may be exploited either in economic or technological terms. For example, concentrations that are currently economically exploitable range from just over twice to several thousand times the average crustal abundance of the desired element (Table 5–1). Crustal abundance is one thing, but the so-called *cut-off grade* or the lowest concentration economically recoverable is far more important as a threshold assessment. Similarly, the impetus imparted to mineral exploration by the use of satellite sensors (Walton, 1977), or to mining techniques by the development of machinery to recover deep-sea nodules, reflects the continually changing definition of what can practically be recovered in terms of technologies.

A mineral *resource* in these terms, is usually recognized as a concentration of a naturally occurring solid, liquid or gaseous material in or on the earth's crust, in such form and amount that economic extraction of a commodity from the concentration is currently or potentially feasible. A resource exists within the terms of this definition only while it can be used to perform a function better or more cheaply than can another substance. In a longer perspective, minerals belong to that category of natural resources known as *non-renewable*: they may be depleted in practical terms when the residual undeveloped mineral, or the dispersed used material derived from the mineral, are so diluted as to make it unfeasible to concentrate them, either in terms of cost, of energy requirements or of environmental disruption. Long-term mineral resource planning and policy making has to be based on three critical parameters: knowledge of which resources are immediately available; the probability of discovering new deposits; and the development of economically viable extraction processes for currently unworkable deposits. Resources must be reassessed continuously in the light of new geological knowledge, developments in science and technology and changes in the economic and political conditions surrounding access to or availability of resources. It is usual to classify known resources from two points of view:

(a) purely geological or physical and chemical characteristics of the metal or ore in place, such as its grade, quality, tonnage, thickness, or depth (thus providing objective scientific information about the resource);   .

(b) analysis of the cost of extracting, processing and using the material in a particular economy at a particular time (a more variable assessment according to time and place, which reflects the costs of technologies of extraction).

To label a material as a *resource* is insufficient: usually a sub-classification is necessary, such as *identified resources* for those resources whose location, grade, quality and quantity are known or estimated from specific geological evidence. That part of an identified resource that meets specified minimum physical and chemical criteria related to current mining and production practices (including those for grade, quality, thickness and depth) is known as the *reserve base*. It represents the in-place demonstrated (measured and indicated) resource from which reserves are estimated and may include those parts of the resources that have a reasonable potential for becoming economically available within planning horizons beyond those that assume proven technology and current economics. The part of the reserve base that could be economically extracted or produced at the time of the determination is a *reserve,* a key concept in the evaluation of mineral resources in the context of the current availability of specific minerals.

The definition of resources and reserves, as well as their classification, made substantial advances in the 1970s (UN, 1979; USGS, 1980; USBM, 1981). The significance of such work is two-fold: it emphasizes the tentative nature of many resource estimates, and it provides a data base useful in discussions of depletion rates. Table 5–2 shows estimated world resources and the reserve base for selected metals and minerals. Pending establishment of criteria for the reserve base, classification of data is

Table 5–2. Reserves and Resources of Selected Metals and Minerals, 1980.

Metal	World Reserve Base	(unit)	Estimated World Resources
Antimony	4,716,400	(tonnes)	Main identified world resources estimated at 5,079,200 tonnes.
Asbestos	87,800,000	(tonnes)	90 million tonnes of identified resources and hypothetical resources of 45 million tonnes.
Bauxite	22,800,000	(thousand dry tonnes)	World resources (reserves plus sub-economic and undiscovered deposits) estimated at 40–50 billion tonnes.
Cadmium	680,000	(tonnes, metal)	World Resources estimated at about 9 million tonnes.
Chromium	3,355,900	(thousand tonnes)	World resources total about 36 billion tonnes of shipping-grade chromite.
Cobalt	3,083,800	(tonnes, metal)	Identified world resources at about 6 million tonnes; large hypothetical and speculative resources in maganese nodules on the seabed in lateritic iron-nickel deposits.
Copper	493,000,000	(tonnes, metal)	Total land-based resources, including hypothetical and speculative deposits, estimated to contain 1,627 million tonnes of copper. Additional 690 million tonnes estimated in deep-sea nodule resources.
Fluorspar	548,735,000	(tonnes)	Identified world resources approximately 100 million tonnes of contained fluorine. World resources of fluorine from phosphate rock estimated at 400 million tonnes.
Gold	31.4	(million kg of metal)	World resources estimated at 62.2 million kilogrammes, of which 15–20 per cent are by-product resources.
Iron ore	105,000	(million tonnes of usable ore, including by-product ore)	World resources estimated to exceed 800 billion tonnes of crude ore, containing more than 235,820 million tonnes of iron.
Lead	157,000,000	(tonnes, lead)	Total, identified, sub-economic world lead resources estimated at about 1.4 billion tonnes.
Magnesium metal/compounds	2,607,625	(thousand tonnes of magnesite)	Virtually unlimited and globally widespread.
Manganese	4,897,800	(thousand tonnes gross weight)	Identified land-based resources very large but irregularly distributed. Very extensive deep-sea resources in the form of manganese oxide deposits.
Molybdenum	9,843,000	(thousand kilogrammes metal)	Identified world resources of about 21 thousand million kilogrammes.

Table continued

Table 5–2. Reserves and Resources of Selected Metals and Minerals, 1980 — cont'd

Metal	World Reserve Base	(unit)	Estimated World Resources
Nickel	54,238,600	(tonnes, metal)	Identified world resources in deposits averaging I per cent nickel or greater are 143 million tonnes of nickel. Large lower grade deposits and deep-sea resources in manganese nodules.
Phosphate rock	133,000,000	(thousand tonnes)	World resources in the thousand millions of tonnes range.
Platinum-group metals (platinum, palladium, iridium, osmium, rhodium, ruthenium)	36,698	(thousand kilogrammes)	World resources estimated at about 99.5 million kilogrammes.
Potash	9,100,000	(thousand tonnes, K_2O equivalent)	Estimated world resources about 140 billion tonnes.
Silver	253	(million kg metal)	Resources about double reserves.
Tin	10,000,000	(tonnes, metal)	Not available.
Tungsten	2,585,520	(thousand kilogrammes tungsten content)	Not available.
Vanadium	15,785,280	(thousand kilogrammes contained vanadium)	World resources exceed 54 billion kilogrammes.
Zinc	240,000,000	(tonnes, metal)	Identified world resources estimated at about 1.8 billion tonnes.

Source: USBM (1981).

based on a judgemental appraisal of current knowledge and assumptions. The table should be interpreted more as an indication of magnitudes of availability of mineral resources in the short and longterm than as a static *fix* of the mineral situation.

The estimates of reserve base are drawn from government and industrial surveys of potentially exploitable deposits, and are constrained by several factors. Typically, such surveys make detailed examinations of resources for quantities no larger than what may be sold over a reasonable investment period: they are therefore limited by the prevailing investment horizons and expected rates of return. They are generally restricted to surface deposits: very little is known about the volume of deep-lying resources. The degree of detail in survey methods differs among the types of mineral: high-value, low-bulk strategic minerals such as vanadium receive different attention than low-value, high-bulk deposits such as phosphate rock. All judgements of warranted expenditures for exploration are affected by whatever are the prevailing anticipations of accumulated demand for the mineral. Thus, the figures for reserve base and resources bear no direct relation to the physical quantities in the Earth's crust. The estimate of copper reserves, for example, may be no smaller in 1980 than it was in 1950.

It is against this background of the occurrence and nature of mineral resources that the major debates of the decade of the 1970s took place, stemming from concern over the increase in aggregate consumption of the materials derived from mineral and other resources. Three types of argument were put forward in the debate. The first, the "Limits to Growth" type, opine that exhaustion of materials could bring about the demise of industrial society as it is now known (Meadows *et al.,* 1972). The second type of argument postulates that industrial societies are in a transition from a "goods" to a "services" economy and that from this will follow a gradual reduction in the rate of materials consumption. The third argument holds that in the past the threat of scarcity has been overcome and there is little evidence that exhaustion threatens or that a transition to a service-oriented economy is necessary: this argument also places emphasis on more efficient ways of obtaining materials in conventional environments, on identifying new materials and new environments, and on the more efficient use and re-use of materials. Much contention surrounded these arguments, and in this context the world mineral situation in the 1970s was, in many ways, similar to the energy situation. In the short-term, difficulties came to be seen as stemming not so much from exhaustion or absolute depletion of mineral resources, as from a recognition of environmental costs involved in the extraction and use of increasingly larger quantities of these resources as industrial raw materials. Similarly, an awareness was growing of the economic and social problems that accrue with the substitution of one particular type of resource for another, and of the political consequences of the uneven geographical distribution of individual mineral resources, as well as of the possession of the means to find and exploit them.

In an absolute sense, there can be no literal "running out" of mineral raw materials. Rather, human development and use of mineral resources effects a redistribution or dissipation of these materials, not a destruction, although patterns of use of particular minerals may make their re-use unfeasible. The continuing process of extraction of the most concentrated and accessible deposits, which are at the same time the most economical to exploit, implies that future mining and processing will become expensive. As a larger volume of associated materials has to be moved and as the energy intensity per tonne of final product increases, direct and indirect environmental impacts will be heightened. Social pressure for more stringent measures to alleviate these environmental impacts, as well as economic feasibility, will provide a growing incentive to recycle particular materials, and, in other cases, to develop and substitute alternatives.

Production of Minerals

MINERAL production encompasses a range of activities, notably physically extracting the resources from the ground, and processing them into forms more amenable for use as industrial commodities. In treating the global output of minerals in gross terms a useful distinction can be made between metallic and non-metallic raw materials: their extraction, processing and use have different impacts on the environment. Like any general appraisal, this distinction obscures some element of overlap between the two categories: for example, bauxite may be processed into metallic aluminium and chromite as well into non-metallic refractory products.

Non-metallic raw materials have two primary uses, either as construction materials or as industrial raw materials. Construction materials comprise natural rock products, such as raw or crushed stone, sand and gravel, and prepared rock products, including cement, plaster, gypsum, clays, silica or asbestos. Industrial raw materials, in turn, can be sub-divided into fertilizer minerals and minerals for chemical and other industrial uses. The most important minerals for use in fertilizer production, as discussed in Chapter 7, are potassium salts and phosphate rock; here, also, the importance of nitrogen as an input to the fertilizer industry should be noted. Among minerals for chemical and other industrial uses are rock salt, sulphur, sodium salts, fluorite, barite and abrasives (such as garnet or diamonds). Selected production data for non-metallic mineral raw materials for the decade 1970–1980 are given in Table 5–3.

Stone, sand and gravel, and raw materials for cement making are most important in terms of volume. These materials are quarried or extracted as closely as possible to the point of consumption, in view of their widespread availability and low value. They are rarely transported over long distances and data on global production are difficult to obtain. Various estimates (Skinner, 1969; Ehrlich, et al., 1977; USBM, 1981) point to a global production of stone of all types of 8 billion tonnes in 1970 compared with 10 billion tonnes in 1980. Comparable figures for sand and gravel are 7 and 8.5 billion tonnes in 1970 and 1980 respectively.

Metallic mineral raw materials have a wide variety of uses and their environmental impacts are consequently much more diverse, particularly at the processing stages of production. Not only must the ores be mined, but the constituent minerals must be separated out and individual metals recovered by smelting or other processes. Table 5–4 shows world mine production of selected major metals and minerals for 1970–1979. Table 5–5 indicates the major producers of selected minerals and metals in 1979, in terms of their percentage share of world production.

Table 5–3. Production of Selected Non-Metallic Mineral Raw Materials, 1970–1980

Material (Unit)	1970	1978/1979	1980[a]
Abrasive (tonnes)	168017	158406	160000
Asbestos (10^3 tonnes)	3797	5278[b]	5057
Barite (10^3 tonnes)	3995	6703[b]	7347
Cement (10^3 tonnes)	568910	829608	920000
Clay building bricks (10^6 units)	91680	100043	110000
Clay roofing tiles (10^6 units)	2966	2820	2850
Clay floor and wall tiles (10^3 square metres)	377252	456281	475000
Diamond, industrial (million carats)	28.7	29.0[b]	30.0
Fluorspar (10^3 tonnes)	4200	4789[b]	4716
Garnet (tonnes)	19008	29858[b]	38548
Gypsum (10^3 tonnes)	51579	74332 [b]	66937
Natural phosphates (10^3 tonnes)	81514	125027	130000
Nitrogen, fixed/ammonia (10^3 tonnes ammonia)	38785	70020[b]	73830
Potash (10^3 tonnes K_2O equivalent)	20013	26345[b]	27505
Slate (10^3 tonnes)	25850	42273	46000
Stone (10^6 tonnes)	3452	7056	7256
Sulphur (10^3 tonnes sulphur)	22162	54834[b]	55000

Sources: Metallgesellschaft (1979); UN (1980); USBM (1975, 1981); World Bureau of Metal
         Statistics (Annual Reports).

[a] Estimate
[b] 1979.

Environmental Impacts of Mineral Production

MINERAL extraction and processing has a wide range of environmental impacts which
can be divided into four main categories: impacts on land, impacts on atmosphere,
impacts on water and impacts on the socio-economic environment of people.

Table 5–4. World Production of Selected Minerals and Metals. 1970–1979 (thousands of tonnes).

	1970	1971	1972	1973	1974	1975	1976	1977	1978	1979
Aluminium	10 260.6	10 945.1	11 647.6	12 727.8	16 817.5	12 335.5	13 202.1	14 327.1	14 745.4	15 221.6
Antimony [c]	67.3	64.8	73.5	73.4	72.2	71.9	69.1	69.1	62.1	63.6
Bauxite	60 631.7	66 660.3	69 212.6	75 365.4	84 252.3	77 280.4	80 662.0	84 601.1	83 954.2	88 017.1
Beryllium conc. (beryl)	6.2	5.3	3.9	3.6	3.2	3.3	2.8	2.4	1.9 [e]	2.4 [e]
Bismuth [b]	3.8	3.8	4.0	3.7	4.8	4.0	3.9	4.0	3.9	4.1
Cadmium	16.4	15.1	16.8	17.5	17.3	15.7	17.3	18.7	17.6	19.0
Chromite	6 053.0	6 434.7	6 100.8	6 695.9	7 478.8	8 229.1	8 611.0	9 801.2	9 579.0	9 600.0 [e]
Cobalt [b]	24.2	25.1	24.8	29.4	30.7	29.4	26.0	29.6	30.8	25.0 [e]
Niobium and Tantalium [ab]	20.4	10.8	15.0	24.4	24.0	15.1	9.8	10.7	11.3	10.7 [e]
Copper [c]	6 350.2	6 448.6	7 047.7	7 501.9	7 665.1	7 345.2	7 856.2	7 982.8	7 873.2	7 935.5
Gold	1.6	1.4	1.4	1.3	1.2	1.2	1.2	1.2	1.2	1.2
Iron (iron ore)	766 593.5	787 110.6	777 750.1	845 702.1	895 388.0	894 493.8	895 000.0	853 500.0	822 000.0	881 000.0
Lead [c]	3 485.4	3 503.1	3 576.6	3 638.0	3 620.7	3 622.0	3 519.0	3 664.3	3 636.2	3 621.8
Magnesium	219.8	232.0	233.6	241.7	248.4	245.2	246.5	255.0	...	...
Manganese ore	18 204.0	21 089.0	20 817.7	21 745.5	22 453.6	24 562.6	24 759.2	22 044.6	21 100.0 [e]	21 800.0
Mercury	9.8	10.4	9.6	9.2	8.9	8.7	7.1	5.8	5.5	5.6
Molybdenum [bc]	82.3	77.6	79.3	81.7	84.2	80.2	86.8	93.4	98.2	104.0
Nickel [c]	666.0	681.9	625.9	682.5	749.7	752.6	769.0	782.2	638.8	698.2
Platinum [d]	131.8	127.0	131.2	160.9	179.0	177.4	186.4	199.0	205.0 [e]	210.0 [e]
Tin [c]	216.6	222.7	231.5	220.5	219.0	219.8	216.8	225.0	233.7	239.1
Titanium-ilmenite [a]	2 820.6	2 581.7	2 415.6	2 706.2	3 192.1	2 919.3	3 185.6	3 690.0 [e]	4 035.0 [e]	3 860.0 [e]
Rutile	416.8	384.5	318.8	349.5	360.8	378.1	427.3	390.0 [e]	425.0 [e]	480.0 [e]
Tungsten [b]	33.8	35.4	38.5	37.9	37.6	38.2	41.7	42.5	47.1	48.4
Vanadium [a]	18.1	18.6	18.4	19.6	18.8	21.0	23.5	29.0	29.4	40.0 [e]
Zinc [c]	5 696.9	5 690.1	5 836.3	6 110.1	6 129.0	6 163.4	6 246.3	6 609.1	6 442.4	6 336.0

Source: Metallgesellschaft (1979); UN (1980); USBM (1981); World Bureau of Metal Statistics (Annual Reports).

[a] Market economies only.
[b] Incomplete total, represents countries for which data available.
[c] Content of ores and concentrates.
[d] Platinum group metals (tonnes).
[e] Estimate.

Table 5–5. Major Mineral Producers in 1979

Mineral/Metal	Share of World Production (in per cent)
Bauxite	Australia (31), Guinea (14), Jamaica (13), USSR (7), Surinam (5), Guyana (4).
Chromite	S. Africa (33), USSR (22), Albania (9), Turkey (7), Zimbabwe (6), Philippines (6).
Cobalt	Zaire (41), New Caledonia (13), Australia (11), Zambia (8), USSR (6), Cuba (5).
Copper	USA (18), USSR (14), Chile (13), Canada (8), Zambia (7), Peru (5).
Gold	S. Africa (55), USSR (25), Canada (4), USA (3).
Iron Ore	USSR (28), Australia (11), Brazil (10), USA (9), China (7), Canada (6).
Lead	USSR (15), USA (14), Australia (11), Canada (9), Peru (5), Mexico (4).
Manganese ore	USSR (41), S. Africa (20), Gabon (9), India (7), Australia (6), China (5).
Molybdenum	USA (63), Chile (12), Canada (11), USSR (10), China (2), Peru (1).
Nickel	USSR (22), Canada (19), New Caledonia (12), Australia (11), Indonesia (5), Cuba (5).
Silver	USSR (14), Mexico (14), Peru (12), Canada (11), USA (11), Australia (8).
Tin	Malaysia (27), Thailand (14), Indonesia (12), Bolivia (12), USSR (8), China (7).
Tungsten	China (28), USSR (19), Bolivia (7), USA (6), Republic of Korea (6), Australia (5).
Zinc	Canada (19), USSR (16), Australia (8), Peru (8), USA (5).

Source: Metallgesellschaft (1979); Mining Journal (1980); USBM (1981).

Direct effects of mining on the landscape, such as surface disturbance, and generation and disposal of wastes tend to be roughly proportional to the quantity of minerals extracted. The extent of the earth's surface disturbed by worldwide mining operations has not been measured accurately. In 1974 the annual movement of soil and rock in the extraction process was believed to be of the order of 2,000 to 3,000 billion tonnes for the world as a whole (Kolesnikov, 1974). The total volume was expected to increase as the proportion of usable ore decreases in many areas and as ore mines deepen and the open pits are extended. An augmentation by a factor of 4 to 6 was considered likely (Lomtadze, 1977). The area of land disturbed by mining of non-metallic and metallic ore minerals was estimated at about 386,000 hectares (ha) per year in 1976, growing to about 924,000 ha per year by 2000 (CEQ, 1980). The land area that will be directly disturbed during the 1976–2000 period is approximately 24 million ha, or 0.2 per cent of the earth's total land surface.

Mining directly disturbs land in a number of ways. According to United States experience over the 1930–71 period, 59 per cent of such land was utilized for excavation and 38 per cent for disposal of mine and mill waste; the remaining 3 per cent either subsided or was otherwise disturbed by underground workings (Paone et al., 1974).

With increase in world production of non-metallic and metallic ore minerals, the question of land use and land rehabilitation becomes increasingly important. The same is true as far as the utilization of more and more lower grade ores is concerned. On the one hand this means that more and more amounts of materials have to be moved and extracted for one unit of metal, and on the other hand there is the problem of waste disposal. Thus not only more land will be disturbed due to the mining activities as such, but increasingly higher amounts of residuals have to be disposed of, much in the form of solid wastes. For example, in 1973 for a US mine production of 290 million tonnes of copper ore, about 680 million tonnes of waste material was moved and discarded. The 245 million tonnes of copper ore milled the same year produced about 5.5 million tonnes of concentrates, leaving some 240 million tonnes of tailings. And the production of 1.6 million tonnes of blister copper at the smelting stage was accompanied by an estimated 2.7 million tonnes of solid waste in the form of slag (USBM, 1976a). These amounts of wastes will markedly increase in the future. It was estimated that for stone, clays, iron ore, phosphate rock and copper, the amount of solid wastes generated in mining and milling will increase from about 12,000 million tonnes per year in 1976 to about 28,000 million tonnes per year by 2000 (CEQ, 1980). Several countries are making use of these wastes. In the Philippines, for example, where mines discharge about 130,000 tonnes of waste daily, experiments are underway to use some of these wastes for cement, ceramics and construction (Miller, 1977).

Reclamation of disturbed land is an important factor in reducing the environmental damage caused by mining wastes. It is believed that about 40–60 per cent of lands disturbed by mining are either in the course of natural restoration or are being reclaimed (Motorina and Ovchinnikow, 1975). During the 1970s numerous steps were taken by governments in developed countries to require reclamation, including revegetation, and the ratio between disturbed and reclaimed lands came closer to a balance. Not more than one-third of the reclaimed lands are used for agriculture and up to one-half of them in the USSR were used for forest cultivation (Zaytzev et al., 1977). During the 1970s greater attention was paid to techniques for the replacement and reclamation of land moved in surface mining (Goodman and Chadwick, 1978; Bugrov and Lutai, 1980; Bradshaw and Chadwick, 1980). However, if surface mining is extended more and more to areas with fragile ecosystems such as the Arctic or permanent frost regions where balances, once altered, are difficult to restore, the rehabilitation of land after mining becomes a particularly severe problem. Progress in rehabilitation will be expensive and slow especially in areas where the soil cover is thin, micro-organisms are delicately balanced, the overburden is high in acidity or salinity and rainfall is sparse (OECD, 1979).

Air pollution generated from mining and processing activities produces serious environmental and health problems. Air pollutants of particular concern are dust, sulphur oxides, nitrogen oxides, hydrogen sulphide and trace metals. Although most of the gaseous effluents are caused by the combustion of fossil fuels used in the mining and processing operations, substantial amounts (for example, of sulphur oxides) go up the stacks of smelters of sulphide-bearing ores. In 1974 U.S. copper smelters emitted about 7,400 tonnes of sulphur oxides daily, about 10 per cent of the nation's total. The copper-nickel smelters of the Sudbury district of Ontario, Canada, emit 2.4 million tonnes of sulphur oxides annually, causing losses of timber with a value of $117,000 per year (CEQ, 1980). Such sulphur oxides contribute more widely to the problems of acid rain (Chapter 2) and to the incidence of respiratory diseases.

Surface and underground water is frequently polluted by effluents of mining and milling operations and by rainfall or stream action on solid mine and mill wastes. Acid mine drainage (produced by reaction of water and air with sulphur-bearing minerals in ore deposits and dumps) discharged into rivers, lakes and streams has detrimentally affected aquatic biota in many regions. The dumping of salt wastes from potash mines in the German Democratic Republic and France has contaminated the Werra River and the Rhine, respectively (CEQ, 1980). In the Philippines, it was reported that the discharge of about 100,000 tonnes of mine tailings per day in the major river systems in the country affected about 130,000 ha of agricultural land. Other examples could be cited from other countries and the trend now is to enforce environmental protection measures to reduce these and other impacts of mining and processing operations. The pressures in some countries for pollution control led to the abandonment of smaller, economically marginal operations and to the concentration of operations in a few larger sites.

Selected Trends and Issues in Mineral Resources in the 1970s

THE following section reviews some of the more pertinent elements of the debate that took place in the 1970s against the background of these global trends. The aspects of the world mineral economy examined below are not an exhaustive treatment of the subject, but are designed to illustrate particular trends that have a bearing on environmental questions.

SEA–BED MINERAL RESOURCES

The potential contribution of sea-bed mineral resources to future production of copper, nickel, cobalt and manganese, and the technological and economic feasibility of the recovery of manganese nodules from the ocean floor, attracted widespread attention in the 1970s (see, for example, Marjoram *et al.*, 1981). Important progress was made during the decade in the study of the distribution and composition of such nodules, particularly in the Pacific Ocean. Ocean mining is still in the stage of research and development, while the political and institutional problems involved are under discussion in such forums as the United Nations Conference on the Law of the Sea. From available data, which are limited by virtue of the proprietary nature of company information and the relatively short history of exploitation, several estimates of mineral resources in nodules have been made. They differ widely because of the paucity of data and differences in the assumptions used. Gluschke et al., (1979) tabulated two estimates made in the 1970s of first-generation mine sites and the metal content of their resources, together with corresponding land-based reserves (Table 5–6). First-generation mine sites are recognized to be areas in which nodules can be exploited with technology now under development, given prevailing economic and legal conditions. If pilot development projects are successful and the outstanding legal problems of an ocean regime can be

Table 5–6. Recent Estimates of First Generation Mine Sites.

	United States Ocean Mining Administration[a]		Archer[b]		Land-based reserves[c]
	Global estimator[d]	Prime-area estimator[e]	Global estimator[d]	Prime-area estimator[e]	
Number of mine sites	185	80	106	44	
Wet-nodule content (billion tonnes)	99	42	57	24	
Dry-nodule content (billion tonnes)	69	29	40	17	
Recoverable metal contents[f] (million tonnes)					
Nickel	190	80	110	47	54
Copper	173	73	100	43	451
Cobalt	39	16	23	10	2.5
Manganese	3,881	1,631	2,250	956	1,800

Source: Gluschke et al. (1979)

[a] Hosler (1976).

[b] Archer (1975).

[c] Based on data by USBM (1977); copper data from UN Centre for Natural Resources, Energy and Transport.

[d] Global estimator: In this approach, the limited data on grade and concentration are considered representative of the whole ocean floor. The data are first weighed on the basis of the relative areas of the various oceans; then the total number of mine sites is determined.

[e] Prime area estimator: A prime area is an area within the sea-floor wherein the occurrences are known or suspected on the basis of geological evidence and theory. In this approach, the more detailed understanding of a specific prime area (for example, the Clarion Clipperton Zone in the Pacific Ocean) is held to be characteristic of other high potential areas. The total number of mine sites are then determined. For both this and the global estimator method, grade and concentration are assumed to be independent on an ocean-wide basis.

[f] Based on a mining recovery of 25 per cent and a 90 per cent processing recovery of nodules containing 1.2 per cent nickel, 1.1 per cent copper, 0.25 per cent cobalt and 25 per cent manganese for ocean resources.

resolved, ocean-floor mining of nodules could begin in the 1980s. For cobalt, nickel and manganese supplies the impact of such mining could be considerable, although in the case of copper the potential contribution of ocean-based resources is felt to be minimal (Table 5–7).

Table 5–7. Potential Contribution of Ocean Mining to World Supply in the Mid-1980s.

	Nickel	Manganese	Cobalt	Copper
	← ————————————(thousands of tonnes)———————————— →			
At 5 million-tonne/y level	75	1,150	10	65
At 10 million-tonne/y level	150	2,300	20	130
Estimated world consumption, 1985 Primary mineral consumption[a] Total consumption[b]	970 1,220	13,400 16,400	38 70	11,500 14,900
Share of world market, Assuming 5 million-tonne/y level (percentage)	7.8 6.1	8.6 7.0	26.3 14.3	0.6 0.4
Share of world market, Assuming 10 million-tonne/y level (percentage)	15.5 12.3	17.2 14.0	52.6 28.6	1.1 0.9

Source: Gluschke et al. (1979).

[a]USBM (1976 b).

[b]UN (1974).

Several problems are inhibiting the exploitation of sea-bed minerals, for example, the application of pioneer and experimental technologies of recovery, serious roadblocks to the agreement of a legal regime and the corollary distribution of benefits, and the introduction of measures to protect against losses by land-based producers. These problems have a direct bearing on the speed with which sea-bed minerals will be developed, as well as impacts on total mineral supply and prices. Not only are there commercial possibilities for manganese nodules from the ocean-floor, but consideration has been given to extraction of sand and gravel, metal sulphides, phosphorite, heavy mineral sands and shells from the outer continental shelf (NAS, 1975 a). From the environmental point of view, however, sea-bed mining represents a new frontier of concern over the impacts of mining activity on marine ecosystems (see also Chapter 3). The environmental impact assessments currently used in conjunction with offshore oil and gas production facilities, and the collection of data on marine ecosystems point to an appreciation of the risks to the environment from undersea technologies. It will be necessary not only to assess impacts such as waste disposal in the oceans but also those associated with land-based processing of these mineral resources.

RECYCLING, SUBSTITUTION AND LOW–GRADE ORES

The potential for recycling and substitution of mineral raw materials received attention in the 1970s, particularly among those who paint a picture of imminent exhaustion of the global resource base. As Landsberg pointed out, however, their role may have been overstated: "Recycling and substitution are the two magic terms that suggest more immediate escapes from scarcity and are on everybody's agenda of remedies" (Smith, 1972; Landsberg, 1976; Page, 1976). Neither recycling nor substitution are new phenomena. Recycling can take the form of re-using mineral materials that have been processed into products and subsequently discarded, or recapturing materials used in processing. The concept of the *minerals cycle* or *materials - energy balance* has spurred a new interest in recycling in its examination of possible constraints on growth posed by shortages of materials or environmental dysfunctions. Briefly, materials cycles require a systems dynamics approach encompassing the gamut of activities involved in the materials system, notably the resources from which materials are created, the processing and transformation of materials, materials use, and the discharges and wastes that accrue with these activities. In other words, resources flow through successive stages of transformation into raw materials and processed materials (primary commodities) and subsequently into industrial and consumer products. Recycling of materials can occur at many points in a resource/material flow, as indeed can environmental dysfunctions. The use of scrap iron in the iron and steel industry and the recovery and re-use of lead from batteries are obvious examples of recycling at the end-use stage of what otherwise would be waste materials. Figure 5–2 shows the extent of recycling of selected scrap metal in the United Kingdom and the United States in 1978 and 1974 respectively. From a comparison with Table 5–4 it will be seen that the amounts recycled in those two countries were in some instances equivalent to a substantial portion of world production of the mineral in that year.

In effect, secondary resource recovery is a form of recycling at the processing stage of resource materials flows, by recovering valuable mineral constituents in metallurgical wastes. An excellent example is offered by the bauxite/aluminium industry. Large amounts of waste dross containing aluminium are generated in the processing of bauxite into alumina and subsequently aluminium, part of which is recovered by a secondary process which, in turn, results in large quantities of salt slag. This slag contains fluxing salts, aluminium metal and aluminium oxide and formerly was put into dumps, thereby causing water pollution problems from the salts in the fluxes. A hydrometallurgical process was introduced, capable of recovering the salt flux and a high proportion of the residual metal for recycling to dross treatment furnaces: in addition the oxide was recycled as a source of alumina in the cement industry. Yet another technique has been developed whereby inert gases replace salt fluxes to avoid oxidation of the aluminium metal during its recovery from dross, thereby curbing toxic pollutant emissions from the fluxes. Another example of process recycling is in the acid and alkaline plating industries, which produce wastes containing copper, nickel, cadmium or chromium: by mixing acid and alkaline wastes under controlled conditions, not only are metals precipitated out for recovery but the resulting filtrates are rendered less potent in terms of their disposal and possible environmental impact as pollutants.

Figure 5–2. Scrap metals recycled; USA data for 1974 and UK data for 1978.

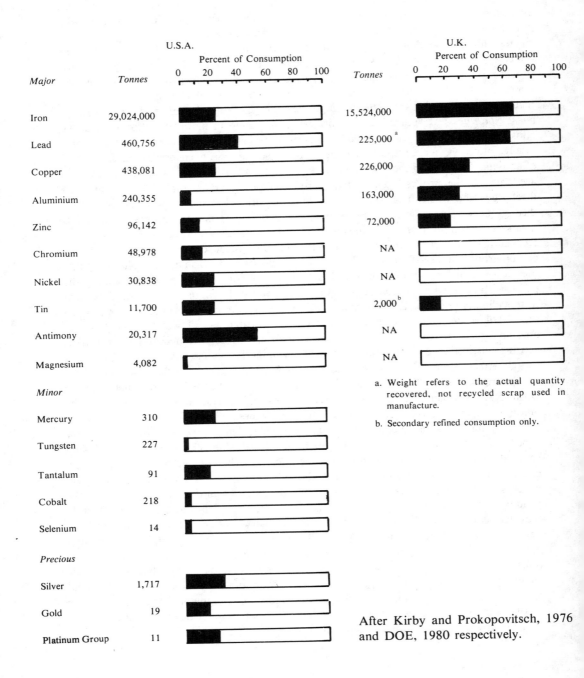

U.S.A.
Percent of Consumption

U.K.
Percent of Consumption

Major	Tonnes		Tonnes
Iron	29,024,000		15,524,000
Lead	460,756		225,000 [a]
Copper	438,081		226,000
Aluminium	240,355		163,000
Zinc	96,142		72,000
Chromium	48,978		NA
Nickel	30,838		NA
Tin	11,700		2,000 [b]
Antimony	20,317		NA
Magnesium	4,082		NA

Minor

Mercury	310
Tungsten	227
Tantalum	91
Cobalt	218
Selenium	14

Precious

Silver	1,717
Gold	19
Platinum Group	11

a. Weight refers to the actual quantity recovered, not recycled scrap used in manufacture.

b. Secondary refined consumption only.

After Kirby and Prokopovitsch, 1976 and DOE, 1980 respectively.

An important consideration in recycling is that the energy input required to re-melt scrap back into production processes is substantially less than that needed in the first place to smelt, reduce or refine ores. For example, in the case of aluminium, the energy requirement for recycled material is some 3–4 per cent of that required to concentrate the metal in usable form from ore: the comparable figures for magnesium and titanium are 1.5 per cent and 30 per cent respectively.

Another way in which new supplies of a particular mineral may be augmented is by substitution. This can take several forms. In some cases, a renewable material can be substituted for one that is non-renewable: more often, abundant materials are substituted for scarcer ones in the composition of industrial outputs. Substitution can also occur in terms of the design of end products or of the processes of production themselves, away from products or processes that are resource — or energy – intensive towards those that are more conservative in mineral resource use.

In one sense the use of lower grade ores is a substitution, not between grades of resources or between different resources, but one in which larger energy inputs substitute for lower ore grades in order to concentrate dispersed material: while this may have been a feasible option in the late 1960s and early 1970s, trends in energy prices have worked against it in the mid-1970s. Higher energy prices dissipated the notion that more abundant minerals such as magnesium or aluminium would necessarily encroach on less abundant ones. For example, although aluminium products have obvious advantages of weight in vehicle manufacture, higher energy costs must now be balanced against these advantages. In reality substitution is an extremely complex set of options, which insofar as mineral resources are concerned demands that all aspects of the economic, technical and socio-political costs of a particular mix of resource use, processing techniques and end-products have to be weighed together. The depletion of mineral resources *per se* need not result in catastrophic problems, with one proviso — that an inexhaustible non-polluting source of energy becomes available, so that low-grade, widely available materials can be substituted for the present higher-grade mineral base of society. Thus, consideration of particular substitutions between particular minerals as raw materials, whether in terms of one mineral being substituted for another ore containing the same metal (e.g. alunite or nepheline instead of bauxite in the aluminium industry), or in terms of the composition of end-products, must be viewed in a wider perspective.

INTENSITY OF THE USE OF MINERAL MATERIALS

A related aspect of the role of mineral materials in a modern economy is the intensity with which they are used, which also has a bearing on their future availability, for it indicates the rate at which reserves are being used. The intensity of materials use shows the relative significance of the different inputs required at a particular time. Table 5–8 shows the per capita use of new materials in the United States in 1972, as an example.

Table 5–8. Use Intensity of Mineral Materials in the U.S.A. in 1972 (kg/capita)

Material	Amount
Sand and gravel	4,091
Stone	3,864
Cement	364
Clays	273
Total non-metallic minerals	8,592
Iron and steel	545
Aluminium	23
Copper	11
Lead	7
Zinc	7
Other metals	16
Total metals	609

Source: Radcliffe (1976).

FUTURE SUPPLIES: "LIFETIMES" OF MINERAL RESOURCES

Economic growth carries with it growth in the physical requirement for material inputs: based on knowledge of current mineral reserves and on the current intensity of materials use in a particular economy, the decade of the 1970s has seen considerable attention devoted to assessment of future mineral supplies. Numerous estimates have been made of the anticipated "lifetimes" of resources of various metals and other commodities: the number and sophistication of such estimates increased during the decade, particularly in conjunction with examinations of the future of the world economy and the spectre of depletion of materials in that economy. Figures indicating such probable mineral lifetimes are useful in planning future strategies or policies to avoid shortages, but they must be considered with great caution: their estimation depends on many assumptions regarding population, demand and supply, future economic growth and technological change, for example, that are themselves subject to wide differences. Resources estimates contain margins of error that dwarf current annual production of individual minerals. Some of the factors to be kept in mind when looking at "lifetime" data for a mineral are:

(a) new deposits are still being discovered;

(b) new processes of extraction and transformation of ores render economic deposits that were held to be uneconomic in the past;

(c) recycling and/or substitution may lower requirements for primary raw materials;

(d) little agreement can be expected regarding the lowest grade of ores (in terms of metal content) that will be mineable in the future;

(e) the impact of the availability of investment capital for the mineral industry on the evaluation of reserves cannot be overstressed;

(f) little is known of mineral resources at depth in the lithosphere;

(g) subjective factors enter into estimates, especially of potential resources, as was demonstrated by Cloud (1977) in a comparison of world figures by Erickson (1973) and the United States Bureau of Mines (USBM, 1976): Erickson's figures for potential resources are 615 times higher than the Bureau of Mines' figures for aluminium, 28.5 times for nickel, 91 times for vanadium, and 13.9 times for zinc, to select extreme differences.

For these and other reasons, all lifetime estimates will remain extrapolations of tenuous reliability. Moreover, in such estimates a distinction is often made between static lifetimes (assuming constant production) and semi-dynamic lifetimes (assuming annual growth rates). To the extent that production of some ores continues to grow, static lifetimes are too high.

The "lifetimes" shown in Table 5–9 are rather low, all but one being less than a century. This creates an initial impression that there may be shortages of some mineral raw materials in the coming decades, if they have not already begun during the 1970s, but for the reasons given above such a presumption is subject to many qualifications. Political considerations may further lower the amounts mined in particular countries at particular times; this may be critical for those metal ores for which there are only a few major producers world-wide.

Table 5–9. Estimated "Lifetimes" for Selected Metal Resources (years)

Metal	Known Reserves (1)	BGR Semidynamic (2)	USBM Estimate (3)	BGR Semidynamic (4)	BGR Static (5)
Aluminium	53	53	63	66	146
Copper	30	34	61	49	58
Lead	29	31	45	50	49
Zinc	18	22	28	32	31
Nickel	42	47	56	73	92
Tin	34	32	82	52	46

Source: Column 1 is from Cloud (1977). Column 2 is a semidynamic estimate of measured and probable reserves by Bundesanstalt für Geowissenschaften und Rohstoffe (BGR). Column 3 is a US Bureau of Mines estimate of potential reserves, from Cloud (1977). Column 4 is a BGR semi-dynamic estimate of measured, probable and potential reserves, and Column 5 the BGR static estimate of measured and probable reserves.

The close agreement between columns 1 and 2 and columns 3 and 4 respectively of Table 5–9 stems from the fact that similar primary sources have been used. Furthermore, columns 1, 2 and 5 refer only to known (identified) resources. There are certainly more to be found, so columns 3 and 4 can be taken as better estimates.

On the other hand, regarding potential (undiscovered, inferred, hypothetical) resources, especially of poorer ores than are currently mined, columns 3 and 4 are rather conservative estimates, so the actual "lifetimes" — at least for most resources — will be longer.

MINERALS IN INTERNATIONAL RELATIONS

Recent trends and issues in mineral resources cannot be assessed without recognition of the importance of minerals in international relations. In the 1970s two aspects of mineral questions were at the forefront of international debate — strategic access to assured supplies by individual countries and the part played by minerals in the North–South dialogue between industrial and developing countries.

The general global trends covered in the preceding sections of this chapter obscure the situation in any individual country at any particular time. Minerals are an integral part of international diplomacy. Each country tries to assure access to external supplies of minerals in those cases where it has neither reserves of its own nor domestic production capacity. Strategic minerals, therefore, are those where the political and economic conditions of availability constrain a particular country's reliance on external sources of particular resource raw materials (NAS, 1975 b). In one sense they are a measure of a country's vulnerability to external political pressures of supply and demand. Table 5–10 shows the United States reliance on such imports of strategic materials for 1980, as an illustration of the link between reliance on imports of particular minerals and particular end-use applications.

The strategic aspects of mineral supplies has been subsumed however, in a wider debate on a new international economic order, the North–South dialogue. Included in this debate have been many of the issues outlined above — renewed concern over depletion, analysis of comprehensive materials cycles rather than of separate mineral/material sectors, problems and prospects for recycling and substitution, investigation of long-term relationships between economic growth and the impact of energy and environmental costs. Minerals, and indeed primary commodities as a whole, tend to be subject to frequent and/or severe fluctuations in supply, demand and price. This situation can be seriously disruptive for producer countries that have economies that are dependent on export of minerals: witness Zambia and its copper resources, which because of a fall in prices in the mid-1970s underwent a severe economic crisis.

Table 5–10. Imports of Strategic Materials, United States, 1980.

Material	Imports as a percentage of apparent consumption	Major sources of imports 1976–1979	Users
Antimony	53%	China, Mexico, Bolivia	Batteries, solders, flame-proofing.
Bauxite	94%	Jamaica, Guinea, Surinam	Packaging, construction, transportation vehicles.
Cadmium	62%	Canada, Australia, Mexico	Electroplating, electrodes.
Chromium	91%	South Africa, Philippines, USSR	Stainless steel.
Cobalt	93%	Zaire, Belgium, Luxembourg, Zambia	Jet engines.
Columbium	100%	Brazil, Canada, Thailand	Alloy steels, cutting tools.
Manganese	97%	Gabon, Brazil, Australia, South Africa, France.	Steel and iron making.
Platinum group metals	87%	South Africa, USSR, United Kingdom	Coatings, catalytic converters.
Tantalite	97%	Thailand, Canada, Australia	Electronics.
Titanium	100%	Australia, India	Titanium sponge products, welding-rod coatings.
Tungsten	54%	Canada, Bolivia, South Korea	Machine tools, alloys

Source: USBM (1981).

Not only is the mineral industry affected, but employment, foreign exchange earnings and development plans can be seriously impaired. Table 5–11 indicates price trends in the decade of the 1970s for selected metals and minerals. Prices converted to constant comparative units were not available. Perhaps the most striking aspect of these trends was their wide fluctuations, a characteristic of the world mineral industry. These price trends have accentuated the debate over access to, development of and the revenues to be obtained from mineral resources, between producers and consumer countries. The key elements under discussion are the investment requirements of the world minerals industry, terms of trade in mineral commodities, the creation of buffer stocks to alleviate the worst effects of the cyclical behaviour of mineral commodity markets, an integrated programme for commodities, export compensation schemes, the channelling of resources into mining ventures and the changing role of transnational corporations vis-a-vis host countries (Brandt Commission, 1980). Environmental policy-making and strategies have to take into account those aspects of the role of minerals in international relations, and in particular their role in the economic development of developing countries, if environmental concerns are to be an integral part of the process of economic development (Sunkel and Fligo, 1980).

Table 5–11. Price Trends for Selected Metals and Minerals, 1970–1980.

Year	Aluminium[a] (cents/lb)	Copper (cents/lb) LME[b]	Copper NY[c]	Lead (cents/lb) LME[d]	Lead NY[c]	Zinc (cents/lb) LME[d]	Zinc NY[c]	Tin (cents/lb) LME[f]	Iron ore[g] (US$/tonne)	Manganese ore[h] (US$/tonne)	Tungsten[i] (US$/short tonne unit WO₃)	Nickel[j] (US$/lb)	Phosphate rock[k] (US$/tonne)
1970	27.9	64.2	57.7	13.8	15.7	13.4	15.3	166.7	11.9	52.7	70.4	1.28	11.8
1971	28.4	49.1	15.4	11.5	13.9	14.0	16.1	158.9	11.5	64.1	49.6	1.33	11.8
1972	26.8	48.6	50.6	13.7	15.4	17.1	17.7	170.8	11.2	61.5	35.4	1.40	11.8
1973	27.2	80.8	58.9	19.5	16.3	38.3	20.8	218.3	15.5	76.3	40.3	1.53	13.8
1974	34.7	93.4	76.7	26.9	22.5	56.3	36.0	371.5	17.2	115.9	80.1	1.74	52.5
1975	39.4	56.0	63.5	18.9	21.5	33.8	38.9	311.6	21.4	139.1	83.3	2.03	68.0
1976	40.4	63.6	68.8	20.3	23.1	32.3	37.5	344.0	20.2	142.1	104.2	2.20	48.5
1977	49.4	59.3	65.8	28.0	30.7	26.7	34.4	489.6	18.9	147.5	170.7	2.30	39.5
1978	60.1	61.9	65.5	30.0	33.7	26.9	31.0	609.0	19.8	141.1	143.8	2.08	35.4
1979	70.3	90.0	92.3	54.6	52.6	33.6	37.3	700.7	24.0	135.0	138.8	2.49	36.4
1980	85.1	100.7	103.3	42.3	42.7	34.3	37.0	776.1	29.1	161.9	145.2	3.41	52.0

Source: Annual averages (1970–1976) for all but nickel are from *Monthly Commodity Price Bulletin, Special Supplement 1960–1976* (March 1977). Other averages for all but nickel are from *Monthly Commodity Price Bulletin* (August 1978 and November 1980). Average for nickel are from *Metals Week*. As compiled in United Nations Committee on Natural Resources; Mineral Resources, Report of the Secretary-General, E/C.7/115, April 1981.

[a] Canadian, delivered United Kingdom;
[b] London Metal Exchange, wire bars, cash;
[c] New York, domestic producer's price;
[d] London Metal Exchange, cash settlement;
[e] United States Prime Western, delivered;
[f] Spot cash;
[g] Canada, Lake Jeannine, concentrates, 65 per cent Fe, c.i.f. North Sea ports (from 1978: Mount Wright concentrates, 64 per cent Fe, c.i.f. North Sea ports);
[h] Mn content, c.i.f. United Kingdom (London);
[i] Wolfram, c.i.f. European ports, basis 65 per cent WO₃;
[j] Major producer, cathode;
[k] Khouribga, 75–77 per cent TPL, f.a.s. Casablanca;
[l] In most cases, average of first 10 months.

Geological Hazards

MOST geological processes, including the formation of mineral bodies, are extremely slow, and even major tectonic movements are measured in the order of centimetres per year. Few of these processes provide changes readily detectable in a decade. From time to time, however, they generate extreme natural events such as earthquakes, volcanic eruptions, and tsunamis (tidal waves), which have an obvious impact. These, with landslides and snow avalanches, constitute the hazards discussed in this section. Such events emphasize the natural variability in environmental systems, remind human communities of the great power of natural forces, and test the abilities of people and nations to respond to them.

As with droughts and heat waves (Chapter 2), and floods (Chapter 4), the social effects of these shifts in the Earth's crust during the 1970s were a product of several factors. Scientific ability to predict the events improved substantially, but their number and magnitude were not strikingly different from previous decades. Human measures reduced vulnerability to losses of life and property in some areas, and increased vulnerability in other areas.

PREDICTION

If the time and magnitude of a rare event like an earthquake can be forecast, it becomes more likely that deaths and injuries and, to a lesser extent, property damage and social disruption can be reduced. Two successes in scientific prediction during the decade held out prospect that the accuracy and reliability of a foundation for such warnings might be improved.

The first successful prediction of a major earthquake was made in the Haicheng area of the People's Republic of China in 1975. Based upon analysis of an array of geophysical and biological precursors, a large urban population was evacuated five and a half hours before the occurrence of heavy shocks of magnitude 7.3 on the Richter scale. Great injury and loss of life was thereby avoided (UNDRO, 1978). Many investigators then believed that the goal of accurate prediction was attainable, although some were pessimistic (Press, 1975). Greater attention was given to designing warning systems to assure effective response to future predictions (UNESCO, 1979). But by the end of the decade the sanguine expectations had not been realized (Kerr, 1978). Notwithstanding large research efforts in Japan, the People's Republic of China, the United States and the USSR, the goal seemed more distant, and a number of massive earthquakes had taken place without warning.

In 1980 a cautious set of predictions based upon earlier studies (Crandall and Mullineaux, 1978) gave warning of the eruption of Mt St Helens in the United States. This reduced the toll of lives taken by the blast, and demonstrated the possibility of forecasting future violent eruptions.

Research on landslide and snow avalanche prediction and the development of associated warning systems continued in Central Europe and North America, and were extended on an experimental basis to high altitude areas in developing countries.

PRINCIPAL EVENTS AND THEIR CONSEQUENCES

There are two common measures of an extreme geophysical event: intensity, which describes its effects, and magnitude, which is stated in terms of the energy released. During the 1970s there were four great earthquakes with magnitudes over 8.0 on the Richter scale, and 136 major earthquakes exceeding Richter 7.0. Their location is shown in Figure 5–3, from which their association with tectonic plate boundaries is evident. Table 5–12 sets out the volume of seismic energy released and shows that the decade experienced somewhat less than the average number of great and major earthquakes, and less than average energy releases (Lomnitz, 1974; von Gehlen, 1980) but was well within the range of variation encountered in the earlier part of the twentieth century.

Table 5–12. Seismic Energies Released Worldwide and Earthquake Deaths During the Years 1970–1980 Compared with Previous Years.

1970–80	Earthquake		Seismic energy (M = 7.0 and more) × 10^{21} ergs	Total seismic energy (× 1.1) × 10^{21} ergs	People killed
	Great	Major			
Total	4	136	5,765.4	6,340	434,667
Average	0.4	12.4	524	576	39,515
For comparison:					
Long-time average	1	18			~10,000
Mean annual value 1904–1952[a]				2,429.3	
Maximum yearly total (in 1906)				12,090.1	
Minimum yearly total (in 1930)				215.1	

Source: von Gehlen (1980).
[a]Lomnitz (1974).

The two earthquakes of greatest magnitude, in West New Guinea in 1971 and the Kermadec Islands in 1976, caused relatively little loss to human life. But the Tangshang earthquake of 27 July 1976 was a catastrophe with an intensity reached only a few times in recorded history. It was estimated to have killed 242,000 people and injured a comparable number, although some estimates put the figures much higher. Previous larger death tolls were in China in 1556 (estimated at 830,000) and in Calcutta, India, in 1737 with 300,000 dead. Overall, there was some evidence in the 1970s suggesting that the human consequences from an event of given magnitude were tending to increase.

Property damage was difficult to calculate because of the inadequacy of much of the data (they were entirely missing for some earthquakes) and because of the difficulty of tracing out the secondary and indirect effects upon household and national economies. No comparative data are available on the environmental consequences, including earthslides, diversion of streams, impairment of dam safety and the like. Rough estimates place the direct property losses for the decade in the neighbourhood of US$6 billion. The annual average was believed to be several times larger than that prevailing in 1926–1950 (Bolt *et al.,* 1975).

Some notion of the dimensions of human suffering generated by these events is conveyed by a description of the effects of the Guatemala earthquake of February, 1976: "More than 3.4 million people out of a total of 5 million (64 per cent) were affected by the earthquake. More than one million persons were left homeless, and more than 222,000 dwelling units were partially or totally destroyed. Of the 1.2 million people left homeless, 350,000 were in the country's largest urban area, Guatemala City. The remainder were largely rural populations living in small towns and villages scattered throughout the earthquake zone. The largest damage impact was on housing" (UNDRO, 1978).

The record for the other geologic hazards is less dramatic but shows a toll of continuing severity. Volcanic eruptions that caused the death of more than nine people each, occurred in six places (Table 5–13). There were at least thirty-six landslides that

Table 5–13. Volcanic Eruptions That Caused More Than 9 Deaths During the Decade 1970–1979.

Date	Volcano	Country	People killed
1971 Sept. 14	V. de Fuego,	Guatemala	10
1971 Dec. 29	Villarrica,	Chile	15
1976 Dec. 23	Nyarangago	Zaire Repub.	38
1979 Feb. 20	V. Sinila, Java,	Indonesia	148[a]
1979 Apr. 29	V. Merapi, Sumatra	Indonesia	80[b]
1980 May 18	Mt St Helens	USA	64[c]

Source: von Gehlen (1980 and personal communication).

[a]killed by poisonous gas.
[b]flooding of 7 villages.
[c]30 known dead, 34 missing.

Figure 5–3. Major Destructive Earthquakes 1970–1979

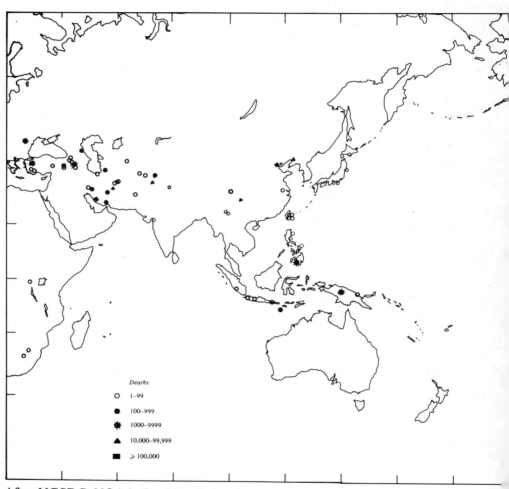

After NGSDC–NOAA, Boulder, Colorado.

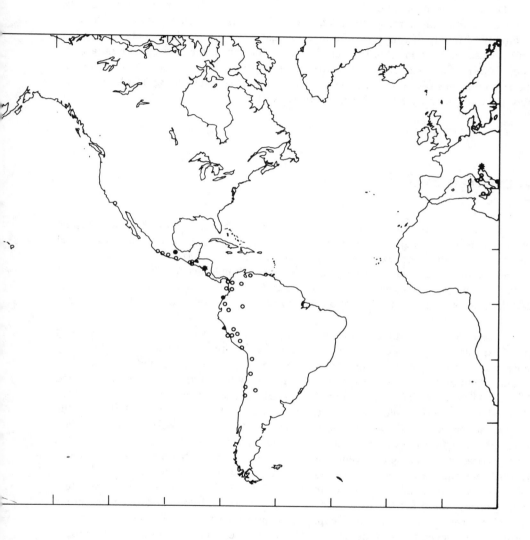

caused more than nine deaths each (von Gehlen, 1980). One of these, resulting from a slide into a lake in Peru, accounted for at least 18,000 deaths. Snow avalanches bringing more than nine deaths each, occurred in at least twelve areas, chiefly in the European Alps (von Gehlen, 1980).

Data on the economic and social consequences of these events are even less satisfactory than those for earthquakes. The full effects of such events as reflected in instability of family life, mental suffering, political strain and environmental disruption, defy precise calculation. One measure is the proportion of the average annual growth rate of GNP that is reduced by the extreme geophysical event: it was estimated that in the five countries of the Central American Common Market during 1960–1974, this may have dropped by about 2.3 per cent (UNDRO, 1979).

VULNERABILITY AND MITIGATION

The apparent trends in some areas toward greater material losses and catastrophic mortality from the recurrence of events of the same magnitude were ascribed to several causes. Population growth encouraged occupation of hazardous areas. Urban concentrations placed larger groups at risk from a single event. The complexities of social organization associated with commercial farming and industrialization made people more susceptible to disruption of services than in folk cultures (Burton, et al., 1978).

Countering those influences were a variety of measures to mitigate possible losses from exposure to geologic hazards. During the 1970s the degree of international co-operation in providing emergency assistance and supporting the rebuilding of disaster-struck communities was enlarged through the activities of the Office of the United Nations Disaster Relief Co-ordinator (UNDRO). As a result there was a better chance that aid to sufferers would appear in the right form at the right time and place as the decade advanced. This was especially important for earthquake victims for whose survival or welfare the aid given in the first few hours may be crucial. Measures to prevent disastrous geological events took shape more slowly. No advances were made towards earthquake or volcanic eruption control, although some success was gained in curbing lava flows, as at Heimay, Iceland, in 1973. In a few areas soil moisture management was practised to reduce vulnerability to landslides and a few mountain tourist enterprises improved their capacity to prevent snow avalanches. Perhaps the most solid achievement was the halting of ground-water pumping in metropolitan areas such as Osaka and New York where depletion has caused land subsidence.

On a wide front efforts were made to reduce the social costs of geologic hazards by mitigating their effects. These measures included plans to deal with the emergency, changes in building design and construction and modification in land use to avoid locating investments in uneconomic sites. The development of earthquake preparedness plans was detailed and highly sophisticated in the Tokyo and Los Angeles metropolitan areas. Both Japan and the United States adopted integrated programmes to mitigate seismic hazards. Many other countries, particularly developing ones, continued to be ill-prepared.

Awareness of the practicability of and need for designing and constructing buildings to withstand earth movement was reflected in the adoption of new building codes. Examples were codes for new dam and highway construction in numerous cities and other places where previous disasters had occurred, such as Skopje, Yugoslavia. Such regulations did not, of course, affect the utility lifelines or older buildings and roads which remained highly vulnerable.

Of greater significance in the long run, as in the case of floods (Chapter 4), were plans incorporated in human settlements policies that located new residential, commercial, and industrial developments away from sites considered especially hazardous due to ground conditions or elevation. These efforts, including microzonation and establishment of seismic safety zones and avoidance of swelling soils, began to find acceptance in Japanese and North American cities. They were adopted only slowly elsewhere except where rapid urban expansion was underway, as in Asiatic coasts subject to tsunami inundation.

In these and other ways the trends toward increased damages and catastrophic events were being partly offset. In the developing countries, however, the overall situation was still deteriorating, the most vigorous efforts being concentrated in the more developed nations of the group.

References

Archer, A. A. (1975), The Prospects for the Exploitation of Manganese Nodules, Paper presented at the CCOP/SOPAC — IOC/IDOE Intern. Workshop on Geology, Mineral Resources and Geophysics of South Pacific, Suva, Fiji, September, 1975.

Bolt, B. A. *et al.* (1975), *Geological Hazards,* Springer Verlag, Berlin.

Bradshaw, A. D. and M. J. Chadwick (1980), *The Restoration of Land,* Blackwell Scient. Publ., Oxford.

Brandt Commission (1980), *North–South; A Programme for Survival,* MIT Press, Cambridge, Massachusetts.

Bugrov, V. I. and T. M. Lutai (1980), Combination of Mining and Recultivation Works in Quarries of Non-Metallic Building Materials, Collected Works of VNII of Non-Metallic Building Materials, N.48, Moscow.

Burton, I. *et al.* (1978), *The Environment as Hazard,* Oxford Univ. Press, New York.

CEQ (1980), *The Global* 2000 *Report to the President,* Council on Environmental Quality, Washington, D.C.

Cloud, P. (1977), Entropy, Materials and Posterity, *Geol. Rundschau,* 66, 678.

Cook, E. (1976), Limits to Exploitation of Non-renewable Resources, *Science,* 191, 677.

Crandall, D. R. and D. R. Mullineaux (1978), *Potential Hazards from Future Eruptions of Mount St Helens Volcano,* US Geological Survey Bull. 1383–C, Washington, D.C.

DOE (1980), *Digest of Environmental Pollution and Water Statistics,* UK Department of the Environment, HMSO, London.

Ehrlich, P. R. *et al.* (1977), *Population, Resources and Environment,* Freeman, San Francisco.

Erickson, R. L. (1973), Crustal Abundances of Elements and Mineral Reserves and Resources, Prof. Paper 820. U.S. Geological Survey, Washington, D.C.

Gluschke, W. *et al.* (1979), *Copper; The Next Fifteen Years,* Natural Resources Forum Library, D. Reidel Publ. Co., Dordrecht.

Goodman, G. T. and M. J. Chadwick, Editors (1978), *Environmental Management of Mineral Wastes,* Sijthoff and Noordhoff, Alphen aan den Rijn, The Netherlands.

Guild, Ph. W. (1976), Discovery of Natural Resources, *Science,* 191, 709.

Hosler, A. F. (1976), *Manganese Nodule Resources and Mine Site Availability,* US Ocean Mining Administration, Washington, D.C.

Kerr, R. A. (1978), Earthquakes; Prediction Proving Elusive, *Science,* 200, 419.

Kirby, R. C. and A. S. Prokopovitsch (1976), Technological Insurance Against Shortages in Minerals and Metals, *Science,* 191, 718.

Kokesnikov, B. P. (1974), Recultivation of Technogenic Landscapes, In *Man and His Surroundings,* Leningrad.

Landsberg, H. (1976), Materials; Some Recent Trends and Issues, *Science,* 191, 637.

Lomnitz, C. (1974), *Developments in Geotectonics*, 5, Global Tectonics and Earthquake Risk, Elsevier Publ. Co., Amsterdam.

Lomtadze, V. D. (1977), *Engineering Geology*, Leningrad.

Marjoram, T. *et al.* (1981), Manganese Nodules and Marine Technology, *Resources Policy*, March 1981, 45.

Mason, B. (1966), *Principles of Geochemistry*, John Wiley, New York.

Meadows, D. H. *et al.* (1972), *The Limits to Growth*, Universe, New York.

Metallgesellschaft, A. G. (1979), *Metallstatistik*, 1968–1978, Metallgesellschaft, Frankfurt A. M.

Miller, A. (1977), Philippines Seeking to Recycle, Reduce Waste in Mining Operations, World Environment Rept. Oct. 24.

Motorina, L. V. and V. A. Ovchinnikow (1975), *Industry and Land Recultivation*, Moscow.

NAS (1975a), *Mining in the Outer Continental Shelf and in the Deep Ocean*, National Academy of Sciences, Washington, D.C.

NAS (1975b), *National Materials Policy*, National Academy of Sciences, Washington, D.C.

OECD (1979), *Interfutures; Final Report of the Research Project in the Future Development of Advanced Industrial Societies in Harmony with that of Developing Countries*, Organization for Economic Co-operation and Development, Paris.

Page, T. (1976), *Economic Basis for Materials Policy*, John Hopkins, Baltimore.

Paone, J. *et al.* (1974), *Land Utilization and Reclamation in the Mining Industry*, 1930–71, US Bureau of Mines, Inf. Circular 8642, Washington, D.C.

Press, F. (1975), Earthquake Prediction. *Scientific Amer.*, 232, 14.

Press, F. and R. Siever (1974), *Earth*, W. H. Freeman and Co., San Francisco.

Radcliffe, S. V. (1976), World Changes and Chances; Some New Perspectives for Materials, *Science*, 191, 700.

Rona, P. A. (1976), Plate Tectonics and Mineral Exploration, *Natural Resources Forum*, 1, 17.

Skinner, B. J. (1969), *Earth Resources*, Prentice-Hall, Englewood Cliffs, N. J.

Skiro, B. (1969), *Earth Resources*, Prentice-Hall, Englewood Cliffs, N. J.

Smith, F. A. (1972), Waste Material Recovery and Re-use. In R. Ridker (Editor), *Population, Resources and the Environment*, Vol. 3 of Research Reports of the Commission on Population Growth and the American Future, US Government Printing Office, Washington, D.C.

Sunkel, O. and N. Fligo, Editors (1980), *Estilos de Desarrollo Y Medio Ambiente en la America Latina*, Fond. Cultura Economica, Mexico City.

UN (1974), *Economic Implications of Sea-Bed Mineral Development in the International Area*, Third Conf. on Law of the Sea, A/Conf. 62/25. United Nations, New York.

UN (1979), The *International Classification of Mineral Resources. Committee on Natural Resources*, E/C.7/104, United Nations, New York.

UN (1980), *Yearbook of Industrial Statistics* 1978 Edition, *Vol.* 2., United Nations, New York.

UNDRO (1978), *Disaster Prevention and Mitigation, Vol.* 3., *Seismological Aspects*, Office of the United Nations Disaster Relief Co-ordinator, Geneva.

UNDRO (1979), *Disaster Prevention and Mitigation, Vol. 7., Economic Aspects*, Office of the United Nations Disaster Relief Co-ordinator, Geneva.

UNESCO (1979), *International Symposium on Prediction of Earthquakes*, UNESCO, Paris.

USBM (1975), *Mineral Facts and Problems*, US Bureau of Mines, Washington, D.C.

USBM (1976 a), *Commodity Data Summaries*, US Bureau of Mines, Washington, D.C.

USBM (1976 b), *Mineral Facts and Problems*, US Bureau of Mines, Washington, D.C.

USBM (1977), *Commodity Data Summaries*, 1977, US Bureau of Mines, Washington, D.C.

USBM (1981), *Mineral Commodity Summaries*, US Bureau of Mines, Washington, D.C.

USGS (1980), *U.S. Geological Survey, Circular No.* 831, Washington, D.C.

von Gehlen, K. (1980), *Lithosphere*, Report Prepared for the United Nations Environment Programme, Nairobi.

Walton, K. (1977), Satellite Remote Sensing of Natural Resources. *Natural Resources Forum*, 1, 215.

Wilson, T. J. Editor (1972), *Continents Adrift*, W. H. Freeman and Co., San Francisco.

Zaytzev, G. A. *et al.* (1977), *Forest Recultivation*, Moscow.

CHAPTER 6

Terrestrial Biota

Over the centuries, mankind has increasingly modified the assemblages of plants and animals (biomes) found in different regions of the continents, and changed the distribution of species and the nature of the ecological interactions between them. This chapter reviews the latest stage in this modification, describes the present state of the major biomes, and notes some of the risks involved in transforming them for agriculture and silviculture. Many of these changes have been an essential component of development, but as a consequence, natural vegetation has disappeared from great stretches of the continents—especially those that, like Europe, are densely populated and highly developed.

Where development has been hampered by poverty or driven by great urgency, the fertility of the land and stability of the soil have been placed in jeopardy. Whole species or populations of plants and animals have disappeared, causing a loss of genetic resources that is not only regrettable from an aesthetic or philosophical point of view but also threatens man's food supply.

The need to secure development while at the same time sustaining the productivity of natural renewable resources and protecting wildlife and genetic diversity was the focus of a major publication at the end of the decade: the World Conservation Strategy, prepared by IUCN in partnership with UNEP and WWF. In a sense, the Strategy can be looked upon as the culmination of more than a century of conservation efforts from around the world.

One of the chief subjects of public concern during the decade was the rate at which the tropical rainforests were being changed – often with considerable loss of fertility. Exact figures of the extent of this destruction were not available by the decade's end, and estimates varied from 7 to 20 million hectares a year; a recent study indicates an average of 11 million hectares a year for tropical forests. Transformation of the rainforests was occurring everywhere they are found, proceeding much further in Africa than in Asia and Latin America.

In tropical deciduous forests, savannahs, grasslands, steppes and areas with Mediterranean climate, another problem was paramount: desertification. This process claimed vast areas in many parts of the world during the decade.

The regions containing temperate evergreen forests and broadleaf deciduous forests – which in North America and Europe include some of the most densely populated and highly industrialized regions of the world – were generally well-managed and remained fertile, although areas with natural and semi-natural plant and animal life are very restricted. Further north the boreal coniferous forest zone was much less affected by man, although it is an important timber source. During the decade fears were expressed that acid precipitation could retard tree growth over wide areas. The sensitivity of coniferous trees to air pollution was well known from laboratory experiments and observations in areas near smelters. But by the end of the decade there was still uncertainty about the extent of such damage in nature.

Although great areas of the Arctic tundra – an ecosystem that provides valuable grazing ground for nomadic tribes – are wilderness, parts of it were threatened and in some cases severely damaged by the search for oil and gas during the decade. Local disturbance and damage have been caused in the Antarctic by visiting tourists and scientists.

210

Islands, mountains and wetlands, ecosystems of special sensitivity and richness of animal and plant life, had their own special problems. The introduction of continental species to islands has in some cases completely transformed the vegetation. Phosphate mining also made a marked impact, as did mass tourism, particularly in the Caribbean. Erosion in mountain areas was accelerated by deforestation, overgrazing, inappropriate cultivation, fire, road building and other factors. Dams and reservoirs sometimes led to flooding in wetland areas, and in other cases to changes due to a lack of water supply. Draining of wetlands was another problem while coastal wetlands were being drastically reduced by agriculture and reclamation for buildings, docks and industrial development.

On the positive side, the decade saw a number of international conventions, that fulfilled recommendations of the Stockholm Conference, go into effect. International conferences were held on desertification and forestry, the number and area of nature reserves increased world-wide, and germplasm banks were established for crop plants and livestock.

Prior to about 40,000 BC humans were probably confined to the "great world island" of Africa and Eurasia, together with Australia and parts of the Indonesian archipelago. Migration into the Americas began about that time, across a land link on the site of the present Bering Strait. The crossing of wider ocean passages to remote islands took place last of all.

Over the centuries, the impact of man on terrestrial biota — the natural living resources of the continents — changed not only as a result of this progressive spread, but also as man's tools and technologies advanced and his needs escalated.

This chapter deals with these natural living resources: the populations of wild plants and animals, the major systems they form (biomes) and their interactions with the non-living factors, conditions and materials of the environment. It concentrates on the changes that have been brought about by recent human impacts. As a result of these changes natural ecosystems and genetic diversity have been reduced in many areas. But many of these recent changes are nonetheless compatible with conservation, in the sense of the management of natural resources for sustained yield. The risks and benefits involved in the transformation of terrestrial ecosystems for agriculture and forestry are discussed.

Changing Impact of Man

IMPACT OF HUNTER–GATHERERS

HISTORICALLY, hunter-gatherers have not made major impacts on the environment because they crop natural populations of animals and plants below sustainable yields. However, the introduction of modern weapons to some groups, especially those who trap animals for trade, has altered this balance, and has sometimes led to serious depletion of the animal populations on which the hunters depend. Over the centuries the numbers of hunter-gatherers have declined. But hunter-gatherer economies still survive in a few areas of the world.

IMPACT OF FIRE

Humans have been using fire for at least 50,000 years. It is still employed to help man hunt wild animals, clear forests, and obtain fuel from charcoal. It continues to be used by shifting agriculturalists to produce, extend or maintain grasslands (UNESCO, 1979). In India's Dekkan, the equilibrium of the good grazing lands is maintained by annual fires, while in Patagonia, South America, and in Otago in New Zealand's South Island, tussock grasslands have increased at the expense of the original *Nothofagus* forests as a result of combined fires and grazing. The frequency of fires helps determine the composition of the forests in part of Tasmania: if they occur only once every 200 years *Nothofagus* species will dominate; if more frequently (10—200 years), *Eucalyptus* will dominate. Fires occurring at less than ten-year intervals lead to disappearance of the forest and eventually to open moors. Repeated fires combined with overgrazing can seriously degrade the environment: this has happened over wide areas of Africa and in the garigue of the Mediterranean sclerophyllous zone. Accelerated run-off and soil erosion sometimes follow fires, depending on local topography, rainfall intensity and other factors.

It is often said, rightly, that fire is a good servant but a bad master. There has been a major change in the last century in the public recognition of the usefulness of fire (Holdgate and White, 1977). Thus while the spectacularly adverse effects of fire have been frequently emphasized in the past, it is becoming clear that controlled burning can be a valuable tool in land management, including the conservation of biological diversity in nature reserves and parks.

IMPACTS OF GRAZING

In pastoral communities, human and animal populations need to be in balance with the carrying capacity of the grazing land. In some arid and semi-arid territories they adjust to changes in the productivity of land by adopting a nomadic way of life, and if nomadism is suppressed the system may break down.

In recent years, improved animal husbandry, water supply and veterinary medicine, and greater demand for animal products have resulted in large increases in populations of livestock in extensive regions of Africa, Asia and Latin America. In the Sahel, herd sizes increased considerably in a series of favourable years in the later 1950s and early 1960s. With the advent of severe drought in the late 1960s and early 1970s, the pasture ecosystems could no longer support the increased animal populations. Great numbers congregated at the wells and proceeded to eat and trample the vegetation for hundreds of square kilometres around (Warren and Maizels, 1977).

Environmental degradation arising from overgrazing has been widespread in arid and semi-arid regions of the Near East, Central Asia, the Sudano – Sahelian belt and the Mediterranean basin for many years. In Nefta in Southern Tunisia, in an area enclosed by a fence for sixty years, vegetation cover was 85 per cent; a comparable area outside the fence had only 5 per cent plant cover (SMIC, 1971). In northern Uganda, overgrazing converted a large woodland rich in flora to a site that now contains thorn-scrub with desert grasses (Jackson, 1977). One consequence of overgrazing is desertification — a process of reduction or elimination of the productive capacity of land that leads ultimately to desert-like formations. About 95 per cent of the land in the arid and semi-arid regions of the world are subject to this process, and even sub-humid areas are susceptible (UNCOD, 1977).

Poor reindeer herding practices can seriously affect the tundra vegetation. For example, on the tundra pastures of the north-eastern European USSR, lichen cover was drastically reduced between 1910 and 1920 due to overgrazing. To correct the situation, a three-year pasture rotation was introduced in some regions of the USSR, with the aim of accommodating by 1980 as many as three million reindeer on a tundra area of about three million square kilometres (km^2) of the northern USSR.

IMPACT OF FOREST CLEARANCE

Forests represent the natural climax vegetation of at least six billion hectares (ha) of the world, and several billion ha more could naturally support woody vegetation. It was estimated that by the mid-twentieth century mankind has reduced the world's original forested area by at least 33 per cent and possibly by as much as 50 per cent (Sommer, 1976; Myers, 1979). Today, closed forests are said to cover some 2.7 billion ha, while a further 1.3 billion ha support some woody vegetation. Forests that once extended over about 33 per cent of Morocco, Algeria and Tunisia had been reduced to about 10 per cent of the total land area by the mid-twentieth century; and by that time also forest cover in China was down to about 8 per cent of the area. Central and western Europe were heavily wooded in prehistoric times, but clearance for agricultural purposes proceeded steadily from Neolithic times onward. In North America the Plains Indians deliberately burned forests to expand the range of the buffalo. Colonization of the New World by white settlers in the sixteenth century, often accompanied by excessive herds of cattle, sheep and goats, accelerated the process of forest destruction over much of the Americas. The expansion of mining and metal working caused much forest alteration in Medieval Europe, and more recently in the New World.

On the steep slopes of the Himalayas, the Andes and East Africa, tree felling and forest clearance — sometimes to altitudes of 2,000 metres — has caused erosion, silting, flood damage and landslides. Forest cover may have been reduced by as much as one million km^2 (Persson, 1977). In Africa, south of the Sahara, shifting cultivation has led to a reduction of original tropical forest by probably more then 100 million ha. In addition to clearance for agriculture, the forests are extensively cut for construction and fuelwood, which is still the dominant source of energy for cooking in most of the developing world (Chapter 12). About 70–80 per cent of the roundwood cut in tropical forests is for charcoal and firewood. LANDSAT observations and FAO–UNEP statistics suggest that reforestation and regrowth are in many areas compensating substantially for such losses (FAO, 1980).

Man has converted extensive tracts of forests to savannah parklands, grasslands and agricultural lands. Along the Transamazon Highway and its associated road system in Brazil, a 20-km-wide belt of forestland, totalling some 360,000 km^2 has been designated for agricultural development. In Central and South America huge tracts of tropical forest have been burned to provide pasturelands. Since 1950 the area of pasturelands and the number of cattle in Central America have more than doubled (Parsons, 1976), and this expansion has been almost entirely at the expense of natural forests. In Amazonia, in the decade from 1966 to 1975, 44,000 km^2 (38 per cent of total deforestation) was accounted for by cattle ranching, and 35,000 km^2 (31 per cent) through smallholder settlement and other agricultural colonization. It is expected that between 1962 and 1985 at least 325,000 km^2 of Latin America's tropical forests will have been cleared for pasturelands.

EFFECTS OF PLANT AND ANIMAL BREEDING AND OF INTRODUCTIONS INTO NEW AREAS

The species of plant and animal that dominate continental ecosystems are not adapted for dispersion across wide oceanic barriers, and this is one reason for the differing floras and faunas of different regions and the unique biotas of many islands. Man, however, has modified this situation and introduced many species to areas outside their natural range, and has selected and bred new strains suited to local conditions. Some tree species have been introduced with beneficial effects: for example, *Pinus radiata* in New Zealand and elsewhere, *Populus deltoides* in Europe, the Near East, Latin America and Far East, *Azadirachta indica* in Africa, *Tectona grandis* in all tropical regions, and *Casvarina* and *Eucalyptus* species in Egypt and Africa. Similarly, staple crops such as potatoes and maize, fruits such as mangoes, vegetables such as tomatoes, and legumes such as soy beans have brought variety and nutritional value to the diets of millions of people in whose countries they were originally unknown. Animal introduction included cows, sheep, horses and zebu cattle. A major development was the introduction of high-yielding varieties of rice, wheat and maize produced by the Green Revolution. These and other increases in productivity are noted in Chapter 7.

Unfortunately many introductions have been made without adequate forethought and in the absence of essential ecological data on the probable impact on native biota. The pheasant *Phasianus colchicus* was introduced to North America from Eurasia without serious side effects. But the house sparrow *Passer domesticus*, introduced in 1950, soon became a serious crop pest in every state (Elton, 1958).

The construction of the Welland Ship Canal between Lake Ontario and Lake Erie allowed the sea Lamprey *Petromyzon marinus* to reach the inner Great Lakes, and by the 1920s it was undergoing a population explosion. The effects were serious and within a decade catches of lake trout (one of several freshwater fish attacked by lamprey) in Lakes Huron and Michigan had declined by well over 90 per cent. However, during the 1970s Coho Salmon, introduced during the previous decades, spread rapidly and became the basis for an important sport fishery in the Great Lakes. In Australia introduction of the European carp *Cyprinus carpio*, which has spread at an unprecedented rate since the 1960s, now seriously threatens the environment of native and introduced sport species in inland waters, mainly because it causes water turbidity which affects the productivity of aquatic plants. The best-known case in Australia of an introduced species is the rabbit *Oryctolagus cuniculus*, which has caused extensive damage to the native fauna and flora on the mainland, and economic loss of major proportions through competition with domestic stock.

During the 1970s, elms (*Ulmus* spp) were virtually eliminated from southern Britain and other parts of north-western Europe as a result of an insect-borne fungal disease, "Dutch Elm disease". It was suspected that the outbreak was triggered by the importation of a more virulent strain of the fungus in timber from North America, where elms had been severely attacked in earlier decades.

There are parallel examples among plants and plant disease. The water hyacinth *Eichhornia crassipes*, the water fern *Salvinia auriculata* and water lettuce *Pistia stratiotes* are examples of inadvertent introductions that are dealt with in Chapter 4. *Leucaena leucocephala* was introduced to the island of Hawaii in the early 1950s, and has now become a serious weed. Similarly *Lantana camara* was introduced to south east Asia, and has now become a pest.

LOSS OF GENETIC RESOURCES

Species extinction is a natural component of the evolutionary process, but some of mankind's activities accelerate it and drain the plant and animal gene pool. The maintenance of genetic diversity is essential for plant and animal breeding programmes.

During the 1970s concern was expressed over the survival of thousands of species of plants and animals. Hunting or collecting animals for food, sport or profit has taken its toll on a number of species, and so too has plant collection for aesthetic or other purposes.

Between three million and ten million species are now believed to exist, but only 1.5 million have been described. According to the *Red Data Books* issued by the International Union for Conservation of Nature and Natural Resources (IUCN), 1,000 species of birds and mammals are currently threatened with elimination. IUCN estimates that 10 per cent of the species of flowering plants are also threatened with elimination or are dangerously rare. The number of entire species threatened with extinction is relatively small; however, the number of provenances (sub-populations) of important or potentially important species threatened with severe genetic depletion or even with extinction is large. The endangered provenances are often found at the limits of the range of a species and it is often these marginal or isolated populations that have developed, through natural selection, specific characteristics such as tolerance to drought or other adverse environmental conditions, that are of great potential value for similar sites.

Destruction of habitats is one of the major reasons for loss of species. This may occur as farmers and villagers gather firewood, or as timber companies destroy forests. It also occurs when grazing practices, ploughing and dam and road building devastate wild habitats. Water and air pollution by toxic chemicals from industrial effluents and pesticides entering inland or coastal waters may also be significant.

CONSERVATION

Conservation embraces measures to protect and to enhance the productivity of the biosphere. Measures affecting agricultural productivity are reviewed in Chapter 7. In the sense of a deliberate government policy to safeguard the living resources of the biosphere and their habitats, conservation is a concern of the past 100–150 years. It has grown steadily in strength and popular support during recent decades, notably during the 1970s. In March 1980 the conservation movement of the 1970s may be said to have reached a peak with the launching of the *World Conservation Strategy,* prepared by IUCN in cooperation with UNEP and the World Wildlife Fund (WWF). As Sir Peter Scott (1980) described it: it was the first time that governments, non-governmental organizations and experts throughout the world had been involved in preparing a global conservation document; it was the first time that it had been clearly shown how conservation of natural diversity can contribute to the development objectives of government, industry, commerce, organized labour and the professions; and it was the first time that development had been suggested as a major means of achieving conservation instead of being viewed as an obstruction to it.

The *World Conservation Strategy* takes into consideration the human impacts outlined earlier and the perils that may threaten the future of the world's life-support systems. It defines three global objectives of living resource conservation:

(a) to maintain essential ecological processes and life support systems;

(b) to preserve genetic diversity;

(c) to ensure the sustainable utilization of species and ecosystems.

The safeguarding of soil, the enhancement of biological productivity by irrigation and drainage and the improvement of plant cultivars and domestic livestock by breeding programmes are all elements in this wider conservation activity.

The Biomes of the World

DEFINITIONS

THE present distribution of species of plants and animals on land is the product of a long history of migration and evolution, influenced by climate and the movement of continents (Darlington, 1957; Good, 1974), and by large-scale human manipulation. As a result the biota of areas with similar climates in different continents are sometimes quite distinct from one another. Biogeographers classify the regions of the world into "realms" or "provinces" on the basis of floristic and faunistic relationships. There is broad agreement about the larger divisions. But we are here primarily concerned with the biotic (plant and animal) formations as they grow and interact and as they influence, and are influenced by, other components of the natural environment and human activities.

There are several systems of classification that take account of communities of species and habitat conditions and provide a framework into which both natural and transformed biotic systems fit. UNESCO (1973) published a system for the classification and mapping of vegetation on a world basis comprising a "comprehensive framework for the more important categories to be used in vegetation maps". This system, based on physiognomy and the structure of vegetation, recognises five formation classes (closed forest, woodland, scrub, dwarf-scrub and related communities, herbaceous vegetation), each including subdivisions. Udvardy (1975), under the combined auspices of UNESCO and IUCN, formulated a classification of the biogeographical provinces of the world in which he recognized eight biogeographic realms (Palaearctic, Nearctic, Africotropical, Indomalayan, Oceanian, Australian, Antarctic, Neotropical) subdivided into 193 biogeographic provinces. Within this phytogeographic frame Udvardy recognizes fourteen biomes. Walter (1979) presented a "classification of the geobiosphere into zonobiomes". This system is used in this chapter. The zonal vegetation types of the zonobiomes are:

      I.   Evergreen tropical rain forest.

     II.   Tropical deciduous forests or savannahs.

    III.   Subtropical desert vegetation.

    IV.   Sclerophyllous woody plants.

     V.   Temperate evergreen forests.

    VI.   Nemoral broadleaf-deciduous forests.

   VII.   Steppe to desert with cold winters.

  VIII.   Boreal coniferous forest (taiga).

    IX.   Tundra vegetation (treeless).

Transitional and intermediate types are known as zonoecotones. To these nine broad zonobiomes, we may add three extrazonal biomes: islands, wetlands and mountains.

Zonobiomes and Their Changes During the Decade

EVERGREEN TROPICAL RAIN FOREST (ZB I)

THREE extensive areas of evergreen tropical rain forest exist in the Amazon river basin, the Congo river basin and the Malay archipelago. Smaller forests are found in Central America, along the coast of the Gulf of Guinea in West Africa, and in humid areas of India, Ceylon and Australia. These luxuriant forests of tall trees are the most complex ecosystems on earth. The quantity of plant biomass is large. Rodin *et al.* (1975) give figures of 600–650 tonnes/ha — the highest for all ecosystems quoted by them. There is relatively little animal biomass, 0.2 tonnes/ha having been calculated for one Amazonian rain forest. The apparently lush, uniform growth of these forests masks a richness in species, variability in composition, fragility and great differences in soil. Some soils are fertile, but the majority are poor, most of the nutrient in the system being held in the trees and other forest organisms, and recycled actively within the ecosystem.

Over the decade 1970–1980 concern increased about the rate at which the tropical rain forest was being altered or destroyed. Exact figures are difficult to obtain: attempts were made by Sommer (1976), UNESCO (1978), Lanly and Clement (1979) and Myers (1979, 1980). These efforts illustrate three problems underlying current attempts to estimate changes in zonobiomes, and those problems are noted here before presenting the estimates for tropical forests or for subsequent zonobiomes.

First, the definitions of "forest" vary and comparisons may be misleading. Thus, some surveys distinguish between "open", "closed" and "woodlands and brush" while others group these categories. Myers defines tropical moist forest as "evergreen or partly evergreen forests, in areas receiving not less than 100mm of precipitation in any month for two out of three years, with mean temperature of 24+ °C and essentially frost free" (Myers, 1980) but includes coniferous and deciduous types with pronounced dry seasons in calculating the total forest area of Thailand. Lanly and Clement make their computations for all closed forests in tropical areas. And over time a change in definition makes it difficult to specify rate of change: in Thailand, again, the remote sensing imagery for 1972 included both productive and non-productive forestlands while 1978 imagery measured only productive forests judged suitable for timber exploitation.

Second, the coverage by surveys is so far incomplete and in many countries is based on very sketchy evidence. For example, out of forty-five countries having tropical rain forest Sommers had evidence from only thirteen and Myers used data from eighteen, accounting for 58 per cent of his estimated total area in tropical forest (Lugo and Brown, 1981). For this reason the assertions as to what has happened to the world's forest area over time are at best highly speculative. Lugo and Brown ventured a comparison of the estimates made for the 1920s by Zon and Sparhawk (1923) with those by Persson (1974, 1975, 1977) for the early 1970s. Although those figures are suspect for the reasons stated above, they suggest a few trends about which there appears to be wide concensus among scientists and foresters. Europe, the USSR, Oceania and North America seem to have enlarged their total forest areas; Latin America's areas have been decreasing; and the area of African closed forests has decreased. These figures say nothing about changes in the quality of the forests, whose measurement is impeded by the third problem of estimation.

This problem arises because the meaning of conversion of a forest stand is a matter of loose connotation. It may signify at one extreme the selective cutting of a forest or at the other extreme the complete destruction of a stand and its replacement by cultivated agriculture or open pasture. In between these extremes a wide variety of transformations may occur. Shifting agriculture, which probably accounts for more tropical forest conversion than any other type of human alteration, may lead to re-vegetation over a period of 15–70 years but the long-term effects on the plants, animals, soil and water of the area are greatly influenced by its natural characteristics, the mode of cultivation, and the length of the cropping cycle. If shifting cultivation is followed by continuous cropping the consequences may be profound. Little is known about the complex biology of these biomes and about the ages and growth rates of their trees (NRC, 1980; Bohrmann and Berlyn, 1981). For the present study the term conversion is used to mean any kind of alteration from human action, and the term destruction is used to mean the virtual obliteration of a stand for productive forestry.

Sommer (1976) estimates the area of the world that could potentially be covered by tropical evergreen rainforest at 1,184 million ha (260 in Africa, 627 in Latin America and 297 in Asia and the Pacific). UNESCO calculates the area at present covered as about 765 million ha (83 million ha in Africa, 557 million ha in tropical America and 125 million ha in Asia). Lanly and Clement estimate the total area of closed forests in the whole tropical world in 1975 at 1,169 million ha. (This figure includes ZB II.) All agree that the past conversion of rain forest has proceeded much further in Africa than in the other two continents.

Estimates of present conversion are even more difficult to obtain, and are based either on all 'tropical moist forests' or all 'tropical forests'. Sommer (1976) calculated a figure of eleven million ha per year (ha/y) for 'tropical moist forest'. The figure of sixteen million ha/y for all tropical forests was widely quoted at the 8th World Forest Congress in 1978. Myers (1980) considers that twenty million ha/y was not unlikely in the mid 1970s, arriving at this figure by assuming that roughly twenty million farm families were clearing one hectare each year per family. He further assumed that about ten million ha/y was destroyed by converting primary forest to permanent cultivation. Seller and Crutzen (1980) estimate that 20–62 million ha/y is being cleared in all biomes for shifting cultivation, and that the destruction rate for virgin forest is 0.5–1.5 million ha/y. In Latin America and the Far East, 5–10 million and 8.5 million ha, respectively, of forest are felled each year (Costantinesco, 1976). The Tropical Forest Resource Assessment Project of the Food and Agriculture Organization of the United Nations (FAO) and the United Nations Environment Programme (UNEP) estimates the annual conversion of closed tropical forests as: 4.1 million ha for Latin America, 2.2 million for Asia, and 1.3 million ha for Africa, for a total of 7.4 million ha. The higher figure of Costantinesco probably includes clearing of secondary growth.

The study of Lanly and Clement reaches more conservative conclusions about future rates of conversion on the bases of a detailed country-by-country analysis of the kinds of change taking place or proposed. According to these authors the natural closed tropical forest may decline from 1,205 million ha in 1970 to 1,026 million ha in 2000, an average of a little less than six million ha/y for *all* tropical forests.

Many observers extrapolate these figures, or even assume that the rates of deforestation will increase, and conclude that the forests of Asia will have disappeared by the end of the century or earlier, and that those of Latin America will not survive for more than fifty years. Such statements do not take full account of the afforestation programmes or the operation of technical and economic factors that affect the rate and type of cutting. Altering forests to expand agriculture (and to produce wood, fibre and energy) need not be detrimental if the fallow period associated with shifting cultivation is sufficiently long, or if the cleared area is converted to a well-managed plantation. Where the area is transformed to permanent farmland, the consequences for species diversity can be catastrophic.

TROPICAL DECIDUOUS FORESTS AND SAVANNAHS (ZB II)

A zone occupied by deciduous or evergreen forests, woodlands, savannahs and grasslands lies between the tropical evergreen rain forest and the subtropical deserts. Proceeding outwards from the evergreen rain forest the natural sequence of vegetation zones is thought to be as follows: evergreen rain forest (ZB I); semi-evergreen rain forest (ecotone ZB I/II); savannah (ZB II); grassland (ZB II); semi-desert (ecotone ZB II/III); deserts (ZB III). This corresponds to trends toward longer and more intense periods of water deficiency. Production in most of this zone is seasonal. In contrast to the tropical rain forest, the fauna is rich and animal biomass much higher, although it varies greatly according to the quality of the grazing.

It is difficult to generalise about changes in this zone as a whole, which is of great importance for agriculture, forestry and animal husbandry, for there are notable contrasts between countries having the same climate and biome type, related mainly to traditional ways of life, population pressure and poverty. The richer countries, such as Australia, have avoided some of the more serious land-use problems; and they are less acute where people are fewer, as in Central Brazil. Nor are these problems confined to the semi-arid parts of the zone: land degradation in some of the mountain catchments of eastern and central Java are quite as serious and intractable as in the Sahel. For a large part of this zonobiome the prevailing land use is shifting cultivation. With a continuous growth of rural populations the period of fallow was curtailed. At the same time, major extensions of cereal cultivation occurred in grassland biomes, and irrigation developed in semi-desert and desert biomes.

Desertification, which has accompanied man's actions throughout history, is still proceeding, apparently at an increasing rate (UNEP, 1977). The *World Desertification Map* (Figure 6–1) shows which areas are particularly susceptible to desertification. The recent droughts in the Sahel of Africa (1968–1972) have dramatized the age-old problems of desert spread. In the Sudan, Ethiopia and Somalia in the east, and in Senegal in the west, extensive areas that were once productive have been added to the territories of the Sahara. It was estimated that deserts expanded southward in the Sudan by 90–100 km in seventeen years (UNCOD, 1977). New areas are being desertified in Brazil, Iran, Pakistan, Afghanistan and the Middle East. Morocco, Algeria, Tunisia and Libya are also affected (Chapter 7).

SUBTROPICAL DESERT VEGETATION (ZB III) AND STEPPE AND DESERT WITH COLD WINTERS (ZB VII)

These two zones are treated together because, to a large extent, the problems and changes affecting them are similar. They are both characterized by low rainfall and the main differences lie in temperature. Arid and semi-arid regions, mapped on bases of bio-climatic features, cover more than one-third of the land surface (UNESCO, 1978). Toward the fringes they grade into less extreme environments, and it is particularly in these ecotones that land-use problems are acute. ZB III occurs on the west coast of Peru, in Mexico, in a limited area in central Australia and in a belt across North Africa and the

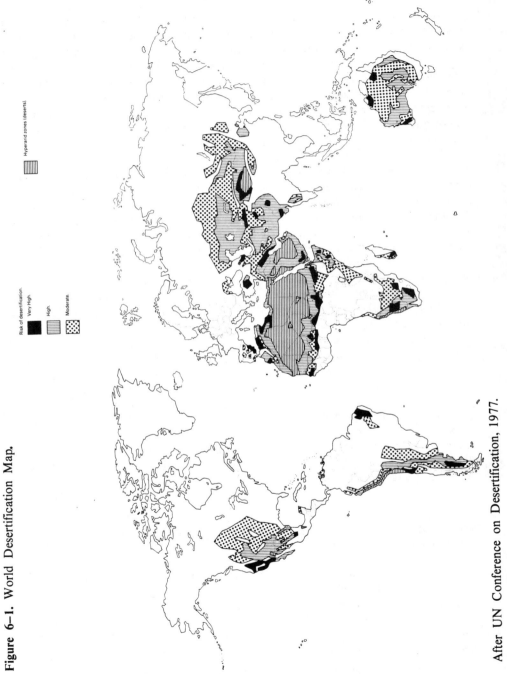

Figure 6–1. World Desertification Map.

Risk of desertification.

Very High.

High.

Moderate.

Hyperarid zones (deserts).

After UN Conference on Desertification, 1977.

Arabian Peninsula, through southern Iran, Afghanistan and Pakistan into north-west India. In Asia it adjoins ZB VII in Jordan, Iraq, Afghanistan and Pakistan. The greater extent of ZB VII is across Central Asia from east of the Caspian into western Siberia and China. Other areas are in eastern South America between latitudes 30° and 40° S and in the mid-western and south-western United States.

Generally speaking, the density and productivity of the vegetation is proportional to the water available. The more favoured areas in North America and Asia have been converted into the world's great grain-growing lands. In the true desert, perennial vegetation is almost confined to areas where moisture (groundwater or run-off water) is concentrated (oases, depressions and dry river beds). The true desert contains many organisms that have special adaptations allowing them to survive in extreme conditions. Such areas have, until recently, been little affected by man. But a number of serious threats have developed in recent decades, notably: exploitation of oil and minerals and the settlements that accompany it; hunting with modern weapons from motor vehicles; and the opening up of new watering-points to which stock are transported by motor vehicles. Further changes are also likely if solar power becomes widely used for large-scale energy production. Tourism poses problems in the Peruvian coastal desert. On the positive side, the extension of oases by irrigation can increase production of food and wood (if salinization is avoided) and there have been great endeavours in irrigating desert lands, for example, in the People's Republic of China and the USSR.

SCLEROPHYLLOUS WOODY PLANTS (Mediterranean) (ZB IV)

This zone includes regions that have hot dry summers, and mild-to-cool wet winters with low evaporation rates. The zonal vegetation is thought to have been forest, dominated by evergreen trees with leaves that are generally leathery (sclerophyll) and small. Few of these forests remain, but sclerophyll trees and shrubs are widespread and abundant.

Sclerophyll forest, and the associated climate, are found in five widely separated parts of the world: the Mediterranean basin, California, central Chile, the Cape region in South Africa, and south west and south Australia. The total area of the zone is only about one per cent of the land surface of the earth, but its importance to human history is great: there is evidence of human occupation around the Mediterranean 500,000 years ago, and the region was the cradle of cereal cultivation and stock-rearing.

The vegetation almost everywhere has been strongly influenced by man. The present vertebrate fauna does not show such a richness or high degree of endemicity as the flora, but the invertebrate fauna is rich.

In Australia there have been a number of changes in land use affecting Mediterranean sclerophyll communities. Among the most important are clearance for temperate zone pastures and cereals, replacement of natural forest by plantations of *Pinus radiata,* and exploitation of native forests for chipboard. The use of machines has accelerated the spread of a fungal disease of *Eucalyptus* (*Phytophthora cinnamomi*).

The situation in South Africa is rather different. The fynbos in Cape Province is being threatened by the increase in urbanization, dam and road building, invasion of introduced wood species (especially three species of *Hakea,* three of *Acacia* and *Pinus pinaster*) and the dissection of the fynbos into small pieces by the extension of agriculture. These pressures, together with the high degree of local endemicity, have threatened many species with extinction: 1,259 of the 1,945 endemic species of southern Africa are actually or potentially threatened species of the fynbos. The fynbos is now the subject of a Fynbos Biome Study, leading to proposals for conservation and management involving nineteen large nature reserves connected by corridors to allow migration: eight of these have already been set up. The Cape Floral Kingdom Project has been started to develop a master plan and build up the necessary public understanding, co-operation and support.

In the Mediterranean basin the ecological balance of centuries, which depended upon conservation of soil and water, is being seriously disrupted. Among the changes that have accelerated in the last ten years are the intensification of agricultural and pastoral uses of the uplands involving scrub clearance, ploughing steep marginal land and increased grazing, fuel cutting and hunting; the intensification and expansion of industrial agriculture; the expansion of urbanization, industry, roads and mining and the rapid development of mass recreation and tourism (Chapter 14).

TEMPERATE EVERGREEN FORESTS (ZB V)

This zone is characterized by well-distributed rainfall and generally warm conditions; a cold season is absent but there may be occasional frost, such as devastated the Brazilian coffee crop in the mid-1970s. The main areas occur in south-east Brazil, the southern part of the eastern United States, and equivalent but broader belts in China, eastern Japan, northwest New Zealand, a band up the east coast of Australia and a small area in southeastern South Africa. The zonobiome is also represented in Portugal, small areas in Chile, the Black Sea coast of Turkey and the northern flank of the Elburz mountains in Iran, running down to the Caspian Sea.

Most areas of warm temperate forest are intensively used. The soils are often erodible and require careful treatment. The accentuated load of sediment in the waters of the Parana river and its Brazilian tributaries emphasizes the need for careful land-use planning, for the retention of forest cover and for comprehensive soil conservation measures.

Many of the natural forests in this zone contain valuable timber trees. But after the best of these have been extracted, it is often considered most profitable economically to remove all the native forest and grow exotics. Very rapid deforestation has proceeded in some countries, followed by planting of *Eucalyptus* spp and *Pinus radiata*. These yield well and can do much to remove pressure from the remaining natural forests. But in some parts of the zone, conservation of adequate areas of indigenous forest is urgently needed. In Paraguay for instance, the forests of the eastern provinces are being removed at the rate of 175,000 ha a year and are unlikely to survive more than another decade. The same applies to the natural forests of the valuable Parana pine (*Araucaria angustifolia*).

NEMORAL BROADLEAF–DECIDUOUS FORESTS (ZB VI)

This zone has abundant precipitation, well-distributed throughout the year, but tending to be higher in summer. There is a marked cold season during which vegetation rests. In the Northern Hemisphere, most trees shed their leaves during winter, but in the Southern Hemisphere evergreen species are more common.

The zone covers much of northwest Europe, the eastern United States, northeastern China, western Japan, southern Chile and eastern New Zealand. It includes some of the most densely populated areas of the world together with some of the most highly industrialized. The equable climate and fertile soils have been particularly favourable to agriculture, through which the productivity of much of the land has been increased greatly. Little natural forest remains except in mountainous areas or on poor soils. Many of the larger vertebrate species, especially the predators, have been eliminated.

This is an area in which competition between different kinds of land use is intense. The growing demand of a relatively affluent population for space for recreation, and the building of roads, towns and factories adds to these conflicts (Chapter 9). The increasing need for plantation forestry to meet demands for wood products is leading, in some areas, to the afforestation of heaths and grasslands considered valuable for grazing, for recreation and for their natural beauty. Grasslands, formerly managed as extensive grazing lands, provide important habitat for the conservation of wild species of plants and animals. This is no longer profitable, and the grasslands are disappearing.

BOREAL CONIFEROUS FORESTS — TAIGA (ZB VIII)

The Boreal forest zone of the Northern Hemisphere extends for nearly 13,000 km from east to west, and lies mostly north of latitude 50° N. There is no comparable zone in the Southern Hemisphere. Extensive areas of these northern forests are dominated by evergreen conifers which are particularly well adapted to the cold winters and short growing seasons. The northern edge of the boreal forest coincides closely with the 10° C July isotherm, but the southern boundary is poorly defined. These forests reach almost to the Arctic coast in relatively sheltered locations such as the lower Mackenzie Valley in Canada. The most northerly trees in the world are stunted larch, spruce and alder on the shores of the Laptev Sea in Siberia at latitude 73° N. The boreal forest of North America is closely related to those of Europe and Siberia, but has an even closer relationship with the sub-alpine forests of the Rocky Mountains and the Sierra-Cascade system.

Extensive areas of the boreal forest in North America and the USSR remain sparsely populated, and even in Nordic countries such areas have the lowest population density in their respective countries.

In Scandinavia and the USSR these areas of low human population density coincide fairly well with the boundary between boreal and mixed forests. It was the nineteenth century before much settlement occurred north of the mixed forest areas. The primary use of the boreal forest is for logging, although in large areas in the north this may not be profitable. In interior Alaska, only about 9 million ha (21 per cent) of the boreal forest is cleared as commercial, of which spruce dominates about 57 per cent.

In recent years concern has been expressed that forest growth may be affected by acid rain. The mixed deciduous/boreal forest around Sudbury, Ontario, Canada, has been severely damaged by sulphur oxides and other pollutants from smelting operations over a period of fifty years. The rate of forest growth appears to have declined in southern Scandinavia and in the north-eastern United States between 1950 and 1970, but it is not possible to verify that this decline is caused by acid precipitation (Abrahamsen et al., 1976; Dochinger and Seliga, 1976; Tamm, 1976). Terrestrial ecosystems are very complex, and since acid precipitation is only one of the many environmental stresses, its impact may enhance, be enhanced by, or be swamped by other factors. Recent experiments indicate that acid precipitation can damage foliage, accelerate cuticular erosion, alter responses to associated pathogens, affect the germination of conifer seeds and the establishment of seedlings, affect the availability of nitrogen in the soil, decrease soil respiration, and increase leaching of nutrient ions from the soil (Abrahamsen et al., 1976; Malmer, 1976; Tamm, 1976). It is possible that acid damage might have been partly offset by the nutritional benefits gained from nitrogen compounds commonly occurring in acid precipitation. Changes already detected in soil processes may as yet be too small to affect plant growth.

The main changes in this zone are those associated with commercial logging. There may be over-cropping in certain parts of Canada and perhaps in northern China. A demand for more domestic timber production is leading to extensive draining of the wetlands in this zone in Nordic countries. Economic development in Siberia (industrial centres, railways, pipelines, commercial logging, etc.) led during the decade to a considerable shrinking of the taiga forest. Conservation measures are now being implemented.

TUNDRA VEGETATION (ZB IX)

Tundra and/or polar deserts occur in both the Arctic and the Antarctic. In the Northern Hemisphere, Low Arctic or High Arctic tundras extend in a circumpolar band across northern North America and Eurasia, and ice deserts are virtually confined to Greenland and the Canadian Arctic islands. In the Southern Hemisphere, the situation is reversed, with virtually the whole of Antarctica covered in ice, and with sub-polar closed vegetation (which differs in many respects from the true tundra) confined to scattered islands.

In high latitudes soil invertebrates contribute an increasing proportion of the faunal diversity. The mammalian fauna of the Arctic is relatively small. In the Antarctic, terrestrial mammals are absent. Land birds are confined to the sub-Antarctic; elsewhere soil invertebrates make up virtually the total land fauna. In contrast, the marine bird and mammal fauna are fairly diverse and very abundant.

Following major oil and natural gas reserve discoveries on the Arctic Slope of Alaska in 1968, there was further exploration activity over wide areas. This led to significant terrain damage in tundra areas, which will probably require many decades to recover. Construction of the trans-Alaska oil pipeline was preceded by that of a gravel highway into what were previously remote wilderness areas. In June 1979, there was a serious rupture in a buried section. At least 2,000 barrels of crude oil polluted about 43 km of the Atigun River, and spread over extensive areas of adjacent low ground. This constituted the first oil pollution of an arctic river ecosystem. Its long-term ecological effects will not be known for some time, but studies are in hand.

In Canada, oil and gas discoveries in the Mackenzie Delta and on some of the arctic islands led to plans for construction of a natural gas pipeline. Deposits of lead and zinc on Little Cornwallis Islands, and iron ore on Baffin Island, are being exploited. In 1978, the Dempster Highway north to Inuvik was open to traffic.

Further developments are to be expected in the Soviet Arctic. In 1974, the largest copper ore deposits in the country were located on the Taimyr Peninsula. At Vrengoy on the Gulf of Ob, the world's largest known natural gas field has been discovered. Both the USSR and Norway have discovered Arctic off-shore and on-shore oil reserves in Svalbard, which will likely be exploited.

In the Antarctic during the peak summer period of 1978/1979, about 2,650 personnel were involved in the Antarctic research programmes of eleven nations, and there were thirty-seven bases, each with up to eighty wintering-over staff. These totals varied little over the decade. In recent years, vessels and aircraft have begun making tourist visits to the area. Repeated visits by tourists in helicopters to the Cape Royds Adelie penguin rookery caused a steep decline in the number of nesting birds. Tourist-use of the Antarctic region is likely to continue, and it poses some threat to the biota, but with proper controls the effects should be localized. A series of specially protected areas has already been set aside under internationally agreed measures for the conservation of fauna and flora (Holdgate, 1970).

Of much greater potential impact would be habitat destruction from development of extractive industries in the Antarctic (Antarctic Treaty, 1979). The Antarctic Treaty Consultative Powers have been considering how to arrange a phased development of mineral exploitation and exploration within their treaty. Japanese scientists announced that they would begin a three-year seismic survey of the Ross, Bellingshausen and Weddell Seas in 1980.

EXTRAZONAL BIOMES – ISLANDS, MOUNTAINS, WETLANDS

Islands

Continental islands are, or have been, geologically part of the adjoining continents and most of them are situated on the continental-shelf areas; their biota usually bear a close resemblance to that of the neighbouring continent. Oceanic islands are independent of continental land masses and are composed of volcanic rocks, or of coralline material built upon volcanic foundations. They are especially numerous in the Pacific.

The native biota of oceanic islands is characterized by the generally small number of species – the smallest, youngest and most remote examples having the fewest species.

A second important feature of all but the youngest oceanic islands is the high proportion of endemic species (i.e. species found nowhere else). In the Hawaiian Islands, for example, over 90 per cent of the native species of flowering plants, 65 per cent of the ferns and approximately 99 per cent of the native insects are endemic. The theoretical relationship between age and size of island, its isolation, and the uniqueness of its biota has interested scientists since Darwin visited the Galapagos, and was the subject of important advances in understanding during the 1970s (e.g. Diamond and May, 1976).

Subsistence harvesting of native fuelwood and the prevention of regeneration by introduced herbivores such as goats, has led to the depletion or even extinction of many insular species: classic examples include St Helena and various southern hemisphere temperate islands (Holdgate, 1967). The destruction of island forests has continued and the vegetation of some islands (e.g. Easter Island) has been transformed to communities dominated by introduced species. The mining of phosphate deposits has also had a marked impact, well exemplified at Christmas Island in the Indian Ocean where it has threatened the world's only breeding population of Abbott's Booby, although a working compromise seems possible at present (Ovington et al., 1981).

The impact of mass tourism has spread to many island groups around the world, particularly in the Caribbean and to other areas such as Fiji, Bali, and the Seychelles. The oceanic islands are often used as civilian and military airfield staging posts. The latter half of the 1970s saw the development of massive oil industry facilities in the Orkney and Shetland Islands, in the latter case after environmental impact analysis (SVEAG, 1976). Facilities for the handling of supertankers have also been constructed in the Canary Islands. In 1979, press reports in Australia indicated that the United States was considering Palmyra Atoll in the Central Pacific as a possible dumping site for nuclear wastes. Such developments bring a continually increasing risk of pollution and of the introduction and establishment of exotic species of plants and animals. A typical example was the introduction of Australian fruit flies to Easter Island and Tahiti by tourist flights.

Mountains

Mountain ranges are characterized by sequences of horizontal belts of vegetation related to the lower temperatures and generally less favourable growing conditions that exist at high altitudes. Mountain ranges occur in all the zonobiomes and the succession of altitudinal belts varies considerably. The tree limit varies from near sea-level at high latitudes to about 4,000 metres in the tropics. Above this there is an alpine belt with dwarf shrubs, herbs and bryophytes, below the zone with permanent snow. Mountain areas, like islands, tend to have numerous endemic species.

Precipitation usually increases at middle altitudes but is less near the summits. There is a belt on many mountains where cloud persists, bringing orographic precipitation and little sunshine; in tropical mountains this is the zone of cloud forest, and in coastal arid lands the zone of mist oases. Higher still there are often strong winds and the distribution of vegetation is related to exposure.

One of the features shared by all mountain areas is instability, caused by their steepness and the intensity of the physical forces of erosion: avalanches, rockfalls and landslips are common, cycles of alternate freezing and thawing are general at high altitudes, and the soil, even under natural vegetation, constantly moves downhill. Many factors contribute to accelerated erosion, including deforestation, overgrazing, inappropriate cultivation, neglect of terraces, fire, overcutting of firewood, road building and over-use by tourists. Some of these are caused by the growth of rural populations, others by the growing affluence and mobility of city populations.

Pressures on the mountain regions in the developing world have intensified in the past ten years, largely due to increasing populations. Large areas of forest are being opened up to shifting cultivation on the eastern slopes of the Andes in Colombia as colonists move down from the plateau on roads opened up for oil exploration. The forests in the Ethiopian highlands are being destroyed at the rate of 100,000 ha/y; they have been reduced from 16 per cent of the land area twenty-five years ago to only 4 per cent now; the forest area in the Himalayas has declined by 40 per cent in the last thirty years. Deforestation is accompanied by overgrazing, over-cutting of fuel wood and extension of dryland cultivation into unsuitable areas.

Paradoxically the problem in certain developed countries is the reverse. Improved communications have made it easier for people to move to the plains or the cities from mountain valleys where the work is hard and relatively unproductive; and so these are becoming depopulated except where tourism is developed. There are serious conflicts in Europe and North America over the growing number of dams and reservoirs in the mountains. This has become a particularly critical issue in Scandinavia.

Wetlands

Wetlands are areas where the water table lies near to, or above, the soil surface. They may be flooded permanently or, as in the flood plains of rivers, from time to time. The water may be rich or poor in nutrients. There are many distinct kinds of wetland depending on the amount, source, seasonality and chemical composition of the water, and upon the nature of the climate.

A number of recent developments have affected inland wetlands. Dams and reservoirs built on rivers and streams have flooded some and denied a supply of water to others. This often causes increased salinity in lakes and inland seas, especially in arid regions. Many wetlands, particularly in northern and western Europe, are being drained. An industry has developed to sell peat for horticulture. Coastal wetlands are being drastically reduced in area not only by agriculture, but by reclamation for building land, docks and industrial development; and the reduced areas that remain are seriously affected by pollution.

Recent Actions to Conserve Terrestrial Biota

INTERNATIONAL INITIATIVES

SINCE its inception in 1948 the work of the IUCN has gradually instilled world-wide awareness of the hazards that threaten species of plants and animals and some of the ecological processes on which the world's life-support systems depend. The International Biological Programme (IBP) established in 1964 by the International Council of Scientific Unions (ICSU) to study "the biological basis of productivity and human welfare", was the first world-wide programme in which biologists of various disciplines worked together (Worthington, 1975). The IBP terminated in 1974. It produced a great wealth of basic information. A series of some forty volumes brings together, in the form of syntheses, the results of these national and international activities. The IBP mobilized the international scientific communities and had a notable impact in sensitizing the world to the dangers that threaten the healthy functioning of the global biosphere. The IBP was for this reason a source of input to the Stockholm Conference and it led directly to the UNESCO-sponsored intergovernmental Programme on Man and the Biosphere (MAB) established in 1971.

There was much national activity during the decade 1970–1980, including conservation legislation and the establishment of national machineries for management of nature reserves. Many actions recommended in the Stockholm Declaration were implemented. These actions were concerned with establishing the conditions in which environmental management considerations can be introduced into international law and national administrations, sensitizing decision-makers and promoting education, training and research. Most important of all, however, was the change in attitude of the World Bank, and several other international and bilateral financing agencies, in altering priorities for investment in development in favour of measures that have environmental components and are ecologically sound.

Conventions and Conferences

Table 6–1 lists international conventions negotiated during the decade that fulfil recommendations of the Stockholm Conference relating to terrestrial biota. In addition to these, reference may be made to: conservation measures within the terms of the

Table 6–1. Multilateral Agreements Affecting Terrestrial Biota

Benelux Convention on the Hunting and Protection of Birds, June 1970, Brussels.

Agreement for the Establishment of a Commission for Controlling the Desert Locust in North-West Africa, November 1970, Rome.

Convention on Wetlands of International Importance Especially as Waterfowl Habitat, February 1971, Ramsar.

Convention on the Prohibition of the Development, Production and Stockpiling of Bacteriological (Biological) and Toxin Weapons, and on their Destruction, April 1972, London, Washington, Moscow.

Convention Concerning the Protection of the World Cultural and Natural Heritage, November 1972, Paris.

Convention on International Trade in Endangered Species of Wild Fauna and Flora, March 1973, Washington.

Agreement on Conservation of Polar Bears, November 1973, Oslo.

Convention on the Protection of the Environment between Denmark, Finland, Norway and Sweden, February 1974, Stockholm.

Agreement on an International Energy Programme, November, 1974, Paris.

Convention on the Protection of the Archaeological, Historical and Artistic Heritage of the American Nations (Convention of San Salvador), June 1976, Santiago.

Convention on Conservation of Nature in the South Pacific, June 1976, Apia.

Convention on the Prohibition of Military or Any Other Hostile Use of Environmental Modification Techniques, December 1976, New York.

Treaty for Amazonian Cooperation, July 1978, Brasilia.

Convention on the Conservation of Migratory Species of Wild Animals, June 1979, Bonn.

Antarctic Treaty of the designation of specially Protected Areas, the adoption of a convention on Antarctic Living Marine Resources, proposals to strengthen the Ramsar Convention on Wetlands at a meeting of the States Parties (Cagliari, Sardinia, November 1980), and the Protocol on Mediterranean Protected Areas.

A number of important conferences during the period also helped to stimulate action and increase awareness. They included the UN conferences on food, population, water, desertification, environmental education, and science and technology. The World Forestry Congress in 1978 devoted one session to the topic of forestry for quality of life. UNEP held a meeting on the tropical rain forest in Nairobi in 1980.

Other International Initiatives

During this decade FAO and the United Nations Development Programme (UNDP) paid much attention to planning for integrated rural development, with increasing emphasis on environmental matters. Much of this activity affects agricultural productivity and is discussed in Chapter 7. More attention is given in this chapter to activities related to preservation of habitat and endangered species. As part of its programme FAO elaborated comprehensive schemes for protected areas (e.g. in Indonesia and Nepal) and for the conservation of genetic resources of crop and forest plants.

UNESCO developed the Man and the Biosphere Programme, whose Project 8, 'the conservation of natural areas and the genetic material they contain' gave added support to the movement to establish a comprehensive network of protected areas, and initiated the concept of biosphere reserves.

IUCN, with the help of UNEP and WWF, in collaboration with FAO and UNESCO, elaborated the *World Conservation Strategy,* launched in March 1980. The follow-up of this document and the implementation of its principles will be among the salient features of conservation during the 1980s. Progress was also made in identifying priorities for work to increase the coverage and improve the management of protected areas, and to stimulate action on threatened species of both plant and animal. The work of the Threatened Plant Committee has been developed entirely since 1973. IUCN established a Species Conservation Monitoring Unit and a computerized data bank on protected areas in Cambridge and Kew. These provide tools for monitoring the status of plant and animal species and protected areas.

Action Concerned with Tropical Forests

In an analysis of threatened vertebrate species recorded in the IUCN *Red Data Book,* Allen and Prescott-Allen (1978) show that out of 295 threatened 'terrestrial' species, 89 are found in tropical forests (68 in rain forests). Almost all of these are threatened by habitat destruction and are concentrated in: Southeast Asia (27), Madagascar (25), South America (19), the Indian Sub-Continent (5), and Mexico and Central America (4).

Examples of events during the 1970s with some bearing on these problems include:

— a number of FAO/UNDP programmes for integrated planning of forest resources, for example in Indonesia, Malaysia and Nigeria;

— The FAO/UNEP pilot project of tropical forest monitoring conducted in Togo, the People's Republic of Benin and Cameroon;

— increasing attention being paid to problems of tropical forest development by the countries in which it occurs, e.g. the appointment of a Minister for Development Supervision and Environment in Indonesia; establishment of a Task Force for the Western Ghats in India; the RADAM Project and allocation of land for various uses in Brazil; and the environmental preamble to the treaty between the Amazonian States;

— the closely planned programme for rural development in west Malaysia;

— the increasing attention of the UN agencies, summed up in the publication of a state-of-knowledge report on *Tropical Forest Ecosystems* prepared by UNESCO, UNEP and FAO (UNESCO, 1978);

— the WWF/IUCN campaign and programme on tropical forests in the mid–70s, and the publication by IUCN of *Ecological Guidelines and Development in Tropical Rain Forests;*

— the preparation of an inter-agency task force report to the President of the United States on a *US Policy, Strategy and Programme for the World's Tropical Forests* (USA, 1980);

— establishment of the International Council for Research in Agroforestry (ICRAF) in Nairobi;

— tentative moves towards an organization of tropical wood exporters.

Extensive plantations have been developed in some areas (for example, of the tropical pines, *Gmelina arborea*, teak and *Eucalyptus* spp), most of them in areas with some seasonal drought. One of the largest is Jari in Amazonia. To be most effective in environmental terms, however, plantations should also attempt to recover the enormous areas that have become degraded to grassland. The 'critical lands' programme in Indonesia has this objective.

There is an encouraging trend toward establishing protected areas. An analysis (IUCN, 1974) of the 1974 United Nations List of National Parks and Equivalent Reserves gave the following figures: tropical rain forests, 13,650,000 ha; tropical areas of high altitudes, 1,500,000 ha. Of these, nearly 6,000,000 ha were in Zaire and none in Amazonia. An analysis of figures prepared by IUCN in 1980 gives a more encouraging picture, with 23,133,000 ha in 223 tropical protected areas. The analysis, according to bio-geographical provinces, is presented in Table 6–2.

Actions in the Tropical Deciduous Forest and Grassland Zone

There has also been a considerable increase in the number and area of national parks and equivalent reserves in this zonobiome. IUCN (1974) listed 33 in the Neotropical realm, 109 in the Africotropical, 24 in the Indomalayan, and 2 in the Australian. Comparable figures in 1980 (Table 6–3) are 82, 139, 51 and 12, totalling more than 58 million ha. A notable advance during the decade was the establishment in India of the network of reserves for the tiger, which have covered all the most important ecosystems in this zone. A few biogeographical provinces are apparently still not represented, including the Malagasy Thorn Forest; the northern grasslands in Australia; and two provinces in Latin America and two in India.

Actions Concerned with Desertification

The United Nations Conference on Desertification, held in Nairobi in 1977, was stimulated by world-wide concern about the rate of deterioration of the world's drylands

Table 6–2. Reserves in Tropical Rain Forest[a]

	No. of Reserves	Area (ha)	Biogeographical Province (Udvardy, 1975)
Africotropical	21	2,680,000	Guinean rain forests
	11	1,181,000	Congo rain forests
Indomalayan	—	—	Malagasy rain forests
	3	376,000	Malabar rain forests
	1	110,000	Ceylonese rain forests
	5	346,000	Bengalian rain forests
	1	2,000	Burman rain forests
	18	1,368,000	Indochina rain forests
	5	13,000	South Chinese rain forest
	9	878,000	Malayan
	9	2,263,000	Sumatra
	10	177,000	Java
	3	47,000	Lesser Sunda Is.
	1	1,000	Sulawesi
	17	824,000	Borneo
	8	219,000	Philippines
	1	13,000	Taiwan
Australian	47	495,000	Queensland coastal
Neotropical	3	93,000	Campuchean
	4	287,000	Panamanian
	4	645,000	Columbian coastal
	18	608,000	Guyanan
	15	10,218,000	Amazonian
	—	—	Maderian
	7	286,000	Serrado Mar
Oceanian	2	3,000	Papuan
	223	23,133,000	

[a]This table is derived from data compiled by the Commission for National Parks and Protected Areas (CNPPA) of IUCN. It includes protected areas that fall within the various biogeographic Provinces of Udvardy. Some protected areas included, or parts of some areas, may fall in other biomes than tropical rain forest, but the figures should give a broad indication of the areas involved. The data are being constantly reviewed and revised by the CNPPA.

and the plight of the people living in them, and particularly by the disastrous Sahel drought of 1968–72.

The areas identified as being at risk of desertification are shown in Figure 6–1. Some of the most seriously affected areas (tropical deciduous forests and grasslands) occur in the drier parts of the zonobiome. But a number of other zones (the sclerophyllous forest, sub-tropical desert and semi-desert, and wintercold steppe and desert) are also prone to desertification.

The Plan of Action to Combat Desertification addressed problems of halting desertification, reclaiming desertified lands, and development of natural resources of deserts. In addition, there were a number of advances in the fields of nature conservation:

Table 6–3. Protected Areas in Zonobiomes

	Realm	No.		Area (ha)	Totals
I.	*Tropical evergreen forest*				
	Oceanian			3,000	
	Africotropical	32		3,861,000	
	Indomalayan	93		6,637,000	
	Australian	47		495,000	
	Neotropical	51	223	12,137,000	23,133,000
II.	*Tropical moist and dry deciduous forests and savannahs*				
	Africotropical	139		42,753,000	
	Indomalayan	51		2,672,000	
	Australian	12		2,487,000	
	Neotropical	82	284	10,448,000	58,360,000
III.	*Subtropical desert or semi-desert*				
	Nearctic	15		1,729,000	
	Palaearctic	4		1,017,000	
	Africotropical	25		19,522,000	
	Australian	28	72	11,311,000	39,579,000
IV.	*Sclerophyllous forest zone*				
	Nearctic	6		440,000	
	Palaearctic	35		662,000	
	Africotropical	4		17,000	
	Australian	47		4,431,000	
	Neotropical	22	114	12,000	5,562,000
V.	*Warm temperate evergreen forest*				
	Nearctic	6		2,175,000	
	Palaearctic	29		1,336,000	
	Australian	22		701,000	
	Antarctic[a]	17		2,229,000	
	Neotropical	16	90	3,491,000	9,932,000
VI.	*Temperate deciduous forest*				
	Nearctic	17		750,000	
	Palaearctic	181	198	6,195,000	6,945,000
VII.	*Winter-cold steppe and desert*				
	Nearctic	11		388,000	
	Palaerctic	47		3,754,000	
	Australian	20		402,000	
	Neotropical	8	86	123,000	4,665,000
VIII.	*Boreal coniferous forest*				
	Nearctic	22		16,832,000	
	Palaearctic	42	64	7,921,000	24,754,000

Table continued

Table 6–3. Protected Areas in Zonobiomes—cont'd.

	Realm	No.		Area (ha)	Totals
IX.	*Tundra (+ arctic desert)*				
	Nearctic[b]	8		81,054,000	
	Palaearctic	10		4,144,000	
	Antarctic	2	20	1,007	85,199,000
	Mountains				
	Nearctic	42		7,608,000	
	Palaearctic	122		6,319,000	
	Africotropical	21		3,903,000	
	Neotropical	38	223	7,735,000	25,565,000
	Islands				
	Palaearctic	8		22,000	
	Africotropical	3		19,000	
	Indomalayan	1		2,000	
	Neotropical	19		1,223,000	
	Oceanian	6	37	113,000	1,379,000
			1,411,		285,073,000

[a]This figure includes all New Zealand protected areas, some of which should be classified elsewhere.
[b]Includes Greenland National Park, 70m ha.
This table is based on data compiled by IUCN. The data have been grouped according to the biogeographical provinces of Udvardy (1975) and each of these has been attributed to a zonobiome. This is an oversimplification and the table gives only a first approximation to the true position.

— the number and surface of protected areas is considerable; all biogeographic provinces are represented except the eastern Sahel (see Table 6–3);

— biosphere reserves (MAB Programme) designed to integrate conservation of habitat and genetic resources with the development of local people have been set up in Durango (Mexico) and in the Touran (Iran);

— the critically endangered Arabian Oryx (*Oryx leucoryx*) has been successfully re-introduced into the Jiddat al Harasis in Oman and the Shaumari Wildlife Reserve in Jordan, after captive breeding in the United States.

— several critically endangered species in the steppeland of the USSR have been restored. They include *Marriota Bobak, Saiga tatarica* and *Gazella subguttorosa*.

Actions in the Temperate Zones

The decade saw the continued growth of a strong environmental movement in the western industrialized countries, which started in the 1960s and acted as precursor to the

Stockholm Conference. Some of the more influential events in the countries of the temperate zone were: European Conservation Year; the National Environment Policy Act and the Endangered Species Act in the United States; and the Countryside Conference in Britain (1970).

The measures for pollution control that were adopted during this period have brought greater benefits to water and to the air of cities than they have to terrestrial biota, largely because the problem for them was more serious. Restrictions on the use of organochlorines have, however, led to the recovery of birds of prey, especially the peregrine falcon (*Falco peregrinus*) in Europe.

New Zealand provides a good example of the way in which temperate-zone problems may be solved. The indigenous forests, especially of the valuable *Podocarpus* and *Agathis*, have been seriously depleted. As a result of public concern, policies have been adopted for the indigenous forests whereby certain areas are totally protected thus saving the endangered Kokako (*Callaeus cinera*). Other areas are reserved for sustained exploitation of native species for high quality timber. This has been made possible by the great success of exotic plantations, especially of *Pinus radiata*.

Action in the Tundra and Ice Desert Zones

In the past decade an increasing area in this zone was set aside for wildlife conservation. In the USSR two reserves for the red-breasted and snow geese were established in the Taimyu Peninsula and Wrangel Island. The population of the wild northern reindeer was doubled, and conservation of polar bears is well supported. In the Antarctic "Specially Protected Areas" have been designated under the Agreed Measures for the Conservation of Flora and Fauna, and the contracting parties to the Antarctic Treaty have discussed ways of preventing environmental damage from possible mineral exploration and exploitation as well as from tourism.

Actions Relating to Islands

One striking success during this decade was the story of Aldabra, the unique raised coral atoll in the Indian ocean that is the home of the old-world giant tortoise, the flightless white-throated rail and many other endemic species. Aldabra was threatened in 1966 by plans to build a staging post for the British and American military. This proposal was abandoned after vigorous opposition from scientific and conservation organizations. Since then, with the active collaboration of the Government of the Seychelles, the Royal Society of London has run a comprehensive research programme there. In 1980 the care of the atoll passed to the Seychelles Island Foundation to ensure that it is protected and used solely for research and education. Other conservation measures were adapted for other island groups. A new wildlife conservation ordinance was enacted on Tristan da Cunha (Wace and Holdgate, 1976). During the 1970s there was extensive discussion of a possible international Convention on Islands for Science and a draft text was prepared for discussion by IUCN. A Convention on the Conservation of Nature in the South Pacific was adopted in 1976. MAB Project 7 addresses the ecology and human impacts on island ecosystems, including studies on the interactions of population, resources, environment and development in Fiji (UNESCO, 1980) and in the Eastern Caribbean.

Actions Relating to Mountains

More support is now being devoted by the World Bank and UNDP to integrated planning for the development and rehabilitation of mountain catchments. A notable example is the FAO/UNDP project in the Solo River Basin in Java. A large World Bank study is beginning on the rehabilitation of the Himalayan catchments. In 1977 New Zealand held a national conference on its mountain problems. As a result the government issued in 1979 a policy statement on mountain lands, the first of its kind. In 1979 also, IUCN, WWF and UNEP published *Ecological Guidelines for Balanced Land Use, Conservation and Development in High Mountains,* which were tested and refined at the New Zealand meetings.

There also were scientific and planning activities in the UNESCO MAB Project 6 on Man and Mountain Ecosystems; the International Workshop on the Development of Mountain Environment organized by the German Foundation for International Development in 1974; and the IUCN meeting also in 1974, on the future of the Alps. A regional centre for integrated mountain development was established in Kathmandu, Nepal, as a co-operative undertaking between Nepal, UNESCO-MAB, the Federal Republic of Germany and Switzerland.

The actual area protected is extremely difficult to assess because many mountain reserves also contain other habitats. Wielgolaski (1980), calculating country-by-country, reached a tentative total of 45 million ha. Added to this there may, however, be areas that are preserved for catchment protection. An important recent addition is the Sagarmatha National Park, covering the Nepalese side of Mt Everest. There has also been a striking increase of protected areas in the Andean countries, from 24 (1974) to 38. But there are still many important mountain massifs that are not covered.

Actions Relating to Wetlands

During the decade there were two particularly significant developments: the growth of public concern, and the Ramsar Convention. Indications of the former were the Council of Europe Wetlands Campaign and the growing body of opinion that all large developments affecting wetlands should be thoroughly assessed for environmental effects. The World Bank is directing more attention to the environmental aspects of projects involving water. It is, for example, financing a comprehensive study of the problems of Himalayan catchments and, in Indonesia, has provided for the establishment of a National Park to protect the catchment area of the Dumoga irrigation project in Sulawesi.

A most significant advance during this decade was the Ramsar Convention (Convention on Wetlands of International Importance, Especially as Waterfowl Habitat, 1971). By mid-1981, this convention had been ratified by twenty-nine countries and four others had signed subject to ratification. A total of 215 sites covering over 6 million ha were listed and protected under the convention. As a result of the recent conference of the Parties (Cagliari, Sardinia, November 1980) it was hoped that the number of countries ratifying this convention would increase, that its coverage might be extended to include other kinds of wetlands and that its regulatory powers might be increased. The Cagliari Conference also proposed measures for strengthening the convention through a protocol and the establishment of a permanent secretariat.

Decisions have been taken recently affecting a number of important wetlands. One is the decision to proceed in a limited form with the proposal to build the Jonglei canal for the benefit of irrigation in the Sudan and Egypt. This would by-pass the wetland of the Sudd where vast volumes of water are evaporated. The other is the decision of the Government of Botswana not to proceed with the proposal to divert the waters feeding the Okavanga delta, a project that would have had profound effects upon wildlife and the way of life of local people. Both these decisions were reached after detailed consideration of the effects of the proposed developments. Another important wetland being examined is near the Kagera river in Tanzania, Rwanda and Uganda. There were also reports that the scheme to divert some of the flows of certain rivers in the USSR that empty into the Arctic Ocean would be carried out with full environmental safeguards and be subject to detailed monitoring.

PROTECTED AREAS AND GENETIC RESOURCES

Three main lines were followed during the decade. They are not new, but they were pursued with renewed vigour and some success. They are: protected areas for blanket protection of ecosystems and species; genetic conservation for selected economic species – crop plants, livestock and forest trees; and concentration on threatened species of plant and animal.

During this period detailed reviews were carried out by the Species Survival Commission of IUCN on the problems of threatened plants and animals. Six hundred and seventy-four species of vertebrates are considered as threatened: 163 fish, 35 amphibians, 75 reptiles, 177 birds and 224 mammals (Allen and Prescott-Allen, 1978). Causes of depletion have been identified as: habitat destruction, 67 per cent; overexploitation, 37 per cent; effect of introduced species, 19 per cent; other causes, 9 per cent (some species suffer from more than one threat).

There has been success in saving several endangered species of plants and animals through protection. *Ranunculus crithmifolius* ssp *paicifolius,* endemic to one locality in New Zealand, increased from 32 individual plants in 1948 to several hundred in 1972. *Orothamus zeyheri* (marsh rose) of South Africa, with only 90 plants in imminent danger of extinction in 1968, now numbers about 2,000 plants. The North American whooping crane (*Grus americana*) a popular symbol of endangered wildlife, increased from 21 birds in 1941 to 119 birds in both wild and captive populations in 1980. The Galapagos fur seal (*Arctocephalus galapagoensis*), thought to be extinct in the 1900s and numbering less than a dozen in the 1930s, is now estimated at about 40,000. Certain species were re-discovered, e.g., *Trochetia melanoxylon,* now propagated in St Helena.

It is hoped that the Convention on International Trade in Endangered Species of Wild Fauna and Flora (CITES) will play a useful part in limiting some forms of over-exploitation, but the main improvement must be expected from protected areas and good land management. Zoos and botanic gardens have an important role in back-up operations. Great progress has been made in stimulating the establishment of protected areas and in developing national policies for nature conservation. Examples are the 142 nature reserves and hunting reserves (total area = 107,783,127 ha) and seven national parks (total area = 410,540 ha) in the USSR (Table 6–4 gives information on most of these reserves), the tiger reserves in India; the chain of reserves in the Andean countries; the Survey of the National Estate in Australia; the Nature Conservation Review in Britain (Ratcliffe, 1977); and the recent decision of the National Council for Physical Planning in Greece to establish nine nature reserves in various parts of the country. The People's Republic of China will carry out such a survey and increase the percentage of its area protected from 0.16 per cent to over 1.0 per cent. In Indonesia five national parks are being developed with buffer zones that set the parks in the framework of integrated land-use, which benefits the local people. UNESCO's Biosphere Reserves now number 193 in 50 countries and cover 50 per cent of the world biogeographical provinces (see also Table 6–3).

Table 6–4. Nature Reserves (Including Game Reserves and National Parks) in the USSR Within the Various Zonobiomes

Zonobiome	Number	Area (ha)
European tundra and Arctic desert	1	795,650
Asian tundra and Arctic desert	2	1,509,570
European taiga	11	1,139,361
Asian taiga	13	1,869,404
Kamtchatkan taiga forests	1	964,000
Broad-leaved forests of temperate zone	6	127,681
Broad-leaved forests of East Europe	25	620,621
Steppes of the temperate climate zone	2	72,980
Steppes of the European part of the USSR	12	492,033
Caucasian steppes	2	13,869
Cold winter deserts	12	1,112,024
Evergreen vegetation of Mediterranean	4	15,685
Desert zone of Aral Sea	1	18,300
High mountains of the Caucasus	33	1,071,182
High mountains of Tien-Shan	14	469,268
High mountains of the Pamir-Altai Region	2	935,095

Source: Data supplied by A. M. Borodin, USSR Ministry of Agriculture.

Plants threatened by habitat destruction are concentrated in islands, especially oceanic islands in the tropics and sub-tropics, tropical rain forests, drylands, the sclerophyllous forest zone, and freshwater wetlands, notably in Europe. Threatened land vertebrates suffering from habitat destruction are mainly found in islands, especially in the tropics, tropical rain forests, wetlands, and tropical dry and deciduous forests. The majority of these are concentrated in the Caribbean, western Indian Ocean, South

Pacific and Hawaiian Islands, and the tropical forests in Southeast Asia, Madagascar and South America.

Ecosystems of exceptional diversity include tropical rain forests, especially those of peninsular Malaysia, Borneo, Sulawesi, Sumatra, the Philippines, New Guinea, Central and South America, and Madagascar (to these might be added the mountain rain forests of Africa); the tropical dry forests of Madagascar; the sclerophyllous forest zone ecosystems of South Africa and Western Australia; and very rich island systems such as New Caledonia, the Hawaiian Islands, and the Canaries and Azores.

Considerable progress has been made in the preservation of microbial genetic resources and a World Data Centre for Microorganisms is established at the University of Queensland, Brisbane (Australia). It holds 441 of the world collections from sixty-five countries. This initiative of UNEP, UNESCO, and several non-governmental organizations is of particular significance, especially in view of the new developments in genetic engineering and bio-technology.

Future Prospects

ALTHOUGH it is possible to recognize general similarities within any one zonobiome, it is evident that local variations are of great significance. Desertification, for instance, is less acute in Australia and in the United States than it is in the Sahel; and the disappearance of rain forest in Indonesia is more rapid and serious than it is in Zaire. For this reason global rates of change, even if accurate data were available, would give little useful information. Where much natural vegetation still remains and population is relatively low, as in Amazonia, Borneo, New Guinea and Central South America, it is still possible to plan the use of the land in such a way that the natural resources of soil, vegetation, water and animals will be used to the best future advantage; there is still freedom to choose. The situation in much of Europe contrasts greatly with this. The land has been fully used for centuries, but because of the temperate climate and the stability of the soils, damage to soil fertility is limited; indeed it has been enhanced in some places. Here there is no new land for exploitation and the increase in the use of the land for one purpose, such as industry or more forest plantations, inevitably means less for some other use. Much Asian land has been enhanced by intricate techniques of terracing, water application and fertilization.

Where the land has been overtaxed for long periods, soil has been lost by erosion and resources depleted by overuse. This is the position in extensive areas of the arid and semi-arid regions of the world (Figure 6–1), and in some very highly populated lands in the tropics such as parts of India and Java. Here the principal task should be to restore wasted resources, maintain ecological processes, and prevent further deterioration.

During the decade since the Stockholm Conference many steps were taken at international, regional and national levels that have a bearing on the condition of terrestrial biota, and a substantial number of the recommendations of the conference were implemented. Progress was made in establishing the conditions in which sound environmental management should become possible, in negotiating international conventions, setting up national and international institutional arangements, holding world conferences on critical issues, increasing the amounts of training and exchange of information, and alerting public opinion. Changed attitudes of multilateral and bilateral institutions for development finance and technical assistance are especially significant. Such events are of fundamental importance for future progress.

A great deal of public attention was focussed on environmental problems during the 1960s and '70s, and they have undoubtedly received greater emphasis among the priorities of governments. However, the fundamental importance of maintaining natural capital is still not fully recognized, and it remains difficult to justify in conventional economic terms the high investment that is needed, for example, for the comprehensive rehabilitation of the Himalayan catchments. There are some indications that these views are changing. But it would be over-optimistic to think that a revolution of attitudes and social and economic organization can be brought about overnight. The necessary measures are complex, and they are very vulnerable to economic and political instability because they require high and sustained standards of planning, management and control.

It is suggested that, with the exception of trade in endangered species, by far the most important problems affecting terrestrial biota are those of land use; and they are concentrated in areas in which the soils and ecosystems are inherently fragile – the tropics, Mediterranean climates, mountains and isolated islands. The effect of changing land practices on climate and on the carbon dioxide balance are still not properly understood and both could be matters of considerable concern.

The effects of pollution on terrestrial biota (discussed elsewhere) are often local, as with fluoride and zinc; although they can also be regional, for example with sulphur and nitrogen oxides in north-west Europe and the north-eastern United States, or global as with the organochlorine pesticides. But, taking a comprehensive view, the importance of pollution for terrestrial biota is much less than that of land-use practices.

FUTURE PRIORITIES

It is evident that pressures on the land will increase in the coming decades and that these can only be met by using the land more efficiently to provide the goods and services required by mankind. If production can be increased in areas that are suitable for it, this will decrease the pressure on those where the best long-term use is protective, or others where a period of rest or rehabilitation is needed. But there are problems also in intensifying the productive uses of the land. Much of the highly productive agriculture of the modern world is very specialized, depending on varieties of plants and animals very well adapted to the conditions of the moment. Its genetic base is dangerously narrow. This disadvantage can be overcome by further planting and animal breeding and by the effective conservation of genetic stocks. While much scientific work is still necessary on the management of natural ecosystems and on the potential uses of unknown plants and animals, the main barrier to progress lies in the difficulty of adapting social and economic systems to a planned use of the land that is self-sustaining yet highly productive. The extent to which this has been achieved in many areas is small in comparison with the need; and it seems to have been wholly successful only where the efforts of people have been harnessed to provide personal care in the management of land.

Terrestrial biota need to be managed in harmony with the basic needs of socio-economic systems, and in most developing countries alleviation of poverty is a major societal objective. Unless development proceeds it will be impossible to reduce pressures in terrestrial biota in extensive tracts of the world. But societies in their quest for economic development and enjoyment of the riches of nature, must come to terms with the realities of resource limitation, including the limited carrying capacities of ecosystems, and must take full account of the needs of future generations. This was the central message of the *World Conservation Strategy*.

The World Conservation Strategy identifies four principal requirements:

(a) The biosphere processes that underlie the functioning of the life support systems need to be maintained (the health of the biosphere is essential);

(b) The ecosystem resources should be managed and harvested within the limits of their productive capacities (over-exploitation should be avoided);

(c) The genetic diversity of wild and cropped biota should be preserved (germplasm resources are most valuable assets);

(d) Conservation of species and habitat should be seen as an integral component of the development of natural resources.

Integration of conservation with development is primarily a national responsibility and needs to be translated into action at field level. Obstacles inherent in socio-political systems, which are especially noted in developing countries, may be reduced through:

— national conservation policies that integrate conservation and development;

— national land-use planning based on ecological surveys of natural resources and land capabilities;

— establishment of national machineries (organizations and legislation) for sustained management of land resources, and development of indigenous scientific capabilities for monitoring and assessing natural resources, training personnel and carrying out research programmes;

— promoting support for the integration of conservation and development and ensuring public participation, especially in rural development.

International assistance should provide support for these national needs and for the national programmes related to them. As the international community shares the global biosphere of the "Only One Earth" recognized at the Stockholm Conference, it is responsible collectively for the maintenance of its health and sustained functioning. Apart from support to international and regional conventions, treaties and protocols relevant to living resources and terrestrial ecosystems, there is need for:

— international programmes for the establishment and management of a world network of biosphere reserves (UNESCO-MAB) and protected areas for science in zonobiomes that are especially important for functioning of the global biosphere, e.g. tropical forests and woodlands;

— an international programme for the conservation of drylands and for combating desertification;

— an international programme for the conservation of genetic resources, including the establishment of world germplasm banks;

— strategies and programmes for conservation of living resources and ecosystems in ecogeographic regions that are shared by neighbouring countries.

References

Abrahamsen G. *et al.* (1976), Effects of Acid Precipitation on Coniferous Forests, In F. H. Braekke (Editor), *Research Report FR–6*, SNSF Project, NISK, Aas, Norway.

Allen, R. and C. Prescott-Allen (1978), *Threatened Vertebrates* (second draft), General Assembly Paper, GA 78/10 Add. 6, IUCN, Gland.

Antarctic Treaty (1979), *Report of the 10th Antarctic Treaty Consultative Meeting*, Department of State, Washington, D.C.

Bohrmann, F. H. and G. Berlyn, Editors (1981), *Age and Growth Rate of Tropical Trees: New Directions for Research*, Bull. No. 94, Yale University, School of Forestry and Environmental Studies, New Haven, Conn.

Costantinesco, J. (1976), *Soil Conservation for Developing Countries*, Soils Bull., 30. Food and Agriculture Organization of the United Nations, Rome.

Darlington, P. J. (1957), *Zoogeography: The Geographical Distribution of Animals*, John Wiley, New York.

Diamond, J. M., and R. M. May (1976), Island Biogeography and the Design of Nature Reserves, In R. M. May (Editor). *Theoretical Ecology: Principles and Applications*, Blackwell, Oxford.

Dochinger, L. S. and T. A. Seliga (1976), *Workshop Report on Acid Precipitation and the Forest Ecosystem*, USDA Forest Service, General Techn. Report NE–26, Northeast. Forest. Experim. Station, Upper Darky, Pa.

Elton, C. S. (1958), *The Ecology of Invasions by Animals and Plants*, Methuen, London.

FAO (1980), *Global Environment Monitoring System*, Pilot Project on Tropical Forest Cover Monitoring, Benin-Cameroon-Togo. Food and Agricultural Organization of the United Nations, Rome.

Good, R. (1974), *The Geography of the Flowering Plants*, Longman, London.

Holdgate, M. W. (1967), *The Influence of Introduced Species on the Ecosystems of Temperate Oceanic Islands*, Proceedings IUCN 10th Technical Meeting, Lucerne, 1966, IUCN Publications, *New Series*, No. 9, 151.

Holdgate, M. W. (1970), Conservation in the Antarctic. In M. W. Holdgate (Editor), *Antarctic Ecology*, Academic Press, London.

Holdgate, M. W. and G. F. White (1977), *Environmental Issues: SCOPE 10*, John Wiley, London.

IUCN (1974), *Biotic Provinces of the World*, Occ. Paper No. 9. IUCN, Gland, Switzerland.

IUCN/UNEP/WWF (1980), *World Conservation Strategy*, International Union for the Conservation of Nature and Natural Resources, United Nations Environment Programme and World Wildlife Fund, Gland, Switzerland.

Jackson, I. J. (1977), *Climate, Water and Agriculture in the Tropics*, Longman, London.

Lanly, J. P. and J. Clement (1979), *Present and Future Forest and Plantation Areas in the Tropics*, FAO:MISC/79/1, Food and Agriculture Organization of the United Nations, Rome.

Lugo, A. E. and S. Brown (1981), *Conversion of Tropical Moist Forests: a Critique*, (in press).

Malmer, N. (1976), Acid Precipitation: Chemical changes in the Soil. *Ambio*, 5, 231.

Myers, N. (1979), *The Sinking Ark*, Pergamon Press, Oxford.

Myers, N. (1980), *Conversion of Tropical Moist Forests*, National Research Council, Washington, D.C.

NRC (1980), *Research Priorities in Tropical Biology*, Committee on Research Priorities in Tropical Biology, National Research Council, Washington, D.C.

Ovington, J. B. *et al.* (1981), *Appraisal and Implications of a Survey* (1979-1980) *of Abbott's Booby on Christmas Island*, Report of the Australian National Park Service, Canberra.

Parsons, J. J. (1976), Forest to Pasture: Forest Development or Destruction, *Revista di Biologia Tropicale*, 24.

Persson, R. (1974), *World Forest Resources*, Research Note No. 17, Royal College of Forestry, Stockholm.

Persson, R. (1975), *Forest Resources of Africa*, Part I: Country Descriptions, Research Note No. 18, Royal College of Forestry, Stockholm.

Persson, R. (1977), *Forest Resources of Africa*, Part II: Regional Analysis, Research Note No. 22, Royal College of Forestry, Stockholm.

Ratcliffe, D. A., Editor (1977), *A Nature Conservation Review*, Cambridge University Press, Cambridge, UK.

Rodin, L. E. *et al.* (1975), *Productivity of the World's Ecosystems*, National Academy of Sciences, Washington, D.C.

Scott, P. (1980), Foreword. In R. Allen, *How to Save the World: Strategy for World Conservation*, Kogan Page Ltd., London.

Seller, W. and P. J. Crutzen (1980), Estimates of Gross and Net Fluxes of Carbon Between the Biosphere and the Atmosphere From Biomass Burning, *Climate Change*, 2, 207.

SMIC (1971), *Study of Man's Impact on Climate, Inadvertent Climate Modification*, MIT Press, Cambridge, Mass.

Sommer, A. (1976): *Unasylva* 28, 112.

SVEAG (1976), *Oil Terminal at Sullom Voe; Environmental Impact Assessment*, Thuleprint, Sandwick, Shetland.

Tamm, C. O. (1976), Acid Precipitation: Biological Effects in soil and on Forest Vegetation. *Ambio*, 5, 235.

Udvardy, M. D. F. (1975), A Classification of Biogeographical Provinces of the World, *IUCN Occ. Paper No.* 18.

UNCOD (1977), *Desertification: Its Causes and Consequences*, UN Conference on Desertification. Pergamon Press, Oxford.

UNEP (1977), *Annual Review*, United Nations Environment Programme, Nairobi.

UNESCO (1973), *International Classification and Mapping of Vegetation*, Ecology and Conservation Series, 6, UNESCO, Paris.

UNESCO (1978), *Tropical Forest Ecosystems: A state of Knowledge. Report by UNESCO/UNEP/FAO*, Natural Resources Research Series, XIV, UNESCO, Paris.

UNESCO (1979), *Tropical Grazing Lands, A State of Knowledge Report by UNESCO/UNEP FAO,* Natural Resources Series XVI, UNESCO, Paris.

UNESCO (1980), *Population Environment Relations in Tropical Islands: the Case of Essential Fiji,* MAB Technical Notes, 13, UNESCO, Paris.

USA (1980), *The World's Tropical Forests: A Policy Strategy and Programme for the United States.* Report to the President by an Interagency Task Force on Tropical Forests, US Government Printing Office, Washington, D.C.

Wace, N. M. and M. W. Holdgate (1976), *Man and Nature in the Tristan da Cunha Islands,* IUCN Monograph No. 6.

Walter, H. (1979), *Vegetation of the Earth and Ecological Systems of the Geobiosphere,* Springer Verlag, New York.

Warren, A. and J. K. Maizels (1977), Ecological Changes and Desertification, in *UNCOD, Desertification: its Causes and Consequences,* Pergamon Press, Oxford.

Wielgolaski, F. E. (1980), MS for World Conservation Strategy Source Book, IUCN.

Worthington, E. B. (1975), *The Evolution of IBP,* Cambridge University Press, Cambridge.

Zon, R. and W. N. Sparhawk (1923), *Forest Resources of the World,* McGraw-Hill, New York.

CHAPTER 7

Agriculture, Forestry and the Environment

More than 450 million people were chronically hungry or malnourished during the decade. For although total food production increased nearly everywhere, it failed to match population growth in many parts of Africa, Asia and Latin America. The annual rates of increase in food production varied from a low of 0.12 per cent for coffee to a high of 6.83 per cent for soybeans. Increases in animal products ranged from 2.98 per cent for meat, to 2.53 per cent for eggs and 1.64 per cent for milk. Some crops suffered a production drop: jute and fibre went down 4.96 per cent, wool by 1.1 per cent. According to the Food and Agriculture Organization of the United Nations (FAO), a 60 per cent increase in food, fish and forest production will be needed just to maintain current consumption patterns to the year 2000 — let alone increase them.

The decade's production increases resulted largely from bringing new areas under cultivation or irrigation. For example, following India's dramatic successes in the Green Revolution of the 60s, more and more land was irrigated. Rangeland management was improved through control of overgrazing in arid lands. However, in some countries agricultural land was being transformed into other uses, thus reducing productive potential. During the decade, in developed countries alone, more than 30,000 square kilometres (km^2) were turned into settlements and roads. World-wide, an estimated 50,000 to 70,000 km^2 was lost to food production in this way.

Soil degradation — erosion, salinization and alkalinization, and chemical degradation — occurred in many parts of the world and caused production losses. Salinization caused abandonment of about the same area that was being reclaimed and irrigated, and was particularly acute in semi-arid and arid regions. Fully half the irrigated soils in the Euphrates Valley in Syria, 30 per cent in Egypt and more than 15 per cent in Iran were believed to be affected by salt or waterlogging.

Desertification continued on a grand scale during the decade: some 60,000 km^2 of land were destroyed or impaired annually as a result of severe and recurrent drought and human exploitation. Large areas of the Sudan, Ethiopia, Somalia, Senegal, Brazil, Iran, Pakistan, Bangladesh, Afghanistan and the Middle East turned into deserts. Between 600 and 700 million people were threatened by this inexorable deterioration. The cures for desertification are well-known, but although a United Nations Conference held in 1977 produced a Plan of Action to Combat Desertification, these cures had not been put into effect in much of the world by 1980.

The decade marked the beginning of what may be a new era in biological production: the bio-technological era. Advances in genetic engineering made possible the production of many valuable substances with the aid of microbes and their enzymes. Production of insulin, interferon and some vaccines was shown to be possible in this way. There were prospects of developing cereal crops capable of fixing atmospheric nitrogen. The Earth's bioproductive systems may in future have to produce not only food, fibre and timber, but also industrial materials and fuel. This would cause increased competition for land.

Concern continued about the side-effects of agricultural chemicals on the environment. Nitrogenous fertilizer production worldwide in 1970/71 amounted to 33,064

250

thousand tonnes and 53,795 thousand tonnes in 1978/79. FAO estimated that by 1985/86 world consumption would be up to about 84 million tonnes. Nitrates from fertilizer residues polluted ground and surface waters, with consequent hazards to aquatic life and human health. Chemical pesticide usage also increased greatly, with adverse effects on some animals, fish and birds. Yet crop losses were so great in some places that there were good arguments for using more pesticides rather than less. At the same time, the demand for increased testing of new pesticides for environmental effects was slowing the introduction of new ones by industry. And meanwhile, pests were developing resistance to the older types in ever-increasing numbers.

During the decade, public concern was expressed about effects of pollutants especially nitrogen and sulphur oxides, acid rain and photochemical smogs, on crop plants, forest trees and livestock. Post-harvest losses of crops also caused concern: losses in rice crops in Southeast Asia were estimated to range up to 37 per cent of the crop. Wastes from livestock and crop residues caused pollution, but methods were being investigated of turning them to useful ends, for example, by biogas production.

As the decade ended, the priorities in agriculture and forestry were clear for the next decade: more action was needed to stop desertification, to conserve soil, to manage forests and water wisely, and to use appropriate methods of cultivation.

Only a small part of the productivity of natural terrestrial ecosystems is used by man. Over history, the development of agriculture and forestry has altered the structure and composition of selected systems so as to increase their yield of food, fibre, timber and other biological products. However, despite their modification by cultivation, irrigation, fertilizer use, plant and animal breeding, control of predators and pests and other management techniques, these systems are (with limited exceptions such as greenhouse horticulture) not wholly controlled by man. The natural processes of the biosphere, and especially climatic extremes like droughts and unseasonable frosts, can still interfere with their production.

In nearly every country, total food production has increased in recent decades. But in many places — especially parts of Africa, Asia and Latin America — it has not matched population growth (Mayer, 1976). In the 1970s, the food situation was critical for vast numbers of people. One estimate put the total who had become increasingly dependent on external supplies for their principal food at one billion, in some 40 low-income countries. Over 450 million were chronically hungry or malnourished (WFC, 1977). The Food and Agriculture Organization of the United Nations (FAO) estimated that a 60 per cent increase in food, fish and forest production would be needed to maintain current patterns of consumption, assuming that the world population rose to 6,300 million by 2000 (FAO, 1977 a). At the end of the decade mankind was facing a pressing need not only to increase world food production but also to make distribution more effective and to improve the security of supply for large numbers of people.

But there were also grounds for hope. The *Global 2000* report suggested that a 90 per cent increase in food production could be achieved using only 2.5 per cent more land than was cultivated in 1978, giving a 15 per cent increase in supply per head (CEQ, 1980). At the end of the decade, FAO foresaw a new agricultural revolution based on biotechnology and on the use of the full capacity of microorganisms as nitrogen fixers in agriculture and as agents of organic syntheses (Saouma, 1979).

Several basic criteria govern the management of ecosystems for sustained productivity. An assured water supply and the maintenance of soil stability and fertility are crucial. The need for protection against damaging pollution is self-evident. A third need is to regulate the crops man takes from the system. If overcropping depletes the nutrients in circulation more than they are replenished by natural processes or by the addition of fertilizers, if pastures are grazed so heavily that palatable forage species can no longer sustain themselves, or if harvested organisms are depleted beyond optimal sustainable yield, the system becomes at best inefficient and unrewarding, and at worst may change through relatively rapid processes of ecological retrogression to one no longer useful to man.

Agricultural and Forest Productivity

LAND–USE CHANGES

Buringh (1981) estimated that in 1975 out of the approximately 13,400 million hectares (ha) of land area not covered by ice the proportions of land in cropland, grassland, forest, non-agricultural use, and in desert, tundra, high mountain or very stony condition were as shown in Table 7–1. The lands were placed in four classes according to potential productive capacity:

high	where there are often two or more crops per year or one crop with high yield (60 per cent of potential maximum).
medium	where there are rather good yields (40–60 per cent of potential maximum);
low	where there are low yields (20–40 per cent of potential maximum);
zero	where the yields are zero or very low (20 per cent).

The estimates allocated about 700 million ha to the high class, 1,100 million to the medium class, and 1,500 to the low class. More than 10,000 million ha yielded little or no return.

Table 7–1. Estimated Use of Ice-Free Land Surface of the World — 1975

Land use:	Land Class				
	High	Medium	Low	Zero	Total
		(millions of hectares)			
Cropland	400	500	600	0	1,500
Grassland	200	300	500	2,000	3,000
Forest land	100	300	400	3,300	4,100
Non-agricultural land	0	0	0	400	400
Other land	0	0	0	4,400	4,400
Total all land	700	1,100	1,500	10,100	13,400

Source: Buringh (1981).

Between 1963 and 1975 there was a considerable expansion in land areas under cultivation in both irrigated and rain-fed systems (developing country figures shown in Table 7–2). The expansion of rain-fed arable lands of developing countries occurred principally in Africa and Latin America. In the former it involved major extensions of cereal cropping into semi-arid margins. In Latin America the advance was partly into forest lands and partly into semi-arid grasslands and scrub lands. Many countries within the steppe and desert and subtropical desert zonobiomes actively expanded their irrigation programmes. The dramatic rise in India's grain production in the late 1960s was a result of bringing more land under irrigation, using improved seeds and increasing the use of fertilizers and pesticides. In 1950, one-fifth of the land in India planted to food grains was irrigated; in 1976 the figure had risen to one-fourth (Mellor, 1976). In Mexico, more than half of the total commercial farm output, as measured in monetary terms, came from land under irrigation, although only about 30 per cent of the cropland was irrigated (Welhausen, 1976). In the developing countries in general, the annual increase in irrigated farmlands was about 2.9 per cent but the figure was only 0.7 per cent for non-irrigated arable land (Holdgate and White, 1977). Projections for the future indicated a rising use of water for irrigation.

The USSR had extensive irrigation and land reclamation projects in the 1970s, especially in the arid and semi-arid areas of the Central Asian Republics. The Kara Kum Canal was one especially significant development. Land-use changes were less pronounced in other developed countries, such as the member nations of the Organization for Economic Cooperation and Development (OECD). The total area of arable and cropland in OECD countries increased by some 2.9 per cent between 1955 and 1965; in 1970 the area was 107.1 per cent of the 1955 level and 106.5 per cent in

Table 7—2. Areas Under Cultivation in Developing Countries[a] (in thousands of hectares)

	Year	Total	Africa	Far East	Latin America	Near East
1. Total Arable	1963[b]	607,724	161,375	254,283	116,453	75,613
	1975	731,451	205,033	264,046	176,756	85,616
	1990	838,572	229,748	282,504	237,628	88,692
	2000	936,374	255,923	297,382	290,483	92,585
2. Arable Irrigated	1963	72,254	1,365	47,461	9,202	14,226
	1975	94,757	3,255	59,171	12,964	19,367
	1990	129,484	5,144	83,453	18,126	22,761
	2000	151,929	6,390	98,343	22,008	25,188
3. Arable Rainfed	1963	535,470	160,010	206,822	107,251	61,387
	1975	636,694	201,778	204,875	163,792	66,249
	1990	709,088	224,604	199,051	219,502	65,931
	2000	784,445	249,533	199,039	268,475	67,398

Source: FAO (1979).

[a]The data are for 90 developing countries, and exclude the People's Republic of China.
[b]1963 data are average of 1961–1965
1975 data are for Calendar year 1975
1990 and 2000 data are projections.

1975 (OECD, 1979). Permanent grassland and forest areas in temperate zonobiomes, however, changed hardly at all. The general pattern of expansion of croplands at the expense of uncultivated wetlands, uplands, coastland and other semi-natural areas concealed considerable variation between countries. In Canada, for example, the growth in arable land by some three per cent between 1965 and 1975 was balanced by a four per cent drop in permanent grassland. During 1967–1975 seventy-four million acres of cropland shifted to pasture, forest and other uses in the United States, and forty-eight million acres shifted from other uses to cropland. These changes were primarily in response to price and production factors (USNALS, 1981).

In the United Kingdom, by contrast, there was a decrease in the area of both arable land and grassland of 2 per cent and 5.5 per cent respectively between 1955 and 1975. But a major re-afforestation programme had raised the woodlands by 1975 to 125.1 per cent of the 1955 area (a 7 per cent increase being reported between 1970 and 1975). In the Netherlands, Luxembourg, Italy and Belgium even greater reductions in arable and cropland were reported. These figures are not precise because of variations in the system of recording between countries (and probably between periods) but they give a general impression of essentially marginal adjustment in areas where the land-use pattern has been broadly established over many decades.

LOSSES OF AGRICULTURAL LAND

Estimates made by Buringh (1981) suggested the losses and degradation of productive agricultural land that might be expected to take place by the year 2000 if the processes of land change working in 1975 were to be continued without alteration. The estimates therein reflected judgement as to the changes believed to be under way in 1975, and assumed that no additional large-scale land conservation programmes would be executed. Buringh recognized that degraded land will in most situations move gradually into a lower class of productivity, and that land that becomes entirely unsuitable for growing crops may be shifted to grassland, forest or other uses. He tried to take stock on a global basis of changes due to non-agricultural use, erosion, desertification, and salinization and alkalinization (toxification). He did not attempt to calculate losses in productivity due to removal of nutrients, soil pollution, silting or reservoirs, or land reclamation. The calculated average annual losses of agricultural land were believed to be of the following magnitudes:

by non-agricultural use	8 million ha
by erosion	3 ,,　,,
by desertification	2 ,,　,,
by toxification	2 ,,　,,

for an annual total of 15 million ha. In addition, it was estimated that part of the forest lands would decline to lower productivity as a result of shortened fallow periods, and that some new croplands would be gained by continuing reclamation. Deterioration of that order does not mean that the entire area of 15 million ha would be lost to agricultural production. There would be shifts from one land class to another and from some uses to others. The way in which those shifts seemed to be taking place is outlined in Table 7—3.

Given the trends believed to be under way in 1975–1980, the total area of high productivity cropland would, according to this projection, diminish in the period 1975 – 2000 by toxification (25 million ha) and by conversion to non-agricultural uses (75 million ha). During the same period about 45 million ha of high-productivity cropland would be reclaimed from forests, making a net loss of 55 million ha in high-productivity land. Through a similar combination of shifts, including loss by erosion and desertification, the area in medium- and low productivity cropland would increase from 1,100 million ha to 1,455 million ha.

These are aggregate figures, and do not reflect the special conditions prevailing in individual countries. For example, an annual loss of 20,000 ha of Egyptian cropland where there are few reserves of potentially reclaimable land is more serious than an annual loss of 1.5 million ha in Brazil where only 5 per cent of the land area is cultivated and as much as 40 per cent is believed to be potential cropland.

There are no thorough surveys of land use and land condition on a world scale. The available data are taken from scattered local and national studies, and the estimates of the global condition are difficult to harmonize with one another. As in the case of the estimates of conversion of tropical forests reviewed in the preceding chapter, firm figures on rates of change are speculative at best. Estimates of changes for selected processes and areas are reported in the remainder of this chapter, but it has not been practicable to reconcile the individual studies so as to arrive at a world synthesis.

It should be noted that scientific understanding of the magnitude and interrelationships of the major processes involved in land transformation is still lamentably incomplete. Much is in doubt, for example, as to how soil erosion, soil compaction, pesticide residues, and fertilizer applications interact to affect cropland productivity. An international study by SCOPE is seeking to bring together the findings on such questions from a variety of national and international research activities.

In the developed countries agricultural land is often taken over by much more aggressive techno-productive systems, including industry, mining and urban development. More than 3 million ha of productive agricultural land appear to have been transformed to settlements and roads during the decade in developed countries alone. Worldwide, this figure may have been around 5 to 7 million ha. In the United States, during 1967 – 1975 approximately 2.8 million ha of cropland shifted to non-agricultural uses (USNALS, 1981). The annual conversion to those uses was about 0.16 per cent of the total stock of cropland and about 0.12 per cent of current and potential cropland combined. However, this included a very heavy commitment to an interstate highway system which was virtually completed during the 1970s. For Japan, the average annual loss of cultivated land to housing and urban services from 1968 to 1974 was about 30,000 ha; if industry and mines, a large highway expansion and forests and parks are included the total approached 55,000 ha — about 0.08 per cent and 0.15 per cent of the land area of Japan respectively (OECD, 1976).

PRODUCTION OF CROPS

Over the world as a whole, cereal production rose from 1,315 million tonnes in 1971 to 1,596 million tonnes in 1978; the production of pulses, fruits, nuts, total meat and milk also increased (Table 7–4). In 1979, however, world cereals production fell, due largely to shortfalls caused by droughts and adverse climate in the USSR, South Asia, and many African countries (USDA, 1980).

The Green Revolution, which began in the 1960s, continued to have a major influence on agricultural trends during the 1970s. It was based on a technological package: high-response varieties (HRV) of wheat, rice, maize and millets; abundant use of fertilizers and pesticides, and irrigation. In the right conditions it resulted in large increases in yields, and when the full package was provided to farmers, along with price-support policies, a rapid increase in crop outputs ensued. The 1980 crops in Bangladesh were particularly rich, after several years of shortages. This was primarily due to irrigation and use of HRV seeds.

Total food production by developing countries rose steadily during the 1970s, but varied greatly from region to region (Table 7–5). In both Latin America and East Asia,

Table 7–3. Projected Changes in World Land Use and Land Productivity, Extrapolating 1975 Trends to 2000

	Land class, cropland			Land class, grassland				Land class, forest land				Non-agr. Land	Other Land
	High	Medium	Low	High	Medium	Low	Zero	High	Medium	Low	Zero		
Land use in 1975	400	500	600	200	300	500	2,000	100	300	400	3,300	400	4,400
Deterioration													
loss by erosion	—	40	—	—	—	—	—	—	—	—	—	—	—
land converted into lower class	—	—	10	—	5	15	—	—	10	—	—	—	—
loss by toxification	25	15	—	—	5	—	—	—	—	—	—	—	—
land converted into lower class	—	—	10	—	—	30	—	—	10	10	—	—	50
loss by desertification	—	—	—	—	10	—	—	—	20	—	—	—	—
land converted into lower class	—	—	—	—	—	5	—	—	—	10	—	—	50
loss by non-agricultural use	75	25	20	30	—	—	—	—	—	—	—	—	—
land converted into non-agr.	—	—	—	—	—	—	—	—	—	—	—	200	—
loss by shifting cultivation	—	—	—	—	—	30	—	25	25	30	—	—	—
land converted into lower class	—	—	—	—	—	10	—	—	25	25	—	—	—
Land reclamation													
for increasing population	25	175	100	—	—	—	—	—	—	—	—	—	—
reclaimed from lower class	—	—	—	—	—	—	—	30	100	—	70	—	—
for replacing lost cropland	20	150	50	—	—	—	—	—	—	—	—	—	—
reclaimed from lower class	—	—	—	—	—	—	—	10	60	80	70	—	—
for replacing lost grassland	—	—	—	—	30	40	—	—	—	—	—	—	—
reclaimed from lower class	—	—	—	—	—	—	—	5	20	25	20	—	—
Land use in 2000	345	745	710	170	320	510	2,000	30	100	230	3,140	600	4,500
Net change, 1975–2000	−55	+245	+110	−30	+20	+10	—	−70	−200	−170	−160	+200	+100

Source: Buringh (1981).

Table 7-4. World Crop Production (in thousand tonne)

	1971	1972	1973	1974	1975	1976	1977	1978	1979
Total cereals	1,315,732	1,278,132	1,375,728	1,345,647	1,377,818	1,487,027	1,476,472	1,595,978	1,553,076
Wheat	354,206	347,320	376,529	364,277	359,688	424,744	390,697	450,059	425,478
Rice Paddy	308,812	295,966	323,196	332,295	358,415	350,456	369,729	386,303	379,814
Maize	306,220	305,167	311,032	293,502	324,801	332,798	346,227	363,927	394,231
Barley	151,346	152,002	168,339	166,767	152,376	186,950	176,280	193,852	172,175
Root Crops	549,743	530,090	573,284	521,277	501,169	512,205	512,170	538,167	547,501
Potatoes	294,352	281,069	316,753	271,104	258,912	262,872	265,635	276,072	284,471
Total Pulses	45,064	45,199	46,434	48,244	46,536	52,329	49,400	50,759	51,873
Vegetables and Melons	286,773	291,010	300,097	300,921	307,782	314,014	324,837	333,391	340,342
Fruits	231,178	228,132	250,656	251,158	256,310	261,781	256,425	267,533	286,979
Grapes	54,246	50,266	63,376	61,553	60,455	60,307	53,444	57,647	67,597
Citrus Fruit	39,708	42,117	45,248	47,434	49,494	50,266	51,994	52,265	55,044
Bananas	34,697	34,832	35,352	33,010	32,607	34,009	35,911	37,824	39,129
Apples	21,175	19,567	22,561	28,480	32,119	32,431	30,637	32,778	35,707
Total Nuts	3,232	3,317	3,541	3,317	3,384	3,365	3,449	3,609	3,662
Vegetable Oils	37,246	36,637	39,888	40,187	43,250	41,424	46,677	48,540	52,963
Sugar (Centrifugal, Raw)	74,704	73,125	77,596	76,137	79,459	83,725	89,747	90,524	88,910
Cocoa Beans	1,598	1,487	1,390	1,552	1,544	1,373	1,429	1,472	1,585
Coffee Green	4,588	4,498	4,113	4,714	4,652	3,553	4,254	4,608	4,972
Tea	1,364	1,482	1,538	1,483	1,547	1,589	1,751	1,796	1,821
Vegetable Fibres	18,970	20,565	21,314	20,065	18,581	18,414	20,408	20,318	20,718
Cotton Lint	12,670	13,588	13,755	13,904	12,281	12,089	13,832	13,115	14,050
Jute and Substitutes	3,344	3,973	4,715	3,210	3,267	3,476	3,745	4,519	4,000
Tobacco	4,539	4,869	4,929	5,301	5,416	5,661	5,530	5,731	5,444
Natural Rubber	3,037	3,017	3,449	3,422	3,522	3,739	3,574	3,684	3,679
Total Meat	108,601	110,970	111,712	121,348	123,246	126,976	131,293	135,478	138,143
Total Milk	398,938	408,029	414,534	425,656	429,678	437,600	449,893	457,056	460,329
Hen Eggs	21,795	22,348	22,435	22,962	23,602	23,929	24,755	25,755	26,558
Wool, Greasy	2,782	2,732	2,573	2,537	2,638	2,596	2,580	2,603	2,676

Source: FAO (1977b; 1980a).

Table 7–5. World and Regional Indices of Food Production (1961–65 = 100)

Region and Country	1961–65	1970	1971	1972	1973	1974	1975	1976	1977	1978	1979
Total production:											
Developed countries—											
United States	100	115	126	126	128	122	134	137	143	144	152
Canada	100	109	130	122	123	112	128	142	144	148	138
Western Europe	100	115	121	121	124	129	125	123	129	136	134
Eastern Europe	100	116	123	132	135	141	138	145	145	150	148
USSR	100	136	135	128	155	144	128	153	148	163	142
Japan	100	110	103	110	110	111	115	109	118	117	116
Oceania	100	121	128	123	127	127	135	138	133	152	142
Developing countries—											
Latin America	100	129	131	130	139	145	152	158	163	168	173
Africa[a]	100	117	120	122	119	125	120	132	129	131	134
West Asia	100	122	127	137	127	141	154	168	166	171	168
South Asia	100	128	126	119	130	124	140	137	150	157	146
East Asia[b]	100	129	132	130	141	147	155	164	167	170	175
World	100	123	127	125	133	132	135	141	144	151	147
Per capita production:											
Developed countries											
United States	100	106	116	114	115	109	119	120	124	125	130
Canada	100	97	114	106		95	106	117	117	110	108
Western Europe	100	109	114	113	116	119	115	113	118	124	122
Eastern Europe	100	111	117	124	126	131	127	133	128	135	133
USSR	100	125	124	116	139	129	113	134	128	140	121
Japan	100	102	94	100	98	97	100	94	101	98	96
Oceania	100	107	111	105	107	105	110	111	106	119	110
Developing countries—											
Latin America	100	107	106	102	106	108	110	111	112	112	113
Africa[a]	100	98	98	97	93	95	96	95	92	91	88
West Asia	100	102	102	107	96	104	110	117	112	113	108
South Asia	100	110	106	97	104	97	107	103	110	113	103
East Asia[b]	100	108	108	104	110	112	116	120	119	119	120
World	100	107	109	106	111	108	108	111	112	115	110

Source: USDA (1980).

[a]Excluding South Africa.
[b]Excluding Japan.

production rose substantially, but in South Asia it barely kept abreast of population growth and in Africa it fell behind. North America, Eastern Europe and East Asia made the larger gains in production per capita. The problem was most acute in sub-Saharan Africa where chronic food shortages arose — and where the export of agricultural commodities was an essential source of foreign exchange (USDA, 1980). Both climate and the instabilities caused by wars in Uganda (affecting Tanzania and Kenya) and Zimbabwe contributed to these problems. Similarly, the difficult food situation in Southeast Asia during the decade clearly reflected the political and military upheavals there.

PRODUCTION OF ANIMALS

Data in Table 7–4 show that total meat production rose by about 29 million tonnes between 1971 and 1979. Milk and egg production rose substantially. These trends were paralleled by a rise in the number of animals used in food production. Cattle numbers rose by 34 per cent in developing countries and 45 per cent in developed countries between 1965 and 1976, and sheep and goats by 32 per cent and 6 per cent respectively (FAO, 1977 b). The increase came about because of greater demand for meat and animal products and improved animal health. In 1976, 1,451 million sheep and goats and 1,214 million cattle, 132 million buffaloes, 123 million horses, mules and asses and 14 million camels were used in agriculture (FAO, 1977b). The greater demand for livestock and poultry, coupled with the desire to make animal husbandry more economical, led to practices of advanced agricultural technology by which large numbers of animals are kept in small areas. Such practices created serious difficulties because of the large amounts of manure that had to be disposed of.

As the chapter on Health reports, the views of nutritionists on man's need for protein (especially animal protein) have changed in recent years. While it is essential to avoid protein deficiency, it is now considered that the lack of total energy intake may be even more serious. The trend towards increased livestock raising, especially in developing countries, may be undesirable if it reduces the use of land for cereal and pulse crops, some of which are rich in proteins. This problem could be reduced if the enhanced animal production can come from land currently closed to stock-raising by disease (e.g. trypanosomiasis) or because the vegetation is not suitable for traditional domestic livestock. Interest remained high during the decade in ways of cropping wild herbivores living on unimproved rangeland. In parts of Africa the meat yield from such animals is considerable (in southern Nigeria 19 per cent of the animal products consumed in 1965/66 came from wildlife).

PRODUCTION FROM FORESTRY

Total roundwood production had been increasing in the 1960s, though at a lesser rate than crop and livestock production, and the lag became greater still in the 1970s. Table 7–6 shows that total forest products increased over the periods 1970–1978. Almost half (47 per cent) of the total world roundwood production was still used as fuel (about 74 per cent in developing countries). The output of industrial roundwood rose in the later part of the decade, and developing countries secured a larger share of the market.

The decade saw advances in technology that in principle permit much more efficient utilization of the forest crop and the use of a wider range of tropical woods in the manufacture of pulp and paper, chipboard, etc. While the area of natural forests was

Table 7–6. World Forest Production (in million m³)

	1970	1971	1972	1973	1974	1975	1976	1977	1978
Roundwood	2,365	2,398	2,402	2,480	2,501	2,449	2,561	2,568	2,601
Developed M.E.	787	790	769	805	797	712	781	781	791
Developing M.E.	918	944	966	966	1,016	1,035	1,081	1,090	1,120
Centrally-Planned	660	664	667	679	688	702	699	697	690
Fuelwood + charcoal	1,090	1,105	1,115	1,125	1,154	1,170	1,202	1,198	1,219
Developed M.E.	75	66	62	59	59	55	57	52	52
Developing M.E.	760	781	792	806	831	850	876	875	895
Centrally-Planned	255	258	261	260	264	265	269	291	272
Industrial Roundwood	1,275	1,293	1,287	1,355	1,347	1,279	1,359	1,370	1,382
Developed M.E.	713	723	707	747	739	657	723	729	740
Developing M.E.	158	163	174	190	185	185	206	215	226
Centrally-Planned	404	407	406	418	423	437	430	426	416

Source: FAO (1980b).

dwindling in the tropics (see Chapter 6), afforestation was expanding and commercial plantations were expected to increase from 4.7 million ha in 1975 to 16.4 million ha in 2000.

Apart from wood products used at home, forest products (sawlogs, veneer logs, sawn wood, etc.) rate high in the exports of many tropical countries. Although less than 6 per cent by volume of wood currently removed from tropical forests is exported, the trade value is about US$4.7 billion annually (FAO, 1979). Wood exports from the tropics increased on average by 7.1 per cent in volume and by 17 per cent in value annually during the 1970s. During the decade, the volume of wood products processed in the tropics before shipment increased from 14 per cent to 19 per cent, and the total value increased from 33 per cent to 43 per cent, indicating growth of wood-processing industries and related employment.

Other products also contributed significantly to export trade. These included a wide variety of latexes, gums, essential oils, medicines, nuts and ornaments. Gum-arabic, for instance, is an important export product for the Sudan. The search for new drugs may expand the scope of these products.

ECONOMIC VALUES OF PRODUCTION

In the decade between 1970 and 1979 the value of agricultural production increased in all regions to varying degrees (Table 7–7). There were accompanying changes in

Table 7–7. Growth in Value of Agricultural Production, 1970–1979[a]

Country/Region	Food Commodities			All Agricultural Commodities		
	Production Index		% Change	Production Index		% Change
	1970	1979	1970–1979	1970	1979	1970–1979
World	100	125	25.0%	100	124	24.0%
Developed M.E.	99	121	22.2%	99	120	21.2%
Developing M.E.	101	127	25.7%	101	125	23.8%
Centrally-Planned	101	127	25.7%	101	127	25.7%
North America	97	126	29.9%	97	125	28.9%
Western Europe	100	118	18.0%	100	118	18.0%
Oceania	99	136	37.4%	100	125	25.0%
Africa	100	116	16.0%	100	115	15.0%
Latin America	102	135	32.4%	101	133	31.7%
Near East	99	132	33.3%	98	129	31.6%
Far East	102	125	22.5%	101	124	22.8%
C.P. Asia	101	137	35.6%	101	136	34.7%
USSR	102	118	15.7%	102	118	15.7%
C.P. Europe + USSR	100	120	20.0%	100	120	20.0%

Source: FAO, (1980 a)

[a] 1969–71 = 100

farming practice, including enlargement of fields, the growing of a single crop over an entire holding, and substantial increases in mechanization with a reduction in labour employed (see for example Figure 7–1). In contrast, arable land per worker decreased in all major regions of the developing world except Latin America (FAO, 1979). The trend towards increasingly intensive agriculture also involves substantial changes in fertilizer and pesticide use, described later, which in turn requires considerable energy inputs. It is estimated that at least 12 per cent of the energy used in the United States went into the chain of food production from farm to distribution. Between 1961–65 and 1976–1978 the average annual growth rate in agricultural output in developed countries was 2.3 per cent, while it was 2.8 per cent in developing market economies. However the growth rate for output per agricultural worker was 5.5 per cent in developed countries.

PROJECTIONS AND FACTORS AFFECTING THE FUTURE

It has often been argued that very large areas of new virgin land could be farmed, especially in the tropics (Kellogg and Orvedal, 1977). But there is debate over how easy

Figure 7–1. Changes in Manpower, Farm Machinery and use of Commercial Fertilizers, 1965–1975 (After OECD, 1979).

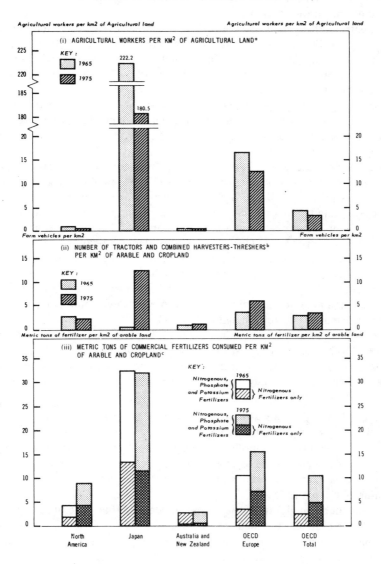

(a) Agricultural land is defined as total arable, crop and permanent grassland.

(b) The data refer to both wheel and crawler tractors used in agriculture and to combined harvester-threshers. The assumption that all tractors are used exclusively on arable and cropland is less satisfactory for countries where such machines play an important role in livestock rearing and forestry.

(c) The data refer to nitrogenous, phosphate and potassium fertilizers. The assumption that they are used exclusively on arable and cropland is less satisfactory for countries where significant amounts of such fertilizers are applied to permanent grassland or forestland.

those soils would be to manage and hence uncertainty over the wisdom and cost of their development (Dassman et al., 1973). The *Global 2000* study (CEQ, 1980), while accepting that the arable area will continue to expand especially in parts of South America, Central Africa and East and Southeast Asia, suggests that the 1971–75 cultivated area of 1.476 billion ha is likely to rise only to some 1.51 billion ha in 1985 and 1.54 billion ha in 2000, partly because of the high cost of development. The study also suggests that competing demands for land for other purposes may well cause a contraction in arable acreages in Western Europe, Eastern Europe, Japan, South Asia, China, North Africa and parts of Central America and East Asia by the early 1990s. Another reason for contraction was demonstrated in the United States where an increase in production was achieved on a smaller area. The projections in Table 7–2 imply a considerably greater rate of further advance.

Buringh projected a gain of 300 million ha for a total area of cropland of 1,800 million ha in 2000 (Buringh, 1981). The FAO (1979) review *Agriculture: Toward 2000* explored various possible paths to agricultural growth, varying the assumptions as to inputs, and suggested that one "normative" scenario for attaining growth in output would derive about 28 per cent from area expansion and 72 per cent from yield increases and more intensive cropping. These projections depend heavily upon expansion of irrigation to increase crop yields and cropping intensity. The FAO report considered an enlargement of irrigated area by 60 per cent might be feasible, but pointed out that a major contribution to production would come from improving existing schemes. Only about one-half of the land under irrigation schemes in developing countries in the late 1970s was believed to be "fully irrigated" (FAO, 1979).

These projections are, however, hampered by imperfect knowledge of the resources available for development. They also depend on assumptions about the likely losses of land through urbanization and soil degradation. Estimates of the world's forest resources also vary widely because they are largely based on extrapolation from scanty observations (Persson, 1977).

Other uncertainties arise because productivity of ecological systems depends so much on climate. The World Meteorological Organization (WMO), in response to the World Food Conference resolutions, established an Agrometeorological Programme, one of whose main objectives is to assist developing countries to apply meteorology to agriculture. But longer-term trends, for example in rainfall and sea level, remain unpredictable (Chapter 2).

It became increasingly apparent during the decade that generalized projections of this type had little practical significance unless supported by detailed investigations of the resources and constraints of individual areas, usually sub-regions of countries. Such analysis was widely encouraged, and began to bear fruit in reports of the type completed by FAO and UNFPA on the potential population supporting capacities of African lands (UN, 1981).

Changes in Bioproductive Systems

SOIL DEGRADATION

THE protection of the soil against hazards of degradation is essential if productivity is to be sustained. Soil deterioration has many causes, but those of immediate concern are inappropriate land-use, erosion, salinization and waterlogging, and chemical degradation.

Erosion is the washing or blowing away of surface soil. It takes place under natural conditions (normal or geological erosion), but is often greatly increased when human activities cause the disappearance of the protective cover of natural vegetation (accelerated erosion). Salinization and alkalinization directly reduce soil fertility and may be caused by accumulation of acid, neutral or alkaline water-soluble salts. The closely-related problem of waterlogging is the state whereby the soil becomes saturated with water within the depth of the active root zone for a period that affects yield and quality of crops. In the mid-1970s the total area of soils in the world affected in some fashion by salt was estimated at 952 million ha (FAO, 1977 a). Chemical degradation may occur if the nutrients in the soil are not replenished to maintain soil fertility, and if soil is contaminated by pollution. In addition land may be lost to agriculture by transfer to other uses.

Wind erosion, overgrazing and other forms of overtaxing the land are active causes of productive soil loss. Soil erosion is a global problem though less pronounced in regions with temperate humid climate. It occurs in both technologically advanced and developing countries, affects both agricultural and forest lands and accounts for major losses in productivity. Deposition of the transported minerals — in fields, rivulets, stream beds, flood plains and finally at the bottom of the sea — is called sedimentation; this also includes chemical precipitation of dissolved components as well as deposition of the remains of animals and plants. Sedimentation may cause environmental problems through the changes it causes in aquatic ecosystems in inland waters and because it reduces the capacity of reservoirs.

In most instances erosion rates are strongly influenced by man's activities. Some estimates of worldwide erosion/sedimentation rates (only a few of those in the literature) are given in Table 7–8. Judson (1968) estimated the mass of material moved annually by all rivers to the ocean "before man's intervention" at 9.3 billion tonnes. That rate "after man's intervention" is given as 24 billion tonnes per year, which means that globally over a long period of time people have increased the erosion rate by a factor of about 2.5 through their activities.

Table 7–8. Estimates of Present Annual Global Rates of Soil Displacement (in billion tonnes per year)

Mass Moved:	Billion Tonnes/y	Reference
Combined solid and dissolved river load carried into oceans	24	Judson (1968)
Consisting of:		
Suspended river solids (without bed load rolling at the bottom)	18.0–18.4	Holeman (1968)
Bed load (estimated at 10% thereof)	1.8	Judson (1968)
Dissolved load	3.9	Livingstone (1963)
Carried by wind from land	0.06–0.36	Judson (1968)
Volcanic debris (into atmosphere)	0.15	Goldberg (1971)
Dust fallout from atmosphere	0.5	Goldberg (1971)
Carried by glacier ice	0.1	Judson (1968)
From extraterrestrial sources (meteorites)	0.00035–0.14	Judson (1968)

At the end of the 1970s the rate of material delivery to the oceans globally was probably about 25 billion tonnes/y. About 15 per cent of this was transported in dissolved form. Some individual rivers carried enormous sediment burdens. The discolouration of the sea off the mouth of the Amazon extends for over 1000 km. The discharge of sediments from the rivers Ganges and Brahmaputra in South Asia is so great that it forms new islands along the southern coasts of Bangladesh and India. Wind transport moves much less material, although Saharan dust is an important factor for the eastern Atlantic Ocean, where it accounts for movements of billions of tonnes per year (Morales, 1979).

By far the largest sediment discharge comes from Asia, according to Robinson (1977), who estimates the inputs in the main regions of the world (in billions of tonnes/y) as:

Asia	14.53
North America	1.78
South America	1.09
Africa	0.48
Europe	0.30
Australia	0.21
Total	18.39

These figures suggest the order of magnitude of current sediment movements. They do no specify the proportion of these average annual loads that result from accelerated soil erosion. But they do suggest that there are significant regional variations in soil erosion and these have a major influence on land productivity patterns.

Various estimates have been made for annual average losses of soil from water and wind erosion in United States (Eckholm, 1976; Biswas and Biswas, 1978). Aggregate figures of that sort are difficult to interpret because of the differences from one small area to another in natural rates of loss and development, type of erosion, distance transported, effect on soil horizon, and productivity of the remaining soil (NAS, 1980). However, these erosion losses were often not accompanied by a decrease in agricultural production or in yields per hectare for major crops. Only a small proportion of the land was abandoned because is was rendered unfit for cultivation. In the USSR, over 70 per cent of agricultural lands are in conditions susceptible to erosion. Five million hectares of land is severely gullied (Zemelnye resoursy, 1973, 198).

The soil erosion problem in the developing countries is estimated to be nearly twice as serious as it is in the United States (Pimentel *et al.*, 1976). For example, accelerated erosion is reportedly affecting 7 per cent of the land in El Salvador, where the silt load in one river basin has increased seven-fold.

History records many instances of massive decline in agriculture (e.g. in Mesopotamia) resulting from the salinization of farmlands and a breakdown of irrigation systems (Jacobsen and Adams, 1978). Excessive irrigation and poor drainage converted many productive farmlands of ancient times into saline and alkaline deserts, and have especially affected the Middle East, Iran, Pakistan, Bangladesh and India. In modern times, the trend in numerous irrigation systems is in the same direction. The area that is now being abandoned is probably about equal to the area currently being reclaimed and irrigated (Holdgate and White, 1977). The problem is particularly acute in semi-arid and arid regions. According to some estimates, between 30 per cent and 80 per cent of all lands under irrigation have been subject to salinization, alkalinization and waterlogging. Salinization is currently affecting large areas of Syria, Iraq, Jordan, Haiti, Mexico, the United States and Afghanistan, and salinization and waterlogging are believed to be serious in 200,000 — 300,000 ha of the world's best land each year (Eckholm, 1975; Worthington, 1977). In the USSR, there are up to 140 million ha of saline soils, and a substantial area of irrigated and irrigable lands is in need of salinity control. Table 7–9 gives details of salt-affected areas in various countries of the world.

The United Nations Conference on Desertification/UNCOD (1977) estimated that one-tenth of the area under irrigation is waterlogged (22 million ha). It is believed that 50 per cent of the irrigated soils in the Euphrates Valley in Syria, 30 per cent in Egypt and more than 15 per cent in Iran are affected by salt or waterlogging (White, 1978). The problems that can affect a large irrigation project are well illustrated in the Indus valley of Pakistan. The water table in many parts of the valley rose from 30 metres to a few centimetres below the surface. Of 5.6 million ha, 3.2 million were affected by the rise in salt level, and 1.4 million ha were no longer being farmed by 1960 (Jackson, 1977). By the end of the decade the process had been reversed over large areas by pumping and other drainage operation. New methods of irrigation e.g. trickle and drip systems, most developed in Israel, improve the efficiency of water use and reduce hazards of waterlogging.

Special problems of saline intrusion are encountered in reclaimed lands of river deltas: this has occurred in Greece, Egypt and the Netherlands. New engineering techniques have been developed in the Netherlands to prevent this hazard. Decline of soil

Table 7–9. Distribution of Salinity and Alkalinity in Countries Most Extensively Affected (Expressed in 1,000 ha)

Area	Solonchaks	Saline phase	Solonetz	Alkaline phase	Total
North America					
Canada	—	264	6,974	—	7,238
United States of America	—	5,927	2,590	—	8.517
Mexico and Central America					
Cuba	—	316	—	—	316
Mexico	242	1,407	—	—	1.649
South America					
Argentina	1,905	30,568	11,818	41,321	85.612
Bolivia	—	5,233	716	—	5.949
Brazil	4,141	—	362	—	4.503
Chile	1,860	3,140	—	3,642	8.642
Colombia	⸳907	—	—	—	907
Ecuador	387	—	—	—	387
Paraguay	—	20,008	1,894	—	21.902
Peru	21	—	—	—	21
Venezuela	1,240	—	—	—	1.240
Africa					
Afars and Issas	59	1,682	—	—	1.741
Algeria	1,132	1,889	—	129	3.150
Angola	126	314	86	—	526
Botswana	1,131	3,878	—	670	5.679
Chad	2,417	—	3,728	2,122	8.267
Egypt	3,283	4,077	—	—	7.360
Ethiopia	319	10,289	—	425	11.033
Gambia	—	150	—	—	150
Ghana	200	—	—	118	318
Guinea	—	525	—	—	525
Guinea-Bissau	—	194	—	—	194
Kenya	3,501	909	—	448	4.858
Liberia	—	362	44	—	406
Libyan Arab Jamahiriya	905	1,552	—	—	2.457
Madagascar	37	—	—	1,287	1.324
Mali	—	2,770	—	—	2.770
Mauritania	150	490	—	—	640
Morocco	42	1,106	—	—	1.148
Namibia	562	—	1,751	—	2.313
Niger	—	—	11	1,378	1.489
Nigeria	455	210	—	5,837	6.502
Rhodesia	—	—	—	26	26
Senegal	141	624	—	—	765
Sierra Leone	—	307	—	—	307
Somalia	1,043	526	3,754	279	5.602
Sudan	—	2,138	—	2,736	4.874

Table 7–9. Distribution of Salinity and Alkalinity in Countries Most Extensively Affected (Expressed in 1,000 ha)– *contd.*

Area	Solonchaks	Saline phase	Solonetz	Alkaline phase	Total
Africa—cont'd.					
Tunisia	990	—	—	—	990
United Republic of Cameroon	—	—	—	671	671
United Republic of Tanzania	—	2,954	—	583	3,537
Zaire	—	53	—	—	53
Zambia	—	—	—	863	863
South Asia					
Afghanistan	2,924	177	—	—	3,101
Bangladesh	—	2,479	—	538	3,017
Burma	634	—	—	—	634
India	2,979	20,243	—	574	23,796
Iran	24,817	1,582	—	686	27,085
Iraq	6,679	47	—	—	6,726
Israel	28	—	—	—	28
Jordan	74	106	—	—	180
Kuwait	209	—	—	—	209
Muscat and Oman	290	—	—	—	290
Pakistan	1,103	9,353	—	—	10,456
Qatar	225	—	—	—	225
Sarawak	—	1,538	—	—	1,538
Saudi Arabia	6,002	—	—	—	6,002
Sri Lanka	180	20	—	—	200
Syrian Arab Republic	—	532	—	—	532
United Arab Emirates	1,089	—	—	—	1,089
North and Central Asia					
China	7,307	28,914	—	437	36,658
Mongolia	3,728	342	—	—	4,070
USSR	11,430	39,662	30,062	89,566	170,720
South East Asia					
Democratic Kampuchea	—	1,291	—	—	1,291
Indonesia	—	13,213	—	—	13,213
Malaysia	—	3,040	—	—	3,040
Socialist Republic of Viet Nam	—	983	—	—	983
Thailand	—	1,456	—	—	1,456
Australasia					
Australia	16,567	702	38,111	301,860	357,240
Fiji	—	90	—	—	90
Solomon Islands	—	238	—	—	238

Source: Szabolcs (1979).

fertility often results from overcropping (nutrient exhaustion), shifting cultivation and repeated burning, which remove nutrients from the system faster than they are replenished by natural processes. This is particularly evident in the tropics.

Considerable progress has been made in developing conservation measures to minimize or prevent soil erosion. Technology and information currently exist to enable much of the soil erosion from both farm and forested lands to be controlled. Farm practices can reduce soil loss by 50–90 per cent and sometimes even by 100 per cent, generally without detriment to high crop yields. Planting trees, including windbreaks and shelter belts, maintenance of grass or cover crops on exposed ground, and controlling grazing markedly reduce losses, especially on slopes. Addition of organic materials to the soil, proper handling of crop residues, tilling along contours and strip cropping are useful preventive techniques. Among the engineering practices that can reduce erosion are the construction of terraces and storm channels, gully control structures, and dams to regulate water flow. Losses in grassland and forest may also be diminished by controlling fires.

FAO has had a long interest in erosion and soil conservation practices. This has included, among other things, a project with UNEP on "A World Assessment of Soil Degradation", an expert consultation held in Rome in November 1976 (FAO Soils Bulletin 33, 1977) and a joint FAO/UNEP consultation on "Assessing Soil Degradation" held in Rome in January 1977 (FAO Soils Bulletin 34, 1977). The USSR gained considerable experience in combating water and wind erosion, illustrated by case studies reported in Biswas and Biswas (1980). An interesting USSR development is buffer-strip cropping, under which crops and pastures are arranged in strips and sowing rates and densities are optimized.

Soils and plants can also be managed by use of proper irrigation and drainage methods to minimize the deleterious effects of waterlogging, salinization and alkalinization. The quality of irrigation water is critical, but desalination to improve its quality is often too expensive to be practical. Use of salt-tolerant plants (cereals such as barley and cotton, vegetable crops such as spinach, date palm and a number of grasses used as forage) may reduce the consequences of salinization. Improved drainage is the measure often employed. The addition of gypsum or sulphur to soil can ameliorate alkalinization.

United Nations agencies have been concerned with the problem for many years. For example, FAO/UNESCO have prepared a map of salt-affected soils, and they have also issued a valuable source book on salinization in relation to irrigation and drainage (FAO/UNESCO, 1973).

Concern by FAO with salinization has also prompted publications dealing with water quality evaluation for irrigation and approaches to solving problems associated with salinization (e.g., Ayers and Westcot, 1976). Effective land-reclamation systems in the USSR have been under construction since the 1960s. These systems depend on protecting the main canals against seepage losses, washing saline soils, chemical treatment of alkaline soils, innovative drainage techniques (including vertical drainage) and irrigation methods (Kovda, 1977).

DESERTIFICATION

The term desert encompasses a wide range of environmental complexes:

(a) rainless deserts, where rainfall is not an annually recurring event;

(b) runoff deserts, where annual rainfall is low (less than 100 mm) and variable;

(c) rainfall deserts, where rainfall is insufficient for sustained crop production (100–200 mm/year);

(d) man-made deserts, parts of the semi-arid steppe country (rainfall 200–350 mm/year) that have been transformed into deserts (desertification) due to man's over-exploitation (Kassas, 1977).

Desertification results from the combined effect of two sets of factors: severe and recurrent drought and human over-exploitation of drylands. It has accompanied man's actions throughout history, and it is still proceeding, apparently at an increasing rate. It is estimated that the productivity of some 60,000 km^2 of land is being destroyed or impaired annually (Eckholm and Brown, 1977). The world desertification map (see Figure 6–1, Chapter 6) shows areas that are particularly susceptible. The Sahara is becoming extended in the Sudan, Ethiopia and Somalia in the east, and in Senegal in the west. Approximately 650,000 km^2 of productive land in the southern portion of the Sahara alone is estimated to have become desert in the last fifty years. In the Sudan, the desert is reported to have advanced southward by 90–100 km in the seventeen years prior to 1975. New areas are being desertified in Brazil, Iran, Pakistan, Bangladesh, Afghanistan and the Middle East. Morocco, Algeria, Tunisia and Libya are also affected. The Earth's drylands population that is eventually threatened totals between 600 and 700 million people while 78.5 million live in areas recently undergoing severe desertification and consequently suffering a decline in agricultural productivity. Fifteen national desertification case studies in twelve countries (Australia, Chile, China, India, Iran, Iraq, Israel, Niger, Pakistan, Tunisia, the United States and the USSR) were presented to UNCOD (Biswas and Biswas, 1980; UNESCO, 1981). The United Nations study on financing the United Nations Plan of Action to Combat Desertification (UN, 1980a) gives a country-by-country estimate of areas affected by desertification; these are summarized in Table 7–10 and in 1980 totalled 27 million ha of irrigated land, 173 million ha of rainfed croplands and 3,071 million ha of rangelands.

In principle, "the cures for desertization have been known for a long time: they consist of the reverse processes, that is, biological recovery . . . of environmental conditions, naturally or artificially induced" (Le Houerou, 1976). Considerable experience in combating desertification has been acquired in the USSR, the United States, Australia, Israel, and elsewhere. But corrective measures are expensive, even though net benefits would exceed costs. The various actions that were planned to follow UNCOD are yet to be fully implemented (Agarwal, 1979). The *UN Administrative Committee on Co-ordination* (ACC) identified four principal obstacles to the

Table 7–10. Arid Lands Affected by Desertification (in thousand hectares)

Continent	Irrigated Land		Rainfed Cropland		Rangeland	
	Total	Area affected by desertification	Total	Area affected by desertification	Total	Area affected by desertification
Africa	7,756	1,366	48,048	39,633	1,182,212	1,026,758
Asia + USSR	89,587	20,572	112,590	91,235	1,273,759	1,088,965
Australia	1,600	160	2,000	1,500	550,000	330,000
Europe (Spain)	2,400	890	5,000	4,200	16,000	15,500
North America	19,550	2,835	42,500	24,700	345,000	291,000
South America	5,389	1,229	14,290	11,859	384,100	319,380
	126,282	27,052	224,428	173,127	3,751,071	3,071,603

Source: UN (1980 a).

implementation of the *Plan of Action to Combat Desertification* set out by UNCOD in 1977:

1. Governments of countries faced with desertification problems or risks appear unable at present to assign sufficiently high priority to desertification control measures, and had only to a limited degree included such measures in their development plans.

2. There is still need to fill gaps in knowledge, particularly concerning integrated inter-disciplinary approaches, including socio-cultural dimensions. Efforts to teach existing knowledge to potential users are far from sufficient.

3. Co-operation within the UN system needs to be strengthened so as to ensure the proper multi-disciplinary approach to projects and to arrange for effective pooling of the efforts and resources of various agencies and bodies.

4. Insufficient financing is seriously limiting the efforts of the UN system to implement the *Plan of Action to Combat Desertification*. There is an urgent need for external sources of finance to increase their assistance to anti-desertification projects.

UNEP established a Consultative Group on Desertification Control which held sessions in May 1978, March 1980, and August 1981, and provided for financial and technical support for a variety of national and multi-national projects. The United Nations Development Programme (UNDP) and UNEP joined in developing the UN Sudano-Sahelian Office which has become an active organ in mobilizing resources for projects in some sixteen countries in the Sudano-Sahelian region.

The UN General Assembly in its consecutive sessions in 1977, 1978, 1979 and 1980 requested the Secretary General to submit to it reports and studies on prospects of additional measures to finance the *Plan of Action to Combat Desertification*. One of these studies concluded that stopping desertification by the year 2000 requires US $4.5 billion annually. This estimate should be read in conjunction with estimates of current annual losses of production due to desertification of US $26 billion (UN, 1980 a).

CHANGES IN RESOURCES MANAGEMENT

Changes from shifting to permanent cultivation

Shifting (swidden) cultivation is an ancient farming system in which the fertility of the soil is maintained by allowing the land to remain fallow for periods of from two to three years. The farmer clears the grassland, bush or forest area, burns the plant material he removes, cultivates the area for a number of years until the yield of crops falls and then abandons the site, allowing fertility to be restored under the unmanaged vegetation that re-colonizes the area.

As populations have increased, the fallow period in shifting cultivation has shortened in some areas, while elsewhere extensive areas have been converted to intensive permanent agriculture, often with unfavourable ecological consequences. Periods of fallow were introduced into early crop rotation systems to allow natural processes of nutrient replenishment to operate, and as an aid to pest and disease control. This was an intermediate stage towards modern intensive cultivation.

Research is now under way in many countries to find how to change from shifting cultivation to permanent cropping systems with a minimum of environmental harm. It is focussing on proper use of chemical and organic fertilizers, devising proper farming systems, applying means of good soil management and introducing mixed cropping and cover crops. The application of these research findings will provide guidance for ecologically sound development in many areas where increased food production is essential.

A good example of such research is the United Nations University study in Northern Thailand (Grandstaff, 1980). Here cultivation on hill slopes poses a threat to soil and watershed managements. The study concluded that the best development approach may be by the improvement of swidden agriculture rather than by its replacement, especially since this is the best means of adjusting technological advances to socio-cultural traditions. The International Council for Research in Agroforestry (ICRAF) was established in Nairobi in 1978 to apply scientific research methods to traditional forms of agriculture that combine trees with food crops, as shifting cultivation does. It maintains agroforestry demonstration plots.

Pasture and rangeland management

Permanent pastures (land used for five years or more for cultivated or wild forage crops) are the most extensive land-use type in the world, covering 3000 million ha (23 per cent of the earth's land surface) (FAO, 1978 a). Other extensive pastures exploited less permanently by nomadic peoples cover most of the arid lands of the world and the tundra. Productivity of pastures ranges from 1 ha supporting 3 to 5 animal units (e.g., on fertile, well-managed pastures in central Europe) to 50–60 ha to support 1 animal unit (e.g., in Saudi Arabia). Grazing lands support most of the world's 3 billion head of domesticated livestock and hence most of the world's production of meat and milk (FAO, 1978 a).

Overgrazing causes extensive destruction of the vegetation in the affected area thereby enhancing the danger of flooding and soil erosion. In many areas farmers are moving onto land that is marginal for agriculture, thereby displacing pastoralists to land that is marginal for livestock (see for instance Van Raay, 1975, for a study on savannah lands in Nigeria). Overstocking is a particularly serious problem in mountain areas such as the Himalayas and the Andes and in semi-arid and sub-humid regions of the Sudanian and Sahelian belt of Africa, North Africa, the Near East, India, Pakistan and Brazil. If continued, extensive grazing beyond the carrying capacity of pasture in arid and semi-arid zones will lead to desertification (Chapter 6). The ecologically sound use of pastures is therefore extremely important. It is being promoted in several countries by an FAO/UNEP programme on Ecological Management of Semi-Arid Rangelands (EMASAR).

Changing hydrology

Irrigation is a major consumer of water in many countries. In many regions, ground water is used for irrigation (Chapter 4). When river water is abstracted for irrigation the rate of water flow in the river is reduced and water quality down-stream may decline. Building reservoirs for irrigation changes the ecosystem of the area impounded for the reservoir. In addition, irrigation increases the water vapour content of the surrounding air, alters the surface runoff characteristics of the land and increases the nutrient level and sometimes the pesticide concentration of the underlying ground water. Concern with the hydrological and other environmental consequences of major irrigation schemes is the basis for the UNESCO MAB Project 4. The WMO has been involved in studies related to evapotranspiration from cropped fields and water requirements of crops, which are aimed at optimum utilization of available water resources.

In contrast, forests often have beneficial effects on water supplies. The runoff of water may be less in managed forested areas than in semi-developed forests. This reduced runoff, in turn, reduces stream flow (Low and Goh, 1972). Studies in southwest Tanzania have shown that forests have much reduced loss of soil and water over the surface than in an area cultivated with an annual grass (Jackson, 1977). Proper plant cover in grasslands may also be beneficial to the hydrology of an area. For example, water was found to penetrate soil more readily and moderate peak water flows were less in an area of northern Uganda with controlled grazing than in a comparable area where the animal grazing was not regulated (Pereira, 1973).

Genetic resource depletion

The *World Conservation Strategy* (IUCN/UNEP/WWF, 1980) noted that:

"The genetic material contained in the domesticated varieties of crop plants, trees, livestock, aquatic animals, and microorganisms — as well as their wild relatives — is essential for the breeding programmes in which continued improvement of yields, nutritional quality, flavour, durability, pest and disease resistance, responsiveness to different soils and climates, and other qualities are achieved. These qualities are rarely if ever permanent. For example, the average lifetime of wheat and other cereal varieties in Europe and North America is 5–15 years. Because of intensive selection for high performance and uniformity, the genetic base of much modern food production has grown dangerously narrow. Only four varieties of wheat produce 75 per cent of the crop grown in the Canadian prairies; and more than half of the prairie wheatlands are devoted to a single variety (Neepawa). Similarly, 72 per cent of the US potato production depends on only four varieties . . . Almost every coffee tree in Brazil descends from a single plant, and the entire US soybean industry is derived from a mere six plants from one place in Asia . . . Unfortunately, while the genetic base of the world's crops and other living resources is narrowing rapidly, the means by which this dangerous situation could be corrected (the diversity of crop varieties and relatives) are being destroyed. Many wild and domesticated varieties of crop plants — such as wheat, rice, millet, beans, yams, tomatoes, potatoes, bananas, limes and oranges — are already extinct and many more are in danger of following them . . . Useful breeds of livestock are also at risk. Of the 145 indigenous cattle breeds in Europe and the Mediterranean region, 115 are threatened with extinction".

The importance of preserving plant germ plasm has been widely recognized in the past decade. The Stockholm Conference stressed it and recommended establishment of a co-ordinating group. Both national and regional genetic conservation programmes now exist, although they are far from adequate in many countries. The Stockholm resolution led to the establishment in 1974 of an International Bureau for Plant Genetic Resource (IBPGR). FAO provides a secretariat for IBPGR, and through CGIAR (the Consultative Group on International Agricultural Research) the international agricultural research institutes, situated in different climatic zones, have begun to maintain or are now maintaining large collections of plant germ plasm. Both UNEP and CGIAR have helped fund these activities. IBPGR is involved in programmes of seed collections, storage and documentation. Various agencies have helped train technicians from developing countries for this work.

FAO, aided by its Panel of Experts on Plant Exploration and Introduction, has been active in stimulating the conservation and testing of plant genetic resources for food production, and there are many national programmes in this area. Concern with the potential loss of tree resources has been expressed by FAO through its Panel on Forest Gene Resources.

Biotechnology

Towards the end of the decade new prospects through biotechnology became apparent: the production of valuable substances, or removal of undesirable materials, with the aid of microbes and their enzymes. Man has always used microbes in fermentation industries. In the early twentieth century these industries developed further to produce chemicals like ethanol and acetone from starch and molasses. The production of antibiotics, enzymes and vaccines followed later. Biotechnological methods were used on a large scale in aerobic and anaerobic waste treatment.

Recent advances have occurred in systems and chemical engineering, automation and genetic engineering, the latter permitting transfer of genetic material from cells from a variety of species with desired characteristics into selected recipient microbes. The microbes then indefinitely produce new individuals with these desired characteristics. A further stimulus resulted from foreseeable oil shortages: the way was opened towards a shift from mineral (non-renewable) resources to renewable agro-based raw materials which could be converted to the desired substances (see Chapter 12).

The decade has thus seen what may be the beginning of the biotechnological era. Examples of the new approach are the large-scale ethanol industry in Brazil, the widespread biogas-producing digesters (Chapter 12), production of selected nitrogen-fixing bacteria (*Rhizobium*) as an inoculant for soil and seed, the production of pest pathogens (e.g. *Bacillus thuringiensis*) for use in biological pest control (in the United States) and the expansion of fodder yeast productions from hydrocarbons, whey and paper industry wastes. Imperial Chemical Industries (UK) started up a factory producing fodder supplement in the form of bacterial cells produced from methanol, while world-wide experimentation on the production of fodder algae from waste has entered the pilot-stage. Although these microbial cells have so far been used only as fodder and fish-food, there are expectations that this protein-rich material, called Single Cell Protein (SCP) eventually could be produced in Southeast Asia in large amounts from rice straw to supplement human food.

The potential of biotechnology as expanded by genetic engineering is generally judged to be high. Already a bacterial strain has been patented capable of degrading a wider range of oil fractions than any strain now known, while biotechnological production of insulin, interferon and certain vaccines have been shown to be possible. Much work has been devoted to the implementation of nitrogen-fixing genes into cereals, which might reduce reliance on nitrogenous fertilizer. Further research is aimed at biotechnological production of hydrogen gas and *in vitro* photosynthesis with enzymes is being attempted.

Thus, while mankind has temporarily profited from its non-renewable oil resources for building up its present chemical industry, it is expected that a return to agro-based raw materials will be inevitable. The bioproductive systems of the earth are therefore becoming exposed to an additional serious pressure: they will not only have to produce food, fibre, fuelwood and timber for a growing world population but also a renewable resource basis for the biotechnological industry, including fuel production. Hence biotechnology will exert an increasing effect on land-use, creating competition for land between indigenous food and cash crops and agro-chemical crops. Furthermore, it will have a prescriptive effect on the kind of plants used, as these must optimally match the criteria the various branches of the new industry impose. Screening of existing economic plants and mould species for these purposes has already begun.

This emerging full "domestication" of the microbial kingdom underlines the need for the preservation of microbial genetic resources in the sense discussed in Chapter 6. This is not only imperative with respect to the many strains now already used for biological nitrogen fixation, pest control and the fermentation industry but especially for new strains resulting from genetic engineering. The microbial populations in the soil, where they fulfil their essential role in nutrient recycling, can also be targets of toxic pollutants. During the decade insufficient attention was paid to this problem.

Environmental Effects of Agricultural Chemicals and Pollutants

AGRICULTURE, forestry and horticulture affect the environment because some of the chemicals used to enhance production or control pests have side-effects on wildlife, aquatic ecosystems or even humans. Conversely, pollutants released to the atmosphere in fuel combustion or by industrial processes can damage crops and trees and reduce production. During the 1970s both these types of interaction continued to cause concern.

FERTILIZERS AND PESTICIDES

Trends in fertilizer use

The increased application of chemical fertilizers supplying the plant nutrients (nitrogen, phosphorus and potassium) is an essential component of modern agriculture. At the start of this century, the total world production of fertilizers was about 2 million tonnes per year. The figure climbed to about 20 million in the 1950s and to more than

100 million in the 1970s (Table 7–11). Changes in world consumption are shown in Figure 7–2, and in further detail by major regions in Table 7–12. It is clear that nitrogen applications have risen especially markedly. In India they increased at an annual rate of 19 per cent between 1959 and 1974 (Mellor, 1976). Nitrogen fertilizer use in Mexico increased from 118,000 tonnes in 1960 to 380,000 tonnes in 1970 and 551,000 tonnes in 1974 (Welhausen, 1976). Fertilizer application in South Asia multiplied with widespread introduction of Green Revolution packages. The number of fertilizer factories also increased.

This increasing use of nitrogen fertilizer is likely to continue. FAO estimates that world consumption will increase to about 84 million tonnes in the 1985/1986 period (FAO, 1978b). The developing countries (70 per cent of the human population) use only about 15 per cent of the world's fertilizers today, but this proportion is certain to change in future (FAO, 1977a).

In developed countries, the consumption of meat and meat products has risen markedly. Animals convert plant protein to animal protein at low efficiency, and hence there has been a parallel increase in the demand for grain and livestock feed concentrates. The change in human dietary habits has therefore led to a substantial rise in fertilizer use.

Environmental problems of fertilizers

Plants rarely use more than 50–60 per cent of the nitrogen in fertilizers (Allison, 1966), or 30 per cent of that in animal manure. The residual nitrogen (nitrate) is liable to pollute ground and surface waters, causing over-enrichment (eutrophication); see Chapter 4, while some may be converted to nitrogen oxides (Chapter 2).

Much work is currently being conducted to determine how to improve fertilizer use and minimize pollution while maximizing food production. In the developed countries means are being pursued to include co-ordinating fertilizer applications with plant need, proper fertilizer placement, better management of irrigation and choosing better fertilizer formulations. One of the more novel methods is to employ fertilizers that slowly release the nutrients; such formulations have been developed but are still expensive. In addition, inhibitors have been devised to slow nitrate formation so that pollution is reduced and there is a greater nitrogen uptake by plants.

Another approach is to improve the efficiency of biological nitrogen fixation, and to extend it to more crop species. The bacteria and algae possessing the capacity to bring about this process are widespread. The association of greatest commercial importance is between leguminous plants and the soil bacterium *Rhizobium*. When working properly, this association can fix large amounts of nitrogen. Projects to expand this type of biological nitrogen fixation in farming systems have high priority in the efforts of international agencies and aid programmes (see the preceding discussion on biotechnology). In the USSR it is estimated that soil bacteria (including nodule bacteria) fix 2.3 million tonnes of nitrogen each year and that soil blue-green algae add 3.4 million tonnes. This biologically fixed nitrogen is almost completely available to the growing plants.

Table 7.11. World Fertilizer Production

	70/71	71/72	72/73	73/74	74/75	75/76	76/77	77/78	78/79
Nitrogenous Fertilizers (thousand tonne N)	33,064	35,031	37,969	40,612	42,487	43,896	46,240	49,331	53,795
Phosphate Fertilizers (thousand tonne P_2O_5)	21,887	23,404	25,914	26,125	27,085	26,126	28,185	29,996	32,363
Potash Fertilizers (thousand tonne K_2O)	17,702	19,307	20,037	22,098	23,578	23,384	25,179	25,760	26,503

Source: UN (1980b).

Figure 7–2. World Fertilizer Consumption (After Data by UN, 1980).

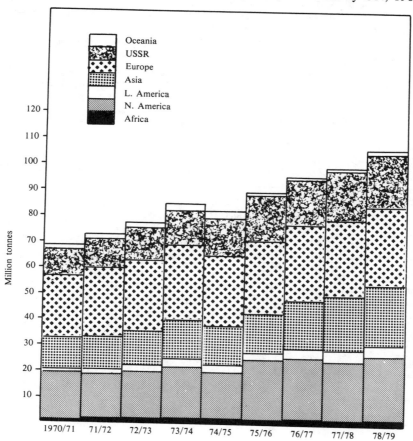

Table 7.12.   World and Major Regional Fertilizer Consumption

	70/71	71/72	72/73	73/74	74/75	75/76	76/77	77/78	78/79
WORLD									
Nitrogenous (thousand tonnes N)	31,540	33,145	35,653	38,567	38,673	42,908	45,039	47,800	51,435
Phosphate (thousand tonnes P_2O_5)	20,719	22,091	23,545	25,229	23,947	25,181	27,333	28,199	30,406
Potash (thousand tonnes K_2O)	16,498	17,403	18,627	20,565	19,659	21,440	23,116	23,171	24,787
AFRICA									
Nitrogenous	823	954	1,062	1,074	1,072	1,251	1,310	1,327	1,389
Phosphate	559	621	672	706	764	824	863	908	915
Potash	257	262	295	309	342	327	339	369	357
NORTH AMERICA									
Nitrogenous	8,420	8,377	8,749	9,767	9,327	11,117	11,537	11,049	11,763
Phosphate	4,940	5,037	5,317	5,440	5,008	5,682	6,024	5,570	6,104
Potash	4,254	4,314	4,598	5,054	4,510	5,238	5,822	5,580	6,297
SOUTH AMERICA									
Nitrogenous	562	596	813	758	829	764	978	1,217	1,210
Phosphate	694	781	1,047	1,165	1,258	1,262	1,601	1,834	1,831
Potash	400	447	570	650	654	665	849	1,103	1,149
ASIA									
Nitrogenous	7,321	7,646	8,554	9,272	9,226	10,005	11,923	13,475	15,162
Phosphate	2,566	3,048	3,401	3,834	3,871	3,783	4,373	4,937	5,733
Potash	1,364	1,385	1,583	1,954	1,990	1,624	1,932	2,156	2,629
EUROPE									
Nitrogenous	9,652	10,251	10,663	11,554	11,314	12,244	12,527	12,953	14,002
Phosphate	7,760	8,102	8,358	8,832	7,962	8,023	8,547	8,660	9,179
Potash	7,475	8,012	8,102	8,706	8,040	8,214	8,357	8,329	8,716
USSR									
Nitrogenous	4,605	5,182	5,606	6,224	6,696	7,339	7,252	7,522	7,658
Phosphate	3,133	3,376	3,516	3,632	4,160	4,728	4,903	5,104	5,360
Potash	2,574	2,788	3,238	3,605	3,884	5,716	5,577	5,400	5,394
OCEANIA									
Nitrogenous	158	138	206	218	208	188	242	256	250
Phosphate	1,067	1,125	1,234	1,619	924	879	1,113	1,185	1,285
Potash	196	194	240	288	238	196	241	234	246

Source: UN (1980 b).

A second type of biological nitrogen fixation is evident in rice fields. Here, blue-green algae (and sometimes the fern, *Azolla,* which contains blue-green algae) grow in the water flooding farmland and make use of atmospheric nitrogen, returning it to the soil-plant system. Recent studies in Asia have demonstrated the quantitative contribution of these organisms. Much greater nitrogen fixation can be obtained by manipulating environmental conditions or microorganisms in the paddy field, and this knowledge, coupled with the paucity or expense of fertilizer in Asia, has prompted international efforts to promote nitrogen fixation in rice culture.

Domestic wastes and sewage sludges

In many developing countries human excreta are traditionally used as a fertilizer. The associated problems of pathogen transmission are familiar (Chapter 10). In the People's Republic of China and elsewhere there were advances during the decade in the composting of these wastes and the production of nutrient-rich effluent that could safely be used in irrigation (Chapter 4). The return of urban organic wastes to the land as sludges after secondary sewage treatment has long been practised in many developed countries. During the decade concern increased over the possible contamination of land with heavy metals (especially if the sewage was derived from industrial as well as domestic sources) and with viruses. Considerable research in Europe and North America was directed towards characterizing sludges and developing codes of practice so that sludges could be used to return nutrients to soil, especially in pasturelands, without the risk of phytotoxicity, persistent soil contamination or hazards to human health.

Pesticides and pest control practices

One estimate (NRC, 1977 a) suggests that 50 per cent of the crop losses now caused by pests could be eliminated by better control practices. This would increase food production from the present 65 per cent of the potential to 82 per cent. Another estimate (Cramer, 1967) is that 30 per cent more food, cotton and other crops could be produced world-wide if they were not destroyed by pests. Even with the best technology, pest damage reduces food production by about one-third in the United States (NRC, 1972).

These damaging pests include insects, microorganisms (both plant pathogens and those that spoil food), nematodes, birds, rats and other rodents and plant competitors (weeds). Mites and ectoparasites of animals such as ticks are also significant. The enormity of the problem of pest control is compounded by the vast array of pest species: more than 1,500 diseases are caused by about 50,000 species of fungi; more than 10,000 insect species are pests; more than 1,500 nematode species damage crop plants. In addition there are about 30,000 weed species of which more than 1,800 are responsible for major economic losses.

There are four basic methods of pest control: cultivation methods (e.g. rotation) which discourage the build-up of pest populations; careful selection of health crop plants (and breeding them for resistance); chemical control of pests using biocides; and deliberate nurture of the natural enemies of pests (biological control). Combinations of these methods, tailored to particular situations, are termed integrated pest management.

Trends in use of chemical pesticides

The period immediately after 1940 saw the rapidly increased use of the insecticides DDT and hexachlorocyclohexane (HCH) and the 'systemic' herbicides 2, 4 – dichlorophenoxy acetic acid (2, 4–D) and 2-methyl-4-chlorophenoxy acetic acid (MCPA). There was a rapid expansion in the range of pesticides approved for use in developed countries in the succeeding years. In the United Kingdom, for example, 63 products were approved for use in agriculture under the Pesticide Safety Precautions Scheme in 1945; in 1960 the total stood at 532; in 1968 at 783; and in 1976, 819 (Sly, 1977).

By the mid-1950s, concern had begun to mount over the side-effects of DDT and other persistent organochlorine pesticides and some organo-metals, especially on birds. In the developed countries, this stimulated action to phase out DDT and other organochlorine insecticides like dieldrin, aldrin and endrin and this trend continued during the 1970s. In England and Wales, the total usage of persistent organochlorines fell from 460 tonnes in 1963 to 300 tonnes in 1967 and 250 tonnes/y in 1970–72 (Royal Commission, 1971, 1974). In 1974 only 22 tonnes of organochlorines were used on arable crops; in 1977 the figure was slightly higher at 35 tonnes (Royal Commission, 1979).

United States figures demonstrate a parallel trend from about 60,000 tonnes in 1963 to 44,000 tonnes in 1967; by 1976 DDT, aldrin and dieldrin had been banned for most uses (CEQ, 1976). These pesticides had also been banned in Scandinavia, Poland, and the Federal Republic of Germany by the end of the decade. However, the value of DDT as a cheap, reliable, persistent and safely handled agent for malarial control has led to the continuing use of some 10,000 tonnes per annum in the developing world through the 1970s, and in some regions, for example South Asia, both production and use rose despite warnings. Concern over this continuing use in the Third World of substances banned in developed countries was reflected in actions like the requirement in 1975 that the US Agency for International Development should not assist the procurement or use of DDT, its congeners, or other pesticides banned in the United States (CEQ, 1976).

As persistent organochlorines have been phased out in developed countries, organophosphorus and carbamate insecticides have replaced them. In 1965, twelve organochlorine insecticides and acaricides were approved for use in the United Kingdom as against five organophosphorus and one carbamate insecticide. In 1975, ten organochlorines remained in the list, but the number of organophosphates had risen to thirty-five. The carbamate insecticides break down relatively quickly in the environment to non-toxic materials, although they are still capable of unwelcome side effects. The organophosphate insecticides vary remarkably in their toxicity between species (which poses problems in screening them). Carbophenothion, approved in the United Kingdom as a winter seed treatment, was shown to be the cause of death in some hundreds of wild geese in 1971 and 1974–75, even though other gramnivorous birds feeding in the same area were apparently unaffected (Stanley and Bunyan, 1979). Malathion has caused considerable damage to fish populations. These materials are also more hazardous to human users than the organochlorines. For these reasons another trend in the 1970s was towards increasingly careful evaluation of such materials before approval, and the development of methods to ensure safe and economical applications.

Crop losses are, however, so severe in some places that there are good arguments for increasing pesticide applications. FAO (1977a) reported that a sample of 38 developing countries applied 162,000 tonnes of pesticides in 1973, and that this represented a 23 per cent increase over the preceding few years. But to reduce serious pest damage FAO estimated that pesticide use would have to be five times greater in the developing countries by 1985 than it was in 1970/71. There is a serious dilemma here, for the cheapest pesticides are the organochlorines, known to accumulate in human fat. The substitution of organophosphorus pesticides brings both higher cost and a need for more carefully trained operators, both of which pose problems.

The increase in the use of herbicides has been a remarkable feature of agriculture in developed countries over the past twenty years. In 1955, 7 types of fungicide and 5 types of contact, soil, or translocated herbicide were approved for use in the United Kingdom (Sly, 1977). In 1965 the figures in the two categories were 20 and 32 respectively, and in 1975, 39 and 78. By 1977 herbicides accounted for the overwhelming bulk of pest control chemicals applied in England and Wales (Royal Commission, 1979), and in 1979, herbicides accounted for 50 per cent of all pesticides applied worldwide (UNEP, 1979).

If herbicides are used correctly, phytotoxic residues do not build up in the soil. Most of their unwelcome environmental effects are due to their impact on desirable plant species and their persistence within agricultural areas. The herbicides 2, 4–D and 2, 4, 5 – trichlorophenoxy acetic acid (2, 4, 5–T), applied in many developed countries in forestry to control woody vegetation, have been alleged to have produced foetotoxic or teratogenic effects on livestock or people due to the presence of a trace contaminant, dioxin.

Changes in pest control practices

The reduction in persistent pesticide use in developed countries has largely been achieved through government action, which has in turn been supported by monitoring programmes that have cast light both on residue accumulation in human and animal tissues and on the resulting alterations in wildlife. Internationally, FAO has been assisting countries to develop schemes for pesticide regulation, for monitoring and for training operators. FAO and the International Atomic Energy Agency (IAEA) have carried out studies on pesticides in soils, plants and food (FAO/IAEA, 1975). In developing countries however, monitoring has not been undertaken widely, and legislation to control pesticides was in the mid-1970s either lacking or inadequate in some forty countries (FAO, 1977a).

The increasing emphasis on testing for possible environmental effects was said to account for between 40 per cent and 60 per cent of the cost of developing a pesticide in the mid-1970s (Roberts, 1975). The rate of introduction of new materials fell in consequence. In the United Kingdom in 1956 the synthesis of about 1,800 chemicals led to one commercial pesticide, but by 1967 the ratio was 5,000 : 1 and by 1976 about 10,000 : 1 (Lewis, 1976). The dilemma to be resolved is between the need to avoid the kind of unwelcome side-effects encountered with earlier pesticides, and the need to avoid delay in finding good substitutes for materials that should be phased out.

Pesticide resistance has been known since 1911 but has developed at an increased rate since 1947 in direct relationship to the increasing use of synthetic products (FAO/UNEP, 1975 UNEP, 1979). The FAO Panel of Experts on Resistance to Pesticides listed 182 resistant strains of insects and mites in 1965; 228 were recorded in 1968 and 364 in 1977 (FAO, 1967, 1968, 1977c).

The classic response to this problem is to change the pesticide, and this is the most practical short-term action in many cases (Mulla, 1977). However, in the longer term, integrated pest control strategies that mix environmental management, breeding of crops resistant to the pest, and chemical and biological control are receiving increasing attention. In parts of the United States this approach has reduced the consumption of pesticide to control cotton pests by more than 50 per cent (Carruth and Moore, 1973). The decade saw considerable advances in understanding of the basic ecology of the man-pest-crop systems (Conway, 1976), and with it an appreciation of the way in which integrated pest control methods can be suited to the biology of the pest. There were also advances in sterile mating techniques, in which one or both sexes of an insect pest is rendered infertile. This technique successfully assisted the control of fruit flies in Mexico and screwworm in the United States (NRC, 1977a). There was also considerable research on chemical attractants and repellents for insects (NRC, 1972). Pheromones (sex hormones) are, for instance, used to attract bark beetles from Norway spruce (Bakke *et al.,* 1977) to locations where they can be killed, thus preventing mating.

EFFECTS OF POLLUTANTS ON AGRICULTURE AND FORESTRY

Nitrogen oxides, sulphur oxides, ozone and peroxyacetyl nitrates (PAN) (components of photochemical smog) all damage the mesophyll cells of leaves, disrupting the chloroplasts and reducing photosynthesis (Ramade, 1977). In biochemical terms, sulphur oxides toxicity may arise through interference with sulphate formation and incorporation in essential compounds like cysteine and methionine (Mudd and Kozlowski, 1975; Treshow, 1978). Ozone may impair protein synthesis through the oxidation of sulphydryl groups, and may also disrupt lipid membranes (Heath, 1975; Treshow, 1978). Particulates, on the other hand, probably act mainly by clogging stomata and forming a crust on the leaf surface. Fluoride and metals deposited on soil are only slightly taken up by plant roots under most conditions, although metals like zinc and aluminium become soluble and absorbable in acid soils (Treshow, 1978). Substances dissolved in irrigation water are especially liable to absorption and even trace concentrations of herbicides can damage crops. However, deposited sulphur may have some beneficial effects on deficient soils and against some fungal pathogens.

The sensitivity of terrestrial organisms to pollutants varies widely between species and according to age, physiological condition, and other factors. Tobacco strains, citrus fruits and coniferous trees are particularly sensitive to ozone and other oxidants (conifers are also sensitive to sulphur dioxide), and show damage when exposed to concentrations of from 2 to 10 parts per hundred million for periods of a few hours (Treshow, 1978; Holdgate, 1979 a, b). Sometimes pollution effects are inconspicuous. Douglas fir (*Pseudotsugu menziesii*) in the vicinity of a source of fluorine have been found with up to 25 per cent less growth even though they showed no signs of damage (Treshow, *et al.*, 1967). Because important commercial plants like maize, cotton, soya beans, lettuce, spinach, tobacco, citrus, grape vines, alfalfa and pines are among those sensitive to one air pollutant or another, serious damage to agriculture and forestry can occur in the vicinity of industrial conurbations.

When photochemical smog in the Los Angeles basin was at its worst, citrus fruits could not be grown within fifty km of the city, and some damage was reported over 3,000,000 ha of California (Leighton, 1966; Thompson and Taylor, 1969). In Canada, white pine was severely damaged or eliminated 24–50 km downwind from smelters (Linzon, 1958; Gordon and Gorham, 1963). Some phytotoxic gases have greater effects in combination than alone; this is true, for example of sulphur oxides, ozone and oxides of nitrogen (Bull and Mansfield, 1974; Capron and Mansfield, 1977), whereas ammonia and sulphur oxide may neutralize one another's effects (Saunders, 1976). Some estimates put the annual cost of air pollution to agriculture in the United States at between $100 million and $500 million in the late 1960s and the 1970s, but all such figures are speculative in the absence of reliable field data (Matthews *et al.*, 1972; CEQ, 1973; NRC, 1977 b).

Airborne pollutants affect animals, especially via areas of gaseous exchange such as the lungs or insect trachea. Ozone, sulphur oxide and PAN act directly on the cells of mucous membranes and cause respiratory disorders in mammals. Particulates are also deposited in various parts of the respiratory tract, causing irritation and in some cases (as with asbestos) more specific illness (Holdgate, 1979 a, b). Fluoride, lead and other metals are, in contrast, largely acquired by animals through ingestion of contaminated herbage. Fluoride is the cause of the best-documented impact of air pollution on domestic livestock, producing acute poisoning and bone damage if consumed in excessive quantity. Fluorosis has been encountered in cattle and sheep grazing land around smelters, brick-works, and other industries (MAFF, 1964) and lead poisoning has occurred in similar situations. In the United Kingdom such poisoning is rare and has declined: only twelve cases of fluorosis were reported in the five years up to 1979 (Royal Commission, 1979), and one of these at least was due to contamination of the vegetation from sewage sludge rather than airborne fluoride. The significance of airborne pollutants to man is discussed in Chapter 10.

The effect of acid rain (Chapter 2) on terrestrial ecosystems is a matter of concern. The rate of forest growth is said to have declined by between 2 and 7 per cent in southern Scandinavia and the northeastern United States between 1950 and 1970, but it is not possible to state unequivocally that this was due to acid precipitation (Sweden, 1972; Dochinger and Seliga, 1976; Tamm, 1976). In one area of the United States acid rain was suspected of causing damage to young spruce trees downwind from a coal-fired power station in Ohio (OTA, 1979). Laboratory studies have shown that acid mist can damage sensitive species and that acidification of the soil can increase the rate of uptake of toxic metals (Shen Miller, *et al.*, 1976; Bourdeau and Treshow, 1978; Treshow, 1978). Other experiments indicate that acid precipitation can accelerate cuticular erosion, alter responses to disease-causing organisms, affect the rate of germination of conifer seeds and the establishment of seedlings, decrease soil respiration and increase the leaching of nutrient ions from the soil (Malmer, 1976; Tamm, 1976). But terrestrial ecosystems are complex, with many living and non-living components, and no firm conclusions could be drawn at the end of the decade about whether significant damage was occurring in nature. Some changes in chemical properties in Swedish forest soils may have been caused partly by acid precipitation (Troedsson, 1980).

Losses in Food Production

POST-HARVEST LOSSES

Harvested crops may be subject to damage (spoilage, partial deterioration) or loss (reduction in useable quantity). These losses occur during transition from the land to the consumer. De Padua (1974) gives the following estimates of post-harvest rice losses in Southeast Asia: harvesting 1–3 per cent, handling 2–7 per cent, threshing 2–6 per cent, drying 1–5 per cent, storing 2–6 per cent, and milling 2–10 per cent. Total losses thus range up to 37 per cent.

Table 7–13 shows estimates of minimum post-harvest losses in food products including durable crops (cereals and legumes) and perishable crops (root crops, vegetables, fruits). These losses are mostly related to harvesting, storage, processing, distribution and pests. Chemicals are extensively used in pest control and in preservation.

Table 7.13. Estimates and Projections of Minimum Post-harvest Food Losses in Developing Countries

	Durables	Perishables
1976 Food Production (million tonnes)	420	255
Estimated minimum loss (%)	10	20
Estimated minimum loss (million tonnes)	42	51
Estimated loss value (US$ billions)	6.9	1.3
1985 Projected Food Production (million tonnes)	472	302
Estimated minimum loss (%)	10	20
Estimated minimum loss (million tonnes)	47	60
Estimated loss value (US$ billions)	7.8	1.5

Source: NAS (1978).

Even with sophisticated technology in the United States, 10–30 per cent of vegetable production is lost between harvesting and consumption. About 10 per cent of the world's harvest of cereal grains, a major component of the global food supply, is wasted. If this figure could be reduced even from 10 to 8 per cent, 22 million tonnes of grain would be saved each year, enough to feed 60 million people. Thus, although considerable uncertainty exists about the extent of the post-harvest losses, general agreement is evident on the enormity of the problem (NRC, 1977 a).

In the past few years, technology to reduce such losses has markedly improved, especially in developed countries. Some of this technology has also been introduced into the developing regions. A variety of traditional microbial fermentation procedures, which not only preserve but often increase protein and vitamin content and enhance taste, are common in Asia and could be developed further (Steinkraus, 1980). But a great deal more remains to be done.

It is evident that in developing countries, where resources are insufficient for development and infrastructure is inadequate, food losses could be minimized — especially in the tropics — by product processing on the spot (canning food and drying vegetables, grain and fruit). This would also help to solve the problem of rural employment in developing countries. Setting up rural food-processing industries would assist the introduction of industrial techniques into agriculture, increase education and improve the infrastructure. Experience in the establishment and management of agro-industrial complexes in the USSR could be helpful to developing countries.

CHEMICAL CONTAMINATION OF FOOD AND LIVESTOCK FEEDS

Chemical contaminants reach food from many sources (UNEP, 1981). Pesticides used in farming often find their way into crops. In addition, veterinary drugs and animal growth-promoting chemicals may pass into meat. Some preservatives (such as sodium nitrite), chemicals and materials contained in packaging (like lead from the seams of side-soldered cans) may also enter the food. Crops may be contaminated by airborne deposition of industrial emissions, or via irrigation water. The current trend to centralize food processing, distribution and handling of food and the greater reliance on large storage facilities can aggravate some of these problems.

Considerable attention has been given to monitoring the amount of pesticides (particularly organochlorines) in food, establishing safe concentrations and finding means of keeping the levels low. This has been an international effort. Government regulations and monitoring, coupled with enforcement of these regulations, have led to a decline in pesticide concentration in food supplies in many countries.

Heavy metals and metalloids, including mercury, cadmium, lead, arsenic and selenium, are among contaminants of food. Many of these are returned to soil with urban wastes that are applied to land.

Sewage sludge, raw sewage, manure and farm wastes used as soil improvers sometimes lead to elevated concentrations of metals in the food supply. Other heavy metals enter the food supply from industrial discharges into watercourses or by direct deposition on the soil. Certain metals (e.g. mercury and tin) are present in pesticide formulations, from which they enter the soil-plant system. Crop plants vary in their ability to take up and accumulate heavy metals, but some can assimilate considerable quantities. In addition, metallic dusts (especially those containing lead) are locally deposited on leaves. If the plant accumulating the metal is not visibly affected it may be used as a food or feed source and hence enter the human food chain.

Fungicides containing mercury have been used widely in agriculture for more than fifty years as a seed treatment to control pathogens affecting seed germination or subsequent growth of seedlings. Several disastrous cases of human poisoning from consumption of treated seed grain have been recorded, the worst killing over 500 people in Iraq in late 1971 and early 1972 (UNEP, 1980). Birds have also been killed from ingesting treated seeds. Mercury-containing fungicides have now been completely banned in many countries, and markedly curtailed in others.

FAO and the World Health Organization (WHO) have been involved in setting international standards for safe food. FAO, WHO and UNEP are developing a Joint International Food and Animal Feed Contamination Monitoring Programme. Through the FAO Panel of Experts on Pesticide Residues and Environment and the WHO Expert Committee on Pesticide Residues, these agencies have been involved in evaluating hazards and extablishing acceptable levels of many pesticides in food. These levels are published in a series of papers issued by FAO. FAO and WHO took action to alert governments when the hazards of mercurial seed dressings were recognized (FAO/WHO, 1974).

LIVESTOCK WASTES AND CROP RESIDUES

In the past decade there was considerable research and development to avoid the pollution that the concentrated animal wastes resulting from intensive livestock husbandry can cause — and where possible to make use of the considerable biological energy and plant nutrient value they contain. The methods developed include land disposal and odour control and storage tanks to hold the wastes until they can be safely discharged or composted. Animal manure remains a vital source of plant nutrients. Manure produced in the United States contains nitrogen equivalent to about 70 per cent of that supplied from chemical fertilizers. In developing countries, cattle manure in 1971 contained about 18, 5 and 14 million tonnes of nitrogen, phosphorus and potassium, respectively (NRC, 1977 a). Processes involving decomposition under controlled conditions to produce methane gas as a farm energy source have been adopted in many countries. These processes lead to the elimination of many pathogens, diminish the odour, reduce the potential for polluting water and produce an end-product still useful as a fertilizer (Chapter 12). Agro-industrial waste waters have, if properly treated, considerable value in irrigation.

Wastes also arise when unused crop portions remain in the field. In the United States, 150–200 million tonnes of such residues are generated each year (Walker, 1977). Worldwide, about 1,700 million tonnes of cereal straw and 50 million tonnes of sugarcane tops are produced annually, and little of it is utilized (NRC 1977 a; UNEP, 1978). Such remains are frequently returned directly to the soil, but in many areas maize, rice and wheat sraw and sugarcane residues are burned, with both a loss of their contained nutrients and the creation of air pollution. One calculation suggests that this process adds more nitrogen oxides to the atmosphere than industry does (Crutzen, *et al.,* 1979). Public pressure to reduce such burning has increased during the decade and some countries have introduced regulations to prevent or control it.

RESIDUES FROM THE FOOD PROCESSING INDUSTRY

Many organic materials remain after a particular food, feed, wood or industrial product is processed. The pulp and paper industry, fibreboard manufacturing and activities related to fish processing are major polluters of rivers, lakes and the air because of the effluents discharged. Canning, dairying and other food processing effluents also cause considerable water pollution because of their richness in organic matter.

Many ways have been developed, some quite recently, to make use of these wastes and to reduce environmental stresses (UNEP, 1978). Remains from the meat industry have found many uses: tallow and grease is obtained from animal fat and animal feed is obtained from unused meat. The whey left after the manufacture of cheese has found use in other dairy products as well as in baking. Left-over maize cobs have been converted to organic acids of industrial importance, oil and bulk filler for formulating animal feeds (Tolba, 1978). In some Asian countries, one-third of the animal blood produced is utilized to make poultry feed and in fertilizers (Bhushan, 1977).

DISEASE

Diseases of farm animals are widespread. They diminish the yields. Diseased animals may also cause illnesses in humans. Furthermore, the extent of certain diseases in developing countries may be so great that the modernization of livestock production is prevented. The destruction of large populations of animals by disease is not a new problem, but only recently have some countries begun to develop extensive programmes to minimize communicable livestock diseases. The relationship between weather and the incidence of animal diseases is one topic in WMO programmes (WMO, 1978) seeking to predict outbreaks of such diseases.

Trypanosomiasis is a special problem. Probably 700 million ha of land in the humid parts of Africa are under-used for raising livestock because of the presence of tsetse flies, which carry African trypanosomiasis. If the disease were under control, probably 125 million cattle could be raised, in contrast to the 7.5 million currently in this region (NRC, 1977 a). The International Laboratory for Research on Animal Diseases (ILRAD) in Nairobi is working to find an economic control of this disease.

Pathogens, including fungi, bacteria, viruses and nematodes, also have a significant impact on crop production and tree growth in the tropics and temperate zones. Many plant diseases can be affectively controlled by developing resistant crop varieties, and some are brought under control by crop rotation, the use of fallow periods, adding organic matter to soil and suitable sanitation procedures. The effects of some are minimized only by the use of fungicides and fumigants.

Future Prospects

MANKIND seems to have exerted four kinds of adverse influences on the land. First is the transformation of land to new uses that cannot be sustained under prevailing economic and technological conditions. The clearest example of this is the expansion of agriculture into areas unsuitable because of either climate or soil. Linked with this is the neglect of the protective vegetation of watersheds and fragile soils. Second is the failure to crop modified ecosystems in a suitable manner, for example taking a sustained yield of timber for fuelwood from natural forest or raising appropriate numbers of cattle, sheep and goats, on grazing land. Third is the erosion of genetic resources as a result of failure to preserve adequate and well-chosen samples of natural populations and ecosystems. And last is the unnecessary reduction of the productive capacity of the land by improperly siting cities, roads and industry, and by pollution caused by industries.

At least four kinds of influence worked toward a more sustainable use of the land. First, in some areas, such as in parts of Western Europe and the United States, the market conditions encouraged management practices that made more efficient and sustainable use of capital resources. Second, dissemination of advances in technology, such as improvements in cereal seeds for the Indian subcontinent or in trickle irrigation for dry areas, made it possible to enhance the productivity of certain terrestrial ecosystems without serious deterioration. Third, the strengthening of national and international activities in support of agricultural research, such as through the Consultative Group on International Agricultural Research (CGIAR) and its network of research stations accelerated the flow of new knowledge about the land and water processes involved. Fourth, government measures to counter unwise transformations of ecosystems found increasing support at national and international levels.

The evolution during the years following the Stockholm Conference of the concepts and principles of ecologically sound development needs to be followed by practical and compatible action on the ground if past mistakes are not to be repeated. New development schemes should be preceded by proper land evaluation. This requires the creation of institutional frameworks for rational land management. The techniques for this have been greatly improved recently, and land evaluation surveys have now been carried out in many developing countries. There are schemes in most parts of the world to demonstrate that productive development of new lands is possible; those of the Federal Land Development Authority in Malaysia are a good example.

The ideal of ecologically sustainable development should include not only good land-use planning and management for productive purposes, but also a sufficient element of preservation, including the safe-guarding of genetic resources and samples of ecosystems (Chapter 6). Schemes are only now being developed and accepted that contain all these elements. The arguments for protection are national, and to persuade local communities they must be accompanied by convincing arguments. Governments, supported by international agencies, have a central role here.

Where the soil resource is deteriorating at an alarming degree, as it is in sectors of the semi-arid zone, the necessity for an integrated approach to managing local resources has only been underlined by the slow progress made during the decade. Long explained in national and international reports, the crucial nature of that need received world attention in the Sahelian crisis and in the judgements offered by the UN Conference to Combat Desertification in 1977. The concrete but pitifully slow progress made in translating conference aspirations into action illustrates the social obstacles encountered in mobilizing local resources to turn the tide.

In parallel with the development of environmentally sound schemes of intensive land management, much can be done to improve the useful crop taken by man from natural forests and grazing lands — and from wild as well as domesticated species. Such lands have the great merit of providing a considerable yield without the intensive input of energy, nutrients, or human management. The ecological principles for their sustained use are far better understood than they were a decade ago. But there is surprisingly little evidence of actual successful management on the ground, especially in developing countries. If — as seems likely — intensive agriculture in future will remain concentrated on the favoured 15–20 per cent of the earth's land surface, it is all the more vital not to squander the more modest but real productivity of the remainder by mismanagement.

The decade since the Stockholm Conference has nonetheless brought real advances in both environmental and institutional terms. Food production in terms of both plant and animal crops has risen. Export evaluation suggests that it will continue to rise even though the balance between production and consumption remains precarious, and food shortages over substantial areas can only be prevented by a trading pattern or aid pattern that shifts surpluses from more favoured regions. Local scarcities seem inevitable, with deeply regrettable consequences in terms both of human suffering and pressure to use land in the short-term emergency in a way that may reduce its future capacity.

Much has been done to curb some of the problems associated with man's use of biological productivity. The pollution hazard of excessive fertilizer applications, and of toxic chemicals that may both reduce crop yields and contaminate human foodstuffs, are better understood and are coming under increasing control. The problems associated with post-harvest losses, mycotoxins and microbial contamination are also receiving attention. A major effort to conserve genetic diversity is in hand. Some interesting and hopeful techniques to make better use of agricultural wastes have been developed. Governments have a central role in such action, and over the past decade many of them have adopted measures that are timely and effective.

The priorities in the decade ahead lie in the developing world, for it is here that the needs are greatest, the pressures most intense, the environment least easy to manage, and the human resources of trained personnel in least supply. Many scientific studies, and some practical demonstration projects indicate what can be done: the overwhelming priority now is for more practical action on the ground in such areas as the fight against desertification, the conservation of soil, the wise management of forests, sound water management, and appropriate agriculture. The least encouraging feature of the past ten years has been the slow pace at which accepted scientific knowledge is being applied.

References

Agarwal, A. (1979), Why the World's Deserts are Still Spreading, *Nature*, 27, 167.

Allison, F. E. (1966), *Advan. Agron.*, 18, 219–258.

Ayers, R. S. and D. W. Westcot (1976), *Water Quality for Agriculture,* Irrigation and Drainage Paper 29, Food and Agriculture Organization of the United Nations, Rome.

Bakke, A. *et al.* (1977), Field Response to a New Pheremonial Compound Isolated from *Ips Typographus, Naturwissen.*, 64, 98.

Bhushan, B. (1977), *Agricultural Residues and their Utilization in Some Countries of South and South-East Asia*, UNEP/FAO/ISS 4/06. United Nations Environment Programme, Nairobi.

Biswas, M. R. and A. K. Biswas (1978), Loss of Productive Soil, *Inter J. Environ. Studies*, 12, 189.

Biswas, M. R. and A. K. Biswas, Editors (1980), *Desertification; Case Studies Prepared for UN Conference on Desertification*, Pergamon Press, Oxford.

Bourdeau, P. and M. Treshow (1978), Ecosystem Response to Pollution. In G. C. Butler (Editor), *Principles of Ecotoxicology: SCOPE* 12, John Wiley, Chichester.

Bull, S. N. and T. A. Mansfield (1974), Photosynthesis in Leaves Exposed to SO_2 and NO_2, *Nature*, 250, 443.

Buringh, P. (1981), *An Assessment of Losses and Degradation of Productive Agricultural Land in the World*. Paper Prepared for the Second Meeting of the Working Group on Soils Policy, Rome, February 1981, Agricultural Univ., Wageningen, The Netherlands.

Capron, T. M. and T. A. Mansfield (1977), Inhibition of Net Photosynthesis in Toronto in Air Polluted with NO and NO_2, *J. Exp. Botany*, 27, 1181.

Carruth, L. A. and L. Moore (1973), *J. Econ. Entomol.*, 66, 187.

CEQ (1973), *Environmental Quality*. Annual Report of the Council on Environmental Quality, Washington, D.C.

CEQ (1976), *Environmental Quality*, Annual Report of the Council on Environmental Quality, Washington, D.C.

CEQ (1980), *The Global* 2000 *Report to the President*, Council on Environmental Quality, Washington, D.C.

Conway, G. R. (1976), Man Versus Pests, In R. M. May (Editor), *Theoretical Ecology*, Blackwell, Oxford.

Cramer, H. H. (1967), Plant Protection and World Food Production, *Pflanzenschutz Nachrichten*, 20, 1.

Crutzen, P. J. *et al.* (1979), *Nature*, 182, 253.

Dassmann, R. F. *et al.* (1973), *Ecological Principles for Economic Development*, John Wiley, London.

De Padua, D. B. (1974), *Post-harvest Rice Technology in Indonesia, Malaysia, the Philippines and Thailand*, International Development Research Centre, Ottawa.

Dochinger, L. S. and T. A. Seliga (1976), Acid Precipitation and the Forest Ecosystems, *J. Air. Pollut. Control*, 25, 1104.

Eckholm, E. P. (1975), *The Other Energy Crisis: Firewood*. Worldwatch Institute, Washington. D.C.

Eckholm, E. P. (1976), *Losing Ground*, W. W. Norton and Co., New York.

Eckholm, E. and L. R. Brown (1977), *Spreading Deserts; The Hands of Man*, Worldwatch Institute, Washington, D.C.

FAO (1967), *Report 1st Session, FAO, Working Party of Experts on Resistance of Pests to Pesticides*. Rep. PL/1965/18. Food and Agriculture Organization of the United Nations. Rome.

FAO (1968), *Report 3rd Session, FAO Working Party of Experts on Resistance of Pests to Pesticides*. PL/1967/M/8. Food and Agriculture Organization of the United Nations, Rome.

FAO (1977a), *The State of Food and Agriculture*, Food and Agriculture Organization of the United Nations, Rome.

FAO (1977b), *FAO Production Yearbook* 1976, Food and Agriculture Organization of the United Nations, Rome.

FAO (1977c), *Report FAO Panel of Experts on Pest Resistance to Pesticides and Crop Loss Assessment*. FAO Plant Production and Protection Paper No. 6, Food and Agriculture Organization of the United Nations, Rome.

FAO (1978a), *FAO Production Yearbook*, Food and Agriculture Organization of the United Nations, Rome.

FAO (1978b), *Annual Fertilizer Review*, Food and Agriculture Organization of the United Nations, Rome.

FAO (1979), *Agriculture: Toward 2000*, Document C 97/24, Food and Agriculture Organization of the United Nations, Rome.

FAO (1980a), *FAO Production Yearbook* 1979, Food and Agriculture Organization of the United Nations, Rome.

FAO (1980b), 1978 *Yearbook of Forest Products*, Food and Agriculture Organization of the United Nations, Rome.

FAO/IAEA (1975), *Origin and Fate of Chemical Residues in Food, Agriculture and Fisheries*, International Atomic Energy Agency, Vienna.

FAO/UNEP (1965), *The Development and Application of Integrated Pest Control*, FAO/UNEP Report AGR/1974/M/8, Food and Agriculture Organization of the United Nations, Rome.

FAO/UNESCO (1973), *Irrigation, Drainage and Salinity*, Hutchinson, London.

FAO/WHO (1974), *The Use of Mercury and Alternative Compounds As Seed Dressings*, Food and Agriculture Organization of the United Nations, Rome.

Goldberg, E. D. (1971), Atmospheric Dust, the Sedimentary Cycle and Man, *Geophysics*, 1, 117.

Gordon, A. G. and E. Gorham (1963), Ecological Aspects of Air Pollution From an Iron-sintering Plant at Wawa, Ontario, Canada, *J. Botany*, 41, 1063.

Grandstaff, T. B. (1980), *Shifting Cultivation in Northern Thailand*, United Nations University. Resource Systems Theory and Methodology Series, No. 3.

Heath, R. L. (1975), Ozone, In J. B. Mudd and T. T. Kozlowski (Editors), *Responses of Plants to Air Pollutants*, Academic Press, New York.

Holdgate, M. W. (1979 a), Targets of Pollutants in the Atmosphere, *Phil. Trans. Roy. Soc.*, London, A 290, 591.

Holdgate, M. W. (1979 b), *A perspective of Environmental Pollution*, Cambridge Univ. Press.

Holdgate M. W. and G. F. White, Editors (1977), *Environmental Issues: SCOPE 10*, John Wiley, London.

Holeman, J. N. (1968), The Sediment Yield of Major Rivers of the World. *Water Resources Res.*, 4, 737.

Jackson, I. J. (1977), *Climate, Water and Agriculture in the Tropics*, Longman, London.

Jacobsen, T. and R. M. Adams (1978), Salt and Silt in Ancient Mesopotamian Agriculture, *Science*, 128, 1251.

Judson, S. (1968), Erosion of the Land, or What's Happening to our Continents? *Amer. Scientist*, 56, 356.

IUCN/UNEP/WWF (1980), *World Conservation Strategy*, International Union for Conservation of Nature and Natural Resources, United Nations Environment Programme and World Wildlife Fund. IUCN, Gland, Switzerland.

Kassas, M. (1977), Arid and Semi-Arid Lands; Problems and Prospects, *Agro-Ecosystems*, 3, 185.

Kellogg, C. E. and C. Orvedal (1977), *Potentially Arable Soils of the World and Critical Measures for Their Use*, US Department of Agriculture, Washington, D.C.

Kovda, V. A. (1977), Soil Loss: An Overview, *Agro-Ecosystems*, 3, 205.

Le Houérou, H. N. (1976), Rehabilitation of Degraded Arid Lands. In A. Rapp. *et al.* (Editors), Can Desert Encroachment be Stopped? *Ecological Bull.*, Stockholm, No. 24.

Leighton, P. A. (1966), Geographical Aspects of Air Pollution, *Geogr. Rev.*, 56, 151.

Lewis, G. E. (1976), Proc. 18th Symposium; British Ecological Soc., p. 237.

Linzon, S. N. (1958), *The Influence of Smelter Fumes on the Growth of White Pine in the Sudbury Region*, Ontario Dept. Lands and Forests and Ontario Dept. of Mines, Toronto.

Livingstone, D. A. (1963), *Chemical Composition of Rivers and Lakes*, US Geol. Survey, Professional Paper 440–G.

Low, K. S. and K. C. Goh (1972), *J. Trop. Geogr.*, 35, 60.

MAFF (1964), *Fluorosis in Cattle*, Animal Diseases Surveys, Report No. 2. HMSO, London.

Malmer, N. (1976), Acid Precipitation; Chemical Changes in the Soil. *Ambio*, 5, 231.

Matthews, W. H. *et al.* (1972), *Man's Impact on Terrestrial and Oceanic Ecosystems*, MIT Press, Cambridge, Mass.

Mayer, J. (1976), The Dimensions of Human Hunger. *Scientific Amer.*, 325, 3, 40.

Mellor, J. W. (1976), The Agriculture of India, *Scientific Amer.*, 235, 155.

Morales, C., Editor (1979), *Saharan Dust; Mobilization, Transport, Deposition; SCOPE* 14, John Wiley, Chichester.

Mudd, J. B. and T. T. Kozlowski, Editors (1975), *Responses of Plants to Air Pollutants*, Academic Press, New York.

Mulla, M. S. (1977), Resistance in Culicine Mosquitoes in California; Countermeasures. In D. L. Watson and A. W. Brown (Editors), *Pesticide Management and Insecticide Resistance*, Academic Press, New York.

NAS (1978), *Post-harvest Food Losses in Developing Countries*, National Academy of Sciences, Washington, D.C.

NAS (1980), *Report of the Workshop on Soil Transformation and Productivity*, Commission on Natural Resources, National Research Council, National Academy of Sciences, Washington, D.C.

NRC (1972), *Pest Control Strategies for the Future*, National Research Council, National Academy of Sciences, Washington, D.C.

NRC (1977 a), *World Food and Nutrition Study*, Vol. 1–3. National Research Council, National Academy of Sciences, Washington, D.C.

NRC (1977 b), *Ozone and Other Photochemical Oxidants*, National Research Council, National Academy of Sciences, Washington, D.C.

OECD (1976), *Land Use Policies and Agriculture*, Organization for Economic Co-operation and Development, Paris.

OECD (1979), *The State of the Environment in OECD Member Countries*, Organizaion for Economic Co-operation and Development, Paris.

OTA (1979), *The Direct Use of Coal*, Office of Technology Assessment, Washington, D.C.

Pereira, H. C. (1973), *Land Use and Water Resources*, Cambridge Univ. Press.

Persson, R. (1977), *Forest Resources of Africa; Part II: Regional Analysis*. Research Note No. 22, Royal College of Forestry, Stockholm.

Pimentel, D. *et al.* (1976), Land Degradation; Effects on Food and Energy Resources. *Science*, 194, 149.

Ramade, F. (1977), *Ecotoxicologie*, Masson, Paris.

Roberts, E. H. (1975), Proc. 8th Insecticide and Fungicide Conference, p. 891.

Robinson, A. R. (1977), *Relationship Between Soil Erosion and Sediment Delivery*, IAHS Public. No. 122, p. 159.

Royal Commission (1971), *First Report of the Royal Commission on Environmental Pollution*, HMSO, London.

Royal Commission (1974), *Pollution Control; Progress and Problems*. Fourth Report of the Royal Commission on Environmental Pollution, HMSO, London.

Royal Commission (1979), *Agriculture and Pollution*. 7th Report of the Royal Commission on Environmental Pollution, HMSO, London.

Saouma, E. (1979), *Statement of the Director General of FAO to the United Nations Symposium on Interrelations: Resources, Environment, Population and Development*, Stockholm, August, 1979.

Saunders, P. J. M. (1976), *The Estimation of Pollution Damage*, Univ. Press, Manchester.

Shen Miller, I. *et al.* (1976), Simulated Acid Rain on Growth and Cadmium Uptake in Soy-beans, *Plant Physiology,* 57, 50.

Sly, J. M. A. (1977), In F. H. Perring and K. Mellanby (Editors), *Ecological Effects of Pesticides,* Academic Press, New York.

Stanley, P. J. and P. J. Bunyan (1979), *Hazards to Wintering Geese and Other Wildlife from the Use of Dieldrin and Carbophenthion as Wheat Seed Treatment.* Proc. Roy. Soc., London, Ser. B., 205, 31.

Steinkraus, K. H. (1980), Food From Microbes, *Bioscience,* 30, 384.

Sweden (1972), *Air Pollution Across National Boundaries; Impact on the Environment of Sulphur in Air and Precipitation.* Sweden's Case Study Presented to the United Nations Conference on The Human Environment, Stockholm.

Szabolcs, I. (1979), *Review of Research on Salt-Affected Soils,* Natural Resources Research No. 15, UNESCO, Paris.

Tamm, C. O. (1976), Acid Precipitation; Biological Effects in Soil and on Forest Vegetation, *Ambio,* 5, 235.

Thompson, C. R. and O. C. Taylor (1969), *Environ. Sci. Techn.,* 10, 934.

Tolba, M. K. (1978), Food Waste, *New Zealand Environ.,* 21, 18.

Treshow, M. *et al.* (1967), Responses of Douglas Fir to Elevated Atmospheric Fluorides, *Forest Sci.,* 13, 114.

Treshow, M. (1978), Terrestrial Plants and Plant Communities. In G. C. Butler (Editor), *Principles of Ecotoxicology:* SCOPE 12, John Wiley, Chichester.

Troedsson, T. (1980), *Ten Years Acidification of Swedish Forest Soils.* Proc. Intern. Conference on Ecological Impact of Acid Precipitation, Sandefjord, Norway, SNSF Project, Oslo.

UN (1980a), *Study on Financing the United Nations Plan of Action to Combat Desertification,* A/35/396, United Nations, New York.

UN (1980b), 1979 *Statistical Yearbook,* United Nations, New York.

UN (1981), *Report on Monitoring of Population Trends,* ESA/P/WP.68, United Nations, New York.

UNEP (1978), *The State of The Environment – Selected Topics,* United Nations Environment Programme, Nairobi.

UNEP (1979), *The State of The Environment – Selected Topics,* United Nations Environment Programme, Nairobi.

UNEP (1980), *The State of The Environment – Selected Topics,* United Nations Environment Programme, Nairobi.

UNEP (1981), *The State of The Environment – Selected Topics,* United Nations Environment Programme, Nairobi.

UNESCO (1981), *Case Studies on Desertification,* United Nations Educational, Scientific and Cultural Organization, Paris.

USDA (1980), *World Food Production,* US Department of Agriculture, Washington, D.C.

USNALS (1981), *National Agricultural Lands Study,* US Gov. Printing Office, Washington, D.C.

Van Raay, H. G. T. (1975), *Rural Planning for Northern Nigeria,* Rotterdam Univ. Press.

Walker, H. G. (1977), *Symposium on Ecology and Agricultural Productions,* p. 169, Univ. of Tennessee, Knoxville, USA.

Welhausen, E. J. (1976), The Agriculture of Mexico, *Scientific Amer.,* 235, 129.

WFC (1977), World Food Council, Document WFC/40, March 1977.

White, G. F. (1978), *Environmental Effects of Arid Land Irrigation in Developing Countries.* MAB Techn. Note 8, UNESCO, Paris.

WMO (1978), *Weather and Parasitic Animal Diseases.* WMO Technical Note No. 159, World Meteorological Organization, Geneva.

Worthington, E. B. (1977), *Arid Land Irrigation in Developing Countries,* Pergamon Press, Oxford.

CHAPTER 8

Population

While world population continued to increase rapidly during the 1970s, the rate of growth diminished slightly. Total population passed 4,400 million in 1980. The proportion living in developing countries then approached 3 out of 4, and the proportion living in cities and towns also mounted.

In the last five years of the decade (1975–80), the annual rate of population increase was 1.72 per cent, while in the first five years of the previous decade (1960–65), it had been 1.99 per cent. The annual rate of increase diminished in all regions of the world except Africa. In fourteen developed countries, human reproduction rates fell to – or below – replacement levels. The importance of these trends is clear, since many environmental problems have their roots in population growth.

Between 1965 and 1975, the birth rates of 94 developing countries declined on average by about 13 per cent, most markedly in Asia and Latin America. However, in Africa there was virtually no fertility decline, and the annual growth rate climbed there by 1980 to 2.9 per cent – the highest of any region. If the rate continues, the African population will double in twenty-four years. Where a drop in birth rates occurred, it was attributed chiefly to a growth in the number of women of childbearing age using modern contraceptive methods, delayed marriage in some regions, a desire to limit births because of such factors as increased childbearing costs, and the reduced roles of children in certain industries and in their economic value to their families.

During the decade the dispute over the relative roles of socio-economic conditions and family planning programmes in reducing birth rates was largely resolved: evidence showed both to be influential and mutually reinforcing. Likewise, the fear that lowered death rates as a result of health programmes would boost population growth in the long term was reduced by accumulating demographic evidence. Family planning programmes were widely adopted, and in 26 developing countries with substantial efforts the birth rates were reported to have declined by 14–40 per cent between 1965 and 1975 (although recent census data suggest somewhat lower declines in some countries).

Despite the moderation of population growth, it continued in many developing countries faster than educational, health, sanitation, transport and other public services could be provided. And international support for population policies began to flag at precisely the time when commitment to family planning was spreading.

Large numbers of people continued to migrate from one country to another during the decade, but the number of unskilled and semi-skilled labourers among them diminished, except to the oil-producing countries of Northern Africa and Southwest Asia, and to the United States. The main migration routes until the early 1950s – from Europe to the Americas, Australia and New Zealand – changed during the 1970s: they now went from developing countries to developed countries and Arab OPEC countries. By 1980 about 2 million workers from Egypt, India, Jordan, Pakistan, the Sudan and elsewhere were temporarily located in oil-rich Northern African and Southwest Asian countries.

Wars and political upheavals added to the stream of people crossing international borders during the 1970s: in the last three years of the decade, on the average 2,000–3,000 *more people became refugees every day throughout the world, and by 1980 they totalled 7,408,300 worldwide – more than three times the number in 1970.*

The decade was marked by a new, broadened view among policy-makers of the interrelationships among people, resources, environment and development. Development came more and more to be seen, as the decade drew to a close, as encompassing not only socio-economic aspects of national activity, but also those related to population, the use of natural resources and environmental management.

During the decade the size, growth rate, distribution and age structure of the world's population changed in several ways that had important relationships to environmental problems. Total population continued to enlarge rapidly but the rate of growth diminished slightly so that it reached 1.72 per cent annually by 1980. While the mean annual rate of increase declined in some areas it continued to rise in two major regions. Crude birth rates declined in most countries, as did death rates, and a keener understanding emerged of the factors influencing growth, and the basic relationships among population, resources, and environment. The chief demographic trends are reviewed here as they relate to total population, regional changes, fertility, mortality, age distribution, migration, and labour force. This is followed by a brief review of changes in knowledge about the interrelations among people, resources, development, and environment.

Demographic Trends of the 1970s

THE human population of the Earth passed the 4,400 million point in 1980, an increase of more than 700 million over the world population in 1970 (Table 8–1). At its current 1.72 per cent rate of increase, a million people are added to the world every five days.

Population growth is at the root of many environmental problems, and information about the size, age, structure, distribution and rate of growth in human populations is therefore of great importance in any evaluation of environmental changes and prospects.

Table 8–1. Population Trends in the Eight Major Areas of the World, 1950–2000, as Assessed in 1980-Medium Variant Projections.

Year	World	Africa	Latin America	Northern America	East Asia	South Asia	Europe	Oceania	USSR
			Population (millions)						
1950*	2513	219	164	166	673	706	392	13	180
1960	3037	275	216	199	816	877	425	16	214
1970	3695	355	283	226	991	1116	459	19	242
1975	4066	407	322	236	1096	1257	474	21	253
1980	4432	470	364	248	1175	1404	484	23	265
1990	5242	635	459	274	1327	1731	499	26	290
2000	6119	853	566	299	1475	2075	512	30	310
			Average Annual Rate of Growth (Percentage)						
1950–1955*	1.76	2.16	2.72	1.80	1.85	1.86	0.79	2.25	1.71
1955–1960*	1.94	2.36	2.78	1.78	1.99	2.24	0.84	2.18	1.77
1960–1965	1.99	2.48	2.80	1.49	1.94	2.40	0.91	2.08	1.49
1970–1975	1.91	2.73	2.54	0.86	1.96	2.36	0.63	1.85	0.95
1975–1980	1.72	2.90	2.45	0.95	1.38	2.22	0.40	1.47	0.93
1980–1985	1.70	3.00	2.38	1.04	1.24	2.17	0.34	1.44	0.93
1985–1990	1.65	3.02	2.28	0.95	1.20	2.02	0.30	1.36	0.84
1990–1995	1.60	2.99	2.15	1.05	1.09	1.90	0.27	1.29	0.70
1995–2000	1.50	2.90	2.02	0.70	1.02	1.72	0.24	1.19	0.64

Source: UN (1981).

*Data prior to 1960 are from UN (1979).

NUMBERS AND GROWTH RATES

In 1970 the world population was estimated at 3,695 million, in 1975 at 4,067 million and in 1980 at 4,432 million (UN, 1981). During 1960–1965 the average natural annual rate of growth for the world as a whole was 1.99 per cent: the figures for 1970–1975 and 1975–1980 were 1.94 per cent and 1.72 per cent, respectively (Table 8–2). The rate is thus down from its recent peak, but not much (Mauldin, 1980). By comparison with the change during 1960–65, the natural increase in 1975–1980 was less by 13.5 per cent. The largest decline in rate of increase was in the more developed countries (–40.3 per cent), and the largest regional increase in that rate was in Africa (+16.9 per cent). The growth rates decreased 29.8 per cent in East Asia, 12.5 per cent in Latin America, and 7.1 per cent in South Asia.

Table 8–2. Average Annual Rate of Population Growth (per cent).

	1960–1965	1970–1975	1975–1980	Percentage Change 1960–1965/1975–1980
World	1.99	1.91	1.72	–13.5
More developed	1.19	0.84	0.71	–40.3
Less developed	2.33	2.32	2.08	–10.7
Africa	2.48	2.73	2.90	+16.9
Latin America	2.80	2.54	2.45	–12.5
N. America	1.49	0.86	0.95	–36.2
East Asia	1.94	1.96	1.36	–29.8
S. Asia	2.40	2.37	2.22	– 7.1
Europe	0.91	0.63	0.40	–56.0
Oceania	2.08	1.85	1.47	–29.3
USSR	1.49	0.95	0.93	–37.6

Source: UN (1981).

Some forward projections suggest the rate of natural increase may drop to 1.65 per cent for the period between 1985 and 1990 (Table 8–1). In 1977 the "doubling" time (number of years in which population doubles) was as high as 693 years for Western Europe (and 173 years for Europe as a whole), 116 years for North America, but only 26 years for Latin America, 29 years for Southeast Asia, and 27 years for Africa. The result is the well-known continuing decline in the proportion of the world's population inhabiting the developed countries of Europe and North America, which in 1965 had almost exactly 30 per cent of the total and in 1980 had about 26 per cent (Figure 8–1).

Within the developing world, moreover, a massive increase in the populations of great cities is expected to take place, with the precise increments depending upon internal migration, birth rates, development policies and many other factors. The prospects and their implications are discussed in Chapter 9.

These and other projections of population are built upon theoretical frameworks of the mechanism of population change, the accumulation of demographic data, and assessments of national and regional situations and of the dynamics of mortality and fertility in closed populations (Frejka, 1981). The projections are not simple extrapolations of past growth. They are complex operations susceptible to wide latitude in judgement and intuition and they use data that vary greatly in reliability from country to country and over time. Accordingly, there are considerable differences among recent projections by the United Nations Population Division, the US Bureau of the Census, and several teams of non-government demographers. The estimates made between 1977 and 1980 by these groups for total world population in the year 2000 ranged between 5,838 million and 6,797 million (Frejka, 1981). The 1980 United Nations Projections for that date spanned a high of 6,340 million and a low of 5,838 million. The figure of 6,119 million in Table 8–1 is for the medium estimate put forward in 1980.

Figure 8–1. Growth of World Population and Shares of More Developed, (shaded sectors) and Less Developed Regions, 1800–2000.

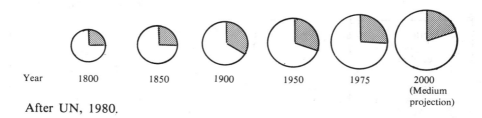

| Year | 1800 | 1850 | 1900 | 1950 | 1975 | 2000 (Medium projection) |

After UN, 1980.

It is instructive to compare these trends with those widely believed to be at work at the time of the Stockholm Conference. In *Only One Earth*, Ward and Dubos (1972) speculated that total world population might be expected to reach 7,000 million by 2,000, a higher figure than the then current United Nations medium projection. An assessment of population prospects one year after the Conference, lowered the 2000 figure. In 1978 the UN medium projection was 55 million less (UN, 1978). By 1980 it had decreased by an additional 78 million to the figure quoted above.

Examining the data in Table 8–1 more closely makes several patterns stand out with respect to population size and growth by region. First, close to three-fourths of the current world population live in the poorest regions, compared to two-thirds in 1950. According to the United Nations projections, the proportion in the developing countries should rise to nearly 4 out of 5 by the year 2000.

A second noteworthy pattern involves a shift in the relative population size of major areas (Figure 8–2). In 1950, East Asia and South Asia had practically equal numbers of people. By 1980, there was a marked increase in South Asia's population as compared to East Asia's, and by the year 2000, South Asia's might well be some 50 to 75 per cent higher. Similarly, Latin America, with nearly the same population as North America in 1950, had 65 per cent more people in 1980, and is expected to have almost twice as many by the year 2000.

FERTILITY AND MORTALITY

Global population growth occurs as a result of the excess of births over deaths. By 1980, most growth was taking place among the same three-quarters of the world's population living in the developing countries. There, previously high crude death rates fell rapidly after World War II and by 1980 were at the comparatively low level of 11.4 deaths per 1,000 population per year (Figure 8–3). Expectation of life at birth for both sexes had increased from 55.8 in 1970–1975 to 57.5 in 1975–1980 with the larger gains in less developed regions (UN, 1981).

Crude birth rates in less developed regions, though beginning to fall rapidly in some cases, were still at an overall average of 33 per 1,000 population annually. As a result, the developing countries' populations were growing at a high 2.08 per cent each year. In the developed regions, the annual growth rate of 0.7 per cent reflected an average birth rate of about 16 per 1,000 and a death rate of about 9 per 1,000 which is expected to increase as the average age mounts.

The more developed regions' already low birth rate sank even lower in recent years, to about 15 per 1,000 population in 1980, less than half the birth rate of the developing regions. Death rates in developed countries also fell to levels about as low as they could go without breakthroughs in conquering chronic diseases that strike mostly in old age — heart disease, cancer, and strokes. In some countries, death rates were rising as the elderly, among whom death is more likely, comprised increasing proportions of the population. Reproduction was at or below replacement level in some 14 developed countries (for example Austria, the German Democratic Republic, the Federal Republic of Germany, Sweden, the USA and the UK). Overall, however, population was still growing in the more developed regions of the world.

Although reliable data to verify trends were lacking for many less developed countries, by 1980 most demographers were convinced that fertility had begun to decline in developing countries as a whole. A study of 20 less developed countries with reasonably satisfactory registration systems showed that more or less substantial decreases in birth rates occurred in all of them after 1960–1965 (UN, 1980). A less precise set of data for 110 less developed countries indicated that between 1960–1965 and 1970–1975 the declines in birth rates were most pronounced in Latin America and least evident in Africa (UN, 1979).

Mauldin and Berelson (1978) estimated that in the decade from 1965 to 1975 the birth rate of 94 less developed countries declined on average about 13 per cent, from about 41 to 35.5 births per 1,000 population with the range between 40 per cent and 0 per cent. They also concluded the decline was most marked in Asia and Latin America (Figure 8–4). Sub-Saharan Africa showed virtually no fertility decline and, with the death rates continuing to fall, population growth in Africa had climbed to 2.9 per cent by about 1980, the highest of any region, meaning a doubling in twenty-four years. Tsui and Bogue (1978) came to the same conclusion: the fertility transition had begun most rapidly for much of the developing world, in such populous Asian countries as China, Indonesia, South Korea, the Philippines and Thailand. They estimate that the world's total fertility rate or average rate of childbearing fell from 4.6 births per woman in 1968 to 4.1 births in 1975. However, in general, the major cause to date has been reduced fertility among

Figure 8–2. World Population Density.

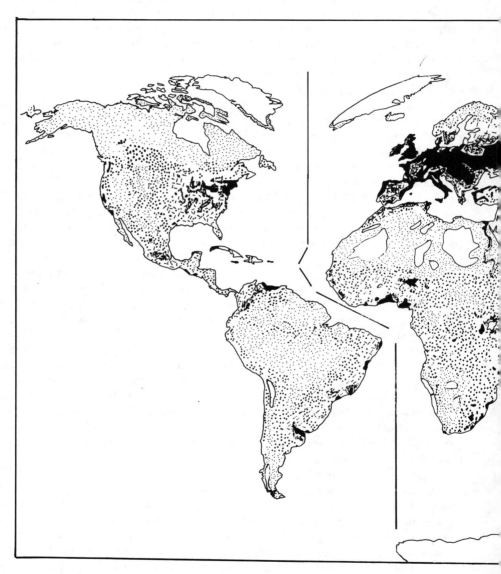

After Rand McNally Atlas with modification.

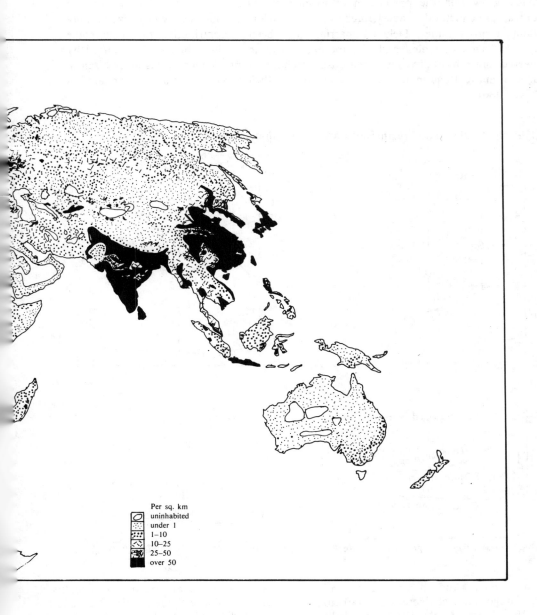

Per sq. km
uninhabited
under 1
1–10
10–25
25–50
over 50

married women, particularly those over age 30. This relates in varying degrees to a fairly steady growth in the proportion of women of childbearing age who use modern contraceptive methods, accelerated in many developing countries by organized family planning programmes. Delayed marriage has been a contributing factor in some countries such as China and Singapore. The desire to limit births is supported by lowered infant mortality, increased costs of child rearing, reduced roles of children in farming and cottage industry, and reductions in their economic value to their families (UN, 1980).

Figure 8–3. Birth and Death Rates and Population Increase.

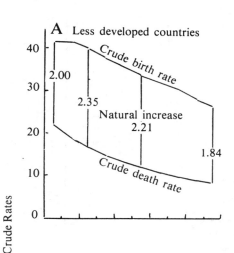

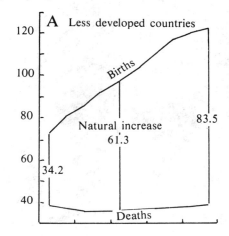

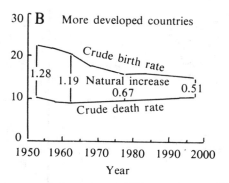

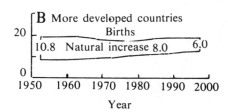

Crude birth and death rates and percentage natural increase, 1950 to 2000 (United Nations medium assumptions).

Average annual number of births, deaths, and population increase, 1950 to 2000 (United Nations medium assumptions).

After, Mauldin, 1980.

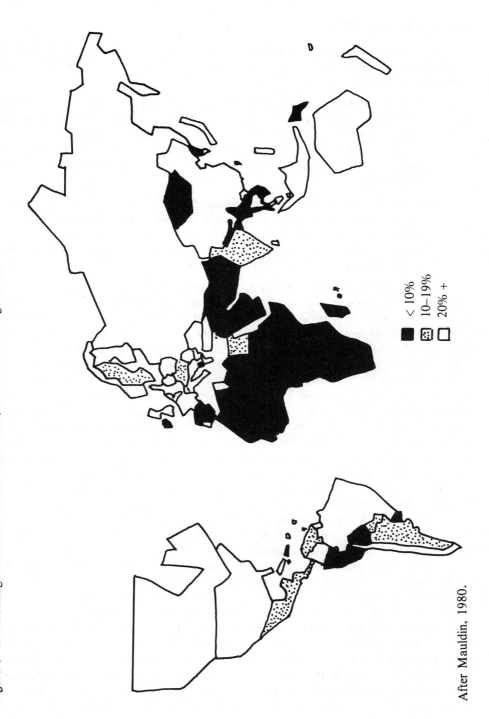

Figure 8–4. Percentage Decline in Crude Birth Rate, 1950–1955 through 1975.

< 10%
10–19%
20% +

After Mauldin, 1980.

FAMILY PLANNING

In the past ten years striking progress was made in undertaking the causes and consequences of high birth rates, and in helping to resolve two controversial and important issues (World Bank, 1980):

(a) The dispute between those alleging that family planning programmes had little effect on birth rates and those claiming that family planning alone could reduce birth rates was greatly narrowed, if not wholly settled. The evidence overwhelmingly suggests that both social and economic conditions and family planning are important in influencing birth rates, and that they are mutually reinforcing.

(b) Accumulating evidence clearly contradicted the fear that health programmes, by lowering death rates, would boost population growth in the long term. Although fertility seemed unresponsive to falling death rates during the 1950s and 1960s, it declined thereafter in many poor countries — partly in response to lower death rates — and population growth began slowing down.

Mauldin (1980) listed 26 developing countries including China, India, Indonesia, the Philippines, Thailand and South Korea with substantial population control efforts and birth rate declines of between 40 per cent and 14 per cent between 1965 and 1975 (Table 8–3). The countries are arranged according to their relative level of per capita income and by the strength of their family planning efforts. Some recent census data suggest the declines were less than estimated in certain of the major countries.

In 1978 China announced a goal of reducing the annual rate of population growth to less than 1 per cent within 3 years, to 0.5 per cent in 1985 and to zero in 2000 (People's Daily, 1979). Another 30 developing countries had some kind of programme. Among the 15 most populous developing countries only Burma is pursuing a pronatalist policy, with a ban on family planning clinics and contraceptive importation. Over 60 countries, with 95 per cent of the population of developing countries, had adopted some kind of programme with different degrees of commitment. However, a number of developed countries, where fertility was below replacement level, adopted targets of modest growth or stability (France, Argentina, Finland and the Netherlands among them) and certain Eastern European countries including Czechoslovakia, the German Democratic Republic, Bulgaria, Hungary and Romania adopted both restrictions on abortion and contraceptives, and financial allowances to encourage child-bearing.

As of 1976, none, of six European countries (German Democratic Republic, Federal Republic of Germany, Luxembourg, Austria, Belgium and the United Kingdom) with stable or declining population had an explicit government policy of stabilizing population. Rather, economic, social and demographic forces converged to bring births in to balance with deaths (UN, 1980). Many countries have shown both that economic and social development itself helps to limit population growth and that public policies can contribute directly to the decline in birth rates. The countries where birth rates recently declined were for the most part those that had managed to spread the economic and social benefits of development widely. Even very poor areas, such as Merala in India, were able to give people new hope for a better life by involving them in the

Table 8–3. Crude Birth Rate Declines (in per cent), from 1965 to 1975 in 94 Developing Countries. (Data are Arranged by Social Setting and Programme Effort.)

Programme effort								
Strong		Moderate		Weak		None		
Country	Decline	Country	Decline	Country	Decline	Country	Decline	Total
High social setting								
Singapore	40	Cuba	40	Venezuela	11	North Korea	*	
Hong Kong	36	Chile	29	Brazil	10	Kuwait	*	
South Korea	32	Trinidad and Tobago	29	Mexico	9	Peru	*	
Barbados	31	Colombia	25	Paraguay	6	Lebanon	*	
Taiwan	30	Panama	22			Jordan	*	
Mauritius	29					Libya	*	
Costa Rica	29							
Fiji	22							
Jamaica	21							
Mean	30	Mean	29	Mean	9	Mean	*	19
Median	30	Median	29	Median	9.5	Median	*	22
Upper middle social setting								
China	24	Malaysia	26	Egypt	17	Mongolia	9	
		Tunisia	24	Turkey	16	Syria	*	
		Thailand	23	Honduras	7	Zambia	*	
		Dominican Republic	21	Nicaragua	7	Congo	*	
		Philippines	19	Algeria	*			
		Sri Lanka	18	Guatemala	*			
		El Salvador	13	Morocco	*			
		Iran	*	Ghana	*			
				Ecuador	*			
				Iraq	*			
Mean	24	Mean	18	Mean	6	Mean	*	10
Median	24	Median	20	Median	*	Median	*	7
Lower middle social setting								
North Vietnam	23	India	16	Papua New Guinea	*	Angola	*	
		Indonesia	13	Pakistan	*	Cameroon	*	
				Bolivia	*	Burma	*	
				Nigeria	*	P.D.R. of Yemen	*	
				Kenya	*	Mozambique	*	
				Liberia	*	Khmer/ Kampuchea	*	
				Haiti	*	Ivory Coast	*	
				Uganda	*	Senegal	*	
						Saudi Arabia	*	
						South Vietnam	*	
						Madagascar	*	
						Lesotho	*	
Mean	23	Mean	14	Mean	*	Mean	*	*
Median	23	Median	14.5	Median	*	Median	*	*

Table continued

Table 8–3.   continued.

Programme effort									
Strong		Moderate		Weak		None			
Country	Decline	Country	Decline	Country	Decline	Country	Decline	Total	
Low social setting									
				Tanzania	*	Laos	*		
				Dahomey	*	Central African Republic	*		
				Bangladesh	*	Malawi	*		
				Sudan	*	Bhutan	*		
				Nepal	*	Ethiopia	*		
				Mali	*	Guinea	*		
				Afghanistan	*	Chad	*		
						Togo	*		
						Upper Volta	*		
						Yemen	*		
						Niger	*		
						Burundi	*		
						Sierra Leone	*		
						Mauritania	*		
						Rwanda	*		
						Somalia	*		
				Mean	*	Mean	*	*	
				Median	*	Median	*	*	
Mean	29	Mean	21	Mean	*	Mean	*	9	
Median	29	Median	22	Median	*	Median	*	*	

Source: Mauldin and Berelson (1978).

*No significant change.

workings of development, improving their health, raising the status and educational levels of women as well as men, and ensuring adequate food supplies for the poor. Where this was done, birth rates tended to fall, while they remained high in some richer developing countries that paid less attention to the needs of the many.

Though rapid population growth puts pressure on public services, the experience of Sri Lanka demonstrates that special efforts to make such services available to all of a developing country's people can actually help retard that growth. Sri Lanka launched a family planning programme in the mid 1960s, but much of the sharp fall in its birth rate from 33 to 26 per 1,000 between 1965 and 1977 is attributed to rapid improvements in education, health, and nutrition. These resulted not from gains in per capita income, but from the country's heavy emphasis on mass-oriented social expenditures (World Bank, 1979).

Rapid population growth also increased unemployment and under-employment in the developing countries, as noted in Chapter 11. According to the International Labour Organization (ILO), the high population growth of the late 1960s and early 1970s will translate into an increase in the developing world's labour force from 1,130 million in 1975 to 1,900 million in the year 2000 (ILO, 1977). If these 770 million new workers are added to some 280 million currently unemployed or underemployed, more than one billion new jobs will be required in the developing world, where job-creating development is proceeding all too slowly.

The magnitude of the rising demands for public services and for employment from the growing population need to be considered along with the apparent reduction in fertility. These reductions may be exaggerated and may not be sustained: moreover, the evidence of declines may generate undue confidence about future population numbers.

There is a risk that if the widespread trends of fertility decline were to create the impression that the population situation is taking care of itself, some of the efforts to continue those trends would be jeopardized. International support for population policies began to flag at precisely the time when the commitment to, and political acceptance of, family planning policies were spreading among developing countries. The needs for population assistance remain great. For example, the United Nations Fund for Population Activities (UNFPA) was able to meet only two-thirds of the requests for assistance it received in 1979 (UNFPA, 1979).

At the end of the decade the world therefore faced a period of profound changes in number, distribution, and age structure of its human population. Using the United Nations' medium projection, increases of the order of those shown in Figure 8–5 were to be expected. Four major regions — Africa, Latin America, East Asia and South Asia — were expected to account for most of the increases.

One of the distinctive changes underway was in the age composition of the populations of the various regions. As indicated in Figure 8–6, the structure of age groups in the developed countries was projected to change chiefly in an enlarging proportion of the total population of age thirty and over. In contrast, in the developing regions, very large increases will occur in the numbers of persons below age fifty-five.

As a result of continuing high fertility and improved survival rates for infants and children there will be larger proportions of young people in or about to enter their childbearing years. This, along with patterns of migration, affects the labour force as discussed above, with implications for industry as presented in Chapter 11.

The projections have major significance for the future distribution of people among rural and urban settings. Rural population enlarged greatly in developing countries during the decade. This led to increased demands for food and fuelwood, and in some places to environmental degradation, as described in Chapters 7 and 12. Large movements from rural to urban areas were spurred by the search for employment, and the requirements for public services expanded accordingly.

Because of internal growth as well as farm-to-city migration, by the year 2000 over half the world's population is likely to be living in towns and cities, as against 39 per cent in 1975. In developing countries that shift to urban areas because of its magnitude and speed, will be far more difficult than it was in the past for the now developed world (see Chapter 9). Between 1950 and 1975, the urban population of developing countries grew by some 400 million people. Between 1975 and 2000, the increase will be close to one billion. The problem is aggravated by the rapid concentration of urban dwellers in very large cities.

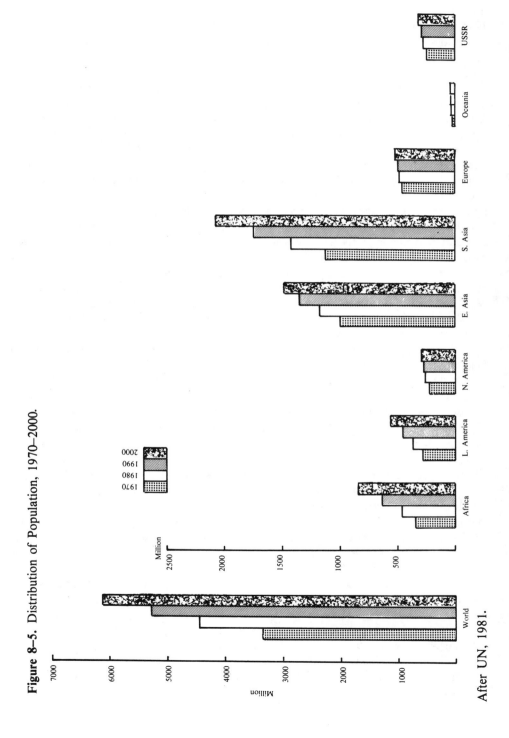

Figure 8–5. Distribution of Population, 1970–2000.

After UN, 1981.

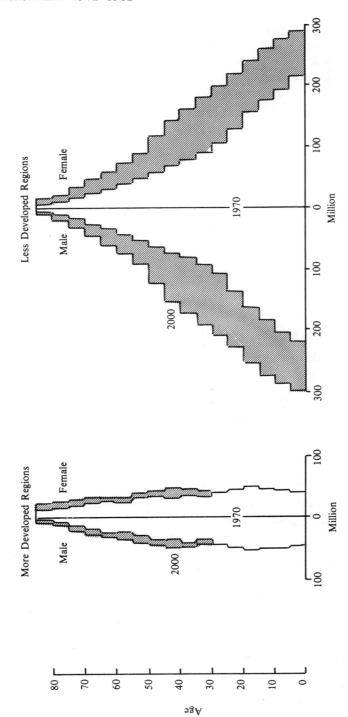

Figure 8–6. Population Growth By Sex and Age Groups, 1970–2000.

After UN, 1979.

In rural and urban areas alike, the population of many less developed countries was growing faster than educational, health, sanitation, transport, and other public services could be provided. Housing was a particularly critical problem, as described in Chapter 9. Health facilities were on a similar tread-mill. Inability of public services to keep up with the demand from growing populations is part of the explanation for the recent slowdown in mortality declines in less developed countries (Van der Tak *et al.,* 1979).

International Migration

THE number of people crossing national boundaries continued to be large in the past decade, and they included both workers and refugees. The migration of unskilled and semi-skilled labour and professional manpower in the preceding decade, which slowed down during the 1970s, was a reflection of imbalances in income and employment opportunities and, to some extent, of constraints on the international flow of capital and trade. The streams of refugees were generated primarily by political upheavals, and to a lesser extent by environmental adversity.

LABOUR

Labour movements were both permanent and temporary. The rich countries that imported workers controlled the number and character of manpower and the duration of its stay: most of the movement was therefore temporary. Much of the demand was structural, coming from industries that could not keep or attract national workers. Although there was demand for more permanent workers, migrant labour in many countries was treated as a temporary workforce. This has created friction and hardship. The movement of migrant workers involves human beings, and its social aspects understandably made it a sensitive and visible issue. These social factors as well as changes in economic balance may help explain why, during the last half of the decade, the flow to Western Europe was reversed.

Although the United States was the primary receiving country as measured by the total number of migrants (in recent years immigration was at an annual rate of 500,000 to 700,000, not counting undocumented migrants from southern neighbours), several other countries attracted a much larger proportion of foreign-born persons to live within their borders. The foreign-born comprise a little less than 5 per cent of the populations of Canada and New Zealand, 20 per cent of Australia's, and more than 50 per cent of those of Kuwait and Israel (Mauldin, 1980).

Until the early 1950s, the main migratory streams were from Europe to North and South America, Australia, and New Zealand, but the direction shifted, and during the decade the two main currents turned toward the industrialized countries from the developing countries and toward the Arab OPEC countries. The number of labourers moving from Portugal, Yugoslavia, Italy, Spain, Turkey, Greece, northern Africa, the German Democratic Republic, Finland and Ireland to western Europe had reached 4–5 million in the 1960s. This movement was reduced and in most cases reversed in the early 1970s. However, the movement to oil-producing areas grew. By 1980 about 2 million workers from Egypt, India, Jordan, Pakistan, the Sudan and other areas were temporarily located in the oil-rich countries of northern Africa and Southwest Asia (UN, 1980).

A second and very different type of migration was the "brain drain". In the early 1960s and 1970s, well over 400,000 physicians and surgeons, engineers, scientists and other skilled people moved from developing countries to more developed ones. The principal sending countries were India, Pakistan, the Philippines and Sri Lanka. Most of the migrants went to the United States, Canada and the United Kingdom, and others to the rest of Western Europe, Australia and the Middle East. This kind of movement has a long history, but never before had it been so extensive, nor based so largely on economic incentives. The brain drain occurred in part because many students and professionals trained in developed countries chose not to return home.

Migration may give benefits to all parties. The sending countries gained from the employment provided to their nationals, from reducing competition for land, and, where there was a return flow, from the training, skills, and experience with resource management acquired by workers who returned. They also benefited from the money sent back by migrants. These remittances have become a big foreign exchange earner for many developing countries where they sometimes match or surpass export earnings from commodities and manufacturers.

Receiving countries also derived benefits from migrant labour which contributed to their domestic product, made their manufacturing industries more competitive and held down costs on construction industries and service sectors. Skilled migrants were particularly valuable as they saved their host countries substantial costs in education and training. On the other hand, the status of migrant workers was often unsatisfactory and precarious. And while some countries of immigration were able to control migrant flows to suit their needs, countries of emigration were at times buffeted by fluctuations in the demand for migrant labour and in remittances, and they lost skilled and semi-skilled manpower they badly needed (Brandt Commission, 1980).

REFUGEES

A different kind of international migration that has become a distressingly regular feature of the modern world and has been disruptive of resource management is the flow of political and religious refugees and people who have been displaced by wars and political upheavals (Chapter 16). It is estimated that in this century some 250 million people have fled their countries (Brandt Commission, 1980).

In recent years the problems assumed an added dimension because refugees often had no intention of staying in the countries of first asylum, nor in many cases did these countries wish to keep and employ them. In the last three years of the decade, an average of at least 2,000–3,000 more people became refugees each day throughout the world (Brandt Commission, 1980). The numbers generated each year, as estimated by the Office of the United Nations High Commissioner for Refugees, are shown in Table 8–4. They grew three-fold during the decade and placed heavy stress upon the resources of the receiving developing countries. The statistics on numbers of refugees moving out of their homelands do not reveal the proportion returning or finding a new home. Some 3 million refugees and displaced persons for whom permanent solutions had not been found in 1980 were in Africa alone, and there were large numbers in various parts of Asia. Altogether, the number of unsettled refugees was estimated to be of the order of 8–10 million.

Some refugee situations were resolved in a relatively short time, as with those from East Pakistan to India during the war that resulted in the establishment of Bangladesh. Most of the 2 million refugees who fled to India were re-settled shortly after the end of the war, as were the additional millions temporarily displaced from their homes (Mauldin, 1980). On the other hand, some refugees, for example the Palestinians, have been displaced for decades with no solution for their resettlement foreseeable in the near future.

Unlike the movements of labourers, which often support more intensive resource management in the receiving country and may relieve underemployment and pressure on scarce resources in the sending country, the waves of political refugees may cause severe and abrupt changes in the environment. Population densities multiply overnight, traditional land systems are disrupted, and markets are disorganized. The newcomers usually are confronted with unfamiliar landscapes and may bring inappropriate techniques for resource use. Thus, in some sectors of the Sahel and in alluvial valleys of Southeastern Asia, the refugee situation worked against conservation practices.

People and Food

UNDERLYING the problems shifts in fertility, mortality, and location of the world's population, was the issue of the capacity to produce food for the growing number of mouths to be fed. From 1961 through 1976, developing countries as a whole improved

Table 8–4. Estimated Number of Refugees.

Regions	1970	1974	1976	1977	1978	1979	1980
Africa	999,083	1,082,140	1,200,000	1,500,000	2,314,800	2,334,000	2,839,000
North America	635,000	648,000	660,000	684,700	776,000	776,000	1,187,000
South America			112,000	108,000	144,483	133,000	173,600
Asia	137,700	49,070	180,000	200,000	653,000	1,241,500	2,314,200
Europe	644,424	553,515	570,000	546,000	519,659	519,900	580,500
Oceania	44,000	38,000	50,000	300,000	314,000	314,000	314,000
World Total	2,460,207	2,370,715	2,772,000	3,338,700	4,721,942	5,318,400	7,408,300

Source: Office of the UN High Commissioner for Refugees.

food production at a faster rate than developed countries, but because of rampant population growth, their per capita food output grew at a much slower pace. The gain in per capita food production averaged a steady 1.4 per cent in industrialized countries during this period.

In developing countries, by contrast, annual per capita gains were already below 1 per cent in the 1960s and nearly vanished in the early 1970s when droughts slashed yields across Asia and Africa. With better weather, increased irrigation, and other investments, agricultural production has since improved in the developing world, particularly in Asia, but the situation remains precarious.

The average daily per capita food intake in the developing countries is nearly half that in the developed regions. As noted in Chapter 7, during 1974–1976 the Food and Agriculture Organization of the United Nations (FAO) estimated, conservatively, that 440 million people constituting 23 per cent of the population of the developing country market economies were chronically undernourished. Surveys indicate that up to 50 per cent of all young children in the developing regions may be inadequately nourished — deprivation likely to lead to lasting physical and mental damage for those who survive.

Many do not survive. As described in Chapter 10, malnutrition-related deaths among children under age five may run as high as 10 million annually (Van der Tak, 1979). If the developing world's population continues to grow by 2.1 to 2.2 per cent a year, the FAO estimates that food supplies available to them must rise by at least 4 per cent annually. This will require either massive imports of food or greatly stepped-up agricultural production. Both have their socio-economic, technological and environmental problems and a solution has to be found through long-range, environmentally-sound planning.

People, Resources, Environment and Development: a Broadened View

AN underlying theme of the 1970s was the recognition that development is a multidimensional concept that encompasses not only economic and social aspects of national activity but also those related to population, the use of natural resources and management of the environment. This view emerged repeatedly in the international conferences on the human environment (Stockholm, 1972), population (Bucharest, 1974), food (Rome, 1974), industrialization (Lima, 1975), employment (Geneva, 1976), human settlements (Vancouver, 1976), water (Mar-del-Plata, 1977), desertification (Nairobi, 1978) and primary health care (Alma Ata, 1978). Although not a novel concept, its implications for environmental research and policies are considerable.

In specific terms, it emphasizes the need to search for causes of seemingly technical problems such as desertification, deforestation and soil degradation among such diverse factors as demographic trends, modes of production, forms of technology and patterns of consumption and earnings, including the prevalence of poverty and income disparities. At the very least, it calls for a systematic extension of current development models and strategies to take better account of interrelationships between population, resources, environment and development. In its most forthright statement it is a call for exploration of alternative life styles as one approach to population policy and environmental management.

This broadened view of development, as noted in Chapter 1, took shape slowly during the decade and by 1981 stood in contrast to a more limited view of man-land relationships that had prevailed in earlier analysis and policy.

The growing attention to interrelationships among people, resources, environment and development stemmed from three basic considerations. First, it became increasingly evident that development efforts at national and regional levels, at all stages of growth and in countries with diverse ideologies and socio-economic-physical structures, affect the productive process in a variety of ways — not all of them beneficial. Second, while such effects involve strong interactions among economic, social, demographic and physical factors, it is difficult to trace out the causal links among them. Third, there accordingly continued to be great uncertainty about the likely long-term impact of development efforts as they affected quality of life and environment. Appraisal had tended to focus on the risks of negative impacts rather than on positive impacts.

It was apparent at Stockholm that countries at different stages of development attach different priorities to objectives. Certainly many developing countries attached the highest priority to economic growth. As noted in Chapter 1, it therefore became important to find ways of achieving such growth without leading to its ultimate collapse because basic environmental factors were neglected. Early global models relating population to resource availability and environmental carrying capacity in single ratios had projected resource and environmental constraints as fixed effective limits to economic growth in the next century. Those models later came to be regarded as inadequate, being too aggregate and simplistic. Research indicated that some resources management policies may promote rather than limit economic growth.

Other factors, such as the uneven geographical distribution of population relative to the available land and the inefficient use of natural resources, entered into the analysis. These broader themes widened the scope of discussion from resource depletion, environmental degradation and population growth to include resource re-distribution and transfer, environmental management designed to improve resource use, the development of appropriate technologies, equity of income distribution, and population movement.

The new view was outlined in a recent report by the Secretary-General of the United Nations submitted to ECOSOC (ECOSOC, 1981). The report drew upon a wide array of efforts, several special symposia and studies and extended the previous studies in three ways. First, it elaborated matters of principal concern to the international community. Second, it identified and reviewed the status of current work. Third, it drew attention to practical measures that could be undertaken at national and regional levels. In suggesting a series of studies of areas where degrading processes had already reached an advanced stage, the supporting recommendations called attention to opportunities presented by energy, drainage basin, and island development. A number of these, such as Himalayan foothill deforestation, Sudano–Sahelian overgrazing, and tropical deforestation, are noted in preceding chapters.

The "interrelationships" efforts marked a major change in the way in which the problems of population were approached, and signalled a more vigorous and integrated attempt to deal with the resulting issues on a global scale. The accomplishments in that direction were meagre at best, but goals were set. The task was summed up dramatically in the following statement:

> "Accommodating future needs and numbers to the earth's natural capacities and resources will give rise to a transformation of human values, social institutions and economic structures on an order which could ultimately approach the Agricultural and Industrial Revolutions. The coming transformation is life-long in duration: a period from a half to a full century. It is enormous in scope: a three-fold increase in world population. And, it is awesome in its implications for change: the need to lower birth rates drastically; the need to provide specially for the poor and the disadvantaged, the upheavals of migration, the expansion in labour force and the growth of metropolitan areas; the need for massive substitutions in primary energy and accompanying adjustments in agriculture and industry; the need to promote intensive, environmentally-sound resource use; and the need to meet the tremendous requirements in the developing countries for food, health, education and housing, or more generally, to be equipped to handle not just "another world but a second and third world on top of this, equal in numbers, demands and hopes" (Cocoyoc, 1974).

POVERTY AND CARRYING CAPACITY

While the world's population increased by unprecedented numbers, there was a rapid increase in average incomes in many countries. These created an extraordinary surge in the demand for renewable and non-renewable natural resources. The emerging patterns of demand were strongly influenced by the glaring disparities in income prevailing among and within countries. Such disparities favoured the production of luxury goods, which are generally resource-intensive and which impede action to make a better life possible for all people. The rising tempo and the distorted pattern of demand raised a complex set of questions about what had come to be known as carrying capacity (a term borrowed from biology, and used to denote the capability of an area of environment to support people at a particular standard of living).

It was argued that the lack of satisfaction of the most basic human needs in some developing countries forces the poor to over-exploit the natural environment, as well as to over-exploit themselves, in desperate attempts at survival. Such situations are aggravated by the fact that poor people are often subjected to the worst environmental degradation, due to undernutrition and bad health conditions. They may be forced to destroy their environment in attempts to delay their own destruction (Gallopin and Berrera, 1979). An analysis of the causes and consequences of environmental degradation associated with poverty showed, for example, that problems arise both from over-use of land and inappropriate crops, and from pollution and misuse of water (Sigal, 1977). An important example is increasing deforestation due to the demand for wood as fuel and to provide farming lands.

Until the social structures that generate poverty are altered, attempts at direct action to help peasants end up with the dilemma that the essential needs for the survival of society may conflict with those essential to the survival of the individual. Efforts to protect the environment under conditions of strong inequality often run up against strong resistance from the people. Poverty may encourage environmental destruction, but amid conditions of blatant inequality it may be impossible to establish a resource management policy based on controls such as protection or limited utilization.

Out of recognition of these and related conditions grew interest in the analysis of the carrying capacity of the resource systems of particular areas. A system in this context refers to the combination of population and resources in any given geographical area: the globe, a multinational region, a country, a subnational region, a metropolis or a village. As carrying capacity is approached, the marginal cost of supporting an additional person or improving the average standard of living rises. The carrying capacity is affected by both internal conditions and external relations. This implies that development strategies, encompassing interrelated sets of goals and policy measures, may make it possible to have a continuing expansion, although environmental scientists would argue that any environmental system must have ultimate outer limits of carrying capacity. The concept offers one means of relating population considerations to development planning and by the end of the decade it had begun to attract appraisal of its methods and applications (IFIAS, 1980; Slesser and Hounam, 1980), through the Working Group on Population and Development Planning of the United Nations Educational, Scientific and Cultural Organization (UNESCO).

MODELS OF POPULATION, RESOURCES AND DEVELOPMENT

During the decade a series of efforts were made to specify the relationship among population, resources, environment and development as a means of indicating the conditions in which environmentally-sound and sustainable development might be achieved. Although, in principle, large-scale models appear to be a way of incorporating a vast array of variables and interdependencies, none of the existing models in their present form is yet adequate as a conceptual framework for the study of these factors.

Cases in point, described in more detail in other UNEP reports, are the Club of Rome Limits to Growth Model, the Leontief World Model, the World Integrated Model (Mesarovic and associates), the SARUM model (used as a basis for the OECD Interfutures study), the Bachue country models sponsored by ILO, the Latin American World Model (the Bariloche model) and the Global 2000 models. But many other more specialized models, emphasizing specific sectors or countries and regions, could be mentioned. The Leontief model, for example, treats population as exogenous. The

Bachue model does not include physical and environmental resources and any limitations on economic growth that may come from that direction.

None of the models adequately depicts environmental concerns. One major deficiency was that they were obliged to extrapolate trends in environmental parameters on the basis of incomplete and tenuous evidence. (This deficiency is revealed in the preceding six chapters of this book in their treatment of such items as air quality, water quality, and soil productivity.) In addition, few of the models are satisfactory in handling substitution possibilities, technological change and other adjustment mechanisms. None of them takes into account uncertainty and risk. However, in fairness to existing models it must be recognized that given the present state of the art no single aggregate model could be constructed to incorporate all such missing elements.

Notwithstanding the fact that the gap between what exists in terms of models and what is desired is large, the complexity of the issues involved makes modelling, even if only conceptual, desirable. The need for specific, quantitative and empirical assessment of relationships was increasingly urgent in the late 1970s. Although the notion of a single master model incorporating all important variables and relationships was not practicable in 1981, research was being directed at further extending and developing existing models to take better account of demographic and physical variables. The prospects for such research were somewhat better at local, regional and national levels than at the global level, particularly because demographic and physical planning models already exist at national and subnational levels. Even so, techniques for interrelating econometric, physical and demographic models were lacking.

References

Brandt Commission (1980), *North-South, A Programme for Survival*, MIT Press, Cambridge, Massachusetts.

Cocoyoc (1974), *UNEP/UNCTAD Symposium on Patterns of Resource Use*, Environment and Development Strategies, Cocoyoc, Mexico.

ECOSOC (1981), *Interrelationships Between Population, Resources, Environment and Development*, E/1981/65, Economic and Social Council, United Nations, New York.

Frejka, T. (1981), *World Population Projections: A Concise History*, Population Council, Center for Policy Studies, Working paper No. 66, New York.

Gallopin, G. and C. Berrera (1979), The Nexus Society and Environment, In G. C. Gallopin (Editor), *Environment and Styles of Development: Some Conceptual and Methodological Issues*, Techn. Res. Project 35, IFDA.

IFIAS (1980), Population, Resources and Society — The Need for Integrative Policies, A paper for UNESCO by the International Federation of Institutes for Advanced Studies, Solna, Sweden.

ILO (1977), Labour Force 1950–2000, Vol. V. International Labour Organization, Geneva.

Mauldin, W. P. (1980), Population Trends and Prospects, *Science*, 209, 148.

Mauldin, W. P. and B. Berelson (1978), *Conditions of Fertility Decline in Developing Countries*, Studies in Family Planning, Vol. 9, No. 5. Population Council, New York.

People's Daily (1979), *People's Daily Newspaper*, Peking.

Sigal, S. (1977), Poverty and Pollution, *Ecodevelopment News*, 1, 5.

Slesser, M. and I. Hounam (1980), *A Methodology for Assessing Carrying Capacity: A Study Undertaken for UNESCO*, Energy Studies Unit, University of Strathclyde, Glasgow.

Tsui, A. O. and D. J. Bogue (1978), Declining World Fertility: Trends, Causes, Implications, *Population Bull.*, 33, 4.

UN (1978), *Concise Report on the World Population Situation in 1977: New Beginnings and Uncertain Ends*, United Nations, New York.

UN (1979), *World Population: Trends and Prospects* 1950–2000, United Nations, New York.

UN (1980), *Concise Report on the World Population Situation in 1979: Conditions, Trends, Prospects and Policies*, United Nations, New York.

UN (1981), *World Population Prospects as Assessed in* 1980, United Nations, New York.

UNFPA (1979), *Report by the Executive Director of the United Nations Fund for Population Activities*, UNFPA, New York.

Van der Tak, J. *et al.* (1979), Our Population Predicament, *Population Bull.*, 34, 5.

Ward, B. and R. Dubos (1972), *Only One Earth: The Care and Maintenance of a Small Planet*, André Deutsch, London.

World Bank (1979), *World Development Report*, World Bank, Washington, D.C.

World Bank (1980), *World Development Report*, World Bank, Washington, D.C.

CHAPTER 9

Human Settlements

The decade of the 1970s marked the mid-point in a gigantic transformation of human settlements patterns. In developed countries, where previously the majority of the world's largest cities were to be found, urban growth began to dwindle, while in developing countries it not only continued to climb rapidly but for the first time produced more huge cities than in the developed regions. In 1950, there was only one city (greater Buenos Aires) in the developing countries with a population over 4 million, whereas in the developed world there were several. By 1975, there were 17 cities of such size in developing countries compared with only 13 in developed countries, and by 1980 the figures were 22 and 16. So rapid was the urban growth rate in developing countries that it seemed certain to double the number of people living in cities by the year 2000.

The direction of urban growth was towards ever larger cities: projections suggest the developing countries will by 2000 have about 61 cities of more than 4 million each, compared with about 25 in the developed regions. Eighteen cities in developing countries are expected to have more than 10 million inhabitants by that year.

Because this growth took place against a background of low incomes, it outstripped these countries' abilities to provide both accommodation and services, and the result was a mushrooming of squatter settlements around the perimeters of vast cities. From 20–80 per cent of urban populations live in these shanty towns.

Despite this urbanization process, the majority of people in developing countries (about 58 per cent) still lived in rural areas by 1980. In India, for example, 575,933, of the 579,052 human settlements were rural ones, and 98 per cent of these were villages with less than 5,000 inhabitants.

Conditions for people living in the growth areas of the developing world scarcely improved during the decade. Rural settlements generally were no better off, while dwellers in squatter settlements and slums were faced with a lack of safe water and waste disposal facilities. Overcrowded housing was a common feature in both rural and urban settings, with three or more persons frequently occupying a single room. Transportation facilities were meagre.

Nevertheless, some important innovations were introduced into the developing countries, and for the first time a positive, citizen-oriented approach was taken towards squatter settlements. Self-help programmes and community development were probably the most significant advances among low income populations, but they were also helped by more flexible building codes and regulations to permit the requirements of these groups to be met. More attention was given to equity in access to employment, shelter and basic resources; the use of indigenous materials in buildings; energy conservation, transportation and land-use problems; and rehabilitation and upgrading of older structures. Citizen participation increased in decision-making about human settlements, with the encouragement of governments. At the national level the emphasis on development policy shifted from maximizing economic growth to improving the quality of life for the poorest.

In developed countries, the major urban issues during the decade were the decline of inner city areas, the need for energy conservation as a result of rapidly increasing fuel

328

costs, and public participation in improving the quality of life. Waste disposal was a growing problem because of increasing consumption of consumer goods and extravagant packaging. Pollution of water courses by garbage dumps and industrial chemicals increased. The change from fast economic growth and suburban expansion to decreasing growth rates, the emergence of environmental concerns, more turbulent social conditions, and strained economic circumstances constituted a challenge that will continue into the 1980s.

The proportion of global population located in human settlements continued to increase during the decade in all major regions. While the absolute increase was greater in rural areas, urbanization proceeded rapidly and a trend toward aggregation of populations in very large cities of the developing regions became pronounced.

This chapter reviews the major changes in settlements in terms of the social, cultural, biological and physical environments they provide. It goes on in the next and principal sections to examine environmental impacts of urbanization and the condition of the people living in settlements during 1970–1980. The variety of public action is then reviewed, and a concluding section suggests trends likely to claim more attention in future.

A human settlement is taken to mean a community — a group of people living in one place. Whether the community is rural or urban, small or large, its development for productive purposes involves a transformation of the natural environment into a man-made environment that includes a variety of structures and institutions designed to meet the community's needs for work, recreation and other aspects of human life. It thus has a natural setting, a physical infrastructure of housing, transport, water, waste disposal and energy sources; and a social infrastructure of political, educational and cultural services.

At the United Nations Conference on the Human Environment held in Stockholm in 1972 and again at the United Nations Conference on Human Settlements (Habitat) held in Vancouver in 1976 the improvement of the quality of human life was seen as the primary aim of settlement policy. There are no easy measures of what in fact happened to the quality of life in those clusters during the decade. More is known about shifts in the size of different types of settlements than in the lives lived there or the satisfactions gained. A few aspects that displayed significant change were: the enhancement of rural communities, sharper recognition of links between rural and urban settlements, the improvement of unconventional settlements of the squatter type, and measures to protect amenities of the natural environment.

Concerns that came to the fore during the 1970s included potable drinking water, improved sanitation and solid waste disposal, and development of spatial patterns to reduce transport needs and make more effective use of energy. Planning to reduce vulnerability to disaster and to make greater use of indigenous construction techniques and local materials also were important concerns.

Changes in Settlement Patterns

THROUGHOUT the world, the single most frequent form of human settlement is the village. Cities and towns are far fewer than villages, isolated farmsteads or herding .camps. The rural population in developing countries in 1980 accounted for about 58 per cent of the total population in these countries. Village populations range from perhaps 100 permanent residents to as many as 10,000. A village is, typically, a bonded group of people sharing in various forms of social organization and productive activity. But there is no widely accepted distinction between rural and urban, and in compiling statistics about settlements the United Nations is obliged to accept different national definitions of an urban place or town or city as contrasted with a rural place.

   The United Nations Commission on Human Settlements* considers rural settlements to be "settlements which are located in a predominantly agricultural area and whose economy depends heavily on agriculture and closely related industries and services" (UNCHS, 1980a). There are two main types: villages and rural towns. The United Nations Population Division used 20,000 as a lower limit for urban settlements but the national definitions differ among themselves. Thus, in India there were estimated to be 579,052 settlements, of which 575,933 were rural, and 98 per cent of those were villages with less than 5,000 inhabitants, with a total population of more than 380 million (UNCHS, 1980a).

   Recognizing the difficulties of exact comparison, the data presented in Chapter 8 (Population) may be broken down to show how the changes of the decade were distributed between rural and urban areas. The urban population of the world is estimated to have grown from some 1,350 million in 1970 to about 1,800 million in 1980 (Table 9–1, Figure 9–1). Whereas in 1970 there were more urban dwellers in the developed regions, the developing regions had more by the end of the decade. All regions

---

* The Commission is the governing body of the United Nations Centre for Human Settlements (UNCHS or Habitat).

Table 9–1. Urban Populations Of The World, 1950–2000 (in millions)

Year	More Developed Regions[a]	Less Developed Regions	Africa	Latin America	North America	East Asia	South Asia	Europe	Oceania	USSR	World Total
1950	449	275	32	68	106	113	105	223	8	71	724
1960	573	439	50	107	133	195	147	266	10	105	1,012
1970	703	651	80	162	159	265	217	318	14	138	1,354
1975	767	794	103	198	171	309	266	344	16	155	1,561
1980	834	972	133	241	183	359	330	369	18	174	1,807
1990	969	1,453	219	343	212	476	516	423	23	209	2,422
2000	1,092	2,116	346	466	239	622	791	477	27	240	3,208

Source: UN (1980).

[a] More developed regions' comprise Europe, the USSR, North America, Japan, Australia and New Zealand and accordingly some of the eight major regions have both developing and developed nations.

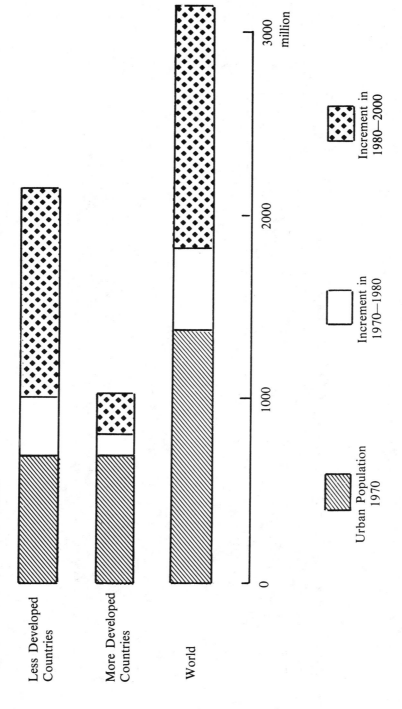

Figure 9–1. Trends in Urbanization.

Less Developed
Countries

More Developed
Countries

World

Urban Population
1970

Increment in
1970–1980

Increment in
1980–2000

0   1000   2000   3000
million

After Data by UN, 1980.

gained in urban population, but as shown in Table 9–2 the average annual growth rates moved in opposite directions between regions. By comparison with the 1960s the growth rates declined in all regions except Africa and South Asia, where they mounted. In total, the proportion of urban population moved from 37.5 per cent to 41.3 per cent while the global urban growth rate remained about the same as in the previous decade.

If the median UN projections prove correct, the proportion of population in urban places by the year 2000 will be over 50 per cent for the whole world, over 78 per cent in developed regions, and over 43 per cent in developing regions (Table 9–3). The total urban population will have doubled between 1975 and 2000. By that time half the population will be urbanized. Thus, the people living in urban settlements in developing regions may be twice as numerous as their counterparts in developed countries. According to these estimates, most of the difference between those two major groupings of countries is due to a more rapid population growth rate in the developing regions (as demonstrated in Chapter 8). It is less attributable to differences in rates of urbanization.

The Tables also show important differences in trends between the eight major area groupings (Figure 9–2). Latin America clearly has a high percentage of its population housed in urban areas compared with South Asia, East Asia and Africa. Because South Asia and Africa are estimated to maintain high growth rates in their urban population, the impact on them of developing urbanization will be much more pronounced relatively, by the turn of the century. East Asia, which includes China and Japan, is expected to continue to have urban growth rates that are less than those in Latin America and declining. The same shifts are apparent when the numbers of rural populations are considered. The directions of these trends and projected trends for the major regions are shown in Figure 9–3.

The features of contemporary urbanization in developing countries differ markedly from those of historical experience. Whereas urbanization in the industrialized countries took many decades, permitting a gradual emergence of economic, social and political institutions to deal with the problems of transformation, the process in developing countries is occuring far more rapidly, against a background of higher population growth and lower incomes (World Bank, 1979). The transformation involves enormous numbers of people: between 1970 and 1980, the urban areas of developing regions absorbed about 320 million people; between 1980 and 2000, the increase is projected to be more than 1000 million.

Such a remarkable increase in urbanization in the developing countries has been accompanied by a rapid expansion of the number of very large cities. Table 9–4 shows the population housed in different sized cities in more-developed and less-developed regions. It is based on analysis of some 1,400 cities that had reached a population of 100,000 at the first of two recent observations. It was estimated that in 1975 there were 95 cities of more than one million inhabitants in the developed regions and 90 in the developing regions; a median projection of growth to the year 2000 showed 155 and 284 in both regions, respectively. In 1950, only one city in the less-developed regions (greater Buenos Aires) had a population over 4 million. In 1960 there were 8 cities that had reached or exceeded that size, compared to 10 cities in the developed regions. By 1980, there were 22 cities in the developing regions with more than 4 million population each, whereas in the developed regions there were only 16 such cities (Table 9–4). It is

Table 9–2. Average Annual Growth Rates Of Urban Populations, 1950–2000 (percentage)

Period	More Developed Regions	Less Developed Regions	Africa	Latin America	North America	East Asia	South Asia	Europe	Oceania	USSR	World
1950–60	2.4	4.7	4.4	4.6	2.3	5.5	3.4	1.8	3.0	3.9	3.4
1960–70	2.0	3.9	4.9	4.2	1.8	3.1	3.9	1.8	2.7	2.8	2.9
1970–75	1.8	4.0	5.0	4.0	1.3	3.1	4.0	1.5	2.7	2.4	2.8
1975–80	1.7	4.1	5.1	3.9	1.5	3.0	4.3	1.5	2.6	2.2	2.9
1980–90	1.5	4.0	5.0	3.6	1.5	2.8	4.5	1.4	2.4	1.9	2.9
1990–2000	1.2	3.8	4.6	3.1	1.2	2.7	4.3	1.2	1.8	1.4	2.8

Table 9–3. Proportions Of Population Living In Urban Areas, 1950–2000 (percentage)

Year	More Developed Regions	Less Developed Regions	Africa	Latin America	North America	East Asia	South Asia	Europe	Oceania	USSR	World
1950	52.5	16.7	14.5	41.2	63.8	16.7	15.7	53.7	61.2	39.3	29.0
1960	58.7	21.9	18.2	49.5	67.1	24.7	17.8	58.4	66.2	48.8	33.9
1970	64.7	25.8	22.9	57.4	70.4	28.6	20.5	63.9	70.8	56.7	37.5
1975	67.5	28.0	25.7	61.2	72.0	30.7	22.0	66.5	73.4	60.9	39.3
1980	70.2	30.5	28.9	64.7	73.7	33.1	24.0	68.8	75.9	64.8	41.3
1990	74.9	36.5	35.7	70.7	77.2	38.6	29.1	73.3	80.4	71.3	45.9
2000	78.8	43.5	42.5	75.2	80.8	45.4	36.1	77.1	83.0	76.1	51.3

Source: UN (1980).

Figure 9–2. Regional Trends of Urbanization.

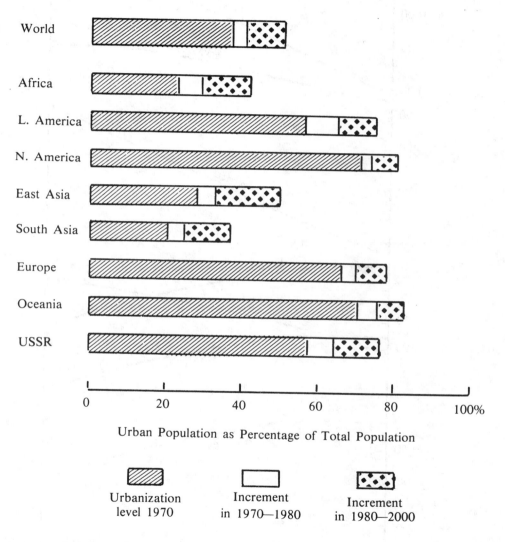

Urban Population as Percentage of Total Population

Urbanization level 1970

Increment in 1970—1980

Increment in 1980—2000

After Data by UN, 1980.

Figure 9–3. Rural Population, 1950–2000, in Major Areas.

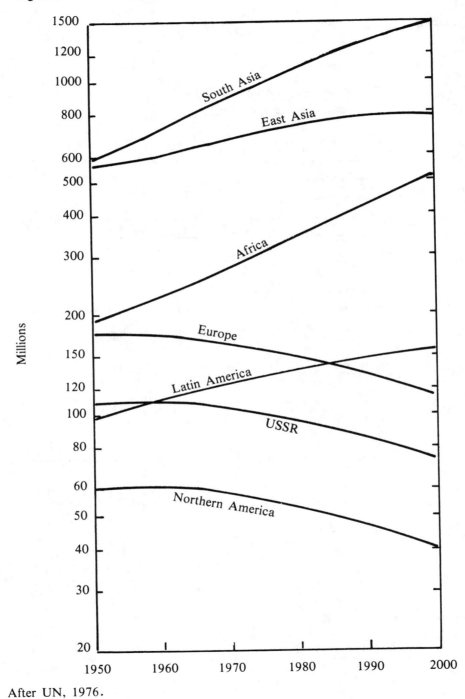

After UN, 1976.

Table 9–4. Population and Number of Cities In a Particular Size Class, 1975–2000
(Population in millions)

Size Class (millions)	1975	1980	1990	2000
More Developed Regions				
Urban Population	767	834	969	1092
4 million +	121	142	171	207
Number of Cities	13	16	19	25
2–3.9 million	72	73	99	96
Number of Cities	26	27	36	36
1–1.9 million	77	99	119	131
Number of Cities	56	74	89	94
Less Developed Regions				
Urban Population	794	792	1453	2116
4 million +	121	170	295	535
Number of Cities	17	22	33	61
2–3.9 million	61	82	144	183
Number of Cities	22	31	50	69
1–1.9 million	73	87	157	213
Number of Cities	51	65	115	154

Source: UN (1980).

estimated that by the year 2000, the developing regions will have about 61 cities of or above this size, compared with about 25 in the developed regions. Eighteen cities in developing countries are expected to have more than 10 million inhabitants by that time. The net additions to city population are even more striking. For example, in every year of the 1970s, Mexico City and Sao Paulo each added more than half a million people, while such cities as Jakarta and Cairo grew by about a quarter of a million people annually. By the end of the century Mexico City could have as many as 32 million inhabitants, Sao Paulo 26 million, and Calcutta, Shanghai, Bombay, Peking, Seoul, Jakarta, Cairo and Karachi over 15 million each.

The pattern of urbanization in much of the developing regions is characterized by a heavy concentration of economic activities and wealth in a few very large urban centres, providing a stark contrast to the economic stagnation and much lower average incomes in many of the peripheral regions. Although average urban incomes are relatively high, poverty remains a serious problem in many cities as well as in the countryside (World Bank, 1979). In Africa and South Asia the proportion of people living in urban areas is not expected to rise above 45 per cent during the remainder of this century. Although some of the world's largest cities exist in South Asia, it is expected to remain the least urbanized region throughout this period.

This shift in the balance between rural and urban sectors is closely linked to industrialization and changing patterns of employment, and to rapid alterations in cultural, social and political conditions throughout the world. There are questions about the causes of urban growth itself — how much is due to natural increase; how much to the balance of immigration into the area compared with movement out; and how much due to removal from rural to urban settlements?

It now appears that the bulk of urban growth in less developed countries is due to the high rates of natural increase in the urban population. Internal migration is a factor but recent analyses show that only about 16 per cent of the difference in urban growth rates between developing and developed countries can be attributed to it. However, this percentage is an average; the high rates of growth of many large cities in developing countries do involve large inward migration.

In developing countries, migration from rural areas has been estimated to be about one-half of the value of rural natural increase, thus leaving positive rates of rural population growth. There is much variability in this generalization both between and within major regions. There are many causes of migration: lack of jobs; lack of assistance to poor farmers; lack of social services and physical infrastructure; and limitations on land ownership. Minimum wage differences are a basic factor in some areas. In developed countries the rate of migration away from rural areas often exceeds natural increase, leading to population decline. Some examples of a reversal of this trend are found in recent census enumerations.

Impacts of Urbanization

HUMAN settlements affect the environment because of the land they occupy, their wider impact on the surrounding region, and the wastes they produce.

IMPACTS ON LAND

The most obvious feature of human settlements is that they are consumers of space: they occupy and use land. The supply of land and its location are mostly fixed; using land for a particular purpose necessarily has an impact on its availability for other uses. Therefore, allocation of land is a conflicting issue in settlement development. Different activities and functions compete for the same land space. Individual and private needs may come into collision with collective land-use requirements, and local, regional and national interests may conflict over the use of land. Agriculture, as well as human settlements, needs land, and the growing demand from both poses problems for the future. More serious is the lack of proper policies and strategies to assure suitable land allocation. At present, only about 2 per cent of the total usable land all over the world is taken up by human settlements.

Despite technological achievements that enable people in developed countries to live and work in high-rise buildings, the most common pattern of urban growth is still urban sprawl. The sheer physical expansion of cities means that peripheral land was converted to urban use at a rapid rate (Clawson, 1971; OECD, 1979). Estimates of annual conversion of cropland to urban, transportation and other uses are given in Chapter 7. As large cities in developing countries continue to grow at great speed, large quantities of agricultural land disappear even though cropping densities may be high. This loss of agricultural and pastoral land was serious in developing countries where the central city has traditionally relied for its supplies on the immediate hinterland. Even in countries like the United States and Australia where food and raw material supplies for cities are drawn from long distances, there were local examples of urban expansion having harmful effects on specialized rural production, e.g. wine growing around Adelaide in Australia, and fruit and vegetable production in California.

REGIONAL IMPACT

As the degree of urbanization increases and as large cities become giant cities, the regional impact of settlements becomes more complex, extensive and intensive. During the decade some important advances were made in establishing the inflows and outflows of materials, energy products, people and wastes from cities. A general ecological method for analyzing this aspect of settlements was developed (UNESCO, 1976), and was applied in a series of studies (see, for example, Numata, 1977, 1981). These emphasized such relationships as those between water supply and land subsidence, effects of suburban growth and wildlife conservation, green-space and aesthetic satisfaction, and health in the zone of interface between sea and land. Material flows in and out of cities were also examined. For example, studies of Hong Kong showed that every day the city needs to bring in 6,000 tonnes of food, 11,000 tonnes of liquid fuel,

9,300 tonnes of raw materials and about 1 million tonnes of fresh water (Newcombe *et al.,* 1978). On the same basis 8,100 tonnes of products are exported each day, together with 820,000 tonnes of liquid sewage and 2,850 tonnes of refuse.

In more conventional terms, there is a good deal of information about the widening impact of city growth on its surroundings, particularly in developed countries. Here large cities coalesced to form urban regions or conurbations. Their demands on surrounding areas were manifold — for recreation, location of ex-urban and peri-urban residences, water supply and large institutional uses unsuitable for urban location but related to the cities. In developing countries the impact was different but substantial and growing for the daily supply of most of the food and much of the material needs of the city. In return the disposal of city waste products was an increasing and emerging problem during the decade for peripheral areas.

WASTE DISPOSAL

The disposal of garbage, solid waste and liquid effluents emerged as a major aspect of urban impact in the 1970–80 decade. But the character of the issue varied between developed and developing countries.

In developed countries, with growing and extravagant packaging of consumer products, the amounts of garbage collected per head were believed to have increased. Traditional methods of disposal — basically by collection, dumping, compaction and land fill — became less satisfactory as a solution (Weinstein and Toro, 1976). Another growing problem was the pollution of water courses by such garbage dumps and the serious contamination sometimes brought about by industrial chemical wastes. A number of measures were taken to deal with the problem. Some cities sought to recycle much of their waste by extracting metals, glass and paper. Some incinerators were built which occasionally and ironically increased the danger of air pollution. Industrial and hazardous wastes were more strictly controlled. And specific waste disposal became a new and specialised feature of local administration in many countries.

In developing countries the issue was different. First, on health grounds it became important to try to arrange some system of waste collection from high density living areas — particularly squatter and similar settlements. In some places these supplemented the complex indigenous arrangements for sorting and recycling all waste. Second, refuse was seen to have potential for fertilizer and energy production. The most extensive and comprehensive example is the system, developed in the People's Republic of China, to use agricultural residues, city garbage and animal and human excreta to produce bio-fertilizers of a liquid or composted kind and biogas as a source of energy (McGarry and Stainforth, 1978). Recent literature has described the system extensively (FAO/UNEP, 1977; see also Chapter 12).

In both types of regions the indiscriminate disposal of toxic wastes from chemical industries took on new importance. As the volume and number of chemical products continued to mount, the difficulties of disposal multiplied, and old dumps were found to pose serious hazards to human health. How many remained undisclosed in urban areas was a cause of speculation.

Conditions of the People

THIS subject can be approached in many ways. One is to examine social conditions and the provision of community services — health, education, security. These are important considerations, but they also represent the areas where the least data and information are available. Another approach is to focus on unconventional human settlements — squatter areas and slums — or evaluate shelter and land cost and use. All these are discussed in the following paragraphs. Water supply and sanitation are dealt with in Chapter 4; transportation in Chapter 13, and energy in Chapter 12.

Few data are available on changes during the decade. Almost all of the statistical information is for one year only, so that trends are difficult to measure. And the scattered reports give more descriptions of urban than of rural situations. In a general review in 1978 the UNCHS agreed that "by and large, the conditions of human settlements and of the poor in developing countries had worsened" (UN/GA, 1979).

The plight of dwellers in slum and squatter areas is part of the broader dilemma of the poor in developing countries, and measures to deal with it are necessarily linked to factors affecting poverty as a whole. The conditions in which such people live are highly diversified, ranging from dilapidated housing in the city proper to improvised and uncontrolled squatter settlements. Beginning in the 1960s attention turned to the problems of these areas, and to possible improvements in relation to national development (UNCHS, 1980c). By 1970 international experience was being compared, and by 1976 at the Habitat Conference the severity of the problems were formally recognized for the first time (Habitat, 1976). The changes in expressed attitudes were not, however, accompanied by clear concensus or by vigorous action in many areas (UNCHS, 1980c).

A number of environmental problems encountered in rural settlements, although they might differ from one country to another, have many common characteristics. Overcrowded housing is common in developing countries, where acute poverty, widespread unemployment and rapid population growth put a strain on all housing. Rural areas suffer from these problems together with a shortage of health and sanitation facilities (WHO, 1973; World Bank, 1980). Lack of community facilities leaves contaminated water in the very heart of the human settlements, and leads to disorganized and mismanaged methods of private waste disposal. Lack of educational facilities is common.

As population continued to grow in most rural areas, housing, water supply and sanitation conditions also worsened. While generally recognized, the difficulties of providing adequate infrastructure and services attracted less attention than the aggravated conditions in urban areas.

Time series data on the quality of life in rural areas in developing countries are hard to come by, but a series of studies commissioned by the United Nations Centre for Human Settlements in 12 developing countries in 1977 revealed that the average urban household income was 30 per cent to 300 per cent higher than the rural average, and more than 500 per cent higher in one country (UNCHS, 1980a). World Bank studies in Brazil, Malaysia and Peru in the early to mid-1970s showed that households classified as below the poverty line accounted for 40 to 55 per cent of the rural populations and only 8 to 13 per cent of the households in metropolitan areas (World Bank, 1977, 1978, and unpublished data).

GROWTH OF UNCONVENTIONAL URBAN SETTLEMENTS

In both developed and developing countries the decade saw the rapid growth of unconventional urban settlements — squatter areas, slums, and, of less importance, mobile home parks. These represent the inability of human settlements to house population growth in terms of permanent accommodation at reasonable standards. But, increasingly, they also represent practical and effective methods of coping with accelerated urbanization.

In developing countries the most obvious phenomenon was the continued expansion of squatter areas. In some cases these reflected growth rates of large cities amounting to hundreds of thousands of people per year with large inward migration. Some countries, such as Singapore, were able to solve the problem and clear the areas by massive public housing programmes, involving the building of new towns, urban renewal and construction of massive high-rise buildings. But in most cases although squatter settlements were not favoured by governments they continued to multiply, and often provided effective community support for families and individuals in urban areas.

About one-third of the urban population in developing countries was believed to live in such areas. For example, early in the decade squatters made up to 45 per cent of the population of Ankara, 30 per cent of the population of Karachi, 20 per cent of that in Manila and about 35 per cent of the population of Caracas (Abrams, 1974). In most areas those proportions increased rather than decreased as the years passed.

In 1980 it was estimated that squatter settlements were growing at twice the rate of urban areas as a whole (UNCHS, 1980c). If those rates of 8 per cent were to continue the squatter settlements would double within ten years. They were growing in a variety of ways, ranging from intensification of old inner-city slums to invasions of peripheral areas in which several thousand families might establish themselves in a matter of days.

On the basis of a global survey undertaken by UNCHS, six problems were found to be widespread among squatter settlement areas (UNCHS, 1980 c):

(1) Land tenure was frequently insecure and haphazard. Land-use controls were generally ineffective, and policies of land registration and acquisition were incomplete.

(2) The residents suffered from health problems, particularly gastro-intestinal and respiratory diseases, related to the environmental conditions and to the heavy demand for shelter. One room per family was common.

(3) Community organization was often based on kinship or place of origin and grew around the resident's needs to obtain service.

(4) Low incomes and weak purchasing power prevailed: underemployment rates reached 60 per cent in some areas. Most heads-of-household worked in the informal sector.

(5) Shelter was generally sub-standard as a result of poverty, insecurity of land tenure, and household investment priorities. Make-shift dwellings of a single room ($6m^2$) housing 5 to 8 people were numerous in some areas. Others had collections of dwellings looking like a transplanted rural settlement. Most buildings had no more than two rooms.

(6) As already noted, public utilities were insufficient and inadequate.

In developed regions, some countries experienced deterioration in inner city areas, including destruction and dilapidation of the built environment. The cost of new construction coupled with sky-rocketing land prices and high interest rates made it all but impossible for young families to acquire new homes; many were forced to rent apartment units or move in with relatives. Special measures were taken in the United Kingdom, some European countries and some parts of North America to cope with these problems. In all cases physical decline was associated with depressed and disadvantaged economic and social conditions experienced by the residents of such areas compared with the rest of the city.

Mobile homes continued to be important in North America as a type of unconventional housing. Many of these were of a high standard, but much more expensive per floor area than conventional housing, and they provided cramped conditions. They were often used as an intermediate stage of housing by families saving for conventional homes.

SHELTER

Data on housing, especially in developing countries, are rare, lacking or sporadic. Most of the information available relates to developed countries. However, an examination of available statistical data reveals that housing conditions as expressed in persons-per-room or deterioration became significantly worse in most developing countries during the 1970s. This is in direct contrast to trends in developed countries. The more relevant reasons are: the rapid growth of population, the migration of rural households to the cities, and significant increases in prices of land and construction materials. Many countries experienced a shortage of the kind of dwelling that the majority of the population needs and a high proportion of vacant housing was priced above the means of the majority. At mid-decade the percentage of households unable to afford the cheapest dwellings available in selected cities ranged between 35 and 68 per cent (Habitat, 1976). It was recently suggested by UNCHS that an international year of shelter for the homeless be organized to focus attention on these needs.

In the Economic Commission of Europe (ECE) region, housing conditions were far better than elsewhere. Between 1961 and 1973, housing construction in Europe as a whole expanded without interruption (ECE, 1980). In 1973, the number of dwellings completed reached 6.1 million (i.e. 8.6 dwellings per 1000 inhabitants). In 1976, the number dropped to 7.3 dwellings per 1000 inhabitants and in 1977 to 7.4 dwellings per 1000. Construction trends during successive five-year periods differed in the various regions of Europe and in many cases offset one another. For example, while the number of dwellings built per 1000 inhabitants reached a peak of 8.8 in 1972 in Western Europe, it declined to 6.4 in 1977. On the other hand, the number of dwellings in Eastern European countries stabilized at about 8.3.

With the increase in urbanization in the 1960s and 1970s, a considerable expansion of building activity in towns took place in Greece, Spain and Finland. In Finland, for instance, 12 dwellings per 1000 inhabitants were built in rural areas in 1974 as against 18 in urban areas; in Spain, 13 dwellings were built in towns as against 4.4 dwellings in rural areas. These trends were even more obvious in the expansion and distribution of construction in the socialist countries. In Bulgaria, the proportion of construction in urban as opposed to rural areas increased between 1960 and 1970 from 60 to 79 per cent, and subsequently to 90 per cent in both 1975 and 1977; in Hungary, the ratio rose from 45 to 55 per cent and then to 63 per cent; in Poland from 65 to 73 and 79 per cent; and in the USSR from 60 to 67 per cent. In Bulgaria, urban housing construction in population terms was six times greater than in rural areas (10 and 1.6 dwellings per 100 inhabitants in urban and rural areas respectively); three times greater in Poland; and four times greater in Romania.

In countries with a higher degree of urbanization a better balance has been achieved in urban and rural construction, and in some cases it has even shifted in favour of the rural areas. This trend became particularly apparent during the years 1971 to 1977. In that period, the proportion of construction in rural areas increased in Belgium from 61 to 67 per cent; in France from 27 to 29 per cent; in the Federal Republic of Germany from 67 to 69 per cent and in the United Kingdom from 25 to 29 per cent. However, the defined "rural" areas probably included many ex-urban and suburban dwellers. In the United Kingdom, the difference in favour of the rural areas in 1973 amounted to 1.6 dwellings (towns 5.1 and rural areas 6.7 dwellings per 1000 inhabitants). A similar trend was noted in the Federal Republic of Germany.

In other regions — the developing regions — excessive overcrowding existed, with a number of countries having more than 40 per cent of their housing occupied at levels of three or more persons per room. Rural areas almost always have more overcrowded housing than urban areas. In Asia, the backlog of needed housing units in urban areas increased from 22 million dwellings in 1960 to 72 million in 1975; in Asia's rural areas, the need for housing units rose from 125 to 219 million in the same 15 years (Van der Tak *et al.*, 1979).

Some flexibility was apparent in helping shortages of housing and was inherent in two developments in residential building activity. In developed countries a wider range of dwelling forms was being provided. Increasingly, building, zoning and planning by-laws were revised to meet the requirements of low income or disadvantaged groups. In developing countries considerable ingenuity was shown in the construction of shelter in unconventional settlements.

In some of the countries with centrally planned economies there were reported to be almost no slums, as in the case of Ulan-Bator, Mongolia (UNCHS, 1980b). There, the planned provision of new housing kept pace with the growing population, although the major problem was reported to be per capita living area.

LAND COST AND USE

One general trend in both developed and developing countries was the increasing cost of land for urban purposes. Some data and information are available for periods during the 1950s and the 1960s and indicate these costs rose at constant prices, in both developed and developing countries (UN, 1975).

The planning of urban expansion and land use in developed countries probably improved. Considerable experience accrued over the years in those processes. Many countries produced a wide variety of policy instruments to enhance performance in land planning, covering land transfer and tenure regulation, public investment decisions, taxes and user charges, zoning and subdivision regulations and transport regulations. In countries with centrally planned economies comprehensive land-use planning was a feature of virtually all new urban development. The same competence is true of some developing countries such as Singapore, but the sheer magnitude of urban growth in many countries meant that its organization and administration were under considerable strain in those areas. While a few countries such as Nigeria and Tanzania undertook to build complete new capital cities the problems of managing land use and land value in the face of rapid expansions were severe.

Public Action

THIS section briefly comments on developments in public policies and programmes concerning the growth and distribution of settlements; how policies involving unconventional settlements changed; the evolution of environmental protection policies in the decade insofar as they relate to human settlements and changes in decision-making processes.

The United Nations Conference on Human Settlements held in Vancouver in 1976 and the subsequent establishment of the United Nations Centre for Human Settlements marked major advances in recognition at national and international levels of the importance of settlements as part of the human environment. They also served to stimulate attention to settlement problems at the national level.

NATIONAL POLICIES ON SETTLEMENT GROWTH AND DISTRIBUTION

These were concerned with:

(1) explicitly identifying the spatial framework which is both a determinant and a consequence of national programmes of economic and social development;

(2) identifying the problems of very large cities and devising policies to deal with or modify their high rates of growth and to avoid congestion and pollution;

(3) recognizing and seeking to correct problems of regional inequities and underdevelopment.

Precisely how far developing and developed countries advanced in these policies is impossible to judge with any assurance. The World Bank identified the pace and pattern of industrial development as the most important element affecting urbanization and spatial concentration (World Bank, 1975). This was amplified and extended by the UN Centre for Human Settlements with the comment that "there is a worsening imbalance in the development of many countries . . . because of inadequate understanding of the function of human settlements, a lack of national settlement policies and a low level of investment in shelter, infrastructure and settlement services." (UNCHS, 1980 b).

At the Habitat Conference and at the World Conference on Agrarian Reform and Rural Development (FAO, 1979) a major shift in emphasis in development policy was recognized. Moving beyond maximizing economic growth, more attention was paid to raising income and improving quality of life for the poorest (UNCHS, 1980 a). The poor are located in rural areas in most developing countries, and the attention might have been expected to shift from manufacturing to agriculture. But as of 1980, studies for the United Nations Commission of Human Settlements suggested that "it does not appear to have led, in most countries, to a logically related shift in settlements policies, from the ongoing emphasis on the problems of the largest urban area to a badly needed concern for conditions in rural settlements" (UNCHS, 1980a).

In developed countries, explicit national settlement policies were variable. Socialist countries and European countries articulated and developed quite complex plans for their nations, cities and regions, although the implementation or sensible modification of these plans when needed was uneven (Gur, 1976). In Canada and Australia the degree of commitment to national strategies of urban and regional development altered significantly over time and with different governments. Thus Australia developed a vigorous and integrated programme from 1972 to 1975, but this was subsequently abandoned.

Recognition of the failure to genuinely improve the welfare of the poor encouraged a number of national and international agencies to make "basic needs" their highest priority in development policy in the less developed regions. This meant greater stress on food, clothing, shelter, health facilities and education in rural areas. These addressed the quality of life in terms of basic services but needed to be supplemented by measures to increase productivity, income, and employment if they were to get at the root causes. The linkage between rural and urban policies was enlarged and was embodied in large-scale programmes in many countries. China has undertaken very extensive schemes in recent years. Brazil has initiated major resettlement programmes.

As a method of stemming rural migration to the cities, the Malaysian Government established a programme for resettlement in land development schemes (UN/ESA, 1978). Instead of moving to towns on the west coast of Peninsular Malaysia, would-be migrants were provided the opportunity to locate in nearby integrated settlements. In addition to giving livelihood to about 300,000 people by 1980, the Government had sought to stimulate other rural and regional developments. In its second five-year development plan Indonesia initiated 81 demonstration projects for rural housing development (UN/ESA, 1978). These included, depending upon the village type, improvements in village infrastructure and environmental sanitation, housing rehabilitation, and stimulation of house building. This form of village development was believed to have increased income and to have widened its distribution.

On the urban side, encouragement of self-help and community development by low income populations probably was the most significant advance in improvement of shelter and neighbourhood conditions. This was fruitful in both central city and squatter areas.

One major problem became more clearly focused during the 1970s: the importance of revision of typical building codes and regulations so as to permit and encourage more flexible standards for building materials and technologies to meet the requirements of low-income groups (Mabogunje *et al.*, 1978). As the 1980s began, it was expected that more countries would move to up-date and rationalize their legislation regarding building zoning and subdivision controls so as to enable their settlements to offer a diversity of contacts, humanity of style, and neighbourliness all too frequently lacking in the planned city of the past.

It became evident during the decade that the conventional financing mechanisms for housing of low-income families did not and could not resolve their difficulties (Habitat, 1976) and that rent controls were a weak tool (UN, 1979). Those approaches "neither accommodate the life-styles, values and savings capacities of the poor nor provide a realistic and efficient attempt to meet the magnitude of the housing finance shortage" (Habitat, 1976). Grassroots initiatives were often thwarted by institutional arrangements and government policies. Innovative efforts to improve the situation were made in such countries as the Dominican Republic, Chile, El Salvador, Upper Volta and the Philippines, but the need for much broader assistance targeted to reach lower-income groups was recognised. A study by the World Bank concluded that a combination of self-help and sites-and-services projects could provide acceptable housing without significant subsidy for at least 80 per cent of the population of most cities, and that many of the lower 20 per cent could be helped with small subsidies (World Bank, 1975). There still remained the very poor whose situation was less tractable.

SQUATTER SETTLEMENTS AND OTHER UNCONVENTIONAL COMMUNITIES

The decade witnessed a change in attitude to the burgeoning squatter settlements of large cities in the developing countries. In 1970, partly inspired by the vigorous but atypical examples of Singapore and Hong Kong, much of the solution had seemed to lie in the massive provision of public housing. But emphasis switched to providing sites and services for squatter settlements. Generally the poor can construct their own shelter, particularly if climatic conditions are not onerous. Where they need help is in providing the necessary services to go with housing.

A recent World Bank report recommended that the public sector concentrate its efforts on improving the supply of public services — not on housing *per se* (World Bank, 1975). But public action needs to go beyond that and some security of tenure for unconventional settlements is needed. This implies institutional and attitudinal changes, which are not always easy. Unconventional settlements need access to the land on which they build their shelter, and relaxed building standards for more conventional settlements: as in general housing for the poor, that implies the opportunity for gradual improvement from one stage to another and not an inflexible commitment to one standard or material.

Another innovation in the decade was the general improvement of slum and squatter settlements, using the aspirations and energy of the people living in them. Such efforts confronted the necessity for housing finance for families and some innovative resources were devised. These flexible and cooperative approaches by governments, public agencies and the communities involved became a distinctive feature of the decade.

Rehabilitation and upgrading generally were seen as the most feasible solutions to pursue. While the public housing approach with its clearance and relocation of communities was seen as effective in a few places, the more gradual upgrading was preferred for several reasons (Van Hyck, 1971; UNCHS, 1980 c). The funding burden was less, people's participation in savings and labour could be mobilized, the development built on rather than destroyed the social fabric of the settlements, and the political and practical disadvantages of relocation — including its removal of people from the informal employment sector — were avoided.

Nevertheless, many governments had not adopted any specific policies for dealing with squatter settlements (UNCHS, 1980 c). Some hoped that the problem would be limited and would in time disappear. Some were overwhelmed by massive urban growth. Others regarded uncontrolled settlements as a part of national development and pursued *laissez-faire* policies. Those that took positive measures either exercised restrictions or provided support.

Several factors contributed to the ambivalence toward squatter settlements (UNCHS, 1980 c). There was lack of agreement on what constituted a squatter settlement and on appropriate standards for them. Competing claims for national development funds were strong and governments had difficulty estimating the full social costs of action and inaction. Technical problems of building materials, skilled labour, land prices and the like impeded remedial programmes. It was difficult to create adequate administrative guidance. And data on housing and related variables was lacking. During the course of the decade it became apparent that one policy in dealing with squatter settlements should be rejected: the policy of automatic slum clearance. The costs of clearance and relocation had proved prohibitive (UNCHS, 1980c).

ENVIRONMENTAL PROTECTION POLICIES

The decade saw the diffusion of strong environmental protection and pollution control policies, as reported in Chapters 2, 4 and 11. This was particularly apparent in developed countries, but important examples also occurred in developing countries such as Brazil, the Philippines and Thailand.

The Organization for Economic Cooperation and Development (OECD) countries formulated forthright principles concerning environmental protection. Of relevance is the strong endorsement of the "Polluter Pays" principle early in the decade. Environmental impact legislation was enacted in many OECD countries and served to enlist public participation in decision-making about development proposals, and to build environmental considerations into such proposals at an early planning stage. This was recognized in a reaffirmation and extension of OECD policy in 1979 (OECD, 1979). Of particular importance were the strong measures developed to deal with noise.

In the socialist countries the principles of environmental protection were closely related to planning of new communities and the industrial activities on which they were based. Thus, protection had its fullest expression in large new industrial complexes, as noted in Chapter 11, and in cities in areas of extreme environmental conditions, as in the hot, dry cities of the Central Asian Soviet republics. The USSR in 1973–75 developed a general scheme for population settlement on three levels: national, regional, and composite or subregional. The regional schemes gave priority to areas of concentrated industrial construction. The scheme also focused attention on the rehabilitation of older city areas, as in Moscow, on the adjustment of urban construction to distinctive landscape-climatic zones, and on integration of regional systems.

Considerable government machinery was established for environmental protection and management. While such legislation and administration had much in common, it is possible to classify environmental protection and management in regard to human settlements as having four overlapping affiliations — with public health, with natural resource development, with a programme of national economic development, or with urban and rural planning strategies. An example of the kind of effort pursued to cope with this complex of considerations at the end of the decade was the project by the UNCHS and the United Nations Environment Programme (UNEP) to provide the basis for guidelines for canvassing environmental aspects of human settlements. Another more concrete activity, involving the Government of Mexico, UNCHS, UNEP and the World Bank, was examining the environmental impact of urban growth in the valley of Mexico.

ADMINISTRATIVE AND INSTITUTIONAL MEASURES

There is no doubt that the recommendations of the Stockholm Conference served to sensitize a number of governments to human settlement problems and issues, including their environmental aspects, and thereby stimulated and accelerated action. Some governments established new agencies, institutions and programmes in this field, and others set up coordinating mechanisms for mobilizing and maximizing the efficient use of resources. It became more apparent that human settlements had to serve as unique focal points for the concentration and extension of community facilities and services, and for the implementation of both public and private sector activities.

No comprehensive review has been undertaken of the responses of different governments to the recommendations of Habitat. But a useful sample survey was undertaken by the International Institute for Environment and Development (Satterthwaite, 1979) of seventeen countries in four developing regions to assess their follow-up actions to the recommendations of the Habitat Conference, divided into the following categories: National Settlement Policy; Land; Shelter; Infrastructure and Services; and Institutions, Management and Public Participation. This shows wide variations in the timing, degree and effectiveness of response, and in each regional grouping there was slow but gradual progress towards the establishment and implementation of national human settlement policies. The environmental problems related to human settlements generally appear to be identified and quantified, though the task of financing and organizing for the massive backlog of improvements required will occupy most governments for many years. Furthermore, the importance of protecting agricultural land from urban encroachment and of promoting integrated rural development appears to be widely recognized among the countries covered in the survey. The survey revealed only two new ministerial-level arrangements specifically charged with human settlements. One of these is Mexico, where the Secretariat for Human Settlements and Public Works (SAHOP) was created in 1976. A general law on human settlement was also enacted in that country, and the Subsecretariat of Human Settlements is the main agency charged with implementing it. The other country with a Ministry of Human Settlements is the Philippines. In other countries, institutional arrangements focus on particular agencies given responsibility for specific aspects of human settlements development. Thus, there are housing authorities, public works ministries and special institutions for planning and administering metropolitan areas and regions.

FUNDING

An evaluation of the funding activities of 15 international and regional financial institutions made in 1976 showed a low volume of assistance to projects related to human settlements. Other types of work were regarded as contributing more directly to economic development. Only 3 of the 15 agencies had direct funding for urbanization and housing in excess of US$100 million (the World Bank, the Inter-American Development Bank and the Asian Development Bank). The average proportion of funds for urbanization and housing in the 3 institutions was only 2.2 per cent of total loans. Considering the fact that more than 200 million urban people were estimated to be living in inadequate shelter and to have no access to conventional urban services, this volume of assistance was judged totally inadequate (Donelson et al., 1979). To be sure, many lending agencies devoted relatively more resources to important elements of infrastructure such as transportation, water supply and waste disposal systems. However, practically all the loans for this purpose went to large and centralized projects relying on modern technology. The assessment revealed that when the total financing of all 15 agencies were considered, US$70.5 billion had been disbursed in the period 1947–1977 for all projects. Of these, only 8.8 per cent went to projects with a direct impact on human settlements. The largest group of projects with a direct impact was for water supply and waste disposal (6.0 per cent), followed by urban transportation and housing (2.2 per cent) and building materials loans (0.6 per cent). Another 8.7 per cent of the agencies' funds went to projects with only an indirect impact on human settlements. All other projects had no measurable impact on human settlements (Donelson et al., 1979).

PUBLIC PARTICIPATION

A final feature peculiar to the decade was the increase in public participation in decision-making about human settlements with governmental encouragement. In developed countries this was partly because of the failure of urban policy and planning to take account of local environmental factors and community interests. In developing countries it was partly because of the need to involve people in the "informal" sector in the constructive direction of their energies to self-help achievement of specific community targets such as new structures or social services. In most countries the character of decision-making changed in that citizens insisted upon — or were allowed — much more influence in crucial decisions (Angel et al., 1976).

In some cases, confrontations occurred on such issues as shoreline protection, industrial pollution, waste disposal sites and technology, storm, drainage and flooding questions, airport locations and noise levels, highways and mass transit, forms of power generation and distribution, maintenance of open space and parks and aesthetic values. The average citizen became better informed about environmental impacts, and many were ready to mobilize against projects they saw as undesirable, infringing on their rights as taxpayers and citizens, or to claim, with growing proof available, that particular projects were unsafe or unhealthy in the short- or long-term. To some extent, as with the case of new airports, nuclear power plants or big dam projects, this active-citizen participation slowed the pace of transformation of many metropolitan areas during the decade.

Sometimes the participation or involvement was token only, but, broadly, governments, non-governmental organizations and individual people became more interactive about proposals. The initiative for discussing and resolving conflicts over environmental matters tended now to come from many of these sources, rather than from governments alone.

Future Prospects

The problems and opportunities provided by human settlements differ in magnitude and kind between developed and developing countries. The developed world is largely urban and some of its countries have taken many decades to achieve their present degree of urbanization. By contrast, developing countries are largely rural and yet are engaged in growth of urban population of a scale and at a rate never experienced before. This is most prominently demonstrated by the emergence of giant cities.

In a sense, the 1970s appeared to be about mid-way in a gigantic transformation. The period saw a tapering of urban growth rates in developed countries, reflecting their lower overall population growth rates and high degree of urbanization. In the developing world, urban populations grew at much higher rates, particularly in Africa, Latin America and South Asia. In both developing and developed regions the linkages between rural and urban settlements were perceived more clearly.

A few common themes were strong in dealing with both urban and rural settlements. Greater attention was given to equity in access to employment, shelter and basic sources. The conservation of energy and the use of new and renewable sources of energy became a more prominent aim (ECOSOC, 1981). Greater emphasis was placed on rehabilitation, renewal and maintenance of existing building stock. The limited evidence of the decade is that rural and urban conditions in developing countries did not improve. There were exceptions in the form of planned developments and experimental programmes. Against this background, it is possible to suggest some prospects for the future that largely reflect trends in developing regions during 1970–80.

The first is in meeting the need for a safe and reliable water supply and for sanitary waste disposal. The 1980s were declared a decade aimed at improving and raising performance here (see Chapter 4). This is a heroic action that promises to improve the condition of a large sector of the poor in both rural and urban settlements.

A second thrust is to deal more positively with unconventional settlements. Considerable progress was made in the 1970s in developing self-help and upgrading programmes for squatter and slum areas. But this kind of action requires institutional changes at times in land tenure, access to housing finance, municipal building standards, organization of community services, development of indigenous construction industries, and larger use of local materials. A continuation of the beginning made in the 1970s will require in addition to funds for basic services, a variety of innovative and imaginative actions and a change in professional attitudes.

A third concern is transportation, discussed in Chapter 13. This is an issue of particular importance to low-income households. As large cities grow rapidly, it becomes vital to organize, reconstruct and reformulate transportation to serve the demands placed upon them. Much can be done to encourage interaction by walking or the use of low-technology means of communication. But the place of cars and buses remains to be defined. This requires sophisticated management and decisions about who pays for what in terms of public and private transport (Churchill and Lycette, 1979). Several countries have developed interesting and progressive attitudes. A variety of policy instruments, as in land development, will be required to bring about the necessary changes, and each city will have its distinctive pattern of requirements and provisions.

In the cities of the developed countries, the issues that emerged in the last decade are conspicuously those of energy use, the decline of inner areas, a decrease in growth rates, and the emergence of environmental concerns linked with developing processes of public participation about decision-making. This accompanied a change from conditions of fast economic growth and suburban expansion. It constitutes a challenge of coordinating growth in an environment of strained economic circumstances, more turbulent social conditions, and the necessity to revive and rehabilitate cities and the quality of life in them by complex processes. These challenges are likely to dominate human settlement concerns in the 1980s.

References

Abrams, C. (1974), *Housing in the Modern World,* Faber and Faber, London.

Angel., S. *et al.* (1976), *The People's Housing Efforts and the low-Income Delivery System in Bangkok,* Asian Institute of Technology, Bangkok.

Churchill, A. and M. Lycette (1979), *Basic Needs in Shelters,* Urban Projects Dept., World Bank, Washington, D.C.

Clawson, M. (1971), *Suburban Land Conversion in the USA,* John Hopkins University Press, Baltimore.

Donelson, S. *et al.* (1979), *Aid for Human Settlements in the Thirld World: A Summary of Activities of Multi-lateral Agencies,* International Institute for Environment and Development, London.

ECE (1980), *Major Trends in Housing Policy in ECE Countries,* Economic Commission for Europe, United Nations, New York.

ECOSOC (1981), *International Co-operation in the Field of Human Settlements: Renewable Sources of Energy for Human Settlements,* United Nations, E/1981/82.

FAO (1979), *Report of the World Conference on Agrarian Reform and Rural Development,* Food and Agriculture Organization of the United Nations, Rome.

FAO/UNEP (1977), *Residue Utilization: Management of Agricultural and Agro-industrial Residues,* Food and Agriculture Organization of the United Nations, Rome.

Gur, O. (1976), Industrial Structure, Urbanization and the Growth Strategy of Socialist Countries, *Quar. J. Economics,* 10, 219.

Habitat (1976), *Report of the United Nations Conference on Human Settlements,* E.76/IV.7, United Nations, New York.

Mabogunje, A. L. *et al.* (1978), *Shelter Provision in Developing Countries,* SCOPE 11, John Wiley, Chichester.

McGarry, M. G. and J. Stainforth, Editors (1978), *Compost, Fertilizer and Biogas Production from Human and Farm Wastes in the Republic of China,* International Development Research Centre, IDRC-TS8e, Ottawa.

Newcombe, K. *et al.* (1978), The Metabolism of a City: The Case of Hong Kong, *Ambio,* 7, 3.

Numata, M., Editor (1977), *Tokyo Projects: An Interdisciplinary Study on The Urban Ecosystem of the Tokyo Metropolis,* Chiba University, Tokyo

Numata, M., Editor (1981), *Chiba Bay Coast Project, Integrated Ecological Studies on the Chiba Bay Coast Cities,* Chiba University, Tokyo.

OECD (1979), *The State of the Environment in OECD Member Countries,* Organization for Economic Co-operation and Development, Paris.

Satterthwaite, D. (1979), *Three Years After Vancouver - Human Settlement Policies in Selected Developing Countries,* International Institute for Environment and Development, London.

UN (1975), *Urban Land Policies and Land-Use Control Measures,* Vol. VII: Global Review, UN Publications Sales No. E.73.IV.II, United Nations, New York.

UN (1976), *Global Review of Human Settlements*, United Nations Conference on Human Settlements, A/CONF.70/A/1.

UN (1979), *Review of Rent Control in Developing Countries*, UN Publications Sales No. E.79.IV.2, United Nations, New York.

UN (1980), *Patterns of Urban and Rural Population Growth*, Department of International Economic and Social Affairs, Population Studies, No. 68. United Nations, New York.

UNCHS (1980a), *Development of Rural Settlements and Growth Centres*, United Nations Commission on Human Settlements, Report HS/C/3/7.

UNCHS (1980b), *Human Settlements and The New International Development Strategy*, United Nations Commission on Human Settlements, Report HS/C/3/4.

UNCHS (1980c), *Upgrading of Urban Slum and Squatter Areas*, United Nations Commission on Human Settlements, Report HS/C/3/8.

UN/ESA (1978), The Significance of Rural Housing in Integrated Rural Development: Report of the Ad Hoc Group of Experts on the Significance of Rural Housing and Community Facilities in Integrated Rural Development, United Nations, New York.

UNESCO (1976), *Task Force on Integrated Ecological Studies on Human Settlements*, MAB Report Series No. 31, United Nations Educational, Scientific and Cultural Organization, Paris.

UN/GA (1979), *Official Records of the General Assembly of the United Nations*, 34th Session, Suppl. No. 8 (A/34/8), United Nations, New York.

Van Hyck, A. P. (1971), *Planning for Sites and Services Programs*, Dept. of Housing and Urban Development, Washington, D.C.

Van der Tak *et al.* (1979), Our Population Predicament: A New Look. *Population Bull.*, 34, No. 5.

Weinstein, A. H. and R. T. Toro (1976), *Thermal Processing of Municipal Solid Waste for Resources and Energy Recovery*, Ann Arbor. Science Publ., Ann Arbor, Michigan.

WHO (1973), *World Health Statistics Report*, World Health Organization, Geneva.

World Bank (1975), *Housing Sector Policy Paper*, World Bank, Washington, D.C.

World Bank (1977), *Meeting Basic Needs in Malaysia, a Summary of Findings*, Staff Working Paper No. 260, World Bank, Washington, D.C.

World Bank (1978), *The Measurement of Spatial Differences in Poverty, The Case of Peru*, Staff Working Paper No. 273, World Bank, Washington, D.C.

World Bank (1979), *World Development Report*, World Bank, Washington, D.C.

World Bank (1980), *Health Sector Policy Paper*, World Bank, Washington, D.C.

CHAPTER 10

Health and the Environment

The heightened environmental awareness of the 1970s extended to human health. For although it was recognized that both environmental and genetic factors interact in disease production, the importance of environmental determinants was emphasized – for example in water supply, urban environmental quality, climate and the pattern of human contacts. Environmental factors play a major role in the transmission of communicable diseases, which accounted during the decade for a large proportion of illness and death in developing countries. In developed countries, quite different kinds of environmental factors played an equally important role in production of the degenerative diseases that predominated there.

Each year during the decade in developing countries, six diseases accounted for the deaths of some five million children. The six were diptheria, pertussis (whooping cough), tetanus, measles, poliomyelitis and tuberculosis. Smallpox was eliminated, and following its success with that disease through vaccination, the World Health Organization (WHO) set up an extensive immunization programme against the other six. Hopes rose that a vaccine might also be developed against leprosy.

Malaria remained the most serious single disease in much of Africa and one of the most significant elsewhere in the tropics. An estimated one million children died from it every year. DDT spraying in the 1950s and 1960s had produced dramatic reductions, but during the 1970s there was a resurgence of the disease. While environmental and economic factors contributed, the most important ones were insecticide resistance in the mosquito, and drug resistance in the parasite.

Schistosomiasis, onchocerciasis and viral diseases remained widespread, and there was marked uncertainty over how best to control many parasitic diseases. The need for urgent scientific advice led to a Special Programme for Research and Training in Tropical Diseases, sponsored by WHO, the United Nations Development Programme (UNDP) and the World Bank. It concentrated on malaria, schistosomiasis, filariasis, trypanosomiasis, leprosy and leishmaniasis.

In developed countries the effects of pollutants on health remained a focus of concern. Classic occupational diseases became rare and attention focussed on long-term exposure to harmful factors in the work-place. Several studies were undertaken on a possible threat not even conceived a decade previously: the health effects that might follow depletion of ozone in the stratosphere (e.g. skin cancer). Controls were introduced to reduce people's exposure to potentially hazardous substances in air, water and food. Metals, organochlorines, PCBs and nitrates and micropollutants in water were monitored carefully. Food contamination also caused hazards in developing countries where mycotoxins remained a problem.

Understanding of the role of environmental and genetic factors in the production of cancer advanced. X-rays, nitrosamines, fungal toxins, pyrrholizidine alkaloids, biological agents and industrial chemicals received particular attention. Some drugs were also implicated, such as diethylstilboesterol, the first drug proved to induce cancer in a human foetus through ingestion of a hormone by the mother.

358

Average per capita food energy supply rose somewhat, but malnutrition remained a major underlying cause of death and illness: in 1974 there were an estimated 98 million moderately or severely under-nourished children in the world, 70 per cent of them in Africa. In developed countries, in contrast, obesity increased, and its role and that of nutrition in promoting cardiovascular disease was explored. The importance of nutrition and life style as determinants of health gained fresh recognition. Health-conscious groups paid increasing attention to exercise, reduction of salt intake and animal fats, and other factors believed to influence cardiovascular disease. The role of smoking as a dominant cause of lung cancer and serious influence on other cancers and coronary heart disease was confirmed, and in the late 1970s there was a slight drop in tobacco consumption in industrial countries. Alcohol and drugs caused increasing concern and the importance of environmental factors in mental health was widely appreciated.

Despite these improvements in understanding of environment-health relationships, there was little improvement in the health of the vast rural and shanty-town populations of many developing countries. Efforts were made to expand health care for such people, but it was clear by 1980 that political commitment and resource availability would be the dominant factors in improvement in the future.

Human health and quality of life are strongly influenced by the environment. Both environmental and genetic factors, however, are involved in the production of disease. While genetic factors usually give rise to congenital diseases and environmental factors to acquired ones, there is often an interplay between the two. For example, an environmental factor (intrauterine infection of the foetus by *Rubella* virus in the first trimester of pregnancy) sometimes predisposes the foetus to a disease classed as congenital (blindness or mental retardation). Or a congenital condition (abnormal haemoglobin) may lead to disastrous complications in a person who suffers an acquired infection of malaria, tetanus or bacterial meningitis. Such combinations of genetic and environmental factors in disease are frequently encountered among populations with high incidences of genetic anomalies inhabiting geographical areas in which communicable diseases are endemic (WHO, 1980).

Epidemiological differences between and within countries can serve as pointers to the role of environmental factors in different regions of the world. These differences may also reflect variations in life-style or cultural practice. For example, the unusually high incidence of oral cancers in India is related to the people's habit of chewing the betel nut, just as the high incidence of skin cancers in Pakistan is associated with the application of hot pots (changri) to the skin.

Studies of peoples who are ethnologically related but live in different parts of the world have strongly incriminated environmental factors in a number of diseases, for example cancer in both childhood and adulthood, hardening (arteriosclerosis) of the coronary and cerebral arteries, and high blood pressure (hypertension). But there is abundant evidence that the environment also plays a role in promoting health. During the decade there were several studies in this field, for example on the effects of high altitude on human health. Differences in disease patterns between inhabitants of areas with different vegetation also gained recognition: for example between people living in the equatorial rain forest belt and those in the savannahs. Temperature also plays a role, as the contrast between disease patterns in tropical and temperate climate attests.

Environmental variations are reflected in seasonal differences in the incidence of diseases in many parts of the world. Some communicable diseases are transmitted much more easily during the rainy season. Temperature, humidity, soil, rainfall and atmospheric conditions are all important factors in the ecology of certain infective and infectious diseases, especially because they control the distribution and abundance of their vectors. Control of these ecological factors therefore provides an important means of interrupting the spread of ill-health.

Although freedom from organic disease is usually considered synonymous with a reasonable state of health, freedom from non-organic disease is equally important. Health demands a sound mind in a sound body. The socio-economic implications of impaired mental health in any population group cannot be ignored. Impaired mental health, like its organic counterpart, can be caused by genetic or environmental factors, or an interplay between both. During the past decade, evidence of the role of biochemical changes in the aetiology (causation) of mental ill health has increased. Some of these biochemical abnormalities could be inherited or induced environmentally. Certain organic causes of mental ill health are certainly due to environmental factors, as with the group of psychoses resulting from infectious agents such as treponematosis or trypanosomiasis. Exposure to heavy metals such as mercury or lead and to certain synthetic compounds may also create a predisposition to brain tumours or abnormal behaviour. The environment therefore has a broad and highly significant influence on the health profile of its inhabitants.

Several intergovernmental bodies are involved in formulating policies for the effective monitoring and control of the environment, and with the interactions between the environment and health. These include the World Health Organization (WHO), the United Nations Environment Programme (UNEP), the United Nations Development Programme (UNDP), the Food and Agriculture Organization of the United Nations (FAO) and the United Nations Children's Fund (UNICEF). Data on world population statistics are available from records of WHO, which published in 1980 a global analysis of the health situation between 1973 and 1977 (WHO, 1980). During the decade there was little improvement in the collection of mortality statistics in many developing countries because the registration of deaths and births had not been made compulsory there. Until this is done mortality statistics will continue to be grossly inaccurate. Morbidity (illness) statistics are even worse in developing countries because of the severe shortage of manpower. Although child mortality and life expectancy figures (Table 10–1) could be used as an indication of the effectiveness with which health care is provided, they are influenced by many variables that differ from one country to another, and even within a country. However, there is clearly a broad relationship between life expectancy at birth and GNP (Figure 10–1).

Table 10–1. Life Expectancy at Birth (both Sexes) by Region, Medium Variant, 1950–1955, 1970–1975, 1975–1980, 1980–1985, 1995–2000, 2020–2025, as Assessed in 1980.

	Life Expectancy at Birth (years)					
	1950–1955	1970–1975	1975–1980	1980–1985	1995–2000	2020–2025
World Total	47.1	55.8	57.5	59.2	63.9	70.4
More developed regions	65.2	71.3	71.9	72.4	73.3	75.4
Less developed regions	42.5	53.1	55.1	57.0	62.4	69.6
Africa	37.4	46.4	48.6	50.8	57.8	67.2
Latin America	51.2	60.7	62.5	64.1	68.1	71.8
North America	69.0	71.4	73.0	73.3	74.1	75.1
East Asia	47.5	63.8	67.6	69.9	72.7	74.8
South Asia	39.5	48.2	50.7	52.8	59.4	68.6
Europe	65.4	71.2	72.0	72.7	74.3	75.7
Oceania	60.8	65.8	65.6	66.7	70.2	73.8
USSR	61.7	69.8	69.6	70.0	71.5	74.6

Source: UN (1981).

In the world as a whole there are three broad groups of diseases that account for a highly significant proportion of illness and death:

(i) communicable diseases;

(ii) degenerative diseases;

(iii) neoplastic diseases (cancers).

The relative frequency of each of these varies according to the socio-economic state of a country and the condition of its environment.

Communicable diseases account for a large proportion of illness and death in developing countries. On the other hand, degenerative diseases such as those of the heart and circulatory system and neoplastic diseases (cancer) account for a large proportion of illness and death in developed countries. It should be noted that these diseases are also widespread in the developing countries, but mortality and morbidity statistics due to them are rarely available.

Infant mortality due to communicable diseases is extremely low in the developed world, while a significant proportion of the adult population there becomes exposed to environmental factors that produce cancer and degenerative diseases. In the developing world, however, where infant mortality is relatively high, a much smaller proportion of people survive long enough to be exposed to agents capable of producing cancer and degenerative conditions. Even those who survive into adulthood may escape because the agents may not be present in the environment. The significant differences between the population pyramids of the developed and developing worlds are therefore partly explicable in terms of their differing mortality and morbidity patterns (Chapter 8).

Figure 10–1. Relationship Between Life Expectancy At Birth and GNP; 1975.

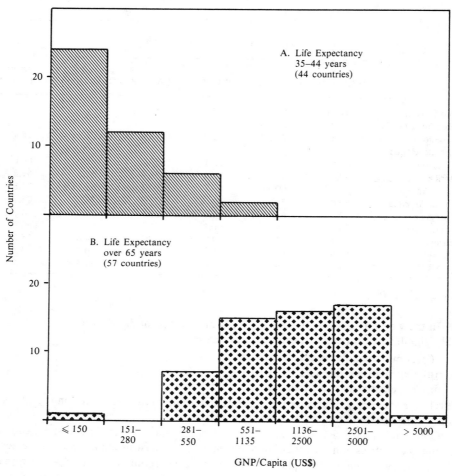

After Data given by WHO, 1980.

Changes in Communicable Diseases during the Decade

ENVIRONMENTAL DETERMINANTS OF COMMUNICABLE DISEASES

The decade was notable for major changes in peoples' perception of health issues. There was a renewed acceptance of the importance of environmental determinants of health, a more positive approach to dealing with the effects of environmental changes on health, and emphasis on coverage of whole populations with basic health care.

The transmission of any infection is influenced by four factors:

(1) The immunological status of the host;

(2) The characteristics of the environment;

(3) The biology of the organisms causing the infection;

(4) The relationship between these organisms and the host.

While infectious diseases are often grouped according to the taxonomic classification of the causative organisms (viruses, bacteria, protozoa, fungi, worms etc.), from an environmental stand-point it is most important to distinguish betwen infections that are maintained wholly in man and those known as zoonoses that are common to man and other vertebrates.

Within these classes the environmental factors likely to be critical vary according to the route or mode of transmission, which can be direct from skin to skin (e.g. in sexually-transmitted diseases); via soil, air, food or water; through a vector (such as a mosquito or snail); or through clothing, bedding etc. All infecting organisms are part of the human environment, but those spreading directly from man to man are less obviously important in discussions of the wider role of the environment.

The most important environmental factor in the transmission of infectious disease is water. It is the habitat of the larval stages of the mosquito vectors of such diseases as malaria, yellow fever and dengue, and of the snails that are alternate hosts of schistosomiasis. It is the medium of transmission of cholera and numerous organisms causing diarrhoeal diseases (bacillary dysenteries). The second major factor is the quality of the urban and residential environment (and especially excreta disposal systems), and the third, the pattern of human movements and contacts. Throughout the past decade, population movements between countries, from rural areas to cities, away from natural disasters, wars and social upheavals, or through nomadic or tourist travel have contributed to the spread of communicable diseases. The risk of epidemics has been enhanced, and the difficulties of disease control increased. Finally, climatic conditions are important to the spread of airborne diseases, while changes in agricultural practices and techniques of animal husbandry (with associated changes in ecological patterns) can affect the distribution of zoonoses and other communicable diseases.

The effect of surface water resource development

.Surface water development for hydropower, flood regulation or irrigation was a major feature of the decade, and had myriad effects on human health. Major schemes (such as the creation of large man-made lakes) altered ecosystems and modified distribution patterns of communicable diseases over millions of hectares (Ackermann *et al.*, 1973; Stanley and Alpers, 1975; see also Chapter 4). The health of the population was affected both during the construction and the operation of a scheme. In the construction phase large numbers of workers were brought together and some were exposed for the first time to locally prevalent diseases. Infections like schistosomiasis, onchocerciasis, filariasis (elephantiasis), malaria and viral encephalitides (Japanese encephalitis, Nyong Nyong fever, St Louis, Western Equine and Murray Valley encephalitides), transmitted by invertebrates that live or breed in water, became rampant in some situations. Irrigation not only increased mosquito and snail habitats but tended to enhance the longevity of adult mosquitoes by raising atmospheric humidity, hence increasing the number of infections each mosquito could cause. Disease problems have been aggravated by inadequately planned housing, food and water supplies for construction workers.

During the decade governments and international agencies increased their efforts to minimize the potential hazards of water developments, though many governments still did not appear to understand that if this is to be done effectively, ecological and epidemiological studies must precede large-scale projects by many years (Stanley and Alpers, 1975). Moreover, while small impoundments and local irrigation schemes collectively had an immense potential influence on disease patterns, because they were too small individually to attract national or international attention, they were generally neglected.

The effects of improved water supply and excreta disposal

The task of providing improved water supplies became increasingly difficult due to population growth, particularly in and around cities. An annual urban growth rate of 4 per cent implies doubled water needs every eighteen years, even at constant per capita use. The extra water is more difficult to obtain, except where improvements benefit from economies of scale. Not only is there more waste water to be handled, but the intensity of pollution in receiving rivers is increased, while, due to water use, the volume of the river-flow available to dilute effluents is less. Such problems affected countries where the growth of cities was much faster and the resources to cope were fewer. Many infectious agents, including those that cause diarrhoea, escape from man via excreta and infect others by ingestion. These faecal-oral infections are of immense public health importance and in the long-run are only controlled by improved water supplies and safe disposal of excreta. The decade was marked by increased efforts to improve these facilities, largely defeated by increases in population, poverty and lack of education – and despite these efforts there was a pandemic spread of cholera. As the decade moved to its close, two major advances showed promise for the future: it was shown that the child mortality of much diarrhoeal disease could be greatly reduced by low-cost methods of oral rehydration, and several previously unknown causes of diarrhoea were identified. These two advances have been harnessed by WHO in its special diarrhoeal diseases programme.

Improvements were made during the decade in both water supply quality and the number of people served. The 1980s have been named the "Drinking Water and Sanitation Decade" and ambitious targets have been discussed (see Chapter 4). However, although the proportion of the population of developing countries with safe water supplies has increased, the absolute number of people unserved appeared greater in 1981 than it was in 1970. Progress in improving excreta disposal was also slow and disappointing during the decade, largely because of the great cost of providing full sewage in the cities of developing countries. Appropriate low-cost technology for handling sewage wastes in such countries, for example using stabilization ponds, was increasingly sought and applied. The application of alternative non-waterborne means of excreta disposal, for example by composting in improved pit latrines, also increased. In East Asia, the use of human excreta as a fertilizer implies that it is an economic resource rather than a waste, although the continuation of this long-established practice has contributed very largely to the transmission of disease-causing organisms. In China and elsewhere, composting and the use of biogas plants made headway (see Chapter 12).

The impact of human migration and behaviour

International air travel contributed during the decade to the rapid spread of sexually transmitted diseases (gonorrhoea, non-specific urethritis, etc.) and to the importation of diseases such as malaria into countries where they were not endemic. Lassa fever* was introduced into temperate countries, and there was a tenfold increase in malaria cases in Britain. Since inter-continental travel time had become less than the incubation period of almost any infection, the whole concept of internationally quarantinable diseases needed reconsideration.

There were eight million people in Africa and Asia under the care of the Office of United Nations High Commissioner for Refugees in 1980. As a result of crowding, malnutrition and lack of health care or facilities, the refugee population continued to fall victim to communicable diseases such as cholera and diarrhoeal and respiratory infections during the decade. The entry of some refugees into forest areas exposed them

---

*After Lassa, Nigeria. A disease caused by Lassa virus characterized by high fever, headache, haemorrhagic signs, and renal and cardiac failure.

to special hazards such as yellow fever, leishmaniasis and scrub typhus. Rural-urban migrations also increased hazards, and imposed considerable strain on the critical infrastructure of available water supplies and excreta disposal systems. Such a situation became worse when breast feeding was abandoned, thus reducing the maternal transmission to the child of antibodies against common infectious diseases.

MAJOR TRENDS IN DISEASE PATTERNS AND ACTIONS

During the decade, communicable diseases continued to cause a high proportion of the sicknesses and deaths in developing countries. Respiratory infections, however, remained a major cause of illness all over the world. In developed countries, where the incidence of major communicable diseases is relatively minimal in the indigenous population, the most taxing problems arose from the importation of diseases by migrants and travellers.

In most developing countries, environmental conditions such as warm climate, food deficiencies, poverty, insufficient and unsuitable water supplies, poor sanitation and the like, favour the spread of diseases caused by parasites and other pathogenic organisms whose life cycles include a period of temperature-dependent development in vectors and intermediate hosts. During the decade there was a noticeable increase in the prevalence of certain communicable diseases of this type, including malaria, cholera, meningitis and dengue haemorrhagic fever. New diseases caused by viruses were also identified and characterized during the decade. The diseases that showed a downward trend during the same period included smallpox, which was eradicated; onchocerciasis, whose transmission was reduced; measles, which was controlled or reduced; filariasis, which showed some reduction, and schistosomiasis, which was controlled by mass chemotherapy in a few developing countries.

Although there were effective measures for the control of communicable diseases, poverty and other socio-economic constraints limited their global application. WHO responded by developing its Expanded Programme of Immunization (EPI), to reduce sickness and death from six target diseases (diphtheria, pertussis, tetanus, measles, poliomyelitis and tuberculosis) by providing immunization against them for every child in the world by 1990. These six diseases accounted during the 1970s for the deaths of about five million children a year in the developing countries, and made a comparable number liable to severe disabilities including blindness, paralysis and mental handicap. In spite of the relatively low cost and ease of delivery of the vaccines, less than 10 per cent of the 80 million children born annually in developing countries received any form of immunization. By 1977, forty-two developing countries in which some 57 million children were born annually were involved in the EPI programme (WHO, 1980). Its success will depend, among other factors, on the extent and quality of primary health care in these countries.

Trends in Particular Diseases

Although parasitic diseases received increased attention during the decade (WHO, 1980), control programmes against specific diseases were rather disappointing, frequently because of human behaviour, ecological adaptation and other environmental factors.

The five bacterial diseases that are of particular epidemiological importance and whose transmission is dependent on human activities and environmental factors are gonorrhoea, leprosy, tuberculosis, meningococcal meningitis and cholera. There was a considerable increase in the incidence of gonorrhoea throughout the world. The emergence of an increased number of resistant gonococcal strains as a result of the indiscriminate use of chemotherapy was particularly disturbing.

Although the prevalence of leprosy remained unchanged, the number of patients receiving treatment increased. Dapsone-resistant strains of lepromatous leprosy emerged making combined chemotherapy necessary as a countermeasure (WHO, 1980). But the laboratory development of a method for culturing the causative bacterium in the nine-banded armadillo (the only animal other than man known to contract leprosy), and so obtaining antigen, brought with it the prospect of possible vaccination and hence of the ultimate elimination of the disease (Storrs, 1971).

Tuberculosis (TB) remained a serious global disease, affecting some 3.5 million people per year and killing over 0.5 million (Bulla, 1977). In more privileged countries the risk of infection declined by as much as 12 per cent per year between 1973 and 1977, but the change was far less marked in developing countries, where the risk was 20–50 times greater (WHO, 1980). Resistance to anti-TB drugs remained a major problem, and by 1981 some evidence cast doubt on the protective value of BCG (*Bacillus Calmette-Guérin*) vaccination in a hyperendemic area.

Epidemics of meningococcal meningitis continued, with long-familiar biennial cycles (WHO, 1977d). Control proved difficult because of drug resistance and antigenic changes. Some promising vaccines were developed during the decade, and began to be employed in field trials. Between 1973 and 1977 the total number of cholera cases reported to WHO declined, but the number of countries affected changed little (WHO, 1980). There were repeated outbreaks in epidemic or pandemic form, especially in western Asia and North-West and East Africa, the *el tor* strain of Vibrio cholerae having largely replaced the classic Bengal form. Endemic foci were becoming established in several areas of the developing world. In 1973 and 1974 over 100,000 cases were reported, but by 1977 the number had fallen to about 59,000 (WHO, 1980). Incorrect notification and inadequate diagnostic facilities probably made all figures under-estimates.

Among parasitic diseases, Bancroftian filariasis appeared to have decreased in prevalence in rural areas of countries where it is endemic, but it was increasingly being transmitted in urban areas by the mosquito *Culex fatigans,* which breeds in polluted water. Leishmaniasis, on the other hand, appeared to be increasing in areas where insecticide was formerly sprayed against malarial vectors. Resurgence of infection followed the cessation of spraying, and local outbreaks were reported from Brazil among workers cutting roads through rain forest.

The geohelminths, predominantly *Ascaris* (roundworm) and hookworms, remained widespread and continued to be a significant cause of illness in developing countries. Generally, chemotherapy against helminths proved consistently ineffective, and very little was known about the immunology of helminth infections, a topic severely neglected both in research and public health terms.

Malaria

Malaria continued to be the most important single disease in sub-Saharan Africa, and one of the most significant elsewhere in the tropics (UNEP, 1978). It remained endemic almost everywhere in tropical Africa, where approximately 290 million people lived in affected areas. By the end of the decade, anti-malarial activities had protected only about 11 per cent of this population, mainly in urban and peri-urban localities. The disease has claimed millions of lives in several countries over recent decades, and continued to account for a very high morbidity and mortality in the non-immune inhabitants of endemic areas. It was the most important single cause of febrile convulsions in children in tropical Africa, and a major cause of death in early life. In Africa approximately 50 per cent of children up to the age of three were infected, and it was estimated that one million children died from malaria every year (WHO, 1980).

In the 1930s, a measure of success was obtained through environmental control of the vector mosquito (*Anopheles*), by draining its breeding sites. In the 1950s and 60s this was followed by DDT spraying, which created malaria-free conditions in countries that could afford it. India and Sri Lanka, for example, witnessed a dramatic reduction in malarial infection. But during the decade there were major reverses and a resurgence of malaria. Between 1973 and 1977 the overall number of reported cases more than doubled (WHO, 1980). In India the incidence of infection rose from 40,000 in 1966 to 1.4 million in 1972 and 6 million in 1976 (UNEP, 1978). Although there was a subsequent decline to around 5 million cases in South-East Asia as a whole by 1978 (WHO, 1980), the situation remained much more serious at the end of the decade than at the beginning. Economic factors contributed to this situation, but a dominant element was the development of resistance to insecticides by anopheline mosquitoes. Both the resistant species and the number of insecticides to which they are resistant increased (UNEP, 1978, 1979 a). Some species of mosquito exhibited multiple resistance, like those that caused an intractable outbreak of over 116,000 cases of malaria in the Cukorova plains of Turkey.

Increasing resistance to DDT, dieldrin and malathion (UNEP, 1979a) progressively excluded these most economical substances from use. Insecticide resistance was also stimulated by agricultural pesticides usage, so that the selection pressure was not under the control of health authorities. This conflict of interest between health and agriculture became difficult throughout the world. It was compounded by the finding that several of the insecticides originally most effective in mosquito control (and which were also cheap) had serious environmental side-effects that led to their prohibition in many developed countries (see Chapter 7).

In the past decade, resistance by *Plasmodium* to important chemotherapeutic agents, including pyrimethamine and chloroquine, became widespread in areas with endemic malaria, and created a major problem. The protection of migrants, tourists and other visitors to such areas, in addition to the treatment of malaria epidemics there, was a matter of great public health concern. Low doses of sulphonamides were used in some substitute mixtures, but if widely employed could increase the risk of sulphonamide-resistant bacterial infections.

Malaria control, whether by insecticides or chemotherapy thus remained in an unsatisfactory state. the best long-term prospect of effective control appeared to lie in the production of a safe, cheap, long-acting chemotherapeutic agent that could be easily administered, or in a safe, inexpensive vaccine. One possibly significant advance during the decade was the development of procedures for culturing the trophozoite and gametocyte stages of the malarial parasite (Haynes *et al.,* 1976; Trager and Jensen, 1976). The extraction of a potent antigen that could be used in the preparation of a vaccine should now be possible.

If efforts to develop a vaccine fail, it may be necessary to fall back on the ancient method of control that used the principle of "species sanitation" — a mixture of drainage, flow modification and other practices to make a habitat less suitable for malarial vectors. Although fish that eat mosquito larvae were being used more widely in the late 1970s, genetic and biological control by agents that produce disease in mosquitoes may also be an effective weapon.

Schistosomiasis

Several forms of this disease remained prevalent. *Schistosoma haematobium,* which occurred in Africa and Western Asia, usually effects the urinary tract; *S. mansoni* in Africa, South America and the Caribbean, the intestinal tract; while *S. japonicum,* confined to Eastern Asia, is a parasite of man and of some domestic and wild animals (UNEP, 1979 a). The disease symptoms arise through host reaction to eggs, worms and their products, and the risk of serious clinical disease rises with the intensity of the infection. For every person with a disabling or lethal lesion (e.g. hepatic fibrosis, bladder cancer, etc), there are many infected people who have few or mild symptoms, or none at all. For this reason it was difficult to state precisely the size of the world's infected human population in the 1970s, but 200 million appeared a reasonable estimate, with another 600 million at risk (UNEP, 1979 a). In several regions where *S. haematobium* is endemic, infection was almost universal by the time children reach school age. Changes in incidence during the decade reflected changes in the physical environment that influence infection, and the tactics developed recently to control it.

The transmission of infection depends on ova from human excreta reaching water containing the relevant snail intermediate hosts, the survivial of the infected snails for over a month while the worm develops, and contact between the human body and water containing cercariae shed from the snails. Any development that facilitates contact between people and water will therefore make the transmission of schistosomiasis more likely. During the decade, the creation of many man-made lakes, fish-ponds and irrigation schemes had just this effect. Particular attention was paid to the impact of large lakes like Lake Volta, where schistosomiasis was widely predicted, but the actual intermediate host snail, *Bulinus truncatus rohlfsi,* was not the one expected to assume this role (MacDonald, 1955). Enormous control efforts were made by a WHO/UNDP team in collaboration with the Government of Ghana, and by 1980 there were indications of falling snail populations and a reduction in the aquatic vegetation that is their habitat.

While attention was concentrated on large lakes, small-scale impoundments, which create at least an equal risk, were neglected. Irrigation schemes increase schistosomiasis transmission most of all both by creating ideal snail habitats and by increasing human contacts with water. Control of the snails can be achieved by lining canals with concrete or covering watercourses, but this is expensive. At the end of the 1960s molluscicides had been shown to be an economic and effective way of controlling schistosomiasis. Chemotherapeutic treatment of the disease was considered too dangerous at community level, and environmental methods were unproved. Since then, the cost of molluscicides has soared and confidence in them has declined, while effective new chemotherapeutic agents (oxamaiquine, matrifonate and praziquautel) have been developed. Physical measures (e.g. pumps and hydrants) and educational measures reduced people's contact with water in many areas and contributed to the reduction in infection. Such a combined approach was markedly successful in China (UNEP, 1979 a).

Onchocerciasis

Onchocerciasis was widespread in parts of Guatemala, Mexico, Venezuela, Northern Brazil, Colombia, Northern Yemen and throughout tropical Africa, being worst in West Africa and the Sahel. The vectors, mainly members of the *Simulium damnosum* complex of black-fly species, breed in rapid rivers. The disease is caused by a nematode worm parasite, *Onchocerca volvulus,* which produces subcutaneous nodules (creating itching and skin changes) and progressive blindness. In some areas up to 20 per cent of villagers aged between 30 and 60 years were blind. In the Volta River basin in 1974, 10 per cent of the population was affected and 70,000 individuals had lost their sight (WHO, 1980). Such high blindness rates in relatively young age groups gave the disease great socioeconomic significance. The severity of the clinical manifestations was much greater in the savannah zones of West Africa than in the equatorial forest regions.

Under the aegis of the Special Programme for Research and Training in Tropical Diseases (TDR), sponsored by WHO, UNDP and the World Bank, an Onchocerciasis Control Programme was created in 1974 and operated for the remainder of the decade. The programme was based on arresting *Simulium* breeding by spraying insecticide from the air, with careful monitoring of the effects on river fauna. Vector control was highly successful in the areas treated, and by 1979 fly-biting and transmission had been reduced and there had been a noticeable decline in the prevalence of the disease among young children. Re-invasion by flies from untreated areas proved the principal problem, since they could travel with the wind for up to 400 km, most were gravid and many carried infective larvae. Extended spraying and the application of larvicides to some of the perennial rivers during the dry season brought improvements. No safe chemotherapeutic agents effective against the adult worm had been developed by 1980, although research continued.

Viral diseases

Six major viral diseases – yellow fever, measles, rabies, smallpox, tick-borne encephalitis and Rift Valley fever – have been encountered in many parts of the world. Smallpox had, however, been totally eradicated by the end of the decade and most of the others had been eliminated from several parts of their former range. However, rabies spread slowly into western Europe during the 1970s through the red fox; there was a major epidemic of infectious hepatitis in Nigeria in 1970, and Rift Valley fever appeared in Egypt in 1977, causing 18,000 infections and almost 600 deaths (Weekly Epidemiological Record, 1978). In temperate developed countries influenza and the common cold continued to cause some deaths and impose high social costs.

Rabies control advanced, with the development of a much safer and more effective human vaccine. Three "new" viral diseases, Lassa fever, Marburg disease and Ebola fever, occurred during the decade in Uganda, Nigeria, Sierra Leone, Liberia, Sudan and Zaire, with relatively high mortality rates (WHO, 1979 a). A further relatively new disease, dengue haemorrhagic fever (first detected in 1953 in the Philippines) remained prominent in several urban centres of Southwast Asia, where it was spread by *Aedes* mosquitoes.

Of the various virus diseases that affect livestock, three (all African in origin) caused considerable concern in the decade. They were African swine fever, African horse sickness and bluetongue. The latter two occurred in several antigenic types and were transmitted by blood-sucking midges (*Culicoides spp*); the first can be spread by ticks or by respiration directly between infected animals. In the 1970s African swine fever spread widely in South-West Europe and northern South America, causing great economic loss.

ACTIONS AGAINST MAJOR DISEASES

The special programme for research and training in tropical diseases

The decade 1970–80 was marked by considerable uncertainty about how best to control many parasitic diseases. Confidence in insecticides as the predominant weapon against vector-borne diseases was shaken, except in onchocerciasis; by the end of the decade it was not known how to cope with resurgent malaria effectively, and there were no safe drugs for the treatment, on a community basis, of onchocerciasis, African or south American trypanosomiasis, or muco-cutaneous leishmaniasis.

The entire world research effort devoted to these diseases was smaller than for several quite rare non-infectious diseases in the Western world. The need for urgent scientific advance led to the WHO TDR programme. This concentrated on malaria, schistosomiasis, filariasis of all types, and trypanosomiasis, because of their great and widespread importance, especially in Africa, and also leprosy and leishmaniasis. Originally the programme was conceived in terms of goal-oriented laboratory research in chemotherapy and immunology, but it was realized early that these cannot be pursued effectively in isolation. Epidemiological studies are essential for deciding the most appropriate deployment of effective drugs and vaccines, and delivery of effective control measures is often a greater limitation than the availability of suitable tools. Malaria for example, cannot be left uncontrolled for a decade of research, and many potentially effective methods, especially in the longer term, are environmental rather than drugs and vaccines. Therefore the programme was made much broader in its approach. Increasing priority was also given to establishing a greater degree of self-reliance among the scientists and research institutions of the countries where the diseases are endemic.

The programme began in 1977 and funding increased from US$ 1.5 million in 1976 to US$ 25 million in 1980. It supports research on better methods of controlling the six diseases, the strengthening of research institutions in the developing countries and also 'trans-disease' research such as epidemiology, biological control of vectors as an alternative to insecticides, and social and economic aspects. Although it would be absurd (and self-defeating) to look for major effects so soon after the inauguration of the programme, it has attracted the attention of the world's scientists to these diseases, and both national and international support has increased.

Diarrhoeal diseases control programme

As the diarrhoeal diseases are also widespread, a programme for control and research on them is also being set up under WHO auspices. Diarrhoeas are one of the top three causes of death from birth to late childhood in many developing countries, often causing half the weanling deaths. Until recently the cause of over half the cases of childhood diarrhoea was not known. The management of severe forms such as cholera require facilities for intravenous infusion, and antibiotic resistance of the known bacterial causes has been increasing rapidly.

Pollution and Health

CONCERN over the impact on human health of chemicals in the environment has increased in recent years (UNEP, 1977, 1978, 1980, 1981). It has become clear, for example, that a number of chemicals act specifically on the heart muscle and thus contribute to the development of heart diseases. Living and working conditions and activities, in conjunction with other stressors, can also cause an increase in morbidity rates of (for example) ischaemic heart disease, metabolic disorders and nervous conditions. Relationships with environmental factors have also come to light, such as that between soft water and the incidence of heart diseases, fluorine deficiency and excessive dental decay, or increased arsenic in soil and water and the enhanced occurrence of cancer. In evaluating human exposure to potentially hazardous chemicals it is therefore necessary to consider all pathways — in air, water, soil and food, and both the home and working environment — and to estimate values for whole-life exposure and exposure at work, as well as doses over short period exposure under various circumstances.

The rate of circulation of many elements through the environment has been greatly increased by man's activities. Korte (1976) estimated that in the mid-1970s over 1,500 substances were produced in quantities exceeding 500 tonnes per year (worldwide), and over 50 substances were produced in quantities over 1 million tonnes. In 1950, world production or organic chemicals was 7 million tonnes, in 1970, 63 million tonnes; and by 1985 it is expected to rise to 250 million tonnes (Korte, 1977). Despite increasingly stringent industrial controls some substances that now occur in negligible concentrations (say less than one part per million (ppm)) may present serious problems to the next and succeeding generations.

Because exposures are more readily documented there, there is much advantage in studying occupationally exposed groups of workers. From such observations it is sometimes possible to construct a dose-effect curve or to estimate a no-effect threshold that can then be extrapolated to the general population. The difficulty is that exposure data are hard to come by, especially for effects with a long latent period; moreover, the working population is not continuously exposed, nor is it a typical cross-section of the community (Duncan, 1979).

By the end of the decade there were only limited direct measurements of the degree to which the general population was exposed to pollutants. Lead levels had been most extensively studied and there was a reasonable set of data on blood lead concentrations. There were also reasonable data for a few other metals and for tissue levels of some organochlorine residues. In most assessments, samples of blood or hair are used because they are easily available; concentrations in these tissues certainly give useful information on exposure, but are not necessarily correlated with total body burden.

A pilot scheme using tissues obtained at autopsy was introduced in the United States and this should provide useful information about the pollutant burden in the community (Colucci et al., 1973). More information is needed, however, about the relationship between dose and effect so that tissue concentrations can be set in perspective. Until this is available environmental standards will continue to be framed on empirical grounds.

Direct measurements are complemented by wider monitoring of the health of the community in a fashion that allows new hazards to be detected and probed by more specific epidemiological surveys. Such analysis depends upon the availability of readily retrievable data. National death-rate statistics and data from cancer registries are obvious sources, but have been disappointing in pointing the way to unsuspected hazards. Data on illness rates are not so easy to come by, but may be gleaned from local hospital, industrial or general practice records or from sickness absence certificates. The most promising approach to monitoring lies in the development of some form of record-linkage system for a random cohort of the population: a pilot scheme has already been introduced in Britain by the Office of Population Censuses and Surveys, with a 1 per cent sample of the 1971 census. If occupational health records are to be used to their best advantage in monitoring, then this will also require some form of record-linkage, especially as some diseases due to chemical exposure may not become evident until after normal retirement.

All such studies demand on the one hand measurement of human response, which will inevitably be affected by a wide range of factors, and on the other a capacity to measure the concentrations of substances in tissues, food, drinking water and the environment, so that exposure, intake, accumulation and elimination can be established. Over the decade, there were great advances in chemical analytical methods. Techniques such as atomic absorption spectrophotometry, gas and gas liquid chromatography and mass spectrometry now allow the estimation of pollutants in nanogram (10^{-9} or one billionth) quantities. The coupling of methods such as gas chromatography with mass spectrometry allows the analysis of extremely complex mixtures of organic compounds. With these methodological advances, it has become possible to set up programmes for monitoring chemicals in the working and general environment and in food, water supplies, human tissues and wildlife (where many bio-accumulator organisms provide valuable samples). It must be stressed, however, that the detection of a potentially toxic substance by such means is not in itself a cause for concern (especially now that the limits of detection are so low). What matters is the total quantity reaching the most vulnerable members of the population by all pathways, and the subsequent acute or chronic effects on health. Only well-designed epidemiological and toxicological studies, and good surveillance of exposed working populations, will ensure early detection of health hazards. Epidemiological studies in particular involve the establishment of correlations between bodies of data that in many countries result from surveys that are the responsibility of different authorities, and it is essential that there is sufficient communication at the design stage to ensure that the results can be linked in a valid manner (Acheson, 1979).

CHEMICALS IN THE WORKING ENVIRONMENT

Over recent decades, industrial hygiene has improved considerably in most industrialized countries, and some of the classic occupational diseases (e.g. acute lead and mercury poisoning) have become relatively rare. Attention is therefore being directed towards detecting smaller and earlier departures from normal, particularly in respiratory and neurological disease. For example, in Britain the number of new cases of pneumoconiosis (a lung disease caused by dust inhalation) is declining; but occupational asthma appears to be on the increase. This is due both to better methods of diagnosis and to the increased number of agents that can induce the disease (over 100 have been implicated). The relationship between occupational exposure and asthma is still often overlooked, however, because the symptoms may not occur until several hours after exposure and the measurement of lung function at the beginning and end of the shift does not always show the anticipated decrement. A more sensitive method of diagnosis is to measure the peak expiratory flow rate throughout the day, including the time spent at home after work (Burge *et al.*, 1979).

As cases of frank neurological disease become rare in industry, more effort is being directed towards discovering subliminal or subclinical abnormalities. There is evidence to show that exposure to some heavy metals and solvents may be accompanied by a slowing in nerve conduction velocity, although the significance of this is by no means clear (Seppalainen *et al.*, 1975). Concern with subclinical change is also finding expression in studies of psychomotor performances (physical activity associated with mental processes) in workers exposed to known neurotoxic materials. These studies involve the administration of a battery of tests of psychomotor, perceptual or intellectual performance to the exposed group, the results of which are compared with those of a control group. In the USSR, behavioural tests on animals have been used for many years to set stringent maximum allowable concentrations for chemicals in the work place. Direct research on the behaviour of people exposed at work has so far been concentrated in some Scandinavian countries and the United States; in Britain a few preliminary studies have been completed. To date, a dozen or so substances have been found adversely to affect performance in psychomotor tests. Most are organic solvents but inorganic mercury has also been implicated (Gamberale, 1975). The changes are generally slight and care must be taken to disentangle the effects of confounding variables such as learning, motivation and mental fatigue. Finally, occupational causes of cancer have been the subject of much detailed research: they are discussed later in this chapter.

CHEMICALS IN THE GENERAL ENVIRONMENT

Potentially hazardous substances reach members of the general population through the air, water, and food. Many of them follow all these routes, making it essential to evaluate the relative significance of each if the overall degree of risk is to be estimated (DHSS, 1980).

Air pollution

Airborne substances can endanger human health (a) by altering the physical properties of the atmosphere, and especially its capacity to screen out ultra-violet radiation (UV–B), (b) by their direct effect when taken into the body through respiratory surfaces, and (c) when they fall out and contaminate food and water. The first two categories are considered here.

During the decade it was suggested that a global health problem may be created by chlorofluorocarbons, which were widely used as refrigerants and aerosol propellants. Worldwide, the production and use of these compounds grew at about 10 per cent per annum up to and including 1974 (NAS, 1976; DOE, 1976) but then began to decline. They dispersed from the atmospheric boundary layer to the stratosphere where they were slowly decomposed by radiation, releasing chlorine-containing radicals that depleted stratospheric ozone and so increased the penetration of UV–B. Mathematical models suggested that if chlorofluorocarbon 11 and 12 usage continued at the 1973 level, there might eventually be a depletion in the ozone layer of about 8 per cent (with an uncertainty range from 2 to 20 per cent) in 100–200 years (UNEP, 1979 b). This will cause an increase in UV–B penetration, the amount of which depends on latitude and season. This radiation can cause skin cancers, a proportion of which are malignant melanomas (see Chapter 2).

One calculation (NAS, 1976), based on an earlier and higher estimate of ozone depletion than that noted above, put the possible increase in melanomas at 15 per cent or a few hundred added deaths per year. But the problem must be judged in perspective. Mortality from melanoma about doubled in the United Kingdom between 1935–39 and 1966–70 and increased tenfold in Connecticut, USA, between 1935–39 and 1966–72, almost certainly as a result of changed social habits, including the mounting popularity of sun-bathing (NAS, 1976).

By contrast with this global, physical effect, most atmospheric pollutants have more restricted toxic effects in areas of high concentration. The most significant sources of air pollution during the 1970s were industry, motor vehicles, domestic fires and power stations. The commonest pollutants were carbon monoxide, oxides of sulphur and nitrogen, hydrocarbon and particulates including heavy metals (Chapter 2). Where motor vehicles were the main source, carbon monoxide, hydrocarbons and nitrogen oxides and the oxidants produced in photochemical smog predominated; close to heavy industry, oxides of sulphur and particulates prevailed. The dispersion of these pollutants in the atmosphere and their effect on terrestrial life are discussed in other chapters.

Smoke particulates and *sulphur dioxide* (SO_2) were the main active agents in traditional fogs like those for which London was once notorious. Where 24-hour concentrations at the same time exceeded 200 micrograms per cubic metre ($\mu g/m^3$) of SO_2 and 150 $\mu g/m^3$ of particulates, adverse effects began to be apparent, especially among elderly individuals with cardiac or respiratory diseases (RCP, 1970; WHO, 1979 b). Most large-scale outbreaks of ill health from this cause belong to a period before the decade under review: they occurred when a layer of stagnant air polluted from domestic and industrial chimneys was trapped beneath an atmospheric inversion layer. In the 1970s, the critical threshold at which adverse effects are observed was rarely exceeded and average annual concentrations were well below this level in industrial cities. The reductions in mortality from chronic bronchitis and emphysema (Table 10–2) may partly reflect this progress. There were some indications (reported in OTA, 1979) that sulphate aerosols could have different and more severe effects than SO_2 aggravating asthma and bronchitis at 24-hour mean concentrations as low as 10 $\mu g/m^3$ (frequently encountered in industrial regions). The balance of evidence however did not point to hazards at the kinds of concentration generally encountered in urban air (WHO, 1979 b).

Table 10–2. Age-standardized Mortality Rates for Chronic Bronchitis and Emphysema for Various Countries, Males Aged 45–74 Years, 1968 and 1977.

	Deaths per 100,000 per year		
	1968	1977	
Australia	126	112	(−11%)
Czechoslovakia	174	148[a]	(−15%)
England and Wales	214	117	(−45%)
Federal Republic of Germany	125	87	(−30%)
Japan	45	27	(−40%)
Mexico	38	48[b]	(+26%)
Netherlands	98[c]	83	(−15%)
Sweden	30[c]	34	(+13%)
United States of America	76	36	(−53%)

Source: Data supplied by London School of Hygiene and Tropical Medicine

[a]1975
[b]1974
[c]1969

Carbon monoxide is not a threat to healthy individuals in the concentrations in which it was generally found in city air (usually less than 6 mg/m³). Increased concentrations were found in the blood of some exposed groups such as traffic policemen: but even in these people, cigarette smoking was for many a more significant source of carbon monoxide then vehicle exhaust emissions (Cole, 1975). However, urban carbon monoxide did in some places reach concentrations potentially hazardous to sufferers from some respiratory and cardiac complaints.

Nitrogen oxides concentrations are high only in the vicinity of sources of pollution, because they are reactive substances and are rapidly removed in the processes generating peroxyacetyl nitrates (PAN), ozone and other oxidants. There were some indications of effects on bronchitics and asthmatics at concentrations above 200 $\mu g/m^3$, and the WHO recommendation was for a maximum permissible 1-hour concentration of NO_2 not to be exceeded more than once per month — of 300–500 $\mu g/m^3$ (WHO, 1977c).

Ozone can cause nose, throat and eye irritation and breathing difficulties in exertion at concentrations around 200–300 $\mu g/m^3$, with more severe symptoms at between 500 and 750 $\mu g/m^3$. There were geographical differences (e.g. between Tokyo and Los Angeles) that may reflect different interactions between air pollutants and also physiological adaption. Epidemiological analyses did not indicate any evident relationship between short-term oxidant exposures and mortality rates (OTA, 1979).

There are a great many *metal particulates* suspended in the atmosphere, almost all in very low concentrations. Of the potentially toxic metals, lead was present in greatest concentrations; levels of 1 $\mu g/m^3$ being typical of inner city areas and except in the immediate neighbourhood of certain kinds of industry, were derived almost exclusively from tetra-ethyl and tetra-methyl lead added as an anti-knock agent to petrol. About 90 per cent of airborne lead probably came from this source. A number of countries imposed restrictions on the amount of lead in petrol during the decade because of the fear that the environmental lead levels might adversely affect the nervous system and behaviour of children, even though some surveys (e.g. JWPLP, 1978) suggest that with an air lead concentration in the vicinity of less than 1 $\mu g/m^3$ lead in air contributes considerably less than 10 per cent to the blood lead. In the USSR leaded fuel was prohibited in urban areas and the same prohibition is proposed in New York City, while in the European Economic Community the permitted range was from 0.40 to 0.15 grammes per litre. The trend generally was towards further reductions or the complete removal of lead. Research on the relationship between lead and behaviour in children continued (Lansdown, 1979; NAS, 1980a).

Air pollution can also occur as a result of accidents. In the decade 1970–80 the most widely publicized such event was the explosion in a chemical factory at Seveso, Italy, in July 1976, that released a cloud of chemicals containing, amongst others, 2,3,7,8-tetrachlorodibenzo-p-dioxin (TCDD). Several hundred people were exposed, and an area of over 3 km^2 was contaminated, over 1 km^2 of it so heavily that the population was evacuated. TCDD is a potent teratogen (i.e. can produce deformities in the foetus) and is foetotoxic (poisonous to the foetus); consequently women in the vicinity who were pregnant at the time were kept under close surveillance. By the decade's end, no foetal abnormalities had been reported (Reggiani, 1978).

Pollution of food and water

Food and drinking water may be contaminated (a) when metals and other airborne particulates settle out on crops, pastures or sources of supply, (b) when chemicals are applied to crops as fertilizers and biocides, and are retained within them or washed off into water courses, (c) when fungi grow on badly-stored food-stuffs and produce toxins there and (d) when potentially toxic substances enter water sources in sewage or industrial discharges. The relative significance of these sources varies with region: in developing countries where over 10 per cent of stored grain may be lost after harvest, mycotoxins are an acute problem, whereas in many developed countries biocides and industrial contaminants cause most concern.

Cadmium, mercury and lead were the most publicized metallic contaminants of food and water during the decade (UNEP, 1980, 1981). Cadmium had previously been incriminated in the outbreak of Itai-Itai disease in Japan, when rice paddy was irrigated with river water containing cadmium (WHO, 1977a). Mercury poisoning has occurred from two main causes: the consumption of grain treated with mercurial fungicide (the largest recorded instance of which caused 500 deaths and 6,000 hospital cases in Iraq in the winter of 1971–72) (WHO, 1976a), and the accumulation of methyl mercury in fish.

This latter phenomenon was the cause of the well-known outbreaks of poisoning at Minamata and Nigata in Japan. It was evident following research that inorganic mercury is readily converted to the highly neurotoxic methyl form by bacteria in the environment, and then readily accumulated by fish, posing a potential hazard to communities with a high component of fish in their diet (technical annex in Holdgate and White, 1977; NAS, 1977; Butler, 1978). A number of governments accordingly ruled that fish containing more than 1.0 or 0.5 ppm mercury may not be sold, and also issued advice on the frequency with which fish should be eaten.

Most individuals derive over half their daily lead intake from food, but the pollution of the soil with this metal is not a major problem because only a small fraction of it is in a form available to plant roots. Particulate lead deposited as fine dust on vegetable leaves is generally removed by washing during food preparation. But in countries where lead water tanks and pipes were used to carry acid (plumbosolvent) water, the metal was found to reach concentrations of up to 2,000–3,000 μg/l at the tap, and pose a potential hazard (WHO, 1977b). When such water was used to reconstitute dehydrated infant food, particular risks could arise, since infants are the most vulnerable members of the community (Käferstein, 1981). Lead from solder could also contaminate food in side-soldered cans.

The problems that can be posed by environmental pollutants derived from industry were well illustrated by the polychlorinated biphenyls (PCBs), used as dielectrics in transformers and capacitors, and as plasticizers in paints and plastics. It was estimated that 1 million tonnes of PCBs had been produced since 1930 and that more than half of this had entered the general environment, where the compounds are extremely persistent. The highest concentration of PCB residues occurs in fish; and small concentrations are present in human adipose tissue (normally less than 1 mg/kg). The only recorded serious episode resulting from the contamination of food with PCBs occurred in Japan in 1968, when more than 1,000 people who had eaten rice oil contaminated with PCBs developed dark pigmentation of the skin, discharging eyes, acne and respiratory symptoms. The disease affected some newborn children since PCBs readily cross the placenta. Recovery from the disease was slow and a number of patients died, although it is not certain whether impurities such as dibenzofurans in the commercial PCB mixture were the primary toxic agents. However, levels in the environment in the late 1970s were clearly not associated with ill-health (WHO, 1976b).

In developed countries there was an increase in the re-use of water for potable supplies during the decade, particularly in densely populated areas. Sewage treatment and chlorination of the water abstracted for supply can prevent the spread of waterborne infectious disease, but this remained an acute problem in many developing countries. In the late 1970s concern centred on the possible presence in potable water of potentially hazardous (especially carcinogenic) organic compounds. The search for these so called micropollutants, including compounds resulting from water supply chlorination, received much attention in developed countries between 1970 and 1980. Epidemiological studies failed to detect any undisputed relationship between the presence of micropollutants and the incidence of cancers, but the subject remained important for research (NAS, 1980 b).

Nitrate in drinking water, which has the potential to cause health problems, may enter the supply either from sewage effluent or from agricultural land, due to the increasing use of nitrogen fertilizer and changing farming practices. The trend over the decade was for increasing nitrate levels in many rivers (e.g. DOE, 1979). Nitrate itself may cause methemoglobinoemia (a blood disorder) in bottle-fed infants if present in excessive quantities in drinking water. The WHO European Standards for Drinking Water required that the nitrate level, measured as nitrogen, should not exceed 11.3 milligrams per litre (mg/l). In some countries, where this level was exceeded, it was necessary to provide a special water supply for infants being fed artifically. Nitrate also caused concern because of its possible conversion to nitrosamines, which had been shown to cause cancer in laboratory animal tests. Nitrosamines, which had been detected in human stomachs, infected urinary bladders, saliva and faeces, had not been incriminated as the cause of any human cancer by the end of the decade.

Chapter 7 discusses in detail the environmental impact of pesticides. Those that caused most concern as far as human health is concerned were the organochlorine compounds. Their relative stability encourages their dispersion throughout the environment, and traces of hexachlorobenzene (HCB), dichlorodiphenyltrichloroethane (DDT) and dichlorodiphenyldichloroethylene (DDE) have been found in human blood, although with considerable national variation (Jenson, 1972). Typical levels of organochlorine compounds in the environment do not cause frank ill health but in the 1960s there were several incidents of mass poisoning from the contamination of foodstuffs during transport or storage. In many Western countries, persistent pesticide use has been reduced and this has been followed by a decline in the amount of residues found in human tissues (Abbott et al., 1972).

Cancer and Environmental Exposure

Tests for carcinogenesis

DURING the decade there was a considerable increase in awareness of environmental agents that are capable of causing cancer (carcinogenic agents). Several publications on the epidemiology of cancer appeared under the sponsorship of a number of international agencies and organizations, including l'Union Internationale Contre le Cancer (UICC), the International Agency for Research of Cancer (IARC) and WHO.

The recent proliferation of new chemicals brought with it a need for extended schemes for screening such materials for potential toxicity and carcinogenicity (the first 24 volumes published by IARC considered 531 chemical compounds; Waterhouse et al., 1970; Muir and Wagner, 1977). Since there is a close correlation between mutagenicity (ability to produce genetic mutations) and carcinogenicity (ability to produce cancer), tests that are positive for mutagenicity were deemed to predict carcinogenic potential, although regulatory authorities were generally not willing to accept negative mutagenicity alone as evidence of safety. Two types of tests for mutagenicity and carcinogenicity were widely recommended and used. These were (a) short-term mutagenesis tests, especially the Ames test (Ames, et al., 1975) and (b) long-term tests, especially animal experiments.

Although no reliable alternatives to long-term tests, which may take up to two years to complete had been developed by 1980, the short-term tests remained useful (especially when two or more different ones were used in combination) for selecting from a large number of chemicals those that were highly suspicious as potential carcinogens and should be subjected to thorough investigation. The fact that a particular chemical exhibits mutagenic activity is a sufficient indication of potential reactivity with DNA. But such tests cannot replace long term bioassays until a satisfactory understanding of the relationship between mutagenicity and carcinogenicity is established and the possibility of false negatives eliminated.

Causes and patterns of cancer incidence

During the decade, considerable progress was made in understanding the process of carcinogenesis and the metabolism of various classes of chemical carcinogens (UNEP, 1977; Garner, 1979). These carcinogens lead to heritable changes in the affected cells. Tumour promotion was generally agreed to be a two-stage process, an initiator causing changes, followed by a promoter which produces dormant tumour cells.

Human exposure to environmental factors such as ionizing radiation, carcinogenic chemicals in air, food or water, or through smoking, alcohol and drugs (chemotherapeutic agents) creates a predisposition to the development of cancer. However, the role of other factors in carcinogenesis cannot be overlooked.

During the decade there was considerable evidence of the importance of genetic factors in carcinogenesis. The relative rarity of certain types of cancer (e.g. testicular tumours and Ewing's sarcoma) in Africans irrespective of their domicile may be attributable to genetic resistance. The immunological status of the host also has a considerable influence on the reaction to potential carcinogens.

The development of immune deficiency may be congenital (e.g. athymic or nude mice or athymic children) or acquired. There was considerable evidence that severe malnutrition or repeated infections, which stimulate the immuno-regulatory system, might reduce the individual's immune response and thus predispose him to malignancies. The relatively high incidence of malignant lymphoma in children in developing countries (e.g. tropical Africa, Iran, Middle East) might be due to these factors.

In the developed world, where malnutrition and repeated infections in childhood were relatively uncommon, the incidence of malignant lymphoma was low but that of leukaemia, which may be related to high levels of radiation among other factors, was high. The incidence of some kinds of cancer may also be modified by the evolution of a protective mechanism. For example, basal cell carcinoma (a skin tumour) is almost absent in Africans, and when it does occur it usually affects albinoes. This suggests the protective effect of melanin against sunlight.

By the end of the decade it was evident that cancer was one of the leading causes of death in the developed world and would become the principal cause there in the very near future if the downward trend in cardiovascular diseases continued unabated. There were considerable differences between the developed and developing worlds in the sites commonly involved in cancer, and these differences appeared environmentally related. In the developed world the commonest sites of cancer were the lungs, colon, rectum, breast and uterine cervix. In most developing countries, the incidence of lung, colon, rectum and breast cancer were extremely low whereas those of cancer of the cervix, liver and lymph nodes were relatively high (Muir, 1975).

ENVIRONMENTAL CARCINOGENS

Environmental carcinogens may be physical, chemical or viral.

Physical carcinogens

The use of X-rays in diagnosis and therapy continued to be the main source of human exposure to radiation. The effects were illustrated by the increased incidence of leukaemia among radiologists, children who were irradiated *in utero,* and patients with ankylosing spondylitis (a form of arthritis affecting the vertebrae) who had been treated with radiation. In all cases there was a quantitative relationship between the dose of irradiation and the risk of developing leukaemia. A latent period of 3 to 4 years after a single heavy dose of radiation was common. Various other cancers, including squamous cell carcinoma, soft tissue and bone sarcomas, and thyroid carcinomas, were reported following X-ray irradiation. Modan *et al.* (1974) reported a significantly higher risk of both benign and malignant head and neck tumours, especially in the brain, parotid gland and thyroid, following the irradiation of children to treat ringworm of the scalp.

X-rays do no exist in the natural environment at the Earth's surface. But there is some natural radioactivity in the environment, including that due to radon daughter products released into dwellings from certain building materials, and they may be expected to cause cancers. This natural background has been augmented slightly by man-made radiation (Chapter 12). Some ultra-violet (UV-B) radiation penetrates the atmospheric ozone screen (Chapter 2) and is capable of causing both benign and malignant skin cancers (including melanomas) in people exposed to the sun for long periods (NRC, 1980). Skin pigmentation is an important defence: in the United States in the 1970s the incidence of malignant melanoma varied from 4.6 to 4.4 cases per 100,000 in white men and women to only 0.9 to 0.7 per 100,000 in black males and females (NAS, 1976).

Chemical carcinogens

It is impossible to review here all potentially carcinogenic chemical substances. During the decade, those that received particular attention included:

(a) nitrosamines;
(b) fungal toxins;
(c) pyrrholizidine alkaloids;
(d) drugs;
(e) biological agents — e.g. vitamins, bile acids and fats;
(f) industrial chemical compounds.

Over a hundred N-nitroso compounds were examined in long-term toxicity tests and many of them were found to induce tumours in animals, the site varying according to the chemical composition. As a result of these findings the use of nitrosamines in industry virtually stopped. Nitrosamines, however, are easily formed by the reactions of amines with nitrate under acid conditions such as occur in the stomach. Nitrite and nitrites are added to food to improve flavour and colour and to prevent the formation of botulunim toxin, and are also present in vegetables; nitrite is produced by bacteria in the human intestine. Mention has already been made of speculation that high concentrations of nitrates in drinking water could increase this process. The extent to which nitrosamines from these various sources cause cancer in man is unknown, but the risk is evident and some precautionary measures have been taken. Regulations have been introduced (in Europe and the United States) to reduce the amount of nitrate added to foods such as bacon and ham. A detailed survey of the state of knowledge has been published by WHO (1978a).

In the 1960s it was demonstrated that an acute toxin (aflatoxins), fatal to poultry, was produced by the growth of the common fungus *Aspergillus flavus* on groundnut meals and other agricultural products (Loosmore *et al.*, 1964). Four aflatoxins (B_1, G_1, B_2, G_2), often occur simultaneously. Aflatoxin B_1 is the most potent liver carcinogen, and one of its two metabolites, aflatoxin M_1, is also carcinogenic and is secreted in milk of animals fed diets containing aflatoxin; it has also been detected in the urine of humans who eat aflatoxin-contaminated food. Several investigators studied the relationship between aflatoxin intake as measured in food and the incidence of primary liver cancer in the total population, and Table 10–3 shows that a reasonably good correlation was established. Aflatoxin B_1 in groundnut oil is destroyed only by heating to 250°C and there appears to be no easy way by which it can be removed from food. Strains of fungi that produce aflatoxin are widely distributed except in areas with cold climates such as Canada and Northern Europe, and all foods are susceptible to contamination. However, rapid drying of crops after harvest, and storage with moisture contents below 10 per cent was shown virtually to eliminate contamination (IARC, 1976).

Plants containing pyrrolhizidine alkaloids toxic to the liver have been used in herbal medicines and "bush teas" in many parts of the world (especially in Asia, Africa and the West Indies) and may have been factors in the high incidence of liver disease in these areas. Contamination of cereal food crops by seeds of these plants has resulted in liver poisoning with many deaths in recent years, and was also responsible for poisoning of livestock in many countries. The alkaloids produce cell damage primarily in the liver, but also sometimes in the lungs and other organs, and some are also carcinogenic.

Table 10–3. Aflatoxin Ingestion and Liver Cancer Incidence in some countries.

Country	Area	Aflatoxin Ingestion (10 ^{9}g/kg/day)	Incidence of Liver Cancer per 100,000 persons per year
Kenya	High altitude	3.5	1.2
Kenya	Mid altitude	5.9	2.5
Kenya	Low altitude	10.0	4.0
Thailand	Songkhla	5.0	2.0
Thailand	Ratburi	45.0	6.0
Swaziland	Highveld	5.1	2.2
Swaziland	Midveld	8.9	3.8
Swaziland	Lebombo	15.4	4.3
Swaziland	Lowveld	43.1	9.2
Mozambique	Inhambane	222.4	13.0

Source: Linsell and Peers (1977); data for Mozambique from Van Rensburg *et al.* (1974).

Drugs may induce tumour growth through several mechanisms, including interference with the body's immune reactions and by agents that act as endocrines or affect endocrine systems (Griffin, 1979). Reports of drug-induced tumours in animal studies are common but evidence in man is rare. This may be because it is difficult to establish a cause-and-effect relationship between a drug and its possible carcinogenic action, since tumours usually appear many years after completion of the implicated course of drug therapy. An example of this long latency is the twenty or more years before the appearance of a tumour known as haemangio-endothelioma of the liver after administration of the drug Thorotrast (232-thorium dioxide).

Tumours tend to develop at sites where there is maximum concentration of the drug. Thus carcinogenic drugs that are excreted via the kidneys reach their maximum concentration in the genito-urinary tract, and it is at this site that tumours are likely to appear (Bengtsson *et al.,* 1968). Similarly, carcinogenic drugs that are metabolized and excreted by the liver tend to cause tumours there. A dose-effect relationship between the amount of drug administered and the incidence of tumours has been demonstrated, for example in chlornaphazine-induced bladder tumour (Laursen 1970).

In the decade under review, several new examples of these kinds of effect came to light, emphasizing the need for careful screening of chemicals before use as drugs. The first confirmed reports of cancers being induced in human foetuses by means of a hormone — diethylstilboesterol* — taken by the mother were published in 1971. Two hundred and twenty-five cases of clear cell adenocarcinoma (a glandular cancer) had been established as having been definitely caused by intra-uterine exposure to diethylstilboesterol (IARC, 1979); new cases were being documented at the rate of fifty per year.

In recent years a number of vascular tumours causing haematomas (blood clots) in the liver have been described in young women taking oral contraceptives. The course of these tumours has been benign except for fatal cases of malignant hepatoma-cellular carcinoma, one in a 22-year-old woman who had been on oral contraceptive therapy for two years. Epidemiological studies have shown a 4– to 10–fold increase in the risk of endometrial carcinoma (cancer of the lining of the uterus) associated with the use of eostrogens in the menopausal and post-menopausal period, for example as hormone replacement therapy (Smith et al., 1975; Gray et al., 1977). Several cases of hepatocellular carcinoma (a liver tumour) have been reported in patients on long-term therapy with androgenic anabolic steroids, and although the link is not established, there is an implication that long-term therapy with C–17–alkylated androgenic-anabolic steroids may carry a risk of induction of liver tumours. The use of anabolic steroids by athletes, to improve performance, is thus extremely unwise. Finally, concern was expressed towards the end of the decade about drugs that could give rise to nitrosamines in the stomach, e.g. Cimetidine (Elder et al., 1979; Taylor et al., 1979; and Hawker et al., 1980) Methapyriline, Disulfiram; and Phenacetin (Bengtsson and Angervall, 1970; McGeown, 1979).

The number of proved occupational carcinogens is small and most occupationally-induced tumours result from past exposure to asbestos. There was anxiety about the possibility that man-made mineral fibres with physical properties similar to asbestos may also be carcinogenic; evidence available by 1980 suggested that they are not (Advisory Committee on Toxic Substances, 1979). A high incidence of some features of asbestos-related disease has, however, been found in some communities with extremely slight exposure to asbestos: for example about 7 per cent of the population in a district in Czechoslovakia were found to have calcified pleural plaques (patches on the membranes that enfold the lung) when their chests were X-rayed (Rous and Studeny, 1970). In the village of Kurain in Turkey (where asbestos was absent but houses were plastered with powdered rock), there was not only a high incidence of pleural calcification, but deaths from pleural mesothelioma were also unusually common (Baris et al., 1978). These reports raise the possibility that fibres other than asbestos may produce effects previously considered almost exclusively to asbestos, and they underline the need to handle fibres of the same size as asbestos with extreme care.

Two other industrial carcinogens, bis-chloromethyl ether (BCME) and vinyl chloride monomer (the basic chemical from which polyvinyl chloride (PVC) is produced) have now been clearly identified. Following the observation of an unusual clustering of lung cancer cases in workers involved in BCME production (Thiess et al., 1973), the chemical was tested in animals and found to cause skin tumours in mice and lung cancer

---

*The hormone was administered to prevent miscarriages.

in rats (Van Duuren *et al.,* 1972). Subsequent investigations showed there is a casual relationship between BCME exposure and lung cancer in man (IARC, 1974) and the manufacturing process has been modified to prevent it. Liver cancer (Angiosarcoma) has been found in vinyl chloride workers with excessively high exposure (Creech and Johnson, 1974; IARC, 1979). The number of cases has remained small, however, and the rigorous control now exercised in the handling of this material should ensure that it remains so. In 1980 there was concern that styrene, which also contains a highly reactive vinyl group, may prove to be carcinogenic, especially as it has been shown to be mutagenic (Vainio *et al.,* 1976). The potential hazards of these and other industrial chemicals have been reviewed in IARC Monographs (1972–1980).

Viral carcinogens

A number of viruses that occur in the environment have been suspected of producing human cancer. The two that have been shown to be causally related to cancer during the past decade are the Epstein-Barr virus, which produces Burkitt lymphoma, and the hepatitis B virus, which produces liver cell cancer (WHO, 1980).

Nutrition and Health

NUTRITION, MORTALITY AND HEALTH

Inadequate nutrition is a self-evident cause of ill health, and a major contributor to the high death rate among infants and young children in developing countries. Surveys made in the last fifteen years have been interpreted as showing that in many countries 30 — 40 per cent of children under 5 are significantly undernourished (i.e. weigh less than 75 per cent of the standard weight for their age) (Keller *et al.,* 1976). In 1974 it was estimated that there were 98 million moderately or severely undernourished children under four in the world, 70 per cent of them in Asia (Bengoa, 1974). The significance of these kinds of statistic is not easy to assess, but in a unique study by Puffer and Serrano (1973) in 16 demographically defined areas of Latin America and the Caribbean, malnutrition was considered to be an underlying or associated cause of over 50 per cent of the 35,000 deaths of children under five who were analysed in detail. However, child mortality depends on many interacting factors, including economic ones (expressed in terms of the adequacy of health services and the quality of housing as well as family incomes), social customs and hereditary influences, and it is generally impossible to isolate and quantify the environmental variables. What is not in doubt is that child and infant mortality varies with social class and the availability of medical services and is generally lower in urban than in rural areas. In Algeria in 1969–71 infant mortality was 50 per cent higher in villages than in cities, and in India the urban rate was said to be 81 and the rural 131 per 1,000 live births. Over the decade there was an improvement in child and infant mortality even in developing countries with a precarious economic balance (Table 10–1; Dyson, 1977; Gwatkin et al., 1979).

There is very little detailed information about trends in nutritional status over the past ten years. However, there has been a substantial increase in average food supply in industrialized countries both in absolute and per capita terms (FAO, 1977). In developing countries, taken as a whole, there has been a more modest increase in production that has just kept pace with the rise in population (see Chapter 7 for detailed statistics of trends in crop production). The main problem in 1980 was the unequal distribution of food within and between countries, and the situation was least satisfactory in Africa and the Far East. Table 10–4 shows that in these regions in 1972–74 the average daily energy supply per head was still only slightly over 90 per cent of the average requirements, while Table 10–5 indicates that nearly 30 per cent of people there were below the threshold of adequate energy intake (if this is set at 1.2 x basal metabolic rate). One of the important developments of the decade was the recognition that energy intake rather than protein supply is the most critical dietary factor for both adults and children, and that whereas protein intake by young children in developing countries was above internationally accepted levels of requirements, there was a substantial deficiency in energy intake. This has important implications for agricultural strategy, since it stresses that while protein and nitrogen content are important, total yield must receive more attention in plant breeding and husbandry.

Table 10–4. Average Daily Energy Supply per Head, as a Percentage of Average Requirement.

	1961–63	1972–74
World	101	107
All industrialized countries	124	132
All developing countries	89	96
Africa	89	91
Latin America	101	107
Near East	93	100
Far East	91	92

Source: FAO (1977).

Table 10–5. Estimated Proportion of People with Daily Energy Intake Less Than the Critical Limit of 1.2 × Basal Metabolic Rate, 1972–1974.

Africa	28%
Latin America	15%
Near East	16%
Far East	29%
*MSA countries	30%
Non MSA countries	18%

Source: FAO (1977).

*MSA – most severely affected.

SPECIFIC NUTRITIONAL DEFICIENCIES

During the decade, deficiencies of Vitamin A, Vitamin D, iron and iodine continued to cause concern in many parts of the world.

Vitamin A deficiency, which occurred mainly in young children and could lead to permanent blindness, was a major problem in India, Bangladesh and Indonesia and occurred less commonly in parts of Africa (particularly south of the Sahara) and in Latin America. WHO (1979c) estimated that there were 9 million blind people in the world, and if 2 per cent of these cases were attributable to malnutrition this would mean 180,000 individuals suffering from nutritional blindness. During the decade there were several important advances in preventive treatment, in India involving large doses of Vitamin A by mouth at intervals of several months and in Central America by adding the vitamin to sugar.

Vitamin D deficiency, which causes rickets, has been virtually eliminated from developed countries but affected 1–2 per cent of pre-school children in India, and occurred moderately to severely in 3–5 per cent of children in the Eastern Mediterranean region of WHO (Rao Someswara, 1974). During the past ten years there were increasing reports of a high incidence of rickets in northern India, the Middle East, Iran and Turkey, and also in Nigeria, South Africa and other areas. Social changes, modifying exposure to sunlight (which produces active Vitamin D in the skin from a precursor), may underly some of these trends. In 1965 osteomalacia (a disease marked by bone softening) was reported to be common in the heavily-veiled Bedouin women of the Negev desert: in 1976, when faces were commonly exposed, there was no evidence of Vitamin D deficiency. The opposite effect was demonstrated in Jamaica. Here young children are usually very lightly clothed and florid rickets (other than renal rickets) used to be virtually unknown, but the disease was described in 1975 in children living in high rise flats who could not easily get outside to play.

Iron deficiency anaemia was extremely common in infants, young children and women (particularly during pregnancy) and reached prevalences as high as 80 per cent in these groups in some countries (WHO, 1975). There were many causes including dietary deficiency, poor absorption from vegetarian diets, reduced absorption due to infection and blood loss caused by conditions such as malaria and hookworm. In the 1970s there were advances in diagnosis, in understanding of the mechanisms of iron absorption, and in prevention through fortifying food — in India, through the addition of an iron compound to table salt.

Iodine deficiency goitre (chronic enlargement of the thyroid), with the cretinism that accompanies it, remained common in many parts of the world, especially in mountainous regions. It affected more men than women. Prevalence was said to exceed 30 per cent in many parts of Africa, to be a problem in 17 out of 26 Latin American countries, expecially in the Andes (Stanbury et al., 1974) and to affect 32 per cent of the population of the southern region of the Federal Republic of Germany. During the decade methods of detection improved and encouraging results were obtained in trials in Ecuador, Zaire, and Papua New Guinea of treatment using a single intramuscular injection of iodized oil in place of the traditional iodized salt.

NUTRITION AND CARDIOVASCULAR DISEASE

The environment plays a large part in the genesis of hypertension (high blood pressure). Although genetic factors are important, they can apparently be over-ridden by favourable environmental factors such as high potassium intake (fruit consumption), absence of obesity, low stress and good hygienic conditions. In isolated communities where hypertension is absent, sodium consumption is also very low (less than 3 g sodium chloride per 24 hours). Evidence incriminating salt as a possible cardiovascular risk factor has increased over the last ten years. A positive association between sodium intake and blood pressure has been demonstrated by comparing different populations.

However there are many dietary and other factors that distinguish populations without hypertension from those in which hypertension exists. The isolated groups in whom blood pressure does not rise with age also tend to have a low energy intake. The relationship between energy consumption and blood pressure is obscure, but a reducing diet that leads to weight loss is associated with a substantial fall in blood pressure, measured as intra-arterial pressure. A reduction in total energy consumption can therefore reduce blood pressure and this may partiallly explain the fall in cardiovascular mortality in populations with impaired food supplies (e.g. in the Netherlands in the Second World War). Total energy restriction will also reduce the levels of other cardiovascular risk indicators such as total serum cholesterol and glucose tolerance.

Obese persons are known to have an increased risk of cardiovascular disease. Excess mortality in overweight subjects is associated with increased hypertension and higher serum cholesterol concentration (Keys et al., 1972). The obese person who (unusually) has normal blood pressure, serum cholesterol and glucose tolerance has the usual life expectancy.

Other dietary factors can be implicated as possible risk indicators with an effect on both blood pressure and cardiovascular death. Such a factor is mineral imbalance: the over-consumption of minerals that are harmful and/or the under-consumption of minerals that are beneficial. Areas with soft drinking water have high cardiovasuclar mortality and Perry and Peterson (1974) have suggested that inapparent metal exposure may be a function of water hardness. Cadmium and other minerals may be toxic to the kidneys and do raise the blood pressure of rats. However, unlike salt and calorie consumption, it is not known whether altering water hardness or reducing cadmium intake will influence any cardiovascular risk factor.

During the last ten years it was realized that the serum concentration of low-density lipoproteins is a risk indicator and that high-density lipoproteins are probably beneficial in increased concentration. Small amounts of alcohol may raise the latter and prove advantageous. The falling cardiovascular death rates in the United States and Belgium have both been correlated with a reduction in saturated fat consumption. However, other changes are occurring in such health-conscious populations, including changes in intake of other foodstuffs and an increase in exercise. Proof was still lacking in 1980 that limiting saturated fats is beneficial.

OBESITY

Obesity is only a health problem if it leads to disability, illness or increased risk of death, and these effects are difficult to quantify. Although serious overweight decreases life expectancy, it is by no means clear why. Obesity predisposes to maturity-onset diabetes, but the evidence linking it to hypertension is controversial and *per se* it appears to be a relatively minor risk factor for coronary heart disease (DHSS/MRC, 1976). It does, however, cause disabilities, including osteo-arthritis of weight-bearing joints, varicose veins, increased surgical and obstetric risks and numerous psycho-social problems. For these reasons it was a serious health problem during the 1970s in industrialized countries and among affluent groups elsewhere, and its prevalance appeared to be increasing. In the United Kingdom, body fat has increased over the past four decades by about 10 per cent in all age groups; in Czechslovakia there was a striking increase in the incidence of obesity in men and women between 1956 and 1972; and in a national survey in Canada more than 60 per cent of people of both sexes aged over forty were said to be overweight. Obesity also increased in some countries in the South Pacific region following dietary changes (especially increased consumption of refined carbohydrates), and the incidence of hypertension, diabetes and gout rose in parallel.

Diseases Associated With Life-Styles

SMOKING, alcohol and drugs all cause significant mortality and social cost, and the decade has seen advances in understanding of their impact and some increase in preventive action.

SMOKING AND HEALTH

Research in the 1950s and early 1960s indicated that cigarette smoking was the principal avoidable cause of death in men. Longitudinal studies from the United States, United Kingdom, Japan and Sweden showed that overall mortality rates were about 70 per cent higher in current cigarette smokers than in non-smokers (USSG, 1964). This amounted to a reduction of 5–8 years in the life expectancy of the average man smoking 20 cigarettes daily, or around five minutes per cigarette smoked (RCP, 1977). About half of this excess mortality was attributable to cardiovascular diseases. The association with lung cancer appeared largely one of simple cause and effect and it was predicted that in the absence of smoking 80–90 per cent of the disease would disappear. Smoking also appeared the most important single cause of chronic bronchitis, but air pollution and other factors also contributed. In coronary heart disease smoking was shown to aggravate greatly the adverse effects of dietary and other features of the 'western' life-style. There was also strong evidence that smoking contributes to the occurrence of cancers of the lip, mouth, pharynx, larynx, oesophagus, bladder, kidney and pancreas, as well as to gastric ulcer.

In the last ten years further evidence confirmed and extended these conclusions (USSG, 1979); associations were also demonstrated with retardation of foetal growth, congenital abnormalities, and increase in absence from work through sickness. Smoking was also found to increase the risk of diabetes, hypertension, thromboembolic risks from oral contraceptives and some environmental and occupational hazards (e.g. from asbestos, uranium, chromium and nickel). Respiratory disease was found to be more prevalent among the children of smoking parents (e.g. Colley *et al.*, 1974). In the late 1970s, there was some evidence that "passive smoking" can also be dangerous rather than just unpleasant to non-smokers. Some measurements recorded concentrations of total suspended particulates of over 260 μg/^{3} in a sample of rooms with a high density of active smokers (CEQ, 1980). And in a study carried out in Japan, it was found that wives who did not smoke but were exposed to their husbands' cigarette smoke developed lung cancer at a much higher rate than non-smoking wives of non-smoking husbands. The risk to non-smoking wives was directly related to the amount their husbands smoked, and that risk was one-half to one third that of direct smoking (Hirayama, 1981).

Table 10–6. Age-standardized Death Rates for Lung Cancer, 1965 and 1975, and Percentage Change.

| Country | Deaths per 100,000 p.a. | | | | | |
| | Men | | | Women | | |
	1965	1975	Change (%)	1965	1975	Change (%)
Australia	34.9	46.0	+32	4.2	7.0	+67
Austria	51.2	50.7	−1	5.8	6.7	+16
Belgium	49.1	67.3	+37	4.3	5.7	+33
Canada	31.4	46.1*	+47	5.0	8.8*	+76
Chile	14.1	18.0	+28	4.7	4.7	0
Costa Rica	6.0	11.6	+93	2.5	6.3	+152
Czechoslovakia	56.4	65.2*	+16	5.6	5.4*	−4
Denmark	37.1	45.7	+23	6.8	10.7	+57
England and Wales	68.5	71.8	+5	10.0	14.6	+46
Finland	61.3	64.1*	+5	3.8	4.2*	+11
France	26.9	35.1*	+30	3.6	3.5*	−3
Germany (FR)	40.4	47.3	+17	5.2	5.1	−2
Greece	30.3	38.2	+26	6.2	6.6	+6
Hungary	35.3	47.1	+33	7.2	8.0	+11
Iceland	9.9	19.5	+97	6.0	11.8	+97
Ireland	30.1	44.2	+47	7.5	13.8	+84
Israel	21.3	24.6	+15	7.9	7.1	−10
Italy	28.6	41.8*	+46	4.4	5.1*	+16
Japan	12.9	19.6	+52	4.6	5.8	+26
Mexico	7.2	9.0*	+25	3.8	3.9*	+3
Netherlands	51.4	71.5	+39	3.4	4.2	+24
New Zealand	35.9	48.7	+36	4.6	10.6	+130
N. Ireland	40.7	52.6	+29	5.9	11.7	+98
Norway	14.1	22.3	+58	2.2	4.5	+105
Poland	27.1	44.2	+63	4.4	5.7	+30
Portugal	10.5	15.1	+44	2.0	3.3	+65
Scotland	75.8	82.7	+9	11.8	15.8	+34
Spain	18.8	26.6*	+41	3.6	4.2*	+17
Sri Lanka	1.0	—		1.0	—	
Sweden	16.5	23.6	+43	5.6	6.0	+7
Switzerland	34.6	47.6	+38	3.2	4.4	+38
Thailand	2.3	5.2	+126	0.8	2.3	+188
United States	37.7	51.0	+35	6.1	12.5	+105
Venezuela	14.1	16.6	+18	6.5	7.0	+8
Yugoslavia	21.7	32.6	+50	4.0	5.5	+38

Source: WHO (1979 d).
*Values for 1974.

During the 1970s, there was little change in average personal tobacco consumption over the world, following an increase in the 1960s (Lee, 1975). Between 1972–74 and 1977 there was a drop from 2.11 to 2.02 kg per person per year in industrialized countries. In the United Kingdom, and probably other developed countries, this was most marked among the professional and managerial section of the population (Capell, 1978). There was also a trend in these countries to reduce tar yields from cigarettes. There was, however, a slight rise in average consumption from 0.79 to 0.81 kg in developing countries. At the end of the decade there was widespread promotion of tobacco products (without any stress on tar yields) and increased tobacco growing in developing countries, where smoking was increasing among the well-to-do and in urban areas, with serious health implications.

Male mortality from lung cancer rose almost everywhere between 1965 and 1975 (Austria was one exception), and while female rates were much lower, they rose swiftly in most countries (but not in Chile, Czchoslovakia, France, the Federal Republic of Germany and Israel) (Table 10–6). Generally, these trends closely paralleled the changes in cigarette smoking some twenty years earlier (WHO, 1979b). Bronchitis mortality, in contrast, appeared to be declining generally in industrialized countries, the greatest improvement being in the United Kingdom where there has been a major reduction in the formerly severe air pollution. Chronic coughing improves rapidly when smoking is reduced (Rose and Hamilton, 1978), and may be expected to follow the tar load to which a population is exposed. Trends in coronary heart disease are more complex (Table 10–7) because they reflect the interaction of many factors. In Japan, for example, mortality has remained low, and declined between 1965 and 1977, despite a large and growing consumption of cigarettes, probably because the low fat content of the national diet prevented the high blood fat characteristics of coronary disease. If the diet becomes more "western" this situation would be expected to change. In the United States,

Table 10–7. Age-standardized Mortality Rates for Coronary Heart Disease in Various Countries for Men Aged 45–74 in 1965 and 1977 and Percentage Changes.

Country	Deaths per 100,000 p.a. 1965	1977	
Australia	969	774	(−20%)
England and Wales	757	761	(+ 1%)
Germany (Federal Republic of)	577	514	(−11%)
Israel	670	593	(−11%)
Japan	190	113	(−41%)
Mexico	119	144[a]	(+21%)
Netherlands	542	566	(+ 4%)
Sweden	578	625	(+ 8%)
United States	978	760	(−22%)

Source: Data supplied by London School of Hygiene and Tropical Medicine.

[a]1974.

Australia, Finland, Belgium and several other countries there was also a decline in coronary mortality rates, possibly as a result of dietary improvement coupled with reduced smoking and reduced tar content of cigarettes.

ALCOHOL AND DRUGS

During the decade, medical and social problems associated with abuse of alcohol and drugs caused mounting concern, especially in developed countries where young people were exposed to high risk. Five classes of substances were involved: sedatives and anaesthetics (including alcohol, barbiturates, various sedatives, volatile anaesthetics, industrial solvents and "glues"); narcotic analgesics (opium, morphine, heroin and various synthetic materials); psycho-stimulants (amphetamine-related drugs, cocaine); cannabis (including Indian hemp, hashish and marijuana) and hallucinogens (LSD, mescaline, etc.). Many of these are long-established materials, but some have created new problems recently, as with the local epidemics of "glue-sniffing" among juveniles in some countries. Action during the decade involved on the one hand improved understanding of the causes and treatment of drug and alcohol problems, and on the other international action to curb trade. A United Nations Fund for Drug Abuse Control (UN Office at Geneva) was set up at the beginning of the decade and by 1979, seventy countries were contributing to the projected budget of US\$ 9,600,000. This Fund has been used to finance the introduction of alternative cash crops in opium-growing regions (especially Afghanistan and Burma). A protocol to amend the 1961 Single Convention on Narcotic Drugs was signed in 1972 and a Convention on Psychotropic Substances signed in 1971. By 1979, 109 states were party to the 1961 Convention, 65 to its 1972 protocol and 55 to the 1971 Convention: the last of these came into force in 1976. The Division of Narcotic Drugs (UN Office at Geneva) publishes a monthly *Information Letter* giving a valuable overview of international developments.

Mental Health and the Environment

MENTAL health is a social concept and can be defined in many ways. But four levels of condition are readily comprehensible: positive mental health, social deviance, psychological distress and severe mental illness. Environmental factors can be involved at any level.

In many countries social deviance and psychological distress appear to have increased over the decade. There was an overall increase in crude suicide rates, and an epidemic rise in deliberate self-harm and attempted suicide among adolescents. Various neurotic disturbances, whose precise manifestation is culturally based and can take the form of possession states or "fits" under some conditions, were shown to be widespread and highly reactive to such environmental factors as poverty, poor housing, unemployment, isolation, boredom, personal problems or physical disease. In some areas outbursts of violent aggression appeared under such conditions: in others such social deviances as delinquency, drug dependence or alcoholism were conspicuous. While overall rates of disturbance did not vary greatly from one area to another, being comparable in rural Sweden (Hagnell, 1966), Canada and Nigeria (Leighton *et al.*, 1963 a, b) there were geographical differences in the types of response that probably reflected differences in the stressors involved. There was some evidence that the incidence of mental disturbance was less in rural areas, where sociocultural integration was more complete, although de-population can impose as severe a stress there as overcrowding does in cities (Cooper *et al.*, 1972). Senile dementia was an increasing problem in many developed countries, as a greater proportion of the population survive to a greater age.

Studies during the 1970s demonstrated that an increase in adverse social pressures may closely pre-date the onset of severe mental illness such as schizophrenia — or provoke a relapse (Leff *et al.*, 1976; Wing, 1977). The symptoms of schizophrenia can also be aggravated by lack of stimuli in the social environment. Environmental factors such as malnutrition, alcohol abuse, social isolation and infectious diseases were increasingly important in the decade as causes of dementia and mental handicap.

During the decade the importance of preventive services and non-institutional medical care in the treatment of mental handicap was increasingly recognized (WHO, 1980). Health education, antenatal care, contraceptive services, genetic screening and improved neonatal health care all contributed in the former area. Field workers were trained to provide psychiatric first aid to Australian aboriginal groups and to treat acutely ill patients in a remote area of Colombia (Climent *et al.*, 1978). In countries with adequate resources, psychiatric institutions were reduced in size and complemented by alternative residential, day, domestic and occupational facilities. Sheltered employment and housing was increasingly available, and care in the community was provided by educational psychologists, community psychiatric nurses and others, and through voluntary and self-help groups. The aim was to promote independence and the maximum use of the patient's talents, as well as to provide appropriate treatment during acute attacks and care and protection if chronic impairments were severe (DHSS, 1975; Deutscher Bundestag, 1975; Joint Commission, 1961). In the future, enhanced understanding of how environmental factors can promote mental handicap and illness should contribute to prevention through wiser community planning and organization.

Future Prospects

THE decade saw considerable improvement in the understanding of health problems and their relationship to environmental factors and changes. However, there was little improvement in the health or social situation of the vast rural and shanty-town populations of many developing countries. Under-nutrition was probably still increasing in 1980, and will not be overcome until storage and distribution and food production systems are improved. Motor vehicle accidents were rapidly becoming a major cause of disability and death in many developing countries (Chapter 13). Travel and population movements were spreading infections (and organisms resistant to treatment) more widely and quickly.

In the industrialized countries the main problems of health policy were how to meet increasing demands at tolerable cost and how to redistribute resources from the hospital sector to community care and preventive medicine. There was also an urgent need for much more effective health education, leading people to take more personal responsibility for their health, and so reduce the burden on the medical profession and public services. Obesity, smoking, alcoholism, drug-abuse and transport accidents were all important, increasing problems best dealt with by informed individual action.

The establishment of a healthy environment demands co-ordinated action by many branches of government. The design of systems for monitoring chemicals in air, food or water supplies, for example, demands understanding of their possible effects on man, since this is crucial to the choice of what substances to monitor, with what degree of precision. Maintenance of a healthy working environment in factories needs to be co-ordinated with the maintenance of environmental quality outside, since it is the total dose of many substances, by all pathways, that determines effects. Housing and settlements planning must be done with health implications in mind. Such co-ordinated action demands a new kind of health official who can investigate, monitor and advise local government on all environmental health problems with laboratory services and central information and advice. Such central services must have epidemiological competence, scanning the health records of large populations in the search for slowly developing problems.

During the last decade the realization grew that systems of health care largely organized around high technology in hospitals were inappropriate to many developing countries. In some developing countries a few large hospitals, most of them in towns, consumed half or more of the annual national health budget (Gish, 1977). In the 1970s more emphasis was therefore placed on extending services through health centres, dispensaries and mobile clinic services. Because access to these services and use of them were still poor over large rural areas, the promotion of primary health care through community or village health workers gained increasing acceptance in the past decade.

The advantages of such auxiliary health workers in terms of costs, their roles and their training have been widely publicized (WHO, 1979 e).

During the decade, it was also increasingly recognized that the health status of communities is largely determined by political, socio-economic, nutritional and environmental factors (World Bank, 1975), and that health services alone can usually bring about only relatively small overall improvements. The International Labour Organization Basic Needs Policy (ILO, 1976) saw access to some health services as one of the essential requirements and asserted that better health would itself help increase production and income in rural communities. This approach ties in closely with the WHO/UNICEF concept of primary health care, and with WHO policy (WHO, 1978 b). Whereas in Europe or North America, primary health care has been equated with services first contacted by a patient, such as general practice, hospital casualty departments and pharmacists, the WHO/UNICEF definition states: "Primary health care is essential health care made universally acceptable to individuals and families in the community by means acceptable to them through their full participation and at a cost that the community and country can afford". The key person is the community health worker who has a brief training and returns to his/her own community.

The main problem confronting the governments of developing countries in 1980 was how to extend this kind of coverage, in the face of built-in-resistance to the redistribution of resources away from hospital services. The national and multinational aid agencies were more sympathetic to rural health programmes and to primary health care than they were ten years earlier, and many countries will probably have to rely on overseas aid for developments in this field.

In recent years, through the efforts of WHO, and of other international organizations, including the World Bank and UNDP, the hopes and aspirations for improved health for developing countries and their peoples have been greatly raised. In 1980 an almost bewildering number of initiatives were competing for limited resources. They included the UN slogan "Health for All by the Year 2000" and the "Drinking Water and Sanitation Decade", the Special Programmes for Research and Training in Tropical Diseases (TDR) and for the Control of Diarrhoeal Diseases. These needed in turn to be viewed against the background of a multitude of longer-standing or less adventurous but not less important initiatives: family planning, maternal and child health, the Expanded Immunization Programme and the like.

Successful and balanced development will depend on the creation of such self-reliance in a country that it can understand and measure its own problems; can make optimal use of its own resources (whether large or small) to solve its problems using all available and relevant knowledge in nationally appropriate terms; can take initiatives to obtain the most appropriate outside technical and financial assistance to solve the problems to which it has given priority; can collaborate effectively on terms of mutual respect with other countries, North and South; and can evaluate the effectiveness of its policies and of the measures taken to implement them. No country can consider it has succeeded in development unless it has assured at least a basic standard of health and nutrition for all of its inhabitants. The basic standard perceived by a population is of course a receding horizon. As the people understand and appreciate the advantages of health care (usually curative more than preventive aspects) they tend to perceive increasing needs and to make ever-increasing demands.

In the 1980s, there will undoubtedly be continuing improvement in some aspects of health in many parts of the world, but there are likely to be many backwaters (particularly among the poor of developing countries) where progress will be slow. Progress will be limited by the availability of resources, by the degree of political will available to distribute them more equitably, and by the capability of each country to identify its own priorities. It will also depend on countries' abilities to develop effective policies, to justify their financing, to implement and evaluate them, and to improve their cost-effectiveness.

The skills required (epidemiology, operational, research, demography, health economics, etc.) are scarce and will remain so unless governments and international agencies are prepared to invest in a few strong bases for research and training, and unless governments are prepared to offer attractive posts for such trained personnel within their structures and to use the skills thus provided to best advantage.

References

Abbott, D. C. *et al.* (1972), Organochlorine Pesticide Residues in Human Fat in the United Kingdom, 1969–71, *Brit. Med. J.*, 2, 553.

Acheson, E. D. (1979), *Record Linkage and the Identification of Long-term Environmental Hazards*, Proc. Roy. Soc. London, B, 205, 170.

Ackermann, W. C. *et al.* (1973), *Man-Made Lakes, their Problems and Environmental Effects*, Amer. Geophys. Union, Washington, D. C.

Advisory Committee on Toxic Substances (1979), *Man-Made Mineral Fibre, Report of a Working Party to the Advisory Committee on Toxic Substances*, HMSO, London.

Ames, B. N. *et al.* (1975), Methods for Detecting Carcinogens and Mutagens with the Salmonella/Mammalian Microsome Mutagenicity Test, *Mutation Res.*, 31, 347.

Baris, Y. I. *et al.* (1978), An Outbreak of Pleural Masothelioma and Chronic Fibrosing Pleurisy in the Village of Kawain/Urgup in Anatolia, *Thorax*, 33, 181.

Bengoa, J. M. (1974), The Problem of Malnutrition. *WHO Chronicle*, 28, 3.

Bengtsson, U. and L. Angervall (1970), Analgesic Abuse and Tumours of the Renal Pelvis, *Lancet*, i, 306.

Bengtsson, U. *et al.* (1968), Transitional Cell Tumours of the Renal Pelvis in Analgesic Abusers, *Scand. J. Urol. Nephrol.*, 2, 145.

Bulla, A. (1977), Global Review of Tuberculosis Morbidity and Mortality in the World (1961–1971), *World Health Statistics Report*, 30, 2–38.

Burge, P. S. *et al.* (1979), Peak Flow Rates in the Diagnosis of Occupational Asthma due to Colophony and Isocynates, *Thorax*, 34, 308.

Butler, G. C., Editor (1978), *Principles of Ecotoxicology*, John Wiley and Sons, Chichester.

Capell, P. J. (1978), Trends in Cigarette Smoking in the United Kingdom, *Health Trends*, 10, 49.

CEQ (1980), *Environmental Quality, Tenth Report of the Council on Environmental Quality*, Washington, D.C.

Climent, C. E. *et al.* (1978), Development of an Alternative, Low Cost Mental Health Delivery System in Cali, Colombia, *Social Psychiatry*, 13, 29.

Cole, P. V. (1975), Comparative Effects of Atmospheric Pollution and Cigarette Smoking on Carboxyhaemoglobin Levels in Man, *Nature*, 255, 699.

Colley, J. R. T. *et al.* (1974), Influence of Passive Smoking and Parental Phlegm on Pneumonia and Bronchitis in Early Childhood, *Lancet*, ii, 1031.

Colucci, A. V. *et al.* (1973), Pollutant Burdens and Biological Response, *Arch. Environ. Health*, 27, 151.

Cooper, J. E. *et al.* (1972), *Psychiatric Diagnosis in New York and London*, Maudsley Monograph No. 20. Oxford University Press, London.

Creech, J. L. and M. N. Johnson (1974), Angiosarcoma of the Liver in the Manufacture of Polyvinyl Chloride, *J. Occup. Med.*, 16, 150.

399

Department of the Environment, DOE, (1976), *Chlorofluorocarbons and their Effect on Stratospheric Ozone.* HMSO, London.

Department of the Environment DOE, (1979), *Digest of Environmental Pollution Statistics No. 2.*, HMSO, London.

Department of Health and Social Security, DHSS, (1975), *Better Services for the Mentally Ill*, HMSO, London.

Department of Health and Social Security/Medical Research Council, DHSS/MRC, (1976), Research on Obesity, A Report of the DHSS/MRC Group. HMSO, London.

Department of Health and Social Security, DHSS, (1980), *Lead and Health, The Report of the DHSS Working Party on Lead in the Environment*, HMSO, London.

Deutscher Bundestag (1975), *Bericht Über die Lage der Psychiatrie in der Bundesrepublik Deutschland*, Drucksache 7/4200, 4201, Heger, Bonn.

Duncan, K. P. (1979), *Occupational Exposure*, Proc. Roy. Soc. Lond., B, 205, 157.

Dyson, T. (1977), Levels, Trends, Differentials and Causes of Child Mortality: A Survey, *World Health Statistics Report*, 30, 282.

Elder J. B. *et al.* (1979), Cimetidine and Gastric Cancer, *Lancet*, i, 1005.

FAO (1977), *The Fourth World Food Survey*, FAO Statistics Series No. 11, Food and Agriculture Organization, Rome.

Gamberale, F. (1975), Behavioural Toxicology: A New Field of Job Health Research, *Ambio*, 4, 43.

Garner, R. C. (1979), *Carcinogen Prediction in the Laboratory, a Personal View.* Proc. Roy. Soc. London, B, 205, 121.

Gish, O. (1977), *Guidelines for Health Planners*, Tri-Med. Books Ltd., London.

Gray, L. A. *et al.* (1977), Estrogens and Endometrial Cancer, *J. Obstet. Gynec.*, 49, 385.

Griffin, J. P. (1979), Drug Induced Neoplasia. In P. F. D'Arcy and J. P. Griffin (Editors), *Iatrogenic Diseases*, 2nd Edit., Oxford Univ. Press.

Gwatkin, D. R. *et al.* (1979), *Can Interventions Make a Difference? The Policy Implications of field Experiment Experience*, A Report to the World Bank. Overseas Development Council — Harvard School of Public Health.

Hagnell, O. (1966), *A Prospective Study of the Incidence of Mental Disorder*, Berlingska, Lund.

Haynes, J. D. *et al.* (1976), Culture of Human Malaria Parasites. *Nature*, 263, 767.

Hawker, P. C. *et al.* (1980), Gastric Cancer After Cimetidine in Patient With Two Negative Pretreatment Biopsies, *Lancet*, i, 709.

Hirayama, T. (1981), Non-Smoking Wives of Heavy Smokers Have a Higher Risk of Lung Cancer; A Study from Japan, *British Med. J.*, 282, 183.

Holdgate, M. W. and G. F. White, Editors (1977), *Environmental Issues; SCOPE Report 10*, John Wiley and Sons, London.

IARC (1972–1980), Monographs on the Evaluation of Carcinogenic Risks of Chemicals to Man. Vol. 1–24, WHO, International Agency for Research on Cancer, Lyon.

ILO (1976), *Employment Growth and Basic Needs*, International Labour Organization, Geneva.

Jenson, S. (1972), The PCB Story, *Ambio*, 1, 123.

Joint Commission on Mental Illness and Health (1961), *Action for Mental Health, Final Report of the Joint Commission*. Basic Books, New York.

Joint Working Party on Lead Pollution, JWPLP, (1978), *Lead Pollution in Birmingham*. HMSO, London.

Käferstein, F. K. (1981), *Heavy Metals in Infant Formulas*, ZEBS. Berichte, 1, Dietrich Reiner, Verlag, Berlin.

Keller, W. *et al.* (1976), Anthropometry in Nutritional Surveillance: A Review Based on Results of the WHO collaborative study on Nutritional Anthropometry, *Nut. Abstr. Rev.*, 46, 591.

Keys, A. *et al.* (1976), Coronary Heart Disease: Overweight and Obesity as Risk Factors, *Ann. int. Med.*, 77, 15.

Korte, F. (1976), Information cited in D. R. Miller, General Considerations, Chapter I of *Principles of Ecotoxicology: SCOPE* 12, G. C. Butler, Editor, John Wiley and Sons, Chichester.

Korte, F. (1977), Occurrence and Fate of Synthetic Chemicals in the Environment. In W. J. Hunter and J. Smeets (Editors), *Evaluation of Toxicology Data for Protection of Public Health*, Pergamon, Oxford.

Lansdown, R. (1979), Moderately Raised Blood Lead Levels in Children, *Proc. Roy. Soc. Lond.*, B, 205, 145.

Laursen, B. (1970), Cancer of the Bladder in Patients Treated with Chlornaphazine, *Brit. Med. J.*, 3, 684.

Lee, P. M., Editor (1975), *Tobacco Consumption in Various Countries*, 4th edition. Tobacco Research Council, London.

Leff, J. P. *et al.* (1976), A Cross-national Epidemiological Study of Mania, *Brit. J. Psych.*, 129, 428.

Leighton, A. H. *et al.* (1963a), *Psychiatric Disorder Among the Yoruba*, Cornell University Press, New York.

Leighton, A. H. *et al.* (1963b), *The Character of Danger: Psychiatric Symptoms in Selected Communities*, Basic Books, New York.

Linsell, C. A. and F. G. Peers (1977), Aflatoxin and Liver Cell Cancer, *Trans. Reg. Soc. Trop. Med. Hyg.*, 71, 471.

Loosmore, R. M. *et al.* (1964), The Presence of Aflatoxin in a Sample of Cotton Seed Cake, *Vet. Rec.*, 76, 64.

MacDonald, G. (1955), Medical Implications of the Volta River Project. *Trans. Roy. Soc. Trop. Med. Hyg.*, 49, 13.

McGeown, M. (1979), In P. F. D'Arcy and J. P. Griffin (Editors), *Iatrogenic diseases*, 2nd edition, 254–286, Oxford University Press.

Modan, B. *et al.* (1974), Radiation-induced Head and Neck Tumours, *Lancet*, i, 277.

Muir, C. S. (1975), International Variation in High-Risk Populations, In J. F. Fraumeni (Editor), *Persons at High Risk of Cancer, An Approach to Cancer Etiology and Control*, Academic Press, New York.

Muir, C. and G. Wagner, Editors (1977), Directory of On-going Research in Cancer Epidemiology, *IARC Scientific Publications*, 17, Lyon.

NAS (1976), *Halocarbons; Environmental Effects of Chlorofluoromethane Release*, National Academy of Sciences, Washington, D.C.

NAS (1977), *An Assessment of Mercury in the Environment*, National Academy of Sciences, Washington, D.C.

NAS (1980a), *Lead in the Human Environment, A Report Prepared by the Committee on Lead*, National Academy of Sciences, Washington, D.C.

NAS (1980b), *Drinking Water and Health*, Vol. 3, National Academy of Sciences, Washington, D.C.

NRC (1980), *The Effects on Population of Exposure to Low Levels of Ionizing Radiation*, National Research Council, National Academy of Sciences, Washington, D.C.

OTA (1979), *The Direct Use of Coal*, Office of Technology Assessment, Congress of the United States; Washington, D.C.

Perry, J. K. and K. L. Peterson (1974), Possible Relationships Between the Physical Environment and Human Hypertension: Cadmium and Hard Water, *J. Prev. Med.*, 3, 344.

Puffer, R. R. and C. V. Serrano (1973), *Patterns of Mortality in Childhood*, Pan American Health Organization Scientific Publication No. 262, Washington, D.C.

Rao Someswara, K. (1974), Malnutrition in the Easter Mediterranean Region, *WHO Chronicle*, 28, 172.

Reggiani, G. (1978), Medical Problems Raised by the TCDD Contamination in Seveso, Italy, *Arch. Toxicol.*, 40, 161.

Rose, G. and P. J. S. Hamilton (1978), A Randomised Controlled Trial of the Effect on Middle-aged Men on Advice to Stop Smoking, *J. Epidem. Comm. Health*, 32, 275.

Rous, V. and J. Studeny (1970, Aetiology of Pleural Plaques, *Thorax*, 25, 270.

Royal College of Physicians, RCP, (1970), *Air Pollution and Health*, Pitman, London.

Royal College of Physicians, RCP, (1977), *Smoking or Health*, The Third Report from the Royal College of Physicians, Pitman, London.

Seppalainen, A. M. *et al.* (1975), Sub-clinical Neuropathy at 'Safe' Levels of Lead Exposure, *Arch. Environ. Health*, 30, 180.

Smith, D. C. *et al.* (1975), Association of Exogenous Aestrogen and Endometrial Carcinoma, *New Engl. J. Med.*, 293, 1164.

Stanbury, J. B. *et al.* (1974), Endemic Goitre and Cretinism: Public Health Significance and Prevention, *WHO Chronicle*, 28, 220.

Stanley, N. F. and H. P. Alpers, Editors (1975), *Man-Made Lakes and Human Health*, Academic Press, London.

Storrs, E. E. (1971), The Nine Banded Armadillo; A Model for Leprosy and Other Biomedical Research, *Inter. J. Leprosy*, 39, 703–712.

Taylor, T. V. *et al.* (1979), Gastric Cancer in Patients Who Have Taken Cimetidine, *Lancet*, i, 1235.

Thiess, A. M. *et al.* (1973), Zur Toxicologie von Dichlorodimethylater — Verdact auf kanzerogene; Wirkling auch bie Menschen, *Zbl. Arbeitsmed.*, 23, 97.

Trager, W. and J. B. Jensen (1976), Human Malaria Parasites in Continuous Culture, *Science*, 193, 673.

UN (1981), *World Population Prospects as Assessed in* 1980, United Nations, New York.

UNEP (1977), *The State of the Environment: Selected Topics*, 1977, United Nations Environment Programme, Nairobi.

UNEP (1978), *The State of the Environment: Selected Topics*, 1978, United Nations Environment Programme, Nairobi.

UNEP (1979a), *The State of the Environment: Selected Topics*, 1979, United Nations Environment Programme, Nairobi.

UNEP (1979b), *The Ozone Layer*, Edited by A. K. Biswas. Pergamon Press, Oxford.

UNEP (1980), *The State of the Environment: Selected Topics*, 1980, United Nations Environment Programme, Nairobi.

UNEP (1981), *The State of the Environment: Selected Topics*, 1981, United Nations Environment Programme, Nairobi.

USSG (1964), *Smoking and Health*, U.S. Surgeon General, U.S. Department of Health, Education and Welfare, Washington, D.C.

USSG (1979), *Smoking and Health. A Report of the U.S. Surgeon General*, U.S. Department of Health, Education and Welfare, Washington, D.C.

Vainio, H. *et al.* (1976), A Study on the Mutagenic Activity of Styrene and Styrene Oxide, *Scandinavian J. Work, Environ. and Health*, 3, 147.

Van Duuren, B. L. *et al.* (1972), Carcinogenecity of Halo-ethers. II. Structure-activity Relationships of Analogs of bis-chloromethyl ether, *J. Nat. Cancer. Inst.*, 48, 1431.

Van Rensburg, S. J. *et al.* (1974), Primary Liver Cancer Rate and Aflatoxin Intake Higher Cancer Area, *S. Afr. Med. J.*, 48, 2508d.

Waterhouse, J. *et al.* Editors (1970), *Cancer Incidence in Five Continents*, Vol. III. IARC Scientific Publications, No. 15, Lyon.

Weekly Epidemiological Record (1978), Vol. 53, 197.

WHO (1975), Control of Nutritional Anaemia with Special Reference to Iron Deficiency, *WHO Tech. Rep. Ser.*, 580. World Health Organization Geneva.

WHO (1976a), *Environmental Health Criteria: 1. Mercury*, World Health Organization, Geneva.

WHO (1976b), *Environmental Health Criteria: 2. Polychlorinated biphenyls and Terphenyls*, World Health Organization, Geneva.

WHO (1977a), *Environmental Health Criteria for Cadmium*, EHE/EHC/77.1, World Health Organization, Geneva.

WHO (1977b), *Environmental Health Criteria: 3. Lead*, World Health Organization, Geneva.

WHO (1977c), *Environmental Health Criteria: 4. Oxides of Nitrogen*, World Health Organization, Geneva.

WHO (1977d), *World Health Statistics Report*, 30, 369–373.

WHO (1978a), *Environmental Criteria: 5. Nitrates, Nitrites and N–Nitroso Compounds*, World Health Organization, Geneva.

WHO (1978b), *Primary Health Care*, World Health Organization, Geneva.

WHO (1979a), Viral Haemorrhagic Fever Surveillance, *Weekly Epid. Rec.* 54, 337–344.

WHO (1979b), *Environmental Health Criteria: 8. Sulphur Oxide and Suspended Particulate Matter*, World Health Organization, Geneva.

WHO (1979c), Advisory Group on the Prevention of Blindness; Data on Blindness Throughout the World, *WHO Chronicle*, 33, 275–183.

WHO (1979d), *Controlling the Smoking Epidemic*, WHO Tech. Rep. Ser., 636.

WHO (1979e), *Training and Utilization of Auxiliary Personnel for Rural Health Teams in Developing Countries*, WHO Tech. Rep. Ser., 633.

WHO (1980), *Sixth Report on the World Health Situation*, World Health Organization, Geneva.

Wing, J. K. (1977), The Management of Schizophrenia in the Community, In G. Usdin (Editor), *Psychiatric Medicine*, Brunner, New York.

World Bank (1975), *Health*. Sector Policy Paper, World Bank, Washington, D.C.

CHAPTER 11

Industry

The 1970s were a traumatic time for industry. An era of remarkable growth, begun after the second world war, came to a close. Fuel costs rose sharply. Disruptions occurred in the monetary system. Inflation reached new heights, and unemployment rose. Construction costs climbed. As a result, by the end of the decade, industry's contribution to gross domestic product was decreasing in most regions of the world.

On top of all these factors another gained prominence during the 70s: an expanding demand for enforcement of higher standards of environmental quality, chiefly in developed countries. Industry, as a source of pollution, came increasingly under scrutiny and criticism. Yet by the end of the decade, industry was seen as only one source of pollutants, and it was recognized that because industrial activities help raise living standards in most countries, controls should not be adopted without regard to their implications for national economic well-being. It was also apparent that wise regulation required a sound scientific understanding of pollutant sources, pathways and impacts.

In the developing world, economic growth was given first priority during the 70s, but with new emphasis on the living conditions of the poor. A United Nations meeting in Peru in 1975 set as a target that the share of developing countries in total world industrial production should rise from the then current 8.6 per cent to 25 per cent in 2000 A.D. As the 1970s passed, that goal was not being met.

The decisions made by industrial managers - whether in the private sector or government - were influenced by two sets of factors that evolved during the decade:

(a) public efforts to improve environmental quality,

(b) industrial efforts to introduce new production techniques, choose alternative materials and treat waste so as to reduce or eliminate harmful effects to people and ecosystems.

Some public efforts took the form of more specific industrial regulations and standards for the work-place and for controlling emissions. Others consisted of experiments with economic incentives and dis-incentives. By 1980 there were the beginnings of systematic analyses of the full range of social costs and benefits of such measures: some of these reviewed the proportion of new investment devoted to pollution control and to possible effect on prices. In socialist countries more attention was paid to integrated siting of new plants so as to reduce the new output of waste.

Industry's own efforts were exemplified by the chemical industry's significant reduction of plant emissions in sulphuric acid manufacture through adoption of new processes, and reductions in mercury consumption in caustic soda production through new control measures. The pulp and paper industry learned how to reduce its discharge rates of effluent by more than half. The petroleum industry reduced its waste water output, the iron and steel industry cut smoke and dust emission, and aluminium manufacturers reduced electric power consumption. The nickel industry recycled tailings water to minimize contamination of public waters and tried to control wind-blown dust from fine tailings through wetting and re-vegetation of worked-out areas. And the lead-zinc industry recycled water for pollution control.

Unfortunately, by the end of the decade, adequate data were not available on the extent to which these improvements were carried out on a world scale, and what the social gains and losses were, but a searching re-appraisal of industry's role in environmental protection was underway.

During the 1970s, industries and governments paid increasing attention to environmental quality concerns, which had taken on new importance in the 1950s and 1960s. These concerns showed in the development and partial adoption of environmentally sound and appropriate technologies, and in a wide range of economic and political measures to encourage such improvements.

This chapter consists of five main sections. The first provides a historical perspective by reviewing industrial* growth and its impacts on the environment before the Stockholm Conference. The second briefly reviews the course of industrialization during the 1970s. The third section, the main part of the chapter, analyzes changes in interactions between industry and environment in developed and developing countries during the decade. It focuses on the technical management measures that were taken by industrial management to control and abate environmental problems. Although a brief account of environmental issues receiving attention in some key industries introduces the section, a general list of issues is not given. Rather, the section concentrates on promising technologies and strategies that have already been implemented and have international relevance and the possibility of wider application. The fourth section examines the principal economic and political factors underlying the choice of improved technologies and management. These include: environmental regulations, standards and norms, occupational health, the economic aspects of environmental control, incentives and dis-incentives, environmental criteria for the location of industry, and environmental impact assessment. One constraint in preparing this chapter was the lack of consistent and reliable international data, particularly for the earlier part of the decade.

The fifth and final section directs attention to the critical role of resource and energy conservation in future industrial development plans and projects, and to the increasing emphasis upon preventative rather than corrective measures to abate pollution.

---

*The term "industry" is used here to encompass the UN International Standard Industrial Classification divisions 3 (manufacture), 2 (mining), and 5 (construction).

Development of Environmental Concerns
in Industry

INDUSTRY and industrialization have long been regarded as key elements in development. They are important to government as major creators of wealth. They are the means of conversion of raw materials into finished products, and a source of foreign exchange and domestic employment. At the same time they have caused many environmental problems. These stem in part from the extraction of raw materials by mining, and from industrial demands for water and energy. A second group of problems arises from the products of industry – especially chemical products – which can have unexpected and unwelcome environmental impacts. A third kind of difficulty – and the most familiar – arises because waste heat, chemical by-products, and waste gases, liquids and solids are discharged to the environment and cause damage or hazard to people, livestock, ecosystems or artefacts.

THE INDUSTRIAL REVOLUTION

During the first phases of the industrial revolution in the United Kingdom, coal played a relatively small role because the mechanical inventions in the textile industry were operated by water power. However, when it was discovered that coal could be used instead of charcoal in blast furnaces and forges for manufacturing iron, industrial development accelerated: between 1720 and 1839, the annual production of pig-iron in Britain grew from 25,000 to 1,347,000 tonnes. At the same time, the smoke that resulted created what came to be known as "The Black Country" of the Midlands.

Steam power was probably the most important discovery of the industrial revolution. In the textile industry, it was first applied to spinning, and then to weaving. The effect was to make the industry independent of woodland and water-power, while the new machinery generated a great increase in the demand for raw cotton. Steam was soon brought into use also for transport. The first steam locomotive was tested in the early days of the nineteenth century, and led to an age of feverish activity in railway building from 1830 onwards. This was a powerful stimulus to the metal industries.

Steam made it easier to use machines for making other machines. The scope and power of the mechanical engineering industry were increased by a series of inventions that created modern steel manufacture. The metal industries were helped further by chemical discoveries that in turn created the chemical industry. The discovery of electricity set in train a further revolution encompassing every aspect of modern life. And because electricity can be transmitted over long distances, it gave industry a wider choice of location than before.

The industrial revolution did not have precisely the same consequences in all countries, but it did produce some common results. It stimulated a major movement of population from rural to urban areas. One country after another was obliged to legislate for the control of factories, and in almost every country, the same problems and the same remedies were discussed. Factory acts regulated hours of work and set minimum wage rates. The rights of trade unions and family endowment were established. Another outcome was periodic mass-unemployment, a consequence of mass-production. It is sometimes said that the industrial revolution substituted unemployment for famine as the nightmare of mankind.

Governments found it necessary from the mid-nineteenth century onwards to introduce an increasing range of controls to curb unwanted environmental impacts. In the United Kingdom, damage caused by hydrochloric acid fumes produced in alkali manufacture led to the Alkali Works Regulation Act of 1863, legislation subsequently extended to embrace air pollution from major industries. Water pollution, too, excited concern in the United Kingdom in the late nineteenth century, and parallel developments took place in several other nations.

THE DECADES BEFORE STOCKHOLM

The 1950s and 60s were a period of impressive industrial development and growth. Prices of basic raw materials and particularly energy remained stable, with crude oil prices constantly below the US$2.00 per barrel level. The colonial era came to an end, and development of the newly independent countries became a focus of world attention. Growth proceeded faster than either the developed or developing countries had experienced in any comparable period before 1950.

During 1960–1975, manufacturing grew more rapidly than other economic sectors, most markedly in the centrally planned economies and the developing countries, with growth rates of 8.7 and 7.4 per cent respectively (UNIDO 1979 a). There were important similarities in the development patterns of most countries, for example in the growth in industry's share of total income (UNIDO, 1979 a).

A broadening industrial base was normally associated with a growing share of heavy industry in manufacturing output. In 1955, heavy industry accounted for almost two-thirds of manufacturing output in the developed market economies, and half in the centrally planned economies. In developing countries the manufacturing share of heavy industry increased from about one-third to nearly one-half. By 1970, heavy industry accounted for two-thirds in both economies.

Between 1950 and 1970, only about 30 per cent of all minerals mined in developing countries were processed there. Efforts to increase local processing of minerals were only partly successful, notably for copper, lead, tin and zinc (Chapter 5). The developed market economies still consumed the bulk of the mineral resources in 1970.

ENVIRONMENTAL IMPACTS

Although the period 1950–70 witnessed significant growth rates in all economic groupings, particularly manufacturing, in many countries these developments were not matched everywhere by concern for environmental impacts. Massive production of goods took place without due regard for either short– or long-term environmental consequences. An increasing quantity of synthetic products (such as plastics) were not readily or safely biodegradable. Volumes of solid wastes increased. "Hard" detergents caused foam on rivers, sometimes blown by the wind to create a nuisance and even a hazard to traffic in adjacent towns. The number and volume of manufactured chemical compounds increased greatly (Table 11–1). Polychlorinated biphenyls (first introduced in the 1920s as transformer fluids), and chlorofluorocarbons, used in increasing quantities as aerosol propellants and refrigerants, accumulated in the biosphere. Organochlorine pesticide residues persisted in wildlife.

Table 11–1. Production of Chemicals and Apparent Consumption Per Capita,[a] Selected Countries, 1963, 1970 and 1975

Production Index (1970 = 100)		Country	Apparent Consumption (US$ per capita)		
1963	1975		1963	1970	1975
—	188	Canada	77[b]	109	285
56	123	USA	160	227	377
37	112	Japan	59	141	294
42[c]	122	Austria	56[b]	121	402[d]
52	269	Belgium[b]	70	154	334
46	136	Finland	—	130	405
50	116	France	80	141	340
48	114	Germany, FR.	130	182	424
38	158[e]	Greece	—	—	—
48	159[d]	Ireland	—	—	—
56[b]	126[b]	Italy	77[b]	115	247
35	120	Netherlands	76[b]	172	294
65	116	Norway	73	134	325
—	—	Portugal	14[b]	47	—
35	275	Spain	39	96	281
58[f]	118	Sweden	89	174	412
58[b]	111[b]	Switzerland	77[b]	155	335
63[b]	116[b]	United Kingdom	113	165	343

Source: OECD (1979 a).

[a]Including man-made fibre

[b]Excluding man-made fibre

[c]Due to changes in measurement method, 1971 = 100

[d]1974

[e]1973

[f]Due to changes in measurement method, 1968 = 100

Lack of understanding of environmental systems lay behind the failure to predict the unwelcome side-effects of many of these otherwise beneficial materials. For example the inert nature of chlorofluorocarbon compounds was looked on as an asset – since it meant that they would not have chemical impacts at ground level – and it was only when it was discovered that their decomposition by strong radiation in the stratosphere released radicals capable of reducing ozone concentrations that concern arose. This growth in understanding was paralleled in the two decades prior to 1970 by acute pollution incidents – only some of which were caused by industry – and mounting public unease, leading to recognition of the need for more thorough screening of new materials and better regulation of industrial activities.

Although many countries then had some legislation on health, sanitation, water and air quality, and the control of nuisances, a number began to draft and promulgate new acts as well as to re-structure their national institutions to cope with these issues. Industry responded by installing more and better pollution control equipment. Much of this had to be fitted to existing plants and gaseous or liquid wastes treated before discharge. The strategy was basically "corrective" since its aim was to reduce or modify the deleterious effects of the pollutants before they reached the receiving media of air, water or soil. There were also efforts to phase out substances such as hard detergents that were causing environmental problems, and to design less polluting processes and equipment. All of this activity was influenced by considerations of economic return from industrial investment and by the incentives and dis-incentives provided by government.

Conditions in the working environment also came under scrutiny. In 1949, the International Labour Organisation (ILO) had issued a "Model of Safety Regulations for Industrial Establishments for the Guidance of Governments and Industy". It had been merely for guidance and did not involve binding obligations but it drew attention to evidence on previously unrecognized occupational hazards. Whilst in a number of countries workmen's compensation laws then existed, they generally related to occupational accidents, or to diseases like pneumoconiosis (black lung disease) and silicosis among miners, masons, metal grinders and some pottery workers, due to the inhalation of fine particulates. Further improvement of the working environment was on the whole directed towards lighting, heating, ventilation and seating with the object of increasing productivity, as a result of time-and-motion studies.

In the mid-20th century occupational cancers began to show up through mortality statistics. The first to come to notice were those mining workers who handled pitch or mixed pitch with coal dust in briquette manufacture, giving rise to the term "pitch cancer". Similarly, "paraffin cancer" was found in shale oil workers, and malignant bladder tumours in dye-stuff industry workers.

These changes were less marked in developing countries for many reasons. First, many newly-independent countries had as a first priority development that would secure their economic base and provide jobs for their expanding populations. Second, it was widely held that the great dispersion and dilution capacity of their environments made stringent controls unnecessary. Third, they were suspicious of the appropriateness of the standards pressed on them by developed countries – and of the motives behind the pressure. In general, industrial development took precedence over environmental matters. As the time of the Stockholm Conference approached however, the broadening environmental debate promoted some changes in this thinking (Chapters 1, 8 and 15).

Developments in the 1970s

DURING the 1970s two groups of forces combined to change the environment-industry relationship. First, economic growth was given first priority in the developing world. In 1975, the Second General Conference of the United Nations Industrial Development Organization (UNIDO) meeting in Lima, Peru, set as a target that the share of the developing countries in total world industrial production should rise from the 8.6 per cent level then prevailing to 25 per cent in 2000. (It was estimated to have reached 9 per cent in 1977). Industrialization was to play a central part in this growth and by 1979 it accounted for 24 per cent and 38 per cent of GDP in low-and middle-income countries. The distribution level reached by the middle-income countries exceeded US$1,000 per capita in 1977 (Table 11–2).

In most developing countries, governments played a crucial role in initiating and supporting early industrialization by investing in transport, infrastructure and public utilities. Policies establishing government-owned and operated industrial enterprises were instituted for diverse reasons. One was the desire to launch and control large capital-intensive plants that otherwise might not have been undertaken by the private sector, or if they were, would require regulation of monopolistic profits. Another was to achieve equitable distribution of income. Still others were to balance the economic power of private industrialists and/or trans-nationals and to obtain a pool of experienced manpower through special training. The pace of structural change in manufacturing was greatest for middle-income countries with a sufficiently large market and an explicit development policy. A large number of developing countries had not reached the threshold of US$700–1,000 per capita income by 1980.

Industrial growth was also stressed in developed countries. Among centrally planned economies the Council for Mutual Economic Assistance (CMEA, 1979) reported that its members shared in 1977 a 12 per cent increase in national income over 1975, while industrial output went up by 12.4 per cent. Higher labour productivity accounted for about four-fifths of the increment in industrial output. In the chemical industry, all CMEA member countries together showed a 7.2 per cent increase over 1976. During the same period, iron and steel industry output grew by 2.8 per cent.

In the early years after Stockholm several events had important impacts on industrial development in most regions of the world. Disruptions in the monetary system, the food crisis, the energy crisis, and expanding armament expenditures contributed to recession, inflation and unemployment.

Table 11–2. Some World Development Indicators

Category of Countries	GNP Per Capita (US $)				Percentage Distribution of Gross Domestic Product											
					Agriculture				Industry				Services			
	1976	1977	1978	1979	1976	1977	1978	1979	1976	1977	1978	1979	1976	1977	1978	1979ⁱ
Low-Income Countries	150	170	200	230[a]	38	37	38	38[a]	24	25	24	24[a]	38	38	38	39[a]
Middle-Income Countries	750	1140	1250	1420	15	15	16	14	37	36	34	38	48	49	50	48
Industrialized Countries	6200	6980	8070	9440	4	4	4	4	36	37	37	37	54	59	59	59
Capital-Surplus Oil Exporters	—	—	3340	5470	—	—	5	2	—	—	65	75	—	—	30	23
Centrally-Planned Economies	—	1160	1190	4239[b]	—	—	—	15[b]	—	—	—	63[b]	—	—	—	22[b]

Source: World Bank (1978, 1979, 1980, 1981).

[a] These values exclude China which is classified in the 1981 World Bank Report with low-income countries; in previous years' reports, China was included with centrally-planned economies.

[b] In the 1981 Report, the World Bank uses "Non-market Industrial economies" to include the following developed centrally-planned European countries: USSR, Bulgaria, Czechoslovakia, German Democratic Republic, Hungary and Poland. The weighted averages, therefore, do not include other centrally-planned economies as in previous years' reports.

Construction costs and average capital investments, for example for US mining and metallurgical projects, showed an average annual increase of about 15 per cent between 1973 and 1975, compared with about 6 per cent annual increase over the 1965 to 1970 period (Boik and Verney, 1976). Within a decade construction costs for projects had doubled, with a consequent slow-down of industrial development. Despite this slow-down, the labour force continued to grow, particularly in developing countries, with average annual increases of 1.9 and 2.4 per cent in low- and middle-income countries respectively (Table 11–3). The 1976 World Employment Conference under ILO auspices drew attention to the major increase in the labour force. It then was estimated that by the year 2000, the total labour force would exceed 2,000 million.

Table 11–3. Average Annual Growth of Labour Force (per cent)

	1960–1970	1970–1980	1980–2000 Estimates
Low-Income Countries	1.7	1.9	2.2
Middle-Income Countries	2.0	2.4	2.5
Industrialized Countries	1.2	1.1	0.6
Capital-Surplus Oil Exporters	2.6	2.8	2.9
Centrally Planned Economies	1.4	1.7	1.2

Source: World Bank (1980).

By the end of the decade, the combination of economic, social and political factors causing recession, inflation, unemployment and under-employment generated pressures to reconsider the whole issue of development, and, in particular, the role of industry. Few doubted that at the closing of the decade after Stockholm the era of remarkable growth achieved after the Second World War had ended.

The second group of forces that appeared during the 1970s to change the environment-industry relationship was the expanding demand for enforcement of higher standards of environmental quality. Industry, as a source of pollution, came increasingly under scrutiny and criticism. Government, industry, international organizations, technical departments in academic institutions and a variety of consumer groups joined in assessing the environmental problems caused by specific industries. As growth slowed and capital costs rose at the end of the period, the need for cost-effectiveness was increasingly stressed. By the end of the 1970s it was apparent that a sound scientific understanding of pollutant sources, pathways, transportation, and impacts was necessary if wise policies were to be drawn up. Industry was recognized to be only one source of many pollutants and the essential consideration was the total dosage people and other targets received from all sources. It was recognized that controls should not be adopted without regard to their implications for national economic well-being because industrial activities are fundamental to the level of living standards in most nations. Technological understanding of what could be achieved at what cost was seen to be crucial.

In 1975, the United Nations Environment Programme (UNEP) established its Industry and Environment Office to provide a forum in which governments, industry, international organizations and international worker federations might discuss the environmental issues of specific industries and devise recommendations for action. A series of seminars and workshops on the environmental aspects of specific industrial sectors were organized. Some results of those meetings and progress in the wider field are described below, first for selected industries that are the principal producers of pollutants, and then for representative changes in technologies. In a later section the changes in economic and political factors affecting environmental decisions by industry are examined.

SELECTED INDUSTRIES

The problems faced by the chemical, pulp and paper, petroleum, iron and steel, aluminium, nickel, and lead-zinc industries illustrate the range of experience. The *chemical industry* made major progress in resource conservation and pollution control during the decade. For example, in sulphuric acid manufacture, the use of double-contact rather than single-contact processes increased conversion from 97.5 to 99.5 per cent, which is equivalent to emission reductions from about 17.5 kilograms per tonne (kg/t) to 3.5 kg/t of sulphuric acid manufactured (ECE, 1977).

New control measures were devised for new chloralkali plants that would reduce the consumption of mercury from an average of 0.2 kg/t to 0.1 kg/t of chlorine produced. In some plants in the Federal Republic of Germany, for example, less than 0.02 kg/t of chlorine is possible. Moreover, a number of new factories avoided using mercury altogether by adopting the perfluorocarboxylic acid membrane process, thus alleviating one of the major environmental problems of chlorine and caustic soda manufacturing (Seko, 1977).

The control of toxic substances and disposal of toxic wastes were issues of growing importance. Member countries of the Organization for Economic Cooperation and Development (OECD) combined to develop appropriate test methods under a Chemical Testing Programme. Increasingly, other countries also considered or implemented measures to control toxic substances. Recognizing the importance of international collaboration, the World Health Organization (WHO), ILO and UNEP agreed to cooperate in an International Programme on Chemical Safety (IPCS). The programme will gradually be broadened to include the effects of chemicals on species other than man, on ecosystems and on natural and man-made resources. In addition, governments and the public were increasingly concerned over the transboundary transport and disposal of hazardous chemical wastes. Awareness of the problem was heightened by highly publicized cases in North America (e.g. the Love Canal incident).

Another issue that had significant impacts on environment and health, but also possibly on trade, was labelling. Although national and regional schemes were available or proposed, none of these was accepted at the international level partly because of the costs involved. While many widely-traded substances have well-known characteristics, it is desirable to disseminate sufficient information on chemical use and disposal to protect the environment and man, while minimizing the effects of divulging trade information. This is particularly important for developing countries, which may unknowingly import chemicals banned in the country of manufacture. Both national and international administrative and institutional measures are needed to ensure that banned substances are not re-packaged, re-labelled and sold without the knowledge of importing countries. A closely related labelling issue concerns language: plant workers, particularly in developing countries, who are responsible for loading, unpackaging, blending, mixing and handling chemical substances, often know only their mother tongue, and cannot understand instructions in other languages.

The *pulp and paper industry* uses large quantities of water, and the costs of waste treatment are affected by the volume of effluent. In older mills, typical water usage was around 180 cubic metres per tonne (m^3/t) of pulp. For a mill constructed in the early 70s, a total liquid effluent discharge of 70 m^3/t of pulp was considered extremely low. However, by incorporating advanced system closure techniques and with proper training of staff, it was found that discharge rates could be lowered to 20–30 m^3/t of pulp.

Treatment of condensates originating from pulp digestion and spent liquor' evaporation is an important measure in reducing pollution. Biological oxygen loads from condensates were reduced in new plants from 10–15 to 2–4; 25–30 to 5–6; and 50 to 10–12 kg biological oxygen demand (BOD_5) per tonne of kraft, softwood sulphite and hardwood sulphite pulps respectively. The principal odour from a kraft mill is from total reduced sulphur (TRS). Absolute TRS emissions were reduced from about 10 to about 0.1–0.5 kg/t of pulp. To reduce energy and water consumption and pollution loads further, the industry was implementing technological developments such as oxygen bleaching and special pulping additives. Pollution control in the industrialized countries focused increasingly on specific hazardous materials, such as organo-chlorines, used to protect industrial products against biological attack.

Research was also undertaken on aquatic species, as a result of eutrophication through nitrogen and phosphorus releases (Betts and Allard, 1979). As greater consideration was given to using non-wood fibres such as bagasse, bamboo, kenafe and hemp, possible environmental problems needed to be assessed. Silica from bamboo pulps and its effects on effluent treatment is an example.

In the *petroleum industry*, refineries with adequate segregation and recirculation achieved a waste water output of less than 0.4 tonne per tonne of crude processed. Until the end of the 1950s, the waste water treatment facilities in most refineries consisted of gravity separators for the recovery of free oil and, sometimes, strippers for the reduction of odour or sour condensates. Most refineries built later include a range of in-plant control measures and waste water treatment units that can meet the following effluent criteria: suspended solids, oil and biological oxygen demand (BOD_5) of 0.012 kg, 0.004 kg and 0.012 kg respectively, per tonne of crude processed. Major air pollutants emitted in a refinery are hydrocarbons, oxides of nitrogen, sulphur oxides, carbon monoxide and particulates. In addition, minor quantities of pollutants such as ammonia and aldehydes may emanate from catalyst regeneration units. Polynuclear aromatics, including benzo-a-pyrene, are found in flue gases.

Hydrocarbon emissions were reduced at distribution points by discontinuing splash loading and following the practice of bottom loading rail and road tankers. For bulk storage of products in the 0.1 to 0.76 bars absolute range in tank farms, hydrocarbon losses were minimized by tanks with floating roofs.

The solid wastes produced in a refinery include catalyst fines from cracking units, coke fines, iron sulphide, filtering media, and sludges from tank cleaning operations, oil-water separators, and biological oxidation processes. Two major options are available for their disposal: incineration is more prevalent. Sludges, emulsion and caustic wastes are stored in separate tanks and pumped to the incinerator where they are burned in the fluid-bed at about 700°C. Spent catalysts that are not worth processing for recovery of valuable components are generally disposed of in secured land-fills.

During the 1970s, much attention was given to means of reducing oil discharges from production platforms and ships. Under the Paris Convention (1974), the maximum permitted concentration of oil in water discharged from platforms was reduced from 100 parts per million (ppm) to 10 ppm. Oil spill contingency plans were adopted nationally, and linked by regional international agreement.

The *iron and steel industry*, in common with many others, found retro-fitting pollution abatement equipment to existing plants to be unsatisfactory. Faced with increasingly stringent standards for pollution control, many manufacturers found it advantageous to re-design their plants or build new ones so as to incorporate improved and profitable techniques. Indeed, manufacturers often may realize economic as well as environmental advantages from making better use of raw materials, reducing coke consumption, recycling water and re-using waste materials, such as slags, in the manufacture of building material.

Dust extraction plants associated with basic oxygen furnaces largely eliminated the steelwork's traditional brown smoke, but some highly toxic fumes were still released. Open storage and transport of dusty materials, such as iron ore, coal, coke and the fluxes needed for iron and steel manufacture, can release wind-blown particulate matter. Careful handling and storage, in moist conditions, reduced the wind-borne drift of fine ore to about 10 kg/t of material stored, even where no spray plant is installed. Gas-cleaning devices installed in the sintering process reduced dust content in discharged gas to less than 150 milligrams per cubic metre (mg/m³). Sulphur oxides formed from sulphur contained in coke fines is also discharged from sintering. Gas de-sulphurization plants need further development to become more economic and efficient.

Water is an essential raw material in iron and steel manufacture. In an integrated mill, the requirement is about 80–200 tonnes per tonne of crude steel. However, since only about 3 tonnes of water per tonne of crude steel are lost, mostly by evaporation, it was possible to reduce the demand to a figure far below the total requirement (IISI, 1978).

The iron and steel industry increasingly used scrap metal in the classical steel-making process and in mini-steel mills using electric arc furnaces. This brought both gains and complications. Recycling by-passes the coking, sintering and blast furnaces stages, but it brings its own environmental hazards, particularly for the workforce. Many of these problems could be solved by cleaner scrap, or its pretreatment. From an environmental point of view, the direct reduction approach to iron production offers certain advantages. It eliminates blast furnace and coking emissions and polluting discharges. However, there is little energy advantage compared with the classical route and direct reduction requires a high-grade quality ore. Natural gas is normally used as the reducing agent and this process was of particular interest where there is an abundance of cheap gas. Also, the direct reduction process enabled economically viable steel production on a smaller scale than the blast furnace route.

In the *manufacture of aluminium* by the reduction process, apart from very high energy use, the process forms toxic fumes, in particular fluorides and carcinogenic tars. Emissions are controlled with electrostatic precipitators and wet and dry scrubbers, and by 1980 the goal for new plants was to allow no more than 1 kg of combined gaseous and particulate fluoride to be emitted per tonne of aluminium produced. Improved production techniques significantly reduced power consumption in the reduction process to an average of 16,400 kilowatt-hours per tonne (kWh/t) and a number of plants were consuming less than 13,700 kWh/t (OECD, 1976), but large capital investment will be required. There is also a tendency for a major shift towards the construction of Prebake rather than Söderberg pots, encouraged by an approximate energy saving of 500 kWh/t and more effective installation of collection and cleaning equipment. In general, the aluminium sector did not find it economically feasible to retrofit adequate pollution abatement equipment to old smelters. Within the working environment of the smelter, in addition to dealing with occupational hazards caused by fluorides, sulphur oxides, dust, heat, and noise, public authorities and the industry were increasingly concerned over polycyclic hydrocarbon emissions.

Aluminium is made by smelting alumina obtained mainly from bauxite. The bauxite residues, from alumina extraction, commonly referred to as "red mud", are generally pumped to ponds or artificial lakes for settling and recovery of some caustic soda. Some authorities were concerned that pond drainage might contaminate ground-water. As it is, such ponds create an ever-growing wasteland around alumina plants, and if the industry expands its activities as projected by the middle of the next century, the volume of residues to be dealt with will have increased some five-fold. Some countries permit dumping red mud at sea under specified conditions. However, this practice was meeting with increasing disfavour by the end of the decade, and this, coupled with the increasing scarcity of resources, provided an incentive to research on new technologies for improved utilization of bauxite residues.

In the *nickel industry*, nitrogenous compounds in mine water and the mine atmosphere are increased when ores are fractured by using a mixture of fuel oil and ammonium nitrate rather than dynamite. Atmospheric concentrations are minimized by ventilation. However, no satisfactory method is available at present to remove nitrogen from mine water. The discharge of this effluent to receiving waters is causing some concern. The nutrient effect of the added nitrogen can be minimized if the receiving stream flow is high enough and dilutes the effluent. Usually the nitrogen content of mine water discharge does not exceed 50 milligrams per litre (mg/1) (Lemmon, 1981). Large volumes of water are required in milling and flotation, and amount to some $3,800 m^3$ per thousand tonnes of ore. The practice of recycling most of the tailings water in order to conserve fresh water and minimize contamination of public waters is now almost universally adopted by the industry. The thiosulphate formed in milling and concentration was successfully treated by allowing sufficient retention time of the waste solutions in an impounded disposal area, where proper conditions of temperature, sunlight, surface exposure and sulphur-oxidizing bacteria oxidize the thionates and polythionates to sulphuric acid. The resulting acid water is neutralized with lime or limestone before discharge. The problem of dusting of fine tailings was a serious one. However, it is now coming under control through wetting the active areas and through re-vegetation of the worked-out areas, forming a green park-like appearance in contrast to the barren, dusty areas of former years. A good vegetation cover will also stabilize tailing basins and prevent acid seepage.

Sulphur oxide emission control is much more complex than particulate emission control, involving the use of expensive treatment plants. Several types of control systems are available but each is limited in the types of off-gas it can handle. Many of the high-volume, low SO_2 — content gas streams from multi-hearth roasters, blast furnaces, and reverb furnaces cannot be handled economically. Development work is continuing on wet scrubbing processes to handle these gases using regenerative and non-regenerative systems. These processes are only in their infancy, and more research and development work is required before they will be suitable for adoption. In order to fix weak SO_2 streams, reduce energy costs and improve working conditions, many smelters changed smelting processes. They include fluid-bed roasters, electric furnaces, flash smelters and continuous smelting.

In the *lead-zinc industry,* water plays an essential role in mining, smelting and processing. Recycling water, especially in arid regions, was the preferred method of pollution control and water conservation. In areas where acid mine drainage is a problem, water is collected and treated prior to recycle or discharge. Where economically possible, many mines preferred to return most of the tailings underground to fill the empty spaces left by slope and cut-and-fill operations. This also overcomes many environmental problems associated with surface disposal. A major concern with surface disposal of lead-zinc tailings was the leachate from tailing ponds. It contains potentially hazardous wastes. In the United States the recommended best available technology was for zero discharge by means of total recycle and impoundment of process water. To achieve this, the segregation and treatment of mine water from process water might be necessary at some locations.

Dust control is important in and around underground or surface mines, and at tailing disposal areas. Dust may be controlled by water or other materials. Once exploratory drilling has been completed, access roads are re-surfaced and sites re-vegetated. Most mines employed extensive ventilation systems. Where possible, water was used as a wetting agent and collected by a drainage system to some central location where the particulate was settled out prior to water re-use for pumping from the mine. Some mines also employed initial grinding or crushing operations underground where mine or surface water was used to control dust during these operations. Dust from tailing heaps was reduced by retaining vegetation and rocks in meadows, through replanting programmes and by using shelter belts and lath fences.

Lead emissions from primary lead smelting include lead-bearing fumes and particulates from manufacturing processes as well as fugitive emissions from concentrate storage, handling, material transfer and leaks. The preparation of lead concentrate for sintering requires careful dust control. Concentrate can be moved via an enclosed conveyor system to control fugitive emissions, and its moisture is maintained around 8 per cent for ease of handling. Wet scrubbers or other collector devices may be employed at transfer points to collect dust for recycling. In sintering, the equipment could be operated with weak gas re-circulation to produce a single strong SO_2 stress acid feed. Particulate, metal vapour, and SO_2 emissions are controlled via the use of electrostatic precipitators, wet scrubbers and acid plants. Wet scrubbers however, represent a potential source of water pollution and require neutralization treatment. Fugitive emissions from sintering can be controlled by good housekeeping, maintenance of equipment and careful monitoring. Adequate ventilation and gas cleaning systems are employed to collect process fumes and dust.

At present, all primary lead smelters employ pyrometallurgy since it represents the least costly and least energy-intensive extractive method. The future of such technology was questioned on account of costs of environmental controls. Much of the current pyrometallurgical practice, according to Kellog (1979), is obsolete because it was designed before environmental control and energy conservation were dominant design criteria.

Sulphur oxides and particulate matter can be simultaneously removed from primary smelters by collecting the strong waste-gas stream containing SO_2 in concentrations sufficient for economic conversion to sulphuric acid or sulphur, or by blending into acid plant gas or process modification. However, metal-laden particulate matter and metallic vapour must be removed first.

During lead processing, a host of certain minor metals may also be recovered. Some of these, such as gold and silver, represent a valuable metal co-product. Other elements, such as arsenic, bismuth, cadmium, and thallium may contribute to environmental problems. The environmental impacts and controls in the extraction and production of lead, zinc and cadmium were reviewed recently by Wixson (1981).

Several other major industries with considerable environmental impacts are discussed elsewhere. Motor manufacturing is considered in Chapters 13 and 14. The environmental effects of agricultural chemicals are discussed in Chapter 7. The agro-industry also provides excellent opportunities for residue utilization, discussed there and in Chapter 12.

A Cross-sectoral Overview

THE ten years after Stockholm saw industry, on both an individual and sectoral basis, make a considerable effort to improve its effluent discharge and its working environment. Part of the improvement was in response to government pressure but much of the effort was linked with increases in production efficiency. Contamination monitoring within the factory and outside became more thorough, as did testing for toxicity, especially of products for human consumption. Nevertheless, considerable problems remained. One was the cost of retro-fitting pollution abatement equipment to old plants which can be prohibitive and may lead to closing down factories, thus exacerbating the growing problem of sectoral or local unemployment and economic recession. Another was keeping down environmental concentrations of potentially toxic substances, whether they arise from factory effluents or consumer products such as lead in petrol, when overall production and consumption were on the increase.

Noise, to which industry was only one contributor, became a major pollutant of the human environment and was on the increase as, for example, traffic volume went up. At an OECD Conference on Noise Abatement Policies, held in Paris in 1980, it was pointed out that 100 million people of the OECD member countries are exposed to daytime outside noise levels considered to be at the upper limit of acceptability (see also UNEP, 1979).

The range of chemical substances produced in industry rose enormously (Table 11–1). As many as 60,000 were on the market by the end of the decade, with up to 1,000 new chemicals appearing each year. In the petrochemical industry, production of synthetic material increased some 350 times since 1940. Quantities of by-products, intermediates and residues are produced in these processes (see, UNEP, 1978 for a discussion on chemicals and the environment).

The pressure for tighter controls on industry — a feature of virtually all countries today — and the mounting costs of compliance with waste disposal regulations, provided an incentive for the use of production residues. But many industrial processes cannot be made totally waste-free, and communities are faced with the need to choose the least damaging and most economic procedures. Sometimes conflicts can arise even when these choices have been made carefully on what appears to be sound environmental and economic logic.

The location of new power plants in rural areas and the adoption of the "tall stack" policy for them and for other industries, contributed to a major reduction in sulphur oxides concentration near the ground, with clear benefits to human health. But there is now concern over the environmental impact of those sulphur oxides washed out in rain at great distances from their points of origin (Chapters 2, 4 and 6). De-sulphurization is costly (especially if retro-fitted to existing plant) and can itself generate slurries of calcium sulphate or solid wastes which require disposal. Washing of power plant plumes is liable to produce acid drainage capable of causing pollution if discharged to rivers. The optimal solution (only applicable to new plants) may be difficult to determine, but might include fluidized-bed combustion, which permits sulphur removal while increasing energy efficiency, or pre-treatment of fuel to remove sulphur (OTA, 1978; Robinson, 1980; Chapter 12). Similar difficult tradeoffs between alternative processes and end-residues arise in many other sectors of industry.

ENVIRONMENTALLY SOUND AND APPROPRIATE TECHNOLOGY

In these and other ways it was demonstrated that industry might be able to reduce its damaging emissions to the environment by adopting, in various combinations, processes and materials that generate fewer potentially damaging substances, better techniques for recovering such substances from liquid and gaseous emissions prior to discharge, and new means of utilizing and re-cycling production residues. The solution adopted inevitably depends on assessment of the harm likely to be done from an emission or discharge (its damage cost), balanced against the benefits the industry producing it confers on the community and the cost of control. If the risk of severe damage is evidently great, stringent controls will be demanded. In less extreme circumstances, the aim will be to introduce controls at an acceptable cost to the consumers, who generally have to pay for environmental protection measures adopted by industry through higher product prices. Improved technologies, giving less pollution at less cost, are clearly important and governments have a role in supporting research and development in this area.

It was recognized by UNIDO and UNEP, as well as by numerous industrial groups, that if the Lima target for industrialization by the year 2000 was to be achieved without environmental degradation, innovative action would be required on a large scale in finding and applying environmentally-sound and appropriate technology. The UNIDO General Conference in 1980 emphasized that the concept of environmentally-sound and appropriate technology was not a narrow, purely economic concept of appropriateness based solely on the capital and labour endowments of a country or region. A three-dimensional view was called for in which the environmental and social dimensions are as important as the economic ones.

The case for such technologies, particularly in developing countries, was not built upon a rejection of industry and the process of industrialization as such; indeed these were agreed to be essential to future prosperity. It was obvious that a great deal could be learned from the successes and failures of industrialization in the developed countries, alongside the simple traditional technologies of the developing world. Six criteria were proposed for selecting environmentally sound and appropriate technologies (Reddy, 1979). These are based on basic human needs and on resource, cultural, societal, human and environmental developments. They began to be applied in a variety of situations.

LOW- AND NON-WASTE TECHNOLOGY

The generally agreed and very broad definition of non-waste technology, as determined by the Economic Commission for Europe (ECE) is "the practical application of knowledge, methods and means, so as — within the needs of man — to provide the most rational use of natural resources and energy, and to protect the environment". In essence, low-waste technology minimizes the creation of harmful wastes, from the extraction of raw materials through the lifetime of consumer goods. It is a "preventive" strategy as distinct from the "corrective" approach, which aims to treat wastes at the end of the manufacturing process, once the product and its consequent wastes have been produced. Experience accumulated during the decade suggested that in many circumstances it is more efficient and less expensive to incorporate pollution preventive measures than corrective techniques.

The proceedings of the ECE (1979) Seminar on "Non-Waste Technology and Production" held in Paris in 1976, include a detailed account, with case studies, of national experiences and policies on the state of non-waste technologies. Thereafter, the ECE, with UNEP's support and the active collaboration of national focal points, began compiling a compendium of promising examples, some of which are set out in Table 11–4. In 1979, ECE adopted, *inter alia,* a declaration concerning low-waste and non-waste technology, and re-utilization and recycling of wastes. This listed ways and means for the application of such technologies and recommendations for national actions and international co-operation, and proposed the creation of a scientific and technical body to deal with such matters.

Because industrial development will continue for a long time to be an important source of wastes notwithstanding these new technologies, it was important to devise methods of re-using waste as secondary raw materials. With this in mind the USSR Government in 1980 published a special decree entitled "On Measures to Further Improve the Use of Secondary Raw Materials in the National Economy", including a system of measures to encourage action by all ministries and departments. An example of the intended action was in the reprocessing of iron furnace slags. The slags are used to produce more than 30 million tonnes of portland cement and other construction materials annually, at an estimated saving of 200 million roubles.

Another example of non-effluent systems in the USSR was the use of closed water circulation schemes in areas where water is scarce or the self-cleansing capacity of rivers is exhausted. The process consists of closed systems for plants, industrial complexes and regions, making use of all material resources and purifying water for re-use. In 1975 the USSR chemical industry recycled 80 per cent of its water. Between 1975 and 1980 total chemical output increased by 76 per cent but the total consumption of fresh water remained at the 1975 level. Within the industry water consumption in producing ammonia was reduced from 32 to 8 m^3/t, and in producing nitric acid from 10 to 0.3 m^3/t. Phosphoric acid production needs for water were reduced twenty-fold. Further examples of the range of technologies that were applied in France are presented in Table 11–5.

Industry is critically involved at all stages of the recycling chain. First, product design and composition is an important factor in efficient recycling: most products were

Table 11.4.   Some Examples of Low- and Non-Waste Technologies

Industry	Traditional Process and Problems	Alternative
Pulp and Paper	*Bleached kraft pulp mills* Water-polluting effluent from wood room, unbleached pulp washings, spent cooking liquor evaporation for condensation and bleach plant.	Rapson process developed in Canada (Rapson, 1977) uses bleach plant effluent and evaporator condensates for pulp washing and in preparing cooking liquor, thus passing chemicals from bleach process to pulping chemical recovery cycle, where organic matter is burned and spent bleaching chemical is recovered as sodium chloride. This is then dissolved and causticized to form liquor for reuse in pulping. All process water from bleach process thus passes through chemical recovery and all chlorine is recovered as sodium chloride. Pulp yield and quality are also improved.
Chemical	*Nitric acid production* Waste gases containing nitrogen oxides.	Process developed in Netherlands (de Reeder, 1980) uses high-pressure acid-resistant steel equipment, recovering more of the oxides as nitric acid, reducing waste gases and greatly reducing energy demand as the reactions used in the new process release heat.
Metallurgical	*Copper Smelting* Traditionally in reverberatory furnace, generating a gas containing sulphur dioxide	New furnace system developed in USSR (UNIPROMED, 1980) blows drier ore concentrate into oxygen-enriched furnace atmosphere. Sulphur combustion generates heat, reducing energy demand. SO_2 – rich (up to 80%) combustion gases recovered as sulphuric acid. Energy consumption reduced.

Source: UNEP

not designed with economic recycling in mind. Products can also be made with fewer materials in the first place, or made to last longer, in some instances with overall increases in cost, but with net gains. Second, through choice of appropriate processes and technologies, waste production in the manufacturing process can be reduced. Third, the reclamation industry in many countries may in itself be profitable and thereby is responsible for a major part of the recovery of waste materials. And finally, the manufacturing industry completes the cycle and makes the basic decisions on whether to use virgin materials or recovered secondary materials. Table 11–6 provides illustrative summaries. Other examples could be drawn from agricultural residues, chemical wastes,

Table 11–5. Costs and Benefits of Non-Waste Technologies (Examples from France)

Process	Company	Cost of operating conventional or destructive pollution control process (French Francs)	Profit of alternative recovery process (French Francs)
Recovery of hydrocarbon in an oil refinery	Raffinerie Flf Feyzin (Rhone)	Investment: nil Operating costs: 2,438,000	Investment: 11,000,000 Operating costs: 2,644,000 Sales of recovered product: 8,000,000 Gross operating profit: 5,356,000
Recovery of Methionine mother liquor by evaporation	Société Alimentaire Equilibrée de Commentry (Allier)	Investment: 9,600,000 Operating costs: 960,000	Investment: 7,000,000 Operating cost: 10,500,000 Sale of recovered product: 13,000,000
Recovery of protein and potassium from a yeast factory	Société Industrielle de la Levure Fala (SILF), Usine de Strasbourg (Bas-Rhin)	Investment: 10,800,000 Operating costs: 1,080,000	Investment: 5,200,000 Operating costs: 860,000 Sale of recovered product: 1,015,500 Gross operating profit: 155,500
Recovery of lead and tin from furnace fumes	Société des Alliages d'Etain et Derives, Montreuil (Seine-Saint Denis)	Investment: nil Operating costs: nil Sale of recovered product: 4,400 Profit: 4,400	Investment: 300,000 Operating costs: 200 Sales of recovered product: 8,930 Gross operating profit: 8,730
Conversion of phosphoric acid waste into plasterboard	Rhone Progil, Les Roches de Condrieu (Isère),Rouen (Seine-Maritime)	Investment: 9,000,000 Operating Costs: 5,000,000	Investment: 35,000,000 Operating costs: 73,000,000 Sales of recovered product: 73,500,000
Water recycle in fiberboard plant	Isorel, Castel jaloux (Tarn-et-Garonne)	Investment: 5,000,000 Operating costs: 500,000	Investment: 2,500,000 Operating costs: 100,000 Sales of recovered product: 350,000 Gross operating profit: 250,000

Table continued.

Table 11–5. Costs and Benefits of Non-Waste Technologies (Examples from France) — contd.

Process	Company	Cost of operating Conventional or destructive pollution control process (French Francs)		Profit of alternative recovery process (French Francs)	
Recycle of effluents in glue and gelatine manufacture	Société des Establissements Georges Alquier Bout-du Pont-de-l'Ain, Mazamet (Tarn)	Investment: Operating costs:	534,000 53,000	Investment: Operating costs: Reduced consumption of chemicals and sale of recovered product: Gross operating profit:	248,000 — 18,000 18,000
Recovery of iron dust in steel works	Sacilor, Gandrange, (Moselle)	Investment: Operating costs:	3,700,000 1,850,000	Investment: Operating costs:	9,800,000 3,250,000
Recovery of plum juice	Establissements Laparre Castelnaud de Gratecombe (Lot-et-Garonne)	Investment: Operating Costs:	768,000 77,000	Investment: Operating costs: Sale of recovered product: Gross Operating profit:	235,000 140,000 247,500 107,500
Recovery of glycerine in a soap factory	Savonnerie de Lutterbach (Haut-Rhin)	Investment: Operating costs:	600,000 60,000	Investment: Operating costs: Sale of recovered product: Gross operating profit:	400,000 101,700 280,000 178,300
Recovery of quarry washings	Société d'Exploitation de l'Entreprise Mirsaint-Lary (Hautes-Pyranées)			Investment: Operating costs: Sale of recovered product: Gross operating profit:	188,000 3,200 11,000 7,800

Source: Ministère de l'Environnement et du Cadre de vie, France (1978).

Table 11.6. Some Examples of Recycling and Residue Utilization in Industry

Industry	Process	Traditional Method	Alternative Method and Benefits
Leather	Tanning	Use of trivalent chromium sulphate producing about 5 kg/m^3 of chromium in effluent.	(a) Treatment of effluent with magnesium oxide, yielding insoluble chromium hydroxide. This reduces chromium in effluent by 99% followed by: (b) Regeneration of hydroxide by solution in sulphuric acid producing chromium sulphate for re-use.
Motor Tyre	Disposal of scrap tyres	Combustion or dumping in landfill	(1) Pyrolysis to gas or oil (2) Carbon black recovery (3) Reclamation of rubber and use in rubber mats (4) Artificial marine reefs and breakwaters.
Agricultural	Intensive livestock or crop production	Combustion of crop residues. Spreading of slurry on land, with risk of pollution of watercourses.	Anaerobic digestion to methane (biogas) (Chapter 12) also giving nutrient-rich liquid effluent suitable as fertilizer.
Iron and steel (blast furnace)	Slag	Dumping	Use as aggregate in construction, as concrete additive, as fine-ground raw material for blast furnace cement.

Source: UNEP.

glass, ferrous metals, mining wastes, non-ferrous metals, plastics, paper, and textiles. In order to encourage and promote more recycling and residue utilization, consideration must be given to institutions, logistics, markets, technologies and incentives. Information should be available on the type of wastes involved, their quality and quantity, when and where they were produced and whether seasonally or all year round. The keys to successful residue utilization are a beneficial use, an adequate market, suitable technology to process the residue under local conditions, and an overall enterprise that is socially and economically feasible. Such enterprises can also bring the benefits of increased employment opportunities and increased local or regional food supplies.

ALTERNATE RESOURCE USE

Scarce resources can be conserved by substituting other more abundant types of resources for them. There are few industrial materials for which there is only one substitution option. For example, minerals are substituted for wood in construction materials: natural rubber is substantially replaced by synthetic rubber; and non-wood, waste paper or hardwoods are substituted for softwoods in pulp manufacturing. Decisions about substitution generally depend on economics. The necessity to consider substitution intensified with the increase in crude oil prices in the 1970s. Besides causing an increase in prices of other resources the oil crisis drew attention to the finite nature of many basic minerals and the vulnerable position of countries that depended on one kind. The choice of resources to be used in the production of a material is based on the quantity and quality of their long-term supply potential, the economics of exploitation, manufacture and use, the energy that must be added to convert them to useful form, environmental impacts and many other social and institutional factors. A substitution strategy does not necessarily imply the total substitution of one form of resource for another, as in the case of energy. A few examples are given in Table 11–7.

Table 11–7. Examples of Substitution of Resources

Industry	Traditional Resource	Alternative Resource
Pulp and paper	Wood	Straw, bagasse (sugar cane waste), bamboo, hemp, reeds. Reed is used in Romania to produce paper, cellophane, cardboard, synthetic fibres, blocks and compressed fibreboard. Alcohol, fuels, insulation material and fertilizer can also be made.
Aluminium	Bauxite Ores	Nepheline-syenite, and alunite ores. Pre-treatment with lime or acid needed and costs exceed traditional Bayer process for bauxite, but residual solid wastes can be used to make cement and construction materials, potentially removing disposal problems with bauxite residues.
Fertilizers	Synthetic fertilizer	Use of agricultural, municipal and some industrial organic wastes as partial substitute.

Source: UNEP.

Changes in Economic and Political Factors

ACCOMPANYING and closely linked with the improvements in industrial technologies were shifts in the policies adopted by public agencies in coping with pollution and in guiding decisions on industrial location and design. These policies and practical measures included regulations involving standards and norms, economic incentives and dis-incentives, and criteria for location and for environmental impact assessment. Basic to much of this action was understanding of the economic factors affecting the adoption and maintenance of suitable technologies. Underlying many of the standards was mounting scientific evidence concerning the effects of specific waste substances on human health (Chapter 10) or ecosystems (Chapter 7).

ECONOMIC ASPECTS OF ENVIRONMENT INVESTMENT

As indicated in Chapter 1, in the days immediately preceding and following the Stockholm Conference, economic development and preservation of the environment were considered by some to pose a dilemma. Environmental issues inevitably have their economic components. Whenever environmental legislation and standards are proposed, questions are asked whether they will cause inflation, increase costs and prices, generate unemployment, bring about plant closures or discourage new investment. Others argue that environmental investments may generate employment and strengthen the resource base of national economies. It sometimes appears that environmental regulations, or any other governmental action, are judged by only one narrow national economic goal — lower prices. As the decade advanced more evidence accumulated concerning the economic aspects of environmental investment and the merits of possible public measures. UNEP (1981) reviews much of this evidence.

Although some estimates were made of changes in production costs owing to environmental regulations, they were not well documented, and comparative studies of changes in different countries were particularly inconclusive. Difficulties in estimation arose because some calculations only included direct costs, and others direct and indirect, and there were other statistical variations. A uniform industrial classification was not adopted. Koo et al. (1979) summarized percentage price increases in the United States due to pollution control (Table 11–8). The estimated price increases varied greatly. Koo et al. suggested that the measured costs of pollution control were possibly upwardly biased, because the input-output computation overstates the cost by not considering input coefficient changes in response to environmental control standards and costs. Moreover, the studies included cost increases in major polluting industries, but excluded any cost savings conferred through increased industrial productivity. A recent report by OECD suggested that the negative effects of environmental regulations on rate of growth were likely to be small, and that overall costs of pollution control measures in developed market economy countries were of 0.75 – 2.0 per cent of GNP (OECD, 1979 a).

Environmental regulations were seen to confer substantial societal benefits including a healthier environment, the employment stimulated through the creation of jobs in the pollution control equipment industry and jobs for those who operate and maintain this equipment. For example, the EAJ (1976) reported that according to the Japan Industrial Machinery Association, orders received in 1972 for pollution control

Table 11–8. Percentage Price Increase in The U.S.A. Due To Pollution Control

	1963 Total	1968–70 Total
Food and related products	1.0	1.0
Steel	2.2	2.2
Paper and paper products	0.4	2.3
Petroleum refining	0.2	4.6
Cement	1.3	–
Primary ferrous metals	–	2.2
Primary non-ferrous metals	1.2	3.1
Leather tanning	0.2	1.4

Source: Koo et al. (1979).

equipment amounted to 270 billion Yen. In 1977, private and government orders increased to 418 billion Yen.

Considerable resources were devoted to pollution control in a number of countries. These included one-time measures for the correction of previously unsatisfactory conditions. In Japan, Iijima (1980) reported that, in 1974, steel, petroleum, thermal power, pulp and paper and chemical industries had a combined capital investment of US$3.3 billion to meet environmental regulations. The investment of these five industries represented approximately 70 per cent of the total investment in environmental preservation by the private sector. For the United States, Gamse and Wood (1978) reported that in 1975, US$5.6 billion, or 5.8 per cent of all industrial plant and equipment investment, was for pollution control. Six capital-intensive basic industries accounted for 77 per cent of all industrial pollution control capital spending, which represented about 13 per cent of their total plant and equipment investment. The industries were electric utilities, steel, non-ferrous metals, pulp and paper, petroleum refining and chemicals. These six industries also accounted for about three-quarters of the energy consumed by all manufacturing. Gamse and Wood showed that on the basis of rough estimates of action needed to meet effluent requirements during the 1975–85 period the electrical utilities would allocate 10.5 per cent of their total expenditure on plant and equipment to pollution control, the chemical industry 11 per cent, pulp and paper 25 per cent, and petroleum refining 25 per cent (in comparison to 22 per cent in preceding years). The American Iron and Steel Institute (AISI, 1980) estimated that between 1966 and 1978, the American steel industry spent 13.1 per cent of its capital expenditure on pollution abatement (US$3.7 billion out of a total of US$28.1 billion). In 1978, the pollution abatement figure was as high as 18 per cent of the total. In an eight year period from 1970, the Japanese steel industry invested about US$5 billion on environmental controls, which accounted for about 15 per cent of the industry's total plant and equipment investment for the same period (Iijima, 1980).

The International Iron and Steel Institute (IISI, 1979) undertook a three year study among its members to assess how much the installation of pollution abatement equipment to meet environmental regulations increased electricity consumption. It concluded that for an integrated steel plant, an average of 45 kWh/t of crude steel is onsumed. However, for three of the plants surveyed, the consumption was more than 120 kWh/t of crude steel, a level the IISI considered to become more general if more stringent regulations are applied.

In 1978, the US Council on Environmental Quality (CEQ) calculated that the total government and private expenditure on pollution control was US$47.6 billion or approximately US$215 per capita. Of this amount, only US$22.7 billion was in response to environmental legislation. The remainder would have been spent without it. This represented approximately a 12 per cent increase, corrected for inflation, over 1977. The central question of the extent to which benefits from these investments were commensurate with the costs was explored in a tentative manner. The CEQ estimated that the most reasonable figure for annual benefits realized in 1978 from measured improvements in air quality since 1978 was US$21.4 billion. Of this total, US$17 billion represented reduction in mortality and morbidity, US$2.0 billion reduced soiling and cleaning costs, US$0.7 billion increased agricultural output, US$0.9 billion prevention of corrosion and other material damage, and US$0.8 billion increases in property values. Another macroeconomic analysis sponsored by the CEQ and the Environmental Protection Agency (EPA) to determine the impacts of pollution control expenditure on economic growth, and likewise subject to considerable question on the suitability of the methods used, indicated that every dollar of pollution control expenditures displaced only 33 to 40 cents of other plant and equipment investment. The impact of pollution control programmes was believed to increase inflation rates by 0.0 to 0.4 per cent per year (Data Resources Inc., 1978).

In the USSR, Kolbassov (1979) reported that in 1978 two billion roubles of capital investments were allocated for environmental protection and conservation. In addition, it was reported that considerable capital investments were made for improvement of technological processes in industry to reduce environmental pollution.

A report by the US Secretary of Commerce indicated that in ten industrialized countries, as shown in Table 11–9, pollution control expenditure was within the range of 0.5 to 2 per cent of their respective GNPs. The OECD found that during the mid-1970s national resources allocated to pollution abatement were nowhere estimated to be higher than 1.7 per cent of GDP (OECD, 1979 a). These figures are, however, sensitive to the method of calculation used and the period considered. At the peak of investment Japan may have spent 7 per cent of GNP on environmental protection. If spread over the life of the plant, such figures are reduced substantially.

A key question in the late 1970s was whether there was a less expensive (or more cost-effective) way to accomplish environmental management objectives. With the world economy in recession, governments became increasingly interested in applying cost-benefit analysis to environmental matters. UNEP's 1979 analysis of the case studies supplied showed three common characteristics in that broad effort. First, no one format or definition described what constitutes a cost-benefit analysis of environmental management. It differs from one country to another and in the sectors covered. The approaches taken differ in the concern expressed for environmental considerations; in the underlying scale of values; in the depth and rigour of the research undertaken; in the scope of the system dealt with and in the period of time that should be considered. Second, nevertheless, the case studies showed a similar analytical approach. The great majority attempted to adapt, with different degrees of success, traditional economic methodologies, oscillating between microeconomics and welfare theory. New and innovative techniques of analysis for environmental economics were lacking. Accordingly, certain case studies concluded that, given the state of analytical tools and technical knowledge, a cost-effectiveness analysis is perhaps a more viable or feasible alternative than cost-benefit analysis. It is, however, possible to envisage situations where both tools could be used to complement each other. Third, costs are relatively more amenable to identification and quantification than are benefits resulting from environmental regulations. Notwithstanding the difficulties, an increasing number of countries attempted to estimate benefits or "damage costs" in terms of monetary values.

Table 11–9. Pollution Abatement costs In Ten Industrialized Countries

Country	Percentage of GNP	Period
United States	0.7–1	1973–1982
Belgium	1.0	1974
Canada	2.0	1974–1980
France	0.4	1974
Federal Republic of Germany	1.8*	1971–1975
Italy	0.6	1971–1975
Japan	1.2	FY 1973
Netherlands	0.5	1974
Sweden	1.0	1974
United Kingdom	1.0	1974

Source: USDC (1975).
*Government estimates for the FRG showed 1.0% for 1970–74, and 1.5% for 1975–79.

REGULATORY APPROACHES

Environmental laws and regulations are adopted and investment in pollution control technologies made in order to protect people and other "targets" from damage considered unacceptable by the communities concerned. Various instruments for obtaining the necessary degree of environmental quality were experimented with or applied during the 1970s. These.included principally: regulations, with accompanying standards and norms; a variety of economic incentives and dis-incentives; guidelines for industrial location and procedures for environmental impact assessment (itself a process of implied cost-benefit analysis). They were undertaken in a variety of combinations in relation to national, environmental and social conditions. Thus, some countries stressed regulations and relatively rigid standards. Others, such as Australia, relied principally on negotiation of voluntary agreements to persuade new enterprises to adjust location and process design to local circumstances and to provide monitoring and appropriate operational changes as the plant starts up.

In the CMEA countries, co-operation in environmental protection included multilateral efforts to solve international problems, and promotion of national measures in conservation, renewal and improvement of natural conditions. This was achieved through joint research in environmental protection, exchange of practical experience, mutual technical, economic and organizational assistance, and international division of labour. A 1979 environmental law in the countries of the socialist community had the following overall characteristics (Kolbassov, 1979):

(a) Fundamental propositions pertaining to society's care of the environment are written down in constitutions;
(b) Legal regulation of the social relations connected with man's action on the environment is ensured on all levels of the government structure — federal, republican, regional and local;
(c) Legal norm-setting for activities connected with environmental protection is accomplished through combinations of laws and by-laws concerning the regulation of conservation and protection of the basic natural elements — the earth, water, forests, flora and fauna, the atmosphere, space;
(d) Emphasis is placed on rules to avert negative changes in the environment, to eliminate existing deformations and to shape new development;
(e) Emphasis also is placed on the mobilization of the entire planning system of the socialist economy to achieve these aims.

The OECD Environment Committee was given the following mandate:

"The Environment Committee will be responsible for:
— examining on a co-operative basis common problems related to the protection and the improvement of the natural and urban environment with a view to proposing acceptable solutions to them, taking into account all relevant factors, in particular economic and energy considerations;
— reviewing and consulting on actions taken or proposed by Member countries in the environment field and assessing the results of these actions;
— providing Member Governments with policy options or guidelines to prevent or minimize conflicts that could arise between Member countries in the use of shared environmental resources or as the result of national environmental policies; the Committee may organize as appropriate, and with the agreement of the countries concerned, consultations to that effect, encouraging wherever appropriate, the harmonization of environmental policies among the Member countries."

One important aspect of regulations that received growing recognition during the decade was enforcement. It matters little how rigorous is the specified standard for an industry's effluents if the regulation is not enforced. Information on statutes or administrative rules are relatively easy to obtain and publish, but information on how these measures are enforced is difficult to come by. The crucial test in terms of environmental quality is how the air, water or soil, and the organisms dependant upon them, are affected.

STANDARDS

Of the different types of standards prescribed for industry, three were of particular relevance:

(a) Product Standards. These set levels of potential pollutants not to be exceeded in the composition of the product (e.g. the sulphur content of fuel oil, lead additives in gasoline), or defined criteria to be met (as for motor vehicle emissions or detergent biodegradability).

(b) Emission/Effluent Standards. These set levels of pollutants not to be exceeded in discharges to air or water. Restriction on the disposal of solid wastes, on noise and on radioactive emissions are similar;

(c) Environmental Quality Standards. These prescribe maximum acceptable concentrations, usually but not necessarily for a given medium — air, water, soil — in a geographical area, irrespective of the sources of discharges. If set following careful analysis of dose and effect, as in the WHO/UNEP Health Criteria Reports, meeting them should ensure the health of people and ecosystems in those areas.

Different countries promulgated different standards during the decade, according to the scientific data at their disposal, subjective judgement and socio-economic conditions. Some set national environmental quality objectives or standards; others relied on product and emission specifications to ensure adequate environmental conditions. Some applied uniform emission standards regardless of the condition of the receiving environment: others sought greatest stringency in the worst conditions but allowed the use of the dilution capacity of air and water elsewhere.

CONTROL MEASURES

By itself, a standard achieves nothing (except a statement of objectives). Effective environmental protection demands a regulatory (or fiscal) approach that ensures that standards are met.

Most governments during the 1970s relied on regulations — that is, the specification in a legally binding statutory instrument of the maximum tolerable emissions from an industry product or process, of the conditions a product was to fulfil or of the way an industrial process was to be conducted. Some placed reliance in some areas on authorized agencies to define these requirements from time to time, as technology advanced. The Alkali and Clean Air Inspectorate in the United Kingdom continued to apply the principle that industrial processes registered under the Alkali Works Regulation Act should adopt "best practicable means"; this being specified by the inspectors in the light of their technical judgement so as to safeguard public health and the environment by securing the maximum degree of pollution control obtainable at an acceptable cost. The latter qualification is important: a degree of control that bankrupts industry was not regarded as practicable within the terms of this definition.

During the decade the OECD adopted the "polluter pays" principle as a common policy. This states that an industry should bear the cost of meeting whatever standards and regulation the responsible government or international group has agreed should apply. In essence it is a no-subsidy policy, arguing that the consumers of a particular industrial product should pay a price for it that included whatever costs had to be incurred in ensuring that its manufacture did not create a hazard to non-consumers or damage to the wider environment.

The member countries of CMEA also joined together to develop multilateral solutions of international problems affecting industry. They adopted a programme of research, information exchange and technical assistance. In 1979 environmental law in the CMEA group had certain common characteristics, including both principles to ensure conservation and planning and regulations for environmental protection (Kolbassov, 1979).

In the developing countries, there was reluctance, at Stockholm and immediately after it, to apply stringent industrial pollution control standards and measures. However, a number of countries, particularly those in the middle income grouping, enacted and implemented legislation for pollution control. These were primarily focused on pollutants and pollutant parameters such as smoke, sulphur dioxide, biological oxygen demand, suspended solids, temperature and pH. Generally, the standards, criteria or norms used were those of the industrialized countries or were adapted from them. What differed were the legal and economic instruments used for enforcement. Towards the end of the 70s, a large and increasing number of developing countries were planning to implement, or were in the process of implementing, legislation on environmental protection, including industrial pollution control.

ECONOMIC MEASURES

Economic instruments provide, in market economies, an alternative to regulations and it has been argued that they are in principle more cost-effective, especially when combined with regulations that prohibit a polluter from exercising the freedom to pay and to discharge water to an extent that jeopardizes public health. The main economic instruments are:

(a) Taxes. Taxation on wastes in proportion to quantity and nature of substances discharged; on users of a resource (e.g. charge for right to discharge to a river in proportion to dispersal capacity used); or on products that have a negative effect on the environment (e.g. motor vehicles, non-biodegradable detergents). One way of giving effect to the polluter pays principle would be to charge an industry in proportion to the estimated potential damage of the wastes it releases.

(b) Subsidies. Used as an aid to relieve the polluter of all or part of the cost of the pollution control measures that must be taken to comply with regulations. The subsidy system has been criticized as lacking in incentives, as being inefficient and unfair, and because it goes against the polluter pays principle, yet subsidies are often employed in environmental policy. Indeed, in some countries industry undertook to abate pollution to "optimum" levels in return for the government sharing the expense. Undoubtedly subsidies can be of advantage in facilitating and speeding up the transitional period when implementing an environmental policy. These were used during the decade in numerous ways.

A recent use of economic incentive was the US EPA's so-called "offset policy", aimed at circumventing the dilemma caused by the non-attainment provisions in the Clean Air Act, which appeared to prohibit new growth in areas already in violation of the primary air quality standards. The policy proposed that new sources seeking to locate in such areas, or existing sources wishing to expand, be allowed to do so provided they obtain offsetting reductions in air pollution from existing sources. By creating a market for pollution and reductions in pollution, the policy was considered to ensure that discharge reductions would be undertaken by those who can do so most cheaply. In this way, it was considered that any given level of environmental quality would be maintained at the least social cost. Of the 45 cases examined in detail by the US Council for Environmental Quality in 1979, 60 per cent of the transactions involved hydrocarbon offsets, 7 per cent sulphur dioxide and 31 per cent particulates. The large majority of new sources desiring offsets were industries expanding existing facilities.

THE SCIENTIFIC FOUNDATION FOR STANDARDS AND REGULATIONS

Standards set to protect the health of people and ecosystems need to be based upon scientific evaluations of the relationship between dose (defined as the product of exposure and time) and effect; these relationships are termed criteria (Chapter 10). Where criteria are not yet established, it is difficult to translate incomplete findings into regulations. This is a problem experienced by industrialized countries, but especially acute in developing countries, with limited qualified manpower. The UNEP's International Register for Potentially Toxic Chemicals (IRPTC) and INFOTERRA Service were developed in part to meet this need.

In order to provide countries with a scientific basis for setting standards, the WHO in co-operation with UNEP initiated in 1973 a programme to develop environmental health criteria. The objectives of the programme are:

(a) To assess existing information on the relationship between exposure to environmental pollutants (or other physical and chemical factors) and man's health, and to provide guidelines for setting exposure limits consistent with health protection, i.e. to compile environmental health criteria documents;

(b) To identify new or potential pollutants by preparing preliminary reviews on the health effects of agents likely to be increasingly used in industry, agriculture, in the home or elsewhere;

(c) To identify gaps in knowledge concerning the health effects of recognized or potential pollutants or other environmental factors, to stimulate and promote research in areas where information is inadequate, and

(d) To promote the harmonization of toxicological and epidemiological methods in order to obtain research results that are internationally comparable.

OCCUPATIONAL HEALTH STANDARDS

The need to protect the occupational health of workers in industry was recognized more widely and appropriate standards were set as the concept of exposure limits for harmful substances evolved (Chapter 10). The concept of maximum allowable concentration — a level not to be exceeded — as well as other concepts such as time-weighted average and ceiling limits were applied where scientific data permitted. In view of the large number of special terms and the different ways in which they are sometimes understood, the ILO promoted use of the generic term "exposure limits". Convention No. 148 (concerning the "Protection of Workers Against Occupational Hazards in the Working Environment Due to Air Pollution, Noise and Vibration") adopted by the ILO General Conference in 1977, required the competent national authority to establish criteria for determining the hazards of exposure to air pollution, noise and vibration in the working environment, and where appropriate, to specify exposure limits on the basis of these criteria; required the competent authority to take into account the opinion of technically competent persons; and required that the criteria and exposure limits established be supplemented and revised regularly, taking into account as far as possible any increase in occupational hazards resulting from simultaneous exposure to several harmful factors at the workplace. As far as possible, under the Convention, the working environment is to be kept free from any hazard due to air pollution, noise or vibration by technical or supplementary organizational measures. Where the measures taken do not bring air pollution, noise and vibration within the limits specified, the employer is to provide and maintain suitable protective equipment and is not to require a worker to work without it. As with other regulations, the effectiveness of these occupational health prescriptions depended in large measure upon their acceptance by employers and their enforcement by the public authorities.

Environmental Considerations in the
Location of Industry

THE developing countries' effort to achieve fast industrial growth and their belief that poverty and underdevelopment were the major causes of environmental problems, may have given the impression that they were providing "pollution havens" to attract industries from industrialized countries faced with stringent standards and regulations. Most transnational corporations operate, however, in another country primarily for economic and market considerations. Operations are concentrated on richer countries and reflect the transnational corporations' preference for the larger and more profitable internal market or for exploiting natural resources. As countries develop, their attractiveness to transnational corporations increases. The major exception is when transnational corporations site affiliates and subsidiaries in export-platform countries as sources for their global systems. Labour and transport costs are more important in those cases than the size of the local market, and though this practice has increased recently, they still account for only a relatively small proportion of the affiliates and subsidiaries of transnational corporations. Data compiled by the United Nations Commission on Transnational Corporations (1978) showed that transnational corporations invested about one-quarter of their foreign assets in developing countries and that in recent years this proportion declined. The transnational corporations' investments in developing countries were concentrated in a few industries and in relatively few countries. In 1976, this amounted to approximately US$287 billion. Very roughly, one-quarter of the assets of transnational corporations was in extractive industries, one-quarter in services of all types, and one-half in manufacturing.

Although relocation of industries in developing countries is mainly based on economic grounds, there are examples which illustrate that relocation has been essentially due to environmental factors (UNEP, 1981). For example, there is a trend to locate new capacities of the Japanese aluminium industry abroad due to environmental considerations, together with the availability of raw materials and cheaper electric power in the host developing countries (Walter, 1975). Difficulties in finding environmentally-sound refinery sites have forced the petroleum industry to look abroad as well, particularly in Indonesia. In the United States of America, a trend is emerging towards relocation of industries producing asbestos, mercury, pesticides and other environmentally-hazardous substances (for example, asbestos factories have been installed in Mexico and Brazil) (Potier, 1979). There may indeed be instances where the relocation of polluting industries in developing countries may contribute to an increase in their GNP, but before this possibility is accepted as valid, the adverse effects of the pollution on other economic sectors and on human productivity need to be examined carefully (CEQ, 1980).

In order to enhance the decisions made in location of new industrial plants a number of general policies and guidelines were drawn up and promulgated at the international level. These sought to specify conditions that should be taken into account in locating a plant, and the procedures worth considering in carrying out an environmental impact assessment (EIA). The International Chamber of Commerce Executive Committee adopted in 1974 Environmental Guidelines for World Industry. One of the stated principles was that "industry recognized that land, air and water are permanent natural resources, which will be utilized for different purposes at different times, and must be protected for further uses. There is special need for better management of non-renewable resources, taking into consideration the interrelationship between environmental considerations and resource availability".

The choice of a site for an industrial project depends upon a wide range of factors. Certain sites may be preferable to the industrial developer insofar as they minimize transport costs for the materials and finished products and/or are located near to power, water and other essential services. Some sites may be preferable to the wider community in terms of the extent to which they may assimilate the environmental impact of particular industrial projects.

Four elements were distinguished as important in environmental site assessment. These are:

— a short list should be prepared of potential sites that offer a genuine choice in relation to the objectives both of the industrial developer and of the general community.
— the sites should be compared in terms of a common set of criteria that help assess the degree to which the impact can be absorbed without unnecessary environmental degradation.
— the assimilative capacity of each site should be related to possible measures of pollution abatement at the plant.
— the socio-economic impact should be estimated with consideration of how public expenditure on physical and social infrastructure may alleviate potentially undesirable effects. Some socio-economic effects, however, may be inevitable once a particular site is chosen.

The organization of non-waste industries makes it especially desirable to assure co-operation among different branches of the same industry at different sites or among several industries occupying contiguous sites. This led to increased attention to possible territorial and industrial complexes of the type developed in the USSR (Zaitsev and Tsygankov, 1979).

The physical environmental criteria that are normally taken into account when siting any plant whether individually or in a complex can be grouped under nine categories: climate and air quality, water, geology, soils, ecology, environmentally sensitive areas, land-use and land capability, noise and vibration, visual quality. The socio-economic environmental criteria can be categorized into population structure, population dynamics, land-use and settlement patterns, labour supply and employment structure, economic production and distribution, and income distribution and consumption. In the UNEP (1980) Guidelines each category of criterion is further divided into a number of sub-elements in screening tables.

ENVIRONMENTAL IMPACT ASSESSMENT

During the decade, formal environmental impact assessment of industrial projects became more important and in many cases a prerequisite for funding and approval. When EIAs were first undertaken the majority were focused primarily on physical impacts. Also, the results were presented in voluminuous statements and reports. EIAs were usually carried out after the project had been planned, designed and on the verge of construction. These factors combined to cast doubt on the necessity and utility of an EIA as well as to cause concern that it was delaying the industrialization process unduly and making construction more costly.

However, the concept of EIA was gradually accepted by a number of nations and financial agencies. It was recognized that by integrating and carrying out the assessment earlier in the planning and feasibility stage, unnecessary delays could be avoided, and alternative processes, raw materials, siting options, and so on, could be evaluated and their environmental impacts identified. Generation of alternatives gave a better basis for decision-making. Another evolution was the inclusion of socio-economic factors in the assessments. Certain countries have introduced what is termed a "scoping process" by which the scope of an EIA is delineated. This is an important step because it allows focussing of manpower and financial resources on areas considered to have a higher priority when conducting an EIA.

An increasing number of countries, both developed and developing, were incorporating and implementing EIAs in their industrial development plans and projects (ECE, 1979; Brandt Commission, 1980). The Declaration of Environmental Policies and Procedures Relating to Economic Development, adopted in New York on 1 February 1980 by the African Development Bank, the Arab Bank for Economic Development in Africa, the Asian Development Bank, the Caribbean Development Bank, the Inter-American Development Bank, the World Bank, the Commission of the European Communities, the Organization of American States, UNDP and UNEP, provided impetus for environmental impact assessments of industrial development projects.

Future Prospects

MANY activities since the Stockholm Conference either met the recommendations adopted at Stockholm or contributed towards their realization. Despite such achievements, important issues remained and require attention and resolution.

Very much at issue was how responsible and accountable industry should be for the use of manufactured products and their impact on health and the environment. Should it be held accountable for the misuse of products and their consequent effect on the environment? Or should industry build in safeguards to reduce environmental and health risks to the minimum or optimum extent possible when designing and manufacturing products? This notion of responsibility raises the related issue of who decides the acceptable levels of risks. Although much progress has been made towards a better understanding of health and environmental risks and the prevention of accidents in industry, improved tools for risk assessment and quantification are still needed. Confidentiality of proprietary information can sometimes lead to information relevant to objective decisions on acceptable risks being concealed. The challenge is to make that information available so that control of the use and disposal of products is achieved, thus protecting the environment and man, while still minimizing trade effects due to the divulgence of information.

Interactions between physical, environmental and socio-economic effects are often difficult to define and quantify, and the way in which they are analyzed has significant political consequences. Because of the deteriorating world economic situation, governments were finding it increasingly difficult to allocate scarce financial resources to the competing needs of education, health and housing, pollution control and environmental protection. Improved cost-benefit analysis tools are needed to assist governments and industry to determine cost and societal benefits so that equitable priorities can be assigned.

On the world scale inflation, recession, unemployment, increases in energy costs, manufactured goods and resources costs, balance of trade, debt repayment and interdependence between developed and developing countries were growing issues. Many models, predictions, scenarios and recommendations had been advanced to help anticipate changes in those aspects of industrialization. Generally, they can be divided into two categories. The first deals with national and international institutional aspects and includes the studies of Tinbergen (1976), Leontief et al. (1977), OECD (1979 b), UNIDO (1979 b) and the Brandt Commission (1980). The other category deals with the type of scientific, engineering, technical and sociological innovations that could be incorporated into industry. All the studies that deal with the institutional aspects of development have emphasized the need to balance and link the interests of developed and developing countries wherever a common denominator can be found. Indeed countries have more interests in common on a medium- and long-range basis than many have so far been able to recognize. The harmonious development of developing countries is in the long-term interest of the developed countries, given that such development plays a central role in their relations. The objectives and strategies of developed countries cannot be confined to purely national levels, and independent of the development of the rest of the world. The internationalization of industry constitutes one of the major aspects of interdependence.

The UNIDO *Industry—2000* study was based on the belief that the restructuring of the world economy requires the restructuring of world industry. Eight major proposals calling for new initiatives in international co-operation were presented: an international industrial finance agency, a commission for international industrial development law, a system for the resolution of industrial conflict, an international patent examination centre, and a manufacturing trade target.

The OECD's *Interfutures* study forsees that the interaction between industry and research, plus the complementarity between industry and services, will progressively alter the concept of industrial activity. Thus a new generation of impetus-giving industries will replace those that were responsible for post-war industrial growth. It also maintains that economic, ecological and cultural interdependence are likely to increase during the latter part of this century.

With regard to technologies for industry, the prospect for more performance at ever-decreasing cost augurs a potential shift in industrial structure. The motive power behind this is the rapid advance in semi-conductor technology, whereby the industry is on the threshold of producing very large integrated circuits. In telecommunications, for example, where digital technology is creating its own revolution, photons — which carry information in the form of light — are increasingly being used interchangeably with electrons, signalling the convergence of fibre optics and computer technology. In the factory, computer-aided manufacturing is already beginning to revolutionize such basic industries as automobile and steel manufacturing. The thrust is seen in decision-making machines in the form of micro-electronic computational power incorporated into products, machinery and industrial processes. Increasingly, such systems will be used to make products simpler, reducing the number of parts, thus using fewer resources and increasing their reliability.

Another change likely to have an impact on industry is in the use of materials. Composites such as polyamides reinforced with graphite, carbon, or plastics will be increasingly used; while metallic glasses, with their high strength and resistance to corrosion, and high-performance ceramics that could replace super alloys in heat engines, could replace traditional materials in fabrications and construction. The driving force in the development of these new materials is fuel costs and the desire for structural-weight reduction.

Another development is in the field of genetic engineering. Gene splicing techniques promise revolutionary breakthroughs in many areas of science and technology, including energy.

Another important but contrasting approach, as noted above, is the use of appropriate, simple and low-cost technologies that make good use of indigenous labour and local materials. Particularly in countries with a larger labour pool, such development may be attractive. The combination of appropriate technology with modern engineering concepts may lead to effective economic solutions for the region in question. The products of manufacture should also be aimed at satisfying the basic needs of the local population. Of particular concern in this regard is the fate of small and medium industries and local craftsmanship, which are important sources of employment. Such units often pollute without control: yet the cost of preventive or corrective measures may jeopardize their existence, and some form of financial and technical assistance may be necessary.

It is important that a broad type of environmental impact assessment be made of all strategies, plans and projects so as to enable potential impacts to be identified — including alternatives for resource- and energy-conservation measures. *The World*

Conservation Strategy (IUCN/UNEP/WWF, 1980) and the *Global 2000* Report's (CEQ, 1980) projections for food, fisheries, forests, non-fuel minerals, water and energy both emphasize the importance of conservation and environmental protection measures in order to enhance and maintain the regenerative capacity of resource bases. The challenge is to find out precisely how the industrial and conservation goals can be harmonized in specific areas.

Resource and energy conservation in industry can be achieved in a number of ways: recycling, residue utilization and low- and non-waste technologies, such as heat pumps and new processes (UNEP, 1978). The concept of producing more with less has been exemplified in a number of studies (see, for example, Leach *et al.* 1979).

The trend is toward conservation measures that enhance environmental quality as well as improve productivity of manufacturing processes. This can be seen in petroleum refineries where added conversion capacities extract more light products from crude; in system-closing in the pulp and paper industry so that excess water is minimized or eliminated; and in the use of double-contact processes in sulphuric acid plants which give higher yield while reducing the oxides of sulphur emitted.

The need for industry to take into account environmental and resource- and energy-conservation considerations has undoubtedly encouraged industrial innovation. Legislation to bring about better environmental management has promoted greater research and development efforts to seek technologies that are more conserving, less polluting and more efficient, and that generate a better environment for the plant worker. The need is to find solutions appropriate to prevailing socio-economic and ecological conditions.

In the last decade much information was published on environmental aspects of industry. This growing body of knowledge needs to be efficiently compiled, collated, stored, retrieved and disseminated to assist decision-making. It may be expected to take advantage of advances in electronics, computers and telecommunications.

The technological means exist for establishing a good communications infrastructure and for assisting countries in environmentally sound development. In developing countries particularly, telecommunications could make a significant contribution by minimizing and preventing the repetition of costly environmental mistakes and speeding up the transfers of sound technologies. Industry can be expected to achieve higher productivity using less resources, including energy and water. Research and development programmes should lead to more efficient manufacturing that utilizes residues and avoids discharging wastes. Great opportunities exist for replacing corrective with preventive technologies.

Governments can encourage such trends by insisting that industries integrate environmental concerns into industrial production. In the face of economic recession governments will be challenged to resist relaxation of their requirements and incentives for cleaner productive processes and for a better environment, whether in the factory or outside it.

References

AISI (1980), *Steel At The Cross Road: The American Steel Industry in the* 1980s, American Iron and Steel Institute, Washington, D.C.

Betts, J. L. and C. A. Allard (1979), *Pollution Abatement Trends for the Pulp and Paper Industry*, Industry and Environment Newsletter, 2,1; United Nations Environment Programme.

Boik, B. C. and L. R. Verney (1976), *Differential Investment and Operating Costs as a Factor of Materials Availability and Price*, Paper presented at Symposium on Materials Adequacy from Minerals – Scarce Raw Materials, August 1976, Atlantic City.

Brandt Commission (1980), *North-South: A Program for Survival*, MIT Press, Cambridge, Massachusetts.

CEQ (1980), *The Global* 2000 *Report to The President*, Council on Environmental Quality, Washington, D.C.

CMEA (1979), *Reports of Various Activities of Bodies of the CMEA in* 1978, Council For Mutual Economic Assistance, Moscow.

Data Resources Inc. (1978), *Macroeconomic Impacts of Federal Pollution Control Laws*, 1978 *Assessment*, Council on Environmental Quality, Washington, D.C.

EAJ (1976), *Quality of the Environment in Japan*, Environment Agency of Japan, Tokyo.

ECE (1977), *Air Pollution Problems of the Inorganic Chemical Industry; Proceedings of a Seminar*, Economic Commission for Europe, Env/Sem, 7/3, Geneva.

ECE (1979), *Seminar on Environmental Impact Assessment*, Economic Commission For Europe, Geneva.

Gamse, R. and D. Wood (1978), *The Economic Impact of Environmental Programmes on US Industry*, US/USSR Environmental Economics Symposium, US Depart. Commerce, Washington, D.C.

Iijima, K. (1980), *Environmental Control Measures in the Japanese Steel Industry*, Industry and Environment Newsletter, 3, 10, United Nations Environment Programme.

IISI (1978), *Environmental Control in the Iron and Steel Industry*, Intern. Iron and Steel Institute, Brussels.

IISI (1979), *Electricity Consumption in The Steel Industry for Protection of the Environment*, Intern. Iron and Steel Institute, Brussels.

IUCN/UNEP/WWF (1980), *World Conservation Strategy*, International Union for Conservation of Nature and Natural Resources, United Nations Environment Programme and World Wildlife Fund. IUCN, Gland, Switzerland.

Kellog, H. H. (1979), Pyrometallurgy: Outlook for the Future, In D. F. Kelsall and J. T. Woodcock (Editors), *Mineral Resources of Australia*, Australian Academy of Technological Sciences, Melbourne.

Kolbassov, O. (1979), The Development of the Socialist Law and Management in the Field of Environmental Protection, In *Environmental Protection in CMEA Member Countries*, Council for Mutual Economic Assistance, Moscow.

444

Koo, A. U. C. *et al.* (1979), *Environmental Repercussions on Trade and Investment,* A Study Prepared for International Labour Organization, Michigan State Univ., Intern. Business and Economic Studies.

Leach, G. *et al.* (1979), *A Low Energy Strategy for The United Kingdom,* International Institute for Environment and Development, Science Reviews, London.

Lemmon, W. A. (1981), *Environmental Aspects of the Nickel Industry, Paper Presented at the UNEP Workshop on the Environmental Aspects of Non-ferrous Metal Industry,* United Nations Environment Programme, Nairobi.

Leontief, W. *et al.* (1977), *The Future of the World Economy – A United Nations Study,* Oxford Univ. Press, New York.

OECD (1976), *Industrial Adaptation in the Primary Aluminium Industry,* Organization For Economic Cooperation and Development, Paris.

OECD (1979 a), *The State of the Environment in OECD Member Countries,* Organization For Economic Cooperation and Development, Paris.

OECD (1979 b), *Facing The Future – Report of the Interfutures Study,* Organization For Economic Cooperation and Development, Paris.

OTA (1978), *The Direct Use of Coal,* Office of Technology Assessment, U.S. Congress, Washington, D.C.

Paris Convention (1974), *Convention for the Prevention of Marine Pollution from Land-Based Sources.* Signed at Paris, 21 Feb. 1974. 13th Intern. Legal Materials, 352.

Potier, M. (1979), Les Implications Economiques de la Lutte contre la Pollution, *Annales des Mines,* August, 1979.

Reddy, A. K. N. (1979), *Technology, Development and the Environment: A Re-Appraisal,* United Nations Environment Programme, Nairobi.

Robinson, F. A. Editor (1980), *The Environmental Implications of Burning More Coal,* The Chemical Soc., London.

Seko, M. (1977), *The Asahi Chemical Membrane Chloro-Alkali Process,* The Chlorine Institute, 20th Chlorine Plant Managers Seminar, New Orleans, L.A.

Tinbergen, J. (1976), *Reshaping the International Order.* A Report to The Club of Rome. E. P. Dutton and Co., New York.

UN Commission on Transnational Corporations (1978), *Transnational Corporations in World Development: A Re-Examination,* E/C/10/38. United Nations, New York.

UNEP (1978), *The State of The Environment – Selected Topics,* United Nations Environment Programme, Nairobi.

UNEP (1979), *The State of the Environment – Selected Topics,* United Nations Environment Programme, Nairobi.

UNEP (1980), *Guidelines for Assessing Industrial Environmental Impact Assessment and Environmental Criteria for the Siting of Industry,* United Nations Environment Programme.

UNEP (1981), *The State of The Environment – Selected Topics,* United Nations Environment Programme, Nairobi.

UNIDO (1979a): *World Industry Since 1960: Progress and Prospects,* United Nations Industrial Development Organization, United Nations, New York.

UNIDO (1979b), *Industry – 2000: New Perspectives,* United Nations Industrial Development Organization, United Nations, New York.

USDC (1975), *The Effects of Pollution Abatement on International Trade.* Third Report of the Secretary of Commerce to The President and Congress. US Department of Commerce, Washington, D.C.

Walter, I. (1975), *International Economics of Pollution,* McMillan, London.

Wixson, B. G. (1981), *Environmental Impacts and Controls in the Exploration and Production of Lead, Zinc and Cadmium.* Paper presented at the UNEP Workshop on Environmental Aspects of Non-ferrous Metals Industry. United Nations Environment Programme, Nairobi.

World Bank (1978), *World Development Report,* World Bank, Washington, D.C.

World Bank (1979), *World Development Report,* World Bank, Washington, D.C.

World Bank (1980), *World Development Report,* World Bank, Washington, D.C.

World Bank (1981), *World Development Report,* World Bank, Washington, D.C.

Zaitsev, V. A. and A. P. Tsygankov (1979), *Mendeleev Chem. J.,* 24, 1.

CHAPTER 12

Energy and The Environment

The 1970s saw a revolution in thinking about energy supplies. No longer were they regarded as cheap, expendable and practically inexhaustible. The "oil crisis" of 1973 led to the realization that fossil fuels were finite, precious, and likely to be increasingly expensive.

World energy consumption rose by about 30 per cent between 1970 and 1978. About 80 per cent of this was in developed countries, where per capita consumption was fifteen times that in developing countries. Oil remained the most widely used fuel. The oil price increases of 1973 and 1979 therefore had severe consequences, especially for developing countries, some of which ended the decade spending 25 per cent to 65 per cent of their hard currency earnings on oil imports.

The changed perception during the decade led people to question how long supplies of non-renewable fossil fuels would last. In 1980 it was estimated that the world's proved recoverable coal reserves would suffice for about 230 years at current consumption rates, but for under 100 years if consumption increased as many people expected – although total resources were much larger. Proved recoverable reserves of oil and gas were smaller: at then current consumption rates, gas supplies would last for about 50 years (but with the estimated additional resources for about 130), while oil supplies, according to two major studies, would fail to meet demand before the year 2000. By the decade's end it was therefore clear that new mixes of energy sources would be needed in future and that energy and energy and environment relationships must be incorporated in national planning.

But there was another fuel crisis during the 70s – a shortage of fuelwood, which (with charcoal and agricultural materials) still provided 30–95 per cent of the total energy used in developing countries. Non-commercial sources were predominant for some 2.5 billion people in regions where animal and muscle power were the engines of agriculture – and such people spent a large proportion of their time looking for fuelwood.

Many developed countries expected to use more coal in the near future, as oil supplies dwindled. In order to prevent environmental damage, research and development sought technologies for fuel pre-treatment, controlled combustion processes and flue-gas desulphurization to ensure that increased coal-burning did not lead to greater sulphur oxides emissions. Ways were also sought to reduce nitrogen oxides production during coal burning, as were methods of curbing environmental devastation from future oil shale and tar sand extraction.

Debate about nuclear power generation, which began in the late 1960s in the United States, was renewed in the 1970s. While nuclear power generation contributed only 0.25 per cent of the ionizing radiation dose received by the average person, controversy increased particularly following some widely publicized reactor accidents and uncertainties over waste disposal practices. The number of nuclear reactors ordered peaked in 1973 and then declined sharply. By 1980 nuclear energy provided about 8 per cent of the world's electrical power, but there was uncertainty about the adequacy of uranium reserves for the future, which was one reason for interest in alternative nuclear fuel cycles.

Renewable energy sources attracted increasing attention during the decade. Hydropower contributed 22 per cent of the world electricity in 1972, and a substantially greater absolute amount (though a slightly smaller share) by 1980. Great hydro potential remained untapped in Africa and Asia. Geothermal, solar, tidal, wave and wind power were less developed but all were studied, while simple solar systems proved their worth in water heating, grain drying and water distillation in developing countries. Biological energy sources also expanded: fuelwood conservation measures were implemented, better techniques for charcoal production developed, and biogas production expanded, especially in Asia. Crop growth for ethanol or methanol production for fuel was expanded.

"The conserver society" became a catchphrase as energy conservation was stressed in developed countries. Several reduced their ratio of energy-use to GNP by over 10 per cent. Increased energy efficiency seemed certain to become a feature of coming decades, but in 1980 development of environmentally acceptable energy mixes remained a research priority.

Energy Consumption and Economic Growth

ALTHOUGH much of the world continued to depend on animal power for motive energy, and on wood, charcoal and animal dung for fuel, an exceptionally rapid increase in commercial energy consumption began in developed countries in the middle of the present century. Between 1925 and 1950 this grew on average at 2.2 per cent per annum. In the following ten years the rate more than doubled (4.9 per cent), and between 1960 and 1970 it reached 5.6 per cent. The total commercial energy consumption in the world in 1950 was about 2,500 million tonnes of coal equivalent* (t.c.e.) while in 1970 it had increased about 2.6 fold to reach 6,500 million t.c.e.

The increase was accompanied by a major change in the composition of primary energy sources. In the 1920s coal accounted for about 80 per cent of the world's total commercial energy consumption, but its share in later years was greatly reduced. The major transition took place in the 1960s (Figure 12–1): although annual consumption of coal continued to mount, in 1950 it met 61 per cent of the world's commercial energy

---

* One tonne of coal contains energy equivalent to 0.688 tonnes of oil, 790 cubic metres of natural gas or 8,140 kilowatt hours (kWh) of electricity (assuming that the energy content of coal is 2.93×10^4 kJ/kg; that of oil is 4.26×10^4 kJ/kg and that of natural gas is 3.7×10^4 kJ/m^3; UN, 1981 a).

Figure 12—1. World Consumption of Commercial Energy.

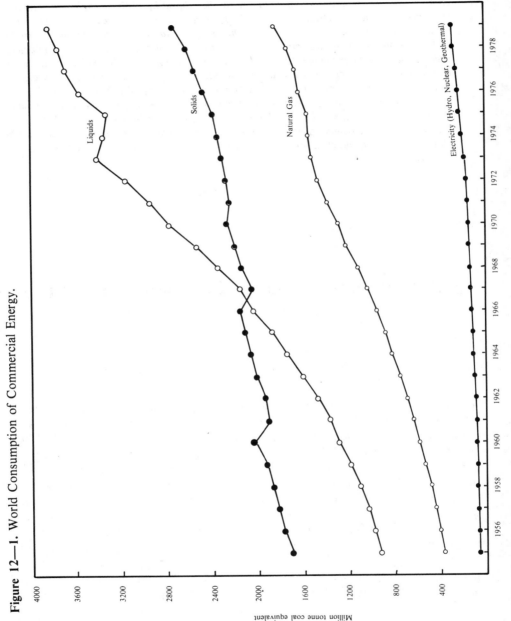

After UN, 1981.

Figure 12–2. Relationship Between GNP and per Capita Commercial Energy Consumption

(Points Represent Individual Countries)

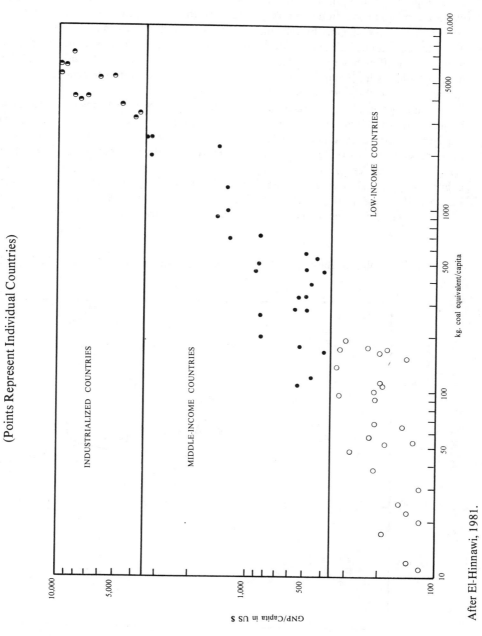

After El-Hinnawi, 1981.

needs, in 1960, 51 per cent and in 1970, 35 per cent. Numerous technological changes gave impetus to this shift in the relative importance of coal and oil. Advances in exploration and production technology improved the supply capacity of the oil industry; improvements in transport by pipelines and tankers added to the advantage of oil as an easily transportable fuel; and the development of refining technology contributed greatly to improving efficiency overall. The result was to stimulate the already widespread use of internal combustion engines, particularly in transport and in power generation, and to further increase the demand for oil.

It has generally been assumed that there is a consistent positive relationship between gross national product (GNP) and energy consumption: as a country's GNP in real terms rises over time, its energy consumption goes up as well. However, the dependence is not absolute or uniform. As Figure 12–2 illustrates, while there is a broad relationship between GNP and energy consumption, there are wide variations in per capita energy consumption between countries having nearly the same GNP per capita. Between 1972 and 1978, GNP per capita in the United States increased about 1.7-fold while the per capita energy consumption remained nearly constant (Figure 12–3).

Figure 12–3. Relation Between GNP per capita and Energy Consumption in the USA, 1972–1978.

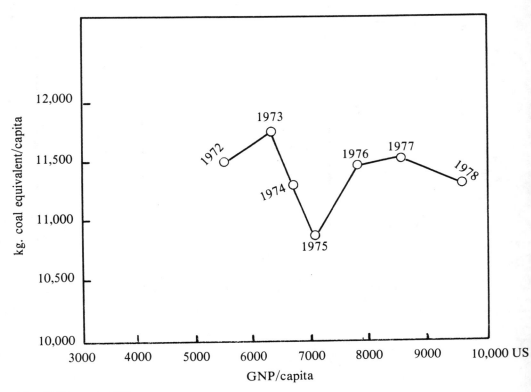

After El-Hinnawi, 1981.

THE ENERGY CRISIS OF THE 1970s

Until the second world war, energy was expensive while labour was cheap. After the war, reconstruction was fuelled in developed countries by cheap oil which powered the rapid technological development that promoted the vigorous economic growth of the

Figure 12–4. Oil prices, 1972–1980.

(a) Prices weighted by production shares
(b) Deflated by manufactured export prices

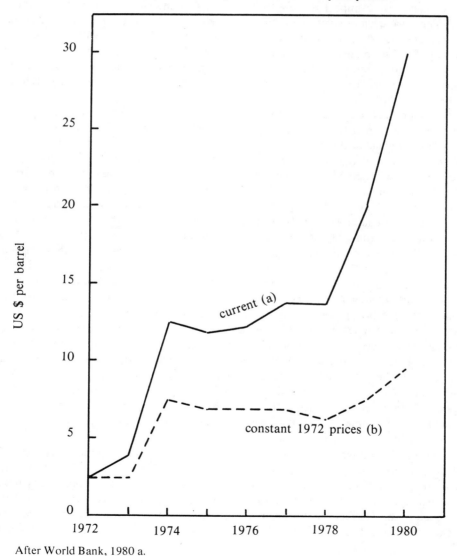

After World Bank, 1980 a.

1950s and 1960s. But in 1973, the world experienced a massive oil-price increase (Figure 12–4). The resulting shock struck a developed world whose national economies were already beginning to exhibit recessionary tendencies (OECD 1979). The oil crisis seriously aggravated a chronic economic disease, caught in the 1960s and caused by increasing competitiveness and economic balance-of-power changes between developed countries, and the economic impacts of greater collective solidarity in the developed world (Malkin 1981). A second major oil price rise began in 1978, further exacerbating the problems, particularly in developing countries, where oil dependence was more widespread and greater than in developed market economies (UN, 1979). At the end of the decade, developing countries were forced to spend 25–65 per cent of their hard currency earnings on imported oil, with disastrous consequences for their development plans. They were, moreover, committed to heavy investments in urban-industrial infrastructure, based on the extravagant oil-use of the 1950s and 1960s, which they could not afford to modify. Added to this the costs of expensive energy had been passed on by developed countries in the higher prices for all goods imported by the developing countries, again seriously affecting their balance of payments and development (Howe and Tarrant 1980).

But many developing countries experienced another energy crisis that threatened their very survival. In 1978 about 1.3 billion people in low-income countries used about 161 kg coal equivalent (kg.c.e.) per person and another 873 million in middle-income countries about 903 kg.c.e. per person, as compared with about 11,370 kg.c.e. per person for the United States (World Bank, 1980 b). Most of the people in these countries, especially those in rural areas relied almost entirely on fuelwood, charcoal, crop-wastes and dung for cooking and heating. Between 30 and 95 per cent of total energy use in many developing countries came from these sources. The eight Sahelian countries were recorded as consuming 84–94 per cent of their total energy as wood (Club du Sahel, 1978). In Kenya where 90 per cent of the population live in rural areas, they depend almost exclusively on fuelwood as their primary source of energy. Fuelwood is also the principal source of energy for cooking and other domestic uses in rural areas (and sometimes urban areas) in many African and Asian countries (El-Hinnawi and El-Gohary, 1981). Most of these countries had population growth rates of 2–4 per cent per year, i.e. doubling times of 35–18 years. Urbanization rates were double this again, a significant factor because urban per capita energy use was several times greater than rural, and charcoal, which was widely used as a fuel, often had to be transported long distances to town so that haulage costs made it very expensive. Population and urban growth thus seriously exacerbated fuelwood shortages which were reaching crisis proportions in many countries (UN, 1981 b). By 1980 food and fuelwood were competing for the same rain-fed land, and the fuel to cook a·meal often cost more than the food in the pot (Club du Sahel, 1978).

The pressure on woodland was exacerbated in the late 1970s by the rising costs of kerosene and propane gas, which passed out of the reach of many people. Villagers were taking up to 30 or 40 per cent of their time to find enough fuel, and their children's school attendance was often curtailed because they had to help. The need to cook food to survive led to the destruction of the remaining trees, even though it was appreciated that this was potentially disastrous. Even the larger industries were beginning to turn to wood and charcoal to avoid paying heavy oil bills. And this drove up fuelwood prices for the rural poor still further. The rising cost of oil and failing availability of wood were therefore, at the end of the decade, two crises of such gravity that they threatened the very existence of several developing countries.

The 1970s ended with wide recognition of a number of important issues including:

(a) the finite nature of non-renewable mineral fuels (especially oil and natural gas);

(b) the ending of the brief period of cheap energy and the need for all economies to adapt to high energy prices;

(c) the importance of developing indigenous energy resources and of establishing new energy 'mixes' to meet the demands for future development;

(d) the importance of the energy-environment relationship;

(e) the growing 'crisis' shortages of wood, crop and animal waste fuels used predominantly in rural areas of the developing world;

(f) the severe foreign exchange difficulties experienced by developing countries as a result of paying for imported oil.

In addition, many developed countries experienced three other phenomena:

(a) 'politicization' of the evaluation of the environmental risks of some energy sources (especially in relation to nuclear power);

(b) acceptance of the importance of increasing the efficiency of energy production and use (energy conservation), in part through stimulating public awareness and participation;

(c) realization that national development plans must incorporate an explicit energy policy.

WORLD ENERGY CONSUMPTION IN THE 1970s

Table 12–1 shows that world total commercial energy consumption increased by about 34 per cent between 1970 and 1979, the rate of increase being less than in 1960–1970 (58.5 per cent). The same trend also characterizes world electricity production, which increased by about 60 per cent between 1970 and 1979*, whereas between 1960 and 1970 it increased by 110 per cent.

* World electricity production in 1970 was 4956×10^9 kWh (of which 74.6 per cent was thermal, 23.7 per cent hydro, 1.6 per cent nuclear and 0.1 per cent geothermal); in 1979 it was 7966×10^9 kWh (70.7 per cent thermal; 21.6 per cent hydro; 7.6 per cent nuclear; 0.13 per cent geothermal) UN (1981 a).

Table 12–1. World Energy Consumption (In 10^6 tonnes coal equivalent (t.c.e.))

Year	Total Commercial Energy	Solid Fuels	Liquid Fuels	Natural Gas	Electricity*
1970	6512	2272	2792	1293	155
1971	6771	2251	2962	1393	165
1972	7088	2270	3165	1474	178
1973	7437	2316	3408	1526	187
1974	7471	2343	3362	1557	209
1975	7529	2397	3348	1561	223
1976	7930	2476	3578	1645	231
1977	8168	2560	3692	1666	250
1978	8395	2612	3768	1738	277
1979	8706	2738	3834	1846	288

Source: UN (1981 a).

*Hydro, nuclear and geothermal

In the 1970s consumption of the world's commercial energy resources was heavily concentrated in the developed market economy countries and the socialist countries of Eastern Europe (Figure 12–5 and Table 12–2). These regions, with about 30 per cent of total world population, accounted for more than 80 per cent of total world consumption of commercial energy. In developing countries the limited commercial energy consumption was concentrated in urban areas, which followed a pattern not unlike that in developed countries (Reddy and Prasad, 1977). This heavy concentration in developed regions was a reflection of their level and type of development. Their transport systems (except in socialist countries) were dominated by privately-owned cars. Their industries were characterized by energy-intensive processes. Communities and individual households had ready access to energy via power grid systems and mechanization had reached not only farms and factories but also offices and commercial facilities. As a result, per capita commercial energy consumption in the Developed Market-Economy Countries in 1979 was about 15 times that of the Developing Market-Economy Countries (Figure 12–6, Table 12–2).

Despite the "crises" of the 1970s, there are indications that wasteful consumption patterns increased in developed countries during the decade. Satellite photographs in 1973 and 1979 show, for example, a major growth in street lighting in the United States during these six years and there have been comparable changes in many other countries.

Parikh (1978) estimated the fuel consumption patterns for the main world regions in 1973 (Table 12–3), concluding that nearly 2.5 billion people in Africa and the Far East depended on non-commercial sources for half or more of their energy. Other recent estimates indicate that non-commercial energy represents 90 per cent of all energy consumed in Nepal (Karki and Coburn, 1977), 83 per cent in Bangladesh, and 48 per cent in India (Henderson, 1975). The detailed pattern of energy allocation was analyzed by Reddy and Subramanian (1980) in a small village in southern India (Pura, with 357 inhabitants). Table 12–4 shows the dominant roles of fuelwood (mostly non-commercial) and of human and animal muscle power.

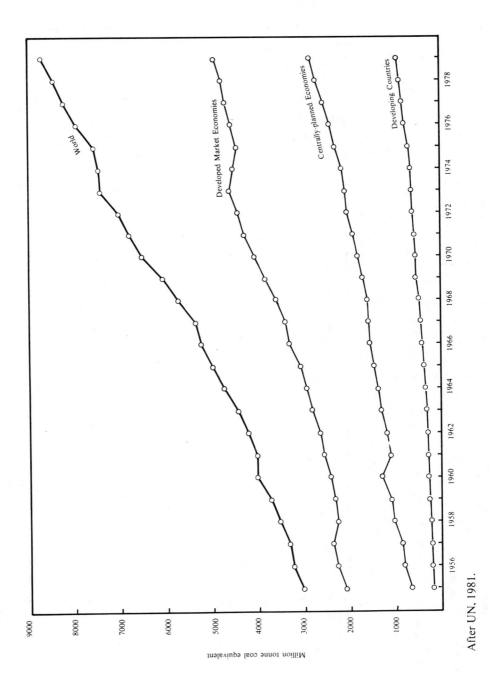

Figure 12–5. Commercial Energy Consumption.

After UN. 1981.

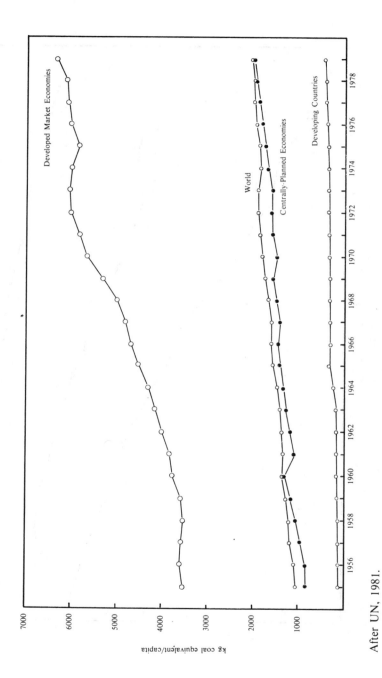

Figure 12–6. Per Capita Commercial Energy Consumption.

After UN, 1981.

Table 12–2. Per Capita Energy Consumption (in kg.c.e.)

	1960	1970	1979
World	1368	1781	2019
Developed Market Economies	3810	5739	6317
Developing Market Economies	211	302	437
Centrally-Planned Economies			
– Europe CP	2797	4123	5522
– Asia CP	592	449	733
OPEC Countries	327	355	565

Source: UN (1981 a).

Table 12–3. Fuel Consumption (in Million Tonnes Coal Equivalent)

	Commercial Fuels	Fuel Wood	Agricultural Waste	Total	Fuel wood + Agricultural Waste as a Percent of total
Africa[a]	66	116	22	204	68
Mid-east	109	5	12	126	13
Far East[b]	247	143	100	490	50
Latin America	304	98	31	433	30
West Europe	1,568	18	6	1,592	2
USSR and Eastern Europe	1,771	43	24	1,838	4
North America	2,723	7	0	2,730	–.
World[c]	7,885	498	167	8,550	8

Source: Parikh (1978).

[a]Excluding South Africa
[b]Excluding Japan
[c]Including Japan, South Africa, Australia, etc.

Table 12–4. Energy Source-Activity Matrix for Pura Village, India (in 10^9 Joules per Year)

	Agriculture	Domestic	Lighting	Industry	Total
Human	33.4	212.6	—	20,8	266.8
Man	(20.9)	(86.2)	—	(17.3)	(124.4)
Woman	(12.5)	(95.4)	—	(3.6)	(111.5)
Child	—	(31.0)	—	—	(31.0)
Bullock	51.9	—	—	—	51.9
Firewood	—	3306.3	—	142.1	3448.4
Kerosene	—	—	72.9	5.9	78.8
Electricity	26.2	—	11.1	3.0	40.3
Total	111.5	3518.9	84.0	171.8	3886.2

Source: Reddy and Subramanian (1980).

Kerosene and electricity (i.e. commercial energy) account for 3 per cent of the inanimate energy used in the village, the remaining 97 per cent comes from fuelwood (which is mostly non-commercial gathered at zero private cost).

Energy and Environment

ENVIRONMENTAL IMPACTS AND CONCERNS

Locally, nationally and sometimes regionally, the environmental aspects of energy production and use were widely debated during the decade. Environmental awareness and anti-pollution campaigns affected the formulation of energy policies in many countries. Perception of the nature and dimensions of the energy problem by scientists, policy makers and the public changed drastically. What were once considered exclusively technical problems amenable to technical solutions came to be recognized as facets of the larger socio-political problems that pervade all society.

Environmental impacts of energy technologies fall into three broad categories:

(a) those that are quantifiable and amenable to comparisons between different technologies;

(b) those that are quantifiable but difficult to compare from one technology to another;

(c) those that are difficult or impossible to quantify.

Some of the parameters that can be quantified – like loss of life or damage to historic monuments and beautiful landscapes – cannot be given a price tag (see, for example, Ashby, 1978; Fischhof et al., 1978; Holdgate, 1979).

In the past more attention has often been paid to direct and immediate impacts on occupational and public health or the physical environment, than to long-term socio-economic and environmental effects. However, by the end of the 1970s, increasing efforts were being devoted to the analysis of these less tangible long-term impacts. Considerable methodological problems were apparent: the criteria for judging and comparing impacts were disputed, the methods for quantifying impacts and costs were poorly developed and in some cases manifestly flawed, and the values placed upon different environmental features and different degrees of protection from various perceived hazards varied within societies and over time (Budnitz and Holdren, 1976; Otway et al., 1978; O'Riordan, 1981). Nevertheless three major conclusions were claimed:

(a) energy technologies have the potential to perturb critical environmental processes as well as threaten human health;

(b) no energy technology is so free of environmental risk that its adoption brings only benefits and no disbenefits;

(c) the uncertainties make it possible to predict with great confidence the environmental consequences of continuing major increases in energy production and consumption (Budnitz and Holdren, 1976).

Holdren (1981) argued further that the disruption of biogeophysical processes might pose a greater threat to human well-being than direct toxic effects. Such uncertainties over the long-term effects of different energy strategies are also manifest in such studies as *Global 2000* (CEQ, 1980), CONAES (1980) and the comprehensive UNEP assessment of the *Environmental Impacts of the Production and Use of Energy* (1981).

The recognition of these gaps in knowledge, and public suspicion that some risks had been seriously underestimated in the past, increased the number of energy-environment battles in the 1970s. Gladwin et al., (1980) drew up an inventory of 803 cases of energy-environment conflict in member countries of the Organization for Economic Cooperation and Development (OECD). One-fourth of the conflicts involved nuclear power plants; 16 per cent oil refineries and petrochemical plants and 12 per cent energy transportation and storage facilities. 60 per cent of these conflicts were in the United States, 12 per cent in the United Kingdom, 5 per cent in Canada, 4 per cent in Japan and 4 per cent in the Federal Republic of Germany. The three issues most frequently disputed were water quality (44 per cent of 220 cases analyzed in detail), air quality (30 per cent) and human health (26 per cent). Air quality issues were most frequent in battles over electric utilities, petrochemical plants and oil refineries. Water quality issues were at stake in 61 per cent of the energy transportation and storage facility conflicts. Concerns of human health and safety were found most frequently in conflicts over nuclear power.

IMPACTS FROM FOSSIL FUEL PRODUCTION AND USE

Fossil fuels (coal, oil and natural gas) are the dominant commercial primary energy sources used world-wide. The environmental impacts of their production, transportation, processing and use are reviewed below. The same main kinds of pollutants are emitted by burning wood, charcoal and other "contemporary" carbonaceous fuels, and the environmental impacts of their use are therefore also described in this section.

Coal, Lignite and Peat Extraction and Processing

The total resources of solid fossil fuels (different types of coal and peat) are estimated at some 11,184 billion t.c.e. Of these about 1,081 billion t.c.e. are 'proved reserves', exploitable in principle with present technology (about 690 billion t.c.e. of these are 'recoverable', i.e. exploitable under existing technological and economic limits). The remainder are 'additional resources' of least foreseeable economic interest, *in situ* (Table 12–5).

Table 12–5. World Resources of Solid Fossil Fuels (Coal and Peat)

	Proved Recoverable Reserves Billion tonnes coal equivalent	Percent	Additional Resources In Place Billion tonnes coal equivalent	Percent
Africa	32.6	4.7	146.5	1.5
America	200.2	28.9	2,970.0	29.4
Asia	116.1	16.7	1,454.1	14.4
USSR	169.1	24.4	4,469.8	44.2
Europe	138.8	20.0	448.2	4.4
Oceania/ Australia	34.4	5.3	613.8	6.1
Total	691.2	100.0	10,102.4	100.0

Source: World Energy Conference (1980)

At present rates of coal consumption (about 3 billion t.c.e. per annum) the proved recoverable reserves of 691 billion t.c.e. would last for about 230 years, while assumed recoverable reserves (taken as 50 per cent of total resources) would last approximately 1,800 years. However, some estimates predict that consumption will rise to 8.8 billion tonnes per annum by the year 2000 and on this basis the proved recoverable reserves would be exhausted by around 2070. The total coal resource is so huge, however, that it is entirely plausible to expect that some of the assumed recoverable reserves will be proved recoverable by then. Coal mining has a number of environmental impacts. Besides accidents in both underground and surface mines, coal-workers are exposed to respiratory diseases (Hamilton, 1977; Morris *et al.,* 1979; UNEP, 1981) and noise. The land area disturbed by coal mining varies according to the depth and geology of the coal-bearing formation and whether it is extracted by strip mining or underground working. Surface mining in densely populated areas has a direct effect on human settlements and infrastructure. Reclamation of strip-mined areas has been successfully achieved in several countries (for example in the Federal Republic of Germany and the United Kingdom).

Both underground and surface coal mining have an impact on water resources. Water flow through mines (especially where the coal and bedrock are rich in pyrite) can result in drainage that is acid, bearing heavy loads of suspended solids, and having high concentrations of metals and other dissolved substances. Such drainage has affected some 10,000 km of water course and 5,000 ha of open water in the eastern United States and has reduced or eliminated aquatic life in many of them (Nephew, 1972; Bradshaw, 1973; OTA, 1979). Acid mine drainage can be controlled, often with great difficulty, by regulating oxygen flow to the pyrite, reducing the water flow in the mine, neutralizing the acid before discharge or purification using ion exchange or reverse osmosis (which is expensive) (OTA, 1979).

Coal conversion processes (liquification and gasification) have two objectives: to convert plentiful coal of different grades into scarce liquid and gaseous fuel and to remove or treat environmentally unacceptable or health-endangering compounds. During the 1970s research on improved processes for obtaining liquid fuels from coal accelerated in several countries.

Oil and Gas

Proved recoverable world oil reserves grew rapidly between 1969 and 1973, but from then until 1979 the total fluctuated without showing a further upward trend (Figure 12–7). The average growth in the decade was about 2.6 billion tonnes, or 3.5 per cent per year. For the same period, world oil production has grown at around 4.1 per cent per year (Figure 12–8). However, during the three years up to and including 1980 the ratio of proved recoverable reserves to production stabilized, discoveries and detailed surveys of resources thus keeping in step with use (*Oil and Gas Journal,* 29 Dec. 1980). As noted in Chapter 5, this ratio reflects investment considerations rather than the physical volume of oil available.

Figure 12–7. Proved World Recoverable Oil Reserves.

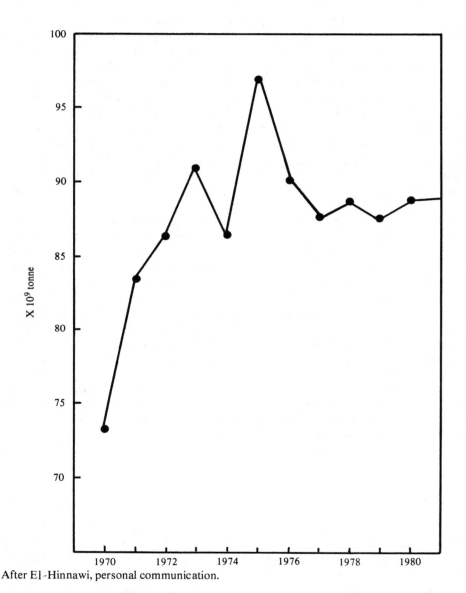

After El-Hinnawi, personal communication.

These reserves form only a small part of the total world recoverable resources of oil (Table 12–6), most estimates of which ranged during the decade between 240 and 360 billion tonnes. Up to the end of 1978 approximately 53 billion tonnes (15 per cent of the total then estimated) had been recovered, and on 1 January 1979 the remaining proved

Table 12–6. Cumulative Production, Reserves, Resources, and Ultimate Recovery for Oil.

Region	Cumulative Production 1.1.79 (Million tonnes)	Per Cent	Proved Recoverable Reserves 1.1.79 (Million tonnes)	Per Cent	Estimated Additional Recoverable Resources (Million tonnes)	Per Cent	Ultimate Recovery (Million tonnes)	Per Cent
Africa	3,750	7	8,040	9	34,000	16	45,790	13
North America	17,520	33	4,480	5	24,000	11	46,000	13
Latin America	7,040	14	7,770	9	12,000	6	26,810	8
Far East/Pacific	1,720	3	2,390	3	12,000	6	16,110	4
Middle East	14,680	28	51,050	57	52,000	24	117,730	33
Western Europe	560	1	2,710	3	10,000	5	13,270	4
USSR, China Eastern Europe	7,530	14	12,700	14	64,000	30	84,230	24
Antarctic					4,000	2	4,000	1
Total	52,800	100	89,140	100	212,000	100	353,940	100

Source: WEC, 1980.

Figure 12–8. World Oil Production, 1960–1979.

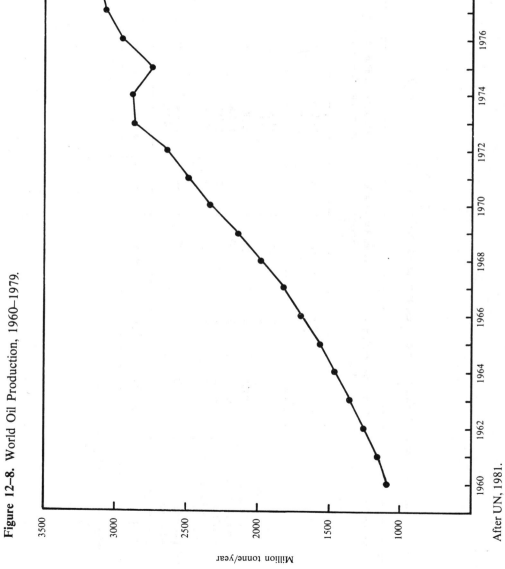

After UN, 1981.

reserves were estimated at 89 billion tonnes (25 per cent) and the additional recoverable resources at 212 billion tonnes (65 per cent) (WEC, 1980). On 1 January 1980 proved recoverable reserves were estimated at 87.9 billion tonnes and on 1 January 1981 at 88.8 billion tonnes (*Oil and Gas Journal,* 1979, 1980).

At the present rate of oil consumption (about 3,000 million tonnes/year) the total world proved recoverable reserves (known on 1.1.1981) would last for only 30 years; i.e. until the year 2010 and the total additional recoverable resources would last for about 70 years. These estimates do not take into account natural gas liquids, the proved recoverable reserves of which are about 1,500 million tonnes and the additional recoverable resources of about 11,600 million tonnes (WEC, 1980).

Table 12–7. World Natural Gas Resources (Thousand Billion (10^{12}) Cubic Metres)

	Cumulative production up to 1.1.79	Proved recoverable reserves on 1.1.79	Estimated additional	"Ultimate recovery"
Africa	0.1	7.3	26	33.4
North America	16.9	7.5	42	66.4
Latin America	1.8	4.7	10	16.5
Far East/Pacific	0.2	3.3	10	13.5
Middle East	1.1	20.5	30	51.6
Western Europe	1.5	3.9	6	11.4
USSR, China, Eastern Europe	5.2	26.9	64	96.1
Antarctic			4	4.0
Total	26.8	74.1	192	292.9

Source: WEC, 1980

Estimates during the 1970s of the ultimate recovery of natural gas range from 200,000 to 300,000 billion cubic metres (m^3). On 1 January 1979 the calculated figure was 293,000 billion m^3 (WEC, 1980; Table 12–7). Of this some 9 per cent had already been recovered, 25 per cent (74,000 billion m^3) was in the form of proved recoverable reserves, and the remainder was estimated additional recoverable resources. Proved recoverable reserves were calculated at 72,000 billion m^3 on 1 January 1980 and 73,900 billion m^3 on 1 January 1981 (figures calculated from *Oil and Gas Journal,* 1979, 1980).

At the present consumption rate of about 1,500 billion m^3 per annum the proved recoverable reserves of natural gas would last for about 50 years and the estimated additional resources for about 130 years.

Oil and natural gas exploration and production have a number of environmental impacts (UNEP, 1981). On land (where about 80 per cent of total crude oil production occurs) large quantities of water are injected into the oil-bearing formation to enhance oil production, and some of this returns to the surface with the oil as an emulsion. Unless separation is carried out very thoroughly, oily discharges can pollute watercourses and harm aquatic life. Offshore, the potential impact of oil spills on marine life was a major cause of concern during the 1970s, and is discussed in Chapter 3. About 50 per cent of all the oil produced in the world each year is transported by sea, and the risk of pollution from this source is another well-known hazard discussed elsewhere (Chapters 3 and 13). Overland, pipelines are the main means of transportation, and the decade witnessed concern over the risks of damage from their failure, especially in Alaska; this topic, also, is reviewed in Chapter 13.

Oil refineries are large industrial installations with air and water emissions, large water requirements for processing and cooling and safety problems due to the risk of explosions and fires. The most important emissions from refineries are airborne effluents (sulphur oxides, organic compounds, nitrogen oxides, carbon monoxide and particulate matter) and liquid effluents. The latter contain a variety of compounds, the most important of which are oil and grease, phenols, ammonia and suspended and dissolved solids. These wastes are normally treated and the effluents discharged from most refineries contain low concentrations of such pollutants (UNEP, 1981).

Oil Shale and Tar Sands

The proved recoverable reserves of oil in oil shales on 1 January 1979 were estimated at 46,260 million tonnes, with additional resources of 292,670 million tonnes. For tar sands the equivalent figures were 40,050 million tonnes and 76,300 million tonnes (WEC, 1980).

The exploitation of oil shale raises both economic and environmental problems. The scale of disruption likely from the very large schemes under discussion in the 1970s would be much greater than in normal surface or underground mining operations. If surface retorting (recovery of oil from shale in a retort vessel) were used, the disposal of large volumes of spent shale would create a further major land disturbance. Air pollution (odours), the accumulation of toxic substances in vegetation, and the contamination of ground and surface water from runoffs would all pose problems. The oil shale industry would have a major demand for clean process water, affecting local water resources, while its effluents would need thorough treatment if they were not to cause damaging pollution. The environmental effects of large-scale tar sands development could also be widespread and severe, involving major land disturbance, pollution and the production of solid wastes. The mine area could be restored, but re-vegetation might well prove more difficult than with coal strip-mines (UNEP, 1981).

Combustion of fossil fuels

The combustion of fossil fuels or of contemporary carbonaceous fuels gives rise to a number of airborne effluents, the most important of which are carbon dioxide, sulphur oxides, nitrogen oxides, carbon monoxide, particulates, organic compounds and trace metals. The quantities of these emissions vary according to the fuel used, its composition and the measures adopted at the power plant to reduce the emissions. Table 12–8 gives a summary of the gaseous emissions (except carbon dioxide and water vapour) and solid wastes produced by the combustion of fossils fuels to generate 1,000 megawatts (MW) of electricity per year.

Table 12–8. Emissions From Fossil Fuel-Operated Power Stations
(in Tonnes/1000 MW(e)y)

		Coal[a]	Oil[b]	Natural Gas[c]
I.	*Airborne Effluents*			
	Sulphur oxides (SO_x)	110,000	37,000	20
	Nitrogen oxides (NO_x)	27,000	25,000	20,000
	Carbon monoxide (CO)	2,000	710	—
	Particulates	3,000	1,200	510
	Hydrocarbons	400	470	34
	Aldehydes	—	240	—
II.	*Solid Wastes*			
	Ash	360,000	9,000	

Source: UNEP (1981).

[a] Assuming power plant burns 3×10^6 tonnes coal; sulphur content 2 per cent; energy content of opal 2.74 $\times 10^7$J/tonne; thermal efficiency of power plant 38 per cent; fly ash removal efficiency 99 per cent; no flue gas desulphurization. Solid wastes: bottom ash + recovered fly ash.
[b] The power plant uses 2×10^6 tonnes residual fuel (1 per cent S, 0.5 per cent ash).
[c] The power plant uses $2.2 \times 10^9 m^3$ of natural gas with energy value of 37,000 kJ/m^3.

These gaseous emissions are of concern because of their potential damage to human health, impairment of agricultural productivity, damage to freshwater ecosystems when deposited in 'acid rain', corrosion of buildings and other artefacts, and effects on climate and on radiation penetration through the atmosphere. All these topics are discussed in Chapters 2, 4, 7 and 10. The important issue here is whether these emissions must necessarily rise as energy demand increases, how far variations in fuel type and circumstances of combustion affect the pattern of impact, and what corrective measures are available.

As Table 12–8 indicates, the output of pollutant per unit of energy produced varies with fuel. Natural gas is normally very low in sulphur, whereas coals normally contain between 1 and 4 per cent sulphur and fuel oils 3–4 per cent (a 3 per cent S oil produces the same SO_x emissions as a low sulphur coal when based on a comparable energy release). Unless remedial action is taken, the increased use of coal in power stations and the home would therefore be likely to increase sulphur emissions, perhaps from 21.3 to 42 million tonnes in the United States and 2.8 to 4.6 million tonnes in the United Kingdom between 1975 and 1990 (OTA 1979; Robinson, 1979). Similarly, fuels differ in their carbon dioxide (CO_2) production, coal producing twice as much CO_2 per unit of electricity generated as natural gas, and one-third more than oil.

During the 1970s considerable efforts were made to develop ways of ensuring that any expansion in coal burning did not aggravate air pollution. There are three ways to reduce sulphur oxides emissions – treatment of fuel before combustion, the use of controlled combustion processes, and de-sulphurization of flue gases – and all were studied although only the third was in widespread operational use during the 1970s. One pre-treatment plant in the United States achieved up to 90 per cent removal of pyrite sulphur from coal through a flotation process (OTA, 1979). Fluidized bed combustion processes offered a promise of effective sulphur removal and enhanced combustion efficiency (but were only applicable to new plants). Several technologies for flue gas desulphurization were tested, including limestone slurry scrubbing, lime slurry scrubbing, manganese slurry scrubbing, sodium solution scrubbing and catalytic oxidation (Cheremisinoff and Young, 1976; Yan 1976). Of these systems, lime-limestone wet scrubbing was by the end of the decade considered a commercial process, but it was not without environmental problems of its own. Assuming coal with a sulphur content of 3 per cent and a scrubber efficiency of 90 per cent, the amount of waste water produced is about 6.1 million tonnes (containing 700,000 tonnes of dissolved and suspended solids) per 1000 MW(e)y. This requires a 7.2–ha, 3m–deep settling pond; the recovered solids require a 10–ha, 6m–deep storage facility (UNEP, 1981). Although these facilities may present problems in densely populated areas, the process is capable of removing nearly 90 per cent of the sulphur oxides from stack gases. This process, or an improved one, in conjunction with some fluidized bed combustion and fuel pre-treatment, is relied on to prevent sulphur oxides emissions in the United States rising proportionally with growth in coal use (OTA, 1979).

Theoretically, it is possible to reduce nitrogen oxides concentrations in combustion gases by modifying the burners or firebox (or both), decomposing nitric oxide and possibly nitrogen dioxide back to the elements oxygen and nitrogen or scrubbing effluent gases. The first approach, which includes fluidized bed combustion, flame temperature reduction, and reduced oxygen availability, appears the most promising. A combination of various strategies had achieved a 40–50 per cent reduction in nitrous oxide emissions from large utility boilers in the United States by the late 1970s. Methods being developed at the end of the decade in Japan and the United States offered a prospect of 85 per cent reduction (OTA, 1979).

A number of technologies were available in 1981 for removing particulates from flue gases (wet collection devices, electrostatic precipitators, improved filters etc.), and it was estimated that their wider use and further improvement might reduce particulate emissions by two-thirds by the year 2000, despite increases in the use of coal. Unfortunately, these devices only remove particles down to one micron in diameter. Finer particles remain suspended and are apt to be carried far from the source and even into the upper layers of the atmosphere.

Combustion of contemporary carbonaceous fuels

In 1978 about 47 per cent of total world wood consumption was for fuel; in some regions, e.g. in Africa it reached 88 per cent (FAO, 1980). This fuelwood came overwhelmingly from local sources, and its collection put growing pressure on woody vegetation near centres of population and caused severe local degradation. The regenerative capacity of the forests was impaired; erosion and wind damage were increased by the reduction in plant cover, and soil fertility was reduced by the removal not only of wood but, in some areas, of dry leaves and litter (UNEP, 1977).

If wood is removed from the forests and burned, and soil organic matter is oxidized faster than the ratio of replenishment, carbon dioxide will be added to the atmosphere. During the 1970s some calculations suggested that these processes might match fossil fuel combustion as a source of CO_2. One estimate put the annual release of carbon from burning fuelwood at 200–400 million tonnes, with 3,600 million tonnes more from oxidation of organic matter following forest clearance as against 5,000 million tonnes from fossil fuel combustion (Bolin et al., 1979).

The direct combustion of fuelwood results in emissions consisting mainly of particulates, condensible organic compounds, carbon monoxide and polycyclic organic matter. Such emissions could cause respiratory diseases and cancer. In a recent study (EPA, 1980) it was found that smoke from wood-burning stoves and fire-places contained 17 priority pollutants, 14 known carcinogens, 4 co-carcinogens and 6 cilia-toxic agents. Although it is only recently that data have become available on emissions from wood stoves (Butcher and Buckley, 1977; Butcher and Sørenson, 1979; EPA, 1980), the available data base and overall understanding is much less than might be desired considering the potential health impact of emissions from wood stoves (Morris, 1980).

NUCLEAR ENERGY AND ITS ENVIRONMENTAL IMPACT

The Growth of Nuclear Technology

Electricity was first generated from nuclear reactors in 1954. The growth in capacity was slow until the early 1960s, but the number of new reactors ordered per year then rose dramatically to a peak in 1973 (Figure 12–9), after which it fell equally dramatically for economic, environmental and social reasons. By March 1979, 186 nuclear reactors with a total capacity of 112 GW* were in operation in 20 countries. In that year, however, the total reactors in operation, under construction, or planned was much larger – 532 in 36 countries, with a capacity of 436,000 GW (Rotblat, 1979). Light Water Reactors (LWRs)– a group including both Boiling Water Reactors (BWRs) and Pressurized Water Reactors (PWRs) accounted for about 90 per cent of this capacity, and will continue to predominate for the remainder of the century (El-Hinnawi, 1980; UNEP, 1981). Over 90 per cent of the nuclear energy generation in operation at the end

*GW = gigawatts = 1 billion (10^9) watts

Figure 12–9. New Nuclear Reactors ordered per year.

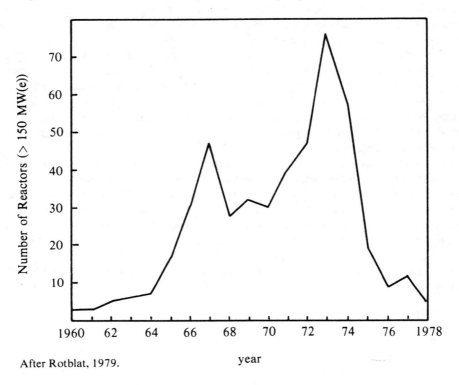

After Rotblat, 1979.

of the decade was in OECD countries; the United States having 4 5.5 per cent of the world total, Europe 28 per cent, Japan 11.8 per cent and Canada 4.9 per cent. The socialist countries had 7.4 per cent and the developing world only 2.4 per cent (Rotblat, 1979).

In 1979 nuclear generation provided about 7.6 per cent of the world's electrical power (UN, 1981 a). The fuel for virtually all these reactors was uranium with its content of fissile U–235 enriched to 2.4–3 per cent, although other fissile materials such as plutonium–239 or uranium–233 were also used. The dependence of this industry on uranium reserves was therefore considerable, although 2 breeder reactors (which produce more uranium than they consume) were operational and 6 more were under construction by the end of the decade (Rotblat, 1979).

Uranium is a fairly common constituent of the earth's crust, with an average abundance of 3.4 ppm. The ores that are mined usually contain 0.1 per cent – 0.2 per cent uranium oxide (U_3O_8) by weight. Uranium can also be recovered from "unconventional" sources: for example, as a by-product of phosphoric acid production, from phosphate rock, marine black shales, coals and lignites, and special types of granites, but on a very limited scale.

In 1977 the nuclear power industry consumed slightly less than 30,000 tonnes of uranium. Table 12–9 gives the projected annual and cumulative requirements of natural uranium, assuming there is no recycling. These cumulative requirements are within known world uranium resources, currently estimated at about 4 million tonnes in the cost category less than US$ 130/kg uranium, but if demand continued go grow, some 9 million tonnes might be required by 2025. There is no certainty that economically exploitable reserves exist on this scale, so that there is a considerable incentive to develop alternative fuel cycles (including reprocessing and the deployment of breeder reactors) as well as to search for new ore bodies.

Table 12–9. World Annual Cumulative Requirements For Natural Uranium, in Tonnes (U)

	1985	1990	1995	2000
Annual	71,000	102,000	134,000	178,000
Cumulative	423,000	873,000	1,477,000	2,276,000

Source: OECD (1978); assuming that the nuclear generating capacity will be 1,000 GW(e) by the year 2000.

The Environmental Impact of Nuclear Technology

The nuclear debate began in the late 1960s in the United States (Surrey and Hugget, 1976; Nelkin and Fallows, 1978). At that time it was mainly technical, embracing such topics as the possible somatic and genetic risks to people exposed to low levels of radiation, the safety of nuclear installations, the impact on particular sites, and the possible environmental risks associated with radioactive wastes. In the 1970s, however, the debate extended to socio-economic problems, including human fallibility, the possible diversion of nuclear material for non-peaceful purposes, and the risks from sabotage and terrorism as well as a more basic disenchantment with centralized decision-making (Chapter 15). Public opposition to nuclear power has in several countries caused delays to plans for the 1970s and beyond.

Effects of Radiation on Man and His Environment

Man has always been exposed to ionizing radiation from various external and internal natural sources, including cosmic and gamma rays, radon and other substances emitted from rocks and building materials, and naturally occurring radioactive substances taken into the body. Exposure to radiation from man-made ionizing radiation such as X-rays is a more recent addition. On average, in the 1970s, a member of the

world population received a whole-body dose of about 1,000 microsieverts (μSv)* per
year of natural radiation and about 700 μSv/y from man-made sources, of which less
than 50 μSv/y was due to radiation from the nuclear power industry (Figure 12–10).
However, there was considerable geographical variation, and while in the United
Kingdom the average dose from the nuclear power industry was about 3μSv/y, the most
exposed members of the population may have received 1,000 μSv/y from this source
(NRPB, 1981, Figure 12–11).

Figure 12–10. Average Radiation Exposure From Different Sources.

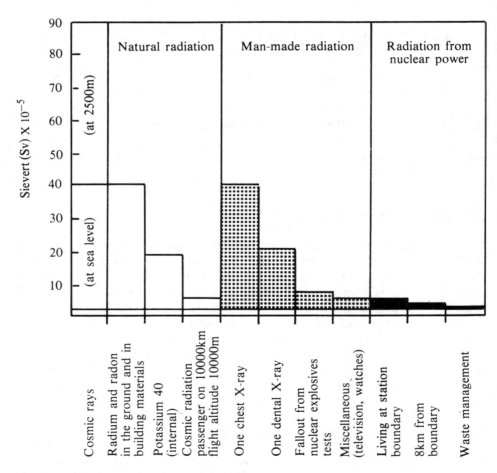

After IAEA/WHO, based on Greenholgh, 1980.

*The unit of radiation dosage: 1 sievert (Sv) = 100 rems

Although our knowledge about the health effects of ionizing radiation has greatly advanced in recent years, the effects of low levels of absorbed radiation have not yet been well defined and have recently been the subject of wide-ranging debate. It is generally assumed that the dose-response relationship is linear, with no threshold (ICRP, 1977; UNSCEAR, 1977). At low doses the relationship is often assumed to be defined by a straight line extrapolating backwards from the observed response at high doses towards the origin. However, the true slope of the curve at low doses is not known and there is also doubt over whether the normal extrapolation over- or under-estimates the true risk (Barnaby, 1980; El–Hinnawi, 1980; UNEP, 1981). Alternative approaches to this problem were evaluated in the BEIR II report in 1980 (NRC, 1980).

Figure 12–11. Average Annual Dose to the Population of the UK (After NRPB, 1981 with modification).

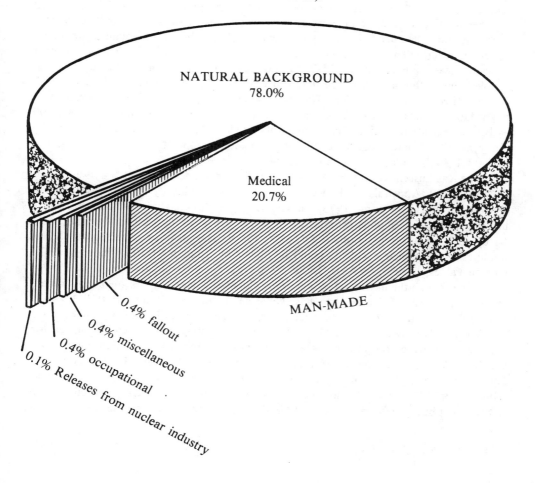

There are two difficulties in establishing the effects of dose-equivalent levels of a few microsieverts per year on the general population. First, no statistically valid epidemiological data are available, nor could they be obtained without a study under controlled conditions on a very large population over several generations. Second, even if correlations did emerge, it would be very difficult to prove cause and effect. Although it is easy to observe deaths and major malignancies such as those that arise from absorbed dose levels above 0.5–1 Gray*, it is more difficult to observe minor incidences of illness in a much larger population such as might result from low-level exposures, and to distinguish them unambiguously from similar illnesses that could be caused by a host of other causes.

Reactor Accidents

Several studies during the 1970s estimated the probabilities of reactor accidents and releases of radioactivity. The most comprehensive was the Reactor Safety Study (also referred to as the Rasmussen Report or WASH–1400) published in 1975. It estimated the probability of a meltdown in a pressurized water reactor as one in 20,000 per reactor per year, and concluded that most meltdowns would not breach the main containment above the reactor. The average individual risk of early fatality from nuclear power plant accidents was computed at 1 in 5 billion per year on average for the 15 million or so people living within 40 km of the first 100 LWRs and 1 in 50 billion per year for the entire United States population. The worst accident, which WASH–1400 estimated might happen once per 10 million years if there were 100 reactors, might cause 3,300 early fatalities, about 10 times that number of early illnesses, additional genetic effects, as many as 57,000 latent cancer deaths in the exposed population over 30 years, and perhaps US$ 14 billion in property damage.

The Rasmussen report estimated roughly a factor of uncertainty of 5 in its estimates (WASH–1400, Appendix 6). However, reappraisals, notably by the Risk Assessment Review Group (Lewis et al., 1978) and CONAES (1980) concluded that several of the uncertainties had been underestimated. The consequences of the various accidents could be up to 3 times more serious (CONAES, 1980). The mean or expected number of fatalities from nuclear accidents could be higher by a factor of 10 or more than the median values given by WASH–1400.

Even though the likelihood of a major accident at a carefully designed, maintained, and managed reactor is small, its precise value is uncertain and is not zero (CEQ, 1980). The public perception of the risk of such accidents is, however, very much greater (Slovic et al., 1979). During the 1970s this public apprehension was stimulated by two reactor accidents that were both larger in scale than "normal" minor operational failures, and widely publicized – at Browns Ferry, Alabama, in March, 1975, and Three Mile Island, Harrisburg, Pennsylvania in March, 1979 (Berger, 1977; Burleson, 1978; Nader and Abbots, 1979). In the second accident some radionuclides were released to the environment but the effects on the health of the population within a 50-mile radius of the

*The unit of absorbed dose: 1 Gray = 100 rad

plant were practically nil (NUREG–0558, 1979). However, the accident greatly increased the public's sensitivity and led to the re-evaluation of safety regulations and requirements in several countries (El-Hinnawi, 1980). In the United States, a special task force identified 23 specific new safety requirements in 12 areas related to reactor operation (NUREG–0578, 1979). In addition the Three Mile Island accident had several economic impacts. The additional safety requirements increased the cost of plants. The repair of the damaged reactor was estimated at about US$ 2 billion. The accident also affected both local and international reactor markets.

Radioactive Wastes

Radioactive wastes are generated in practically all areas of the nuclear industry as liquids, solids, or gases with wide-ranging radiation levels. The bulk are formed at the front-end of the nuclear fuel cycle, which includes mining and milling, while the more radioactive wastes occur at the back-end of the cycle, which includes reactor operation and fuel reprocessing. Among the former type of wastes, inactive mill tailings can lead to the exposure of people to radiation but can be greatly reduced by adequate design of the tailings pond and by the use of a clay cover (UNEP, 1981). Wastes at the back-end of the nuclear fuel cycle are generally classified as low-intermediate–and high-level, and wastes contaminated with transuranic elements. Low-level and intermediate wastes are normally disposed of by shallow land burial or by dumping in the deep ocean in specially designed containers. High-level and transuranic wastes must be conditioned and subsequently disposed of, normally in a solidified form, at a suitable repository.

Such material is sufficiently persistent and hazardous to life to require special long-term isolation. During the decade there was much research on the vitrification of high level wastes, or solidification in synthetic rock slabs, so as to facilitate handling in transport to central storage and disposal sites and on the potential of different rock strata on land and different areas of the deep sea bed as sites for permanent repositories (Kenneth-Hare and Aikin, 1980). The Swedish Nuclear Fuel Safety Project (Kärn–Bränsle–Säkerhet, KBS, 1978) reported on possible deep disposal in crystalline rock; this was the object of searching review by the U.S. National Academy of Sciences (NAS, 1980). However no disposal techniques have yet been generally agreed to be fully satisfactory (CEQ 1980). Similarly, while the de-commissioning of nuclear reactors and other installations at the end of their operational lives is technically feasible, the estimated costs are high and many problems remain to be overcome (El-Hinnawi, 1980).

NON—BIOLOGICAL RENEWABLE SOURCES OF ENERGY

Water and wind power have been used for centuries as local sources of energy, and large hydropower schemes have been developed throughout the present century. But the 1970s saw increasing interest in geothermal, solar, tidal and wave power, in new technology for harnessing wind energy, and in ocean thermal energy conversion (OTEC) technologies. Reviews of renewable energy systems and their environmental effects were undertaken by UNEP (1981) and by El-Hinnawi and Biswas (1981).

Hydropower

Of all renewable energy sources, hydropower was furthest developed by 1970 and retained its lead during the decade. In 1970 it provided 1,175 billion kWh/y (23.7 per cent of world electricity production) and by 1979 the capacity had risen to 1,721 billion kWh/y although this represented only 21.6 per cent of world supply (UN, 1981 a). Table 12–10 sets out the installed capacity and output in 1978, and estimates of potential region by region, and illustrates that while the resources in Europe and North America were 75 per cent developed, only a small proportion had been tapped in Oceania, Asia, and especially Africa.

Table 12–10. World Hydropower

	Potential available 95% of time (thousand kW) (1)	Potential output 95% of time (million kWh/y) (2)	Present installed capacity (thousand kW) (3)	Current annual production (million kWh/y) (4)
Africa	145,218	1,161,741	11,437	49,663
Asia	139,288	1,114,305	59,773	245,096
Europe (incl. USSR)	102,961	827,676	177,797	620,676
N. America	72,135	577,086	111,402	434,035
Latin America	81,221	649,763	38,582	176,845
Oceania	12,987	103,897	9,578	31,669
World Total	553,810	4,434,468	408,569	1,557,984

Source: UNEP (1981).

Hydropower developments have substantial environmental impacts (UNEP, 1981; Biswas, 1981). Large storage schemes displace settlements, the upheaval and resettlement causing considerable social effects: they modify agricultural and transport patterns and they have effects on regional health (Chapter 10). They can also stimulate fisheries (Chapter 4). Downstream, river flow is modified and hydropower is commonly an element in multi-purpose water management projects. Small schemes, while they may increase the incidence of waterborne diseases, otherwise have generally beneficial effects and minor environmental impacts. The experience of the past decade has been that small hydropower systems can be an important component of development, but that the potential impact of all schemes needs thorough evaluation in advance.

Geothermal Energy

Although the upper crust of the earth stores an enormous amount of heat energy – equivalent to the output of some 70,000 times the world's recoverable coal reserves (UNEP, 1981, Ellis, 1981) – only localized concentrations of this heat are economically exploitable. Iceland pioneered the process, using geothermal hot water to heat buildings in Reykjavik in 1943. By 1980 geothermal sources were used for space heating in the United States, the USSR, New Zealand, Japan, Hungary, and France as well as Iceland. Hot geothermal waters were used extensively in horticulture, especially in the USSR which had some 25 million m^2 of greenhouses heated in this way.

There was also about 2,472 MW of installed geothermal electrical generating capacity by mid 1981. Projections suggested that by 1985 there would be about 4,239 MW of electricity generation and 10,000 MW non-electrical use, rising to 50,000 MW and 100,000 MW respectively by the year 2000, when geothermal energy might meet 0.8 per cent of global primary energy demand (Ellis, 1981).

Geothermal energy is tapped by withdrawing steam or hot water from subterranean reservoirs. The energy must be used as heat, or converted into electricity, near to the point where it is tapped, so the entire fuel cycle from extraction to transmission is located at one site. In environmental terms this is advantageous in minimizing land requirements. Moreover, geothermal power stations do not generally need an external source of cooling water, since they condense and recycle the steam produced. Adverse environmental impacts can come from land subsidence, hydrogen sulphide (the main atmospheric pollutant emitted causing problems through its unpleasant smell rather than its toxicity) and liquid effluent containing heavy metals and salts. These can cause pollution if discharged to surface watercourses. Waste water may be disposed of by re-injection or treated by de-salination (the water being re-used) or by evaporation: the choice of method depends on local hydrological conditions, the quality of the water, the economics of recovery of water and salts, and environmental regulations (UNEP, 1981, Ellis, 1981).

Solar Energy

The sun's energy powers the living world. About 1.2×10^{17} watts (or 10^{18} kilowatt-hours) is received annually at the surface of the Earth (UNEP, 1981). However, only a tiny fraction of this energy is tapped directly for human use. The systems employed are both active and passive, centralized and decentralized. Solar collectors that heat water for domestic use, generally supplemented by fossil fuel heating, have sold widely in developed countries in temperate regions. By 1979 there were some 2 million installed in Japan and 70,000 in Australia (UNEP, 1981, Pheline, 1981). Low-energy-consuming houses combining passive solar gain (heating obtained by orientation of the dwelling with regard to the sun), high insulation, solar collectors for water heating, and sometimes very large heat-storage reservoirs so that surplus energy absorbed in summer can be drawn upon in winter, have been built in a number of places in Europe and North America, although mainly for demonstration and experiment. "Active" systems involving photovoltaic cells to generate electricity have been incorporated in some of these buildings.

Simple solar water heating and water-distillation systems, solar cookers and solar grain-drying cribs have been developed, and at the end of the decade photovoltaic cells were being produced at a cost that indicated that they could soon be acceptable for widespread use in developing countries. Experience with solar cookers (cheaply available in India as early as the 1950s) suggests that overcoming social traditions may be a major barrier to the use of such devices.

Centralized use of solar systems for electricity generation was also planned and there had been proposals for very large satellites with several square kilometres of intercepting surface that would beam the energy they collected down to large receiving antennas on earth in the form of microwave radiation.

Solar energy use usually has only slight environmental impacts. Where it is combined with good design and insulation to reduce consumption of other forms of energy it is environmentally beneficial, especially in reducing pollution. Some changes in housing design and layout are needed to maximize passive gain. In developing countries solar stills, driers and other devices can bring real improvements in quality of life. Centralized solar power plants require land areas comparable to those needed for conventional thermal power stations (and antenna arrays to receive energy beamed from satellites would be very extensive), but much of this land can be used for other purposes as well.

Wind Energy

The total potential global wind energy is of the order of 1,200 million MW (Sørensen, 1979 a, 1979 b). It can only be tapped economically, however, at a limited number of sites. During the decade wind-energy machines in the 5–100 kilowatt range were used increasingly for water pumping, flour milling and electricity generation in rural areas. Larger (100 kW–5MW) machines were also being developed. The rate of growth of this form of renewable energy utilization is likely to depend more on cost and public acceptability than on technology.

One estimate (Merriam, 1978), is that the world-installed wind generation capacity may rise from 500,000 kW in 1985 to 10 million kW in 1990 and 200 million in the year 2000, with corresponding energy outputs per year of 1.5 billion, 30 billion and 900 billion kWh hours (in 1979 the total world electricity production was 7,966 billion kWh according to UN, 1981 a). Coastal areas have the greatest potential (Table 12–11).

Wind power systems can have a number of environmental impacts (Sørensen, 1981). Large arrays along coasts (especially areas of high natural beauty could be visually intrusive and reduce the attraction of the area for tourism. Concern has also been expressed over associated noise, interference with telecommunications and risk of accidents.

The Oceans

The theoretical wave power of the oceans is enormous, but as with wind and geothermal energy, the extractable fraction is small (Merriam, 1978). Similarly, although

Table 12–11. Estimate of Coastline Wind Potentials

Region	Assumed Coastline (10^6m)	Est. coastline wind potential (TWh* per year)	Electricity consumption (1978) (TWh per year)
North Amnerica	46	754	2,400
South America	22	604	300
Oceania	20	780	150
USSR	11	494	1,000
Asia (except USSR)	42	701	1,000
Europe (except USSR)	24	1,051	2,000
Africa	27	534	200

Source: Sørensen (1979 b); consumption figures have been rounded.
*TWh = terawatt hours
1TW = billion (10^9) kilowatts

about 60 billion watts is potentially available at sites where tidal stations could be built, no more than 10—25 per cent of this could be converted to electricity (WEC, 1980). A third theoretically large oceanic energy source is thermal energy conversion (Lavi and Lavi, 1979). The overall potential of the oceans as an energy resource was reviewed by Goldin (1980).

By the end of the 1970s a number of devices for harnessing wave energy were under study, although the only installed systems were those generating around 70–120OW to power buoys. The installations under development included floating oscillating devices, rectifiers in the inter-tidal zone, and fully submerged systems responding to the variable head of pressure above them. Because none was in operation at the end of the decade their potential environmental impacts are not easy to determine. However, none would release waste heat or polluted effluent, alter water salinity or demand freshwater for operation. But they would calm the sea by acting as wave-breakers and would also be extensive physical intrusions into the marine environment, causing both ecological changes and some loss of amenity (UNEP, 1981; Said Ahmad and El-Hinnawi, 1981).

One major tidal power system was built during the 1970s on the Rance in France. Others (like the Severn Barrage in England) were under investigation (Department of Energy, 1981). Such schemes could have large potential ecological effects, modifying the flow and salinity of the waters draining into them, affecting the concentration of pollutants and altering tidal patterns: they would also demand large volumes of construction materials, could be visually intrusive, and could influence the pattern of transport both by affecting port operations and by the construction of major road links on the barrages.

Such impacts can only be evaluated scheme by scheme, but it cannot be assumed that harnessing tidal power is environmentally beneficial simply because a renewable resource is tapped. The same applies to ocean thermal energy conversion, of which prototype devices were tested during the 1970s. These could cause temperature and salinity changes, and local chemical pollution from anti-fouling paints (Said Ahmad and El-Hinnawi, 1981).

The acceptability of Wind, Solar and Small-Hydro Sources

A general criticism levelled against renewable energy sources (wind, solar, mini-hydropower) is their slow degree of penetration of the rural sector because of cost disadvantages, especially when compared with diesel power or a grid as a source of electricity. Contradictory results from different analyses probably arise because costs depend on factors such as fuel price and price of renewable systems, which vary from one country to another. A joint U.S. National Academy of Sciences – National Science Research Council of Tanzania study carried out in August 1977 (TNSRC, 1978) suggested that small-scale renewable technologies were able to compete with diesel power or grid (Table 12–12) under the conditions of the comparison (production of up to 1 kWh/person/day for a remote Tanzanian village of about 300 people).

Table 12–12. Electricity Costs For a Typical Tanzanian Village

			Annual Supply (000 kWh)	Capital Cost[a] (US$/kW)	Unit Cost (c/kW)
1.	*Extend existing grid (20 km)*				
	500–kW supply: load factor	2.5%	110	2,180	29
	(including generating costs)			(2,000)	44
		25%	1,100	same	3
				same	6.7
2.	*Mini-hydro (no storage)*				
	60–kW supply: load factor	20%	110	560–1,375	6–13
		60%	330	same	2–4
3.	*Mini-hydro (with storage)*				
	15–kW supply: load factor	83%	110	3,080–3,920	11–13
4.	*Diesel generator sets*				
	Fuel at $0.25/liter				
	10 sets at 6 kVa each				
	60–kW supply: load factor	20%	110	5,320	29
		60%	330	same	12.5
5.	*Windmills (with storage)*				
	30–kW supply: fits wind regime		110	4,380	25
6.	*Future solar cells (with storage)*				
	Cell cost $0.5 per peak watt,				
	expected after 1985				
	60–kW supply: fits solar regime	·	110	1,100	10

Source: TNSRC (1978).

[a] All capital cost amortized over expected equipment lifetime at 10 per cent per year interest charges.

BIOLOGICAL ENERGY SOURCES

Measures to Enhance Woodland Productivity

The dry weight of all living plant matter on the Earth's land surface has been calculated by Rodin et al., (1975) as about 2,400 billion tonnes, and by Lieth and Whittaker (1975) at 1,800 billion tonnes. The annual production rate is calculated at about 170 billion and 118 billion tonnes dry weight per year by these authors respectively. The latter is equivalent to about 10 times the present total world energy consumption from all commercial sources. However, much wood is cut non-commercially for fuel (Chapter 7) (Openshaw, 1978; Arnold 1979). Production and use varies geographically and in many developing countries harvesting exceeds replenishment so that the forest capital is being depleted. Under these circumstances, it is not surprising that ways of sustaining fuelwood production were emphasized during the decade.

Two approaches seemed promising: using fuelwood more efficiently, and developing managed plantations. As burnt at present, fuelwood is not an efficient fuel. Cooking on an open, slow-burning fire requires about five times as much energy as cooking on a kerosene stove (Eckholm, 1975). A study in Indonesia found that on the usual type of fuelwood stove, 94 per cent of the heat value of the wood was wasted (Singer, 1971). Simple improvements in stove design cut this loss by about 20 per cent. Cutting the wood some weeks before use and then drying it in the open air reduced the loss by a further 10 per cent, and a new type of cooking pot, partly sunk into the stove, cut heat loss by an additional 30 per cent. Numerous political, cultural, historic, economic and technical factors combined to slow the design and widespread use of efficient stoves (Joseph, 1979).

The logical immediate response to the fuelwood shortage, one that will have many incidental ecological benefits, is to plant more trees in plantations, farms, along roads, in shelter belts, and on unused land throughout the rural areas of the poor countries. For many regions, fast-growing tree varieties are available that can be culled for firewood within a few years, especially if the trees are coppiced. Some species could provide fodder and food crops as well as fuel. Leguminous species would improve the soil at the same time by fixing atmospheric nitrogen. While competition for land makes fuelwood planting difficult in heavily cultivated areas, some means of producing sufficient amounts on a sustainable basis is essential to rural economies in developing countries.

During the 1970s there was a move towards the growth of crops and fast-growing trees for their energy value. Eucalyptus was used in Australia and parts of the United States (Mariani, 1978; Hall, 1979). In the Philippines, Leucaena acidophila (giant "ipil-ipil") was favoured. One study showed that a 10,000 ha plantation would supply a 75 MW steam power station (Semana, 1979). In Indonesia, 34,000 ha of red kaliandra (produces up to 33 tonnes of wood per hectare per year) have been established (Silitonga, 1979). Trial plantings of alder, willows and poplars were made in Europe and elsewhere, and the use of coppicing and selective breeding to increase productivity examined (Klass, 1978).

Production of Charcoal and Other Fuels by Pyrolysis

The conversion of wood into charcoal has been known since the dawn of civilization. In primitive earth kilns, 100 kg of wood yields only 10–15 kg charcoal, and although weight for weight this has 2–2.5 times the energy content of wood, 70–80 per cent of the energy in the initial wood is lost. Modern steel kilns increase the charcoal yield to 30–35 kg from the same amount of wood. If the volatile liquids can be collected, these can also be used as fuels (UNEP, 1981). Charcoal offers several advantages over wood as a fuel. It is easier to transport, store and distribute; it is more efficient in burning and less polluting. Attention is now being paid to the pyrolysis of urban refuse, straw, leaves and other woody and vegetable wastes, the char being compacted into briquettes. However, this is not the only, or necessarily the best way of using these materials. Pelletized and briquette fuels made directly from dried agricultural and organic wastes are likely to be more energy efficient, and producer gas is another potential product.

Producer Gas

The rising price of oil has led to a renewal of interest in producer or generator gas, a low–BTU gas evolved when a restricted air stream is passed over heated wood, charcoal, coke or other carbon sources (Kjellstrom, 1981). The gas, principally carbon monoxide and hydrogen, is then burned in an internal combustion engine. Conversion efficiencies are higher than in direct combustion. This system was widely used on trucks and buses in Europe during the Second World War. Charcoal and coke produce the cleanest gas requiring least filtration from organic tarry residues and so are most suitable for use in trucks and tractors. Wood can be used successfully for stationary power producers, where cumbersome filtration equipment is acceptable. During the 1970s, several developing countries recognized the value of producer gas, which seems particularly satisfactory for remote oceanic tropical islands like the Seychelles, where waste coconut shells form an excellent fuel and where the cost of diesel transport is very high.

Biogas Production

The anaerobic digestion of animal and vegetable matter yields a mixture of about 2/3 methane and 1/3 carbon dioxide with small amounts of hydrogen, nitrogen, organic sulphides and hydrocarbons, commonly known as biogas (gobar gas or marsh gas). During the past fifty years, some authorities in Europe and North America have built anaerobic digesters to treat their sewage and many have used the resulting biogas ("sewage gas") as a source of energy. In 1951, 48 sewage treatment plants in the Federal Republic of Germany provided more than 16 million m^3 of biogas, about 3.4 per cent of which was utilized for power production, 16.7 per cent for digester heating, 28.5 per cent passed into the municipal gas supply system and 51.4 per cent was converted to vehicle motor fuel (Tietjen, 1975). Several small installations for producing biogas from manure were built in Europe (e.g. in Germany and France) to solve the problem of fuel shortage during the Second World War. There were a few scattered small biogas plants in some developing countries in the 1950s, but the main thrust to develop them came in the late 1960s and early 1970s. In India more than 36,000, mostly small-scale, gobar gas plants had been built by 1975-76; by 1980 the total was 80,000 and 20,000 were being installed annually. The largest number of biogas installations was in the People's Republic of China, where more than 8 million plants existed in late 1979, (El-Hinnawi and El-Gohary, 1981). Hundreds of small-scale biogas plants have been installed in the Philippines, Bangladesh, Indonesia, Sri Lanka and in several African countries. In developed countries they have been built at intensive livestock-rearing units where they provide power on the farm and prevent pollution of drainage water.

The production of biogas is a "package" (UNEP, 1981; El-Hinnawi and El-Gohary, 1981). It yields energy for cooking, lighting, internal combustion engines and electricity production. The effluent and sludge remaining after digestion is a nutrient-rich fertilizer. The anaerobic digestion eliminates most of the parasites and pathogenic organisms found in the manure. Pollution is reduced both because organic effluent to watercourses is cut down and air pollution through incineration avoided. Biogas is also a more efficient fuel than wood and its use therefore reduces deforestation. Small-scale plants are environmentally beneficial: large-scale ones also can be, but they suffer from land-requirement problems, the need to collect and transport organic waste and to treat waste-waters, and if industrial or urban wastes are involved, from toxic contamination (UNEP, 1981).

Alcohol

Ethanol (ethyl alcohol) can be produced through fermentation of sugarcane, cassava, corn, sweet sorghum, and other crops. Sugarcane is the most efficient in terms of net energy yield. Methyl alcohol (methanol) can also be produced (for example from wood) but is less promising (World Bank, 1980 c); increasing quantities were however being produced in Brazil (CTP, 1980 a). Pilot-scale studies on ethanol were underway in several countries in the late 1970s and production programmes had begun in others, the largest being the Brazilian National Alcohol Programme (Yang and Trindade, 1978; Trindade, 1980). In 1975, the alcohol consumption in Brazil was 414,000 m³ (of which 35.6 per cent was used as fuel alcohol, the rest in chemical and pharmaceutical industry). It reached 2.4 million m³ in 1978, 60 per cent being used in gasoline blends. The target in 1980 was to increase this amount to 10.7 million m³ (of which 73 per cent would be used as fuel alcohol) by 1985 (Trindade, 1980).

Up to 20 per cent alcohol can be blended with gasoline without any changes in present-day internal combustion engines. Ethanol and vegetable oil can also be blended in diesel fuel. Modified engines can be run on neat ethanol and the Brazilian target is for 2.5 million of these (17 per cent of the national total) by 1985 (CTP, 1980 b). Savings in crude oil follow: in Brazil a combination of measures led to a reduction in the gasoline fraction of refined products from 30.5 per cent in 1970 to 22.5 per cent in 1978 (CTP, 1980 b). Alcohol also increases the octane rating, rendering lead anti-knock additives unnecessary. The production of alcohol from fuel crops raises a number of important issues however: land area requirements; fertilizer, water and pesticide requirements; the pressures on soil productivity and above all the possible competition with food production (El-Hinnawi and El-Gohary, 1981). In addition, the fermentation process produces large amounts of potentially polluting effluents containing organic and mineral matter (stillage). However, it is technically feasible to convert stillage into marketable products such as fertilizers and feed additives or into methane, as a supplementary energy source, by anaerobic fermentation.

Other Energy Crops

Other potential crops include algae, grasses and fast-growing "weeds" as well as familiar agricultural crops like sugarcane and sorghum. Algal growth in shallow ponds can achieve about 3 to 5 per cent solar energy conversion efficiency under good conditions (Hall, 1979). In California average yields of algae exceeding 100 kg/ha per day (dry weight) (or 36.5 tonnes/y) have been obtained – enough to produce about 50,000 kWh of electricity. Blue-green algal culture promotion and improvement for biogas production was one of the features of an FAO/UNDP Regional Project in Asia and the Far East begun in 1978. Processing for methane production would follow a route comparable to that for producing biogas from organic waste, and have the same ancillary benefit of fertilizer production. Other plants, including *Hevea braziliensis* (rubber plant), *Euphorbia* and *Avalois* species, produce natural hydrocarbons for which they could be grown (Calvin, 1979; Hall, 1979).

Oils expressed from seeds of sunflower, oil palm, grape, castor bean, rape and mustard, after degumming, have been successfully used as a substitute for diesel fuel, either pure or mixed in various proportions with diesel, kerosene or petroleum. The residue after pressing can be used as a high quality animal feed. The energy efficiency of production appears to be several times better than ethanol. Rape-seed oil has been used in pilot field trials in tractors in Sweden and grape-seed and sun-flower seed oils were, at the end of the decade, beginning to be used in tractors in Australia and South Africa respectively.

THE IMPACT OF ELECTRICITY GENERATION AND TRANSMISSION

Electricity generation in large centralized installations, whether using fossil fuel or nuclear power, has several environmental impacts. The laws of thermodynamics make it inevitable that about 60 per cent of the heat energy generated is "waste" and unless it can be used as low-grade heat to warm buildings nearby, it has to be released into the environment. Combined heat and power schemes were developed in many countries during the 1970s, but are most suited to medium-sized power stations in urban areas, and not to large fossil fuel or nuclear installations that are commonly built away from centres of population. Waste heat may be discharged to the air, where it can affect local climate (Chapter 2) or to fresh or marine waters with the ecological effects described in Chapter 4. It can also be used to boost plant production in horticulture or agriculture, if warmed water is used for irrigation in winter. Fish and shell-fish production might also be enhanced if warm water discharged from power stations is used in aquaculture (Biswas, 1980; UNEP, 1981).

Other impacts arise from electricity transmission. It is much more costly to place transmission lines underground (where access for maintenance is also more difficult) and in the 1970s this was done mainly in areas of particularly outstanding landscape quality. Generally above-ground transmission lines were built, their length naturally being related to the type of power station and its location. Hydropower schemes, usually being remote from the consumer, require especially long lines. The main impact of such lines comes from their visual intrusion, but they also restrict agriculture on swathes of land 30–120 m wide and may cause some interference with nearby radio and television reception.

It has been postulated that the lines may affect bird behaviour (especially water fowl), perhaps because they sway or hum in the wind: other hypotheses involve the effects of electrical fields. However, comprehensive reviews during the 1970s conclude that the latter have no significant biological effects (Kaufman and Michaelson, 1974; Bridges, 1975; 1977; Biswas, 1980). Similarly, calculations show that electrical (corona) discharges from power lines will cause only a negligible amount of ozone production. On the positive side, where lines traverse forests they produce useful fire-breaks and also provide permanently maintained clearings bearing herbaceous or scrub vegetation, which increases ecological diversity and provides grazing for herbivores.

Energy Conservation

BEFORE the 1970s it was assumed that a steady increase in energy supplies was an essential concomitant of economic growth, and the national energy supply industries vied with one another in expanding their markets. Investment in supply capacity was inevitably determined centrally by a small number of large investors among whom governments are prominent and hence have a direct interest in sales and pricing policy. In contrast energy demand is the collective expression of a large number of users. During the 1970s, when constraints on the current or future supply of several forms of energy became apparent, a number of policies changed. For example, the previous tendency to give a price discount to large consumers was, in several countries, replaced by one giving cheaper supplies to small users. Governments also intervened to encourage more efficient energy policies, by reducing waste both in energy production and use. Energy conservation can be defined as the strategy for reducing energy requirements per unit of industrial output or individual well-being without affecting the progress of socio-economic development or causing disruption in life style (Schipper, 1976).

In temperate developed countries most energy is used in heating and lighting industrial and domestic buildings. Industrial processes, transport and agriculture are the other main users. During the 1970s it was demonstrated that substantial savings could be achieved through appropriate building technologies and the use of energy-efficient equipment for heating, air-conditioning and lighting. In Sweden, for example, space heating requirements were 30–40 per cent lower per square metre of space in homes and commercial buildings than in the United States, the difference being ascribed to greater efficiency in energy use (UNEP, 1978). Passive solar heating was made use of by planning building developments for maximum solar interception. Combined heat and power schemes reduce waste heat emissions from power stations and reduce domestic fuel demands and consequent urban pollution. Heat re-cycling through the use of heat exchangers to recover heat from the outward channels of controlled ventilation systems, and heat pumps that reclaim heat from waste warm water provide further examples.

Half the direct energy spent on lighting in the late 1970s was superfluous, and most lights operated inefficiently. Incandescent bulbs convert only one-twentieth of the energy in electricity into light; fluorescent bulbs convert one-fifth and some are also cheaper. There is no fundamental theoretical reason why a much higher conversion efficiency of electricity into light should not be attained. In the late 1970s, improved light bulbs that cut electricity consumption by 60 per cent were developed (UNEP, 1978).

Substantial energy savings have been made in transport and more can be achieved – by improving engineering, increasing load factors, switching increasing volumes of traffic to more efficient modes and by changing transport habits. During the late 1970s, light automobiles with greatly improved fuel economy became increasingly common in many countries. Conservation efforts in the transport sector often bring unexpected secondary benefits. For example, the reduction of the maximum permitted highway speed in the United States (which was intended to increase fuel efficiency), had the additional benefit of increasing automobile tyre life and, more important, reducing highway accidents and deaths. These matters are discussed further in Chapter 13.

In industry, substantial savings of energy have been achieved through technological innovations. The steel industry provides several examples. Hot coke is usually quenched with water in the United States, thus dissipating its heat while producing air and water pollution. In Europe and the USSR, coke is cooled with a recycled inert gas, and much of its heat is recaptured to perform useful work (Hayes, 1976). Aluminium refining is an exceedingly energy-intensive operation, and the industry has therefore situated its major installations near sources of cheap energy like large hydro-electric facilities. Technical advances in the traditional refining process can reduce energy requirements by more than a fifth.

Consumption of energy in agriculture has increased in the past few decades largely as a result of technical innovations to increase food production. During the 1970s energy costs emerged as a major factor in agriculture. Renewable sources of energy can contribute to the adjustment now required. Wind power for irrigation pumping, solar energy for heating greenhouses and drying grain, and low-grade geothermal resources for greenhouses can contribute to savings in the utilization of fossil fuels. Simple, on-the spot biogas production from animal and agricultural residues can also make a significant contribution.

No short list can exhaust the possibilities for substantial conservation of energy. Most goods could be both manufactured and made to work more efficiently. A variety of energy-saving measures have been recently adopted by various countries, including fiscal measures, regulations and standards, encouragement of action by common means (public transportation, total energy systems), public education and research and development.

Policies designed to encourage efficient use of energy will probably have to incorporate many of these' measures. Some industrialized countries have succeeded in reducing the ratio of energy use to GNP: between 1973 and 1977 this fell by 16 per cent in Japan, 13 per cent in France, 12 per cent in the Federal Republic of Germany, 10 per cent in the United States and Italy, 9 per cent in Canada and 7 per cent in the United Kingdom. Moreover, Japan and Western Europe have held their absolute volume of petroleum use constant since 1973 and the United States has done so since 1978 (World Bank, 1980 b). While the means available differ, the developing countries have even more to gain from efficient energy use.

Future Prospects

UNTIL recently, national development plans were centred on economic objectives like rapid industrial development, capital-intensive GNP growth, and increases in living standards. Production was widely oriented towards energy-intensive industries like plastics and petrochemicals, and towards the mechanization of agriculture, and between the mid-1960s and early 1970s there was a decline in the efficiency of energy use in many countries. Economic growth was indeed stimulated by the expansion of energy use and by increasing petroleum consumption. With the cost increases of the 1970s these conditions changed. In future, rapid economic growth rates will be contingent to a substantial degree on the price and availability of energy resources. Energy "demand" will be scrutinized increasingly stringently and more emphasis placed on energy "need" (Howe and Tarrant, 1980).

While most governments have responded vigorously and expeditiously to the energy "crisis", policy formulation and implementation is seriously handicapped by a wide range of uncertainties, including:

1. The magnitude of total energy demand as well as its profile, which results in "high" and "low" estimates for the year 2000 differing by a factor of three or more;

2. The quantity, location, and availability of various energy sources under different circumstances, including future prices;

3. The difficulty of assessing accurately the technical, environmental and economic aspects of various alternative energy systems within a time frame relevant to policymakers today;

4. Interrelations between economic development planning and energy policy, including industrial location, rural electrification, urbanization and transition from non-commercial to commercial fuels;

5. The constraints imposed upon the selection of energy development strategies by the need to manage wastes such as reactor fission products, uranium and coal mine tailings, and emissions from fossil fuel combustion;

6. Changing social attitudes to risk, and changing personal preferences affecting conservation and transport and the acceptability of environmental damage.

Various computations of future world primary energy demand have been made in the past decade: the most important are those by the Workshop on Alternative Energy Strategies (WAES, 1977), World Energy Conference (WEC, 1980), the World Bank (1979, 1980 b), OECD (1979), the Global 2000 Study (CEQ, 1980), and the International Institute for Applied Systems Analysis (IIASA, 1981 a, b, c). They suggested requirements of between 9,000 and 11,000 million tonnes of oil equivalent (m.t.o.e) per year in 1990 and not very great differences in 2000 (the IIASA high projection was for 11,860 m.t.o.e. and the low projection, 9,574 m.t.o.e. in that year, rising to 25,115 − 15,774 m.t.o.e. in 2030). Many of these studies also developed scenarios to balance future energy demand and supply (e.g. WAES, 1977; WEC, 1978; IIASA, 1981 a, b, c), but the question of how to develop an environmentally-sound and appropriate energy "mix" (which will vary from one country to another) remained unanswered at the end of the decade. However, during the 1970s a series of efforts to develop environmentally acceptable policies was made (e.g. Ford Foundation, 1974; World Coal Study, WOCOL, 1980).

Both the WAES (1977) and WEC (1978) studies indicated that the supply of oil would fail to meet demand before the year 2000. IIASA (1981 a, b, c) came to nearly the same conclusion but indicated that unconventional oil (from oil shales, tar sands, oil produced by enhanced recovery, from deep offshore wells etc.) would stretch the supply to meet demand until about 2020, after which the "gap" would have to be filled by synthetic liquid fuels produced from coal. In most developed countries an increase in coal use in utilities, cement, steel, pulp and paper and other industries is expected during the next twenty years.

The future shortage in oil supplies has particularly serious implications for those developing countries lacking indigenous energy resources and with weak financial resources. Their domestic energy requirements are expected to continue growing with the increasing pace of industrialization and development. Their share of world energy consumption is expected to rise by at least 50 per cent of current levels by 2000 (Howe and Tarrant, 1980; World Bank, 1980 a, b). Commercial energy is expected to substitute increasingly for non-commercial. The means to ensure energy supplies for development is, therefore, of critical importance for developing countries and for the world as a whole. The response will vary with national circumstances. In countries with indigenous energy resources, control of depletion rates and planned transitions to new energy mixes as reserves are exhausted, will be critical. In all countries technology will have a major role in improving the efficiency of resource utilization, conservation and the prevention of avoidable environmental damage. Research and development will be crucial. Various national inquiries have spelled out research needs (e.g. Australia, 1979, which stresses alcohol production from crops, coal liquifaction, oil shale utilization and the study of associated environmental impacts). Developing countries face severe difficulties in meeting all these challenges, and in securing the transfer of appropriate technology (UNCTAD, 1980).

There has been so much discussion about the future potential of renewable energy that it is important to question whether it can be deployed at the scale required to service a modern urban society. In an analysis of future West European demand, Lyttkens and Johansson (1981) took as their starting points the calculated requirement of 15,000 TWh by 2030 according to Colombo and Bernadini (1979) or 10,000 TWh according to Lovins (1979). Lovins assessed the breakdown of end-uses as:

Heat	100°C	44 %
	100–600°C	11%
	600°C	12%
Liquid fuels		23%
Electricity		10%

Lyttkens and Johansson attempted to match the latter breakdown of 10,000 TWh against possible renewable supplies. They concluded that even on this scale, a future based on renewables seemed feasible (Table 12–13). But although most of the technology required is available, much of it is as yet unproven. Perhaps the biggest problem is cost, which will not come down until increased mass-scale demand stimulates market forces. In developing countries, decentralized systems involving small-scale power generation units and local schemes – some very simple – for tapping solar, water and wind energy and for producing biogas, seem likely to be an increasing feature.

If new technology is to be efficient and to avoid environmental damage, much of it will need to be sophisticated and the result will be to increase the cost per unit of energy produced. Large capital resources will be needed if there is to be environmentally sound development at an acceptable rate in the developing world, and this is bound to place new strains on the world economy. These prospective costs, coupled with increasing public understanding of the energy-environment system, could well help to bring about beneficial changes in energy consumption per capita, reducing waste. Public demand for pollution control can itself be beneficial in stimulating research and development and bringing costs down because such equipment is manufactured on a larger scale. Some pollution control systems (like fluidized bed combustion) also bring benefits in efficiency of energy production. All of these costs and benefits will require careful appraisal in arriving at viable national and international policies.

If growth in energy supply in future is to be achieved without unacceptable damage to environment, research, planning, the wise use of new technology, conservation and the decentralized adoption of systems for using renewable energy sources are all likely to be needed. The precise mix will inevitably vary nationally and regionally, and the development of solutions will be a major task for the 1980s.

Table 12–13.   Capacity of Renewable Energy Sources to Meet Forecast Demand in Western Europe.

Demand (TWh)	Use	Renewable Sources	Supply (TWh)
4,400	Space and Water heating	Solar heat from flat collectors	4,100
		Hydro, wind, wave and tidal (via electricity grid)	300
1,100	Industrial process heat at 100°C — 600°C	Solar heat from concentrating collectors	600
		Waste heat from biomass conversion processes	300
		Hydro, wind, wave, tidal via electricity grid	200
1,200	Industrial process heat, over 600°C	Solar heat from concentrating collectors	200
		Hydro, wind, wave, tidal via electricity grid	1,000
2,300	Liquid fuel	Biological sources	4,600
1,000	Electricity	Solar thermal energy conversion (1,400); hydro, wind, wave and tidal (800); and industrial generation of electricity (300)	2,500

Source: Lovins (1979); Lyttkens and Johansson (1981).

References

Arnold, J. E. M. (1979), Wood Energy and Rural Communities. *Natural Resources Forum*, 3, 229.

Ashby, E. (1978), *Reconciling Man with The Environment*, Stanford Univ. Press, Stanford, California.

Barnaby, F. (1980), The Controversy Over Low-Level Radiation, *Ambio*, 9, 74.

Berger, J. J. (1977), *Nuclear Power – The Unviable Option*, Dell Publ. Co., New York.

Biswas, A. K. (1980), Non-Radiological Environmental Implications of Nuclear Energy. In E. El-Hinnawi (Editor) *Nuclear Energy and The Environment*, Pergamon Press, Oxford.

Biswas, A. K. (1981), Hydro-electric Energy. In E. El-Hinnawi and A. K. Biswas (Editors), *Renewable Sources of Energy and The Environment*, Tycooly Intern., Dublin.

Bolin, B. *et al.* (1979), *The Global Carbon Cycle: SCOPE* 13, John Wiley and Sons, Chichester.

Bradshaw, A. D. (1973), Ecological Effects. In *Fuel and The Environment*, Institute of Fuel, London.

Bridges, J. E. (1975), *Biologic Effects of High Voltage Electric Fields*, Electric Power Research Institute, Palo Alto, California. Rept. 381–1.

Bridges, J. E. (1977), *Environmental Considerations Concerning the Biological Effects of Power Frequency (50 or 60 Hz) Electric Fields*. Proc. JEEE, Paper F77–256–1.

Budnitz, R. J. and J. P. Holdren (1976), Social and Environmental Costs of Energy Systems, *Annual Review of Energy*, 1, 553.

Burleson, C. W. (1978), *The Day The Bomb Fell*, Prentice-Hall, New Jersey.

Butcher, S. S. and D. I. Buckley (1977), A Preliminary Study of Particulate Emissions from Small Wood Stoves, *J. Air Poll. Control Assoc.*, 27, 4, 346.

Butcher, S. S. and E. M. Sørenson (1979), A Study of Wood Stove Particulate Emissions, *J.Air Poll. Control Assoc.*, 29, 7, 724.

Calvin, M. (1979), Petroleum Plantations and Synthetic Chloro-plasts. *Energy*, 4, 851.

CEQ (1980), *The Global* 2000 *Report to President of the USA*. Council on Environmental Quality, Washington, D.C.

Cheremisinoff, P. N. and R. A. Young (1976), Control of Fine Particulate Air Pollutants, Equipment Update Report, *Pollution Engin.*, August, 22.

Club du Sahel (1978), *Energy in the Development Strategy of the Sahel*, West Africa Development Bank, Ministries of Co-operation of France, the Netherlands and the Federal Republic of Germany.

Colombo, U. and O. Bernadini (1979), *A Low Energy Growth* 2030 *Scenario and the Perspectives for Western Europe*. Report prepared for the Commission of the European Communities, EEC, Brussels.

CONAES (1980), *Energy in Transition* 1985–2010. Final Report of the Committee on Nuclear and Alternative Energy Systems. National Academy of Sciences, Freeman and Co., San Francisco.

493

CTP (1980 a), *Methanol as a Fuel.* CTP Newsletter, 5, 1. Centro de Tech. Promon, Rio de Janeiro.

CTP (1980 b), *Biomass Energy Technology Development Programme Reviewed.* CTP Newsletter, 5, 1. Centro de Techn. Promon, Rio de Janeiro.

Department of Energy (1981), *Tidal Power from the Severn Estuary.* Vol. 1, Energy Paper No. 46. HMSO, London.

Eckholm, E. (1975), *The Other Energy Crisis: Firewood,* Worldwatch Institute, Paper 1.

El-Hinnawi, E., Editor (1980), *Nuclear Energy and The Environment,* Pergamon Press, Oxford.

El-Hinnawi, E. (1981), The Promise of Renewable Sources of Energy, In E. El-Hinnawi and A. K. Biswas (Editors), *Renewable Sources of Energy and the Environment,* Tycooly Intern., Dublin.

El-Hinnawi, E. and A. K. Biswas, Editors (1981), *Renewable Sources of Energy and the Environment,* Tycooly Intern., Dublin.

El-Hinnawi, E. and F. El-Gohary (1981), Energy From Biomass. In E. El-Hinnawi and A. K. Biswas (Editors), *Renewable Sources of Energy and the Environment,* Tycooly Intern., Dublin.

Ellis, A. J. (1981), Geothermal Energy. In E. El-Hinnawi and A. K. Biswas (Editors), *Renewable Sources of Energy and The Environment,* Tycooly Intern., Dublin.

EPA (1980), *Preliminary Characterization of Emissions From Wood-Fired Residential Combustion Equipment,* US EPA–600/7–80–040, Washington, D.C.

FAO (1980), 1978 *Yearbook of Forest Products,* Food and Agriculture Organization of the United Nations, Rome.

Fischhoff, B. *et al.* (1978), Handling Hazards, *Environment,* 20, 16.

Ford Foundation (1974), *A Time To Choose: America's Energy Future,* Ballinger Publ. Co., Cambridge, Massachusetts.

Gladwin, T. N. *et al.* (1980), *Patterns of Energy-Environment Conflict Within OECD Nations* 1970–1978. Study Prepared for OECD, Environment Directorate, Organization For Economic Co-operation and Development, Paris.

Goldin, A. (1980), *Oceans of Energy,* New York.

Greenhalgh, G. (1980), *The Necessity for Nuclear Power,* London.

Hall, D. O. (1979), Solar Energy Use Through Biology, *Solar Energy,* 22, 307.

Hamilton, L. D. (1977), *Alternative Sources of Energy and Health,* CRC Forum on Energy, CRC Forums, Cleveland, Ohio.

Hayes, D. (1976), *Energy: The Case for Conservation,* Worldwatch Paper 4, Worldwatch Institute, Washington, D.C.

Henderson, P. D. (1975), *India: The Energy Sector,* Oxford Univ. Press, New Delhi.

Holdgate, M. W. (1979), *A Perspective of Environmental Pollution,* Cambridge Univ. Press, Cambridge.

Holdren, J. P. (1981), Energy and The Physical Environment: The Generation and Definition of Environmental Problems, In G. T. Goodman *et al.* (Editors), *The European Transition From Oil,* Academic Press, London.

Howe, J. W. and J. J. Tarrant (1980), *An Alternative Road to the Post-Petroleum Era: North-South Co-operation*, Overseas Development Council, Monograph 14, Washington, D.C.

ICRP (1977), *International Commission on Radiological Protection*, Publication No. 26, Pergamon Press, Oxford.

IIASA (1981a), *Energy in a Finite World*, Executive Summary. International Institute For Applied Systems Analysis, Laxenburg, Austria.

IIASA (1981b), *Energy in a Finite World; Paths to a Sustainable Future.* Ballinger Publ. Co., Cambridge, Massachusetts.

IIASA (1981c), *Energy in a Finite World: A Global Systems Analysis*, Ballinger Publ. Co., Cambridge, Massachusetts.

Joseph, S. (1979), *Problems and Priorities in Developing Wood Stoves*, Report prepared for FAO, Food and Agriculture Organization of the United Nations, Rome.

Karki, A. B. and B. A. Coburn (1977), *The Prospect of Biogas as one of the Sources of Energy in Nepal*, 10th World Energy Conference, Istanbul, Sect. 4.6–3.

Kärn-Bränsle-Säkerhet, KBS (1978), *Handling of Spent Fuel and Final Storage of Vitrified High Level Reprocessing Waste*, Stockholm.

Kaufman, G. E. and S. M. Michaelson (1974), Critical Review of the Biological Effects of Electric and Magnetic Fields, In *Biological and Clinical Effect of Low-Frequency Magnetic and Electric Fields*, Thomas Publ. Co., Springfield, Illinois.

Kenneth Hare, F. and A. M. Aikin (1980), Nuclear Waste Disposal: Technology and Environmental Hazards, In E. El-Hinnawi (Editor), *Nuclear Energy and The Environment*, Pergamon Press, Oxford.

Kjellstrom, B. (1981), *Electricity Generation from Agricultural Residues Using the Gengas System: State of the Art* (in press).

Klass, D. L. (1978), *Energy from Biomass and Wastes*, Symposium on Energy from Biomass and Wastes, Paper No. 1. Institute of Gas Techn., Chicago.

Lavi, A. and C. H. Lavi (1979), Ocean Thermal Energy Conversion, *Energy*, 4, 833.

Lewis, H. W. *et al.* (1978), *Risk Assessment Review Group*, Nuclear Reg. Comm., NUREG/CR-400, Washington, D.C.

Lieth, H. and R. H. Whittaker (1975), *Primary Productivity of the Biosphere*, Springer-Verlag, Berlin.

Lovins, A. (1979), Re-examining the Nature of the ECE Energy Problem, *Energy Policy*, 7, 178.

Lyttkens, J. and T. B. Johansson (1981), Renewable Energy in Western Europe – Potential and Constraints, In G. T. Goodman *et al.* (Editors), *The European Transition From Oil*, Academic Press, London.

Malkin, D. (1981), The International Economic Context: Constraints and Prospects, In G. T. Goodman, *et al.* (Editors), *European Transition From Oil*, Academic Press, London.

Mariani, E. O. (1978), *The Eucalyptus Energy Farms as a Renewable Source of Fuel*, Symposium on Energy From Biomass and Waste, Paper. 2, Institute of Gas Techn., Chicago.

Merriam, M. F. (1978), Wind, Waves and Tides, *Annual Review of Energy*, Vol. 3, 29.

Morris, S. C. *et al.* (1979), In *An Assessment of National Consequences of Increased Coal Utilization*, US Dept. Energy T1D–2945, Vol. 2, Washington, D.C.

Morris, S. C. (1980), *Health Aspects of Wood Fuel Use,* Brookhaven Natl. Lab. Upton, New York.

Nader, R. and J. Abbotts (1979), *The Menace of Atomic Energy,* Norton and Co., New York.

NAS (1980), *A Review of the Swedish KBS–II Plan For Disposal of Spent Nuclear Fuel,* National Academy of Sciences, Washington, D.C.

Nelkin, D. and S. Fallows (1978), The Evolution of The Nuclear Debate, *Annual Review of Energy,* 3, 275.

Nephew, E. A. (1972), Healing Wounds, *Environment,* 14, 12.

NRC (1980), *The Effects on Population of Exposure to Low-Levels of Ionizing Radiation* (the BEIR II Report), National Academy of Sciences, National Research Council, Washington, D.C.

NRPB (1981), *Living With Radiation,* National Radiological Protection Board, Chilton, Oxfordshire, UK.

NUREG–0558 (1979), *Population Dose and Health Impact of The Accident at the Three Mile Island Nuclear Station,* US Nuclear Regulatory Commission, Washington, D.C.

NUREG–0578 (1979), *TMI–2; Lesson Learned,* Task Force Status Report and Short-term Recommendations, US Nuclear Regulatory Commission, Washington, D. C.

OECD (1978), *Nuclear Fuel Cycle Requirements,* Organization for Economic Co-operation and Development, Paris.

OECD (1979), *Interfutures; Final Report of the Research Project on the Future Development of Advanced Industrial Societies in Harmony with the Developing Countries,* Organization for Economic Cooperation and Development, Paris.

Openshaw, K. (1978), Woodfuel – A Time for Re-assessment, *Natural Resources Forum,* 3, 35.

O'Riordan, T. (1981), Social Attitudes and Energy Risk Assessment, In G. T. Goodman *et al.* (Editors), *The European Transition From Oil,* Academic Press, London.

OTA (1979), *The Direct Use of Coal,* Office of Technology Assessment, Congress of the United States, Washington, B.C.

Otway, H. J. *et al.* (1978), Nuclear Power: The Question of Public Acceptance, *Futures,* 10, 100.

Parikh, J. (1978), Energy Use for Subsistence and Prospects for Development, *Energy,* 3, 613.

Pheline, J. (1981), Solar Energy, In E. El–Hinnawi and A. K. Biswas (Editors), *Renewable Sources of Energy and The Environment,* Tycooly Intern., Dublin.

Reddy, A. K. N. and K. K. Prasad (1977), Technological Alternatives and The Indian Energy Crisis, *Economic and Political Weekly* (India), Special No. August 1977, 1496.

Reddy, A. K. N. and D. K. Subramanian (1980), *Integrated Energy Systems for Rural Development – An Indian Approach,* 11th World Energy Conference, Munich, Vol. 1B, 551.

Robinson, F. A., Editor (1979), *Environmental Effects of Utilizing More Coal,* Royal Soc. of Chemistry, London.

Rodin, L. E. *et al.* (1975), *Productivity of the World's Main Ecosystems,* Proc. 5th General Assembly Special Committee IBP, National Academy of Sciences, Washington, D.C.

Rotblat, J. (1979), Nuclear Energy and Nuclear Weapon Proliferation, In *Stockholm International Peace Research Institute (SIPRI), Nuclear Energy and Nuclear Weapon Proliferation,* Taylor and Francis, London.

Said Ahmad, M. T. and E. El–Hinnawi (1981), Energy From The Sea, In E. El–Hinnawi and A. K. Biswas (Editors), *Renewable Sources of Energy and The Environment,* Tycooly International Publishing Ltd., Dublin.

Schipper, L. (1976), Raising the Productivity of Energy Utilization, *Annual Review of Energy.* 1, 455.

Semana, J. A. (1979), Energy Plantations for Steam Power Plants, Proc. Workshop Biogas and Other Rural Energy Resources, Suva. ESCAP, *Energy Resources Develop. Ser. No. 19,* ESCAP, United Nations, Bangkok.

Silitonga, T. (1979), *The Possibility of Kaliandra Wood as a Source of Energy,* Proc. Workshop Biogas and Other Rural Energy Resources, Suva. ESCAP, *Energy Resources Develop. Ser. No. 19.* ESCAP, United Nations, Bangkok.

Singer, H. (1971), *Improvement of Fuelwood Cooking Stoves and Economy in Fuelwood Consumption,* Food and Agriculture Organization, Rome.

Slovic, P. *et al.* (1979), Rating the Risks, *Environment,* 21, 14.

Sørensen, B. (1979 a), *Renewable Energy,* Academic Press, London.

Sørensen, B. (1979 b), *Wind Energy – An Overview,* UNITAR Conference on Long-Term Energy Resources, Montreal 1979, United Nations Institute For Training and Research, New York.

Sørensen, B. (1981), Wind Energy, In E. El–Hinnawi and A. K. Biswas (Editors), *Renewable Sources of Energy and The Environment,* Tycooly Intern., Dublin.

Surrey, J. and C. Huggett (1976), Opposition to Nuclear Power, *Energy Policy,* 286.

Tietjen, C. (1975), From Biodung to Biogas, In W. Jewell (Editor), *Energy, Agriculture and Waste Management,* Ann Arbor Science, Ann Arbor, Michigan.

TNSRC (1978), *Workshop on Solar Energy for The Villages of Tanzania,* Tanzania National Scientific Research Council, Dar-es-Salaam.

Trindade, S. C. (1980), *Energy Crops – The Case of Brazil,* Inter. Conf. on Energy from Biomass, Session I., Brighton, UK.

UN (1979), *An Overview of the World Energy Situation,* United Nations Economic and Social Council, New York.

UN (1981 a), 1979 *Yearbook of World Energy Statistics,* UN Publications E/F.80.XVII.7, United Nations, New York.

UN (1981 b), *Report of the Technical Panel on Fuelwood,* UN Conf. New and Renewable Sources of Energy, A/Conf.100/PC/34. United Nations, New York.

UNCTAD (1980), *Energy Supplies for Developing Countries,* United Nations Conference on Trade and Development, Geneva.

UNEP (1977), *The State of The Environment – Selected Topics,* United Nations Environment Programme, Nairobi.

UNEP (1978), *The State of The Environment – Selected Topics,* United Nations Environment Programme, Nairobi.

UNEP (1981), *The Environmental Impacts of Production and Use of Energy,* Study Director: E. El—Hinnawi, United Nations Environment Programme, Tycooly International Publishing Ltd., Dublin.

UNSCEAR (1977), *Sources and Effects of Ionizing Radiation,* United Nations Scientific Committee on the Effects of Atomic Radiation. United Nations, New York.

WAES (1977), *Energy: Global Prospects* 1985–2000, Report of the Workshop on Alternative Energy Strategies. McGraw—Hill, New York.

WASH–1400 (1975), *Reactor Safety Study (The Rasmussen Report),* US At. Energy Comm., Washington, D.C.

WEC (1980), *World Energy Resources* 1985–2020, World Energy Conference. IPC Science Techn. Press, Guildford, UK.

WOCOL (1980), *Coal-Bridge to the Future,* Report of the World Coal Study, Project Director C. L. Wilson, Ballinger Publ. C., Cambridge, Massachusetts.

World Bank (1979), *World Development Report* 1979, World Bank, Washington, D.C.

World Bank (1980a), *Energy in the Developing Countries,* World Bank, Washington, D.C.

World Bank (1980b), *World Development Report,* World Bank, Washington, D.C.

World Bank (1980c), *Alcohol Production from Biomass in the Developing Countries,* World Bank, Washington, D.C.

World Energy Conference (1980), *Survey of Energy Resources,* 11th World Energy Conf., Munich.

Yan, C. J. (1976), Evaluating Environmental Impacts of Stack Gas Desulphurization Processes, *Environ. Sci. Techn.,* 10, 54.

Yang, V. and S. C. Trindade (1978), *The Brazilian Gasohol Programme,* Symposium on Energy from Biomass and Waste, Paper No. 42, Institute Gas Techn., Chicago.

CHAPTER 13

Transport

Transport continued to be an essential component of development during the 1970s, and there were parallel trends in developed and developing countries, although with substantial contrasts. For example, animal power remained important in developing countries – two-thirds of Indian rural transportation depended on it, and improved carts and harness design there were matters of moment. Pedestrian travel remained a dominant mode of travel in urban areas even in developed countries, where cycling may have increased during the 1970s.

Railway freight transport increased in both developed and developing countries, although unevenly from country to country. Passenger travel increased in some countries but declined in others. Trains were improved in speed and comfort.

But the dominant feature of the world transport scene was the continuing rapid growth in the use of motor vehicles, especially passenger cars. During the decade, the cost of private motoring in terms of energy consumption, pollution, congestion and noise led some governments to attempt to put a brake on it by supporting public transport – including unconventional paratransit systems. The pace of technical development of vehicles that were quieter, less polluting, safer, and more economical users of fuel accelerated in response to mounting environmental concern and to the energy crisis.

Other kinds of transport also expanded. In 1977, 27 per cent more goods were moved by pipeline in the United States and western Europe than in 1970. Inland water traffic increased. There were 20 per cent more sea-going ships at the end of the decade than at the beginning, and a 77 per cent increase in tonnage. The size of oil tankers increased dramatically. Between 1970 and 1979 the number of passenger-kilometres in air travel more than doubled.

The impact of this growth was considerable. Motorways in countries of the Organization for Economic Co-operation and Development (OECD) more than doubled in length, while other main roads were extended by about 12 per cent. Substantial areas of farmland were lost, and large amounts of raw material consumed (according to one estimate, building the world's 200 million passenger cars consumed 6 months total world production of the metals used). Energy consumption by transport doubled in some countries, and accounted for 15-33 per cent of total national energy use in OECD states. Transport remained the largest single source of marine oil pollution.

Road accidents continued to be a serious consequence of transport growth: about 250,000 people were killed every year during the decade. Fatalities declined in some countries, but in many others – notably developing countries – accident rates increased because of increasing traffic and lack of training and safety measures.

The adverse environmental and social effects of transport were moderated in a number of ways during the decade. Vehicles were improved to meet higher pollution abatement, noise, energy consumption and safety standards. Transport management routed vehicles, ships and aircrafts in ways designed to reduce accident risk, noise and nuisances. Education and training were used to influence people's behaviour and their perceptions of risk.

One anticipated problem did not arise: the reduction of stratospheric ozone by supersonic aircraft ceased to be a matter of great concern, partly because such aircraft did not fly in the numbers expected.

At the end of the decade, the main problem lay in achieving an efficient balance between transport modes, in improving energy efficiency and preparing for new fuels in the post-oil era, in continued reduction of accidents and pollution, and in ensuring that effective public transport systems were maintained even in the many developed countries where private cars seemed certain to remain the dominant mode of travel.

Transport Modes and Systems

FROM earliest times, transport has had a vital influence on the evolution of civilizations. Ancient trade routes stimulated the growth of many of today's cities and influenced the development of cultures and nations. Today, transport is well recognized as an essential ingredient of social and economic development. But whereas in the past transport systems developed more or less spontaneously in accordance with social need and technical and economic opportunity, today there is an increasing emphasis on deliberate planning because of the enormous amount of resources transport consumes and the impact it has on the quality of life, the environment, and the pattern of industrial and economic activity.

This chapter is concerned with changes during the 1970s in the numbers of vehicles of all kinds employed in moving people and goods, their impacts on the environment, and the resources consumed in civil transport activities.

Transport is a complex system. Figure 13–1 summarizes some of the main components that have been studied in detail. The relative apportionment of investment between major modes – aircraft, shipping, railways, motorized road travel, and the older systems powered by animals and man – vary geographically and are continuously changing over time. In many developing countries, draught and pack animals remain the principal means of conveying goods over short distances, while personal travel is predominantly on foot (in some cases, by cycle).

Broadly speaking the sequence that characterized countries whose development began over a century ago is being repeated today in developing countries – from human and animal power through railways and public road vehicles to private cars. However,

Figure 13–1. Some of the Main Interactions in Transport.

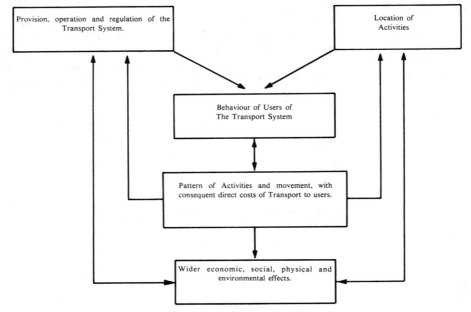

After Allsop, 1980 with modification .

the rail mode is often omitted and stress placed deliberately on rural road programmes and dependable motorized transport. Road transport has itself changed greatly in recent decades due to advances in vehicle technology, giving more efficient energy use; better power-weight ratios, producing less environmental impact; and better highway design.

Transport has four main kinds of impact on the environment. First, it consumes land for roads, railways, harbours, airports and associated facilities (Figure 13–2). Second, it consumes resources (especially minerals and metals) in vehicle and infrastructure construction, and substantial amounts of energy. Third, most forms of transport generate pollutants, which are discharged to air or water, and many also cause noise and vibration. Finally, transport accidents are a substantial cause of human death and disability, especially when heavy traffic flows in areas that were not designed for motor vehicles, such as the cities of developing countries, or when human judgement is impaired by alcohol.

For these reasons, transport planning and control is now recognized as an essential element in environmental management. Transport planning seeks to relate road and rail patterns to developing social needs, separating industrial and residential areas and so minimizing noise, air pollution and other adverse influences on people's living space. Since the pioneer studies of Davie (1937) it has been recognized that lines of communication are of crucial importance in shaping the pattern of development of industry and residential areas in cities. Industry has tended to locate near lines of water or rail transport, and low-grade housing to cluster about it, while the more affluent

Figure 13–2. Transport – Land Relationship.

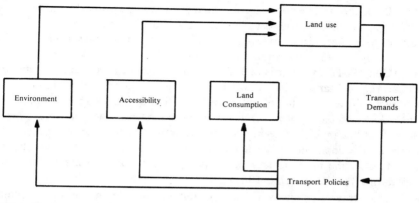

After Simkowitz *et al.*, 1979.

residential zones have spread along the main axes of road communication, often in a radial pattern (Hoyt, 1939; Robson, 1971). In theory, therefore, the deliberate control of transport corridors should be a means of guiding the broad pattern of urban development. Transport planning is also concerned to ensure the distribution of food and other essentials and of industrial products at the lowest cost. Transport management endeavours to enhance safety and quality of life and sustain efficiency through routing and controlling the speed, direction and spacing of aircraft, shipping and road vehicles. Its aim is to do this in such a way that energy is not wasted and the risk of accidents, damage to historic buildings and urban centres, and intrusion in residential areas and cherished environments, is minimized.

Trends in Transport During the 1970s

TRANSPORT ON LAND

Pedestrians, cyclists and animals

THERE are no global statistics of the changes during the past decade in the simplest and oldest methods of land transport – walking (whether carrying loads or not), riding and using pack animals, or using animal-drawn carts. In the rural areas of developing countries, these clearly remained the most important forms of travel – and indeed the sole methods in many remote and mountainous regions. In India in 1980, 50 per cent of the 500,000 villages were not yet connected by roads passable by motor vehicles. Animal-drawn vehicles were used widely in such areas, being economical for loads of 0.5–2 tonnes over short distances, even when the utilization rate was as little as 50 days per year, partly because the draught animals could be harnessed to power other activities (UN, 1981). Two-thirds of Indian rural transportation was by animal-drawn vehicles carrying perhaps 15 billion tonne-km of freight per year. Even in urban areas, animal-drawn vehicles were important, about 3 million of India's 15 million carts being in towns. Considerable improvements in cart and harness design were considered possible and although a decline in the relative importance of animal transport was predictable as development proceeded and road networks capable of use by motor vehicles extended, the mode clearly had a major contribution to make in developing countries during the 1980s (UN, 1981).

Pedestrian travel remained one of the dominant modes in the urban centres of developing, and indeed developed countries in the 1970s. In the United Kingdom, for example, the 1972/73 National Travel Survey indicated that walking accounted for 40.8 per cent of all trips – a higher percentage than private cars (40.6 per cent) (Rigby, 1977). By 1975/76, however, the percentage of journeys made on foot had fallen to 35 per cent, the decline being spread fairly evenly across the whole range of travel purposes including education, recreation, shopping and work (Hillman and Whalley, 1979). Cycling also remained important, especially in those urban areas favourable to it because of gentle gradients, equable climate (Quenault and Head, 1977), compactness (cycling is most useful in towns under 8 to 10 square kilometres (km^2) in area) and the construction of segregated cycleways (not all of which, however, followed the most direct routes). In the Netherlands cycling was the dominant mode in terms of number of trips (Hoekwater, 1978): in Denmark 46 per cent of adults and almost all children over six years old described themselves as cyclists (Laursen, 1978). In the United States 35 per cent of adults used bicycles in the mid-1970s, but perhaps half of them only very infrequently (Kaplan, 1977), and the same was true in the United Kingdom, where cycling accounted for only 2.8 per cent of all recorded trips and only 33 per cent of cycle owners used them several times a week (Rigby, 1977; Stores, 1978). Cycling remained of major importance in many developing countries (e.g. China) and cycle-propelled taxis were also important in many Asian cities, but data on frequency and trends were not available. There was some anecdotal evidence that one consequence of the rise in energy costs during the decade, coupled with the consciousness that regular exercise is a factor predisposing against cardiovascular disease (Chapter 10; Taylor, 1979) was a marginal increase in pedestrian and cycle travel in Western Europe and North America, while in other parts of the world these two modes were probably declining.

Railways

As the first, and for many years the only system of mechanized, fast, long-distance overland travel, railways expanded rapidly in Europe and North America during the nineteenth century. Substantial networks and some long-distance lines appeared also in

South America, the Indian sub-continent, Asia and Africa. Subsequently, there was a reduction in railroad mileage in many parts of Europe in the face of competition from road vehicles, primarily because the latter are more flexible in their ability to take goods and people from origin to destination without trans-shipment and following routes and time schedules determined by the user. However, between 1970 and 1977 there was an increase in both the total and percentage of freight transported by rail in 12 European countries. In other parts of the world, including the USSR, South America and Oceania, there was also a marked increase in railways goods traffic during the 1970s, some of which may have been due to the commissioning of new lines. These trends are shown in Table 13–1 (which compares freight transported by different modes during the period) and Figure 13–3, which demonstrate a considerable growth in goods transported by rail in the world as a whole despite the very slight increase or stabilization in North America, Europe and Africa. There were also international diferences in the trends in passenger rail travel. In France, for example, this increased from 41 billion passenger-kilometres in 1970 to 52 billion in 1977, and a similar trend was reported in some developing countries including Algeria (UN, 1979). However, in the Federal Republic of Germany, the United Kingdom, Czechoslovakia and the United States there was a decline in passenger travel by rail in this period, due to a switch to other modes.

Table 13–1. Freight Movement by Mode in Selected Countries (in billion tonne-km).

	Road	Rail	Inland Waterways and Coastal Shipping	Pipeline	Total
1970					
Twelve European[a] Countries	408	244	173	62	887
Australia	24	33	66	—	123
Japan	136	63	151	—	350
United States	602	1,126	466	629	2,823
1977					
Twelve European Countries	538	212	175	82	1,007
Australia	37[b]	59	—[c]	—	
Japan	143	41	202	—	386
United States	810	1,215	538	797	3,360

Source: UN (1979); IRF (1980).

[a] Belgium, Denmark, Finland, France, Federal Republic of Germany, United Kingdom, Italy, Netherlands, Norway, Spain, Sweden, Switzerland.
[b] 1976 figure.
[c] No data available since 1971.

Railway technology has changed substantially in recent years. In most developed countries coal as the main locomotive fuel was replaced by oil (diesel) or electric propulsion long before the 1970s, but electrification continued to expand in many countries during the decade. Improvements in locomotive and rolling stock design culminated in the aerodynamically improved, high speed trains of which Japan's Shinkansen system is perhaps the best known. Wheel-on-rail technology proved capable

Figure 13–3. Growth in Railway Traffic.

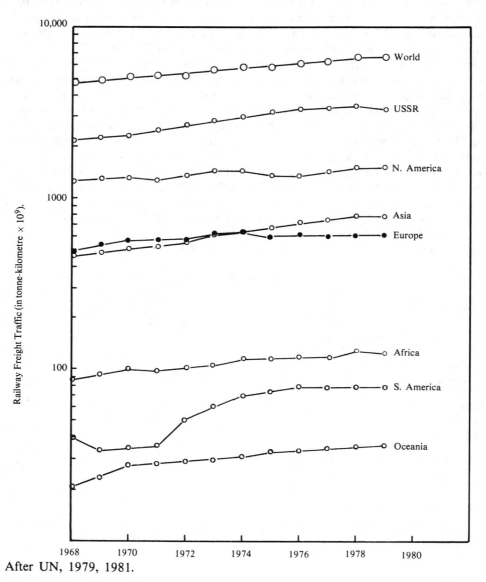

After UN, 1979, 1981.

of providing trains running at 150–225 km/h on improved track shared with slower freight and passenger units: this was one of the reasons more advanced systems of high-speed travel involving special track (e.g. tracked hovercraft or systems with magnetic suspension) were not adopted, despite their theoretical attractiveness. One analysis suggested that there might, however, be openings for very high-speed rail systems of this kind in the most densely populated parts of Europe.

There were also advances in rail track design, with general adoption of continuously-welded rail, sometimes mounted on continuous concrete bases. In most developed countries, railways became much less labour-intensive with the adoption of new signalling systems and automated warning and gate systems at road crossings. Comfort for rail passengers was improved, with widespread adoption of air-controlled rolling stock, commonly fitted with interior loudspeaker systems allowing better passenger information.

Another area of development was mass passenger transport in urban areas. Various systems were built, of which the Bay Area Rapid Transport System (BART) in San Francisco is perhaps the best known. Underground systems were built or extended in many major cities, including Washington DC, London, Brussels and some in the Soviet Union. In the USSR, electrification of the urban public transport system was a major feature of the decade, affecting 198 cities with populations exceeding 140,000. In 1969 these cities had 200 km of regularly-used electrified underground, moving 2.3 billion people annually; by 1979 the figures were 300 km and 3.7 billion respectively (Vestnik Statistiki, 1980). Light railroad (tramway) systems also extended in many countries after a period when they had been largely replaced by buses, partly for reasons of energy economy. For example, in the USSR tramway lengths increased from 8.3 thousand to 9.1 thousand km between 1970 and 1979, moving 8.0 billion and 8.3 billion people in those two years.

Road vehicles

The dominant feature of the world transport scene in the 1970s was the continuing rapid growth in motor vehicles, especially passenger cars. Figure 13–4 indicates that in 1970 there were some 185 million cars in the world (in 1960 there had been only about 100 million), and that this figure grew at about 5 per cent per annum, reaching 360 million in 1977.

There was a considerable regional variation (Figure 13–5). In the United States, where the first-car market became almost saturated during the decade (OECD, 1979b), growth was only at about 2.2 per cent. In Western Europe, most countries had annual increases around 5 per cent, while in Japan it was 14 per cent. Per unit of population, the number of cars was highest in North America, Oceania and Europe (Figure 13–6).

This increase in vehicle numbers was paralleled by rises in both passenger-kilometres travelled and tonne-kilometres of freight transport by road. Among countries of the Organization for Economic Cooperation and Development (OECD), there was a five-fold increase in the former in Japan between 1965 and 1975, and over 100 per cent increases in the United States, Finland, Italy, Norway, Spain and Turkey (OECD, 1979 b). Road freight rose by over 30 per cent in the sample of European countries included in Table 13–1 between 1970 and 1977, and by 34 per cent in the United States; Japan and Australia had experienced rapid growth between 1965 and 1970.

Many factors influence the rate of growth in car ownership, but it is fairly closely related to overall economic growth, per capita wealth, cultural attitude and availability of leisure. Although some studies (e.g. Leach, 1973) predict a slowing in the growth rate in developed countries, partly as a result of rising energy costs but also because of changes

Figure 13–4. Growth in World Motor Vehicles.

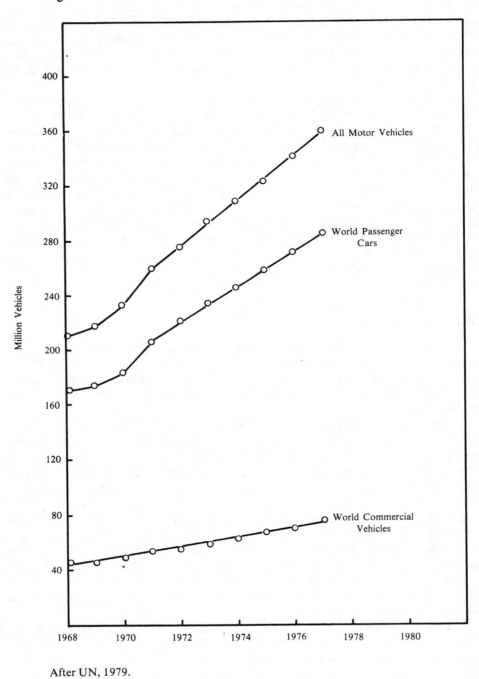

After UN, 1979.

in preferred life-style, substantial increases appear likely, especially in Europe and Japan where the second– and third-car markets have only recently begun to develop (OECD, 1979 b). In many developing countries, especially where public transport systems are inadequate, a sharp increase in car ownership is predictable.

The trend away from public transport to privately owned motor cars has been so universal a concomitant of economic growth in so many countries as to appear almost inevitable. However, during the 1970s the relatively high cost of mass private motoring, in terms of energy, pollution, congestion and noise, led some governments to take steps deliberately to curb the trend, both by the increasing subsidization of traditional public transport modes and the introduction of unconventional new ones. Bus systems were improved, in many cases with World Bank support, in (for example) Abidjan, Bombay,

Figure 13–5. Regional Growth of Passenger Cars.

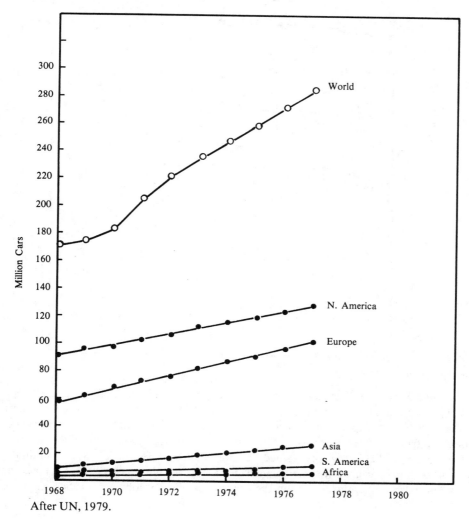

After UN, 1979.

Figure 13–6. Growth of Passenger Cars/1000 population in different regions.

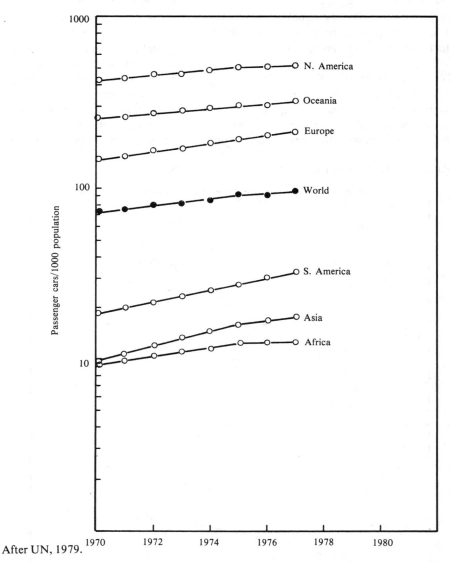

After UN, 1979.

Tunis and a number of Brazilian cities, both through modernization of the bus fleets and new highway and traffic engineering systems (World Bank, 1979). In the USSR there was a substantial expansion in urban bus transport, the length of city networks expanding from 87.6 thousand km in 1970 to 126 thousand km in 1979. Electrification in the form of trolley buses also gained popularity (Vestnik Statistiki, 1980). In addition, various so-called paratransit systems, intermediate in vehicle size between a private car and a normal bus, have grown up in the urban areas of developing countries, many of them initially in an unregulated or even illegal form. The vehicles may be mini-buses, shared public taxis, or other shared small vehicles. Examples include the *dolmas* in Turkey, the *service* in Lebanon, the *samlor* or *silor* in Thailand, *peseros* in Mexico, *matatus* in Kenya and *jitneys* (*jeepnies*) in the Philippines. These systems are often very responsive to passenger demand, relatively inexpensive, and able to work alongside buses or other public transport vehicles. In many cities they have been organized and regulated to improve safety and reliability without sacrificing their beneficial features. However, the failure to provide public or para-transit facilities was acute in some developing country cities where large sectors of the labour force in outlying and squatter settlements were obliged to walk long distances to their places of work.

Para-transit systems have also grown up in many developed countries. An OECD study (1977) identified 485 individual projects in various cities, including demand-responsive bus systems, dial-a-ride mini-bus or car services summoned by telephone, taxi-derived para-transit operated in a similar way, collaborative para-transit involving car and van pools with volunteer drivers, and publicar systems which include self-drive taxis, auto-taxis and very short-term car rental arrangements. The rate of increase in such systems was greatest in the United States and Canada, where the number grew by over 35 per cent between 1967 and 1974. Not all such systems have succeeded (dial-a-ride, for example, proved uneconomic and attracted few patrons in many experiments), but the trend is likely to continue.

Road transport systems were also the scene of considerable technical development and improvement during the decade. The energy crisis gave an impetus to improved fuel economy, which was widely achieved through better engine design, aerodynamically sound body shapes, and weight reductions. Small diesel engines, with markedly better fuel economy than petrol engines of comparable size, made inroads into those markets where a marginal reduction in acceleration and top speed was acceptable. Electric road vehicles were the subject of much research and interest, and a number reached the experimental stage, but although improvements were made in the design of conventional lead-acid batteries and several new battery types were under study, the poor energy densities of batteries relative to petrol and the short range and high capital cost of such vehicles militated against their widespread adoption.

In parallel with these trends in engine design and vehicle weight there were other advances that materially improved safety of both occupants and others involved in accidents. These included anti-fade and anti-lock braking systems for freight vehicles and systems to prevent jack-knifing in articulated units. Body designs were modified to reduce the danger of injury to pedestrians in collisions, and to dissipate energy more efficiently on impact. Seat belts were fitted to most new passenger cars in developed countries, and passive restraint systems (such as air bags) remained a topic for research and development. Micro-electronic systems came into increasing use to improve vehicle performance (thereby saving energy), aid fault diagnosis, and improve the information to drivers. Pollution emissions and noise were reduced (as described in later sections).

Pipelines

During the 1970s, pipelines were used on an increasing scale to transport gas, petroleum, coal and other bulk products, and solids in slurry form. In 1975 nearly

Figure 13–7. Total length of Oil pipeline in Europe.

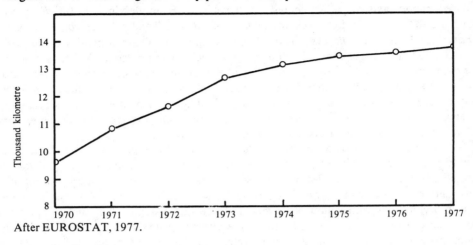

After EUROSTAT, 1977.

Figure 13–8. Merchant Shipping Fleets.

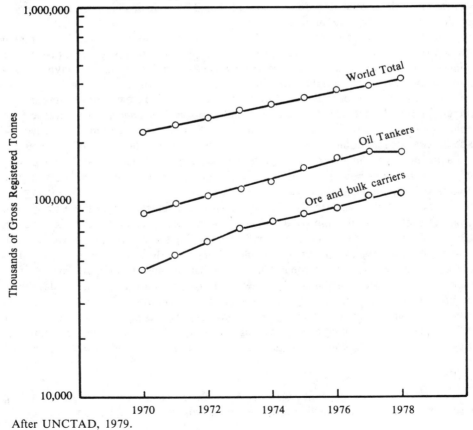

After UNCTAD, 1979.

140,000 km of such pipelines existed or were planned in the world (Hale, 1978; UNEP, 1980). In the European communities there was a 43 per cent growth in the oil pipeline network over the 7 years 1970 – 1977 (Figure 13–7), and by 1980 it extended for some 15,000 km. Table 13–1 gives figures for the goods transported by pipeline in 12 European countries and the United States over the same period, indicating a rise of 27 per cent from 691 to 879 billion tonne-kilometres. In 1976, pipeline transport accounted for 24 per cent of all freight movement (in tonne-kilometres) overland in the United States, as against 14.9 per cent in the USSR, 17.6 per cent in the Netherlands, 6.8 per cent in the

Figure 13–9. Growth of International and Domestic Air Passenger Traffic.

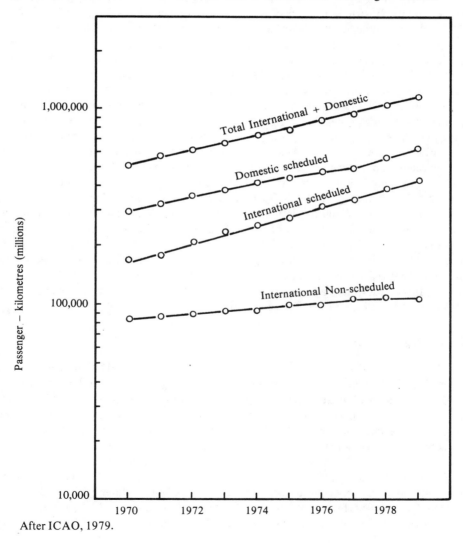

After ICAO, 1979.

Federal Republic of Germany, 5.8 per cent in the German Democratic Republic and 4.6 per cent in the United Kingdom (O'Reilly, 1974; EUROSTAT, 1977; UN, 1979). However, if the data are expressed in tonnes moved rather than tonne-km, pipelines appear less important because they are predominantly a long-distance mode.

Inland waterways

Major inland rivers have been important transport corridors since prehistoric times, and remain so in many countries today. Navigation on the Rhine, the Main, the Seine and its tributaries, and the Danube system, for example, forms an important component in the freight transport system of Europe. The great potential of the trans-European east-west waterway linking the Black Sea and the North Sea had been recognized as far back as 1920, and its construction, which involved 13 riparian countries, continued during the 1970s with an estimated completion date of 1985. Engineering works have opened the lower reaches of many river systems to small vessels capable of navigation in the coastal seas, while combined barge and ship systems, such as barge-aboard-catamaran (BACAT) or lighter-aboard-ship (LASH), have been developed to allow small craft designed for river traffic to be conveyed across intervening stretches of open sea.

As Table 13–1 shows, the combination of inland waterways and coastal shipping remained an important means of freight transport in Europe, Japan and the United States during the 1970s, and grew considerably in the two latter countries. In Europe, although total traffic remained steady, international waterborne freight increased. It is not easy to separate the inland waterway and coastal shipping components of the statistics, but in the European Economic Community (EEC) in 1977 there were some 32,000 "units" of inland shipping compared with 18,000 sea-going merchant vessels (EUROSTAT, 1977).

There were great variations in the national importance of inland waterways. In the Federal Republic of Germany 22.4 per cent of all tonne-km of freight used this mode: in the Netherlands 56.7 per cent, the United States 16 per cent, the USSR 5 per cent, France 6.02 per cent, the German Democratic Republic 3.2 per cent and in the United Kingdom under 0.5 per cent. The United Kingdom has substantial coastal shipping but most of its inland waterways are narrow and shallow and during the decade were increasingly being transformed for recreational use.

TRANSPORT AT SEA

During the 1970s, there was a substantial growth in the world shipping fleet, some 43 per cent of which in terms of tonnage was made up by oil tankers (UNCTAD, 1978, 1979). The number of vessels increased by 20 per cent and the tonnage by 77 per cent during the decade. Figure 13–8 indicates the main trends and Table 13–2 the shipping tonnages of the main nations involved. In terms of cargo transported, crude oil and oil products constituted some 66 per cent of world seaborne trade during the decade. Between 1960 and 1977 the total of crude and products transported rose from 449 to 1,700 million tonnes (Table 13–3). In 1977 there were nearly 7,000 tankers, totalling about 340 million dead weight tonnes (dwt) as against 3,500 totalling 37 million dwt in 1954 (IMCO, 1978). The size of vessel has increased dramatically, the largest in service in 1954 being around 30,000 dwt whereas in 1980 there were several ships exceeding

Table 13–2. Merchant Shipping (Registered Tonnages; in thousand tonnes) in the 1970s.

Country/Group	1970	1971	1972	1973	1974	1975	1976	1977
EEC (9 countries)	54,625	58,221	61,186	63,714	66,693	72,001	74,958	73,792
United Kingdom	24,689	26,108	27,727	29,237	30,642	32,184	31,927	30,481
Norway	18,826	21,178	23,269	23,355	24,580	25,847	27,593	27,368
Greece	10,675	12,732	15,258	19,218	21,682	22,451	24,962	29,433
CMEA Countries	12,959	13,622	14,660	15,111	16,119	17,674	19,451	20,473
Liberia	33,193	38,432	44,364	49,824	55,246	65,760	73,402	79,804
Panama	5,517	6,128	7,630	9,417	10,810	13,352	15,249	18,890
Other Flags of Convenience	1,885	2,616	3,738	6,529	8,157	8,882	10,338	9,650
United States	17,856	15,496	14,378	14,742	13,632	13,672	13,937	14,264
Japan	25,173	28,363	33,346	35,142	36,974	38,042	39,968	38,346
World Total	211,887	229,831	254,514	275,225	295,973	325,622	354,502	374,707

Source: EUROSTAT (1977).

The United Kingdom figures are also included in the EEC totals, while smaller shipping nations are not recorded separately: the world total is not, therefore, the sum of the columns.

500,000 dwt. Between 1975 and 1980, however, the annual growth in oil transportation slowed and became approximately stable.

Table 13–3. World Movement of Oil by Sea (in million tonnes)

	Crude	Products	Total
1960	305	144	449
1965	567	180	747
1970	1,033	230	1,263
1973	1,404	291	1,695
1974	1,387	269	1,656
1975	1,273	235	1,508
1977			1,700

Source: IMCO (1978); UNEP (1981).

Figure 13–10. International and Domestic Air Transport of Goods in the 1970s.

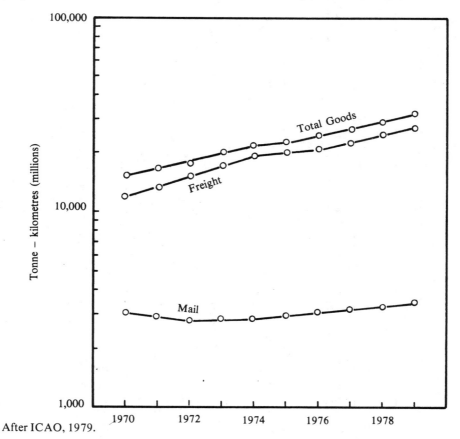

After ICAO, 1979.

AIR TRANSPORT

There was a marked increase in civil air transport during the decade: in 1970 the total number of international (scheduled and non-scheduled) and domestic passenger-kilometres was about 500,000 million; by 1979 it had more than doubled to reach 1,160,000 million (Figure 13–9). International flights made up about 42 per cent of all scheduled traffic in 1979 as against 35 per cent in 1970. International non-scheduled traffic fell from 32.4 per cent of all international passenger traffic in 1971 to about 19 per cent in 1979. This decrease was mainly due to the success of scheduled airlines in competing for the personal and leisure travel market.

Air freight in 1970 was about 12 billion tonne-km; and by 1979 it had more than doubled to reach 27.8 billion tonne-km. Air mail transport remained nearly constant however (3 billion tonne-km in 1970 and about 3.4 billion tonne-km in 1979) (Figure 13–10). International freight traffic constituted about 54 per cent of all air freight traffic in 1971, increasing to 67 per cent in 1979. On the other hand, international air mail traffic remained at about 42.5 per cent of all air mail traffic (ICAO, 1979).

This marked increase in civil air transport was made possible through great technological advances in navigation and aircraft design and construction in the 1970s (an increased number of wide-body aircraft were put into operation and the first generation of supersonic aircraft was introduced), and major airport construction and expansion.

The Impact of Transport on the Environment

THE CONSUMPTION OF RESOURCES

Land

OVER the five years 1975–1979 there was general growth in road networks around the world: some examples are given in Table 13–4. Between 1965 and 1975 the total length of motorway roads in OECD countries increased from 39,722 to 89,961 km, (OECD, 1979 b). There was a smaller, but still significant, increase in the length of the network of other main roads (16.7 per cent for countries with comparable data for the 2 years). In the United States in 1974, 11.4 million hectares (ha) (1,2 per cent of the total land area) were devoted to transport: of this 9.3 million ha were under roads, 1.3 million ha used by

Table 13–4. Total Road Networks (in thousand km)

Country	1975	1976	Year 1977	1978	1979
Federal Republic of Germany	464	470	474	480	482
United Kingdom	344	346	348	349	351
Poland	298	301	300	299	298
United States	6,175	6,206	6,223	6,252	—
Mexico	188	193	200	207	212
Brazil	1,428	1,489	1,502	1,545	—
Japan	1,068	1,079	1,088	1,097	1,106

Source: IRF (1980).

There are differences between countries in the base of these statistics, which makes international comparison difficult.

railways, and 0.8 million ha by airports (Frey, 1979; UNEP, 1980). The taking of agricultural land for transport is inseparable in most statistical series from the general loss to urbanization. In the United States this is estimated to have reached 420,000 ha per year during 1967–75 (CEQ, 1977), and totalled 0.8 per cent of all farmland in the decade 1960–70. Japan also lost a substantial fraction of its agricultural land during the decade (OECD, 1979 b). Towards the end of the decade, motorway construction programmes were nearing completion in many developed countries, so that the rate of land consumption would be expected to fall during the 1980s.

Raw materials

The construction of aircraft, rail and especially road vehicles and their associated infrastructure consumes a large amount of raw materials. One estimate suggests that in 1970 the metals (which constitute more than 85 per cent of a vehicle's weight) contained in the approximately 200 million passenger cars in the world, accounted for about six months of the world's production of those metals (UNEP, 1977 a). It was also estimated that the motor vehicle industry in the United States consumed some 20 per cent of annual steel production, 7 per cent of copper, 13 per cent of nickel, 35 per cent of zinc, 50 per cent of lead and some 50 per cent of rubber. The cost of these raw materials and the critical situation of world reserves of some of them stimulated an interest in increasing the lifetime of motor vehicles and in using alternative abundant materials in their manufacture. For example, there has been an increase in the use of plastics, light alloys and aluminium in the motor vehicle industry during the last 20 years (UNEP, 1977 a) and this trend is likely to continue. Recovery and recycling of material from wrecked vehicles has also increased in several countries. With 10 to 12 per cent of the total vehicles in each country becoming unserviceable each year (the average life of a car is estimated to be 11 working years, although wide variations occur from one country to another), recycling provides a valuable means for conserving the raw materials used by the motor vehicle industry.

Energy

Over the past ten years, energy consumption by transport increased greatly in many countries, doubling in some (Table 13–5). Among OECD countries, it accounted in 1980 for between 15 and 33 per cent total energy consumption. In western Europe and the United States, 95 per cent of the total energy demand for transport was met by liquid fuels, and almost all the remainder by electricity (ECE, 1976). In eastern Europe solid fuels were used more extensively, meeting about 38 per cent of the energy demand, while liquid fuels accounted for 55 per cent and electricity, 7 per cent. In most developed countries road vehicles accounted for between 70 and 85 per cent of the petroleum used by transport, over half of this going to automobiles in urban areas. In developing countries road vehicles took an even higher share (about 90 per cent) of the liquid fuels used by transport.

Table 13–5. Energy Consumption in the Transport Sector in Some Selected Countries (in million tonne oil equivalent).

	1960	1973	1976	1980	1985
United States	234	406	426	476	484
Japan	12	40	43	59	75
Federal Republic of Germany	16	33	36	36	40
Sweden	2.8	5.2	5.6	6.1	6.6
United Kingdom	21.1	30.8	30.5	35.0	36.0
Spain	4.0	11.3	13.7	14.3	16.5

Source: OECD (1978 a); 1980 and 1985 figures are forecasts.

Energy is also used indirectly by transport in the refining and movement of fuels, the manufacture and repair of vehicles, the construction and maintenance of highways, ports and airports and their associated facilities and the operation of parking and traffic management systems. One study in the United States concluded that these indirect uses could account for as much as 40 per cent of the total energy used by the average automobile.

Railroads and waterways are commonly stated to be more efficient than aircraft or automobiles in their use of energy (Rice, 1972). For example, the average automobile with 1 to 2 passengers typically consumes 2 to 4 times the energy per passenger-kilometre of a well-loaded bus or train. However, these average figures are misleading unless the substantial ranges of variation are also considered. For example one set of official data on fuel consumption in passenger cars (UK, 1980) indicates a range of between 7 and 25 seat-km per litre. There are also wide variations according to speed and journey type, with distance per unit of fuel used halved in urban conditions and falling by 40 per cent as speed rises from around 40 km/h to 110 km/h. Temperature, vehicle load, driving style and maintenance also introduce marked variations. Similar variations apply to public transport modes (except that driving styles have less impact on fuel use in diesel-engined vehicles) and may easily swamp the difference between mode averages. In certain circumstances the automobile becomes more efficient, and there are many journeys that cannot conveniently be made by any other means.

Overall costs

The combination of resource, energy and other costs gives an indication of the overall expenditure required to provide transport by different modes, and Table 13–6 summarizes the outcome for urban areas. The figures are subject to the same criticism as average energy figures, and are only illustrative, but they do emphasize the advantage in resource terms of public transport so long as it is well-used. The table also emphasizes the low cost of provision for pedestrians and cyclists.

POLLUTION

Air pollution

Table 13–7 sets out the main gaseous pollutants emitted by road vehicles without pollution control systems. In addition, diesel engines (especially poorly maintained ones under load) emit fine particles as dark smoke (Ember, 1979). Diesel-engined railway locomotives contribute the same pollutants as diesel road vehicles but on a much smaller scale because of their lesser numbers. If organic (tetra-ethyl or tetra-methyl) lead is added to petrol as an 'anti-knock' agent, about 90 per cent of the metal is emitted in the form of inorganic compounds, reaching concentrations of up to 1 microgram per cubic metre ($\mu g/m^3$) in urban air. Total emissions of many of these pollutants increased during the 1970s in many countries because the rise in the number of vehicles was not matched by pollution controls. The extent to which such trends are significant within the total air pollution situation evidently depends on the relative importance of vehicles and other sources. The incomplete combustion of fuels by motor vehicles is, for example, the main source of carbon monoxide emission, which rose during the early 1970s in Finland, France, Sweden and Switzerland (OECD, 1979b), and over the decade as a whole in the United Kingdom (DOE, 1980), but fell in the United States and Canada where stringent emission standards were imposed at an early date. Airborne lead, too, is mainly derived from vehicle emissions, except in close proximity to certain types of industry. Nitrogen oxides and hydrocarbons, on the other hand, have many sources, and while emissions of one or other of them (or both) rose over the period 1970–1975 in Japan, Canada, the United States, Finland, France, the Federal Republic of Germany, the Netherlands, Norway, Sweden and the United Kingdom, the trend cannot be blamed solely on motor vehicles (the rise in hydrocarbons, indeed, is probably mostly due to solvents and fuel handling) (OECD, 1978b; 1979 a, b).

Table 13–6. Illustrative Costs of Urban Travel by Different Modes.

	Speed (km/h)	Persons per metre-width per hour	Track capital costs Per hour US cents per km	Track capital costs Per person US cents per km	Track maintenance costs Per vehicle US cents per km	Track maintenance costs Per person US cents per km	Vehicle operating costs Per vehicle US cents per km	Vehicle operating costs Per person US cents per km	Total costs per person US cents per km
Footway, 1.2 metre wide	3.4	336	1.2	0	0	0	0	0	Negligible
Bicycle track, 1.2 metre wide	12.9	137	31.1	0	0.19	0.19	0	0	0.19
Urban street, 7.3 metre wide, mixed traffic									
Car with driver only	24.1	8.8	74.5	2.5	0.25	0.25	8.1	8.1	10.9
	16.1	15.6	74.5	1.5	0.25	0.25	9.1	9.1	10.8
Taxi with 4 passengers	19.3	36.6	74.5	0.6	0.25	0.06	8.4	2.1	2.8
	13.8	61.0	74.5	0.4	0.25	0.06	9.6	2.4	2.8
Minibus with 10 passengers	16.1	45.8	74.5	0.5	0.4	0.06	12.4	1.2	1.8
	12.1	76.3	74.5	0.3	0.4	0.06	14.9	1.5	1.9
Bus with 30 passengers	13.8	91.5	74.5	0.25	0.6	0	31.1	1.1	1.3
	10.8	152.5	74.5	0.12	0.6	0	37.3	1.2	1.4
Urban street, 13.4 metre wide, mixed traffic									
Car with driver only	24.1	11.9	74.5	1.93	0.25	0.25	8.1	8.1	10.2
	16.1	16.8	74.5	1.37	0.25	0.25	9.1	9.1	10.7
Taxi with 4 passengers	19.3	48.8	74.5	0.5	0.25	0.06	8.4	2.1	2.7
	13.8	67.1	74.5	0.3	0.25	0.06	9.6	2.4	2.7
Minibus with 10 passengers	16.1	58.0	74.5	0.4	0.4	0.06	12.4	1.2	1.7
	12.1	85.0	74.5	0.25	0.4	0.06	14.9	1.5	1.8
Bus with 30 passengers	13.8	125.0	74.5	0.19	0.6	0	31.1	1.1	1.2
	10.8	167.8	74.5	0.12	0.6	0	37.3	1.2	1.4
Urban expressway (capacity per metre width is independent of width)									
Car with driver only	64.4	54.9	559	3.1	0.25	0.25	6.8	6.8	10.2
Taxi with 4 passengers	64.4	219.6	559	0.75	0.25	0.06	7.0	1.7	2.5
Minibus with 10 passengers	64.4	366.0	559	0.5	0.4	0.06	10.6	1.1	1.6
Bus with 40 passengers	64.4	610.0	559	0.25	0.6	0	26.7	0.7	0.9
Metro (22,500 passengers per hour)	33.8	518.5	2,733	1.6	26.7	0.43	23.0	0.4	2.4
Urban railway (22,500 passengers per hour)	48.3	518.5	994	0.56	26.7	0.43	23.0	0.4	1.4

Source: World Bank (1975); recalculated to SI Units.

Table 13–7. Representative Composition of Exhaust Gases (Heavy Vehicles), in parts per million (ppm) by volume

Pollutant	Idling	Accelerating	Cruising	Deceleration
Petrol engine:				
Carbon monoxide	69,000	29,000	27,000	39,000
Hydrocarbons	5,300	1,600	1,000	10,000
Nitrogen oxides	30	1,020	650	20
Aldehydes	30	20	10	290
Diesel engines:				
Carbon monoxide	Trace	1,000	Trace	Trace
Hydrocarbons	400	200	100	300
Nitrogen oxides	60	350	240	30
Aldehydes	10	20	10	30

Source: Cottee (1978).

The critical factors governing the dispersion and reactions of these substances in the atmosphere have been reviewed in Chapter 2, while their effects on man are discussed in Chapter 10 and on terrestrial life in Chapter 7. Any direct effect on man, other organisms or structures clearly depends directly on the concentrations to which these targets are exposed, and the duration of exposure, and this is in turn influenced by dispersion – itself susceptible to modification by urban and highway design and traffic management. High concentrations of carbon monoxide, for example, can occur in congested narrow streets, garage forecourts, tunnels and other confined spaces, but are unlikely in wide streets with free-flowing traffic and good ventilation (Reed, 1976). Congested urban centres in developing countries, as in Bangkok, Cairo, Ibadan and other Nigerian cities (Oluwande, 1979), can, however, pose special problems. On the other hand, the photochemical reactions involving hydrocarbons and nitrogen oxides, which generate oxidant smog, take place when there is a sunlit stagnant or slow-moving air mass over a city as a whole, and this problem is not susceptible to amelioration through highway design and traffic engineering.

Aircraft, especially those flying in the lower stratosphere, are also a cause for concern because of the pollutants they emit. Any jet aircraft burning typical jet fuel releases large amounts of water vapour together with carbon monoxide, carbon dioxide, nitrogen oxides, sulphur oxides and particulates. These appear initially in the jet plume behind the aircraft. In the troposphere, natural turbulence and precipitation swiftly disperse and remove them. But in the stratosphere they persist near to the altitude of injection, where the global dynamics of the atmosphere (Chapter 2) spread them, in a few weeks, through the latitudinal zone into which they were released.

As Chapter 2 indicates, such contamination could contribute to reactions that affect stratospheric ozone concentrations and hence the screen against ultra-violet radiation (Grobecker et al., 1974; Crutzen, 1974; NAS, 1975; NAS, 1976). The water droplets and aerosols released could also affect heat transfer to and from the earth, and hence influence climate (Grobecker et al., 1974). There is some evidence of increased cloudiness, and reductions in radiation reaching the ground, in some areas of North America, Switzerland and the USSR below aircraft flight routes (Lamb, 1977).

In 1970–1971 it was thought possible that several hundred civil supersonic transport aircraft would eventually fly in the stratosphere, and that these would be sufficient to reduce the average global ozone cover by 10 per cent or more. While military aircraft continue to make a number of stratospheric flights, the abandonment of civil supersonic projects has removed this immediate threat. A report by the World Meteorological Organization (WMO), prepared in collaboration with the United Nations Environment Programme (UNEP) and the International Council of Scientific Unions (ICUS), concluded that "currently planned supersonic transport aircraft due to their lower flight altitudes of 17 km and their limited number (30 – 50 projected) are not predicted to have an effect that would be significant or that could be distinguished from natural variations" but that "a large fleet of supersonic aircraft flying at greater altitudes is predicted to have a noticeable effect on the ozone layer" (UNEP, 1977 b). The use of chlorine-containing gases in the United States space shuttle could lead to a very small (0.1 per cent) decrease in ozone.

The subsonic fleet also presents a problem for the future. As it grows, it is likely also to fly at higher altitudes. If there are no controls, the nitrous oxide emission index for future subsonic aircraft engines may be larger than today's value (the emission index for widebody jets is already 2.5 times larger than that for 707/DC–8 class aircraft). Because subsonics fly near the tropopause, where the residence time of contaminants is known with less certainty than that higher in the stratosphere, the calculation of stratospheric pollution effects by subsonic aircraft are more uncertain than those for SSTs.

Noise and vibration

Although significant progress has been made in the last 30 years in reducing mechanical and exhaust noise from road traffic, motor vehicles remain a major source, mainly because of the growth in traffic. Although one Japanese survey (EAJ, 1978) indicated that transport noise (including noise from aircraft) only accounted for 5 per cent of complaints overall, other studies there and in the United Kingdom, France, the Federal Republic of Germany, Norway and Sweden have stressed its seriousness as a social problem, especially in urban areas (NSIBR, 1968; O'Reilly, 1974; UNEP, 1979). One study (O'Reilly, 1974) concluded that in that year between 19 per cent and 45 per cent of the United Kingdom's urban population lived in roads with traffic flows that produced undesirable noise levels, and predicted that by 1980 the proportion would be in the range 30–60 per cent. An OECD survey (1979 a) indicated that in the mid–1970s between 10 and 20 per cent of the population in OECD countries lived in areas exposed to outdoor noise levels above 65 dBA – considered the upper limit of acceptability. Railway noise is also a serious local problem, for example along the Shinkansen system in Japan (EAJ, 1978). Traffic also generates vibration that is not only disturbing but may damage old and frail buildings. Figure 13–11 summarizes the system within which traffic noise operates.

Figure 13–11. The Traffic Noise System.

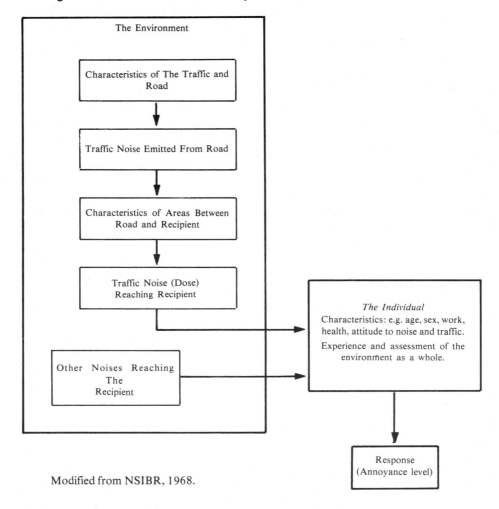

Modified from NSIBR, 1968.

Unlike the very high noise levels sometimes experienced in industry, traffic noise does not normally pose a risk to health or hearing. It is unlikely to be a common cause of the sudden gastric, cardiovascular, neurological or hormonal changes reported in some subjects exposed to sudden and unexpected noise (UNEP, 1979). But it can undoubtedly impose stress, disturb sleep (especially if irregular) and cause severe annoyance. The aged, sick, and people with certain psychological disturbances, as well as children aged between 4 and 6 are particularly sensitive (UNEP, 1979). Noise insufficient to interfere with normal speech or routine tasks may impair group activities in schools, conference rooms or concert halls (O'Reilly, 1974). As traffic has grown and extended into new areas during the 1970s, such problems are likely to have become more widespread despite measures to quieten vehicles and insulate property.

Aircraft noise is a notorious social problem around major airports and below busy flight paths, although it disturbs fewer people in total than traffic noise (OECD, 1979b) (Table 13–8). During the past decade it has become worse in some places, especially where residential development has been permitted to expand in areas of high noise intensity. In other areas it has been alleviated by sound proofing, controls on aircraft and the development of new, large-capacity aircraft with quieter engines.

Land, freshwater and marine pollution

Chapter 3 describes the sources and effects of oil released into the marine environment, indicating that marine transportation accounted for about 45–55 per cent of all direct pollution of the sea with oil. If the considerable contribution of transport to urban run-off and airborne dispersal is added, there can be little doubt that it is by far the main source of this type of pollution. Tanker accidents account for only about 10 per cent of all the oil releases attributed to shipping (and thus 5 per cent or less of all oil entering the sea); the total annual spillage contributing between 50,000 and 250,000 tonnes per year in the period between 1970 and 1978, with no significant trend (see Table 3–10). The progressive increase in tanker size has however brought with it an increase in the amount that can be discharged in a single accident: the escape of 220,000 tonnes from the *Amoco Cadiz* was the worst such event on record. Less massive but insidiously damaging emissions can come from the discharge of oily ballast water and tank washings, although these have been considerably reduced by the adoption in new vessels of segregated ballast, the construction of facilities to receive and clean ballast water at terminals, the 'load-on-top' procedure and the use of crude oil rather than sea water to wash tanks. Other spills arise from fractures of pipelines, valve failures and human error at terminals, where chronic pollution has brought about some well-documented ecological changes (Baker, 1976).

Oil spills have also occurred from pipelines mostly affecting the land or freshwater environment. Losses have been a very small fraction of the total oil transported. In Europe, for example, in 1972 the total throughput of oil in 15,000 km of pipeline was 433 million m^3, and of this 2,700 m^3 was spilled in 21 incidents. More than 1,800 m^3 was recovered, and the net loss of 900m^3 represented 0.0006 per cent (or 6 tonnes per million) of the total amount transported. No potable water was polluted (CONCAWE, 1974). These high standards have been sustained despite the extension of the pipeline network during the 1970s, and apply also in other regions. The Trans-Alaskan pipeline, from Prudhoe Bay to Valdez, was constructed only after lengthy environmental evaluation, and while one rupture has affected the freshwater environment of a major river, the total oil shed in all incidents was a very small fraction of that transported.

The impact of road transport on roadside vegetation in the United Kingdom was reviewed in 1978 (Colwill, *et al.,* 1979). This study highlighted the positive contribution of new road systems to the habitat for plant and invertebrate species, reviewed the impact on such vegetation of pollution from traffic, and highlighted a problem common to many developed countries with cool climates – the effects of large quantities of de-icing salts used to keep surfaces free of snow and ice in winter. In the United States about

Table 13–8. Population Exposed to Aircraft and Road Traffic Noise, Selected Countries or Regions, mid-1970s (per cent).

Noise Level in Leq (dBA) outdoor measures	Aircraft Noise % of national population exposed to given levels[a, b]				Road Traffic Noise % of national population exposed to given noise levels[b]											
	United States[c]	Canada[d]	Japan[c]	Europe[e]	United States[a]	Japan[f]	Belgium[f]	Denmark[f]	France[f]	Germany[f]	Netherlands[f]	Norway[a]	Spain[f]	Sweden[a]	Switzerland[f]	United Kingdom[g]
≥55 Sleep can be disturbed if windows are open.	13	2	3	3	40	80	68	50	47	72	..	22	74	41.5	66	50
≥60 Sleep and conversation can be disturbed if windows are open.	5	1	1	1	18	58	39	..	32	46	30	12	50	25	28	27
≥65 Sleep and conversation can be disturbed even if windows are closed.	2	1	0.5	0.2	6.4	31	12	20	14	18	7.4	5	23	12.5	12	11
≥70 Sleep and conversation disturbance; possible complaints.	0.6	0.3	0.2	0.05	1.8	10	1	..	4	4	1.6	2	7	..	1	4
≥75 Possible long-term danger for hearing ability	0.2	0.1	0.1	0.01	—	1	—	..	0.5	—	0.1	—	1	..	—	1

Source: OECD (1979 b).

[a] Expressed in Leq over 24 hours.
[b] Data refers to various years in the early Seventies for different countries. Since many measurements and surveys do not give results in Leq, equations relating Leq and other indices have been used. The margin of error due to national estimates, different years, and to this transformation are probably very important, especially at lower level of noise (± 10%).
[c] For all airports.
[d] For 5 major airports (Edmunton, Montreal, Ottawa, Toronto, Vancouver).
[e] For 34 airports. Broad assumptions were made concerning densities around some airports.
[f] Expressed in Leq over the period 6–22 h.
[g] Expressed in Leq over the period 6–24 h, England only.

9 million tonnes of such salts were used in 1970 alone, and the quantity was estimated to be doubling every five years (McConnell and Lewis, 1972). In Europe, applications varied considerably with climatic variation, but in the United Kingdom and the Federal Republic of Germany there was, if anything, a downward trend in applications between 1967–68 and 1971–72 (Thompson, *et al.,* 1979). Such salts not only affect roadside vegetation, killing sensitive trees and bushes, but are removed in runoff to affect ground-water and nearby water-courses. A substantial amount is also removed by the traffic and some of this remains on vehicle underbodies and can accelerate corrosion.

Emissions from road vehicles using gasoline to which tetra-ethyl lead has been added contribute particluate lead to dust on the ground. Much of this material is deposited within about 100 m of the highway but the finer particles are widely dispersed through the atmosphere and the upward curve of emissions is conspicuous in ice and snow cores from Greenland and other remote sites (Murozumi, *et al.,* 1969). During the decade new evidence accumulated on the health hazards of lead, and the deleterious effects of nitrates dispersed from automobile exhausts (NAS, 1980). Concern also grew over the hazards from the conveyance of toxic, explosive and radioactive materials by rail and road, especially after several accidents involving such loads.

THE SOCIAL IMPACTS OF TRANSPORT

The benefits of improved transportation systems to the community are obvious. They play a crucial role in development. The safe and inexpensive movement of large numbers of people over long distances has been a major determinant of the growth of tourism over the decade (Chapter 14). Unfortunately, the growth in road transport in particular has also brought a severe social disbenefit through increased accidents.

The World Health Organization (WHO) estimates that a quarter of a million people are killed and several million injured every year in road accidents, a considerable proportion being pedestrians. Table 13–9 shows the total of fatal and non-fatal transport injuries in the United Kingdom between 1968 and 1978, indicating that road accidents accounted for the vast majority. These totals remained more or less constant during the decade, and since this was a period when traffic volume grew considerably, they indicate an improvement in safety in terms of accidents per vehicle- or passenger-kilometre. Detailed analysis also confirmed that motorcyclists ran more than twice pedal cyclists' risk of fatal injury and twenty times car drivers' risk, that commercial and public service vehicles were safer still to travel in; and that motorways were the safest roads (Sabey and Taylor, 1980; Holdgate, 1981). Air travel, in terms of either gross fatalities per 100,000 passengers or fatalities per unit of distance, was about six times safer than road travel (Stratton, 1974), and rail was also a low-risk form of travel. In the United States, the decade of the 1970s saw a reduction in road fatalities (from 53,000 in 1970 to 48,000 in 1978) (Bick and Hohenemser, 1979), and this was the experience in other developed countries as well. In some other countries, however, there were considerable changes in accident rates between 1975 and 1979, and the situation deteriorated, especially in some developing countries (Figure 13–12; IRF, 1980). The death rate per million vehicle-

Table 13–9. Road, Rail and Air Casualties in the United Kingdom 1968–1978.

	1968	1969	1970	1971	1972	1973	1974	1975	1976	1977	1978
Road											
Deaths	6,810	7,365	7,499	7,699	7,763	7,406	6,876	6,366	6,570	6,614	6,831
Injuries	342,398	345,529	355,869	344,328	351,964	346,374	317,726	318,584	333,103	341,447	342,964
All Road Casualties	349,208	352,894	363,368	352,027	359,727	353,780	324,602	324,950	339,673	348,061	349,795
Rail											
Deaths[a,b,c]	334	352	381	373	328	306	360	416	382	401	449
Injuries[a,b,c]	6,497	7,114	6,692	6,390	6,245	6,464	6,218	5,725	5,304	5,301	5,758
All Rail Casualties	6,831	7,466	7,073	6,763	6,573	6,770	6,578	6,141	5,686	5,702	6,207
Air flights[d]											
Deaths	53	–	–	63	118	–	–	–	63	–	–
Injuries[e]	40	8	5	4	20	2	4	9	–	–	1
All Domestic Air Flight Casualties	93	8	5	67	138	2	4	9	63	–	1

Source: Department of Transport, UK (1978).

[a] Includes staff employed by National Carriers and Freightliners Ltd.
[b] Includes all killed and injured except railway staff on railway premises.
[c] Includes suicides and attempted suicides.
[d] On scheduled passenger services of UK airlines.
[e] Requiring hospital treatment.

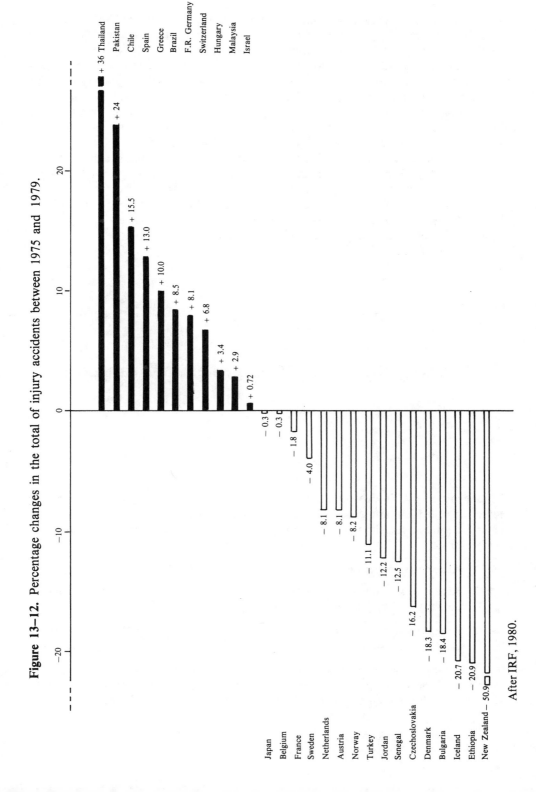

Figure 13–12. Percentage changes in the total of injury accidents between 1975 and 1979.

After IRF, 1980.

kilometres in many developing countries is about six times that in the United States. In cities like Caracas, Bangkok and Cairo, with narrow and congested streets, pressure for road space has meant such encroachment on the pavements that space for pedestrians barely existed and walking and cycling were dangerous and unpleasant (UNEP, 1980). The number of traffic accidents markedly increased in many developing countries during the 1970s because of this increase in traffic density and a lack of adequate training and safety measures. Moreover, people were not the only victims: a survey in the United States indicated that 120,000 deer and 1,200 other large wild animals were killed each year, in addition to many thousand domestic pets (UNEP, 1980).

Transport accidents not only cause pain and suffering: they impose a major cost on the community. Such costs are hard to estimate (the value put on life and the assumptions about the cost of pain and grief are clearly arbitrary and controversial) but one analysis (Sabey and Taylor, 1980), put the cost at £1,600 million per annum in the United Kingdom alone. The social losses involved are a major incentive to improve vehicle and traffic engineering and driver education.

The Regulation and Management of Transport

THE report of the Stockholm Conference identified urban transport as an important topic and called for various actions to plan and manage traffic so as to reduce its adverse environmental and social impacts. During the decade there have been developments in three areas:

(1) Action to improve the efficiency and safety of vehicles;

(2) Action to improve the corridors over or through which vehicles move, and to direct, space and manage them better;

(3) Action to inform, train and educate people so as to enhance the efficiency and safety of transport.

The primary aim of those designing new ships, aircraft, rail or road vehicles must be to achieve efficiency in operation. In the late 1970s, economic use of energy had become a vital concern. But it remained essential that such vehicles were as safe as possible – both for those who operate or travel in them and those liable to be hurt if an accident happened. A fourth need was to make them cause as little noise as possible, and minimal pollution when operated normally or when involved in an accident. These features inter-relate; a lightweight road vehicle, for example, generally uses less energy than a heavy one, but may be more dangerous to travel in, and may lose its energy economy if extra devices have to be added to prevent air pollution.

ACTIONS TO IMPROVE VEHICLES

Actions to reduce pollution from motor vehicles

Differences between countries in the severity of air pollution problems, differing national judgements about the scientific evidence for the adverse effects of various substances, and variations in the economic resources available, all contributed to the wide variation in the stringency of control over emissions from motor vehicles in the 1970s. But there was widespread recognition that while more precise scientific information was desirable, the potential damage to health and environment was such that reductions in pollution should be sought at once, especially in areas where traffic density is high. Moreover, the mobility of vehicles meant that they had to be designed to produce acceptable emissions wherever they might go – hence the standards adopted were those appropriate to urban centres.

The recognition that hydrocarbons and oxides of nitrogen emitted from petrol-driven motor cars were the precursors in the reactions leading to photochemical (oxidant) smog, first identified as an acute problem in the Los Angeles area (Chapter 2), was one reason why the first and most stringent vehicle emission standards were adopted in the United States. The initial goal was that by 1975 emission of carbon monoxide and hydrocarbons from new cars should be reduced to 14 per cent and 4 per cent respectively of the levels from uncontrolled cars (CEQ, 1970), with a reduction of nitrogen oxides to 15 per cent of the emission from uncontrolled vehicles one year later. These were being reconsidered in 1981. Canada applied the same standards as the United States for 1974 and for 1975 adhered to the United States test procedure but with higher limit values than in the United States. The Federal Republic of Germany adopted a programme for the gradual reduction of the noxious substances in exhaust emissions by spark-ignition engines to 1/10 of the average 1969 values by 1980 (FRG. 1980). Australia and Sweden introduced for 1976 onwards requirements that were applied in the United States for 1973 cars. Japan also adopted a stringent control programme. The member states of the European Economic Community applied ECE Regulation No. 15, as did Austria, Czechoslovakia, Norway and Switzerland. In the United States, the need to protect catalytic converters from damage has led to the removal of lead from petrol, while in the EEC the maximum permissible concentration of the metal is in the range 0.40 to 0.15 grammes per litre.

One of the main problems in comparing requirements for vehicle exhaust emissions and the results of their enforcement in different countries and areas, quite apart from differences in enforcement, is that the measurement methods and test procedures, including driving cycles, were still not fully harmonized by 1981. While test procedures must take account of local conditions such as driving habits, infrastructure and traffic conditions, there was a need for agreement, in acceptable international forum, at least on the equivalence of the methods used for measuring pollutant concentrations. This remained an important prerequisite for wider international harmonization. Wherever possible, variations in the technical legislation applying to motor vehicles also needed to be eliminated, since these increased production costs, could waste resources, and created non-tariff barriers to trade.

Another problem encountered in the 1970s was the deterioration of emission control systems after vehicles came into use – whether as a result of poor initial design or inadequate maintenance. In the United States at the very start of the emission control programme it was found that cars that in the summer of 1968 complied with federal standards for carbon monoxide and hydrocarbon emissions were a year later emitting on average 20 per cent and 8 per cent more of these gases respectively than the standards permitted, and by 1970 the divergences had increased to 25 per cent and 10 per cent (CEQ, 1970).

Aircraft emissions have not been subject to similar controls. But the International Civil Aviation Organization (ICAO) published a circular on the certification procedures for subsonic turbine engines and planned to issue mandatory requirements for control of smoke, vented fuel and certain gaseous emissions from future subsonic and supersonic turbojet and turbofan engines, as an annex to the Convention on International Civil Aviation. Studies on the possible operational control of aircraft engine emissions were also in progress.

For shipping, the Inter-Governmental Maritime Consultative Organization (IMCO) is the international organization responsible for technical matters. In February 1978 it passed regulations requiring new oil tankers to have segregated ballast and systems to minimize pollution during tank cleaning, and in the same year it adopted more stringent regulations for inspecting and certifying tankers and training their crews. IMCO has also concerned itself with the development of safer and more accident-proof systems for ship design and for handling hazardous cargoes, including explosives, compressed and liquified gases, inflammable materials, poisons, corrosive materials oxidizing agents and radioactive substances.

Actions to reduce noise

Many countries have adopted regulations to control maximum permissible noise levels for the different categories of motor vehicles. Table 13–10 sets out the limits adopted in 1977 by the EEC. Beyond this, tentative goals for 75 dB for cars and light trucks and 80–82 dB for heavy vehicles were set, to be met by advances in engine, fan, gearbox and transmission by the mid-to-late 1980s if technical developments permit. The 1977 figures are of the same order as those adopted in the USSR in 1974 (84 dBA for cars, 85–92 dBA for public service vehicles according to size) (Harris, 1979).

Table 13—10. EEC Automotive Noise Legislation (sound pressure levels in dB at 7—5 m).

	1977	1980/82
Passenger car	82	80
Van/light truck	84	81
Medium truck	89	86
Heavy truck	91	88

Source: Cottee (1978).

Measures to reduce noise from aircraft have also been agreed upon. In September 1968, ICAO adopted a resolution that has led to specifications under which modern jet aircraft are 16 to 20 EPN dB quieter than those in common use in the later 1960s. Retro-fitting the older aircraft would be the quickest, but an expensive means of bringing about a speedy improvement (OECD, 1975). In the United States new regulations will, however, require that all aircraft regardless of production date meet the 1968 standards by the mid-1980s (CEQ, 1977).

Actions to promote the efficient use of energy

The rise in energy prices during the 1970s stimulated efforts to reduce vehicles' fuel consumption. Newly developed lighter vehicles with improved engines made a considerable contribution: many 1980 four-seater cars used between 5 and 7 litres per 100 km at constant 90 km/h, while consumption in the 8—10 litre range were not uncommon a decade earlier. (On the long-term, reductions of 45 per cent in fuel consumption were in 1981 predicted for large cars.) Some countries imposed maximum speed limits of around 90—100 km/h as an aid to economy. High taxation on fuel, publicity, the encouragement of car sharing, traffic routing to avoid congestion and schemes to divert travellers to public transport were all used in various countries. Efforts were made to increase the occupancy levels of buses and trains and to reduce empty running by freight vehicles as a means of significant energy saving. It was estimated that in the EEC a combination of such measures could reduce predicted fuel demand in 1985 by 10 per cent to 15 per cent.

Actions to enhance safety

There is no doubt that the motor vehicle of 1981 was inherently safer than its predecessor, as a result of improvements in design such as the elimination of interior features liable to cause injury on impact, the better shaping of vehicle fronts to reduce danger to pedestrians in accidents, energy-dissipating bodywork, reinforcement against collapse in the event of roll-over, anti-lock and anti-fade brakes, safety tyres and many other systems. In addition, seat-belts and other occupant-restraint systems have come increasingly into use, backed by regulations in many countries. These improvements are the outcome of research and testing programmes that absorbed considerable effort in developed countries during the 1970s. In the United States the use of seat belts and other restraints was said to have produced a 50 per cent to 70 per cent reduction in accident death rates, although their use was not compulsory everywhere (Department of Transport, USA, 1978). In Australia, the enforcement of seat-belt regulations was reported to have cut deaths and injuries among car occupants by 20 to 40 per cent (Grime, 1979). Unfortunately, comparable progress had not occurred in developing countries, where safety measures were much less common.

Such devices have been supplemented by improvements in highway design. The importance of these is well illustrated by Sabey and Taylor's (1980) analysis, which indicated that better road engineering might prevent 20 per cent of accidents, incidentally in a highly-cost-effective fashion. Some of these measures, like the realignment of road junctions, could show a 400 per cent economic rate of return in the first year.

Road transport is not the only mode to show advances. Aircraft in 1981 undoubtedly had a better safety record than those of a generation earlier, as a result of improved design, instrumentation and ground control. This advance has not been recognized widely, probably because the increased size of passenger aircraft has also meant that the total fatality list in the rare accidents that have occurred has been alarmingly large.

ACTIONS THROUGH TRANSPORT MANAGEMENT

Operational controls take many forms. They include routing vessels and aircraft so as to minimize the risk of collision and avoid noise to people on the ground. They include the management of road traffic to assure that vehicles flow as smoothly, quietly and efficiently as possible. They should obviously include effective regulation enforcement – something often done inadequately at present. They also include difficult issues such as striking the right balance between private and public transport. So long as occupancy rates are fairly high, public passenger transport systems are more energy-efficient and have less environmental impact – but as communities become wealthier people want their own cars, and public transport becomes unprofitable. Analysis by OECD (1979 b) has shown how varied this problem is from one country to another, but also that there are ways of encouraging the use of public transport (including educational efforts).

Efficient road vehicle management systems advanced considerably during the decade. Traffic-responsive lights and computer-based control systems allowed faster urban traffic flows and hence enhanced efficiency and energy conservation. Segregation of traffic flow and improved signs and road markings enhanced safety. Schemes to confine town centres to pedestrian uses were adopted and refined around the world as a way of preserving the environment in city centres and historic areas (OECD Road Research, 1973; OECD Environment Committee, 1974, 1975). These schemes were most successful in small to medium-sized towns, and their application to large cities without substantial disruption of the motorized modes still raised problems at the end of the decade. Progressive refinement of pedestrian schemes had resolved difficulties over goods deliveries and public transport access but several socio-economic impacts (especially affecting the residents and traders in these centres) needed further evaluation (Taylor, 1979). Another development was the provision in some countries of special facilities for cyclists (for example, separate cycle lanes). However, the design of such systems needs care. It was observed that in certain cases they were not used because their disbenefits – perhaps in terms of greater distance for a journey – were apparently perceived as outweighing the gains in safety and environmental quality (Alexander, 1975; Zaidel et al., 1977).

Locational control is a component of national land-use planning, and must be carried out as part of a strategy for the development of settlements and industries. A new transport corridor will often stimulate development along its length, and have a long-term impact that cannot always be foreseen when it is first built. It is wise, accordingly, not just to construct new routes (or to improve old ones) to meet present needs, but to evaluate what the future consequences may be. The consequences will reach beyond the urban and industrial environment and the farming communities whose produce will reach markets more easily. A major environmental impact of modern transport has come through tourism reaching remote areas (Chapter 14), bringing with it new pressures on wildlife and placing severe stresses on local human communities. The ecological and human consequences are not easy to foresee, and cost-benefit analyses are extremely difficult. Traffic routing away from residential areas and better road network planning also aid in reducing people's exposure to pollution and noise. By-pass construction can reduce traffic flow through towns and villages with populations under 10,000 by as much as 50 per cent, greatly reducing noise, vibration, dirt and air pollution and bringing major benefits to the quality of life of residents (Mackie, 1981). Codes for urban design to attain defined noise standards have been developed.

Planning and management systems have also been developed to reduce noise exposure around airports. Three approaches have been combined. The first is to impose controls on take-off and landing and to restrict the number of noisy aircraft using an airport (particularly at night). By the end of the decade Schiphol (the Netherlands) and the major airports in the Federal Republic of Germany permitted night operations only by those aircraft that meet the ICAO noise standards. In some countries e.g. Japan, France and the Netherlands special "jet fees" were charged on domestic jet flights, the proceeds being used to compensate local residents.

A second approach consists of minimizing contact between human activities and airport noise through the co-ordination of airport planning with regional and local land-use policy. This approach can be implemented most easily in the case of new airports situated in areas not yet intensively developed. However, even around existing airports possibilities arise to re-zone heavily noise-impacted areas over a period of time so as to minimize exposure of private dwellings, schools, hospitals and recreation areas. Re-zoning may involve heavy costs in purchase and clearance of residential houses but in some cases it may be possible to convert existing structures and areas, for instance into airport-related activities, industrial parks or sports stadiums.

Land can be acquired or restrictions imposed on private housing construction at the outset, to establish a buffer zone between a new airport and surrounding development. This was done for Montreal's Mirabel airport, where an area of 360 km^2 was acquired although only 82 km^2 were needed for the airport itself, and for the Charles de Gaulle airport at Roissy, Paris, where a prohibition was imposed on the construction of private dwellings, schools and hospitals within the zone of the most intense noise (OECD, 1975). At previously existing airports, such as Zurich and Geneva, the problem of incompatible land uses near the airport was dealt with by legislation. In Scandinavian countries certain criteria were laid down by the Ministries of the Environment for existing and future land uses and their compatibility with different noise levels.

The third approach concentrates on providing protection against noise at its point of reception. Sound-proofing of private dwellings, hotels and offices may prove to be the only way of dealing rapidly with noise disturbance around existing airports where land development has already seriously encroached upon the buffer zone. This technique was used with Heathrow (United Kingdom), Schiphol (the Netherlands) and the German Federal Republic airports. At Heathrow more than 4,000 dwellings in the most exposed areas have been sound-proofed since 1966. However, sound-proofing remains an incomplete measure as it does nothing to improve the outdoor environment.

Where noise levels still remain unacceptably high in spite of all remedial efforts, a solution of last resort is to compensate home owners for the property's loss in value due to noise. In turn, the airport acquires a "noise easement" on the property. In the United States, where compensation has been used it has amounted to roughly 20 per cent of the value of the property.

Planning is also important in reducing the risks of marine pollution by oil which often arises more from loading and unloading facilities on shore than from shipping. Terminals have often been constructed in or near ecologically sensitive coastal areas, such as estuaries. The installation may make valuable fish nursery grounds useless. Whether the terminals service a large petroleum refinery or a pipeline for conveying oil to distant places, the risk of an oil spill always exists in the transfer of oil from tanker to shore facility. Even in the absence of acute, large-scale oil spills, there is often the long-term chronic effect of continuing small spills and leaks. For these reasons, increasing attention was paid during the 1970s to the selection of sites for deep-water oil ports. An environmental risk index for such siting was developed for the east coast of Canada (Canada, 1978). A similar activity was underway in 1980 for site selection on Canada's west coast, where there was a need for a terminal that would accept crude petroleum conveyed by tanker from Valdez, Alaska, and transmit it through a pipeline to areas of high demand in the midwestern and southern United States.

ACTIONS THROUGH EDUCATION AND TRAINING

Analysis in the United Kingdom shows that the road users there were solely responsible in 65 per cent of road accidents and contributed to a further 29 per cent (Sabey and Taylor, 1980). Perceptual errors (imperfect observation, inattention or misjudgement) and mistakes in executing a manoeuvre accounted for 60 per cent of these incidents. In many countries the risk is further increased by alcohol consumption. False perception of risk may be one reason why many road users do not attach their seat-belts in countries where this is voluntary.

Publicity campaigns and the impact of energy crises can bring about short-term improvements in individual driving behaviour and in safety measure observance. But sound education and training are the foundation for responsible, safe use of transport. During the decade considerable advances were made in understanding the foundation of perception and attitude and in the development of educational and information methods.

Future Prospects

THE major problems surrounding transport in the future in developed countries are likely to include achieving a proper balance between different modes, and especially ensuring that people's understandable desire for their own cars does not so undermine public transport systems that the very young, the very old, the poor, and those who for other reasons cannot run their own transport are severely hampered. As increased energy costs reduce the use of private vehicles in some countries it will be important that public transport has been maintained in condition to accommodate new loads. There will also be continuing concern over land appropriation for highways and airports, the risks from hazardous goods transported in ever-increasing volume, and traffic intrusion into town centres and areas celebrated for their history, natural beauty or wildlife. A very real conflict between conservation and tourism has already developed in some national parks and ecologically vulnerable areas and such problems are likely to become more frequent.

Within the next fifty years oil supplies are likely to diminish, and alternative fuels for transport will have to be found. New kinds of engine and vehicle may well appear. There have been suggestions that hydrogen may become the new aircraft fuel. In towns, there may be an increasing role for electric vehicles – which are quiet, non-polluting, and reasonably efficient for short journeys (especially those involving frequent stops and starts). Synthetic liquid hydrocarbon fuels made from coal provide another alternative. Railways powered by electricity generated from nuclear sources may take over more of the long-haul overland market. These are, to a considerable degree, matters of speculation. What is clear is that the futures of transport and energy are inseparable, and that the international community will in the future, as today, be concerned with the harmonization of standards for design, operation and environmental impact. There is a pressing need to evaluate the future prospects now – before short-term pressures become overwhelming.

There remain some major uncertainties which demand research. One is the real impact on humans of noise and of some pollutants emitted by transport. The seriousness of carbon monoxide and lead pollution from petrol-driven cars, for example, is still a matter of dispute. Another is the extent to which the transport technologies of developed countries can be transferred to the developing world. Although there is a great deal of relevant experience, more research is needed to provide good and economical guidelines for transport planning and development (including environmental impact assessment). Accidents cannot be totally avoided; they will inevitably occur from time to time, especially with the great increase in transport in terms of load or of distances. Greater efforts are therefore needed to reduce the occurrence of such accidents through more stringent transportation rules and procedures nationally, regionally and internationally. This applies to transport by land, sea or air of all goods, and in particular of those toxic substances likely to affect the environment when spilled.

In developing countries there is a pressing need to extend highway and railway systems, and to develop effective public transport. Lessons learned in developed countries, especially regarding energy and resource conservation, need careful application. The new transport systems must be integrated and co-ordinated. In parallel, major efforts will be needed to educate road users in safety if a further, sharp deterioration in accident statistics is to be avoided.

References

Alexander, R. (1975), Pros and Cons of Bike Lane Striping, *Traffic Engin.*, 45, 6, 18.

Allsop, R. E. (1980), *Transport Studies and the Quality of Life*, Environmental Planning, A., 12 339–356.

Baker, J. M., Editor (1976), *Marine Energy and Oil Pollution*, Applied Science Publishers, Barking.

Bick, T. and C. Hohenemser (1979), *Target; Highway Risks*, Environment, 21, 16.

Canada (1978), *Potential Pacific Coast Oil Ports: A Comparative Environmental Risk Analysis,* Dept. Fisheries and Environment, Canada.

CEQ (1970), *Environmental Quality*, Report of the Council on Environmental Quality, Washington, D.C.

CEQ (1977), *Environmental Quality*, Report of the Council on Environmental Quality. Washington, D.C.

Colwill, D. M. *et al.*.Editors (1979), *The Impact of Road Traffic on Plants*, Transport and Road Research Lab. Report SR 513, Crowthorne, U.K.

CONCAWE (1974), *Spillages from Oil Industry Cross Country Pipelines in W. Europe*, Report 1/74, Conservation of Clear Air and Water Inter, Study Group of Oil Companies (CONCAWE), Den Haag, Netherlands.

Cottee, B. (1978), *Road Transport and the Environment*, Long Range Planning, 11, 39.

Crutzen, P. J. (1974), *Estimates of Possible Variations in Total Ozone Due to Natural Causes and Human Activities*, Ambio, 3, 201.

Davie, M. R. (1937), The Pattern of Urban Growth. In G. P. Murdock (Editor), *Studies in the Science of Society*. New Haven.

Department of Transport, (1978), *Transport Statistics, United Kingdom* 1968–78, HMSO, London.

Department of Transport, (1978), *United States Department of Transport News*, August 1978, DOT 12278, US Government Printing Office, Washington, D.C.

DOE (1980), *Digest of Environmental Pollution Statistics*, Department of Environment, HMSO, London.

EAJ (1978), *Report of the Environment Agency of Japan for* 1978, Tokyo.

ECE (1976), *Increased Energy Economy and Efficiency in the ECE Region*, (E/ECE/883/Rev.1), Economic Commission for Europe, Geneva.

Ember, L. (1979), *The Diesel Dilemma*, Environment, 21, 17.

EUROSTAT (1977), *Statistical Yearbook*. Transport, Communication, Tourism. Statistical Office of the European Communities, Brussels.

Frey, H. T. (1979), *Major Uses of Land in the United States,* 1974, Agriculture Economic Report No. 440, US Department of Agriculture, Washington, D.C.

FRG (1980), *Environmental Policy in the Federal Republic of Germany,* Federal Republic of Germany, Bonn.

Grime, G. (1979), *The Protection Afforded by Seat Belts,* Report SR 449, Transport and Road Research Laboratory, Crowthorne, UK.

Grobecker, A. J. *et al.* (1974), *The Effects of Stratospheric Pollution by Aircraft,* Executive Summary, Depart. Transport, Washington, D.C.

Hale, D. (1978), *World Pipeline Outlook,* Pipeline and Gas Journal, January 1978.

Harris, R. V. (1979), *Urban Transport and Related Environmental Issues,* United Nations Transport Programme, ESA, United Nations, New York.

Hillman, M. and A. Whalley (1979), *Walking is Transport,* Policy Studies Institute, London, XLV, No. 583.

Hoekwater, J. (1978), In M. Taylor, *Pedestrians and Cyclists,* OECD Seminar on Urban Transport and the Environment, Organization for Economic Co-operation and Development, Paris, 1979.

Holdgate, M. W. (1981), *Risk in the Built Environment,* Phil. Trans. Roy. Soc., London (in press).

Hoyt, H. (1939), *The Structure and Growth of Residential Neighbourhoods in American Cities,* Washington, D.C.

ICAO (1979), *Annual Report of the Council,* Intern. Civil Aviation Organization, Montreal, Canada.

IMCO (1978), *The International Conference on Tanker Safety and Pollution Prevention – 1978,* Inter-Governmental Maritime Consultative Organization, London.

IRF (1980), *International Road Statistics,* International Road Federation.

Kaplan, J. A. (1977), *Riding Patterns of the Regular Adult Bicyclist,* Transportation Engineering, 48, 7, 40.

Lamb, H. H. (1977), *Climate, Present, Past and Future,* Methuen, London.

Laursen, J. G. (1978), *Accidents Involving Cyclists and Moped Riders in Denmark,* P.T.R.C., 6th Summer Annual Meeting, 10–13 July, Univ of Warwick.

Leach, G. (1973), *The Motor Car and Natural Resources,* Organization for Economic Co-operation and Development, Paris.

Mackie, A. M. (1981), *Environmental Effects of Traffic Changes as a Result of Bypass Construction in Ten English Towns,* Paper presented to Planning and Transport Research and Computation Conference, Warwick Univ., UK, July 1981.

McConnell, H. H. and J. Lewis (1972), *Add Salt to Taste,* Environment, 14, 38.

Murozumi, M. *et al.* (1969), *Chemical Concentration of Pollutant Lead Aerosols, Terrestrial Dusts and Sea Salts in Greenland and Antarctic Snow Strata,* Geochim. Cosmochin Acta, 33, 12, 47–94.

NAS (1975), *Environmental Impacts of Stratospheric Flight,* National Academy of Sciences, Washington, D.C.

NAS (1976), *Halocarbons; Environmental Effects of Chlorofluoromethane Release,* National Academy of Sciences, Washington, D.C.

NAS (1980), *Lead in the Human Environment,* National Academy of Sciences, Washington, D.C.

National Swedish Institute for Building Research, NSIBR, (1968), *Traffic Noise in Residential Areas*, Report 36E, National Swedish Institute for Building Research, Stockholm.

OECD (1975), *Airports and the Environment*, Organization for Economic Cooperation and Development, Paris.

OECD (1977), *Para Transit in the Developing World*, Organization for Economic Cooperation and Development, Paris.

OECD (1978a), *Energy Conservation in the Transport Sector in the IEA*, OECD/IEA, Paris.

OECD (1978b), *Photochemical Oxidants and Their Percursors in the Atmosphere*, Env (78) 6, Organization for Economic Cooperation and Development, Paris.

OECD (1979a), *Urban Transport and the Environment*, Organization for Economic Co-operation and Development, Paris.

OECD (1979b), *The State of the Environment in OECD Member Countries*, Organization for Economic Cooperation and Development, Paris.

OECD Environment Committee (1974), *Streets for People*, Organization for Economic Co-operation and Development, Paris.

OECD Environment Committee (1975), *Better Towns with Less Traffic*. Organization for Economic Cooperation and Development, Paris.

OECD Road Research (1973), *Techniques of Improving Urban Conditions by Restraint or Road Traffic*, OECD Symposium Proceedings, Organization for Economic Cooperation and Development, Paris.

Oluwande, P. A. (1979), *Automobile Exhaust Problems in Nigeria*, Ambio, 8, 1, 26—29.

O'Reilly, M. P. (1974), *Some Examples of Underground Development in Europe*, Transport and Road Research Lab. Suppl. Report 592. Crowthorne, UK.

Quenault, S. W. and T. V. Head (1977), *Cycle Routes in Portsmouth*, Transport and Road Research Lab. Suppl. Report 317, Crowthorne, UK.

Reed, S. B. (1976), *Pollution from Road Vehicles*, Environ. Health, Feb. 1976, 36.

Rice, R. A. (1972), *Systems Energy and Future Transportation*, Techn. Review, 74, 31.

Rigby, J. P. (1977), *An Analysis of Travel Patterns Using the 1972/73 National Travel Survey*, Transport and Road Research Lab. Report 790, Crowthorne, UK.

Robson, B. T. (1971), *Urban Analysis; A Study of City Structure*, University Press, Cambridge.

Sabey, B. E. and H. Taylor (1980), *The Known Risks We Run: the Highway*, Transport and Road Research Lab. Report SR 567, Crowthorne, UK.

Simkowitz, H. *et al.* (1979), *Land Use, In Urban Transport and Environment*, Organization for Economic Cooperation and Development, Paris.

Stores, A. (1978), *Cycle Use in Great Britain*, Transport and Road Research Lab. Report 843, Crowthorne, UK.

Stratton, A. (1974), *Safety and Air Navigation*, Journal of Navigation, 27, 4.

Taylor, M. (1979), *Pedestrians and Cyclists*, OECD Seminar on Urban Transport and the Environment, Organization for Economic Cooperation and Development, Paris.

Thompson, J. R. *et al.* (1979), The Implication of De-icing Sheets for Motorway Plantings in the UK, In D. M. Colwill et al. (Editors) *The Impact of Road Traffic on Plants*, Transport and Road Research Lab. Report SR 513, Crowthorne, UK.

UK (1980), *Official List of Results of Fuel Consumption Test on Passenger Cars*, UK, HMSO, London.

UN (1979), *Statistical Yearbook* 1978, United Nations, New York.

UN (1981), *Report of the Ad Hoc Group on Animal Power*, A/CONF.100/PC 39, UN Conf. New and Renewable Sources of Energy. United Nations, New York.

UNCTAD (1978), *Review of Maritime Transport*, 1977, United Nations Conference on Trade and Development, Geneva.

UNCTAD (1979), *Review of Maritime Transport*, 1978, United Nations Conference on Trade and Development, Geneva.

UNEP (1977 a), *Environmental Aspects of Motor Vehicle and Its Use*, Industry Programme, United Nations Environment Programme, Nairobi.

UNEP (1977 b), *The State of the Environment: Selected Topics* – 1977, United Nations Environment Programme, Nairobi.

UNEP (1979), *The State of the Environment : Selected Topics* – 1979, United Nations Environment Programme, Nairobi.

UNEP (1980), *The State of the Environment : Selected Topics* – 1980, United Nations Environment Programme, Nairobi.

UNEP (1981), *Environmental Impacts of Production and Use of Energy*, Study Director : E. El-Hinnawi, Tycooly International Publishing Ltd., Dublin.

Vestnik Statistiki (1980), *Automobilniy Transport, Seviya* 4, Passazhinskiye Perevozki Autotransport on KYP2N.

World Bank (1975), *Urban Transport: Sector Policy Paper*, The World Bank, Washington, D.C.

World Bank (1979), *World Development Report*, 1979, The World Bank, Washington, D.C.

Zaidel, D. *et al.* (1977), *Factors Affecting the Use of Pedestrian Overpasses*, The Voice of the Pedestrian, vii, 61—77.

CHAPTER 14

Tourism

The number of international tourist arrivals increased over the decade by more than 100 million: from 180 million in 1971 to 286 million in 1980. By the end of the decade international travel was a major concern of many countries, contributing a substantial share of their national income.

But while tourism brought much foreign exchange to countries in need of it, part of the foreign exchange went abroad to pay for the goods and services used by tourists. Similarly, while tourism undoubtedly provided jobs for local employees, it cost their countries a good deal to create those jobs: for example, it was calculated that in Tunisia between 1965 and 1971 the cost of creating a job in the hotel industry was between US$13,300 and US$20,300.

The social effects of tourism were also mixed. Sometimes tourism resulted in dislocation of residents of an area and damage to their economic interests. Sometimes it caused inflation and changed life-styles among local people, or challenged their cultural beliefs. It had both good and bad effects on the arts, on the one hand resulting in production of articles without artistic merit, while on the other revitalizing dying crafts.

The environmental effects of tourism were legion. The need to attract tourists led in some places to protection of the physical environment, historic sites and monuments, and wildlife. But the mass movement of tourists also transformed many areas and brought irreversible environmental damage. Tourist facilities marred many coastlines, while the tourists themselves choked the narrow streets of historic towns and crowded picturesque countrysides. The insatiable curiosity of the tourist damaged fragile ecosystems on islands, coastal lands and mountains, and contributed to the pollution of coastal waters. In some areas tourists left behind a trail of litter, erosion and forest fires.

In many areas during the 1970s the limits of desirable tourist influx were being reached, so that planning was a challenge for the 80s. The environmental damage that was caused during the decade was often the result of poor planning of individual tourist schemes and poor planning for growth. It was clear that such damage was counter-productive for the industry itself.

A key principle advocated by those who sought a balance between tourism and the environment (Manila Declaration, 1980) was that the type and scale of tourist development should be related to the carrying capacity of tourist resources. Assessment of such capacity – and balancing the level of tourist activity within it – were thus seen as crucial means of preventing environmental damage in future. For by the end of the decade, tourism's impact on both the physical and the sociocultural environment was substantial and widespread, and expected to increase. The prime planning initiative was seen to rest with national governments, but because tourism is world-wide, there would have to be collaboration on both a regional and an international scale in order to find a balance between tourism on one side and environment on the other.

World Trends

TOURISM in the decade of the 1970s became a major industry, with widespread economic, socio-cultural and environmental aspects. Its growth was extremely rapid internationally, especially during the latter half of the period (Figure 14–1), with international tourist arrivals increasing from 180 million in 1971 to 286 million in 1980. So important had international tourism become by 1980 that a World Tourism Conference held that year in the Philippines issued a declaration, adopted by 107 states, called the *Manila Declaration*. This declaration sought, in the light of the experience of the 1970s, to balance the obvious economic advantages of tourism with the need to conserve the heritage of its signatories. It emphasized that the needs of tourism must not be satisfied in a fashion prejudicial to the social and economic interests of the population in tourist areas, to the environment or, above all, to natural resources and historical and cultural sites, which are the fundamental attraction for tourism. It stressed that these resources are part of the heritage of mankind, and national communities and the entire international community must take the necessary steps to ensure their preservation.

Table 14–1 gives details of the growth of tourism in various regions of the world (see also Figure 14–1). Europe accounted for 72.8 per cent of the international tourist traffic in 1980, the Americas for 18.4 per cent, East Asia and the Pacific for 5.3 per cent, Africa for 2.0 per cent, the Middle East for 1.0 per cent and South Asia for 0.5 per cent. Between 1971 and 1980, there was a marked increase in East Asia's and the Pacific's share of world tourism (from 2.2 per cent to 5.3 per cent) and a slight decrease in the European share (from 75.3 per cent to 72.8 per cent). The absolute numbers of international tourist arrivals in the Middle East and South Asia appear to have fallen between 1978 and 1980.

In addition to international tourism domestic tourism (i.e. journeys that do not cross national boundaries) grew in scale. It is estimated that global domestic tourism totals about four times the volume of international tourism (Aguirre, 1978). Although the

Table 14–1. Structure of International Tourism Arrivals in Different Regions (in thousands)

Region	Traffic	1971	1972	1973	1974	1975	1976	1977	1978	1979	1980 [a]
Africa	Total arrivals	2,657	3,190	3,438	3,018	3,140	4,100	4,500	4,900	5,300	5,800
	Intra-regional	561	556	709	808	840	492	1,101	1,235	1,389	1,450
	Inter-regional	2,096	2,634	2,729	2,210	2,300	3,608	3,399	3,665	3,911	4,350
Middle East	Total arrivals	3,631	3,843	3,753	4,936	5,140	3,600	3,500	3,800	3,600 [b]	3,000
	Intra-regional	2,839	2,912	2,905	3,500	3,650	1,682	1,980	2,701	2,788 [b]	2,300
	Inter-regional	792	931	848	1,436	1,490	1,918	1,520	1,099	812 [b]	700
South Asia	Total arrivals	960	1,071	1,232	1,239	1,289	1,700	1,970	2,100	2,000	1,500
	Intra-regional	273	286	286	178	179	313	386	449	462	350
	Inter-regional	687	785	946	1,061	1,110	1,387	1,584	1,651	1,538	1,150
East Asia and Pacific	Total arrivals	3,952	5,147	6,611	7,448	7,800	9,200	10,200	12,000	13,800	15,000
	Intra-regional	1,784	2,558	3,651	4,178	4,300	5,336	7,155	8,018	8,681	9,200
	Inter-regional	2,168	2,589	2,960	3,270	3,500	3,864	3,045	3,982	5,119	5,800
The Americas	Total arrivals	31,757	35,305	33,366	36,116	36,700	43,500	45,100	47,500	49,500	52,500
	Intra-regional	29,405	32,194	29,558	30,863	31,200	37,000	38,100	39,500	40,700	42,000
	Inter-regional	2,352	3,111	3,808	5,253	5,500	6,500	7,000	8,000	8,800	10,500
Europe	Total arrivals	130,863	168,115	166,676	165,541	166,090	165,000	178,300	189,000	196,000	208,000
	Intra-regional	112,195	146,068	146,013	147,499	148,000	142,700	147,500	158,100	157,800	164,300
	Inter-regional	18,668	22,047	20,663	18,042	18,090	22,300	30,800	30,900	38,200	43,700

Source: Data provided by World Tourism Organization.
Total arrivals: arrivals from countries of the region and arrivals from other regions.
Intra-regional: arrivals from countries of the region.
Inter-regional: arrivals from countries of other regions.

[a] provisional estimates
[b] estimates

Figure 14–1. Growth of International Tourism.

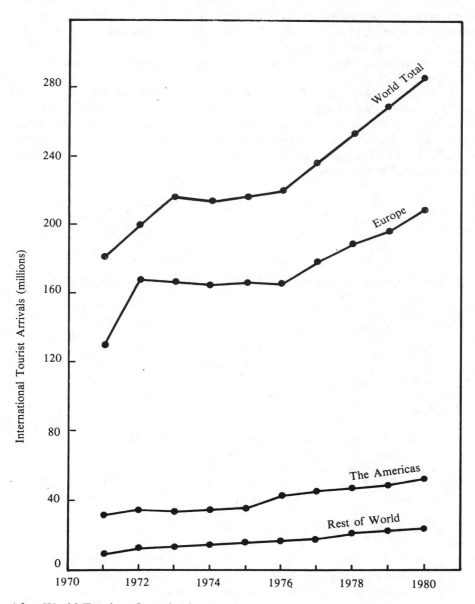

After World Tourism Organization.

majority of this domestic tourism falls within countries in the developed world, many developing countries have begun to generate their own.

Developments in the USSR and the CMEA (Council for Mutual Economic Assistance) countries illustrate several of these points. Between 1972 and 1979 domestic tourist totals in the USSR rose from 42 to 63 million whereas international tourists visiting the country increased from only 2.3 to 4.0 million. In the smaller CMEA countries international tourist arrivals, in contrast, substantially exceeded domestic travel (Table 14–2).

At the end of 1977, about 70 per cent of the world's international tourists came from 20 countries. First among these was the United States (14.7 per cent) followed by the Federal Republic of Germany (10.7 per cent), France (8.5 per cent), the United Kingdom (6.5 per cent), Canada (5.5 per cent), the Netherlands (3.8 per cent) and Belgium (2.8 per cent). Japan, Australia and Sweden generated an increasingly high rate of tourism over the preceding 5 years.

Table 14–2. Growth of Internal and International Tourism in CMEA Countries

		1972	1979
USSR	Domestic	42.2	62.6
	International	2.3	4.0
Bulgaria	Domestic	0.5	1.0
	International	3.0	5.0
Hungary	Domestic	0.8	1.1
	International	3.6	—
German Democratic Republic	Domestic	1.5	1.9
	International	16.0	17.1
Poland	Domestic	3.1	4.9
	International	8.8	10.7
Romania	Domestic	1.1	1.8 (1978)
	International	2.9	4.5
Czechoslovakia	Domestic	0.9	1.1
	International	11.5	19.4

Source: Norodnoye Khozyaistvo SSSR V 1972. Moscow, Statistika, 1973.
Norodnoye Khozyaistvo SSSR V 1979. Moscow, Statistika, 1980.
Natsional'nye Statsticheskoe Exegodniki Stran-Chelenov CEV Statisticheskiyae Exegodniki Stran-Chelenov CEV,.

"International" refers to foreign visitors to these countries.

Economic and cultural aspects

INTERNATIONAL tourist receipts (receipts of countries in the form of consumption expenditures, i.e. payments for goods and services, made by foreign tourists out of foreign currency resources and excluding international fare payments) rose five-fold in 10 years. They were US$18,200 million in 1970, US$28,800 million in 1975, US$65,000 million (about 5 per cent of international trade) in 1978, and US$92,000 million in 1980, and as an aggregate world total did not reflect fluctuations in economic conditions in the countries of origin.

International tourist receipts make a major contribution to the national income of many countries, representing for example, 14 per cent of the national income of Malta, 10 per cent for Spain, 9 per cent for Cyprus, 8 per cent for Austria, 7 per cent for Tunisia and Morocco and 4 per cent for Mauritius and Jordan (WTO 1977). International and domestic tourism together make, in many countries, large contributions to regional and local economies and to employment. This economic dimension provides a major impetus to the continuing growth and geographical spread of tourist facilities.

It should be noted, however, that although tourists' expenditure contributes to the national income, part of the foreign exchange pays for the cost of importing goods and services used by tourists, some of the costs of capital investment in tourist amenities, such as hotels and vehicles, payments to foreign travel agents, royalties, etc. and promotion and publicity expenditure abroad. Therefore, the overall balance of payments contribution of the tourist industry varies from one country to another and is generally difficult to determine accurately.

Tourism has undoubtedly contributed to employment, and can help significantly in providing jobs. But the tourist industry is not so labour-intensive as is generally thought. In Tunisia, it was calculated that during the period 1956 to 1971 the cost of creating a job in the hotel industry was between US$13,300 and US$20,300, and in manufacturing industry, approximately US$12,700 (Bugnicourt, 1977). Therefore, the degree to which tourism should be supported in any particular country with a view to job-creation, as compared with investment in other sectors, must depend on the circumstances and resources of that country. A significant characteristic of the tourist industry in most countries is its seasonality — the wide difference between the high and low tourist seasons. The proportion of labour laid off in the off-season varies widely from country to country but averages about 25 per cent. Those affected are principally the lowest-paid and least-skilled workers (UNEP, 1979).

On the other hand, Manning (1976) reports that tourism in Bermuda provides, directly or indirectly, three-quarters of all jobs: one in six workers is employed by the hotels alone. The abundance of jobs results in the widespread practice of working at more than one job and at the lowest employment rate. Tourism may also offer particular employment opportunities for women in activities like cleaning and washing (Thurot, 1975).

The infrastructural costs of tourism constitute the heaviest investment for the industry: ports, airports, roads, water and electricity supply, public health, sewage disposal and so forth. However, many of these facilities and services contribute profits to other sectors and, especially in the case of basic transport improvements, may contribute significantly to higher output. Allocation of costs and benefits to particular sectors is not therefore straightforward. It is easier where a complete region or area is being developed primarily for tourism, or when a facility like a road exclusively for tourist traffic is being installed.

Tourism may compete with other developments for space, and providing for it should be an integral part of national land-use planning, taking environmental criteria into full consideration. Once established, there is pressure to preserve and protect recreational areas against encroachments through proper legislative or institutional arrangements. For instance the USSR introduced a Health Resort Regulation in 1973, under which territories defined as health resorts, or having a health resort potential, are protected within a zone in which all activities that may affect their quality are banned. Industries incompatible with the requirements of the health resort are removed, e.g., mining was stopped in the Mineralnye Vody area (the Caucasus).

The development of tourism may, in certain circumstances, contribute to pressures on the general level of prices. Its inflationary effect varies considerably from one country to another. Although the main effects are encountered in the accommodation sector, in some countries they may extend to basic items, including food and clothing, creating local socio-economic problems (UNEP, 1979).

In broad terms, one may expect that domestic tourism would raise fewer issues of social or cultural impact than international travel, because the tourist within his (her) own country will normally share the same social and cultural tradition as the people of the area he (she) visits. But international tourism may bring into close proximity (as 'host' and 'guest') people of different race, colour, religion and social and cultural tradition; in developing countries there may also be wide, and conspicuous, disparities in income level between the average tourist and the average local resident.

The social impact of tourism on receiving areas is largely a direct counterpart of its economic impact. Tourism brings income and employment into an area. Saglio (1976) describes the benefits that have accrued from the experimental project for "integrated village tourism" that has been pursued in Senegal since 1971, as follows:

> "the profits, used prudently, have permitted the co-ordinated development of village activities and the integration of the tourism operation in the village economy . . . it has been possible to utilize the profits for other activities such as vegetable farming, raising livestock, fishing and crafts. This has in turn enabled many young people to find jobs locally and has effectively deterred migration to the cities".

By contrast, Green (1976) reports that in Africa the gains from tourism may not be concentrated among the initial residents of an area. Frequently these people suffer from dislocation of their existing patterns of production, lack of attention to their direct needs, and loss of land. Development of tourist complexes often involves extending game parks, banning hunting by savannah and forest peoples, relocating fishermen away from homes and markets, and clearing out unsightly evidence of poverty (such as squatter villages) near tourist sites. This may be damaging, even in narrow economic terms, to the poorest and weakest of the initial residents.

Similar effects can be seen in developed countries, with tourism acting both as a stimulant to the economy of ailing regions and as a dislocating factor. In the Federal Republic of Germany tourism development in rural areas is considered an important means of bringing relief to depressed agricultural regions. Attempts are made, through investment in the tourist sector, to diversify rural economies and improve the employment available there. By increasing the attractiveness of an area, it is hoped that the drift from the land will be slowed down, halting selective migration and social erosion (ECE, 1976). In Scotland, however, it is reported that the demand for second homes (a form of tourism) can force up the price of housing and put local people — particularly young workers — at a serious disadvantage. The evidence of places like Galloway and Strathspey — where second-home demand has consumed the stock of vacant housing — shows that this aspect of economic impact needs careful thought (DART, 1977). In the Federal Republic of Germany, special areas have been set aside for second homes, so as to avoid this conflict.

Allied to such socio-economic effects of tourism are those related to life-style and culture. Particularly in less developed countries, the life-style and cultural stance of visitors may be markedly different from the host community's and have a strong effect upon them. For example, Greenwood (1976) reports of Fuenterrabia in Spain that "over time, local people have come to adopt a style of life markedly similar to that of the middle-class tourists they have seen . . . (But) continual contact with outsiders who are rude, rich and idle is particularly offensive to the young Basques. Their reaction is a combination of defensiveness, hostility and attempted social invisibility. They mimic the consumption patterns of the tourists, dropping all external signs of their Basque culture". Haulot (1974) speaks of the 'banalization of customs' that follows the development of tourism; the transformation people undergo when they become tourists, 'seeing themselves like the people in the latest advertisements'; and the effect this introduced world-scale uniformity has upon the customs of the host countries. In some countries, there has been grave concern about the moral impacts of tourism (Nettlefold, 1975).

Tourism is seen by some as representing a form of 'neo-colonialism' (Haulot, 1974; Nettlefold, 1975; Bugnicourt, 1977). Bugnicourt notes that some developing countries may divert valuable resources to ensure that tourists find the same amenities in their countries as they have at home. For example, at Djerba in Tunisia in 1974, 20 per cent of the water in the main supply network went to the large hotels, although 80 per cent of the dwellings in Djerba had no running water.

The Seminar on the Social and Cultural Impacts of Tourism (1976) sponsored by the United Nations Educational, Scientific and Cultural Organization (UNESCO) and the World Bank revealed examples of both the damaging and beneficial impacts of tourism upon the arts. Among the former were the mass-production of small carved heads, without artistic merit, in the Ivory Coast and the transformation of meaningful religious or community ritual into a performance for outsiders. On the other hand, tourism provided a re-vitalization of dying crafts, such as jewellery and leatherwork in Tunisia, or textiles and glass in Malta, and encouraged performing arts and folklore, such as Creole music in the Seychelles. Thurot (1975) points to the role of tourism in helping to salvage cultural values:

> ". . . the value attached by the foreigner to the evidence of the cultural past, which has become foreign, makes the citizens of the host country aware of the idea of historical and cultural continuity, which can help to enhance their present culture. There are many examples: the earliest is obviously that of Greece in the nineteenth century, which witnessed the extraordinary conjunction of national independence, the rise of tourism and the great archaeological discoveries of Schliemann — all this in a country where popular culture hardly looked any further back than the fall of Byzantium. The most recent case is the resurgence of Indian culture in South America, where there was every reason to believe it was completely extinct."

Environmental Aspects

UNSPOILED countrysides, especially outstanding scenery such as coastlines, lakes and rivers, islands or mountain regions, and historical sites and monuments constitute the stock of natural and man-made resources for tourism and recreation. Until recently such amenities were taken for granted. In the 1970s, however, it became increasingly apparent that these resources are, to a large extent, fragile, with limited resilience and carrying capacity. The *Manila Declaration* (1980) stated that, "Tourism development at both the national and international level can make a positive contribution to the life of the nation provided the supply is well planned and of a high standard and protects and respects the cultural heritage, the values of tourism and the natural, social and human environment."

Tourism has positively benefited the environment by stimulating measures to protect physical features of the environment, historic sites and monuments, and wildlife (UNEP, 1979). In the Central African Republic, the opening to visitors of Saint-Floris National Park permitted effective protection of wildlife, the income from tourism allowing proper maintenance of trails and rangers' camps, and the very presence and movement of tourists keeping poachers at bay. Peters (1978) claimed that if Perdjari park in Benin were not exploited for tourism, the possibility of developing it in the future might be lost. The historic and cultural heritage that determines the attractiveness of a country to tourists encourages the authorities to protect it: witness the many examples of cultural salvage operations stimulated by tourism and sponsored by UNESCO (Lonati, 1969; Thurot, 1975). The Traditional Settlement Project of the National Tourist Organization of Greece rehabilitates and develops traditional settlements throughout the country, not in the sense of turning them into museum pieces but as means of societal development. Tourist facilities are provided through reconstruction of traditional buildings and the promotion of local activities and the cultural heritage. The project thus has the dual objective of local community development and tourism promotion.

Many other efforts have been made, at both national and international levels, to provide for systematic protection of old towns, villages and groups of buildings of historic and artistic interest (UNESCO has supported and sponsored a great deal of this important work).

Several villages and health resorts were created, or improved, for the purpose of tourism. Examples in Britain are the sea-side resorts of Eastbourne and Brighton and the spa towns of Bath, Cheltenham and Buxton, whose architectural and environmental qualities have made them a recognized part of the country's historic heritage (BTA, 1975). A project at Ixtapa, on the Pacific coast of Mexico, involves not merely the creation of a new tourist resort (complete with international airport), but the comprehensive environmental improvement of the adjoining town. This improvement includes the installation of water supplies and a sewage system, paved roads and electricity supplies, tree-planting, coastal protection and mosquito control, all of which should markedly improve local levels of health, sanitation and amenity. Similar programmes are taking place in six tourist-destination towns in Tunisia; at Kotu on the coast of Gambia; at La Petite Côte in Senegal; at Cox's Bazar beach in Bangladesh; and in the Kyongju province of Korea. This Korean project illustrates a further dimension of the link between tourism and the environment; the project includes creation of a new reservoir that will not only serve the town and tourist development in Kyongju, but also provide irrigation for nearby farming areas.

The counterpart to these positive effects is the negative impact tourism can have on the physical environment. Tourism involves the movement and accommodation of people, often in large numbers, and is thus a major cause of transport development and urbanization. Mass tourism necessitates the development of access roads, hotels, restaurants, shopping and entertainment facilities and other services. In the process, the major tourist sites are inevitably transformed: at best only their natural attractiveness or innocence will be lost, but at worst, major and often irreversible environmental damage will be caused by a rush to build tourist facilities on the most attractive sites, by speculative land and building booms (recreational urbanization) and by major inroads into the local ecology through the development of tourist infrastructure and services. Countless hotels, roads, cable-cars and other facilities provided for the tourists may ruin the beauties of the sea coast (Cohen, 1978).

Inhabitants of historic cities and old villages are often distressed to find their narrow streets choked with tourist traffic, and their picturesque squares and market-places turned into car parks for visitors. The influx of traffic creates noise and air pollution, the latter made worse by the local transport infrastructures developed to support tourism. Elsewhere, urban and industrial development can lead to pollution that damages tourist goals, as at the Acropolis in Athens (Chapter 2). Parts of the Mediterranean coasts are considered by some to have had their natural charm and character brutalized by the massive and standardized tourist development. In many countries, the building of corniche roads has led to the ribbon development of highly scenic coastlines (ETC, 1974). In Ireland, the United Kingdom, Denmark and the Netherlands, recreational pressure of domestic tourists has caused erosion of dunes and heavy loss of coastal vegetation. Most seriously threatened, perhaps, are the fragile ecosystems of some of the islands in the Caribbean, the Pacific and the Indian Ocean, which have recently been opened for tourism.

Widespread concern has been expressed about the pollution of coastal and inland waters by tourist development or activity. Tourism is not, of course, the only cause of such pollution, which may result from untreated wastes from towns, industries, agriculture or shipping. But tourist development in many areas undeniably contributes to the pollution — and in turn, the pollution can have damaging effects upon tourism. Thus, in the summer of 1972, local authorities on stretches of the coasts in parts of Europe were obliged to declare the sea unfit for bathing because of pollution. Although this pollution was not principally caused by tourism, it was certainly made worse by untreated sewage from tourist resorts, by effluents from thousands of tourist yachts and by the seepage of sump oil from thousands of tourist cars. As well as preventing bathing, the pollution damaged sea-life (Haulot, 1974; Haulot et al., 1977). Tourist development has also contributed to the pollution of the Mediterranean and has in turn been seriously affected by it (ETC, 1974; Tangi, 1977).

Such pollution is primarily caused by inadequate investment in infrastructure or by lack of control over effluents, such as have affected Acapulco in Mexico and the Spanish island of Ibiza (ECE, 1976). Conversely, the pollution can be prevented or cured by investment and stringent controls. Pollution abatement and sewage disposal policies, after being financed and implemented efficiently, have resulted in improvements in water quality in lakes and rivers. For instance, people can bathe in Lake Maelaren and even in the very centre of Stockholm, where public beaches are open (OECD, 1976).

Negative impacts of large-scale movement by tourists include noise levels in popular resorts and near airports, traffic congestion, a heavy call on non-renewable energy sources, and the human and material cost of traffic accidents (Aguirre, 1978). Even in more remote areas, where tourist travel is by non-mechanical means, resource degradation and exhaustion can occur. In some US national parks and wilderness areas, backpackers or canoeists have left behind trails of litter, erosion and occasional forest fires (Garrett, 1978). In the Khumbu valley of Nepal, tourists travelling on horseback have contributed in their search for fuelwood to the attrition of tree-cover and hence to upland erosion and valley flooding.

The environmental problems connected with tourism and recreation development in mountain areas, and in particular the Alpine region, were much discussed during the decade (e.g. UNESCO MAB Project No. 6). While tourism plays a major role in mountain area economies, ecosystem damage has in some instances reached a critical level, thus impairing the future of tourism itself, unless effective counter-measures are taken. Widely appreciated and important values of these areas for tourism and recreation, especially natural scenic grandeur and relatively low population densities, are gradually being compromised. According to a study by the Council of Europe (1974), about 150 million visitor nights are spent each year in the European Alps, and in high season native and tourist population density may reach 1,800 inhabitants per square kilometre, higher than that of many industrialized districts. The physical impact consists of serious detrimental effects to the mountain system — soil, vegetation, wildlife and water balance. Another hazard arises if new buildings and communication systems are inadequately planned and are set up in avalanche, landslide and rockfall areas. A comprehensive evaluation is now being made of the effects involved in the change from mountain economies, based entirely on agriculture and forestry, to economies relying on tourism and industrial development.

Historic monuments and sites constitute a particular category of man-made resources for tourism. They share with many natural assets the characteristic of having a limited capacity that cannot be exceeded without destroying the fabric that constitutes their attraction. Uncontrolled mass tourism is in this respect a serious threat. Damage to a number of historical sites due to mass tourism was reported in Greece, the United Kingdom and other countries during the 1970s (Cohen, 1978).

Future Prospects

THE foregoing analysis reveals a picture of increasing tourist activity during the 1970s with both negative and positive impacts. It is clear that in many areas the limits of desirable tourist influx are being reached, and planning and management for a new balance will be a challenge in the 1980s. Those meeting it will be helped because during the 1970s the factors determining whether impact of tourism on the physical and socio-cultural environment of the receiving country or area will be beneficial or damaging were more clearly defined. The most important appeared to be the nature and carrying capacity of the receiving area; the type, intensity and pattern of tourist development; the approach to planning, design and management; and the ideology and types of tourists.

Where environmental damage was caused by tourist developments, it was most often due to poor planning of individual tourism schemes and of the overall growth of the industry. In some cases the increase in visitors outpaced infrastructure development. Such damage is ultimately counter-productive for the industry itself. Authorities have sometimes been inclined — perhaps under commercial pressure, perhaps from inexperience — to take a short-term or limited view of planning, with the result that a later generation or a particular segment of society pays an undue price in environmental damage. As for any other sector, it is the responsibility of the government and the public authorities to ensure that there is proper planning and supervision of developments, with due regard to the assessment of likely environmental impacts, so that profits for the industry are not made at the cost of wider environmental and social loss.

A key principle advocated by those who seek a balance between tourism and the environment is that the type and scale of tourist development and activity should be related to the carrying capacity of tourist resources (Dower, 1965; ECE, 1976; DART, 1976).   Such an idea has an obvious relevance to, say, the airlines or water supply systems serving a particular tourist resort. But the principle applies equally to the social system and to the physical or cultural resources that may form the basic attraction to the tourist. The social system — the population and its workforce — may absorb and serve a certain number of tourists before strains begin to appear. The physical resources, such as beaches, ski slopes or African game reserves, may take a certain load of tourist activity, but show signs of deterioration if that load is exceeded. Assessment of carrying capacity, and the balancing of levels of tourist development and activity with that capacity, are thus crucial means of preventing environmental damage, protecting resources and securing the continuance of tourism itself on a "sustained yield" basis.

Such an assessment can be helped by the use of systems analysis, as illustrated by the Obergurgl case study undertaken by the International Institute for Applied Systems Analysis (IIASA) and the Austrian national MAB programme (Holling, 1978; IIASA, 1979). The knowledge of businessmen, scientists and government officials was combined to develop a model of human impact on the alpine ecosystem, and to identify potential areas of conflict. The study predicted a maximum size for the resort, forecast future social problems, and indicated solutions. Figure 14–2 shows the main components in the analysis.

By the end of the 1970s, tourism was no longer a marginal issue: it had become a major and integral part of world economic, social and physical development. Its impact on the physical and socio-cultural environment was substantial and widespread, and expected to increase. In the decades ahead, the prime initiative must still rest with governments, which are in the best position to appreciate the needs, interests and resources of their countries and to ensure that tourism is kept in balance with them. But the world-wide nature of tourism and the interest in mankind's physical and socio-cultural heritage add an international dimension. This will take the form of cross-border collaboration between neighbouring governments where tourist resources cross national boundaries, collaboration on a regional scale, as in tackling Mediterranean pollution or wildlife management in Africa, and efforts on a global scale to help governments in the search for a balance between tourism and other economic activities on one side and environment on the other.

Figure 14–2. Components of the Obergurgl Model.

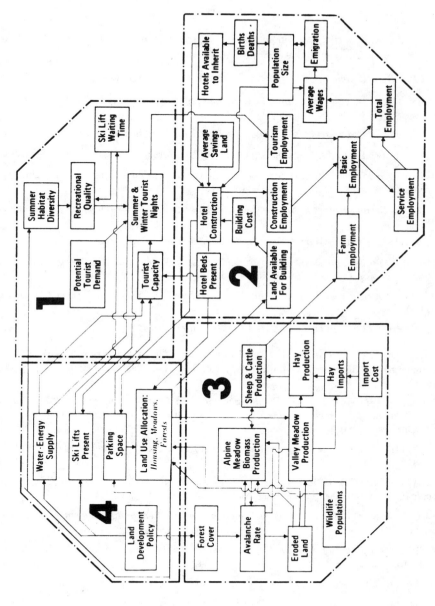

After IIASA, 1979.

References

Aguirre, I. (1978), *Tourist Saturation and the Distribution of Tourist Flows*, WTO/IATA Conference on Tourism and Air Transport, Mexico.

BTA (1975), *Resorts and Spas in Britain*, British Tourist Authority.

Bugnicourt, J. (1977), Tourism with no Return, *Development Forum*, v, 5. United Nations, New York.

Cohen, E. (1978), *The Impact of Tourism on the Physical Environment*, Ann. Tourism Res., v, 2.

Council of Europe (1974), *Endangered Alpine Regions*, Nature and Environ., Ser. 6, Strasbourg.

DART (1976), *Hadrian's Wall: A Strategy for Conservation and Visitor Services*, Dartington Amenity Research Trust, Totnes, Devon, UK.

DART (1977), *Second Homes in Scotland*, Dartington Amenity Research Trust, Totnes, Devon, UK.

Dower, M. (1965), *Fourth Wave; The Challenge of Leisure*, Civil Trust, London.

ECE (1976), *Planning and Development of the Tourist Industry in the ECE Region*, Economic Commission for Europe, United Nations, E. 76.II.E.4.

ETC (1974), *Tourism and Conservation; Working Together*, European Travel Commission, Dublin.

Garrett, W. E. (1978), *Grand Canyon; Are We Loving it to Death?* National Geogr. Mag., 154, 1.

Green, R. H. (1976), *Towards Tourism Planning in African Countries*, UNESCO/World Seminar on the Social and Cultural Impacts of Tourism, Washington, D.C., Oxford Univ. Press.

Greenwood, D. J. (1976), *Tourism Employment and the Local Community; a Case Study of Fuenterrabia, Spain*, UNESCO/World Bank Seminar on the Social and Cultural Impacts of Tourism, Washington, D.C.

Haulot, A. (1974), *Tourisme et Environnement; La Recherche d'un Equilibre*, Marabout SA., Verviers.

Haulot, A. et al. (1977), *L'Occupation Touristique d'une Bande Côtiere et Ses Consequences Ecologiques*, Commissariat General Au Tourisme De Belgique.

Holling, C. S., Editor (1978), *Adaptive Environmental Assessment and Management*, John Wiley, Chichester.

IIASA (1979), *An Adaptive Approach to Environmental Management*, Executive Rept. No. 1, Inter. Instit. Appl. Systems Analysis, Laxenburg.

Lonati, R. (1969), *Dimension Culturelle du Tourisme*, Rev. de l'AI.I.T., Monaco.

Manila Declaration (1980), *World Tourism Conference, Manila*, 1980, World Tourism Organization, Madrid.

Manning, F. E. (1976), *Tourism and Bermuda's Black Clubs; a Case of Cultural Revitalization*, UNESCO/World Bank Seminar on the Social and Cultural Impacts of Tourism, Washington, D.C., Oxford Univ. Press.

Nettlefold, R. (1975), Cultural Impact, Some Reflections for the Young. In *Caribbean Tourism: The Cultural Impact of Tourism,* Caribbean Tourism Research Centre.

OECD (1976), *Tourism Policy and International Tourism in OECD Member Countries,* Organization for Economic Co-operation and Development, Paris, See also; OECD (1980): The Impact of Tourism on the Environment.

Peters, M. (1978), *Developpement du Tourisme en Relation avec la Faune et les Parcs Nationaux dans le Nord du Benin,* Food and Agriculture Organization of the United Nations, Rome.

Saglio, C. (1976), *Tourism for Discovery: A Project in Four Villages of Lower Casamance, Senegal,* UNESCO/World Bank Seminar on the Social and Cultural Impacts of Tourism, Washington, D.C., Oxford Univ. Press.

Tangi, M. (1977), *Tourism and the Environment,* Ambio, vi, 6, 339.

Thurot, J. M. (1975), *Impact of Tourism on Socio-cultural Values,* Report prepared for UNESCO by Centre d'Etudes du Tourisme, Aix-en-Provence.

UNEP (1979), *The State of the Environment: Selected Topics,* United Nations Environment Programme, Nairobi.

WTO (1977), *Tourism Compendium,* World Tourism Organization, Madrid.

CHAPTER 15

Environmental Education
and Public Understanding

The United Nations Conference on the Human Environment, convened in Stockholm in 1972, provided an impetus for renewed interest in environmental education during the 1970s. In response to the Stockholm Recommendations, the United Nations Educational, Scientific and Cultural Organzation (UNESCO) and the United Nations Environment Programme (UNEP) set up an International Environmental Education Programme which aims at promoting exchange of information and experiences in the field of environmental education. Workshops, symposia and studies were held during the 70s to deal with various aspects of environmental education, and pilot projects were established in seventeen countries throughout the world. A set of guiding principles for a worldwide programme in the field was drawn up at an international workshop held in Belgrade in 1975. Two years later the first Intergovernmental Conference on Environmental Education was held at Tbilisi in the USSR.

Courses were designed from primary levels through graduate schools. But because environmental issues differed in each country, educational approaches varied too: in primary school, for example, formal environmental education was introduced as a subject in some countries, while in others it was an added component of existing subjects such as nature study or hygiene. Similar approaches were made in secondary schools, but sometimes experimental and field studies were added. Universities helped secondary school teachers formulate courses through seminars and discussions.

At the beginning of the decade courses in environmental education were not popular: less than 2 per cent of university students in countries of the Organization for Economic Co-operation and Development (OECD) were enrolled in them. But by 1979 the interest had grown: 350 students graduated in environmental science every year in the United Kingdom alone. In the United States, 27 universities offered a degree or a major in environmental engineering in 1978–1979, compared to only 4 offering degrees before 1970. Undergraduate enrolment in such courses climbed from less than 300 students in 1971–1972 to more than 1,000 in 1976–1977. But the rising trend seemed to slow by the end of the decade. Environmental education courses for university students in developing countries were not eagerly sought after. A principal factor affecting enrolment was employment: opportunities were greatest where environmental impact assessment and environmental management were most frequently found.

Public participation in environmental affairs increased during the decade. Some of this interest was spurred by the efforts of the media to cover the field. But media coverage was uneven, because it responded to the public's consciousness of environmental problems and to accidents and special events.

Environmental awareness increased most in wealthier and better-educated populations, and was stimulated by books and films as well as newspapers, magazines and the electronic media. In areas where surveys were conducted, they seemed to show that people's attitudes towards environmental issues changed. While remaining concerned about pollution, they became more alert to the scarcity of some natural resources, the *necessity for conservation and the relation between environment and development. Public organizations affected the decision-making process in a number of countries, particularly in connection with nuclear power development. Referendums were held in the United States, Sweden, Switzerland and Austria to decide issues relating to nuclear power stations as a result of the intensity of public feeling. Sweden's parliament approved a cessation of chemical spraying of forests for a year, pending a solution of problems caused by the sprays, and pressure from environmental groups contributed to the reduction of elimination of lead from gasoline in a number of countries.*

On the whole, progress was apparent in both environmental education and public awareness of environmental issues during the decade. Consensus emerged on educational methods and the challenge now is to translate these into action. As this is done, public understanding of environmental issues can be expected to improve.

As a follow-up to the recommendations of the United Nations Conference on the Human Environment, convened in Stockholm in 1972, the United Nations Educational Scientific and Cultural Organization (UNESCO) and the United Nations Environment Programme (UNEP) launched an International Environmental Education Programme which aimed at promoting the exchange of information and experience in the field of environmental education. Within the framework of this Programme, an International Workshop on Environmental Education was held in Belgrade in 1975. The Workshop drew up the Belgrade Charter: A Global Framework for Environmental Education. The Charter proposed a number of guiding principles of environmental education programmes (*Connect,* 1976; UNESCO, 1977a). Environmental education, said the Belgrade Charter, should:

— consider the environment in its totality – natural and man-made, ecological, political, economic, technological, social, legislative, cultural and aesthetic;
— be a continuous life-long process, both in school and out of school;
— be interdisciplinary in its approach;
— emphasize active participation in preventing and solving environmental problems;
— examine major environmental issues from a world point of view, while paying due regard to regional differences;
— focus on current and future environmental situations;
— examine all development and growth from an environmental perspective;
— promote the value and necessity of local, national and international co-operation in the solution of environmental problems.

Two years later, the first Intergovernmental Conference on Environmental Education organized by UNESCO and UNEP was held in Tbilisi, USSR. The

Conference declared (UNESCO, 1978):

> Education utilizing the findings of science and technology should play a leading role in creating an awareness and a better understanding of environmental problems. It must foster positive patterns of conduct towards the environment and the nations' use of their resources. Environmental education should be provided for all ages, at all levels and in both formal and non-formal education. The mass media have a great responsibility to make their immense resources available for this education mission. Environmental specialists, as well as those whose actions and decisions can have a marked effect on the environment, should be provided in the course of their training with the necessary knowledge and skills and be given a full sense of their responsibilities in this respect. Environmental education, properly understood, should constitute a comprehensive lifelong education, one responsive to changes in a rapidly changing world. It should prepare the individual for life through an understanding of the major problems of the contemporary world, and the provision of skills and attributes needed to play a productive role towards improving life and protecting the environment with due regard given to ethical values. By adopting a holistic approach, rooted in a broad interdisciplinary base, it re-creates an overall perspective which acknowledges the fact that natural environment and man-made environment are profoundly inter-dependent. It helps reveal the enduring continuity which links the acts of today to the consequences for tomorrow. It demonstrates the interdependencies among national communities and the need for solidarity among all mankind. Environmental education must look outward to the community. It should involve the individual in an active problem-solving process within the context of specific realities, and it should encourage initiative, a sense of responsibility and commitment to build a better tomorrow. By its very nature, environmental education can make a powerful contribution to the renovation of the education process . . .

The Tbilisi Conference was the culmination of the first phase of the UNESCO–UNEP International Environmental Education Programme, which, aims at providing information useful to policymakers and planners of environmental education through referral, coordination and research services. In addition to the environmental education newsletter *Connect*, published quarterly in English, French, Spanish, Russian and Arabic, the programme established a computerized data base containing a series of directories of institutions, organizations, individuals, projects, activities and periodicals dealing with environmental education. The first directories (in English, French and Spanish) were published in 1977; *Institutions Active in the Field of Environmental Education* and the *International Directory of Individuals in Environmental Education*. At the operational level the UNESCO–UNEP programme provided financial and technical assistance to pilot projects in a number of regions of the world (Table 15–1). The great variety of these 17 projects shows the breadth of the field of environmental education.

During the decade several regional projects (workshops, symposia, studies) dealt with various aspects of environmental education. A UNESCO seminar-workshop was held in Montevideo Uruguay, 17–28 November 1975, to develop modules for science education using environment as an integrating theme. A workshop held in Chosica, Peru, 1–19 March 1976, launched an experimental one-year programme of environmental learning, integrating teachers, students, government officials and community representatives. The few countries that implemented this programme – Cuba, Panama, Peru and Venezuela – applied a realistic problem-solving approach in school communities.

Table 15–1. Pilot Projects in Environmental Education (UNESCO–UNEP International Programme).

AFRICA	Ghana	Development of multimedia materials on environmental education components, for primary school teachers in Sub-Saharan Africa.
	Kenya	The Kiambu High School project for development of an integrated environmental science education programme for Kenya secondary schools.
	Senegal	Environmental education pilot project for the adult population in Africa.
ARAB STATES	Jordan	Pilot project on water pollution and purification in the Ghore area of Jordan Valley.
	Egypt	Environmental education for youth clubs and associations.
ASIA AND OCEANIA	Afghanistan	Design, development and implementation of instructional materials in environmental education for primary schools.
	Indonesia	An environmental education experiment using an integrative approach in Jakarta primary schools.
	Mongolia	Non formal environmental education for the general public and for specific social groups.
LATIN AMERICA AND THE CARIBBEAN	Colombia	Education programme for the conservation of the ecological balance and renewable natural resources of Colombia.
	Guatemala	Pilot project to organize the first four years of primary education around environmental problems.
	Panama	Environmental education as a component of the work study programmes of general basic education centres.
	Peru	Experimental environmental education project for adaption to the third-year programme of Peruvian secondary education.
	Venezuela	Environmental education for secondary schools.
EUROPE AND NORTH AMERICA	Ukrainian SSR	Methodological interdisciplinary research concerning the integration of school and society in the sphere of environmental education.
	Canada–USA	A two-nation regional environmental education programme based on the shared marine environment of the Pacific Northwest.
	France	Interdisciplinary methodological research concerning the acquisition of knowledge, values, attitudes and skills related to the environment by secondary schools students.
	United Kingdom	In-service training of European educators in urban environmental studies and research.

Source: Connect (1978).

An International Centre for Training in Environment Sciences for Spanish Speaking Countries (CIFCA) was set up in 1975 as a joint UNEP–Spanish Government project, and has since then organized more than 80 seminars. Since 1977 the Economic Commission for Latin America (ECLA) and the Latin American Institute for Economic and Social Planning (ILPES) have held yearly courses and seminars, related to environment, development and planning.

In 1976, regional meetings of experts on environmental education were held in preparation for the Tbilisi conference in Brazzaville (Africa), Kuwait (Arab countries), Bangkok (Asia), Helsinki (Europe), Bogota (Latin America) and St Louis, Missouri (North America). A seminar on environmental education was held in Prague, Czechoslovakia, 1–3 February 1977, for experts from the member states of the Council for Mutual Economic Assistance (CMEA). The main theme was environmental education in university studies and the training of environmental specialists. UNEP and the Association of African Universities held a workshop on environmental education in Nairobi in 1978 (UNEP–AAU, 1978). A workshop on environmental education for Latin America was held in San Jose in 1979 (UNESCO, 1980a); studies addressing regional and international aspects of environmental education included: Capurro (1979) for Latin America; Morris (1976) and Harvey (1977) for Europe; and Saveland (1976) and Shaffer (1978) for global aspects.

The extensive discussions that took place at these meetings seemed to indicate that the principal functions of environmental education were to develop:

— awareness of, and sensitivity to, the total environment and its allied problems;
— knowledge of the total environment, its associated problems and the responsible presence of humanity in it;
— attitudes, social values and strong feelings of concern for the environment, and the motivation to participate in its protection and improvement;
— skills to solve environmental problems;
— ability to evaluate environmental measures and education programmes in terms of ecological, political, economic, social, aesthetic and educational factors;
— participation to help develop a sense of responsibility and urgency regarding environmental problems so as to ensure appropriate action to solve them.

Piecemeal perceptions of the environment were thus being replaced by more comprehensive views due to the visible impact of fast-growing populations, high-intensity agriculture, modern transport systems, and the increasing demand for energy and industrialization. Such a comprehensive outlook was not always reflected in educational programmes for young people.

To achieve this breadth of coverage, it was seen that environmental education needs to be planned nationally. Several studies addressed this issue during the decade. Stapp (1976) gave guidelines and a suggested process for developing a national environmental education strategy. Schoenfeld (1975) recommended some fundamental changes in national environmental education strategy. Greenhall and Womersley (1977) discussed key issues in the development of environmental education in Australia.

Declarations of aims for environmental education were fully recorded during the decade. It was more difficult to measure the actual changes in curricula, classroom teaching methods and teaching materials, and their effects upon students. On the other hand there were a number of polls that sampled changes in public opinion on environmental issues, and there was evidence of increasing involvement of citizen groups in public decisions affecting environmental quality.

Environmental Education at the Pre-Primary and Primary Levels

ENVIRONMENTAL education starts at home and in its immediate neighbourhood. Activities, particularly group activities, are important at this stage. Manipulative skills are developed through helping in the home and at play. Some informal training is received in personal hygiene, and problems of food and water contamination. In rural areas it is easy to develop a sensitivity to the cycle of seasons and the elements of nature. A child's perception of the environment develops into a hybrid consisting partly of formal schooling in nursery schools, temples, churches, and other pre-primary institutions, and partly of informal education at home. At the pre-primary level the basic objective is to address the child's emotional orientation to nature and to the environment of home and neighbourhood. This level is followed by more formal schooling at the primary school (ages 5/7 – 11/14).

In more fortunate urban societies in developing countries some nursery and kindergarten schools existed during the decade, and trained teachers were available. In advanced countries, however, pre-primary and primary schools were much better developed and equipped so that elements of social interaction, hygiene and nutrition were often introduced through organized play and co-operative activities. Gadsby (1975) described the advantages of wetlands as habitats for environmental education, while Green (1977) gave guidelines for preparing nature trails for education purposes.

The need for adequate teacher training and appropriate teaching materials was strongly felt in both developed and developing nations. Eighty-one per cent of the countries responding to a 1975 UNESCO–UNEP questionnaire placed teacher training at the top of their list of priorities (UNESCO, 1977b). Shortages of teaching materials occurred in most developing countries: seventy-three per cent of countries responding to the questionnaire listed them as of high priority.

Mental alertness toward the environment seems to develop in most children at the age of 9/10 years. They can appreciate the interactions of man and nature and the relationship between hygiene and nutrition and are ready to accept the demonstrations of such interrelationships. These ages provide a most challenging task for teachers and curricula designers, activity planners and teaching educators. Teachers of these age groups often need a choice of resource materials, help and counselling services.

During the decade, a number of authorities grappled with the problems of developing curricula for primary schools. Collins (1977) provided a model for developing a short course in environmental education for use at this level. Reid and Shaw (1975), Garigliano and Knape (1977) and Lines and Bolwell (1978) dealt with these problems from various sides. Several studies took the module approach to introducing environmental education into primary schools. Bottger (1975) introduced environment as a subject for the school curriculum: a syllabus on "rubbish, from where to where". A year later (1976) she introduced another subject – car exhaust fumes that foul the environment – as a syllabus for the second school year. Kasler *et al.* (1975 – 1976) outlined a syllabus on waste disposal for primary grades.

Formal environmental education was introduced as a subject in primary school curricula in some countries; in others it was introduced as an added component of existing subjects: hygiene, nature study and population education. Examples of the former approach are in Bangladesh and Hungary. Examples of the latter can be found in Canada, Costa Rica, Denmark, Japan, Niger, Pakistan, Qatar and Switzerland, among others. Environmental knowledge may be incorporated in almost all disciplinary subjects. Jain (1976) described the incorporation of social, ethical and environmental values into biology in India's elementary and secondary schools, whereas Hoffman (1978) showed that environmental education could be connected with literary education.

The diversity of the environment, particularly of large countries, required each teacher to frame his teaching to suit local conditions. Lack of training, teaching materials and guidance made the developing country teacher's tasks more arduous than his counterpart's in the developed nations. Textbooks and primers from developed countries were often used in developing countries. Teachers did not find in them the tools they needed as they did not often reflect local or national situations. At the end of the decade there were several efforts to produce more effective indigenous teaching materials. Chile, for example, was publishing textbooks, articles and other documents. Colombia had its own audio-visual aids. And Honduras was distributing booklets, video tapes, radio programmes, posters and story books on environmental subjects.

Environmental Education at the Secondary Level

STUDENTS enter secondary schools between the ages of 11 and 14 and leave between ages 16 and 19. They thus enter as children and leave as adolescents. Secondary school students are usually receptive and strongly motivated, and are capable of assimilating an environmental education that is (*a*) value-oriented, (*b*) community-oriented, and (*c*) concerned with human well-being.

Considerable progress was made during the decade in formulating guidelines and policies for environmental education at secondary levels. The basic formulations in several countries in Asia were elaborated from the schematic descriptions given by Alles (1975). Two approaches developed:

(*a*) to underline the environmental aspects of each element of the student's learning processes,

(*b*) to bring in environmental education as a synthesis of the various elements of the secondary school curricula through an integrative study of interrelations.

These are similar to approaches in the primary school. But developments during the decade seem to indicate that experimental and field studies may be part of the secondary school environmental education. Madders (1975) and Bergstedt *et al.* (1976) explained and gave examples of laboratory work; Kominski (1975) and Varley (1975) described environmental field studies.

In most developing countries, secondary schools providing environmental education faced shortages of resource materials and suitably trained and perceptive teachers. The phenomenal growth of the school-age population in many developing nations accentuated these difficulties.

Since secondary education was often oriented to traditional disciplines, there was little room for teachers to make use of integrative environmental elements. Multidirectional environmental knowledge implies a diversity of skills. In developed countries at the later stages of secondary schooling, students were often brought into contact with some of the skills that form the basis of training for environmental technicians. Some efforts also were being made in developed countries to bring to formal education a study of some of the interrelationships and interactions within nature, in order to develop some understanding of ecology. In some countries the emphasis was on introducing environmental aspects into school science courses and integrating these later. In most developing countries, however, apart from broadly-based biology facilities, training in pollution measurements or ecology rarely existed at school.

Several universities in Europe, Canada and the United States held seminars and discussions, involving secondary school teachers, through which secondary school courses in environmental sciences were formulated. Among these were those formulated at the University of Tours in France which established a centre (CESA) supported by the OECD. Much of the material developed there was incorporated successfully into secondary school teaching in France. A similar impact was made by the University and Technical Institute at Lund in Sweden, and by the British Environmental Education group.

The courses designed at the University of Waterloo, Canada, and the University of Wisconsin, Green Bay (USA), introduced during the decade, tend to emphasize one of two approaches:

1. Students should get involved in out-of-school activities, problem-solving and community activity related to environmental problems.

2. Students should concentrate on basic environmental facts such as ecology, resource distribution, population dynamics, and the problems of hunger and starvation.

In secondary schools in the USSR and Eastern Europe various aspects of nature protection were incorporated in biology, geography, physics and chemistry curricula. In these schools environmental subjects took about ten per cent of the teaching time. Schools in several countries (e.g. Canada and the Federal Republic of Germany) did not teach environmental science as a separate subject but incorporated environmental topics into disciplinary subjects.

Several developing countries introduced environmental science into the secondary school in a variety of ways. Conservation of natural resources was an item in school curricula in India (NCERT, 1977); in Bangladesh college students participated in out-of-school environmental awareness programmes; and a certain amount of "learning by doing" encouraged students' outdoor activities in the Philippines, Malaysia, Mexico and Kenya.

Environmental Education at the University and Professional (Tertiary) Level

FEW college-level institutions twenty-five years ago considered developing courses designed to make students environmentally literate. There was, however, an increased awareness of environmental education after the establishment in 1948 of the International Union for Conservation of Nature (IUCN), and its Commission on Education in 1949 published several studies on environmental education and conservation. Similarly in Europe, OECD initiated an investigation of basic university curricular needs, including those of environmental education. This was followed by several symposia such as those on Conservation Education in Lucerne, Switzerland (1966); the Conservation of Renewable Natural Resources in Bariloche, Argentina (1968); the European working group on Environmental Conservation Education in Ruschlikon, Switzerland (1971); and the OECD Workshop in Berne, Switzerland (1971).

After the Stockholm Conference, several other conferences and workshops followed, including some organized by CIFCA, which has carried out a co-operative programme with Spanish and Latin American universities on the establishment of advanced environmental studies. These activities culminated in, but did not cease with the Tbilisi Conference (1977), which laid the foundations of current thinking about tertiary level environmental education. Several of these conferences made it clear that there is a need for environmental literacy among university graduates, since many important decisions on resource utilization and local projects are in the public domain. These need understanding and a long-term perspective by both civic leaders and ordinary citizens.

While general environmental programmes open to all students were found by a survey to be practically non-existent in OECD countries as a whole in 1971, by 1979 Pethen (1979) found that there were 350 graduates in Environmental Science produced annually in the United Kingdom alone, with a marked rise in the period since 1973. Schoenfeld and Disinger (1978) described 45 case studies of environmental programmes in colleges and universities in the United States. These included undergraduate general studies, graduate and professional programmes, basic and applied research and extension education. Fenner (1977) summed up deliberations of a symposium (Canberra, September 1976) held by the directors of environmental education programmes in various Australian universities. Vandenhazel (1976) described and compared environmental programmes in the Federal Republic of Germany, the Netherlands and the United Kingdom.

Short multi-disciplinary over-view courses, offered part-time or evenings and open to large numbers of students and working people, stimulated both the learners and the teachers at many universities in North America and Europe. These courses were criticized occasionally because their treatment tended to be superficial and sometimes their multi-disciplinarity made them bewildering. Subject matter was often grouped under broad topics such as energy, ecology and social systems to reduce the fragmentary nature of the course. While the interest of European universities led to the establishment of a number of courses in environmental sciences, they were not popular: less than 2 per cent of all university students in OECD countries were enrolled in some form of environmental course in 1971. This figure is estimated to have increased only marginally since then.

Strong pressures and deeply-rooted traditions encouraged the higher education system to be narrowly vocational because university-level education was largely aimed at filling job vacancies. This was a strong conservative force. The other difficulty was the disciplinary inertia of the university system. However, universities in Sweden, the USSR and the Federal Republic of Germany responded substantially to environmental challenges and initiated a variety of environmental studies and research.

In the USSR four main themes were stressed: the introduction of ecological principles into specialist college courses, the establishment of new professional specializations such as environmental rehabilitation, broad training in the conservation and wise use of environmental resources, and improvement in existing courses on environmental topics.

Many universities offer courses that aim at promoting environmental awareness, and there is a trend towards increasing these types of courses. However, the number of students enrolling in environmental courses in OECD countries showed no significant increase during the decade. In the United States the curve of student numbers in university environmental courses also began to flatten out. The Bangladesh University of Engineering and Technology had special environmental science courses within the degree curriculum. But in most developing countries, general courses on environmental sciences for university students did not seem popular. One reason, applicable to most developing countries, was the problem of graduate employment. Manpower requirements and future employment opportunities were usually not available, and universities could not plan adequately for courses at specialized professional levels, including environmental sciences. This was compounded by the attitude of employers who did not appreciate applicants who took such courses.

The great variety of possible approaches to environmental education can be interpreted as constituting the exploratory phase of environmental education. Detailed studies by Swann and Stapp (1974), Emmelin (1975) and Newbould (1976) indicated not only great diversity but also the many purposes and aims involved. Some of these aims were divergent. Guy *et al.* (1978) presented a compendium of environmental education in 57 universities and 24 polytechnics in the United Kingdom. This compendium made reference to 250 programmes (122 first degree, 99 postgraduate degrees and 29 others).

POSTGRADUATE STUDIES

Postgraduate education in environment in several universities offered programmes in:

    (*a*) environmental planning and resource development;

    (*b*) environmental impact studies;

    (*c*) teacher training;

    (*d*) investigation of specific ecological disturbances and environmental degradation;

    (*e*) specialized systems analysis and operations research techniques applicable to environmental systems;

    (*f*) training in research and investigation methodologies of various pollutants and ecotoxic agents.

Postgraduate programmes in environmental studies were offered by several universities in developed countries, e.g. Australian institutions offered eleven M.Sc. degree courses in environmental science; Patterson (1980) quoted the *Register of Environmental Engineering Graduate Programmes* in the United States in 1974 as comprising sixty-nine institutions providing for M.Sc. programmes and fifty-nine for Ph.D. programmes; Guy *et al.* (1978) cited numerous postgraduate courses in the United Kingdom.

The United Nations University (Tokyo) and its world-wide network of associated institutions set up a programme on natural resources and environment that has produced a series of in-depth studies on arid lands, coastal lands, high mountains, and tropical forests.

PROFESSIONAL LEVEL

University specialist education in environmental areas needs to be adapted to the social and economic situation of each country. Uniform solutions are not practicable. Distinctions are necessary and often important in the structure and content of courses for individual industrialized or developing countries. UNESCO published reports on the environmental education of engineers (*Report of the Working Group Meeting of Caracas, Venezuela, in* 1979, and *Environmental Education for Engineers: Current Trends and Perspectives,* 1979) that were indicative of the variety of perceptions and approaches. The major aim of university environmental education at the professional level is not only to help students develop a broad conceptual framework, but also to develop specialized knowledge and technical skills. For example, the skills of water protection engineers, afforestation ecologists, urban planners and earth resources conservationists can be applied to resource management, environmental and ecological problems due to urbanization, industrialization, forestry, and intensive agriculture. It was suggested that a new type of professional with a basic training in a specialization who, in addition, has a strong inter-disciplinary background in environmental sciences, would be needed. Such trained environmentalists could provide to decision-making bodies a broad perspective of the likely social, economic and environmental consequences of various actions. Australian institutes of higher education already offer seven undergraduate degree courses in environmental studies.

In many countries lawyers are increasingly assuming a role in environmental issues. Legal experts specializing in these matters at national and international levels will obviously need some background in the environmental sciences in order to understand the principles underlying legislation, and many universities have begun to incorporate environmental studies in their legal degree courses.

Engineers have a special role in creating, modifying and developing the environment of man. The training of engineers is primarily concerned with technical abilities and the capability to apply advances in science and technology. But some economic knowledge is needed to enable the engineer to ascertain the economic viability of his projects, and some understanding of environmental science is equally important. The appreciation of the need to incorporate environmental sciences in the training of engineers is a recent development. The engineer was formerly seen as a person trained to address the environment in purely physical terms: a challenge to be harnessed or an obstacle to be surmounted. Hidden costs showed the inadequacy of this perception, and the need for introducing a core element of environmental knowledge in the training of engineers became evident.

The UNESCO–UNEP International Programme on Environmental Education and Training of Engineers included an international multidisciplinary working group that dealt with this aspect of environmental education from March 1977 to March 1979. *Environmental Education of Engineers: Current Trends and Perspectives* (UNESCO, 1979) reports on the findings of the group. The studies surveyed:

1. Experiences in introduction of environmental science into engineering curricula in Brazil, Colombia, France, the Philippines, the United States and Venezuela;

2. Curricula for environmental engineering at the undergraduate level in Peru and the United Kingdom and at the postgraduate level in Japan, Mexico, Switzerland, the United Kingdom, the United States, Hungary and the Netherlands.

This survey shows clearly the widespread development of this aspect of environmental education during the decade.

In a review of environmental engineering education in the United States, Patterson (1980) noted that in 1978–79, twenty-seven universities offered either a degree or a major in environmental engineering compared to four offering degrees before 1970. Undergraduate enrolment climbed from less than 300 students in 1971–72 to more than 1,000 in 1976–77. He noted that "the past two decades, 1960–1980, have been a period of transition for the environmental engineering profession and for university programmes in environmental engineering". Among the four sub-disciplines (air quality engineering, industrial hygiene engineering, solid waste management, water quality engineering) water quality engineering dominated. But Patterson noted that during 1950–65, at fifty-six institutions, 2,305 post-graduate degrees were awarded to water quality engineering students and only eighty (3.3 per cent) to air quality engineering. In 1978 graduate student enrolment included: 1,467 in water and wastewater, 216 in water resources, 185 in air pollution, 15 in solid waste, and 696 in environmental sciences and environmental management.

Teacher Training

TEACHERS' training tends to be in scientific disciplines. The problem of developing teachers' sensitivity to the environment existed in all continents, but was particularly acute in developing countries where the low status and salaries of secondary school teachers did not make the teaching career attractive. An added difficulty was that the number of students in each class in most developing countries tended to be too high and did not allow for carrying out group training programmes, which are necessary components of environmental education.

While progress was made in some developed countries in introducing flexibility into curricula and by short-term teacher training in summer programmes, much still had to be done at the end of the decade to achieve an integrated environmental approach to what were otherwise rather fragmented science and social science curricula. Current teacher training is not oriented or sensitized towards physical and socio-cultural environmental issues or community involvement of the teacher. Issues of pollution, urban wastes, urban development, pesticide and water management (in rural areas) and population education and attitudinal problems require the teacher's involvement to enable him to function adequately. Motivated and well-trained teachers can introduce the idea of the interaction of technology with the environment through examples in the neighbourhood. Developmental projects that have recently been started or are continuing can provide examples. Irrigation projects, urban projects, road-building, provide exercises for observing impact of such projects on the environment.

In many countries the secondary school provides through vocational training an acquaintance with technology. Environmental aspects of such technology could be a valuable component of this training.

Teacher training includes (i) in-service training and (ii) pre-service training of teachers joining environmental education programmes in teacher training institutes or universities.

For certain categories of in-service training, IUCN, UNESCO and UNEP organized summer schools, mainly for secondary school teachers. The International Biological Programme training course for teachers, sponsored by IUCN and the Netherlands government was an effort of nine countries to deal with environmental education at primary and secondary levels in Europe. A new successful in-service training approach was the teacher centres developed in many countries, e.g. Japan, the United Kingdom, the Netherlands, Nigeria, the Philippines, India, Mexico and the United States. The centres helped design new training programmes that included environmental training for secondary school teachers (e.g. Lamy *et al.* 1975; Vander Smissen, 1975; Marsh, 1976; Bowman and Disinger, 1977; NCERT 1977). Another approach was in-service training through short, one-to-two-week workshops and courses focused on particular topics.

There also were journals such as: the monthly *Environmental Education Report* (United States), the bimonthly *Eccentric* (Environmental Studies Centre, Bowling Green State University, Ohio, USA), the *Journal of Environmental Education* (USA) the *Journal of Environmental Education and Information* (UK) and the quarterly *Review of Environmental Education Developments* (UK), which are teacher-oriented. Another effort to educate and update teachers on new environmental education resources was the 'clearing house' mechanism. Examples were the *Directory of Environmental Literature and Teaching Aids* (DELTA), the *Catalogue of Curriculum Resources* published by the Science Teachers' Association of Ontario, Canada, and the Educational Resources Information Centre (ERIC) which disseminated information and kept it updated by feeding materials and resource information to participating groups and teachers.

Education and Public Participation

PARTICIPATION enhances learning: this is true whether the action is in field work or in other efforts for environmental change. However in many types of action taken by environmental groups, during the decade, the educational limitations were evident. The lack of in-depth analysis of a problem and the emotional and simplistic nature of the message sometimes undermined the endeavour.

The media provided valuable support to environmental action. Activities such as "Earth Day" or "World Environment Day" focused attention on problems and processes that otherwise went largely unattended. The governments of Australia, the Netherlands and Greece have provided funds to community and public interest groups concerned with the conservation of nature and protection of the environment.

Participation in environmental planning is a special case of environmental action that has great educational potential. But during the decade there was increasing debate over what constitutes effective and appropriate means of community participation. A particularly instructive example of participation in environmental management came from Colombia (Santander, 1975). A comprehensive programme with many highly developed features was devoted to environmental education and management and aimed at peasants, fishermen, forest workers and other rural groups. The aim was to introduce conservation of natural resources and to stop over-fishing, erosion and over-exploration of forests. An important feature was the direct involvement of the people concerned.

During the decade environmental education addressing consumers and households gained special importance, in for instance, Recommendation 16 of the Tbilisi Conference (UNESCO, 1978, 1980b). Formal consumer education was included in many home economic courses, while non-formal education used various means available for consumer information, including labelling and the media. The aim was to bring home to people two facts: that consumption inside and outside households was an important source of pollution, and that the cost of observing environmental standards for goods fell on the consumer and the taxpayer.

Public participation in environmental affairs also gained strength through the expansion of the voluntary conservation movement. Nature conservation societies and associations in many countries became active and influential institutions. In the United States, voluntary groups supported by individual contributions and private foundations undertook large-scale programmes of education and of legal advocacy. Apart from their direct influence on individual developments they challenged assumptions about national life-style.

In Japan education against environmental disruption (Kogai) and the citizens movement against pollution started in the 1960s. Parliament requested *Kogai* education to be introduced to schools in 1971. Ever since it has become an integral part of education at all levels (Numata *et al.* 1974). In Western Europe, political parties have pressed environmentalist arguments.

NON-FORMAL ENVIRONMENTAL EDUCATION

Environmental problems involve all citizens. Out-of-school youth often participated in tree planting, nature conservation, wildlife protection (as in the wildlife clubs in Kenya, Tanzania, Uganda, Mauritius and Zambia). In developed countries, there were organized attempts to develop environmental knowledge and skills among youth. For example, the 4–H Clubs and the Youth Conservation Corps in the United States; Boy Scout, Rover Touring Clubs, and Youth Camps in Australia, New Zealand and Europe; and the Blue and Green Patrols in the USSR contributed substantially in creating interest and promoting environmental protection activities by youth. The corresponding situation in developing countries ranged from fairly strong, coherent and ecologically conscious movements (e.g. Thailand, where a campaign for environmental reform by youth led the government of Thailand to enact the National Environmental Quality Act of 1975) to very limited interest in environmental issues.

The Open University in the United Kingdom and some universities in the USSR, the United States and France experimented with environmental courses in evening classes for out-of-school and working people. Comparable programmes are needed in the developing countries.

THE MEDIA AND PUBLIC EDUCATION

Several authors (see, for example, Sandman, 1974; Emmelin, 1977; Schoenfeld, 1977; Parlour and Schatzow, 1978) discussed the role of media content on public environment education. Mass media can perform an effective educational function. The relationship between education levels and the educational impact of the media is obviously important in the communication of scientific information, e.g. on environmental problems, where levels of understanding could be expected to depend upon pre-formed receptivity to such information.

Sandman (1974) discussed the role of news media in relation to public education (imparting knowledge, skills and motivation) and pointed out that "their effectiveness as environmental educators is greatly diminished by their inattention to environmental skills, and their delivery of persuasive content (advertising) into the hands of the environmental exploiters."

However, in motivating people, the educational role of the media may be more important. Surveys of attitudes towards pollution control and specific environmental problems showed a reasonable correlation between general awareness of a given problem and the news coverage given to that problem. When surveys were followed by any form of testing of factual knowledge about a problem, however, the sharp limits of the educational role of the media were clear (Emmelin, 1977). The Swedish experiences with mercury contamination of fish may serve as a useful illustration. The problems received great press coverage and were exclusively related to mercury in fresh-water fish. A large proportion of the press coverage dealt with differences of opinion between scientists involved, related to the Japanese Minamata case and similar matters. The National Institute of Public Health issued recommendations both on maximum allowable concentrations and on what species to avoid or to consume in limited amounts. In spite of front-page press coverage in most Swedish dailies, subsequent investigations revealed an almost general ignorance of the exact content of the recommendations. A temporary drop in the sale of all sorts of fish — including frozen cod from the North Atlantic — was the most noticeable effect of this educational effort.

Another example is the eutrophication of Canadian lakes, which received extensive coverage in the media; yet the Canadian public's understanding of the issue remained extremely limited (Parlour and Schatzow, 1978). The tendency of the media to concentrate on the impact rather than the content of an environmental message, the emotional and sometimes inaccurate nature of their presentation and the focus on events rather than processes may (among other characteristics) explain the media's limited educational value.

The Tbilisi Conference on Environmental Education (1977) stressed in its documents and recommendations the role of the mass media. It is true that in the decade of the 1970s an increasing number of popular books (fiction and non-fiction) dealing with environmental issues (oil spills, nuclear blackmail, nuclear accidents, etc) were published, but the audience of such books is mainly the literate medium-to-upper economic class of society.

During the decade the number of scientific journals dealing with environmental and conservation topics increased ten-fold: 13 (environment) and 164 (conservation) in 1969–70 and 686 (environment) and 486 (conservation) in 1977–80*. This trend is partly a component of the scientific publication explosion, and partly a reflection of the increasing interest in environmental literature.

The popular media did not lag behind. From being a virtually unknown term to the newspapers of the 1940s and the 1950s, "environment" came in the 1960s and 70s to dominate headlines and leading articles that took up hundreds of column inches. In the

*G. F. White (Personal Communication)

United States in 1957–59 only 68 environmentally-oriented articles appeared in periodicals, but in 1967–69 226 were published (Figure 15–1). The overall increase in the 16 years after 1953 was a little over 470 per cent. Since 1970 coverage has fluctuated with dramatic upsurges following events like the wreck of the tanker *Amoco Cadiz* in 1978, the Three Mile Island nuclear power plant incident and the oil-well blowout in the Gulf of Mexico in 1979. Articles dealing with environmental topics in *The New York Times* increased from less than 200 in 1960 to more than 1600 in 1970 (Figure 15–2). The number fell to less than 700 in 1979. In a similar survey, Schoenfeld (1980) reports a comparable trend.

The decade also witnessed an increasing number of films dealing with environmental issues, some of which attracted a considerable audience and have been of some educational value (for example, *The Towering Inferno*, illustrating the hazards of modern tall buildings; *Earthquake; Meteor*, illustrating the dangers of the military build-up in space; The *China Syndrome* illustrating the risks of nuclear energy and the attitudes of the nuclear industry). Similarly, many television films were produced to relay messages about environmental issues.

Perceptions and Attitudes

Public awareness of environmental hazards has, until recently (the early 1960s), been initiated mainly by "trigger events."

For example, public concern for atmospheric quality was mainly a result of such disastrous smog episodes as those in London (1952), which caused more than 4,000 deaths and New York (1963) which caused 800 deaths.

It can be argued that economic growth was one of the causes of the surge in environmental awareness and concern that was a feature of the 1960s in the developed countries. People's awareness of environmental issues increases as they become wealthier and better educated, and in the United States the rise in concern between 1971 and 1978 was marked (Figure 15–3). The publication of *Silent Spring* (Carson, 1962) was followed by a series of other writings by concerned scientists that stimulated public awareness (e.g. Ehrlich and Ehrlich, 1970; Commoner, 1971), and also by a series of considered scientific evaluations and recommendations for action. The latter were exemplified by two US reports: *Restoring the Quality of our Environment*, from the US President's Science Advisory Committee (1967) and *Man's Impact on the Global Environment* (SCEP, 1970).

The public's attitude towards the environment changed considerably in the decade after Stockholm. While remaining concerned about pollution, people became more alert to the scarcity of some natural resources, the necessity for conservation and the relationship between environment and development. Already in the 1960s and later in the 1970s public concern about pollution was an important variable motivating the flurry of pollution legislation and administration (White, 1966; Althoff and Greig, 1977).

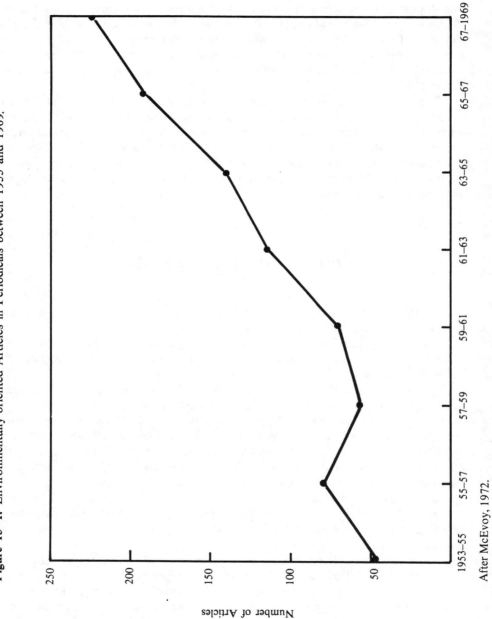

Figure 15–1. Environmentally oriented Articles in Periodicals between 1953 and 1969.

After McEvoy, 1972.

Figure 15—2. New York Times Articles Dealing with Environmental Topics. Articles listed under "Geographical Areas — Environmental problems" are not included.

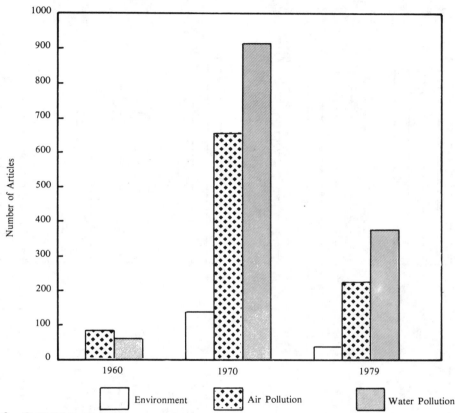

After G. F. White, personal communication.

Polls carried out, for example, in the United States (Althoff and Greig, 1977) showed that the respondents exhibited a great deal of concern about the environmental issue, a relatively low level of trust in governmental and industrial efforts to solve the pollution problem, a relatively low level of dedication to environmental protection, and some degree of commitment to personal aid in solving the pollution problem. Bowman (1977), in a study of the opinion of Wyoming students about environment, pointed out that although the students recognized that society faced a severe environmental crisis and that the country's institutions might not be able to cope with it, they had not accepted the ecologist's view that it was necessary to restructure the consumption and production pattern of the modern technocratic state. Results of a survey of public opinion on environmental issues in the United States (CEQ, 1980) indicated that "Although the state of environment is no longer viewed as a crisis issue, strong support to environmental protection continues".

Figure 15–3. Awareness of Environmental Issues.

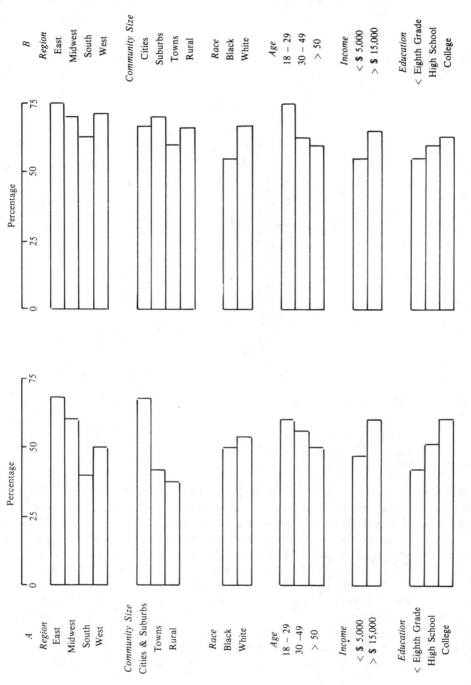

A: People feel that water pollution is serious as local problem in 1971.

B: People feel that water pollution is serious as a national problem in 1978.

After White, 1980.

An opinion poll in the nine member European Economic commission (EEC) countries in 1976 showed that the protection of nature and control of pollution was ranked third overall in importance after action against unemployment and inflation, and was generally perceived as slightly more important than the provision of more housing and the protection of the consumers. It was regarded as much more important than the strengthening of military capacity or the control of multi-national corporations (Euro-Barometre, 1976).

In the years immediately preceding the Stockholm conference and the decade thereafter, anti-pollution groups and conservation-minded organizations appeared in many countries, developed and developing. Several of these groups affected the decision-making process in the United States, Canada, Japan and several European countries. Their most remarkable activity in the 1970s was in connection with nuclear power development (see Surrey and Hugget, 1976; Nelkin and Fallows, 1978; and El-Hinnawi, 1980). At the beginning of the 1970s the nuclear debate was mainly "technical" and the scientific community was concerned chiefly with how to ensure the safe operation of nuclear installations. Soon, however, the debate extended to socio-economic problems. These politicized the debate and brought the basic issue of the acceptability of this energy source into question in several developed countries.

Several referendums took place, for example in California in the United States, and in Sweden, Switzerland and Austria to decide issues relating to nuclear power stations. Irrespective of the results of these referendums, they reflect the magnitude of the environment movement of the 1970s.

Many other examples exist of the success of environmental groups in highlighting environmental issues and affecting the policy-making process. For example, Sweden's parliament approved a cessation of chemical spraying of forests either from the air or the ground for a period of at least one year, pending a long-term solution to the problem caused by such sprays. The decision was taken after heavy and continuing pressure from environmental groups (WER, 1980). Following a public outcry that a fungicide was affecting the health of 80,000 sugarcane field workers, the production of Merapicine-3, a mercury-based fungicide, was suspended in Brazil (WER, 1980). Pressure from environmental groups also contributed to the reduction or elimination of lead from gasoline in the European Economic Community, Australia, Hong Kong and elsewhere.

Although environmental groups in developing countries were not as strong and well-organized as those in industrialized countries, active concern about some environmental issues was evident: for example, public opposition to nuclear power in the Philippines; public discussion about site selection of a nuclear power plant in Egypt (WER, 1980); and public concern about deforestation and soil-loss in Kenya and other countries. In some countries the government was active in promoting conservation and public awareness of environmental issues. In Kenya, for example, the government sought to ban hunting and trade in ivory, and mounted campaigns for better forest management and soil and water conservation. In the Philippines, afforestation programmes and energy conservation were promoted mainly by the government. In many cases the public responded as a result of increased awareness of the dimensions of the problems due to the continuous catalytic role of the mass media. An instance of a popular movement, consisting mainly of shepherds and farmers, is the *chipko* in India which seeks to prevent tree felling by timber contractors in Himalayan hillslopes.

Media space devoted to environmental matters in the United States and other developed countries rose and fell through the 1970s. In some places where media coverage declined, public concern also tended to drop, but in others the articulated interest in environmental matters remained high. According to one study, people in Canada in late 1971 were only about half as disturbed about pollution as they were in 1970, and by 1972 only 6 per cent of Canadians viewed the subject as a major national problem — their attention being diverted to energy, unemployment and inflation, which were then receiving emphasis in the press (Parlour and Schatzow, 1978). In the United States it was different, for public support for the protection of the environment steadily increased during the 1970s and only in the 'gasoline crisis' of 1979 did people begin to concede that energy and environmental goals might not be achievable simultaneously (EPA, 1979).

Even then, the reaction was more towards accepting a slower rate of economic growth so as to protect the environment (58 per cent of one sample) rather than the relaxation of environmental standards so as to achieve economic growth (a view held by only 20 per cent). Some studies seem to indicate that upper income groups tended to be more concerned about environmental issues than the poor. If publicity declines at the same time as economic recession intensifies, a change may be expected in the values people put on their environment.

The issues are in many respects those of environmental risk assessment (Kates, 1978). As noted in Chapter 10, people run the risk of ill health or death from a wide array of hazards in their environment. Some of these are involuntary, as with the children who suffer from diarrhoeal disease associated with a polluted habitat. Some are voluntary, as with smoking. Most are the product of human decisions and environmental factors, as with the decisions to occupy vulnerable areas in zones of high economic activity (Chapter 5) or to rely on different transport technologies (Chapter 13).

In all cases there are problems of identifying the risk, of estimating its severity to the particular people involved, and of placing a value on the benefits and costs to be incurred.

Two aspects of this complex process were given greater attention and were partly clarified during the decade. On the one hand the analysis of risk was advanced to explore the scientific ground on which the dangers of contagious disease, smoking, building on an earthquake fault zone, driving a motorcycle, or living downwind of a nuclear power facility might be calculated. The complexities of such analysis were refined and some of the pitfalls recognized (Whyte and Burton, 1980; Royal Society, 1981; MURS-NAS 1981).

On the other hand, it was recognized that the way in which people perceive and value the effects of such environmental interventions may have no direct relation to the technical computations. Different groups of people see the risk in different lights and are influenced by their own experience, involvement, sense of efficacy in dealing with the situation and numerous other factors (O'Riordan, 1971). Hence, the role of education may be large in affecting how people use scientific information in making their choices or in supporting or opposing public programmes.

Future Prospects

TEN years after Stockholm and less than two decades to the end of the century, the environmental education situation gave evidence of considerable progress. Environmental education was accepted in the school system almost universally, even if it was not always equally effectively carried out. Environmental education and research had found a place in many universities. The initial debate about what constitutes environmental studies had been in some measure resolved, mainly through widening the concepts. The general declarations of the past decade now need to give way to development of practical courses.

These courses should have two aims: to make people more aware of their environment and to enable them to develop and manage it wisely, with appreciation of the risks involved. In the first area, the need is to promote an ecological view of man, so preparing society for the next century of challenges and to contribute, as the UNESCO General Conference (Belgrade, 1980) put it "to the improvement of individual and collective behaviour concerning the human environment and to the perception of its quality".

As a new generation of teachers, trained in integrated environmental studies and with practical experience, gradually finds a place in the universities and schools, these courses should improve. But the process of evolution will need continual guidance. Comparative studies and evaluations of environmental education courses should be initiated, to provide feedback and ensure continuing improvement and adaption of the courses to meet rapidly changing socio-economic situations. Education, and environmental education is no exception, has comparatively long lag-times between influence and response. This is illustrated by the familiar slow diffusion of new scientific knowledge and has been one factor hampering effective dialogue between those involved in development and environment, particularly in the developing countries.

On the positive side there will be increasing numbers of people, mainly in the younger age groups, who will receive some environmental education during school and college. The sophistication and skill of their approaches to resource-use and environmental issues will be greater than it is now.

The decade saw the formulation of consensus on the main structure and methods of environmental education. The challenge now is to translate these into action, taking full account of the necessity to reconcile environmental and development goals and to compare realistically the opportunities and risks of alternative courses of action. To do this successfully, excessive formalization of environmental education should be avoided and flexibility maintained.

Public awareness will be enhanced by this advance in environmental education. The perception of risks and benefits in the short-and-long-term should be improved and the gap narrowed between estimates based on scientific objectivity and concerns based on human preferences and values. The recent expansion of citizen groups, the youth movement, and societies concerned with wild life conservation, the protection of natural beauty and the historic heritage of the human environment may have reached its peak in some countries but is likely to continue and to become increasingly articulate and well informed. It is likely that the environment will continue to figure in national politics in some countries, as one foundation for an alternative way of life. Because uncertainty is inevitable in any systems so complicated as those of the environment, disputes are equally predictable. But the future of mankind as a whole can only benefit from an increase in the scale and quality of popular environmental understanding.

The media have a crucial part to play in these developments. In the past decade they have done much that has been of great benefit. Television in particular has given millions of people sight of places and human situations they can never visit, and has done much to promote understanding in developed countries of problems in the developing world. But there is evidence that, in many parts of the world, standards of accuracy have not always been sufficiently high, and media have been more disposed to publicize problems than successes. By promoting balanced understanding the media can do much to improve the prospects for the world environment.

References

Alles, J. (1975), Mediation in Learning: The Changing Scene in Asia, *Prospects*, UNESCO, 5.

Althoff, P. and W. H. Greig (1977), Environmental Pollution Control: Two Views from the General Population, *Environment and Behaviour*, 9, 441.

Bergstedt, C. *et al.* (1976), Der Experimentelle Zugang zu Problemen des Umweltschutzes, *Biologie in der Schule*, 25, 7/8, 315.

Bottger, E. (1975), Das Thema 'Umwelt' im Sachunterricht des 2-Schuljahers: die Unterrichtseinheit 'Mull, Woher-wohin?', *Sachunterricht und Mathematik in der Grundschule*, 3, 7, 332.

Bottger, E. (1976), Autoabgase Verschmutzen und Vergiften die Umwelt: Skizze einer Unterrichtseinheit für das Zweite Schuljahr, *Sachunterricht und Mathematik in der Grundschule*, 4, 9, 440.

Bowman, J. S. (1977), Public Opinion and the Environment, *Environment and Behaviour*, 9, 3, 385.

Bowman, M. L. and J. F. Disinger (1977), *Land Use Management Activities for the Classroom*, ERIC Information Analysis Centre for Science, Mathematics and Environmental Education, Ohio State University, U.S.A.

Capurro, L. F. (1979), *Formacion de Docentes en Educacion Ambiental para Escuelas Primarias y Secundarias en Instituciones para Profesores en Formacion o en Servicio*, UNESCO Regional Office for Education, Santiago, Chile.

Carson, R. (1962), *Silent spring*, Fawcett Publications, Greenwich, Conn.

CEQ (1980), *Public Opinion on Environmental Issues: Results of National Public Opinion Survey*, Council on Environmental Quality, Government Printing Office, Washington, D.C.

Collins, M. A. J. (1977), How to Develop and Test Your Own Curriculum, *Science and Children*, 14, 6, 11, National Science Teachers Association, Washington, D.C.

Commoner, B. (1971), *The Closing Circle*, Alfred Knopf, New York.

Connect (1976), *Environmental Education Newsletter*, UNESCO, Paris, Vol. 1, 1.

Connect (1978), *Environmental Education Newsletter*, UNESCO, Paris, Vol. 3, 2.

Ehrlich, P. R. and A. H. Ehrlich (1970), *Population, Resources and Environment: Issues in Human Ecology*, Freeman and Co., San Francisco.

El-Hinnawi, E., Editor (1980), *Nuclear Energy and The Environment*, Pergamon Press, Oxford.

Emmelin, L. (1975), Environmental Education at University Level, *Ambio*, 6, 4, 201.

Emmelin, L. (1977), Environmental Education Programmes for Adults, In *Trends in Environmental Education*, UNESCO, Paris, 177.

EPA (1979), *Environmental Outlook* 1980, *Executive Summary*, Environment Protection Agency, EPA/600/8–80–003, Washington, D.C.

Euro-Barometre (1976), Importance Attached to Various Issues in EEC Countries, *Euro-Barometre*, No. 5.

Fenner, F. (1977), Environmental Studies in Australian Universities, *Search,* 8, 4, 122, Australian and New Zealand Association for the Advancement of Science, Sydney, Australia.

Gadsby, B. (1975), Environmental Education at the Wildfowl Trust, *J. Biological Ed.,* 9,3–4, 114.

Garigliano, L. J. and B. J. Knape (1977), *Environmental Education in the Elementary School,* National Science Teachers Association, Washington, D.C.

Green, R. (1977), *Guidelines to the Preparation of Nature Trails,* Australian Conservation Foundation, E. Melbourne.

Greenhall, H. E. and J. C. Womersley, Editors (1977), *Development of Environmental Education in Australia - Key Issues,* Curriculum Development Centre, Canberra.

Guy, K. *et al.* (1978), *Environmental Education in United Kingdom Universities and Polytechnics: A Compendium,* Report No. 8, Monitoring and Assessment Research Centre (MARC), London.

Harvey, J. G. (1977), Interdisciplinarity in Environmental Sciences, *Interdisciplinarity,* 19–22, Society for Research into Higher Education, UK.

Hoffmann, B. K. (1978), Specifickyum moznostem litararni vychovy pri vychove k peci zivotni prostredi na prvnim stupni, *Komensky,* 102, 5, 276., Ministerstvo skolstve ve Statnim pedagogickem nakladatelstvi, Brno.

Jain, S. C. (1976), Value-oriented Education in Indian Schools Through Biology Teaching, *Biology and Human Affairs,* 41, 2, 100. British School Biology Council, London.

Kasler, A. *et al.* (1975–1976), Okonomische Probleme des Umweltschutzes am Beispiel der Abfallbeseitigung: Unterrichtsversuche für die Grundstufe, *Sachunterricht und Mathematik in der Grundschule,* 3, 12, 587. (1975); 4, 1, 18 (1976).

Kates, R. W. (1978), *Risk Assessment of Environmental Hazard: SCOPE 8,* John Wiley, Chichester.

Kominski, J. W. (1975), Forming an Ecology, *Club New Era* (Cambridge, UK), 56,16.

Lamy, S. *et al.* (1975), A Conference Model for Global Environmental Education, *J. Env. Educ.,* 2, 48.

Lines, C. J. and L. H. Bolwell (1978), *Teaching Environmental Studies,* Ginn, Aylesbury (UK).

Madders, M. (1975), Ecosystems in the Laboratory, *School Science Review,* 56, 197, 685. Association for Science Education, Hatfield, U.K.

Marsh, J. A. (1976), The Preparation of Teachers for Environmental Science, *South Pacific J. of Teacher Educ.,* 14, 2, 109.

McEvoy, J. (1972), The American Concern with Environment, In W. R. Burch *et al.* (Editors), *Social Behaviour, Natural Resources and the Environment,* Harper and Row, New York.

Morris, J. W. (1976), *European Curriculum Studies in the Academic Secondary school, No. 10: Geography,* Council of Europe, Council for Cultural Co-operation, Strasbourg.

MURS-NAS (1981), *Evaluation des Risques et Processus de Decision.,* M.U.R.S. and National Academy of Sciences, Paris (in press).

NCERT (1977), *Organization of Training Programmes For Primary Science Teachers: A Suggested Model,* National Council of Educational Research and Training, New Delhi, India.

Nelkin, S. and S. Fallows (1978), The Evolution of the Nuclear Debate, *Annual Review of Energy*, 3, 275.

Newbould, P. J. (1976), *Environmental Eduation At University Level: Trends and Data*, OECD/CERI, Paris.

Numata, M. *et al.* (1974), *Proceedings of the International Symposium on Environmental Education*, Chiba University, Japan.

O'Riordan, T. (1971), Towards a Strategy of Public Involvement, In W. R. Sewell and I. Burton (Editors), *Perceptions and Attitudes in Resource Management*, Department of Energy, Mines and Resources, Canada.

Parlour, J. W. and S. Schatzow (1978), The Mass Media and Public Concern for Environmental Problems in Canada, 1960–1972, *Intern. J. Environmental Studies*, 13, 9.

Patterson, J. W. (1980), Environmental Engineering Education: Academia and an Evolving Profession, *Environ. Sci. Techn.*, 14, 5, 524.

Pethen, R. W. (1979), First Destinations of Graduates from First Degree Environmental Science Courses 1977, *Inst. Env. Sci. News-sheet*, 4, 2, 5.

Reid, A. J. and N. J. Shaw (1975), Environmental Education: Conceptual Approaches, *Primary Education*, 6, 5, 11. East Melbourne, Australia.

Royal Society (1981), *The Assessment and Perception of Risk*, The Royal Soc., London.

Sandman, P. M. (1974), Mass Environmental Education: Can the Media do the Job? In J. A. Swann and W. B. Stapp (Editors), *Environmental Education*, John Wiley, New York.

Santander, J. (1975), The Psychology of Protective Behaviour, *J. Safe. Res.*, 10, 58.

Saveland, R. N., Editor (1976), *Handbook of Environmental Education with International Case Studies*, John Wiley, Somerset, New Jersey.

SCEP (1970), *Study of Critical Environmental Problems: Man's Impact on the Global Environment*, MIT Press, Cambridge, Mass.

Schoenfeld, C. (1975), National Environmental Education Perspective, *J. Env. Educ.*, 7, 2, 9.

Schoenfeld, C. (1977), Role of Mass Communication in Environmental Education, *J. Env. Educ.*, 8, 3, 60.

Schoenfeld, C. (1980), Assessing the Environmental Reportage of the Daily Press: 1965–1979, *J. Env. Educ.*, 11, 3, 31.

Schoenfeld, C. and J. Disinger, Editors (1978), *Environmental Education in Action II: Case Studies of Environmental Studies Programs in Colleges and Universities Today*, ERIC Clearinghouse for Science, Mathematics and Environmental Education, Ohio State University, USA.

Shaffer, B. E. (1978), *International Environmental Education: General Perspectives, Communications and Program Status in Selected Countries*, Colorado State Dept. of Education, Colorado.

Stapp, W. B. (1976), *Suggestions for Developing a National Strategy for Environmental Education*, ENDEV Africa-2, UNESCO, Paris.

Surrey, J. and C. Hugget (1976), Opposition to Nuclear Power, *Energy Policy*, 286.

Swann, J. A. and W. B. Stapp, Editors, (1974), *Environmental Education: Strategies Towards a More Livable Future*, John Wiley, New York.

UNEP-AAU (1978), Workshop on Environmental Education and Training in African Universities (Summary Report). UNEP/WG.21/25, Feb. 1979.

UNESCO (1977a), The International Workshop on Environmental Education; Belgrade, October 1975. Final Report, ED-76/WS/95. UNESCO, Paris.

UNESCO (1977b), Needs and Priorities in Environmental Education: An International Survey, Intergovernmental Conf. on Environmental Education, Tbilisi, October 1977, UNESCO/ENVED 6.

UNESCO (1978), Intergovernmental Conference on Environmental Education, Tbilisi (USSR), Final Report, ED/MD/49. UNESCO, Paris.

UNESCO (1979), Environmental Education of Engineers: Current Trends and Perspectives, SC-79/WS/21. UNESCO, Paris.

UNESCO (1980a), Workshop on Environmental Education for Latin America, ED.80/WS/87. UNESCO, Paris.

UNESCO (1980b), Environmental Education in the Light of the Tbilisi Conference, *Education on the Move*, 3, UNESCO, Paris.

US President's Science Advisory Committee (1967), *The World Food Problem*, US Gov. Printing Office, Washington, D.C.

Vandenhazel, B. J. (1976), *Environmental Education and Field Studies: Programmes in Three Selected N.W. European Areas*. Faculty of Education, Nipissing University College, North Bay, Ont., Canada.

Vander Smissen, B. (1975), *Research Camping and Environmental Education*. Pennsylvania State University, College of Health and Physical Education 508.

Varley, M. E. (1975), *Ecology Projects: An Innovation – Teaching at a Distance*, 2, 27. Open University, Milton Keynes, Bucks, UK.

WER (1980), *World Environment Report*, 6, Nos. 8, 12, 13, 14.

White, G. F. (1966), Formation and Role of Public Attitudes, In H. Jarrett (Editor), *Environmental Quality in A Growing Economy*, John Hopkins, Baltimore.

White, G. F. (1980), Environment, *Science*, 209, 183.

Whyte, A. V. and J. Burton, Editors (1980), *Environmental Risk Assessment: SCOPE 15,* John Wiley, Chichester.

CHAPTER 16

Peace and Security

Wars, and the threat of war, were constant features of the decade. Between 1945 and 1979 some 81 nations were involved in 130 civil and regional conflicts causing widespread suffering and disruptions. By the closing months of 1980 the international situation was such that many people feared an outbreak of global dimensions. The wars that were fought left environmental destruction behind, as wars always do, and those that merely threatened gave rise to fears of even greater destruction. These fears created tensions that diminished the possibilities of international co-operation in defining and solving environmental problems, and competed for scarce resources that could have been used for development.

During the 1970s the cost, in human and material terms, of the relics of past wars, received increasing attention. Surveys revealed that one country alone had removed 58.5 million mines from 2.5 million square kilometers of its territory after the second world war, another suffered 3,800 fatalities and 8,000 injuries. In Southeast Asia, social organization, agriculture and forest vegetation had been severely damaged, and were taking many years to recover.

By 1980 global military expenditure was thirty times as great as it had been at the turn of the century, and four times as great in constant money terms as in 1964. The rate of increase was a little less in the 1970s than it had been in the previous decade, and it grew less rapidly than total GNP. But the share attributable to the developing countries (which could least afford it) grew particularly rapidly. Armaments trade increased by about 15 per cent each year between 1970 and 1975. The oceans, the stratosphere and space were increasingly militarized and the military absorbed about 40 per cent of all the world's expenditure on research and development. In 1978, an average of one military satellite was launched every three days. And weapons systems, technically refined to a high degree, became ever more sophisticated and destructive.

Despite widespread condemnation of nuclear weapons, 469 nuclear devices were exploded between 1970 and 1980, 41 of them in the atmosphere, where they produce the greatest amount of radioactive fallout. However, as a result of the Partial Test Ban Treaty, environmental radionuclide concentration on the whole was lowered. But weapons testing continued to appropriate substantial land areas, and concern over the proliferation of nuclear technology and transport of nuclear materials increased.

A number of studies were carried out during the 1970s on the potential effects of nuclear war. These suggested that a major conflict would kill 200 to 300 million people and destroy most of the economic resources of the superpowers. Climatic and other environmental changes would be likely, and fallout would affect the whole world.

The destructive power of conventional weapons also grew. By 1980, aircraft carrying high explosive cluster bombs or grenade clusters could deliver an attack comparable in devastation to that of a tactical nuclear guided missile with a 1 kiloton warhead. It was clear that chemical and biological weapons could also produce severe environmental effects, especially when used to destroy forests and other vegetation in tropical areas with fragile soils, or semi-arid areas poised on the brink of desertification.

> *There was also concern over the possibility of using environmental modification as a weapon. Practices feasible by 1980 included the artificial creation of fog, cloud cover, hail, snow or rain in limited areas; the destruction of dykes and irrigation works and the pollution of water supplies; the destruction of permafrost areas; the stimulation of landslides and avalanches; and the destruction of vegetation and soil cover.*
>
> *The United Nations took many disarmament initiatives in the 1970s, but its total expenditure on this work in 1979 was equivalent to only 0.002 per cent of world military expenditure. Several major multinational agreements were signed, one prohibiting environmental modification for hostile purposes, and the United States and the USSR adopted the first SALT Treaty. But at the end of the decade the arms race still remained a serious threat to humanity and the environment.*

Human societies are founded upon co-operation. But competition between groups is also a human characteristic, intensified from time to time by environmental disruption and population growth. There is room for much debate over how far such basic ecological factors underlie conflict today, when the immediate reasons for war are almost always stated in economic, political, ideological or even religious terms.

During the 1970s, environmental issues became more and more important in the internal policies of many states and in international affairs. Development today requires more security and confidence than in the past because of the scale and cost of many vital programmes. War and the preparations for war are inimical to development because they squander scarce resources and destroy the international confidence that is essential to the improvement of the environment at regional level. While war may have brought incidental benefits in some fields by accelerating technological innovation, it has contributed few of the technical skills needed for environmental development.

Recognition increased during the decade of both the hazards posed by modern weapon systems and the need for peaceful international relations as a foundation for environmental development and human prosperity. The United Nations Charter (UN, 1945) takes as its starting point the need to maintain peace and security through the suppression of acts of aggression and through the settlement of international disputes in conformity with the principles of justice and international law.

But the charter also envisaged, and the United Nations Organization over the past thirty-five years has pursued, more positive action. It has been recognized that peace and security require the fulfilment of the other great principles enunciated in the preamble to the charter: social progress, better standards of life, freedom, fundamental human rights, the dignity and worth of human individuals and the equal rights of men and women and of large and small nations,

Environmental Impacts of War

THE economic and social burdens of preparations for war, the relationship between disarmament and development and the environmental effects of military activity have been reviewed in a series of United Nations reports and in publications outside the United Nations system (UN 1971, 1978 a, b, c, 1980; UNEP, 1980; Robinson, 1979 a; SIPRI 1976 a, 1977, 1980 a). These reviews suggest that the subject is best analyzed under three headings:

1. The environmental consequences of current and past wars:
    (i) hazards from unexploded weapons;
    (ii) physical and biological effects of damage to soil and landscape;
    (iii) human suffering resulting from the disruption of social systems.

2. The environmental impacts of preparations for war:
    (i) indirectly, through the diversion of resources from environmental development;
    (ii) through the impact of the armaments industry;
    (iii) directly, through weapons testing and military operations;
    (iv) through the proliferation of nuclear technlogy.

3. The hazards of possible future warfare:
    (i) The possible impacts of conventional warfare;
    (ii) the possible impacts of nuclear war;
    (iii) the possible impacts of chemical and biological warfare;
    (iv) the possible impacts of environmental modification.

To set the analysis in context, the scale of warfare itself over recent decades needs to be recalled. Between 1945 and 1979 there were some 130 civil and regional wars, involving some 81 nations, most of them developing countries (SIPRI, 1976b, 1979; UNEP 1980). The civilian deaths attributed to some of the larger of them, with World

War II figures for comparison, are shown in Table 16–1. Apart from great human suffering and an astronomical waste of resources, at least 12 of the 130 conflicts caused considerable environmental damage (Westing and Lumsden 1979; SIPRI, 1980a). In 1980 there was further serious destructive warfare in the Middle East, South-East Asia and Africa, involving about eight countries.

Table 16–1. Civilian Deaths and Displacements in Some Recent Major Wars.

War	Civilian Deaths		War Deaths as percentage of total population	Civilian Displacement
	Estimated Number	As % of all War Deaths		
World War II[a]	29,868,000	58	4	
Korean War 1950–53	560,000	42	0.2	
Algerian War of Independence 1954–62	~500,000		~5	2,000,000
Nigerian Civil War, Biafra 1967–70	~1,500,000		~18	
Bangladesh War 1971	1–3 million		>3	10 million
Second Indochina War	700,000	38	0.7	
Kampuchean Insurrections of 1975–77	1–2 million		>12	

Source: SIPRI (1980 a).

[a] The most stricken countries were Poland, in which 17.5% of the population were killed, Yugoslavia (11.3%), USSR (10.8%), Germany (9.3%), Austria (5.4%), Hungary (4.4%), Romania (3.6%), Czechoslovakia (3.1%), Greece (2.9%), Japan (2.8%), Albania (2.8%) and the Netherlands (2.6%). All others lost under 2% each.

ENVIRONMENTAL CONSEQUENCES OF CURRENT AND PAST WARS

In a recent UNEP survey (UNEP, 1980), forty-four governments reported on the environmental effects of the remnants of war. One Government reported that it had cleared 14,469,600 land mines left behind after the Second World War, and that clearance was continuing at the rate of 300,000 to 400,000 a year. Many thousands of shells, bombs and other munitions had to be dealt with in various countries. The country most seriously affected reported that these remnants of war had killed 3,834 people, most of them children, and injured 8,384 others, of whom 6,783 were children. In the five years up to 1979, thirty to forty people had been killed there each year and fifty to eighty injured. Some 460 disposal personnel had been killed and 655 injured. Coastal states reported parallel difficulties with marine mines, dumped ammunition and wrecked ships (some containing explosives).

Further detailed information was provided at a special symposium held in 1981 on the Material Remnants of the Second World War on Libyan Soil (especially in papers by Cestac, 1981 and Ceva, 1981), although the meeting was largely concerned with questions of legal liability. The symposium revealed that in the USSR, 58.5 million mines were removed from some 2.5 million square kilometres (km²) after World War II; in France, 13 million mines, 23 million shells and 600,000 bombs were cleared in thirty-five years after 1945, mostly from coastal zones (Cestac, 1981). The financial costs of such clearance are great: Cestac indicated that the annual budget of a 60–man team in Libya is approximately US$400,000 for personnel and equipment.

Such problems have recurred following the Second Indochina War of 1961–75, which is calculated to have left some 150,000 — 300,000 unexploded munitions in the combatant territories. Removal of unexploded weapons is not only costly but often is hampered by a lack of records of where mines were laid. Moreover many developing countries lack both the skills and resources to devote to such operations and argue that where other countries were the belligerents the latter should bear the costs of environmental restoration (see, e.g., Blischenko, 1981; Miggiani, 1981; Basso, 1981).

Concrete road-blocks, gun emplacements, abandoned airfields and other installations are still a conspicuous feature of many former battle zones, defacing the landscape and reducing its attractiveness for tourism. Less conspicuous but more demanding is the loss of soil and vegetation, which is only slowly restored, and disruption of agriculture. During the Second World War ten nations suffered a short-term reduction in agricultural productivity of about 38 per cent: recovery proceeded at about eight per cent per annum. In the Second Indochina War, several countries that were formerly exporters of rice became heavily dependent on imports, and in some cases on famine relief.

In South Vietnam, chemical herbicides destroyed some 1,500 km² of mangrove forest and caused some damage to about 15,000 km² more; several hundred thousand hectares were disrupted by bomb craters (Somerville, 1970; SIPRI, 1979, 1980 a; UNEP, 1980). Much of the nutrient in those areas is held in the standing crop of trees and the thin humus layer at the soil surface, and is likely to have been lost in solution in run-off; the exposed soils are liable to both erosion and, in some areas, conversion to laterite rock. Even where this does not happen, recovery can be expected to be extremely slow. Other areas of tropical forest affected by recent wars, for example in Kampuchea, are at risk in a comparable way.

Robinson (1979 a) analyzed the types of ecological impact that various military activities impose on ecosystems. The most fundamental and persistant effects arose when vegetation disruption was accompanied by massive soil erosion, and by alterations to the hydrological regime and to the likely pattern of plant succession. There is no guarantee under such circumstances that the original ecosystem will be restored. Major ecological changes of this kind are especially likely in tropical forest regions and semi-arid areas and also in polar tundra zones where recovery from any disturbance is very slow.

The defoliant – Agent Orange – used in Vietnam was a mixture of 2, 4 – D (2, 4 – dichlorophenoxyacetic acid) and 2, 4, 5 – T (2, 4, 5 – trichlorophenoxyacetic acid), and contained up to 100 parts per million (ppm) of a contaminant, dioxin (2, 3, 7, 8 –

tetrachlorodibenzo-p-dioxin or TCDD). The latter substance is known to be highly foetotoxic (toxic to the foetus) and teratogenic (capable of producing abnormal offspring) in laboratory experiments, and there were allegations that it caused genetic and bodily defects and liver cancer in the exposed human population (UNEP, 1980; Nader *et al.*, 1981).

Tragic though such cases are, it was the widespread social disruption and the uprooting of large numbers of people that created the most persistent human effects of past wars. About seventeen million (or one-third of the regional population) were displaced in the Second Indochina War, most of them from rural areas (Table 16—1). Those displaced flocked to the cities: one estimate suggests that the population of ten of the major areas in South Vietnam outside Saigon trebled during 1963—71 (Lumsden, 1975). In the short term, such refugees not only experience personal suffering and economic loss, but exert severe pressures on the areas to which they migrate. The destruction of farmlands and villages inevitably hampers their rehabilitation, which is further hindered by their physical weakness, the accumulation of disease, and the disruption of their social groupings. Following the ending of conflict, the first priority is rightly seen as the re-establishment of social order and the care of human victims of war: resources to combat soil erosion or afforest denuded areas are likely to be lacking and the problems seen as lower in priority.

ENVIRONMENTAL IMPACTS OF PREPARATIONS FOR WAR

Consumption of limited resources

The statistical data on national military expenditure vary widely because of inconsistencies in the activities included under this heading and the virtual impossibility of estimating the costs of supporting an associated civil labour and industrial effort consistently (Sivard, 1980). For this reason no figures for individual national outlays are given in this Chapter; the statements about overall global expenditure that follow are based on estimates by the Stockholm International Peace Research Institute (SIPRI), which are generally intermediate between other estimates.

By the end of 1970s, global military expenditure had increased 30–fold since 1900. It had quadrupled since 1946 (Figure 16–1). Although the rate of increase, at 2 to 2.5 per cent per annum in real terms, was somewhat less over the decade 1970–80 than between 1960–70, (when it averaged 3 to 3.5 per cent) the upward trend continued, (SIPRI, 1981). In 1980 this expenditure was well over US$450 billion per annum in 1978 dollars – approaching US$1 million per minute – and if the current trend continues could reach US$650 billion a year at 1978 prices by the year 2000 (SIPRI, 1978, 1979, 1981). There were some indications during 1980 that the annual rate of expenditure on armaments had begun to increase again and was rising faster than world economic growth (SIPRI, 1980 b).

Figure 16–1. World Military Expenditure.

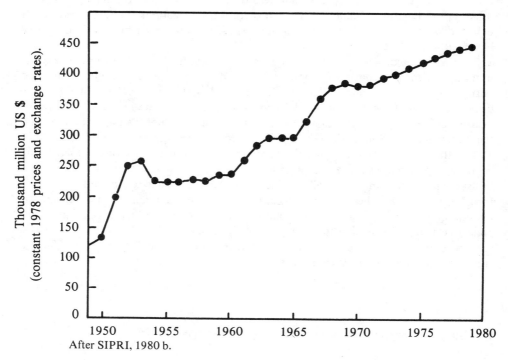

After SIPRI, 1980 b.

This military expenditure varied between regions and nations. However, it is likely that the share attributable to the developing countries (Latin America, Africa and Asia excluding China and Japan) increased particularly rapidly during the decade, both in gross terms and in terms of military expenditure per head. Much of this growth was attributable to countries in oil-rich or especially conflict-ridden regions. But developing country military expenditure was small when viewed in a world context: in 1979 over two-thirds of world spending on armaments was by those same six developed countries that had held the lead throughout 1965–75, with the USA and USSR having by far the largest shares (SIPRI, 1980b, 1981: Sivard, 1980).

The 1970s also saw a great growth in trade in conventional major weapons (combat aircraft, armoured vehicles, missiles and warships). During the early 1960s this grew at around 5 per cent per annum: in the second half of that decade it reached 10 per cent and between 1970 and 1975 it ran at around 15 per cent. Seventy-five per cent of this trade consisted of deliveries from industrialized countries to the developing countries (Figure 16–2). The total value was put at US$21 billion in 1978 (SIPRI, 1981; Sivard, 1981). These imports accounted for about a quarter of the estimated total developing country military expenditure in this period.

The oceans, stratosphere and space have become increasingly militarized. During 1978, 112 military satellites were launched – about 1 every 3 days. Between 1957 and the beginning of 1979 a total of 1,601 military and part-military satellites were launched.

Figure 16–2. The importers and exporters of major weapons, 1970 – 1979.

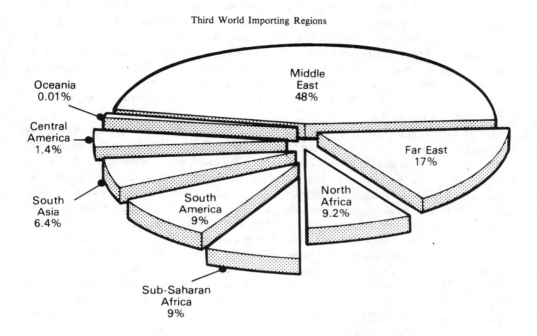

Third World Importing Regions

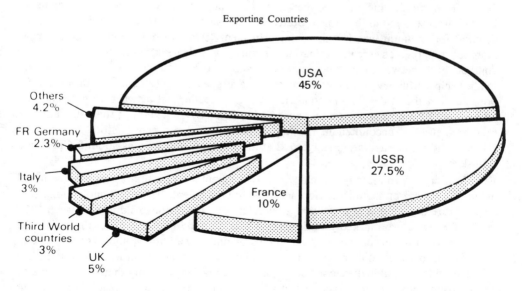

Exporting Countries

After SIPRI, 1981.

(non-military satellites accounted for only 15 per cent of the global total) (SIPRI, 1979). They were used mainly to aid navigation, for target identification and for surveillance (the latter useful in verifying arms control agreements: UNEP, 1980). Several hundred nuclear-powered submarines carried a number of ballistic missiles, estimated at more than 1,600 by the United Nations (1980) but more than 5,000 by Sivard (1981), and the sophistication of anti-submarine warfare increased greatly. The environmental effects of military vessels are not regulated by current international conventions. An increasing number of military supersonic aircrafts were flying in the stratosphere, but as Chapter 2 reports, there were insufficient data to assess their environmental impacts in a meaningful way.

These activities involved vast human and natural resources. About 60 million people, equivalent to the entire labour force in manufacturing industry in Europe outside the USSR, were engaged in military or related occupations. Moreover, many of these were highly qualified people: one estimate suggested that military research and development absorbed scientific and technological capabilities ten times as great as were available in all the developing countries together (UN, 1971). About 400,000 highly qualified scientists worked in military research, and military Research and Development was absorbing about 40 per cent of all world research and development expenditure (UN, 1978 a). These figures need to be seen in the wider context of human needs and human resources. Total global military expenditure as a percentage of total GNP declined at a compound rate of 2.1 per cent between 1969 and 1978, although these figures were considerably influenced by the decline in US expenditure following the Vietnam war (USACDA, 1979a). This reduction was, however accompanied by increasing sophistication and destructiveness of weapon systems, and a parallel increase in the quality of rare natural resources (including metals) consumed by the arms race. Some raw materials, including copper, lead, zinc and bauxite were especially in demand for military uses, and in the United States in 1972 more than 40 per cent of the national demand for titanium was in this sector (Huisken, 1975). Competition for scarce raw materials regarded as essential to national security was clearly itself a potential source of conflict, both between developed countries and in the wider context of North-South relationships. Military resource consumption averaged 5–6 per cent of total output in both developed and developing countries over the decade (and between 25 per cent and 28 per cent of central government expenditure) (USACDA, 1980). In the United States military activities accounted in the mid-1970s for 7–8 per cent of total energy use (Hveem, 1978): extrapolation suggests that the worldwide figure was about 3.5 per cent (Huisken, 1975).

Military expenditure is especially of environmental concern if it competes with and jeopardizes environmental development and management. There are indications that expenditure on health and education grew relative to military expenditure between 1970 and 1978 but more markedly in developed than in developing countries (Table 16–2). There is room for argument over the details behind these figures, and over the general relationship between military expenditure and other national investment (although there is some evidence that in developed countries with a market economy there was an inverse relationship between the percentage of GNP devoted to military expenditure and that devoted to domestic investment in the civil sector) (Figure 16–3). These data do not

Table 16–2. Public Expenditure on Education, Health and Foreign Economic Aid
(Expressed in Billion Constant 1977 US$).

	Education		Health		GNP		Military Expenditure	
	1970	1978	1970	1978	1970	1978	1970	1978
Developed countries	255.0	374.2	125.7	231.0	4900	6490	312.4	344.7
Developing countries	38.0	67.0	13.3	22.5	1143	1858	69.9	102.0
World	293.0	441.2	139.0	253.5	6043	8348	382.3	446.7

Source: USACDA (1980). Other authors, e.g. Sivard (1980) cite different figures but present a
similar trend.

support the supposition that high military expenditures strengthen a nation's economy,
as had been postulated by some (Baran and Sweezy, 1966). If anything, they suggest that
such expenditures serve to dampen the economy, as has been postulated by others
(Smith and Smith, 1980). What is not challengeable is the fact that the increase in
military expenditure took place at a time when 1,500 million people (about 35 per cent of
the world's population) had no effective medical services, nearly 450 million were
undernourished, about 650 million lacked drinking water supply services (Chapter 4)
and about 450,000 children died each month from infectious diseases (Chapter 10).
About 800 million people were illiterate, and nearly 250 million under the age of 14 did
not attend school (SIPRI, 1978).

ENVIRONMENTAL RISKS FROM THE WEAPONS PRODUCTION INDUSTRY

There were no separate statistics for the environmental pollution caused by the
industries producing military equipment. Since military expenditure accounted for 5–6
per cent of GNP, crude extrapolation might suggest it contributed a comparable
percentage of the total pollution attributable to industry. However, the weapons industry
handles some materials that are particularly hazardous. These include explosives, rocket
propellants, highly toxic chemicals and fissile materials. The heavy industries associated
with defence construction include some that have been major polluters, and in which
technological change has been slow. The risk of dangerous accidents and the general
pollution burden are therefore likely to be higher than a simple statistical comparison in
expenditure terms suggests (Kaldor, 1976). Accordingly, segregation and special
protection of the facilities handling the most dangerous materials is normal for reasons of
public safety as well as military security.

Figure 16–3. Military Expenditure and Productivity.

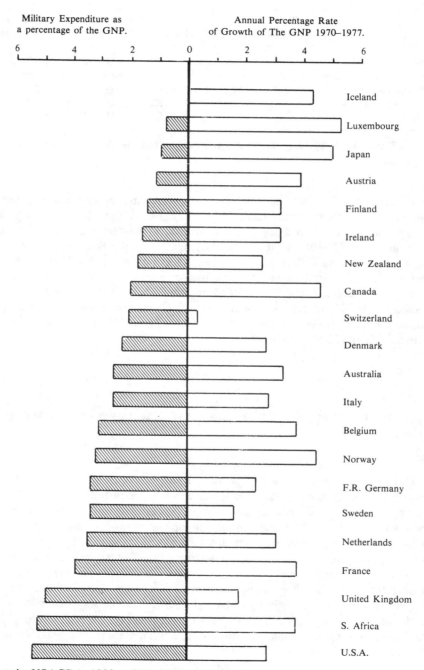

After data by USACDA, 1980 and World Bank, 1980.

Direct impact of weapons tests and military activities

Between 1970 and 1980 there were 469 nuclear explosions, mostly to test weapons: 41 were in the atmosphere despite the prohibition by the Partial Test Ban Treaty (SIPRI, 1981). Since 1945, about 595 devices have been exploded in at least five major deserts, 132 of them above ground (SIPRI, 1980 a). With the increase in the nuclear arsenal, there have been growing fears of possible accidents during transport, manoeuvres or even routine maintenance, as well as of deliberate sabotage.

The environmental effects of a number of nuclear tests have been monitored. Blasts, thermal radiation and nuclear radiation are all important, the latter causing both somatic effects (like cancer) and possible genetic changes (mutations). In the Mohave Desert (Nevada, USA) with explosions in the 10–70 kiloton range, the zone of central destruction of almost all life extended for 70–200 ha; the outer zones of severe ecological damage and detectable damage covered 400–1300 ha and up to a maximum 3250 ha respectively (SIPRI, 1977). Species varied considerably in their sensitivity, simpler organisms like algae or insects surviving radiation doses many hundreds of times greater than those which would kill vertebrates or advanced plants like forest trees (Whicker and Fraley, 1974). Within three to four years pioneer plant species invaded the central zones, with slow ecological recovery also in the outer zones. The overall pattern resembled that following other kinds of major physical disturbance of the desert ecosystem in being slow and likely to require decades for completion. There can only be speculation about possible long-term ecological changes resulting from genetic modifications in the irradiated populations.

On Pacific Islands, with a far more favourable environment, vegetation recovery appeared to have followed the normal and much more rapid successional course. In such sites, however (as would be expected) certain radionuclides, including caesium–137 and strontium–90, appeared to have incorporated in the local bio-geochemical cycles: recent studies showed abnormally high amounts of both, and of plutonium, in the bodies of Bikini islanders (Robinson, 1979 a). The full biological effects of these impacts may not be established for a considerable time.

Because of these concerns, radioactivity from world-wide fall-out was monitored regularly in many countries. The success of the Partial Test Ban Treaty was reflected in generally falling levels of radio-nuclides in rain, and in milk (which gives a useful indication of the combined influence of deposition from the atmosphere and the cumulative deposit in the soil). In the United Kingdom the annual average concentration of caesium–137 in milk fell from 1.7 Becquerel per litre (Bq/1) in 1966 to 0.62 Bq/1 in 1970 and 0.15 Bq/1 in 1977 (DOE, 1978). These figures are probably representative of a reassuring general trend.

There is less information about the environmental impact of other kinds of advanced weapons testing. Some ecological surveys were made of sites where biological weapons were tested (Robinson, 1979 a), although very few results have been published. At one site, however, anthrax spores remained viable in the soil at least thirty-six years after testing ceased. Chemical weapons were tested in arctic, arid, tropical, temperate and insular situations, but again few results of surveys of their ecological impact were published. However, much information is available about the impact of chemical weapons used in past wars.

Considerable land areas were set aside for military training and weapon testing. In the United Kingdom almost 20 per cent of the total land area was in some way used for military purposes at the height of World War II (Ministry of Defence, 1973), but this had fallen to 1.27 per cent (3065 km²) by 1972. Two-thirds of this latter area was in use as training areas and ranges. Military activities can stress the affected ecosystems through soil disruption, habitat destruction and pollution – but they also protect areas of wild habitat such as heathlands from conversion to agriculture or forestry and as such were regarded as important agents of wildlife conservation in some parts of lowland Britain (Harrison, 1974; Duffey, 1974). However, in the United Kingdom as in other densely populated countries, there was pressure for return of land from military to civilian use, and much military training now takes place abroad. In North America military use affects Arctic habitats, which are more fragile than those of temperate regions (Murrman and Reed, 1972). In the Federal Republic of Germany positive efforts have been made to train and use the armed forces in peacetime to protect the environment, and in 1980 the Government of the Federal Republic convened an International Seminar on the Environmental Impacts of Defence Activities in Peacetime.

Various other environmental impacts of peacetime military activitivies have been identified or postulated. The electromagnetic field created by large antenna arrays used in extreme low frequency communications systems allegedly affected migrating birds (Larkin and Sutherland, 1977). The transport of weapons brings with it the risk of accident, and there were accidents or incidents involving nuclear weapons every few months (Leitenberg, 1977). None of these led to the actual functioning of a mass-destruction weapon, but some led to contamination. One nuclear warhead, ruptured off Greenland, contaminated marine organisms over a wide area with plutonium (Aarkrog, 1971).

PROLIFERATION AND RISKS FROM THE CIVIL NUCLEAR POWER INDUSTRY

The Treaty on the Non-Proliferation of Nuclear Weapons (NPT), which entered into force in 1970, is concerned with preventing the wider dissemination of nuclear weapons and the technology for their manufacture. By March 1979 it had been ratified by 107 nations, and signed by 8 more. (Rotblat, 1979; Goldblat, 1979). But concern over the risk of proliferation remained – partly because of the failure of many states (including some with nuclear technology) to become parties to the NPT, and partly because of the absence of safeguards to prevent transfer of nuclear technology from the nuclear power industry to nuclear weapons manufacture.

By 1980, military stocks of fissile material roughly equalled those held by civil industry. But it was realized that if nuclear power generation expanded as some projections suggested with reprocessing of spent fuel and possibly the introduction of breeder reactors, the quantity of fissile material in transit (especially plutonium) could become considerable, bringing with it risks of theft or sabotage. For these reasons, it was suggested that the growth of the civil nuclear power industry could be a threat to peace and security and to the environment if there were inadequate safeguards over material in transit. Although the proliferation of nuclear weapons among governments determined to acquire them would not be prevented by stopping the development of nuclear power, the latter might accelerate weapons proliferation (CEQ, 1980, CONAES, 1980).

Various technical measures could reduce the risk of theft (or rather, make it harder to use fuel materials for weapons manufacture) but safe-guards and effective institutional arrangements are urgently needed to protect the environment and prevent weapons proliferation. The International Nuclear Fuel Cycle Evaluation (INFCE) has recently identified the sensitive points in the nuclear fuel cycle that could lead to diversion of nuclear material for purposes other than power production. It also identified and analyzed a number of means (technical, improved safeguards and institutional arrangements) to minimize the danger of misuse of fuel cycle facilities for the acquisition of nuclear weapons, without jeopardizing energy supplies or the development of nuclear energy for peaceful purposes (INFCE, 1980).

The Environmental Hazards of Possible Future Wars

THE 1970s saw a worldwide increase in concern about the dangers posed by warfare to the biosphere and to the future human civilization. This concern was based on a growing understanding of the potential hazards of new types of warefare and a re-assessment of the risks of conventional warfare in the light of experience with conflicts that occurred in that decade.

POSSIBLE IMPACTS OF CONVENTIONAL WARFARE

The Southeast Asian conflicts demonstrated that pre-occupation with the risks of nuclear, chemical, biological or environmental weapons could all too easily divert attention dangerously from the considerable probability of the outbreak of further conventional warfare. Such warfare, these conflicts demonstrated, could be enormously destructive. The destructiveness of conventional weapons continued to increase during the decade, and by 1980 aircfaft carrying high explosive cluster bombs or grenade clusters could deliver an attack comparable in devastation to that of a tactical nuclear guided missile with a one kiloton warhead (Table 16–3). Such weapons, furthermore, were widely available on the world market.

Table 16–3.   The Potential Lethal Impact of Some Modern Weapons

Type of weapon	Lethality index[a]
Light machine gun	21 000
Medium howitzer high explosive shell	890 000
Shoulder-fired flame-rocket launcher	1 200 000
Fighter-bomber with napalm firebombs	1 900 000
Tactical guided missile, HE/frag bomblet warhead	7 200 000
Multiple rocket launcher, HE/frag rockets	12 000 000
Bomber with blockbuster light-case HE bombs	52 000 000
Fighter-bomber with HE/frag cluster bombs	150 000 000
Heavy bomber, with HE/frag grenade clusters	207 000 000
Tactical nuclear guided missile, 'mininuke' warhead	60 000 000
Tactical guided missile, 1 kiloton nuclear warhead	170 000 000
Tactical guided missile, 20 kiloton nuclear warhead	830 000 000
Strategic guided missile, 1 megaton warhead	18 000 000 000
Strategic guided missile, 25 megaton warhead	210 000 000 000

Source: Robinson (1979 b).

[a] Lethality index based on Dupuy (1964), Taking into account rate of fire, number of potential targets per strike, relative probability of killing or incapacitating target, effective range, accuracy, reliability and mobility.

HE: High explosives.

POSSIBLE IMPACTS OF NUCLEAR WAR

During the 1970s a number of studies were made of the potential effects of nuclear war (e.g. NAS, 1975; USACDA, 1979b; OTA, 1979; UN, 1980). These analyses suggested that a major war between the two nuclear superpowers, involving the use of a greater part of their nuclear arsenals, would kill some 200–300 million people and destroy the greater part of the economic resources of both countries. But as the United Nations evaluation stresses, the consequences would not be restricted to nuclear-weapon states. Fallout radiation from a large nuclear war would affect the whole world (although predominantly the hemisphere in which the war was fought).

Fallout from a total explosive yield of 10,000 megaton would cause some five to ten million additional deaths from cancer over the next 40 years. Genetic damage would appear with about the same frequency as lethal cancer, half of the defects appearing in the two generations immediately following the war and the remainder in subsequent generations (UN, 1980; UNEP, 1980; SIPRI, 1979, 1980 a).

The environmental effects of such a conflict have also been analyzed (NAS, 1975; UN, 1980). Detonations totalling 10,000 megaton might (especially if the individual explosions were large) inject substantial quantities of nitrogen oxides into the stratosphere, leading to substantial ozone depletion. A quantity of dust comparable to that ejected in the eruption of Krakatoa might also be injected. Measurable climatic changes, perhaps involving mean annual temperature reductions of the order of 0.5 – 1.0°C might result, with effects on agriculture that would further hamper the processes of recovery. If there was a major increase in ultra-violet penetration, this might damage sensitive crops as well as increase skin cancers in man. Natural ecosystems would undoubtedly be affected, although instabilities on a global scale are unlikely and recovery could be expected to be fairly complete after some twenty-five years.

Table 16–4 summarizes the main impacts of a 1 megaton nuclear explosion in an urban area (USACDA, 1979 b). Table 16–5 lists the impacts of two other sizes of explosion on vegetation and vertebrate fauna in a rural environment. Westing (1978) calculated that a one kiloton neutron bomb detonated 200 metres above ground would cause death to a wide range of micro-organisms over an area of 40 ha, to many insects over 100 ha, to amphibians and reptiles over 330 ha and to mammals and birds over 490 ha.

Table 16–4. The Environmental Impact of a One-Megaton Nuclear Explosion

Distance (km)	Effect
2.4	Reinforced concrete multistorey buildings destroyed. Most people killed instantly.
4.6	Concrete buildings destroyed. Spontaneous ignition of clothing. Third-degree flash burns to exposed skin.
6.7	Brick and wood frame houses destroyed. Spontaneous ignition of clothing. Third-degree flash burns to exposed skin.
7.8	Spontaneous ignition of clothing and other combustion materials. Third-degree flash burns to exposed skin.
9.9	Third-degree flash burns to exposed skin.
13.6	Moderate damage to brick and wood frame houses.

Source: USACDA (1979 b).

The data in Table 16–5 are for the 24–hour period after the detonation of a nuclear device. Of the total radiation energy released by such an explosion, 10–15 per cent would remain undissipated by the end of that period. This would exert a chronic ecological effect because the main radioisotopes involved – notably caesium–137, strontium–90, carbon–14, hydrogen–3 and iron–55 – would enter biogeochemical cycles. While, therefore, the potential effects of nuclear weapons were generally assessed in relation to human populations, it was recognized that their environmental effects could be of comparable long-term significance (UN, 1968; NAS, 1975; SIPRI, 1977).

Table 16–5. Some Effects of Ground-Burst Nuclear Weapons Within 24 Hours of Detonation

Type of damage	Area over which damage may occur (ha)	
	20–kiloton atomic bomb	10–megaton hydrogen bomb
Craterization by blast wave[a]	1	57
Vertebrates killed by blast wave[b]	24	1 540
All vegetation killed by nuclear radiation[c]	43	12 100
Trees killed by nuclear radiation[d]	148	63 800
Trees blown down by blast wave[e]	362	52 500
Vertebrates killed by nuclear radiation[f]	674	177 000
Dry vegetation ignited by thermal radiation[g]	749	117 000
Vertebrates killed by thermal radiation[h]	1 000	150 000

Source: Robinson (1979 a).

[a] Refers to dry soil. A sub-surface burst could craterize four times as large an area as a surface burst. Nuclear warheads exploding above the surface would produce no craters at all if the burst were sufficiently high, but the nuclear and thermal radiation effects would then extend over larger areas.
[b] Refers to areas over which the transient over-pressure, would be likely to exceed 345 kilopascal; this being the over-pressure for about 50 per cent lethality among large mammals, including man. These figures are, in fact, augmented by reflected over-pressures which (depending upon height of burst, terrain, etc.) can more than double the total (so-called Mach front) over-pressures experienced at any distance.
[c] Refers to areas over which the early radiation dose would be likely to exceed 70 kilorad.
[d] Refers to areas over which the early radiation dose would be likely to exceed 10 kilorad.
[e] Refers to areas over which the transient wind velocity at the shock front, ignoring the Mach front, would be likely to exceed about 60 metres per second. Such a wind would be likely to blow down about 90 per cent of the trees in an average coniferous forest or a deciduous forest in leaf.
[f] Refers to areas over which the early radiation dose would be likely to exceed 2 kilorad.
[g] Refers to areas over which the incident thermal radiation would be likely to exceed 500 kilojoules per square metre for the atom bomb or 1,000 kilojoules per square metre for the hydrogen bomb if the weapons were detonated on a clear day having a visibility of 80 km.
[h] Refers to areas over which, on a clear day of 80 km visibility, the incident thermal radiation would be likely to exceed that which would have a 50 per cent lethality for exposed pigs (380 kilojoules per square metre for the atom bomb and 750 kilojoules per square metre for the hydrogen bomb).

POSSIBLE IMPACTS OF CHEMICAL AND BIOLOGICAL WARFARE

Chemical and biological warfare agents could also have serious environmental consequences since they involve, in effect, deliberate pollution by the release of toxic chemicals or harmful micro-organisms. Of the two, chemical weapons were of greater military interest at the end of the decade. One of their more likely uses is against the environment, to destroy vegetation and crops, and the herbicides used would probably differ from commercial ones in combining high toxicity with persistence. Chemical deforestation in tropical areas with fragile soils, or vegetation destruction in semi-arid areas already poised on the brink of desertification, could create widespread erosion and long-term damage, as experience in the wars in South-East Asia showed (SIPRI, 1976 a; Robinson, 1979 a).

The potential lethal impact of anti-personnel chemical weapons is considerable: a tactical guided missile with a nerve-gas warhead could have a "lethality index" of 91,000,000 – more than the smallest size of tactical nuclear guided missile (Robinson, 1979 b).

Anti-personnel chemical and bacteriological weapons are banned under international agreements, but research and development of the former have continued,

Table 16–6. Hostile Environmental Modification Techniques Feasible in 1980 (often under limited conditions only)

Basic natural systems	Type of effect	Military significance	Remarks
Atmosphere	Dispersion of cloud cover or fog	Ensures visibility in combat areas, airfields and naval bases	Effective in limited areas as a tactical device
	Artificial creation of fog or clouds	Impedes surveillance by the enemy, and protects against light radiation from nuclear explosions	Effective in limited areas, under certain weather conditions as a tactical device
	Artificial creation of hail, snow or rain	Damage to communications equipment and certain types of military equipment	Effective at certain altitudes in limited areas as a tactical device
Inland Waters	Changes in local water balance (destruction of dykes and irrigation works)	Impedes combat operations and logistical support	Effective on a tactical scale
	Action to affect the physical properties of water resources (pollution, infection)	Impedes combat and supply operations, disrupts operations in logistic areas	
Continental Ecosystems	Action to affect permafrost areas	Destroys road networks and airfields, damages water systems	Possible for certain areas
	Stimulation of avalanches and landslides	Destroys road networks and impedes military operations	Possible only in limited areas as a tactical device
	Destruction of vegetation or soil cover	Impedes activities of enemy forces, disrupts agricultural activities	Effective as a tactical device

with the production of so-called binary devices in which two relatively safe materials were stored separately but mixed to form a lethal combination when a weapon was routed to its target. On the biological side, the effects of deliberately disseminating quantities of up to a dozen species of highly virulent pathogenic bacteria are uncertain. Much would depend on whether they were employed against crop species, livestock or man, and on how long they sustained themselves in the wild, but the agricultural and ecological balance could be disturbed for a long time (UN, 1969; WHO, 1970: SIPRI, 1976 a, 1977; UNEP 1980).

POSSIBLE IMPACTS OF ENVIRONMENTAL MODIFICATION

Seeking to damage an enemy by disrupting his environment is an ancient practice, but such 'scorched earth' tactics have generally been employed by retreating armies or those facing defeat. More recently there have been speculations about the use of environmental modification as an offensive weapon (Goldblat, 1975; Jasani, 1975; Barnaby, 1976). Methods of modifying weather were being developed during the 1970s for peaceful purposes, but obviously had military potential. Table 16—6 lists some of the forms of environmental manipulation that were feasible by the end of the decade. Other, more speculative, but theoretically possible variants include the creation of hurricanes and tsunamis, while the creation of floods, earthquakes and electrical storms and the stimulation of volcanic eruptions have been discussed but remain highly problematical (WPC, 1979). Such activities could conceivably be used, not as overt acts of war but as means of surreptitiously weakening a competing or potentially hostile state (UNEP, 1980, Whittow, 1980).

The Responses of the International Community

THE UNITED NATIONS AND DISARMAMENT

DISARMAMENT has been a continuing pre-occupation of the United Nations since its foundation, and its activities between 1945 and 1975 have been reviewed in two publications (UN, 1970, 1976). The first General Assembly sought for ways of eliminating atomic weapons and 'all other major weapons adaptable to mass destruction' (UN, 1946). In 1970 U Thant, the then Secretary-General of the United Nations, reviewed progress and concluded that:

> "The rewards consist mainly of a limited number of measures of arms control and disarmament, achieved during the last decade. Efforts to make substantial progress towards general and complete disarmament – the goal that the Members of the United Nations unanimously accepted in 1959 – have not borne fruit. While progress in disarmament has been slow, science and technology – in particular nuclear technology – have advanced at a formidable pace. Tremendous material resources and human creativeness have been applied to destructive rather than constructive purposes; and despite repeated assurances to the contrary, the world becomes less secure with every new generation of more sophisticated weapons."

These words were no less apt in 1980 despite several important United Nations initiatives during the 1970s. These included the devotion of the 10th Special Session of the General Assembly in 1978 to disarmament, with the production of a final document that introduced major reforms into the negotiating machinery and established a programme of action (UN, 1978 a). The General Assembly, the UN Disarmament Committee (constituted in 1952), the Committee on Disarmament and the Advisory Board on Disarmament Studies (both established in 1978) and the UN Centre for Disarmament were all involved in these efforts. The 1980s were designated a Second Disarmament Decade, and a Second Session on Disarmament was scheduled for 1982.

The 1970s brought some partial measures of varying practical significance, and also a series of bilateral arms control agreements among some of the states possessing nuclear weapons. The most important of these was undoubtedly the Strategic Arms Limitation Treaty (SALT) I of 1972 which put a five-year interim ceiling on the strategic arsenals of the United States and the USSR and limited their anti-ballistic missile systems. In 1979 a second SALT Treaty, constructed on the basis of strategic nuclear equivalence between the two powers, and providing for the limitation of various categories of arms, was signed: however it had not been ratified by mid—1981. These treaties were seen by some as hopeful signs, but disarmament on any significant scale existed at the end of the decade only as a future objective. In 1979 the United Nations was expending some US$10 million per annum on disarmament efforts — a sum equivalent to 0.002 per cent of world military expenditure (Bhagat, 1979).

Outside the United Nations several other intergovernmental groups are active in this field, including a number of bilateral USA–USSR working groups; the trilateral USA–UK–USSR negotiations on a comprehensive nuclear weapon test-ban treaty; the Conference on the Mutual Reduction of Forces and Armaments and Associated Measures in Central Europe (based in Vienna); and an Agency for the Prohibition of Nuclear Weapons in Latin America (based in Mexico City).

DEVELOPMENT BETWEEN 1970 AND 1980

Table 16—7 lists the principal international agreements on disarmament or weapon limitations in force in 1980. It is clear that four of the ten were concluded during the decade under review, while one more – the Treaty on the Non-Proliferation of Nuclear Weapons – entered into force in that period.

The 1971 Sea Bed Treaty (Hopmann, 1974; Ramberg, 1978) prohibits the emplacement of nuclear and other weapons of mass destruction on or in the sea-bed outside 12-mile territorial limits. It thus seeks to prevent an arms race developing in an environment upon which military activities have not yet grossly encroached, and has obvious inter-relationships with the continuing evolution of the Law of the Sea. The 1972 Biological Weapons Convention prohibits the development, production, retention, stockpiling or acquisition of microbial or other biological agents, or toxins from whatever source, of types and in quantities that have no justification for peaceful purposes. It also prohibits weapons and delivery systems for such agents or toxins (Goldblat, 1972; Lambert and Mayer, 1975). The 1972 Anti-ballistic Missile Treaty is a bilateral agreement between the United States and the USSR on the numbers and locations of anti-ballistic missile defences (Newhouse, 1973).

The 1977 Convention on the Prohibition of Military or any Other Hostile Use of Environmental Modification Techniques differs from the others in being specifically 'environmental'. The states party to the convention agree not to engage in military or other hostile use of environmental modification techniques having widespread, long-lasting or severe effects as the means of destruction, damage or injury to any other state party. These definitions contain evident ambiguities that have been the subject of debate (Goldblat, 1977). 'Widespread' was agreed by the UN Committee on Disarmament to mean 'Encompassing an area on the scale of several hundred square kilometres'; 'long-lasting' to imply a duration of several months; and 'severe' to mean 'involving serious or significant disruption or harm to human life, natural resources or other assets'. These definitions do not however, appear in the text of the treaty. There has also been debate over what is meant by 'environmental modification techniques'. These have been defined in the Treaty to refer to any technique for changing, through the deliberate manipulation of natural processes, the dynamics, composition or structure of the Earth, including its biota, lithosphere, hydrosphere and atmosphere, or of outer space.

The *State of the Environment 1980* report (UNEP, 1980) listed several further relevant measures. These included a Protocol added in 1977 to the Geneva Convention of August 1949 prohibiting 'methods or means of warfare which are intended, or may be expected, to cause widespread long term and severe damage to the natural environment'. A further Article stresses the need to take care in warfare to protect the natural environment, and prohibits attack against the natural environment by way of reprisals. Starvation of civilians as a method of warfare is prohibited, as is action to attack, destroy, remove or render useless objects indispensable to the survival of the civilian population such as food-stuffs, agricultural areas for the production of food-stuffs, crops, livestock, drinking water installations and supplies and irrigation works.

States party to the 1972 Convention Concerning Protection of the World Cultural and Natural Heritage undertake 'not to take any deliberate measures which might damage directly or indirectly the natural heritage situation on the territory of other states parties' (UN, 1972). The need to protect the environment in times of conflict is also stressed in various United Nations and bilateral agreements, including resolution 2603 A (XXIV) of the General Assembly. This declares it contrary to the generally recognized rules of international law to use in any armed conflict any chemical agents that might be employed because of their direct toxic effects on man, animals and plants. Likewise, the resolutions adopted by the UN Conference on Desertification express concern over the serious acceleration of desertification that war might cause.

Future Prospects

THE short list of international treaties and agreements in Table 16–7 is supplemented by a series of seven agreements that were either in process of negotiation or awaiting ratification at the end of the decade (Table 16–8), and a startlingly long list of items on the disarmament agenda of the United Nations.

In 1980 nine General Assembly resolutions gave specific responsibilities to the Committee on Disarmament for actions ranging from comprehensive disarmament and the cessation of the nuclear arms race to the prohibition of radiological, chemical, and new weapons of mass destruction. Twenty eight other resolutions on many aspects of general and regional disarmament, nuclear weapon-free zones, arms limitation and good neighbour relations between states were also adopted. Six special conferences (including two special sessions of the General Assembly on Disarmament) were called for between 1975 and 1982. In 1980, ten topics in the general area of arms limitation or disarmament were the subject of reports being prepared by the Secretary General in response to resolutions. As UNEP (1980) concluded, "there are some obvious contradictions in the attitude of the World Community to the whole question of military activity. On the one hand, the numerous conventions, treaties and agreements, provide clear evidence of a widespread desire to prevent the more devastating forms of warfare. On the other, the evidence of mounting military expenditure around the world implies a lack of conviction in the practicability of disarmament, or even of holding forces and arsenals at constant size."

The lack of confidence, indeed, appeared more marked at the end of the decade under review than it did at the beginning, and there were signs that the great powers were on the brink of a new upswing in military expenditure, including investment in tactical and

Table 16–7. The Principal International Arms-Regulation or Disarmament Agreements Currently in Force

Title of agreement	Signed	Entered into force	Number of states party[a]
Protocol for the Prohibition of the Use in War of Asphyxiating, Poisonous or Other Gases, and of Bacteriological Methods of Warfare	1925	1928	96
The Antarctic (de-militarization) Treaty	1959	1961	20
Treaty Banning Nuclear Weapon Tests in the Atmosphere, in Outer Space and Under Water	1963	1963	111
Treaty on Principles Governing the Activities of States in the Exploration and use of Outer Space, including the Moon and Other Celestial Bodies	1967	1967	80
Treaty for the Prohibition of Nuclear Weapons in Latin America	1967		27
Treaty on the Non-Proliferation of Nuclear Weapons	1968	1970	111
Treaty on the Prohibition of the Emplacement of Nuclear Weapons and Other Weapons of Mass Destruction on the Sea Bed and the Ocean Floor and in the Subsoil Thereof	1971	1972	68
Convention on the Prohibition of the Development, Production and Stockpiling of Bacteriological (Biological) and Toxin Weapons and on Their Destruction	1972	1975	87
US–Soviet Treaty on the Limitation of Anti-Ballistic Missile Systems	1972	1972	2
Convention on the Prohibition of Military or Any Other Hostile Use of Environmental Modification Techniques	1977	1978	27

[a] As of 31 December 1979. Source of Table: United Nations. The full texts of the multilateral treaties are to be found in the United Nations (1978 c) and USACDA (1977).

strategic weapons useful for fighting a nuclear war rather than deterring one. The Third World was becoming involved in an escalating arms trade, the super-powers were taking actions that could lead to their military involvement there, and scarce raw materials were increasingly in contention.

It is obvious that the questions of disarmament, development and environmental protection are closely linked. Development cannot proceed at the required pace, or a healthy environment be guaranteed, if scarce human and material resources are absorbed by a widening and constantly escalating arms race. Moreover, development and environment are threatened by the armaments, and especially the nuclear weapons, already stockpiled; and the use of these, whether through error, intent or sheer madness, would severely jeopardize mankind's very existence and bring ecological disruption to vast areas of the globe.

One of the most urgent tasks is to arrest the technological spiral at the centre of the arms race. Another is to remove the present obstacles to effective negotiations for the control of strategic weapons. But these are only a first step towards reversing the process and liberating resources through major reductions in world military expenditure. Such a reversal would release vast financial, technological and human resources for more productive uses, including environmental improvment, in both developing and developed countries.

Table 16–8. International Arms-Regulation or Disarmament Agreements Under Active Negotiation or Awaiting Entry Into Force in 1980

A comprehensive nuclear-weapon test ban treaty	Multilateral discussions continued after conclusion of the Partial Test Ban Treaty in 1963. Negotiations on a trilateral USA–UK–USSR basis commenced in 1977.
A chemical weapons convention	Multilateral discussions commenced in 1968. A USA–USSR joint initiative for eventual submission to the Committee on Disarmament was under active bilateral negotiation from 1977 to 1980.
Mutual reduction of forces and armaments and associated measures	Exploratory negotiations between the participating states of the North Atlantic and Warsaw alliances began in 1973.
USA–USSR Treaty on the Limitation of Underground Nuclear Weapons Tests (Threshold Test-Ban Treaty)	Signed in 1974; awaiting ratification.
USA–USSR Treaty on Underground Nuclear Explosions for Peaceful Purposes	Signed in 1976; awaiting ratification.
USA–USSR Treaty on the Limitation of Strategic Offensive Arms (SALT II)	Signed in 1979; awaiting ratification.
A radiological-weapons convention	Under active negotiation within the Committee on Disarmament on the basis of a joint USA–USSR proposal submitted in 1979.

References

Aarkrog, A. (1971), Radioecological Investigations of Plutonium in the Arctic Marine Environment, *Health Physics*, 20, 31–47.

Baran, P. and P. Sweezy (1966), *Monopoly Capital*, New York.

Barnaby, F. (1976), Towards Environmental Warfare, *New Scientist*, 69, 981, 6–8.

Basso, L. (1981), Advisory Opinion, Symposium on Material Remnants of the Second World War on Libyan Soil, Geneva, 28 April – 1 May 1981; Paper UNITAR/EUR/81/WR/10 GE. 81–00846.

Bhagat, S. (1979), How much to Spend on Disarmament? *Disarmament Times* (New York: NGO Disarmament Committee), Vol. 2 Nos. 3 and 4.

Blischenko, I. P. (1981), The Legal Basis of Claims for Damage to the Environment Resulting from Military Action, Symposium on Material Remnants of the Second World War on Libyan Soil, Geneva, 28 April – 1 May 1981; Paper UNITAR/EUR/81/WR/1 GE. 81–00674.

CEQ (1980), *The Global* 2000 *Report to the President*. Council on Environmental Quality, Washington, D.C.

Cestac, R. (1981): The Technical Aspects Related to Material Remnants of War in Libyan Battlefield. Symposium on Material Remnants of the Second World War on Libyan Soil, Geneva, 23 April – 1 May 1981; Paper UNITAR/EUR/81/WR/3 GE. 81–00683.

Ceva, L. (1981), The Influence of Mines and Minefields in the North African Campaign of 1940–43, Symposium on Material Remnants of the Second World War on Libyan Soil, Geneva, 28 April – 1 May 1981; Paper UNITAR/EUR/81/WR/2. GE. 81–00677.

CONAES (1980): *Energy in Transition,* 1985–2020, Final Report of The Committee on Nuclear and Alternative Energy Systems, National Academy of Sciences, Freeman and Co., San Francisco.

DOE (1978): *Digest of Environmental Pollution Statistics,* Department of Environment, HMSO, London.

Duffey, E.A.G. (1974): Lowland Grassland and Scrub: Management for Wildlife, In A. Warren and F. B. Goldsmith (Editors), *Conservation in Practice*, J. Wiley and Sons, London.

Dupuy, T. N. (1964), *Appendix in Historical Trends Related to Weapon Lethality,* Report prepared for US Army Combat Development Command by Historical Evaluation Research Organization, Washington, D.C. US Techn. Inf. Serv. No. AD 458, 760–763.

Goldblat, J. (1972), Biological Disarmament, *Bull. Atomic Sci.*, 28, 4, 6–10.

Goldblat, J. (1975), The Prohibition of the Environmental Warfare, *Ambio*, 4, 5–6, 186–190.

Goldblat, J. (1977), The Environmental Warfare Convention: How Meaningful Is It? *Ambio*, 6, 4, 216–220.

Goldblat, J. (1979), Implementation of the Non-proliferation Treaty, In SIPRI (Stockholm International Peace Research Institute), *Nuclear Energy and Nuclear Weapon Proliferation,* Taylor and Francis, London.

Harrison, C. M. (1974), The Ecology and Conservation of British Lowland Heaths., In A. Warren and F. B. Goldsmith (Editors), *Conservation in Practice*, J. Wiley and Sons, London.

Hopmann, P. T. (1974): Bargaining in Arms Control Negotiations: The Seabeds Denuclearisation Treaty, *International Organization*, 28, 3, 313–343.

Huisken, R. (1975): The Consumption of Raw Materials for Military Purposes, *Ambio*, 4, 5–6, 229–233.

Hveem, H. (1978), *Conflict and Control Over Strategic Resources*, International Peace Research Institute, PRIO Publication S13/78, Oslo.

INFCE (1980), *International Nuclear Fuel Cycle Evaluation, Vol. 9*, International Atomic Energy Agency, Vienna.

Jasani, B. (1975), Environmental Modification–New Weapons of War? *Ambio*, 4, 5–6, 191–198.

Kaldor, M. (1976), Technical Change in Defence Industry, In K. L. R. Pavitt (Editor), *Technical Innovation and British Economic Performance*, MacMillan, London.

Lambert, R. W. and J. E. Mayer (1975), *International Negotiations on the Biological Weapons and Toxins Convention*, US Arms Control and Disarmament Agency, Pub. 78, Washington, D.C.

Larkin, P. R. and P. J. Sutherland (1977), Migrating Birds Respond to Project Seafarer's Electromagnetic Field, *Science*, 195, 777–779.

Leitenberg, M. (1977): Accidents of Nuclear Weapons Systems, In *SIPRI (Stockholm International Peace Research Institute) Yearbook* 1977, 52–85, MIT Press, Cambridge, Massachusetts.

Lumsden, M. (1975): Conventional War and Human Ecology, *Ambio*, 4, 5–6, 223–228.

Miggiani, M.A. (1981); The After Effects of War Waste Left by Belligerent States During the Second World War on the Libyan Soil: General Legal Aspects. Symposium on Material Remnants of the Second World War on Libyan Soil, Geneva, 28 April – 1 May 1981; Paper UNITAR/EUR/81/WR/10 EE. 81–00846.

Ministry of Defence (1973): *Report of the Defence Lands Committees (1971–73)*, HMSO, London.

Murrman, R. P. and S. Reed (1972): *Military Facilities and Environmental Stresses in Cold Regions*, US Army Corps of Engineers, Cold Regions Research and Engineering Laboratory, Special Report No. 173, Washington, D.C.

Nader, R. *et al.* (1981): *Who's Poisoning America?* Sierra Club Books, San Francisco.

NAS (1975): *Long-Term Worldwide Effects of Multiple Nuclear Weapons Detonations*, National Academy of Sciences; National Research Council, Washington, D.C.

Newhouse, J. (1973): *Cold Dawn: The Story of SALT*, Holt Rienhart and Winston, New York.

OTA (1979), *The Effects of Nuclear War*, Office of Technology Assessment, Congress of the United States, US Government Printing Office, Washington, D.C.

Ramberg, B. (1978), *The Seabed Arms Control Negotiations: A Study of Multilateral Arms Control Diplomacy*. University of Denver, Graduate School of International Studies, Monograph Series in World Affairs.

Robinson, J. P. (1979 a): *The Effects of Weapons on Ecosystems*, United Nations Environment Programme Studies, Vol. 1, Pergamon, Oxford.

Robinson, J. P. (1979 b), Qualitative Trends in Conventional Munitions: The Vietnam War and After, In M. A. Kaldor and A. Eide (Editors), *The World Military Order*, MacMillan, London.

Rotblat, J. (1979): Nuclear Energy and Nuclear Proliferation, In SIPRI (Stockholm International Peace Research Institute), *Nuclear Energy and Nuclear Weapon Proliferation*, Taylor and Francis, London.

SIPRI (Stockholm International Peace Research Institute), (1976 a), *Consequences of the Second Indochina War*, Almqvist and Wiksell, Stockholm.

SIPRI (1976 b), World Armaments and Disarmaments, *SIPRI Yearbook*, 1976. MIT Press, Cambridge, Mass.

SIPRI (1977), *Weapons of Mass Destruction and the Environment*, Taylor and Francis, London.

SIPRI (1978), *Armaments or Disarmaments: The Crucial Choice*, SIPRI, Stockholm.

SIPRI (1979), World Armaments and Disarmaments, *SIPRI Yearbook*, 1979. Taylor and Francis, London.

SIPRI (1980a), *Warfare in a Fragile World: Military Impact on the Human Environment*, Taylor and Francis, London.

SIPRI (1980b), World Armaments and Disarmaments, *SIPRI Yearbook*, 1980. Taylor and Francis, London.

SIPRI (1981), World Armaments and Disarmaments, *SIPRI Yearbook*, 1981. Taylor and Francis, London.

Sivard, R. (1980), *World Military and Social Expenditures*, World Priorities Inc., Leesburg Virginia.

Sivard, R. (1981), *World Military and Social Expenditures*, World Priorities Inc., Leesburg, Virginia.

Smith, R. and D. Smith (1980), *International Resource Cost of Armaments: Macro–and Micro–Economic Perspective*, Report to UN Group of Experts on the Relationship Between Disarmament and Development, United Nations, New York.

Somerville, N. (1970), They Shall Inherit the Earth. In B. Weisberg (Editor), *Ecocide in Indochina: The Ecology of War*, Harper and Row, New York.

UN (1945), *Charter of the United Nations;* see also: *Yearbook of the United Nations* 1971. UN Publications, E.73.1.1, United Nations, New York.

UN (1946): United Nations General Assembly Resolution I (1) of 24 January 1946.

UN (1968): *Effects of the Possible Use of Nuclear Weapons and the Security and Economic Implications for States of the Acquisition and Further Development of these Weapons*, UN Publications, Sales No. E.68.IX.I, United Nations, New York.

UN (1969), *Chemical and Bacteriological (Biological) Weapons, and the Effects of their Possible Use*, UN Publications, Sales No.E.69.1.24, United Nations, New York.

UN (1970), *The United Nations and Disarmament* 1945–70, UN Publications, Sales No. 70.IX.I., United Nations, New York.

UN (1971), *Economic and Social Consequences of Arms Race and of Military Expenditure*, UN Publications, Sales No.E.72.IX.16, United Nations, New York.

UN (1972), *United Nations Juridical Yearbook,* UN Publications, Sales No. E.74.V.I., United Nations, New York.

UN (1976), *The United Nations and Disarmament* (1970–75), UN Publications, Sales No. 70.IX.1., United Nations, New York.

UN (1978a), *Economic and Social Consequences of the Arms Race and Military Expenditure,* UN Publications, Sales No. 78.IX.1, United Nations, New York.

UN (1978b), *The United Nations Disarmament Yearbook,* Vol. 3. United Nations, New York.

UN (1978c), *Status of Multilateral Arms Regulations and Disarmament Agreements,* UN Publications, Sales No. E.78.IX.2, United Nations New York.

UN (1980), *General and Complete Disarmament,* Comprehensive Study on Nuclear Weapons A/35/392, 12 September 1980, United Nations General Assembly, New York.

UNEP (1980), *The State of the Environment - Selected Topics* 1980, United Nations Environment Programme, Nairobi.

USACDA (1977), *Arms Control and Disarmament Agreements,* US Arms Control and Disarmament Agency, Publication 94, Washington, D.C.

USACDA (1979a), *World Military Expenditures and Arms Transfers* 1979, US Arms Control and Disarmament Agency, Publication 100, Washington, D.C.

USACDA (1979 b), *The Effects of Nuclear War,* US Arms Control and Disarmament Agency, Washington, D.C.

USACDA (1980): *World Military Expenditures and Arms Transfers,* 1969–1978, US Arms Control and Disarmament Agency, Publication 108, Washington, D.C.

Westing, A. H. (1978): Neutron Bombs and the Environment, *Ambio,* 7, 3, 93–97.

Westing, A. H. and M. Lumsden (1979), Threat of Modern Warfare to Man and His Environment: An Annotated Bibliography, Paper in *The Social Sciences,* No. 40, UNESCO, Paris.

Whicker, P. W. and L. Fraley (1974): Effects of Ionizing Radiation on Terrestrial Plant Communities, *Advances in Radiation Biology,* 4, 317–336.

Whittow, J. (1980), *Disasters: The Anatomy of Environmental Hazards,* Allen Lane, London.

WHO (1970), *Health Aspects of Chemical and Biological Weapons,* World Health Organization, Geneva.

World Bank (1980), *World Tables 2nd Ed.,* John Hopkins University Press, Baltimore.

WPC (1979), *Peace, Disarmament and the Environment,* Report of Commission on the Environment, World Peace Council, Helsinki.

CHAPTER 17

Conclusions

THIS Study is set out to review the changes in the world environment and in human understanding of it during the 1970s, to evaluate the significance of those developments, and to provide a foundation for international and national action in the years ahead.

The first general conclusion is that the data base is of very variable quality. Although this Volume contains a large number of tables and diagrams (and many more could have been provided) there are startling gaps and a special lack of reliable quantitative information about the environment in the developing world. This must be remembered when projections of the future state of the world environment are examined: many are based on only the scantiest of evidence about what, in fact, has been happening.

On the world scale, there are measurements of the major meteorological elements, of carbon dioxide and ozone concentrations in the atmosphere, of atmospheric turbidity and of precipitation chemistry. The distribution of exposure to ionizing radiation is now reasonably well-known and information on food contamination by some metals and organochlorine compounds is available from an increasing number of countries. There are also reasonably complete records of the surface distribution and flow of fresh waters. The state of other environmental resources is less fully documented. A preliminary assessment of the state of tropical forests and the factors affecting them has been completed recently. There are also some good regional monitoring programmes, like those on various seas and for long-range transport of atmospheric pollutants in Europe and in North America, but these are not numerous.

In spite of these data, it is difficult, in many cases, to undertake accurate environmental assessments. For example, it is premature to say with certainty whether worldwide climatic warming has begun (or is likely). There is still not enough evidence to permit confident judgements of possible human influence on stratospheric ozone. Although UNEP, other organizations and national governments have promoted some good programmes of regional marine monitoring, there are no reliable global data on the pollution of the oceans and seas. The amount and condition of ground waters is another area of uncertainty. On land, in spite of the recently completed preliminary assessment of tropical forests, there is conflicting evidence on the scale and rate of deforestation. There are general local and /or regional figures for the extent of deserts, rangelands, farmlands and other major land-use categories but detailed information about their condition — and rates of degradation — are rarely available.

The information about some major human activities that affect the environment is rather better. Food production and fishery statistics are extensive, even if uncertainties remain about the state of the ecosystems on which fish and whale stocks depend.

CONCLUSIONS

623

Demographic data on human populations and on birth and death rates are fairly complete and there are also good records of energy production and use, and of the scale of many major industrial activities and trade flows. But even in such areas as vital to mankind as health and disease, deficiencies in the data base for developing countries hamper the assessment of priorities for action, or of success and failure.

There are many reasons for this situation. One is a lack of agreement on the parameters whose monitoring should receive priority. In the course of preparing this volume the editors attempted to list a small series of indicators that would be especially useful in judging the state of man and environment around the world, but found that there were not enough well-documented ones to warrant inclusion in the final text. A second cause of incompleteness is a lack of universally agreed methods. There are other factors: what matters is the consequence that the world community has not yet achieved one of the major goals of the Stockholm Conference — the compilation, through a global programme of monitoring, research and evaluation, of an authoritative picture of the state of the world environment. Even an imperfect series of environmental statistics, drawing together what we have (and, through its manifest inadequacies, providing a stimulus to better observation) would be an improvement on the present situation.

A second general conclusion concerns the essential unity of the world's environmental system, despite the great geographical and biological diversity of its components. A major review by SCOPE (Bolin, in press), has shown how close the linkages are between the global cycles of carbon, nitrogen, phosphorus and sulphur both on land and in the sea. Human actions have been influencing all of them on an increasing scale. In 1980, the annual release of carbon dioxide to the atmosphere from burning fossil fuels was about 10 per cent of the amount being used by green plants in photosynthesis. In the past century about 10 per cent of the land surface had been transformed into agricultural land, and this has caused a major movement of nitrogen compounds and other nutrients from the soils to the rivers and lakes, and ultimately to the sea. In 1980 the formation of nitrogen oxides and nitrate in the processes of fuel combustion and fertilizer manufacture was about half of what the biosphere produces naturally. More sulphur oxides were entering the atmosphere, mainly from fossil fuel combustion, than were being exchanged naturally between the air, land and oceans as a result of the decay of dead organic matter. All these human impacts were tending to increase, and bulk larger in proportion to the natural components of the cycles, and it was clear that the modification of any one cycle by man would affect the others. In this sense, life on earth functioned as one global ecosystem, but great uncertainty remained over the nature and rate of long-term adjustment of the components of this system in response to these alterations in major biogeochemical cycles.

The data that were available in 1980 suggest (establish would be too strong a word) that the implications of the rise in atmospheric carbon dioxide concentrations do need to be taken seriously — especially because most national energy plans assume an increase in carbonaceous fuel combustion. While major uncertainties remain, a global warming from this cause need not be entirely harmful on the world scale. One current speculation implies that it might increase rainfall in the Mediterranean, the steppes of the southern USSR, and much of East Africa, but make other areas including the cornlands of the mid-western USA more arid. For the very reason that some of these changes would demand major socio-economic adjustments, it is important to know about such developments in advance, which is why the expanded programmes of research in this area are vital.

Although a number of studies suggested that it must still be regarded as a potentially serious problem, there was no instrumental evidence of change in the ozone layer during the decade. Certainly worries over the impact of high flying aircraft, an active concern at Stockholm, can now be seen in a more balanced perspective. On the other hand the suggestion made at Stockholm that acid rain could be a serious environmental problem has gained wide acceptance. In two considerable areas the reality of the phenomenon is firmly established, and the associated changes in freshwater ecosystems have been documented although the precise nature of any ecological impact on terrestrial systems is far from clear. International co-operation in responding to these problems has been given high priority in Europe, where a regional Convention has been negotiated.

Urban air pollution — whether of smoke, sulphur dioxide or the gases involved in forming photochemical smog — appears to have responded to controls in many developed countries over the decade. However, it is a disturbing fact that in the great and growing cities of the developing world these problems are intensifying. Calcutta today has smoke problems as bad as those of London in 1952/53. And developing countries lack the means to curb many of these emissions especially since inefficient combustion of wood, charcoal or animal dung in the home, or poorly maintained automobiles, are a source of a high proportion of pollutants.

In the seas, the dominant problems appear to be those of mismanagement of resources that people have traditionally looked on as a "free good". World fisheries landings increased during the decades, but it is a sobering thought that in 1980 they may well have been fifteen to twenty million tonnes less than they would have been had management been more competent. The extension of coastal state jurisdiction during the decade, and international agreement on stricter fishery limits may help eventually, but only if there is scientific monitoring of stocks, understanding of the factors regulating numbers, and effective enforcement. It is also disturbing to see from these pages how uncertain the estimates of potential fishery resources are — ranging in the case of Antarctic krill from speculations in the early 1970s that this species alone could double world fishing harvests to demands for extreme caution lest the entire southern oceanic ecosystem be disrupted.

This review suggests that on the global and regional scale fisheries and marine ecosystems have not yet been damaged significantly by pollution. Certainly such unambiguous proof of acute damage as exists is highly localized — around oil refineries and industrialized estuaries, bays and coastal zones where numbers have been reduced and many species eliminated. Even land locked and contaminated seas like the Baltic or Mediterranean show no sign of decline in marine productivity. Oil production is a nuisance, a bird-killer and a threat to coastal shellfish and tourism and it has grown during the decade but cannot be proved to have had any serious impacts on a wide scale. Yet many marine scientists feel uneasy about taking such negative evidence at its apparent face value. They argue that even if concentrations are low, the contamination of the sea is increasing: that chronic effects could appear slowly but then be virtually irreversible, and that the most stringent precautions are therefore essential. In the present state of uncertainty there are good reasons for treating such arguments with respect, and for sustaining monitoring and research.

The inland waters of the world are a resource vital to human well-being. Not only do they provide a great essential for life directly, but the quality and quantity of their supply is crucial to the other basic essential — food. The continuing growth of world population and acceleration in water use had by 1970 already begun to strain the water resources of some areas, even in humid regions, and the problems were aggravated by pollution and the continued prevalence of water-borne disease.

During the 1970s, withdrawals of water for use in the home, industry and agriculture continued to increase, although in many developed countries more slowly than in the preceding decade. Statistics remained uneven, but domestic water supplies barely kept pace with population growth in many developing regions and waste water disposal services fell behind in many areas. Unless progress accelerates, the targets of the Drinking Water and Sanitation Decade will be unattainable and problems will grow especially in the squatter settlements on the fringes of tropical cities.

There were improvements in river management, flood prediction, and the management of irrigation systems to prevent salt accumulation in the soil. Pollution control also advanced in the urban and industrial areas of developed countries, but the ecological problems created by sulphuric and nitric acids deposited in rain in north-west Europe and Eastern North America became more serious. Ground water quality also deteriorated in many areas, and statistics for this section of the freshwater resource remained inadequate.

The solid earth beneath our feet is the literal foundation of civilization. In the past decade much has been learned of its slow but irresistible movements, by which the pattern of lands and seas is set, and through which also the location of zones rich in minerals is determined. Something, too, has been learned of how to forecast the sudden devastations by earthquakes and volcanoes which — in statistical terms — occurred with below average frequency and magnitude in the decade yet included one of the most killing events on record. This is an area where research toward better predictive methods could avert great suffering. On a more prosaic note, the mineral resources of the lithosphere are the foundation of many industries and much play has been made of their impending exhaustion. This review emphasizes three crucial points: that it is the quality and accessibility rather than absolute quantity of mineral reserves that matters; that it is often uneconomic to prove the existence of recoverable reserves for more than thirty years ahead, and that the proportional use of one mineral rather than another or the balance between recycling and extraction from the ore depends on economic and political factors rather than any crude notion of absolute availability or exhaustion. Because the time scale on which major investments in energy generation or industry has to be planned is now very long, may exceed the period for which it has been considered necessary to prove reserves, and may vary between alternatives which need to be examined together (as between nuclear power and fossil fuel developments), integrated planning at national level is becoming increasingly essential.

The life of the land is grouped into wild and managed ecosystems — the latter forming agricultural and forest resources, although the distinction is not sharp and many grazed rangelands are semi-natural in character. In the decade both world food yields and the demand for food rose and all the projections implied continuance of the trends. Many agricultural areas increased their productivity, through the use of high yielding varieties developed during the Green Revolution and through better husbandry (but at the cost of higher energy use). But food availability per head dropped in Africa and parts of Asia, so that the overall picture concealed serious regional problems. The scientific data implied that in future more intensive use of the better, more fertile lands was likely to be more rewarding than winning new farms from the wilderness. They also provided much evidence of the waste of environmental resources through soil loss, desertification, salinization and other consequences of poor management. Over large areas of the developing world, too, the demand for wood as the dominant energy source was coming into conflict with the need for farmland, and over-cutting of shrub and forest was jeopardising soil stability on the steep hills. The problems of the developing world, where short term hunger and cold drove people into land-use practices that were bound to lead in the longer term to greater misery emerged acutely during the 1970s and stand starkly in this volume.

The wild ecosystems of the land were in retreat in many areas. Forests were cleared for agriculture and energy on a scale that was the subject of dramatically contradictory estimates. Genetic resources were perceived to be at risk, and the subject of some energetic conservation measures in the marine and freshwater environments as well as on land. But at the same time the decade saw the wide acceptance of the central message of the World Conservation Strategy — that conservation in its widest sense is concerned with sustaining and enhancing the biological productivity of the planet through processes of ecologically sound social development; and that only within a positive approach of this kind, which raises standards of living and education, can resources be found for the protection of the richness of wild nature. The decade saw many advances in this protection.

Looking back to the Stockholm Conference it is clear that humanity's perception of the natural world has changed. In 1972 problems tended to be seen individually, simplistically, and overwhelmingly from a developed western country's standpoint. In 1980 much has been learned about the subtle complexity of environmental systems. The inevitability of variation, the need to expect the unexpected (and allow room for it) and the interlocking of phenomena are widely accepted. It is now appreciated that all environmental systems are subject to natural change, that human action commonly modifies its rate and direction, and that few changes are irreversible — although the time scales and efforts required to achieve reversal vary widely. So is the fact that while some great global problems exist or may come to exist, pollution control, adequate food production and environmental resource conservation do not pose insuperable problems for developed countries — irrespective of whether they have market or centrally planned economies. Here, the means for environmentally sound development exist and the question is whether they are being applied. But problems basic to life — affecting food, fuel, soil and water — are central to many developing countries and often force them into courses of action that cannot fail to damage their futures in the longer term.

This dichotomy between developed and developing countries emerges with great force in the second half of this book, which is about the human rather than the natural world. It begins with population — another of the great preoccupations of the early years of the decade. The figures confirm that the developed countries, generally speaking, are no longer experiencing a population explosion. Their numerical increase is slowing, and birth and death rates coming into balance with a respectable life span between. In the developing world, birth rates have begun to decline in some countries with unexpected rapidity but there is bound to be dramatic population growth with its attendant environmental pressures, for decades to come. And this growth is especially great in the cities, many of which are topping the ten million mark and expanding in a chaos of unplanned, under-serviced housing. In the next decade the populations in urban areas will double, and many of these new citizens will live in squatter settlements of this type.

The health of mankind in the decade reflects this dichotomy also. In the developing world infectious diseases remain great killers, the six most serious of them taking the lives of five million children every year, and parasitic diseases remain rampant. More parasites and bacteria are becoming resistant to an increasing number of drugs and pesticides, and this is a particularly serious problem in controlling malaria. While the average expectation of life at birth improved steadily almost everywhere during the 1970s, there are many developing countries where it is still less than fifty years, and only a relatively small proportion of the population lives long enough to be troubled by the diseases of the developed world — coronary heart disease, hypertension and cancer. It is an irony that the very success of medicine in developed countries in warding off infections in childhood, and latterly in curbing heart disease, should lead their citizens inexorably toward a situation in which the worst feared of ailments – cancer – should also be the commonest form of death. This review suggests that the greatest challenges for environmental medicine in 1980 lay in the less developed regions, especially to curb parasitic infections and the diseases of squalid settlements, rather than in the developed countries where all the indications were that environmental factors were not a major cause of premature mortality and where a major challenge to medicine was to overcome social and behavioural problems and to adapt the pattern of health care more closely to the needs of people.

It is clear that, given sufficient investment and sound planning, most industrial development need not be a hazard to the environment. The events of the decade have confirmed that industry can be competitive and productive without creating damaging pollution – and that the margin of cost added in meeting acceptable standards is of the order of 1 or 2 per cent of GNP in those developed countries that have made estimates. Good planning and design are essential because it is almost always far cheaper and better to build pollution avoidance or pollution control into an industrial plant at the outset than to fit it afterwards. There were encouraging signs during the decade that some developing countries were resisting moves to make them "pollution havens" where industrial development was rendered cheap at the cost of environmental devastation. But this review stresses the complex interaction of technology, economics and public preference in such development. Recycling and low and non-waste technologies are attractive in principle (and gained some ground in the decade) but not all wastes are necessarily polluting and not all recycling clean, and the adoption of a technology to prevent or abate pollution must depend on whether it is necessary to prevent unacceptable damage and hazard. Keener insight into environmental economics emerged as one requirement for the future. Alongside it came recognition of the major influence of the world economic system on the environment.

The energy crisis loomed large during the decade. Oil ceased to be the cheap, secure, universally available fuel. Developing countries whose plans depended on it for urban and industrial use found that price rises imposed a crippling balance of payments burden. At the same time, wood (and charcoal) remained the staple fuels for much of the world and securing supplies from depleted woodlands was taking an alarming proportion of the time of many poor people, hampering their own development and the education of their children. Women bore an especially heavy share of this burden. For developed countries, the energy crisis was more of an inconvenience than a disaster but the decade revealed considerable uncertainties about how to cater for the future: how far expanded use of coal was tolerable in view of the carbon dioxide and acid rain problems, how the considerable potential contribution from conservation could best be realised, how far nuclear power offered a safe alternative, and what the role of new renewable sources might be. These uncertainties, and the economic pressures provoked an unprecedented wave of re-evaluation of national policies and of long-term planning.

Transport of people and goods is an essential component in the life of society and its importance grows as industry and trade develop. In the 1970s human and animal muscle power still moved goods in much of the developing world, but all forms of mechanized transport grew despite the pressure of energy costs. In developing countries reliable and cheap means of moving goods and people by road proved an important prerequisite for development, and soaring petroleum costs bore especially hard. In market economy developed countries personal road transport continued to grow at the expense of rail and other public transport modes, and ways of maintaining the latter at occupancy rates that realized its potential energy efficiency and gave an adequate service to those without their own vehicles were a focus of attention. As the decade came to an end, research and development of transport systems that were efficient, non-polluting and safe was a priority in many countries. Road casualties continued to take a heavy toll of life in many nations, especially in cities of the developing world that were not built for motorized traffic, and air pollution from badly maintained internal combustion engines also created serious environmental problems there at a time when controls were easing such problems in many developed countries.

During the decade tourism gave an increasing number of people in developed countries first hand experience of environments in other lands and climatic zones. But the process also threatened valuable coastal environments and had disruptive effect on some local communities even though it brought them economic benefits. In a few places, development for tourism consumed resources that would have improved the standard of services for much larger numbers of local people.

The development of environmental education proceeded in many lands, and public awareness was enhanced by it and by the mass media. The latter have an important part to play in the development of a balanced understanding of the environment, and during the decade there was a slow but welcome trend in reporting away from excessive enthusiasm for "scare stories" and towards more perceptive appraisals and the reporting of successes. This is important because the resources available to the world community for sound environmental development are limited, and money spent on reducing a small risk to which the public has been sensitized by alarmist reports is liable to cut into the sums available for developments that will remedy less spectacular but more all-pervading hazards.

This problem of limited resources is illustrated most graphically in the field of military expenditure, which rose considerably during the decade, especially in developing countries, and accounts for a staggering sum of money per annum. The reversal of the arms race and its underlying spiral of costly technology would do much to release resources needed to assure the future of mankind and the human environment.

International and regional actions to protect and to develop the environment increased greatly during the decade. UNEP, in co-operation with UN bodies and many regional and non-governmental groups made real advances. Several joint programmes and activities of different organizations, did much to restore damaged environments and enhance the human condition. Many Conventions were agreed and vastly more expert reports were issued. Yet with all this, it is difficult to contend that the international system is yet as efficient as it should be. The ratio of words to action is weighted too heavily towards the former. And despite the evidence that people's perception of environmental problems has improved, it is less clear that many groups have adapted their life styles in response.

Overall, three features of the decade stand out. First, the technology or organizational means to avoid or solve many of the problems identified in developed countries in the 1960s and early 1970s is now known, as is the cost of implementing the various options. What is now required is implementation. But that does not mean that research on the traditional problems should stop. Moreover, it is overwhelmingly evident from this review that the crucial difficulty in many areas is the lack of resources in developing countries and a lack of information about what is happening there. Cheaper, more cost-effective solutions adapted to the needs of those countries are urgently needed, for example for providing energy. The importation of technology evolved in developed countries under different social and economic conditions often will not do. Research is equally vital to define and develop solutions to emerging new problems, before undue damage is done or resources wasted, for example through the loss of productive soils. Better environmental monitoring and assessment are equally essential if such problems are to be recognized, and the success or failure of actions to protect the environment defined.

A second major advance of the decade lay in people's understanding of environmental systems, and in the recognition that environmental and economic systems are inseparable. The physical sectors of lithosphere hydrosphere, atmosphere and biosphere cannot be isolated from the social and technical spheres of humanity. The rapid changes in relationship between nations following the end of the colonial era were still progressing, and the decade ended with the north-south dialogue at the centre of the world stage. As the Brandt Commission recognized, continued economic growth in the developed world may well depend on the progress made by the developing countries: as the World Conservation Strategy emphasized, this progress is likely to be the only means whereby developing countries gain the resources for environmental conservation. Yet the "north-south" division is itself a simplification. Within both such arbitrary groups there are countries at many stages of development with different economic and social priorities. Environmental conditions vary also. It is not enough to deduce that poverty defiles the environment in many developing regions: it is necessary to know exactly how this happens – and how over-consumption creates other threats elsewhere. The complexity of the socio-environmental mosaic must not be forgotten in the quest for a broad, general picture.

The Stockholm Conference established that certain environmental problems needed to be studied globally or regionally. The experience of the past decade has confirmed that such an approach works reasonably well where the aim is the collection of information and its assessment as a basis for national action. During the 1980s, international co-operation is likely to be needed for global and regional environmental, monitoring and its extension by the adoption of authoritative, critical assessments. Co-operation will also be important for continued development of less polluting technology that is cost-effective and suited to the developing world, for action to combat soil degradation and provide guidance on the ground to people endeavouring to develop land in areas vulnerable to erosion and diminishing productivity, for continued efforts against desertification, for the improvement of the human environment through better planning of settlements and services, for action against the diseases that degrade the lives of so many people and for action to conserve world genetic resources. But experience also shows that international action is more difficult where the need goes beyond information collection, analysis and dissemination and involves joint management of commercially important resources, especially where national interests conflict. Advances in this area will be slow, but remain important in the 1980s. To avoid wasted effort it is important that the limitations as well as prospective benefits of an international action are evaluated when it starts, and that the action has an agreed function that is visibly beneficial (as was the case with agreements in the field of telecommunications, and in regional seas pollution control).

Finally, the 1970s emphasized that the great problems of the world environment have political roots. Stable administrations, supported by popular consensus, are needed if long-term environmental developments are to proceed, and resources are not be dissipated in strife and the preparations for war. This review shows that despite serious local disruption, the world environment is not in imminent danger of disintegration. But it needs thoughtful, committed management which can only be achieved in an atmosphere of peace, security and stability.

One of the major contrasts between the early 1970s and 1980s that has become conspicuous in the course of compiling this review has lain in this area of attitude towards the capability of human institutions. At the Stockholm Conference it was generally assumed that the world's system of national governments, regional groupings and international agencies had the power to take effective action, and that the limiting factors were scientific, and economic. By the early 1980s there was less confidence in the capacity of national and international managerial systems to apply known principles and techniques, or in the effectiveness with which international debates lead to action to improve the well-being of people on the ground. The capacity of any existing economic system to bring about the necessary social and environmental developments has been challenged in many quarters (especially following the energy crises of the 1970s). Restoration of confidence and consensus in these areas may be the greatest challenge for those seeking to improve the world environment during the 1980s.

Reference

Bolin, B. *et al.* (in Press), *The biogeochemical cycles and their interactions.* SCOPE Report No. 24, John Wiley and Sons, Chichester.

Index

Acid rain, 20, 38-41, 58, 61, 142-144, 285-286
Acidification of lakes, 142-144
Acid mine drainage, 187
Air pollution control, 59-61
Air pollution and health, 375-378, 520
Air transport, 517
Agricultural productivity, 252
Agricultural land, 255-256
Alcohol: fuel, 485-486
Alcoholism, 394
Alkalinization, 255, 265-267
Aluminium industry, 418
Animals: production of, 260-261
Appropriate technology, 422
Aquaculture, 154-156
Atmosphere, 21-24; carbon dioxide in, 47-50; composition, 22; events, extreme, 55; heat released into, 29; physical structure, 22-24; trace metals in, 41-43; water vapour in, 29
Atmospheric trends, 30
Attitudes: public, 579-584
Awareness: public, 579

Biogas, 484-485
Biota: fresh water, 152-153; impact of man on, 212-217; impact of hunter-gatherers on, 212; impact of fire on, 212; impact of grazing, 213; impact of forest clearance, 213; multi-lateral agreements, 231; terrestrial, 210
Biotechnology, 276-277
Biomes, 217; classification, 218
Birth rates, 305

Cancer, 380-386
Carbon dioxide, 20, 22-23, 25, 47-51, 54, 58, 62-63, 76
Carbon monoxide, 33
Carcinogens; chemical, 383-386; physical, 382; viral, 386

Carcinogenesis, 380
Cardiovascular diseases, 389-390
Charcoal, 484
Chemical industry, 415
Chemicals: in food, 287-288; in general environment, 375; in working environment, 374
Chlorofluorocarbons, 24, 44-45, 63
Cities: growth of, 330-337
Climate: adverse, 54-55; alterations, 47, 51; anomalies, 54; changes, 51-54, 57; forecasts, 58, 54; models, 26; prediction, 58; system, 25-27
Coal, 462-463
Coastal zone development, 104-105
Communicable diseases, 363-372
Coniferous forests, 225
Conservation, 216
Conservation: of energy, 487-489; of terrestrial biota, 230-241
Crops: energy, 483-486; production, 256-259; residues, 288-289
Cultivation: shifting, 273; permanent, 273
Cyclists, 503-504

Deciduous forests, 225
Density of population, 306
Desalination, 130
Desertification, 221, 222, 233, 267, 271-273
Desert vegetation, 221
Development indicators, 412-413
Diseases: cancer, 380, communicable, 361, 363-372; degenerative, 361; diarrhoeal, 372; heart, 393; Itai-Itai, 378; malaria, 368; mental, 394-395; Minamata, 378-379; neoplastic, 361; onchocerciasis, 370; schistosomiasis, 369; viral, 371
Drought, 54-55, 127-129
Drugs, 394

Earthquake, 199-201
Ecodevelopment, 7
Energy: alcohol, 485; biogas, 484; charcoal, 484; coal, 462-463; conservation, 487-489; consumption, 449-452, 455-460; crisis, 453-455; crops, 483; environmental impacts, 460-462; fossil fuels, 468-470; fuelwood, 471-483; future prospects, 489-492; geothermal, 479; hydropower, 478; natural gas, 467; nuclear, 471-477; ocean, 480-481; oil, 463-468; oil shale, 468; renewable sources, 477; solar, 479; tar sands, 468; wind, 480
Environmental awareness, 579
Environmental carcinogens, 382-386
Environmental education, 562-567; non-formal, 577; post-graduate, 572-573; pre-primary level, 567; primary, 567-568; professional, 573-574; secondary, 568-570; teacher training, 574-575; university, 570-572
Environmental impact assessment, 440
Environmental movement, 4, 5
Environmental regulations, 432-437
Environmentally-sound technology, 422
Estuaries, 81
Eutrophication, 139-140, 153
Evaporation suppression, 130
Evergreen tropical forests, 218-220

Family planning, 310-313
Fertility, 305
Fertilizers, 277-281
Fish: freshwater, 154-156; marine, 98-102
Fisheries, 98-102, 154
Floods, 127-129
Food contamination, 378-380
Forest: clearance, 213; productivity, 252, 260
Forest: coniferous, 225; deciduous, 221, 225, 233; evergreen tropical, 218-220; temperate, 224; tropical rain, 218, 232
Fossil fuels, 468-470
Freshwater biota, 152-153
Fuelwood, 471, 483

Genetic resources, 215, 239, 275
Geological hazards, 199
Geothermal energy, 479
Grazing, 213
Green Revolution, 256
Groundwater, 126-127, 159-160; pollution, 146-147

Heat islands, 47
Human health, 357; effect of pollution on, 372-380
Human settlements, 327; changes in, 330; funding of, 351; land use, 345; national policies, 346; rural, 336; shelter, 343-345; unconventional, 342-343, 348; urban, 331-335, 337-338
Hydrology, 274
Hydropower, 478

Industry, aluminium, 418; chemical, 415; environmental impacts, 408–415; iron and steel, 417; lead-zinc, 419; location, 438–439; nickel, 418; petroleum, 416; pulp and paper, 416;
Inland navigation, 138, 514
International migration, 316
Irrigation, 133–135
Islands, 227, 237
Itai-Itai, 378

Labour: force, 414; migration, 316
Lakes, acidification of, 142–144 man-made, 156–158
Lands, arable, 253–254; arid, 253; degradation, 255–256, 265–267, 271; disturbance, 186; use, 252–254, 345
Life expectancy, 361, 362
Lithosphere, 172–205
Livestock wastes, 288
Low-grade ores, 191
Low-waste technology, 423–427
Lung cancer, 391

Malaria, 368–369
Man-made lakes, 156–158
Marine development, 105–109; environment, conventions for protection, 105–109; metals in, 82–85; oil in, 90–92; pesticides in, 85–88; pollution of, 79–82, 92–98; radioisotopes in, 88; mammals, 88, 102–103; pollution, 79–88, 92–98, 525; resources, 98–101; transportation, 90–92, 525;
Mediterranean, 81, 83, 86; vegetation 223
Mental health, 394–395
Migration: international, 316; labour, 316; refugees, 317
Minerals: future supplies, 194–196; low-grade ores, 191; metallic, 184; non-metallic, 183; production, 183–184; sea–bed, 188–190; resources, 177–182;
Mining: acid mine drainage, 187; air pollution, 187; environmental aspects, 184–188; land disturbance, 186;
Mitigation of hazards, 204–205
Mountains, 228, 238

Natural disasters, 204–205
Natural gas, 467
Natural hazards, 59, 199
Nickel industry, 418
Nitrate: haze, 37; in precipitation, 41;
Nitrogen dioxide, 23, 26, 34
Noise, 523
Non-metallic menerals, 183
Non-waste technology, 423–427
Nuclear energy, 471–477
Nutrition, 386–390; deficiencies of, 388

Obesity, 390
Oceans, 73; biological features, 75–78; chemical contamination of, 79–88; chemical features, 75–78; mineral exploitation, 89, 188–190; physical features, 75–78; sources of pollution in, 80, 525
Occupational health, 437
Oil, 463–468
Oil Shale, 468
Oil Spills, 90–91, 96–98
Onchocerciasis, 370
Ores, low-grade, 191
Ozone, 24; layer, 20, 24, 44–46, 63

Particulate matter, 20, 34–36
Pasture management, 274
Pedestrians, 503–504
Permanent cultivation, 273
Pest control, 281–284
Pesticides, 281–283
Petroleum industry, 416
Photochemical oxidants, 20, 36–37, 284–285
Physical carcinogens, 382
Pipelines, 511–514
Plate tectonics, 174–176
Population, 299; birth rates, 308; death rates, 308; demographic trends, 301; family planning, 310–313; fertility, 305; growth rates, 303–304; migration, 316; mortality, 305; refugees, 317; resources and development, 320, 323
Post-graduate education, 572–573
Post-harvest losses, 286–287
Primary education, 567–568
Professional education, 573–574
Public attitudes, 579–584
Public awareness, 579
Public participation, 576
Pulp and paper industry, 416

Railways, 504–507
Rangeland management, 274
Recycling, 130, 191–193
Refugees, 317
Renewable sources of energy, 477
Resource substitution, 427–428
Road-vehicles, 507–511
Rural settlements, 336

Salinization, 139, 255, 265, 267
Sanitation, 137
Schistosomiasis, 369–370
Sclerophyllous forests, 223
Sea-bed minerals, 188–190
Sea water, 77
Shared water resources, 158, 160–161
Smoking, 391–394
Soil degradation, 265–271
Solar energy, 479

Stockholm Action Plan, 8–11
Stockholm Conference, 6–8, 11
Stratosphere, 24, 29, 44–46, 63
Sulphate aerosol, 35
Sulphate haze, 37
Sulphur oxides, 20, 26, 32–36, 284

Taiga, 225
Technologies: appropriate, 422; environmentally-sound, 422; low-waste, 423–427; non-waste, 423–427; recycling, 191–193
Temperate forests, 224
Thermal pollution, 141
Tourism: 543; cultural aspects, 549–552; economic aspects, 549–552; environmental aspects, 552–555; world trends, 545–548
Transport, 499; air, 517; animal, 503–504; cyclists, 503–504; energy requirements, 519–520; impact on environment, 517; inland waterways, 514; marine, 514, 525; modes, 501–503; noise, 523; pedestrians, 503–504; pipelines, 511–514; railways, 504–507; road vehicles, 507–511; sea, 514–515; social impacts, 527–530; vibration, 523
Tropical deciduous forests, 221, 223
Tropical rain forests, 218, 232, 234
Troposphere, 22–24, 26, 32
Tundra, 226, 237

Ultraviolet radiation, 24, 29, 45–46
Urban population, 330–332
Urbanization, 332–333, 336, 338–341

Vibration, 523
Volcanic eruptions, 201

Warfare: chemical, 608–609; consumption of resources, 597; conventional, 605; disarmament, 610–615; environmental impacts, 594–595; environmental modification for, 609; expenditure, 597–601; nuclear, 606–608; remnants of, 595–597
Waste disposal, 340
Wastewater treatment, 144–146, 151
Water: demand, 131–133; domestic, 135–137; global balance, 126; industry, 135; irrigation, 133–135; management 147–152; pollution, 140–147, 150, 378–380; quality, 139; recycling, 130; resources, 124–125, 160–161; supplies, 129–131; withdrawal, 131–133
Waterlogging, 265, 267
Weather: anomalies, 54; forecast, 64; modification, 129; prediction, 58
Wetlands, 229, 238
Wind energy, 480
World Conservation Strategy, 3, 12, 210, 216, 232, 243, 275, 443

Zonobiomes, 218–229, 235